EVERYBODY'S QUOTING IT!
EVERYTHING IS HERE!
THE COMPLETE
UNABRIDGED
SUPER
TRIVIA
ENCYCLOPEDIA

has 800 pages 99/100% pure unadulterated entertainment. It's a collector's delight, a gambler's treasury, a crosswordnik's cache. Here's the book that remembers everything you can almost, but not quite, recall. It's the bestseller that's all things to all people—informative, interesting, fun, funny, provocative—a magnificent answer to all arguments about minutiae. For example, the answers to those cover questions:

1. My Shawl   2. All Quiet on the Western Front   3. William Lee   4. Tony Baretta   5. Foxy Loxy ate Turkey Lurkey, Goosey Loosey, Ducky Lucky, Henny Penny and Chicken Little.   6. Lord Greystoke   7. Zsa Zsa Gabor   8. Hedda Hopper   9. P. T. Barnum   10. Mae West

*TQ—Your Trivia Quotient
is scored this way:
10 right—You're sensational!
7 to 9—Superior, definitely superior.
5 to 6—A delicate balance.
4 or less—You're much too serious.
You .... to read . . .

Books by
Fred L. Worth

*The Complete Unabridged Super Trivia
Encyclopedia Volume I*

*The Complete Unabridged Super Trivia
Encyclopedia Volume II*

Thirty Years of Rock 'n' Roll Trivia

Published by
WARNER BOOKS

THE COMPLETE UNABRIDGED SUPER TRIVIA ENCYCLOPEDIA

by
Fred L.
Worth

WARNER BOOKS

A Warner Communications Company

Dedication

Four hundred twenty-two people were reported to have died on U.S. highways during the Labor Day weekend of 1977. Jerry Fried, the original editor of this book, was one of those statistics. The manuscript for this book was with him at the time, as he was delivering it to the publisher. Without his help and patience this book would not be. We'll miss him.

To the memory of Jerome Fried.

"Trifles make perfection and perfection is no trifle":
   Michelangelo

Mayor La Trivia:
   Character played by Gale Gordon on "Fibber McGee and Molly" radio show

The March of Trivia:
   Routine featured on radio's "The Fred Allen Show"

"We all have a girl and her name is Nostalgia":
   Ernest Hemingway

Acknowledgments

I want to thank the numerous people who helped me with this new edition. Special thanks to my wife Susan (the fastest typist in the west), David Strauss, Auriel Douglas, James Worth, Michael Uslan (*The Comic Book Revolution*), Ralph Albi, David Glagovsky, Ben Fernandez, Garry Owens, Flo Fried, Charles Powell, Gwillim Law, Jerry Shoemaker, B. Baxter Matheny, Frederick H. Ferguson III, Darlington Brooks, Bill Mesler, Tim Murphy, Dave Hooley, R. Ted Hunt, Roger C. Dutton, Gerald Lizenbery (cq.) and to so many others—Thanks.

A Note to the Reader

No attempt has been made to compile sports records; there are just too many, and there exist a sufficient number of books on most aspects of sport. A few key people, events, and feats are included, nevertheless.

No attempt has been made to compile the roles of actors in movies or on television—the list would be much too long and dull; the roles and personalities mentioned herein are those that are the most popular or unusual in nature.

Some seeming errors will have crept in, a result of differences of opinion of authors or sources on some point of fact. I have found in many cases that something appearing in a book or play version will have been changed in the movie or television adaptation, adding to confusion. An attempt has been made to make this work as valid as possible; therefore, movies or TV, having wider audiences, have been preferred over plays and books. The inference is not that one is "better" than the other, but rather than the "fact" is more widespread through the more popular of the media.

It should be noted, among other things, that couples mentioned as being married may no longer be together; that dates for movies given in sources are sometimes dates of completion and sometimes dates of release—there is great ambiguity in source material; that the arrangement of the book depends to a large extent on the compiler's own feeling, so far as under what name or letter of the alphabet information appears. Some cross-referencing has been done, but obviously the book would have gotten out of hand if everything had been sewed up tight and leakproof. Note also that numerical entries, for example "221B Baker Street," lead off in the letter of the alphabet in which the spelling of the number falls, i.e. "221B" is under "T" for "Two." These numerical entries are followed by capital letter combinations that do not form words ordinarily pronounced, for example "TBI" and "T.C." Then follow normal alphabetical entries for the given letter of the alphabet.

Introduction

In the 1965 movie *The Agony and the Ecstasy* Rex Harrison, as Pope Julius II, asked Charlton Heston "When will you make it end?" Heston, who portrayed Michelangelo, the great artist painting the Sistine Chapel, replied "When it is finished!"

I hope it never does end because a work like this hasn't any. My definition and comprehension of *"What is Trivia"* keeps changing through the years. Once I was satisfied to just know the names of the Seven Dwarfs. Now, who played their voices, which was the only one that didn't have a beard, and what musical instruments they played are "trivia musts." The thirteen elves in Tolkien's *The Hobbit* are now becoming popular trivia items, as is *Star Wars!* The best definition of trivia that I keep coming back to is that it is nothing more than American Folklore. If you were to offer a course in trivia, the educational community would balk. Teach the same material under the title of *American Folklore* and your students would learn a lot about their own and their parents' heritage.

This book was written with a double purpose: one, to compile in one reference work a collection of interesting and trivial facts; and second, to collect interesting and perhaps not so trivial facts, facts that are difficult to find. If, therefore, tragic events are mentioned, no minimizing of the event is intended, for they are not meant to be considered trivial per se but fall under my second purpose.

The sources for a book like this are endless, which is as it should be. Trivia is everywhere.

I hope the book answers at least a few of the questions

9

about some particular item or items. As new sources are tapped, and as time produces new trivial facts, more entries will surely be included within the scope of this work. Constant revision probably will be necessary. To this end, I welcome correspondence suggesting new areas, new concentrations. Likewise, any inaccuracies will be ironed out in subsequent printings, and I ask that such inadvertent errors be called to my attention: a note to me at my publishers' will do the trick.

This personal statement would be incomplete without my giving thanks to those who kept the faith. My thanks go too to my editor, Jerry Fried, who brought some light into darkness and without whose help this book might better have been called an encyclopedia of chaos.

When I first began working on *The Trivia Encyclopedia*, I was a novice in the realm of trivia. After four years of research, I realized how much *more* there is to dig for. Will I ever find out who played Robby the Robot, or who held the flashlight on *NBC's Sunday Mystery Movie?* In time, maybe I'll find these and more answers. But until then, it's a kick to keep searching, for I know it'll never end. One great man noted that he learned more about so many other subjects when he was in pursuit of another. Until my next edition *Think Trivia* and be wary of people who answer, "So what?"

FRED L. WORTH

Preface

Little did I, or the publisher, realize the interest the *The Trivia Encyclopedia* would provoke. I've received letters from all over the country, the vast majority suggesting new entries and correcting minor inconsistencies. To those people who wrote, I thank you. Any work this size is bound to contain slight imperfections, and thanks to the readers, these have been eliminated.

I even received information from a college professor who taught a course in trivia. Numerous new entries have been sent by the readers. Those new entries have been included in this, the new edition titled *Super Trivia*. Entries in *The Trivia Encyclopedia* have been enlarged and new entries have expanded the book to its present size. About the most difficult problem I have encountered is trying to keep up with the teams in various sports leagues. Since they come and go so fast, it is difficult to have a current list. No doubt the lists will have changed by publication date.

FRED L. WORTH
(No relation to the comic strip character Mary Worth who was originally named Apple Worth, but that's another story)

A

A

The Scarlet Letter, an "A" embroidered on Hester Prynne's dress, meaning "adulteress" (*The Scarlet Letter* by Nathaniel Hawthorne)

A.

Mutt's initial when the comic strip "Mutt and Jeff" began in 1907. Bud Fisher, the original artist, titled it "A. Mutt." On June 7, 1908, Russ Westover killed off A. Mutt, only to bring him back to life. His full name, later: Augustus P. Mutt

A1ANA2

Lawrence Welk's California automobile license plate

A-1 Detective Agency

Jack, Doc, and Reggie's agency (radio series "I Love a Mystery"). Their secretary: Gerry Booker. Motto: "No job too tough, no mystery too baffling"

A 7397664A

Number of the $10. gold certificate that led to the arrest of Bruno Hauptmann (see 4U13-41)

A & M

Record company founded by recording artist Herb Alpert and Jerry Moss. The studio is on the grounds of the Charlie Chaplin studio (1919–1940) at 1416 N. La Brea, Los Angeles

A & P

Great Atlantic & Pacific Tea Company: grocery store chain begun in New York City in 1859. Founded by George Hartford.

A & W

(Root beer stands; oldest food franchis (1922) Barons are Roy Allen and Fred Wright

A. A. Fair

Pen name of Erle Stanley Gardner

ABC Powers

Argentina; Brazil; Chile

A. B. C. D. E. F.

American Boys Club for the Defense of Errol Flynn: defenders of Errol Flynn when accused by teenagers Betty Hansen and Peggy Satterlee of rape. Trial: January and February 1943, William F. Buckley Jr. was a member of A.B.C.D.E.F.

ABO Blood Groups

A; B; AB—universal recipient; O—universal donor

ANL 709

Arizona license plate number of Marion Crane's 1955 Ford: 1960 movie *Psycho*. She later traded it for a 1957 Ford (California license NFB418 in Gorman.

ASTA

British license plate of Nick and Nora Charles' (Craig Stevens and Jo Ann Pflug) Rolls Royce (1975 TV movie "Nick and Nora")

AU1

License plate number of (18K gold) Rolls Royce Phantom 337 owned by Auric Goldfinger (Gert Frobe) (1964 movie *Goldfinger*)

AXE

Government organization for which Nick Carter works: detective novel series *New Adventures of Nick Carter*

Abbey Road

Apple Record's 1969 Beatle album. Its cover helped further a rumor that Paul McCartney had died in a car accident as far back as 1966. On the cover McCartney is walking barefooted and with his eyes closed. A Volkswagen parked nearby has the license plate number LMW 28IF, supposedly indirectly saying that Paul would have been 28 *if* he had lived. The rumor, of course, proved false. "Abbey Road" was the last album the Beatles recorded together although "Let It Be" was released later.

Abbot

Head of the Friars Club, founded June 1907; Wells Hawk was first Abbot

Abbot and Costello

William "Bud" Abbott and Louis Cristillo: comedy team in radio, then (after 1940) movies. The team split in 1957.

Their "Meet" movies:

Meet Frankenstein, 1948 (in Great Britain, . . . *Meet the Ghosts*) The monster: Glenn Strange

Meet the Killer Boris Karloff, 1949

Meet the Invisible Man, 1951 The Invisible Man: Arthur Franz

Meet Captain Kidd, 1952 Captain Kidd: Charles Laughton

Meet Dr. Jekyll and Mr. Hyde, 1953 Dr. Jekyll: Boris Karloff

Meet the Keystone Kops, 1955

Meet the Mummy, 1955 The Mummy: Edwin Parker

Abel, Colonel Rudolf

Russian spy exchanged February 10, 1962 for F. Gary Powers, U-2 pilot

Aberdeen Express

British train robbed of 7 million dollars (in British currency) on August 8, 1963, in what was called The Great Train Robbery

Abraham Lincoln

Frigate on which Ned Land, Professor Pierre Aronnax, and Conseil were when it was rammed by the "Nautilus" (Jules Verne's *20,000 Leagues Under the Sea*)

Absolute Zero

−273.16°C, which equals −459.69°F

Academy Awards

Pictures:

Rocky, 1976

One Flew Over the Cuckoo's Nest, 1975

Godfather II, 1974

The Sting, 1973

The Godfather, 1972

The French Connection, 1971

Patton, 1970

Midnight Cowboy, 1969

Oliver!, 1968

In the Heat of the Night, 1967

A Man for All Seasons, 1966

The Sound of Music, 1965

My Fair Lady, 1964
Tom Jones, 1963
Lawrence of Arabia, 1962
West Side Story, 1961
The Apartment, 1960
Ben-Hur, 1959
Gigi, 1958 (9 Oscars, 9 nominations)
The Bridge on the River Kwai, 1957
Around the World in 80 Days, 1956
Marty, 1955
On the Waterfront, 1954
From Here to Eternity, 1953
The Greatest Show on Earth, 1952
An American in Paris, 1951
All About Eve, 1950
All the King's Men, 1949
Hamlet, 1948
Gentleman's Agreement, 1947
The Best Years of Our Lives, 1946
The Lost Weekend, 1945
Going My Way, 1944
Casablanca, 1943
Mrs. Miniver, 1942
How Green Was My Valley, 1941
Rebecca, 1940
Gone with the Wind, 1939
You Can't Take It with You, 1938
The Life of Emile Zola, 1937
The Great Ziegfeld, 1936
Mutiny on the Bounty, 1935
It Happened One Night, 1934
Cavalcade, 1932/1933*
Grand Hotel, 1931/1932*
Cimarron, 1930/1931* (Only Western to win)
All Quiet on the Western Front, 1929/1930*
The Broadway Melody, 1928/1929*
Wings, 1927/1928* (silent)

Songs:
"Evergreen," 1976
"I'm Easy," 1975

---

*Award year: August 1 to July 31

"We May Never Love Like This Again," 1974
"The Way We Were," 1973
"The Morning After," 1972
"Theme from Shaft," 1971
"For All We Know," 1970
"Raindrops Keep Fallin' on My Head," 1969
"The Windmills of Your Mind," 1968
"Talk to the Animals," 1967
"Born Free," 1966
"The Shadow of Your Smile," 1965
"Chim Chim Cher-ee," 1964
"Call Me Irresponsible," 1963
"Days of Wine and Roses," 1962
"Moon River," 1961
"Never on Sunday," 1960
"High Hopes," 1959
"Gigi," 1958
"All the Way," 1957
"Whatever Will Be, Will Be," 1956
"Love Is a Many-Splendored Thing," 1955
"Three Coins in the Fountain," 1954
"Secret Love," 1953
"High Noon," 1952
"In the Cool, Cool, Cool of the Evening," 1951
"Mona Lisa," 1950
"Baby, It's Cold Outside," 1949
"Buttons and Bows," 1948
"Zip-A-Dee-Doo-Dah," 1947
"On the Atchison, Topeka and the Santa Fe," 1946
"It Might As Well Be Spring," 1945
"Swinging on a Star," 1944
"You'll Never Know, 1943
"White Christmas," 1942
"The Last Time I Saw Paris," 1941
"When You Wish upon a Star," 1940
"Over the Rainbow," 1939
"Thanks for the Memory," 1938
"Sweet Leilani," 1937
"The Way You Look Tonight," 1936
"Lullaby of Broadway," 1935
"The Continental," 1934

Academies

United States Air Force: Colorado Springs, Colorado

United States Army: West Point, New York
United States Coast Guard: New London, Connecticut
United States Merchant Marine: Kings Point, New York
United States Navy: Annapolis, Maryland

Ace

Bruce Wayne's dog, that took on the identity of Bat Hound (comics)

Ace

Cowboy actor Tim McCoy's horse (Western films). McCoy later rode Baron

Ace Drummond

Newspaper comic strip created by Captain Eddie Rickenbacker (drawn by Clayton Knight): later (1936) a movie serial starring John King

Acme Packing Company

The company which provided uniforms for the first Green Bay Packers football team

Acme Saloon

Bar in El Paso where John Wesley Hardin was shot from the rear and killed by John Selman, a policeman, August 19, 1895. Hardin was rolling dice; his last words were "four sixes to beat"

Acropolis

Hill in Athens, Greece, on which the Parthenon, the temple of Athena, patron goddess of the city, is located

Acuff, Roy

Cowboy singer, leader of Smokey Mountain Boys: member of Country Music Hall of Fame. Finished first as most popular singer (Frank Sinatra, second) in World War II poll of U.S. servicemen in Europe.

Adair, Paul "Texas Red"

World's foremost oil-well-fire fighter: played by John Wayne in the 1969 movie *Hellfighters* as Chance Buckman

Adams, John

President of the United States; father of President John Quincy Adams: only father-son presidential pair. John Adams lived longest of the presidents, 90 years, 247 days

Adjutant

Longest lived dog: 27 years old (1936–1963), a Labrador retriever, in England

Admiral Benbow

Inn at Black Hill Cove owned by Jim Hawkins' widowed mother (Robert Louis Stevenson's *Treasure Island*)

17

Admiral Harriman Nelson
   Commander of the 1983 nuclear submarine "Seaview" (TV series "Voyage to the Bottom of the Sea"): played by Richard Basehart

Adventure
   Captain Lemuel Gulliver's merchantman ship in his later adventure in the land of the Houyhnhnms (rational, intelligent horses) (Jonathan Swift's *Gulliver's Travels*)

Adventure Galley
   Captain William Kidd's ship

Aerodome
   Samuel P. Langley's unsuccessful 1903 airplane, which twice crashed into the Potomac River

Agent 3030
   Secret Service agent Vesper Lynd, lover of agent 007, James Bond. She turns out to be a double agent (*Casino Royale*)

Ahdet Bay
   Secret identity of Im-ho-tep, the Mummy (1932 movie *The Mummy*): played by Boris Karloff

Ain't It Gruesome
   B17 in which Clark Gable flew a mission over Germany, August 1943

Air America
   Airline owned and operated by the CIA

Aircraft Carriers, United States*
   CV-1: Langley (ex collier Jupiter), commissioned March 20, 1922, sunk by Japanese
   CV-2: Lexington (ex battle cruiser CC-1), lost in battle of Coral Sea
   CV-3: Saratoga (ex CC-3)
   CV-4: Ranger, first carrier built from keel up, commissioned Feb. 25, 1933
   CV-5: Yorktown, sunk by Japanese submarine in battle of Midway
   CV-6: Enterprise, called "Big E"
   CV-7: Wasp, deliberately sunk by U.S.S. Lansdowne
   CV-8: Hornet, deliberately sunk by U.S.S. Dustin and U.S.S. Anderson
   CV-9: Essex
   CV-10: Yorktown (ex Bon Homme Richard), called "The Fighting Lady"

CV-11: Intrepid
CV-12: Hornet (ex Kearsage), recovered Apollo II capsule after Armstrong's first moon walk
CV-13: Franklin, called "Big Ben"
CV-14: Ticonderoga (ex Hancock)
CV-15: Randolph
CV-16: Lexington (ex Cabot)
CV-17: Bunker Hill
CV-18: Wasp (ex Oriskany, collided April 26, 1952, with U.S. destroyer Hobson; 176 died
CV-19: Hancock (ex Ticonderoga)
CV-20: Bennington
CV-21: Boxer
CV-22: Independence (ex Amsterdam, light cruiser CL-59)
CV-23: Princeton (ex Tallahassee, CL-61), sunk deliberately by U.S.S. Reno
CV-24: Belleau Wood (ex New Haven, CL-76)
CV-25: Cowpens (ex Huntington, CL-77)
CV-26: Monterey (ex Dayton, CL-78)
CVL-27: Langley (ex Fargo, CL-85; ex Crown Point)
CVL-28: Cabot (ex Wilmington, CL-79)
CVL-29: Bataan (ex Buffalo, CL-99)
CVL-30: San Jacinto (ex Newark, CL-100; ex Reprisal)
CV-31: Bon Homme Richard
CV-32: Leyte (ex Crown Point), explosions aboard in Boston, Oct 16, 1953, killed 37
CV-33: Kearsage
CV-34: Oriskany, used in 1954 movie *The Bridges at Toko-Ri*, and called the Savo Island
CV-35: Reprisal
CV:36: Antietam
CV-37: Princeton
CV-38: Shangri-La
CV-39: Lake Champlain (Jack Lemmon stationed on)
CV-40: Tarawa
CV-41: Midway
CV-42: Franklin D. Roosevelt (ex Coral Sea)
CV-43: Coral Sea
CV-44: construction cancelled January 11, 1943
CV-45: Valley Forge
CV-46: Iwo Jima
CV-47: Philippine Sea (ex Wright)

CV-48: Saipan

CV-49: Wright

CV-50-55: construction cancelled March 27, 1945

CVB-56-57: construction cancelled March 28, 1945

CV-58: United States; construction cancelled April 23, 1949

CVA-59: Forrestal, fire aboard off North Vietnam, July 29, 1967; 134 died

CVA-60: Saratoga

CVA-61: Ranger

CVA-62: Independence

CVA-63: Kitty Hawk: appeared in final scenes of 1966 movie *Lt Robin Crusoe, U.S.N.*

CVA-64: Constellation, fire aboard in Brooklyn Navy Yard, Dec. 19, 1960; 50 died

CVA(N)-65: Enterprise, explosions Jan. 14, 1969, off Hawaii; 27 died

CVA-66: America

CVA-67: John F. Kennedy

CVA(N)-68: Chester W. Nimitz, largest mobile man-made structure

CVA(N)-69: Dwight D. Eisenhower

CVA(N)-70: Unnamed

Air Force One

The plane of the President of the United States, stationed at Andrews A.F.B.

Airline Pilots' Creed

"In God we trust, everything else we check"

Airplane Crashes

March 31, 1931: Knute Rockne

August 15, 1935: Will Rogers and Wiley Post

January 16, 1942: Carole Lombard

March 22, 1958: Mike Todd

February 3, 1959: Killed (in a Beech Bonanza, N3794N) were rock 'n' roll singers Buddy Holly, J. P. Richardson (The Big Bopper), Ritchie Valens. Just before takeoff Waylon Jennings of the Crickets gave up his seat to Richardson. Pilot was Roger Peterson. Flight was from Mason City, Iowa, to Fargo, N.D. At Fargo, young Robert Velline (later known as Bobby Vee) helped fill the empty bill

---

*CV, aircraft carrier; CVA, attack aircraft carrier; CVB, large aircraft carrier; (N), nuclear-powered

March 5, 1963: Killed in a Piper Comanche were country-and-western singers Patsy Cline, Lloyd "Cowboy" Copas, Harold "Hawkshaw" Hawkins. Pilot was Randy Hughes

July 31, 1964: Jim Reeves

December 10, 1967: Otis Redding

August 31, 1969: Rocky Marciano

May 28, 1971: Audie Murphy

September 20, 1973: Jim Croce

November 29, 1975: Graham Hill

Airports
Other than named after city served:

Will Rogers, Oklahoma City	National, Washington, D.C.
General Mitchell, Milwaukee	Midway, Chicago
Lindberg Field, San Diego	Weir Cook, Indianapolis
Friendship, Baltimore	Hobby, Houston
Dulles, Washington, D.C.	Jetero, Houston
Stapleton, Denver	Standiford Field, Louisville

Blue Grass Field, Lexington-Frankfort

Akron, Ohio
Location of annual All-American Soap Box Derby

Akron and Macon
Sister-ship dirigibles (ZRS-4 and ZRS-5). *Akron* crashed off the New Jersey Coast April 4, 1933: 73 died. *Macon* crashed at sea off the California coast February 12, 1935: 2 died

Alamesa State Prison
Detention facility where inmates are incarcerated (TV series "On the Rocks")

Alamo
188 men died after 10-day defense of the Alamo against more than 4000 Mexicans under Antonio Lopez de Santa Anna; included among the dead Texans were William Barret "Buck" Travis, James "Jim" Bowie, Davy Crockett. Over the Alamo's door, the inscription reads: "Thermopylae had its messengers of defeat. The Alamo had none."

Alan Brady Show
Television program for which Rob Petrie (Dick Van Dyke), "Buddy" Maurice Sorrell (Morey Amsterdam), and Sally Rogers (Rose Marie) wrote and which Mel Cooley (Richard Deacon), Brady's brother-in-law, produced (TV series "Dick Van Dyke Show"): Alan Brady played by Carl Reiner

Albatross
   Pirate ship of Captain Geoffrey Thorpe (Errol Flynn) (1940 movie *The Sea Hawk*)

Albert
   Alligator who lives in the Okefenokee Swamp (comic strip "Pogo" by Walt Kelly)

Albertina
   DC6B airliner that crashed September 18, 1961, 10 miles west of Ndola Airport, Northern Rhodesia, killing United Nations Secretary General Dag Hammarskjold

Alcan Highway
   Dawson Creek, British Columbia, to Fairbanks, Alaska: officially called the Alaska Highway, opened November 21, 1942

Aleta
   Queen of the Misty Isles. Sweetheart, then wife of Prince Valiant (comic strip "Prince Valiant")

Alexander
   Dagwood and Blondie's son, originally called Baby Dumpling: born in the comic strip of April 15, 1934

Alexander Throttlebottom
   U.S. vice president under President John P. Wintergreen (George Kaufman-Morris Ryskind musical play—music and lyrics by the Gershwins—*Of Thee I Sing* and sequel *Let 'Em Eat Cake*)

Alexander Waverly
   Head of Policy and Operations (Section I) for U.N.C.L.E. (TV series "The Man from U.N.C.L.E."): played by Leo G. Carroll

Alfred
   Brude Wayne's (Batman's) butler (one of the few persons who knows his secret identity) Alfred's last name is Pennyworth and he has a brother Wilfred. Alfred played in 1943 movie serial by William Austin, and on TV by Alan Napier

Alfred E. Neuman
   Mad magazine's "What Me Worry?" hero. First appearance on *Mad* cover #30 in 1956. Original in an undated, untraceable "comic" postcard of many years before

Algernon
   Mouse friend of Charlie Gordon (Cliff Robertson) (1969 movie *Charly* made from novel *Flowers for Algernon* by Daniel Keys)

Algy

Sidekick of detective Bulldog Drummond: played by Charles Butterworth, Claude Allister, and Reginald Denny, among others

Alias Smith and Jones

Television Western series about the adventures of two fugitives from the law, leaders of the Devil-Hole Gang

Name	Alias	Actor
Hannibal Heyes	Joshua Smith	Pete Duel, Roger Davis
Jed "Kidd" Curry	Thaddeus Jones	Ben Murphy

Alice

George Gobel's wife (TV show): played by Jeff Donnell and Phyllis Avery. Gobel's real wife's name is Alice

Alice

Brady family housekeeper (TV series "The Brady Bunch"): played by Ann B. Davis

Alice and Henry Mitchell

Dennis the Menace's mother and father: played on TV by Gloria Henry and Herbert Anderson

Alice Cooper

Stage name of rock singer Vincent Furnier

Alice Harper

Girl who married Joe Cartwright (TV series "Bonanza"): played by Bonnie Bedelia

Alice in Cartoonland

One of Walt Disney's first cartoon series: first was "Alice's Day at Sea," released March 1, 1924

Alice in Wonderland

Novel (*Alice's Adventures in Wonderland*, 1865) by Lewis Carroll (real name: Charles Lutwidge Dodgson)

Several times made into movies, especially in 1933 by Paramount and in 1951 as a cartoon feature by Disney. There was a 1950 British puppet version. 1933 movie starred Charlotte Henry as Alice (role originally assigned to Ida Lupino), Gary Cooper as the White Knight, Edward Everett Horton as the Mad Hatter, W. C. Fields as Humpty Dumpty, Richard Arlen as the Cheshire Cat, Cary Grant as the Mock Turtle, Jack Oakie as Tweedledum, Edna Mae Oliver as the Red Queen, Louise Fazenda as the White Queen, Charles Ruggles as the March Hare, Sterling Holloway, Roscoe Ates, Leon Errol, and many other "name" actors in miniature or "cameo" roles

Other Alices: 1903—May Clark; 1931—Ruth Gilbert; 1951—Carol Marsh (French); 1976—Kristine De Bell (an x-rated musical starring a former *Playboy* cover girl)

Alice May
Derelict vessel used in cremating Sam McGee ("The Cremation of Sam McGee" by Robert W. Service)

Alice Rutherford
Maiden name of Tarzan's mother before she married John Clayton, Lord Greystoke (Edgar Rice Burroughs' Tarzan series)

Alice's Restaurant
Established by Alice May Brock in Stockbridge, Mass. 1969 record album and resultant movie. Arlo Guthrie made both record and movie; Pat Quinn was movie Alice.

Alicia
Blind girl friend of the Thing (Ben Grimm, of the Fantastic Four)

Allen
Popular comedians: Fred, Gracie, Marty, Steve, Woody, and Barbara Jo (Vera Vague)

All-American Soap Box Derby
First run in Dayton, Ohio, 1934: moved to Akron, 1935. Ages of contestants 11-15. First girl to win, 11-year-old Karen Stead (1975), her left arm in a cast

All that Money Can Buy
Movie version (1941, directed by William Dieterle) of Stephen Vincent Benet's "The Devil and Daniel Webster." James Craig played the farmer Jabez Stone; Walter Huston played the Devil, Mr. Scratch, who bargained for his soul; Edward Arnold played Daniel Webster, who pleaded successfully for Jabez' soul with a jury of scoundrels and renegades from American folklore and legend

Allen's Alley
Fred Allen's radio show featured its inhabitants: Senator Beauregard Claghorn (Kenny Delmar); Titus Moody (Parker Fennelly); Ajax Cassidy (Peter Donald); Mrs. Pansy Nussbaum (Minerva Pious); Falstaff Openshaw (Alan Reed); Senator Bloat (Jack Smart); Socrates Mulligan (Charles Cantor); Pierre Nussbaum (never seen or heard)
Catch lines: Claghorn, "That's a joke, son," Moody, "Howdy, Bub"; Nussbaum, "You're expectin' maybe . . ."

Alley Oop

Caveman who fluctuates between modern and prehistoric times: comic strip (debut of Alley Oop Aug. 7, 1933) by Vince T. Hamlin. The prehistoric kingdom of Moo is ruled by King Guz (or Guzzle), whose daughter Wootie is enamored of Alley Oop, who in turn loves (and later marries) Oola. Oop's pet is the dinosaur Dinny. Dr. Wonmug is the scientist who controls the time machine. A pop song of the 1960s by the Hollywood Argyles was titled "Alley Oop."

Alou brothers

Baseball players: real last name, Rojas:
Matty (December 22, 1938)
Felipe (May 12, 1935)
Jesus (March 24, 1942)
All three played outfield for San Francisco Giants September 22, 1963, against the Mets at New York

Alpha

Dolphin trained to speak English by George C. Scott (1973 movie *The Day of the Dolphin*)

Alphabet, spoken

Words used to differentiate letters in voice transmission over radio (also called phonetic alphabet)

Current usage			World War II usage		
Alpha	Lima	Whiskey	Able	Love	Whiskey
Bravo	Mike	X-Ray	Baker	Mike	X-Ray
Charlie	November	Yankee	Charlie	Nan	Yoke
Delta	Oscar	Zulu	Dog	Oboe	Zebra
Echo	Papa		Easy	Peter	
Foxtrot	Quebec		Fox	Queen	
Golf	Romeo		George	Roger	
Hotel	Sierra		How	Sugar	
India	Tango		Item	Tear	
Juliet	Uniform		Jig	Uncle	
Kilo	Victor		King	Victor	

Also Sprach Zarathustra

Symphonic poem (1896) by Richard Strauss, part of which was used as thematic music in 1968 movie *2001: A Space Odyssey*

Altair IV

The forbidden planet in the constellation Aquila (1956 movie *The Forbidden Planet*)

Alvin

David Seville's delinquent chipmunk (see Chipmunks)

Amalgamated Broadcasting System

Radio network founded by Ed Wynn in 1933, lasting only a few months

Amanda (Grayson)

Mr. Spock's human mother, wife of Vulcan ambassador Sarek (TV series "Star Trek") : played by Jane Wyatt

Amigiri

Japanese destroyer that on August 2, 1943, in Blackett Strait, Solomon Islands, rammed and sank PT-109, which was commanded by Lt. John F. Kennedy. Kennedy's commander in the Solomon's was John Mitchell, who was later attorney-general under Richard M. Nixon

Amazon Plane

Wonder Woman's invisible robot jet airplane, originally a propeller plane (comic book)

Amberjack II

President Franklin D. Roosevelt's 45-foot sailboat

America

National hymn ("My Country 'Tis of Thee") of the United States: words written in 1832 by Samuel Francis Smith; music same as "God Save the King (Queen)"

America

Fokker trimotor plane, piloted by Thomas Acosta and Bernt Balchen, in which Admiral Richard Byrd crossed the Atlantic (1927)

America

Winner of international yacht race, August 22, 1851, defeating the British yacht "Aurora" by eighteen minutes; hence America's Cup. Before this, it was called the Queen's Cup.

American Bandstand

Philadelphia television (WFIL-TV) dance program MC'd by Dick Clark after July 1956. Most popular couple during the 1950's: Justine Corelli and Kenny Rossi. Theme song: "Bandstand Boogie" by Les Elgart

America's Boy Friend

Nickname of Charles "Buddy" Rogers, husband of Mary Pickford, "America's Sweetheart"

America's Sweetheart

Nickname of Mary Pickford," also called The Girl with the Curl. She was Canadian-born Gladys Smith, married

Douglas Fairbanks, Sr., and Charles "Buddy" Rogers. Oscar, 1928/29 for *Coquette*. Debut: *The Warrens of Virginia*, by William DeMille, whose brother Cecil aso appeared in the play

American Baseball League

Eastern Division:
  Baltimore Orioles
  Boston Red Sox
  Cleveland Indians
  Detroit Tigers
  New York Yankees
  Milwaukee Brewers
  Toronto Blue Jays

Western Division:
  California (Anaheim) Angels
  Chicago White Sox
  Texas (Arlington) Rangers
  Minnesota (Bloomington) Twins
  Kansas City Royals
  Oakland Athletics (A's)
  Seattle Mariners

American Basketball Association (*defunct 1976*)

Eastern Division:
  Carolina (Greensboro, N.C.) Cougars
  Kentucky (Louisville) Colonels
  Memphis Tams
  New York (Carle Place) Nets
  Virginia (Norfolk) Squires
  St. Louis Spirits
  San Antonio Spurs

Western Division:
  Dallas Chaparrals
  Denver Rockets (Golden Nuggets)
  Indiana (Indianapolis) Pacers
  San Diego Conquistadors (Sails)
  Utah (Salt Lake City) Stars

American Basketball League (*1961–1962*)

San Francisco (Saints)
Pittsburgh (Rens)
Kansas City (Steers)
Cleveland (Pipers)
Los Angeles (Jets)
Chicago (Majors)

Washington (Tapers)

Hawaii (Chiefs)

American Bicentennial Novel Series

Created by John Jakes: *The Bastard; The Rebels; The Seekers; The Furies; The Titans; The Warriors*

American Express Card

Used same card number (040 072 493 b 100 AX) for various people, including William E. Miller, who had been 1964 candidate for U.S. vice-president (TV commercials)

American Gothic

Painting by Grant Wood (completed 1930): the two who posed were Nan Wood Graham, the artist's sister, and the family dentist, Dr. Byron McKeeby

American Graffiti

Nostalgic 1973 movie about the year 1962 ("Where were you in '62?"), produced by Francis Ford Coppola. It is the movie being shown aboard Columbia Airlines flight 409 in the 1974 movie *Airport '75*

American Hockey League (*1968–1969*)

Cleveland (Barons)

Rochester (Americans)

Springfield (Kings)

Buffalo (Bisons)

Quebec (Aces)

Providence (Reds)

Baltimore (Clippers)

Hershey (Bears)

American La France

Biggest builder of fire engines in the United States (later known as Ward La France)

American universities

Order of establishment:

Harvard	Massachusetts	1636
William and Mary	Virginia	1693
Yale	Connecticut	1701
Pennsylvania	Pennsylvania	1740
Princeton	New Jersey	1746
Washington and Lee	Virginia	1749
Columbia	New York	1754

America's Favorite Lovebirds

Twentieth Century Fox's title for their movie couple Charles Farrell and Janet Gaynor

Ames Billiards
>New York City pool hall where "Fast" Eddie Felson (Paul Newman) beats Minnesota Fats (Jackie Gleason) (1961 movie *The Hustler*)

Ames Brothers (Urick brothers)
>Ed (played Mingo in TV series "Daniel Boone"); Gene; Joe; Vic: popular 1950s vocal group, sang with Russ Morgan's orchestra

Amigo
>Bobby Benson's golden palomino (radio)

Amity Island
>Setting of Peter Benchley's 1976 movie *Jaws:* actually filmed on Martha's Vineyard

Amos 'n' Andy
>On radio (1928–1943) played by Freeman Gosden and Charles J. Correll (Amos Jones and Andrew Halt Brown): last broadcast Nov. 25, 1960. Radio: Amos, Gosden; Andy, Correll; George Stevens, Lightnin', both Gosden; Henry Van Porter, Correll; Sapphire Stevens, Ernestine Wade; Madame Queen, Harriette Widmer; Ruby, Elinor Harriot
>
>TV: Amos, Alvin Childress; Andy, Spencer Williams; George Stevens, Tim Moore; Lightnin', Nick O'Demus; Sapphire, Ernestine Wade; Algonquin J. Calhoun, Johnnie Lee; Sapphire's mother, Petunia Smith, Amanda Randolph

Amos Mouse
>Mouse in "Ben and Me" (1954 Walt Disney cartoon): he helped Ben Franklin invent

Amy Fowler
>Quaker bride of Marshal Will Kane (1952 movie *High Noon*): played by Grace Kelly

Amy Moore
>First person to receive one million dollars from the millionaire (John Beresford Tipton) (TV series "The Millionaire"). She received the money from Tipton's bank executive Mr. McMahon (not from Michael Anthony, the agent who later gave out the money). Amy Moore returned the money

Amy Prentiss
>San Francisco female chief of detectives (NBC Sunday Mystery Movie series) played by Jessica Walter

Anabelle

Heifer given to the team completing its side of the barn first (1954 movie *Seven Brides for Seven Brothers*)

Anaheim, Azusa, and Cucamonga

Three stops called out by the train station announcer (Mel Blanc) for departing trains (radio's "The Jack Benny Program")

An-An

Moscow zoo's giant panda

Ananias Club

Club of which all members are liars: founded by Theodore Roosevelt

Anastasia and Drizella (Tremaine)

Cinderella's two step-sisters (Walt Disney cartoon feature movie): voices by Lucille Bliss and Rhoda Williams, respectively

Anatevka

Russian village in musical play *Fiddler on the Roof*

Anatomy of a Murder

Novel by Robert Traver (pen name of Michigan Supreme Court Justice John D. Voelker), read by Ringo Starr in 1964 Beatles movie *A Hard Day's Night*. Also 1959 movie with James Stewart and Lee Remick in which lawyer Joseph Welch of the Army-McCarthy hearings played Judge Weaver

Anchorman

Lowest man in Annapolis graduating class (low score in marks)

Andamo

Mr. Lucky's gambling partner (TV series "Mr. Lucky"): played by Ross Martin

Anderson

Name of family of which Robert Young and Jane Wyatt played father James and mother Margaret (TV series "Father Knows Best"): on radio, Margaret played by June Whitley and Jean Vanderpyl. Children: Betty (TV, Elinor Donahue; radio, Rhoda Williams), Bud (TV, Billy Gray; radio, Ted Donaldson), Kathy (TV, Lauren Chapin; radio, Norma Jean Nilsson)

Anderson, Shelley

First winner (1974) of the Annual Unofficial Miss Las Vegas Showgirl Pageant, hosted by Steve Allen. Shelley turned a lamp off and on to the time of music as her talent

Anderson quintuplets

Born April 26, 1973; Roger, Owen, Scott, Kay, Diane

Andersonville

Largest confederate military prison during the Civil War, in Georgia. More than 13,000 Union prisoners died there, mostly of neglect. Major Henry Wirz, commandant, was the only Civil War soldier executed for war crimes *Andersonville*, fictional novel by MacKinlay Kantor, won 1956 Pulitzer Prize

Andrew Bond

James Bond's father (James' mother's maiden name was Monique Delacroix)

Andrew John

Name of boy born to Rosemary (Mia Farrow) (1968 movie *Rosemary's Baby*). The Satan worshippers named him Adrian

Andrews

Fred and Mary, Archie's parents (Archie Andrews comic strip)

Andrews Sisters

Singing group at one time with Leon Belasco band: Maxene, La Verne, Patty. Patty was once married to Marty Melcher, who later married Doris Day

Androcles

Removed the thorn from the lion's foot and was later spared by the same lion. The story is from Aesop's fables, with the moral: "One good deed deserves another"

Andy

Mark Trail's Saint Bernard (comic strip/radio series)

Andy Hardy

Son of Judge James Hardy (See Judge Hardy) of the small town of Carvel. Andy was hero of a long series of movies in which he was played by Mickey Rooney. Sister: Marian (played by Cecilia Parker); Aunt Milly played by Sara Haden and Betsy Ross Clarke. In the first movie, his sister Joan was played by Julie Haydon, but that was her only appearance in the series. The Andy Hardy movies, from MGM, were:

A Family Affair, 1937
You're Only Young Once, 1938
Judge Hardy's Children, 1938
Love Finds Andy Hardy, 1938

Out West with the Hardys, 1938
The Hardys Ride High, 1939
Andy Hardy Gets Spring Fever, 1939
Judge Hardy and Son, 1939
Andy Hardy Meets a Debutante, 1940
Andy Hardy's Private Secretary, 1941
Life Begins for Andy Hardy, 1941
The Courtship of Andy Hardy, 1942
Andy Hardy's Double Life, 1942
Andy Hardy Steps Out, 1942
Andy Hardy's Blonde Trouble, 1944
Love Laughs at Andy Hardy, 1946
Andy Hardy Comes Home, 1958

Angels (orders)

Highest to lowest rank:

Seraphim
Cherubim
Thrones
Dominations (or Dominions)
Virtues
Powers
Principalities
Archangels
Angels

Animals

Collective words ("an army of frogs" or "a bale of turtles")

Army—frogs
Bale—turtles
Band—gorillas, jays
Barren—mules
Bed—clams, oysters
Bevy—quail, swans
Brace—ducks
Brood—chicks
Bury—conies
Business—ferrets
Cast—hawks
Cavvy—extra cowboy mounts
Cete—badgers
Charm—goldfinches, hummingbirds
Chattering—choughs
Clamor—rooks
Cloud—gnats
Clowder—cats
Cluster—cats
Clutch—chicks
Clutter—cats
Colony—ants, gulls
Congregation—plovers
Convocation—eagles
Covert—coots
Covey—quail, partridge
Cry—hounds
Down—hares
Draught—fish
Dray—squirrels

Drift—swine
Drove—cattle, sheep, hares, oxen
Exaltation—larks
Field—racehorses
Flight—birds
Flock—sheep, geese, bustards, camels
Gaggle—geese
Gam—whales
Gang—elks
Grist—bees
Herd—curlews, elephants, animals
Hive—bees
Horde—gnats
Host—sparrows
Hover—trout
Husk—hares
Kindle—kittens
Knot—toads
Leap—leopards
Litter—pigs, cats, dogs
Murder—crows
Muster—peacocks
Mustering—storks
Mute—hounds
Nests—vipers, pheasants
Nide—pheasants
Nye—pheasants
Pace—asses

Pack—hounds, wolves
Pair—horses
Plump—wildfowl
Pod—seals, whales walruses
Pride—lions
Remuda—extra cowboy mounts
Run—poultry
School—fish
Siege—cranes, bitterns, herons
Shoal—fish, pilchards
Skein—geese
Skulk—foxes
Sleuth—bears
Sounder—boars, swine
String—racehorses
Spring—teals
Swarm—bees, eels
Team—ducks, horses
Tribe—goats, monkeys
Trip—goats, wildfowl
Troop—monkeys, kangaroos, lions
Volery—birds
Watch—nightingales
Wedge—swans
Wing—plovers
Yoke—oxen

Young:

Ass—hinny, foal
Bear—cub
Beaver—kitten
Bird—nestling
Cat—kitten
Cattle—calf
Chicken—poult, chick
Coffish—codling
Cow—calf
Deer—fawn
Dog—pup

Duck—duckling
Eagle—eaglet
Eel—elver
Elephant—calf
Fish—fry, fingerling
Fox—cub, kit
Frog—tadpole
Goat—kid
Goose—gosling
Grouse—poult
Hare—leveret

Hawk—eyas
Hen—chick, pullet
Horse—colt, filt, filly, foal
Insect—nymph, pupa
Kangaroo—joey
Lion—cub
Monkey—baby
Moose—calf
Otter—whelp
Oyster—spat
Peafowl—peachick

Pig—shoat, piglet, farrow
Rabbit—bunny, leveret
Rhinoceros—calf
Seal—pulp
Sheep—lamb
Swan—cygnet
Tiger—cub
Turkey—poult
Whale—calf
Wolf—cub, whelp
Zebra—colt

Ann Darrow

King Kong's *femme fatale* (in a one-sided romance) (1933 movie *King Kong*): played by Fay Wray. For the 1976 remake, Barbra Streisand, Valerie Perrine, Bette Midler, and Cher were suggested for the part of Dwan, but it was finally played by Jessica Lange

Anne Howe

Wife of prize-fighter Joe Palooka (comic strip/movies): played on radio by Elsie Hitz and Mary Jane Higby

Annie Fanny

See Little Annie Fanny

Annihilations

Emperor Ming's robot soldiers (movie serial *Flash Gordon*)

Annihilus

Evil ruler of the Negative Zone, enemy of the Fantastic Four (Marvel Comics)

Anniversaries

1st—paper
2nd—cotton
3rd—leather
4th—fruit, flowers
5th—wood
6th—sugar, candy
7th—wool, copper
8th—bronze, pottery
9th—pottery, willow
10th—tin
11th—steel
12th—silk, linen

13th—lace
14th—ivory
15th—crystal
20th—china
25th—silver
30th—pearl
35th—coral
40th—ruby
45th—sapphire
50th—gold
55th—emerald
75th—diamond

Answer Man, The

Albert Mitchell (radio series)

Antelope

Ship, wrecked at sea, from which Lemuel Gulliver is washed ashore on Lilliput (Jonathan Swift's *Gulliver's Travels*)

Anthony Alucard

Count Dracula's son (1943 movie *Son of Dracula*): played by Lon Chaney, Jr. (Alucard is Dracula spelled backwards)

Apartments

12D—The Jefferson family ("The Jeffersons")

D—Mary Richards ("Mary Tyler Moore Show")

9E—Rhoda Gerard's apartment ("Rhoda")

2B—Rhoda's sister Brenda's apartment ("Rhoda")

27—Mike and Jill Danko ("The Rookies")

88—Maxwell Smart ("Get Smart")

312—Sam McCloud ("McCloud")

3B—Lucy and Ricky Ricardo ("I Love Lucy")

Ape Movies

Based on Pierre Boulle's novel *Planet of the Apes*:

Planet of the Apes (1968)

Beneath the Planet of the Apes (1970): title chosen over originally suggested "Planet of the Apes Revisited" and "Planet of the Men"

Escape from the Planet of the Apes (1971)

Conquest of the Planet of the Apes (1972)

Battle for the Planet of the Apes (1973)

Roddy McDowall as Cornelius (later as the chimpanzee Caesar) starred in all but the second picture. Kim Hunter was the only actor to appear (as Dr. Zira) in all of the first three

1974 TV series, "Planet of the Apes," starred Roddy McDowall. There was also a TV cartoon series by that title

Apex Broadcasting Company

Radio station (WXYZ) where Alan Scott (The Green Lantern) worked as a radio engineer (comic books)

Apollo

Great Dane given by Richard Wentworth (The Spider) to his girlfriend, Nita van Sloan (comics)

Apollo 1

Space capsule in which Virgil "Gus" Grissom, Edward White, and Roger Chaffee were killed when a fire occurred inside the craft on the ground, January 27, 1967, at Cape Kennedy launching pad 34.

Apollo 11 Crew

First man-moon landing, July 20, 1969: Neil Armstrong and Edwin Aldrin walked on the moon's surface; Michael Collins remained with the command ship. The initials of the three astronauts are the same as those of Adam, Abel, and Cain, first men on earth

Apollo 12

Second mission to the moon: landed on October 27, 1969. Commander Charles "Pete" Conrad stated as he placed his foot on the lunar surface, "Whoopee! Man, that may have been a small one for Neil, but that's a long one for me!" (See Armstrong, Neil A.)

Apollo 17

Moon flight on which Steve Austin (Lee Majors) was an astronaut (TV series "Six Million Dollar Man")

Apple

The Beatles' record company. Address: 3, Saville Road, London, W. 1, England. "Hey, Jude" was the company's first single. The label shows a Granny Smith apple

Appleby, U.S.S.

Naval destroyer (TV series "Ensign O'Toole")

Appleton, Iowa

Setting of TV series "Apple's Way"

April Dancer

The girl from U.N.C.L.E. (TV series starring Stefanie Powers)

April 2, 1912

Birthdate of Ellery Queen (TV series starring Jim Hutton)

Aquacade

Word coined by entrepreneur Billy Rose: registered by him as a trademark

Aqualad

Aquaman's partner (comic book character): he was born March 6

Arbadella

Amos's daughter (radio's "Amos 'n' Andy"): played by Terry Howard. On TV played by Marie Ellis

Arcaro, Eddie

Only jockey to win the Triple Crown twice: 1941, on Whirlaway: 1948, on Citation. In addition, he won the Kentucky Derby on Lawrin (1938), Hoop Jr. (1945), and Hill Gail (1952). He won the Preakness and Belmont 6 times each

Archangels

In Christian belief: Michael, Chamuel, Raphael, Gabriel, Uriel, Zadkiel, Zophiel (Jophiel)

Archerfish

U. S. submarine, under command of Commander J. F. Enright, that sank 59,000-ton Japanese carrier *Shinano*, November 29, 1944. It took 4 years to build the carrier, which was on her maiden cruise; two hours after launching she was sunk

Archie

Bartender (radio series "Duffy's Tavern"): played by Ed Gardner. Catch line: "Duffy's Tavern, Archie speakin'. Duffy ain't here. Oh, hello, Duffy."

Archie Andrews

Student at Riverdale High School, hero of comic strip "Archie" created by Bob Montana. Premiered in Pep Comics #22, December 1941 on radio played by Charles Mullen, Burt Boyer, Bob Hastings, and Jack Grimes. TV cartoon series: "Archie's Funhouse" (1968–70) "Archie's TV Funnies" (1971–73). The group from the show, The Archies, had the number one song in 1969: "Sugar Sugar"

Archie Goodwin

Nero Wolfe's assistant and narrator of his stories. Birthday: Wednesday, Oct. 23, 1912, in Ohio. 180 lbs., 6 ft. tall, 9 shoe. On radio, played by Louis Vittes, Gerald Mohr, and Everett Sloan; in movies, by Lionel Stander to the Nero Wolfe of Edward Arnold and Walter Connolly

Archie Justice

Archie Bunker's name through the first two pilot films of TV series "All In The Family"

Archie Leach

"The last person to say that to me was Archie Leach, just before he cut his throat!": said by Cary Grant, whose real name is Archibald Leach, in 1940 film *His Girl Friday*

Archimedes

Merlin's owl (Disney cartoon feature movie *Sword in the Stone*): voice of Junius Matthews

archy

Cockroach who types by falling from height onto each key, thus no capitals (created by columnist-author Don

Marquis: 1927 and after). His friend is the cat Mehitabel. In the play *Shinbone Alley*, Mehitabel was played by Eartha Kitt, archy by Eddie Bracken

Argo
Ship on which Jason and the Argonauts sailed in quest of the Golden Fleece (Greek legend)

Argonaut
Mike Nelson's private boat (TV series "Sea Hunt")

Argos
Odysseus' dog (Homer's *The Odyssey*)

Argus
Giant with 100 eyes (Greek mythology)

Argus, H.M.S.
First aircraft carrier, Royal Navy, 1918

Arion
Hercules' horse: given by him to Adrastus

Aristotle
Pugsley Addams' pet octopus (TV series *The Addams Family*)

Arizona, U.S.S.
Only United States battleship still in commission (sunk at Pearl Harbor, 1941, now a memorial)

Ark Royal
English Lord High Admiral Charles Howard's flagship in the battle against the Spanish Armada in 1588 (a later "Ark Royal," a British aircraft carrier, carried the planes credited with sinking the German "Bismarck" in May 1941 and was herself sunk in November 1941 by a German submarine in the Mediterranean)

Armistice Day
November 11, 1918, end of World War I; observance begun 1926; observed from 1954 to 1970 as Veterans' Day in late October

Armstrong, Henry
Holder of three boxing titles simultaneously: Featherweight champion (1937–1938); Welterweight champion (1938–1940); Lightweight champion (1938)

Armstrong, Neil A.
First man to walk on the moon (July 20, 1969). Apollo 11 LM (lunar module) landed 4:17:20 P.M. EDT. Armstrong's EVA (extra-vehicular activity) on surface 10:56:20 P.M. EDT; Aldrin on surface 11:14 P.M.

EDT. Armstrong's words: "That's one small step for a man, one giant leap for mankind."

Armstrong of the S.B.I.

Radio series about the adventures of Jack Armstrong (the All American boy) after he grew up: S.B.I.-Scientific Bureau of Investigation

Army rank

Generals	
General of the Army—	5 stars
General—	4 stars
Lieutenant General—	3 stars
Major General—	2 stars
Brigadier General—	1 star

The rank of General of the Army has been held by George C. Marshall, Douglas MacArthur, Dwight D. Eisenhower, Henry H. Arnold and Omar Bradley

Arnie Aardvark

First mate on Boner's Ark (comic strip "Boner's Ark")

Arnold

Pet pig (TV series "Green Acres"): winner of TV PATSY, 1967, 1968, 1969. Owned by Ziffel (Hank Patterson)

Arnold

Fred Flintstone's paperboy (TV cartoon "The Flintstones")

Arnold, Kenneth

Filed the first official flying saucer sighting, June 24, 1947, while flying near Mt. Rainier

Arnold's

Milwaukee drive-in restaurant at 2115 Lake Avenue where the gang hangs out (TV series "Happy Days"): Arnold is played by Pat Morita

Arrangement in Grey and Black

Original name of the painting "Whistler's Mother" or "The Artist's Mother" by James McNeill Whistler: in the Louvre, Paris

Arrow, The

Al Capone's 32-foot cabin cruiser, kept at his Florida villa

Arrowsmith

Novel by Sinclair Lewis (1925), one of two novels buried in the 1939 New York World's Fair time capsule. (The other novel: Margaret Mitchell's *Gone with the Wind* (1936)

Ars Gratia Artis
"Art for Art's Sake": motto of MGM films, created by Howard Dietz, appears in the circle above the lion's head. Original motto: The Lion Roars. Unofficial MGM slogan, also by Dietz. "More Stars than there Are in Heaven."

Arsène Lupin
French detective, originally a jewel thief, in novels by Maurice Leblanc: played in movies by Earle Williams (1917), Lionel Barrymore (1932), Charles Korvin (1944), Robert Lamoureaux (1957), Jean-Claude Brisby (1962). In two 1910 German movies, Lupin is the archenemy of Sherlock Holmes. The first Lupin novel was *The Exploits of Arsène Lupin* (1907)

Artemus Gordon
Jim West's partner, a master of disguise (TV series "The Wild, Wild West") : played by Ross Martin

Arthur Godfrey and His Friends
(TV series)
Announcers
Tony Marvin
His Friends:
Janette Davis, Bill Lawrence, Julius La Rosa (fired on the air on October 19, 1953 after singing "I'll Take Manhattan," because "He lacked humility"), Marion Marlowe, The Mariners, Lu Ann Simms, Carmel Quinn, McGuire Sisters, Chordettes, Haleloke
Theme Song:
"Seems Like Old Times"
Orchestra:
Archie Bleyer's (Bleyer was dismissed along with La Rosa)

Arthur's
New York City pool hall where "Fast" Eddie Felson's thumbs are broken for hustling pool (1961 movie *The Hustler*)

Artistry in Rhythm
Stan Kenton's theme song

Artoo Detoo
Princess Leia's small robot (R2-D2) (1977 movie *Star Wars*): played by 3'8" Kenny Baker

As the Stomach Turns
Soap opera take-off (TV series "The Carol Burnett Show")

Ashenden
British spy created (1928) by W. Somerset Maugham in novel *Ashenden; or The British Agent*

Ashford, Emmett Littleton
First black umpire (after 1966) in major league baseball (American League)

Asp, The
Silent henchman of Daddy Warbucks (comic strip "Orphan Annie")

Assassinations, U.S.

Assassin	*Assassinated*
John Wilkes Booth	Abraham Lincoln (1865)
Charles J. Guiteau	James Garfield (1881)
Leon Czolgosz	William McKinley (1901)
Giuseppe Zangara	Anton J. Cermak (1933)
Dr. Carl A. Weiss	Huey Long (1935)
Lee Harvey Oswald	John F. Kennedy (1963)
James Earl Ray	Martin Luther King, Jr. (1968)
Sirhan Sirhan	Robert Kennedy (1968)

Asta
Wire-hair terrier of Nick and Nora Charles (Movie/TV *The Thin Man*): played by Skippy in movies and winner of 1960 TV PATSY. In novel by Dashiell Hammett described as a Schnauzer

Astaire-Rogers movies
Flying Down to Rio (1933)
The Gay Divorcee (1933)
Roberta (1935)
Top Hat (1935)
Follow the Fleet (1936)
Swing Time (1936)
Shall We Dance? (1937)
Carefree (1938)
The Story of Vernon and Irene Castle (1939)
The Barkleys of Broadway (1949)
Dorothy Jordon was to have been Astaire's partner in *Flying Down to Rio* but she married producer Merian C. Cooper instead

Aston Martin DB-5
James Bond's battleship gray gadget-packed automobile issued to him by Q Branch: in the novel *Goldfinger* by Ian Fleming it is a DB-3. The three revolving license plates are: BMT 216A, 4711 EA 62, LU 6789. Some of the

car's gadgets (*Goldfinger* 1964, *Thunderball* 1965) are: Bullet-proof windows, front-mounted machine guns, rear oil dispenser, smoke screen, passenger seat ejector, rear bullet shield, extending wheel spinners

Astraea
Roman galley upon which Judah Ben-Hur was a slave oarsman (#41) (Lew Wallace's *Ben Hur*)

Astro
The Jetson's family dog (TV cartoon series "The Jetsons"): voice is Don Messick's

Astrodome
Roofed athletic stadium in Houston, Texas (location of Lyndon B. Johnson Spacecraft Center of NASA, hence the Astro-prefix) available for football (Houston Oilers of NFL), baseball (Houston Astros of National League), basketball (Houston Rockets of NBA), tennis (Billie Jean King defeated Bobby Riggs here), etc.

Athenia
Cunard liner, first ship sunk by enemy action in World War II, September 4, 1939. There were 292 U.S. citizens among the 1,400 passengers

Atlantic City, New Jersey
Location of all the streets mentioned in the game of Monopoly (American version). Site also of the Miss America Pageant (since 1921)

Atlantis
Legendary island in the Atlantic Ocean west of Gibraltar believed by Plato to have sunk into the ocean.

In comic books, Atlantis is the home of Sub-Mariner and the place where Aqualad was born

Atlantis
World War II German raider disguised under a number of foreign flags: piloted by Captain Bernhard Reger (1960 movie *Under Ten Flags*): played by Van Heflin

Atlantis
World's largest yacht, built (1974) by Aristotle Onassis' brother-in-law Stavros Niarchos: Onassis' yacht "Christina" had been the largest

Atom, The
Secret identity of Al Pratt (5′ tall): debut in All-American Comics #19, October 1940. Also, secret identity of scientist Ray Palmer: debut in Showcase Comics #34, October 1961

Atom, The

Secret identity of Ivy University professor Raymond Palmer (DC Comic Books). Debut: Showcase Comics #34, October 1961

Atomic Annie

First atomic cannon, United States, 1953

Attucks, Crispus

Negro-Indian leader killed in the Boston Massacre (March 5, 1770), a Black hero of the twentieth century

Crispus Attucks High School, Indianapolis, was attended by Oscar Robertson, who set many basketball school records there

Augie-Doggy

Doggie Daddy's puppy son (TV cartoon series "Huckleberry Hound"): voice of Daws Butler. Always addresses his Daddy as "Dear old Dad"

Auguste C. Dupin

Detective created by Edgar Allan Poe for the 1841 story "The Murders in the Rue Morgue," often called the first detective story

AuH$_2$O

"Goldwater," Senator Barry Goldwater's 1964 election slogan

Auld Lang Syne

Guy Lombardo's theme song; earlier he used "Comin' thru' the Rye." First broadcast from Roosevelt Grill, New York, 1929; now heard every New Year's Eve from the Waldorf-Astoria

Aunt Bee Taylor

Sheriff Andy Taylor's aunt (TV series "Andy Griffith Show"): played by Frances Bavier

Aunt Bluebelle

Lady who sells Scott Towels (TV commercials): played by Mae Questel, who has also done the voices of Betty Boop, Olive Oyl and Li'l Audrey

Aunt Clara

Samantha's absent-minded witch-aunt (TV series "Bewitched"): played by Marion Lorne

Aunt Em

Dorothy's aunt Emily (L. Frank Baum's *The Wizard of Oz*): played by Clara Blandick in 1939 movie, a role for which May Robson was first considered.

Aunt Harriet

Dick Grayson's aunt and Bruce Wayne's housekeeper. She is ignorant of their secret identity, Batman and Robin. She was played on TV by Madge Blake

Aunt Jemima

Brand name of popular syrup and pancake mix. Nancy Green was the original Aunt Jemima, at the Chicago World's Exposition of 1893. Radio series starring Harriette Widmer

Aunt Polly

Tom Sawyer's aunt (Mark Twain's novels *Tom Sawyer* and *Huckleberry Finn*): played in 1973 movie *Tom Sawyer* by Celeste Holm

Aurora Australis

The Southern Lights

Aurora Borealis

The Northern Lights

Australia

Capital: Canberra

State	Capital
New South Wales	Sydney
Queensland	Brisbane
South Australia	Adelaide
Tasmania	Hobart
Victoria	Melbourne
Western Australia	Perth
(Northern Territory	Darwin)

Autobiography of Alice B. Toklas, The

Autobiography of Gertrude Stein (1933). *What Is Remembered* is the actual autobiography of Alice B. Toklas

Automobile movie titles

1956: The Solid Gold Cadillac
1965: Yellow Rolls-Royce
1967: The Gnome-Mobile
1968: Chitty Chitty Bang Bang
1969: The Love Bug
1973: Herbie Rides Again

Autry, Gene

Cowboy star "America's Favorite Cowboy" (1907—   ) with his horse Champion. Made the singing cowboy popular. One of the owners of the American-League California Angels; owner of the Golden West radio network; owner of Flying A Production Company.

Theme: "Back in the Saddle Again"

Movie debut: *In Old Santa Fe* (1934)

Avalon

Isle of the blest, or dead, where King Arthur went after his death

Avenger

Captain Peter Blood's pirate ship (1935 movie *Captain Blood* with Errol Flynn)

Avenger, The

Leader of Justice, Inc.; real identity: Richard Henry Benson (adventure series by Kenneth Robeson, actually by Paul Ernst). Crew: Algernon "Smitty" Heathcote (6'9" tall), Fergus MacMurdie, Nellie Gray. First novel in series: *Justice Inc.* (1941)

Avengers, The

John Steed (Patrick Macnee); Mrs. Emma Peel (Diana Rigg); Tara King (Linda Thorson) (TV series made in Great Britain). Honor Blackman as Mrs. Cathy Gale was Macnee's first partner, then Elizabeth Sheppard, then Diana Rigg, and finally Linda Thorson

Avengers

Marvel comic book heroes of the 1960s. The group members have been The Hulk, Thor, Iron Man, Ant-Man, Wasp, Captain America, Giant-Man, Wonder Man, Hawkeye, The Scarlet Witch, Swordsman, Mantis, Moondragon and the Beast

Aviation Hall of Fame

At Dayton, Ohio

Orville and Wilbur Wright were first two elected (1962)

Awards

First place: blue ribbon; gold medal

Second place: red ribbon; silver medal

Third place: white ribbon; bronze medal

Axis Countries

World War II: Japan; Germany (includes Austria); Italy; Thailand; Bulgaria; Hungary; Romania; Finland

Axis Sally

Rita Louise Zucca (Italy); Mildred E. Gillars (Germany). The Japanese propaganda equivalent was Tokyo Rose

Ayesha

She Who Must Be Obeyed. "She" is queen of the Amahaggar people in the land of Kor (H. Rider Haggard's novel *She*)

B

B Bar B
> Bobby Benson's ranch in the Texas Big Bend country (H Bar O ranch while Hecker's H-O cereal was the sponsor)

BAR
> Browning Automatic Rifle

B. D.
> Character with no full name in Gary Trudeau's comic strip "Doonesbury": named after Yale quarterback Brian Cowling

B. O. Plenty
> Bob Oscar Plenty, ex-criminal who in 1946 married Gravel Gertie (Dick Tracy comic strip): their daughter is Sparkle

B. P. O. E.
> Benevolent and Protective Order of Elks, founded in 1868: headed by the Grand Exalted Ruler

B & W Trucking Company
> Trucking company owned by Vince Wolek (Anthony Ponzini) on the daytime serial "One Life to Live"

BDRX
> Television station in Bedrock (TV series "The Flintstones")

BMT 216A
> British license plate number on James Bond's Aston-Martin DB5 (movies: *Goldfinger, Thunderball.*) The two other numbers of the rotating license plate are 4711EA 62 and LU 6789

BR549

Phone number of Samples Sales (Junior Samples' Used Autos) (TV series "Hee Haw")

b.v.d.'s

Men's underwear: name from initials of the firm of Bradley, Voorhees, and Day

Baba-Looey

Quick Draw MacGraw's little sidekick burro (TV cartoon series): voice of Daws Butler

Babbitt and the Bromide, The

Dance scene featuring Fred Astaire and Gene Kelly (1946 movie "Ziegfield Follies"). Both Babbitt and Bromide are "square" types, the first from the writings of Sinclair Lewis, the second from Gelett Burgess

Babe

Paul Bunyan's blue ox, 42 ax handles and a plug of chewing tobacco between the ears. Found during the winter of the blue snow.

Babe, The

Nickname of George Herman Ruth (1893–1948). Babe was the nickname of other ballplayers and athletes, too, like Babe Pinelli, National League infielder and later umpire, as well as of Oliver Hardy and other actors and actresses

Babe Ruth Day

April 27, 1947, celebrated at Yankee Stadium

Babieca

El Cid's horse

Babs

Chester Riley's daughter (radio/TV series "The Life of Riley"): on TV played by Lugene Sanders (with William Bendix) and Gloria Winters (with Jackie Gleason); on radio, by Sharon Douglas, Barbara Eiler, and Peggy Conklin

Babs Gordon

Daughter of Commissioner Gordon and real identity of Batgirl (comic book series)

Baby

Pet leopard whose favorite song is "I Can't Give You Anything But Love, Baby" (1938 movie *Bringing Up Baby* also starring Cary Grant): real name of leopard is Nissa

Baby Birds

A nickname of the Baltimore Orioles baseball team

Baby Dumpling

Alexander's nickname as an infant (Dagwood and Blondie's son): played in movies by Larry Simms, on TV by Stuffy Singer and Peter Robbins, on radio by Leon Ledorix, Larry Simms, Jeffrey Silver, and Tommy Cook

Baby Huey

Large cartoon goose with a voracious appetite (Harvey comic books). An Army helicopter has been nicknamed "Baby Huey"

Baby LeRoy

LeRoy Overacker, baby actor who appeared with W. C. Fields in *Tillie and Gus* (1933), *It's a Gift* (1934), *The Old-Fashioned Way* (1934)

Baby Roo

Kanga's baby kangaroo (Winnie-the-Pooh stories)

Baby Snooks

Four-year-old character played on stage and radio by Fannie Brice. In the 1936 Ziegfield Follies, Bob Hope played her father, Lancelot Higgins; on radio, it was Hanley Stafford (real name, Alfred John Austin)

Bacall-Bogart movies

To Have and Have Not (1945)

Two Guys from Milwaukee (1946)

The Big Sleep (1946)

Dark Passage (1947)

Key Largo (1948)

They were scheduled to make *Melville Goodwin, U.S.A.* prior to Bogart's death (The movie's title was changed to Top Secret Affair with Kirk Douglas and Susan Hayward)

Bachelor at Large

Comic strip created by Paul Morgan (Tab Hunter) (TV series "The Tab Hunter Show")

Back in the Saddle Again

Gene Autry's theme song, composed by Autry and Ray Whitley

Backstage Wife

"The story of Mary Noble, a little Iowa girl who married Larry Noble, handsome matinee idol, dream sweetheart of a million other women, and her struggle to keep his love in the complicated atmosphere of backstage life" (radio series "Backstage Wife")

Backus, Jim
Voice of Mr. Magoo; the rich Herbert Updike of the Alan Young radio show; Joan Davis' husband, Bradley J. Stevens, on TV's "I Married Joan"; and many other roles in movies and other media, notably Thurston Howell III on the TV series "Gilligan's Island"

Backwards
Three events won by moving backwards
1. Tug of war
2. Back stroke (swimming)
3. Rowing

Bacteria
Warring nation of which Benzino Napaloni (Jack Oakie) is dictator: ally of Tomania (1940 movie *The Great Dictator*)

Bader, Douglas
World War II British ace who had lost both legs before the war. Played by Kenneth More in 1956 movie *Reach for the Sky*

Badges

	Wearer	*Actor*	*in*
1	Investigator John St. John	Jack Warden	TV series "Jigsaw John"
3	Egbert Sousé	W.C. Fields	1940 movie *The Bank Dick*
17	Private eye Oliver Hardy	Oliver Hardy	1945 movie *The Bullfighters*
25	Detective Alex Bronkov	Jack Palance	TV series "Bronk"
26	Police Captain Wade Griffin	Lorne Greene	TV series "Griff"
29	Officer Stan Laurel	Stan Laurel*	1933 movie *The Midnight Patrol*
82	Officer Oliver Hardy	Oliver Hardy*	1933 movie *The Midnight Patrol*
106	Officer Mulligan	James Burke	1937 movie *Dead End*
150	David Toma	Tony Musante	TV series "Toma"

609	Plainclothes detective Tony Baretta	Robert Blake	TV series
714	Sergeant Joe Friday	Jack Webb	TV series "Dragnet"**
723	Officer Gunther Toody	Joe E. Ross	TV series "Car 54 Where Are You?"
744	Officer Pete Malloy	Martin Milner	TV series "Adam-12"
903	Officer Anthony X. Russell	Henry Fonda	1968 movie *Madigan*
1432	Officer Francis Muldoon	Fred Gwynne	TV series "Car 54 Where Are You?"
2208	San Francisco Chief of Detectives Amy Prentiss	Jessica Walter	TV series "Amy Prentiss"
2211	San Francisco Detective Harry Callahan	Clint Eastwood	1971 movie *Dirty Harry*
2430	Officer Jim Reed	Kent McCord	TV series "Adam-12"
4866	Los Angeles Police Department Officer Tom Porter		TV series "Adam-12"
5369	Officer James Aloysius O'Malley	Pat O'Brien	1937 movie *The Great O'Malley*
5466	Officer O'Hare	Jack Carson	1944 movie *Arsenic and Old Lace*
5618	Officer Charles Kane	James Whitmore	1968 movie *Madigan*
19076	Frank Serpico	Al Pacino	1973 movie *Serpico*
20747	New York City Detective Joe Leland	Frank Sinatra	1968 movie *The Detective*

---

*Their police car call sign is Car 13
**Series called "Badge 714" in reruns

Baer Brothers

Heavyweight boxers: Max (Maximilian), champion 1934; Buddy. Both became movie actors; Buddy wrestled a bull in 1951 *Quo Vadis?* and later served as sergeant-at-arms of California State Senate

Baer quintuplets

Born January 5, 1973: Douglas, Elizabeth, Leslie, Thomas, Vickie

Baker Street Irregulars

Organization (one of several such under various names) of Sherlock Holmes enthusiasts: founded in 1933 by Christopher Morley, and named for the group of Holmes' aides, headed by Wiggins who appeared in the Arthur Conan Doyle Sherlock Holmes stories. Two of the most famous members were Franklin D. Roosevelt and Harry S. Truman

Balkan states

Present: Yugoslavia, Albania, Greece, Romania, Bulgaria, European Turkey

Baldy

Large trained raven that appeared in the 1963 movie "The Birds"

Ballad of Cat Ballou

Sung by Nat King Cole, with Stubby Kaye as his fellow shouter (1965 movie *Cat Ballou*)

Ballad of Paladin

Theme song of TV series "Have Gun—Will Travel" starring Richard Boone: sung by Johnny Western

Baloo

Bear in Rudyard Kipling's *The Jungle Book*. In Walt Disney's 1966 movie, his voice was that of Phil Harris

Baltimore and Potomac Railroad Station

Washington, D.C., site of the assassination of President James A. Garfield by Charles J. Guiteau, July 2, 1881. Garfield lived for 80 days in which time he signed one extradition paper. He died September 19, 1881

Balto

Dog that led a sled team through a blizzard to Nome, Alaska, in the winter of 1925, to bring serum to halt an epidemic among the Eskimos (sled driver was Gunnar Kaasen). A statue of Balto by F. G. Roth stands near the zoo in Central Park, New York

Baltz, Stephen
   11-year-boy who survived the midair collision over New York City between a United DC8 and a TWA Super Constellation December 16, 1960. Stephen later died, bringing the total dead to 140. (6 died on the ground). Sir Edmund Hillary was to have flown in the United jet but missed his flight.
Bambino, The
   Nickname of Babe Ruth
Banana Nose
   Nickname of jockey Eddie Arcaro
Banana Splits
   Bingo, a gorilla (voice: Daws Butler)
   Drooper, a lion (voice: Allan Melvin)
   Fleagle, a dog (voice: Paul Winchell)
   Snorky, a baby elephant (voice: Don Messick)
   They live in Hocus Pocus Park, where their cuckoo clock always reads 6:55 (The bird is called Kookie). Their theme is "Tra-la-la Song." Fleagle is the only one who doesn't wear glasses
Bandari
   Native tribe living in Bengali jungle with the Phantom (comic strip and books)
Band of Renown
   Name of Les Brown's orchestra
Band of a Thousand Melodies
   Larry Funk's orchestra
Banjo
   Lucky Jenkins' horse (Hopalong Cassidy movies). Jenkins is played by Russell Hayden
Banjo Eyes
   Nickname of comedian Eddie Cantor
Bank of Italy
   Name of Bank of America before the founder, Amadeo P. Giannini, changed it
Bannister, Roger
   First person to break 4 minutes for the mile: 3:59.4, May 6, 1954, Oxford, England, in a meet between British AAA and Oxford University. Race paced by Chris Brasher and Chris Chataway. Bannister wore the number 41 on his jersey that day
Bara, Theda
   Silent movie actress, nicknamed The Vamp: real name

Theodosia Goodman (1890–1955). Bara is "Arab" spelled backwards and Theda is an anagram for "death"

Barbara Anne
Presidential yacht used by President Dwight D. Eisenhower

Barbara Ross
Kidnapper (Susan Dey) who shot and wounded Steve Keller (Michael Douglas) on Montgomery Street in San Francisco (TV series "The Streets of San Francisco")

Barbarella
Heroine of French comic strip drawn by Jean-Claude Forest. She lives in the 401st Century. In the 1968 French-Italian movie portrayed by Jane Fonda

Barbarians
Comic book muscular super-hero barbarians (Marvel Comics)
Ka-Zar, Lord of the Hidden Jungle
   (Zabu is his sabertooth tiger)
Kull, The Destroyer
Thongor, Warrior of Lost Lemuria
Conan, The Barbarian
Gulliver Jones, Warrior of Mars

Barbe, Jane
Woman whose recorded voice has given the time over the telephone since 1964. She also says, "I'm sorry, but the number you have dialed . . ."

Barbie
Teenage doll created by Jack Ryan, Zsa Zsa Gabor's sixth husband and manufactured by Mattel, Inc. Her friends are Kelly, Skipper, Francie, P.J., and Ken, her boyfriend

Barbours
Family who lived in Sea Cliff district of San Francisco (radio series "One Man's Family"). The family settled there in 1879

Bar-B-Q
Sign in front of Arizona cafe in which killer Duke Mantee holes up for a time (1936 movie *The Petrified Forest*)

Bard of Avon, The
Nickname of William Shakespeare

Bard of Ayrshire, The
Nickname of Robert Burns

Barkley

Family (TV series "The Big Valley") living on the Barkley Road, 4 miles outside Stockton, California

Victoria, Mother (Barbara Stanwyck)

Jarrod, son (Richard Long)

Nick (Nicholas), son (Peter Breck)

Eugene, son (Charles Briles)

Heath, son (Lee Majors)

Audra, daugher (Linda Evans)

Tom Barkley (1813–1870), Victoria's deceased husband, was father of all the children

In one episode Audra kills the man (Handy Random, played by James Whitmore) who killed the man who killed her father, Tom

Barlow, Howard

Conductor of the Voice of Firestone Orchestra (radio)

Barnabus Collins

Resident of Collinwood in Maine (TV daytime serial "Dark Shadows"): a 200-year-old vampire played by Jonathan Frid

Barnaby Jones

Private investigator (TV series "Barnaby Jones"): played by Buddy Ebsen. His office number: 615; his phone number: 467-7935

Barnard, Dr. Christian

Performed first successful heart transplant. Capetown, South Africa, December 3, 1967, on Louis Washkansky, who lived for 18 days

Barney Google

Novelty tune recorded by its composer, Billy Rose, in 1923: title from cartoon character by Billy DeBeck and later Fred Lasswell. Barney's horse was Spark Plug

Barnum, P. T.

Phineas Taylor Barnum (1810–1891), American showman

His most famous exhibits and clients: Jenny Lind, General Tom Thumb, Jumbo the Elephant, the Siamese Twins (Chang and Eng), the Bearded Lady (Josephine Clofullia), Commodore Nutt, Wild Man of Borneo, The Feejee Mermaid, Joyce Heth. Called The Prince of Humbugs, Barnum is credited with saying, "There's a sucker born every minute." In the 1934 movie *The Mighty Barnum*, Wallace Beery played Barnum

Baron, The

Reformed British jewel thief John Mannering (detective novels by Anthony Morton, whose pen name is John Creasey). First novel: *Meet the Baron* (1937) of 47 books. Played on TV by Steve Forrest.

Barracuda

Submarine commanded by Commander Paul Stevenson (1959 movie *Up Periscope*)

Barrymore

Family name of actors Lionel (1878–1954), Ethel (1879–1959), John (1882–1942): they played together only in the 1932 movie *Rasputin and the Empress*. Father: Maurice (1845–1905), born Herbert Blythe

Barsoomian

Inhabitant of the planet Mars (native name, Barsoom), (Edgar Rice Burroughs' John Carter Martian series)

Bartley House

1,200-room New York hotel of which Kathleen "Katy" O'Connor is assistant manager to James Devery (TV series "The Ann Sothern Show") Katy was played by Miss Sothern, Devery by Don Porter

Barton, Clara

Founder (July 1, 1881) of the American Red Cross Society

Bar-20 Ranch

Hopalong Cassidy's cattle ranch near Crescent City

Baseball commissioners

Kenesaw "Mountain" Landis (1920–1944)
Albert "Happy" Chandler (1945–1951); Ford Frick (1951–1965); General William Eckart (1965–1969); Bowie Kuhn (1969–   )

Baseball Hall of Fame

Cooperstown, New York: opened June 12, 1939
First 5 members elected (1936): Ty Cobb (222 votes), Babe Ruth (215), Honus Wagner (215), Christy Mathewson (205), Walter Johnson (189)

Baseball stadiums, major leagues

City	Team	Stadium
Atlanta	Braves	Atlanta Stadium
Baltimore	Orioles	Memorial Stadium
Boston	Red Sox	Fenway Park
California	Angels	Anaheim Stadium
Chicago	Cubs	Wrigley Field

Chicago	White Sox	White Sox Park
Cincinnati	Reds	Riverfront Stadium
Cleveland	Indians	Municipal Stadium
Detroit	Tigers	Tiger Stadium
Houston	Astros	Astrodome
Kansas City	Royals	Royals Stadium
Los Angeles	Dodgers	Dodger Stadium
Milwaukee	Brewers	Milwaukee County Stadium
Minnesota	Twins	Metropolitan Stadium
Montreal	Expos	Jarry Park
New York	Mets	Shea Stadium
New York	Yankees	Yankee Stadium
Oakland	Athletics	Oakland-Alameda County Coliseum
Philadelphia	Phillies	Veterans Stadium
Pittsburgh	Pirates	Three Rivers Stadium
St. Louis	Cardinals	Busch Memorial Stadium
San Diego	Padres	San Diego Stadium
San Francisco	Giants	Candlestick Park
Seattle	Mariners	The Kingdome
Texas	Rangers	Arlington Stadium, Arlington (near Dallas-Fort Worth)
Toronto	Blue Jays	Exhibition Stadium

Basil Hallward

Young artist who painted the picture of Dorian Gray in Oscar Wilde's novel

Basketball Hall of Fame

At Springfield College, Springfield, Mass., where Dr. Naismith invented the game. Opened February 18, 1968, to the public. First elected member was Dr. Forrest Clare "Phog" Allen

Bass, Sam

American western outlaw. Played in movies by Howard Duff (*Calamity Jane and Sam Bass* 1949); Nestor Paiva (*Badman's Territory* 1946); William Bishop (*The Texas Rangers* 1951); Leonard Penn (*Outlaw Women* 1952); Rex Marlow (*Deadwood 76* 1971)

Bastille Day

July 14: France's national holiday. The Bastille, a Paris prison, was stormed and taken this day in 1789

Bates Motel

Motel near town of Fairvale where Marion Crane (Janet Leigh) is stabbed to death on Saturday, Dec. 12, 1959, in the shower of cabin #1 (of 12 cabins) (1960 movie *Psycho*)

Batgirl

Secret identity of Babs Gordon, daughter of Commissioner Gordon (comic book series): played on TV by Yvonne Craig. First appearance: D.C. Comics #359.

Batman

Secret identity of Bruce Wayne (played in TV series by Adam West; on radio by Stacy Harris, Gary Merrill, and Matt Crowley; in 1950s movie serial played by Robert Lowery), Debut: Detective Comics #27, May 1939; Batman Comics, Spring 1940 (created by Bob Kane). His sidekick is Robin. In 1943 movie serial *The Batman*, Batman was played by Lewis Wilson, Robin by Douglas Croft. In the 1949 movie serial *Batman and Robin*, Robert Lowery was Batman, John Duncan was Robin. Adam West was Batman in the 1966 movie *Batman and the Fearsome Foursomes*

Batman's enemies

In TV series "Batman":

Foe	Played by
Catwoman	Julie Newmar (also Eartha Kitt; first by Lee Meriwether)
The Joker	Cesar Romero
The Penguin	Burgess Meredith
The Riddler	Frank Gorshin, John Astin

Batter

6 ways a batter can get on base without getting a hit: error; base on balls; catcher drops third strike; hit by pitch; fielder's choice; interference by catcher

Batting helmets

Introduced in major league baseball by the Brooklyn Dodgers in 1941

Battle Hymn of the Republic, The

Words written by Julia Ward Howe in 1862 to the tune of "John Brown's Body"

Battle of Bunker Hill
Actually took place (June 17, 1775) on Breed's Hill, where the Bunker Hill monument is located, across the Charles River from Boston: "Don't shoot until you see the whites of their eyes"

Battle of the Century
Superman vs. the Amazing Spider-Man On the suggestion of a young reader DC Comics and Marvel Comics produced a $2.00 comic book in February 1976 in which the pair battled to a draw

Battle of the Coral Sea
First modern naval engagement (first carrier battle) in which surface ships did not exchange a single shot or sight each other visually (May 7-8, 1942)

Battle of New Orleans
January 8, 1815: fought two weeks after the Treaty of Ghent had been signed ending the War of 1812. U.S. forces under Andrew Jackson defeated British under Edward Pakenham

Battle of New Orleans
Popular song by Johnny Horton: banned on Canadian radio when Queen Elizabeth II visited Canada in 1960

Battle of the Sexes
Tennis match, Houston Astrodome, Sept. 20, 1973, in which Billie Jean King defeated Bobby Riggs 6–4, 6–3, 6–3 before 30,492 spectators (largest live audience for tennis) and television viewers in 37 countries: Riggs had swept the Wimbledon championships in 1939, 4 years before Mrs. King's birth

Battle of the Sexes
Match race between Ruffian, a filly (winner of 7 out of 7 starts), and Kentucky Derby winner Foolish Pleasure, held July 6, 1975, at Belmont Park, New York. Ruffian fell during the race, breaking her right leg, and had to be destroyed the next day

Batwoman
Secret identity of Kathy Kane (comic books): debut in DC Comics #233. Batgirl is another (and later) character

Baxter
Name of family for whom Hazel Burke is housekeeper and maid (cartoon/TV series "Hazel"). Ted Key created the cartoons in the *Saturday Evening Post*. On TV Hazel was played by Shirley Booth; George Baxter (Mr. B) by

Don De Fore, Dorothy by Whitney Blake, Harold (Sport) by Bobby Buntrock

Baxter Building
New York City heacquarters of the Fantastic Four (comic book series)

Bay City
City where TV serial "Another World" takes place

Bayport
The Hardy Boys' home town. They live on the corner of High and Elm Streets. They attended Bayport High School

Bazooka
Large musical instrument made of a kitchen funnel and some pipe, invented by Bob Burns in his comedy skits on radio. The name was later applied to a World War II weapon

Be My Love
Mario Lanza's theme song: first sung in the 1950 movie *The Toast of New Orleans*

Be Prepared
Boy Scout's motto

Beach Boys, The
Rock 'n' Roll group: among its members have been Brian Wilson, Carl Wilson, David Marks, Al Jardine, Bruce Johnston, Mike Love, Dennis Wilson (Glen Campbell was a substitute for a short time and Daryl Dragon and Toni Tennile of the Captain and Tennile were both once members). The group founded Brother Records

Beagle, H.M.S.
Ship on which Charles Darwin made his scientific voyage (1831–1836) to Patagonia and the Pacific and thence around the world back to England

Beagle, Boys, The
Foes of Scrooge McDuck (Walt Disney character). Uniform numbers of original members: 671-176, 617-716, 176-671. Others later were SS-666, Strike 3, D103, 1-176, 186-802 (Grandpa)

Beal, Frank P.
Inventor of paddle tennis: late 1940s

Beam Ends
Errol Flynn's first novel, completed in 1937. Other novel: *Showdown* (1946). His autobiography is titled *My Wicked, Wicked Ways* (1959)

Bean, Judge Roy
"The Law West of the Pecos": played by Walter Brennan in 1940 movie *The Westerner* and by Paul Newman in 1972 movie *Judge Roy Bean*. In a TV series, Edgar Buchanan played the part. In real life, Roy's brother Josh Bean was first mayor of San Diego, California

Beanie
Office boy of the *Daily Planet*, under Jimmy Olsen (radio series "Superman"): played by Jackson Beck

Beany and Cecil
Puppet show based on characters created by Bob Clampett. Beany is the boy with a propeller hat, his sidekick is Cecil, the seasick sea serpent
(1950s puppet show; 1961–62 cartoon series) Other puppets: Caboose Goose, Captain Huff 'n Puff, Hunny Bear, D. J. (Dishonest John), Hopalong Wong

Bear Band Jamboree
Walt Disney characters:
Five Bear Rugs Band: Zeke, Zeb, Ted, Fred, Tennessee (Sammy sits with his teddy bear)
Entertainers: Henry, the M.C.; Wendall, Big Al (sings "Blood on the Saddle"), Trixie.
Liverlips, Terrance, Gomer, Teddi Barra (sings on a swing)
Sun Bonnet: Bunny, Bubbles, Beulah

Beatles
George Harrison (Feb. 25, 1943–   )
John (Winston) Lennon (Oct. 9, 1940–   )
(James) Paul McCartney (June 18, 1940–   )
Ringo Starr (Richard Starkey) (July 7, 1940–   ), who replaced Pete Best as drummer
Previous members: Pete Best, Stu Sutcliffe (who died in Hamburg, Germany), Tommy Moore, Norman Chapman
The Beatles had more (20) number one records than any other artist or group. They were the backup group for Tony Sheridan in Hamburg, and called the Beat Boys. Other earlier names: Quarrymen, Johnny and the Moondogs, Silver Beatles, The Rainbow.
Their first hit was "Love Me Do" (Oct. 1962). First appearance in U.S. on Ed Sullivan Show, Feb. 9, 1964 (Neilson figured 73,700,000 viewers); they sang "She Loves You" and "I Want to Hold Your Hand." McCartney's wife

Linda and Lennon's wife Yoko Ono were both born in Scarsdale, N.Y., and attended Sarah Lawrence College

Beatles' movies
A Hard Day's Night (1964), *Help* (1965; original title, "Eight Arms to Hold You"), *Yellow Submarine* (1968), *Let It Be* (1970); *Magical Mystery Tour* (for TV, 1967)

Beatrice
Stuart McMillan's mother (TV series *McMillan and Wife*): played by Mildred Natwick

Beau James
Nickname of New York City Mayor Jimmie Walker: title of his biography (1949) by Gene Fowler. Portrayed in 1957 movie *Beau James* by Bob Hope

Beauregard
Pappy of Bret and Bart Maverick (TV series "Maverick"): played by James Garner

Beauregard
Beauregard Chaulmoogra Frontenac de Montmingle Bugleboy, bloodhound in Pogo comic strip

Beauregard, Jr.
Sleeping hound dog (TV series "Hee Haw")

Beautia
Captain Marvel's girlfriend, daughter of Dr. Sivana, the World's Wickedest Scientist. Her brother is Magnificus

Beautiful Dreamer
Favorite song (by Stephen Foster) of Mighty Joe Young (1949 movie *Mighty Joe Young*) and of Walter Mitty (Danny Kaye) in 1947 movie *The Secret Life of Walter Mitty*

Beauty
Horse ridden by Joan Crawford in 1954 movie *Johnny Guitar,* by Clark Gable in 1952 movie *Lone Star,* and by Elizabeth Taylor in 1953 movie *Giant*

Becky Sharp
Heroine of William Makepeace Thackeray's *Vanity Fair.* Title of first full Technicolor film (1935) in which Miriam Hopkins played Becky. In this film Thelma Catherine Ryan, later Mrs. Richard M. Nixon, played as an extra

Becky Thatcher
Tom Sawyer's girlfriend

Bedrock
Home-town of the Flintstones (TV cartoon); population 2560; town paper *Bedrock Gazette*

Beer Slogans

Hamms—America's Classic Premium Beer

Olympia—It's the Water

Coors—Brewed with Pure Rocky Mountain Spring Water

Schlitz—The Beer That Made Milwaukee Famous

Black Label—The World's Leading Internationally Brewed Beer

Budweiser—King of Beers

Piel's—The Light Beer of Broadway Fame

Beer that Made Milwaukee Famous

Schlitz beer, but originally the slogan was Miller Beer's. It was coined by the father of actor Robert Stack

Beery brothers

Actors: Noah (1884–1946) and Wallace (1889–1949; born and died on April Fool's Day). Noah Beery, Jr., was prominent in movies and TV. Wallace won an Oscar in 1931/32 for *The Champ*

Beetle Bailey

GI in Mort Walker cartoon strip (begun 1950). His eyes are never shown. He is the brother of Lois Flagston, of the "Hi and Lois" strip, drawn by Addison (a pen name of Mort Walker). On TV cartoon series, Howard Morris is Beetle's voice

Believe It Or Not!

Newspaper cartoon of unusual, hard-to-believe facts from throughout the world first drawn by Robert L(eRoy) Ripley in 1918. His first published drawing appeared in the New York *Globe* December 19, 1918. "Believe It Or Not!" became a radio program on NBC in 1930. There have been many spin-off features. Ripley first planned to call the facts "Chumps and Champs" as they originally involved sport feats

Bell X-1

First airplane (officially) to exceed the speed of sound, flown October 14, 1947, by Major Charles E. Yeager. Plane nicknamed Glamorous Glennis

Belle

Lorenzo Jones' wife: played by Betty Garde and Lucille Wall

Bellerophon, H.M.S.

Ship on which Napoleon made his formal surrender, July 15, 1815, after Waterloo. Captain Maitland commanding, off the port of Rochefort

Bellus

Star that collides with and destroys the Earth August 12. 42 people escape in a rocketship to the planet of Bellus, named Zyra (1951 movie *When Worlds Collide,* from 1932 novel of same title by Edwin Balmer and Philip Wylie, in which the new planet is Bronson Beta)

Belts, Judo

White belt (lowest), Brown belt (3 grades), Black belt (10 degrees)*

Ben Gunn

Pirate marooned on Treasure Island (not by Captain Flint, but by another unnamed pirate): he dug up the treasure. The first thing he wanted when he saw Jim Hawkins was a piece of cheese (Robert Louis Stevenson's *Treasure Island*)

Ben-Hur

Novel by General Lew Wallace published 1880 while he was Governor of New Mexico territory. (The movie of 1959 has won the most Oscars with 11). The title role has been played in the movies by Ramon Novarro (1925) and Charlton Heston (1959)

Benjamin

Bobbie Lee's rag doll which Billy Joe McAllister accidentally dropped off the Tallahatchee Bridge (1976 movie *Ode to Billy Joe*)

Bennett

Family name of actresses Constance, Joan, and Barbara. Father: Richard (1873–1944)

Bennett, Floyd

Pilot who flew Admiral Richard Evelyn Byrd over the North Pole (1926). When Byrd flew over the South Pole, he dropped an American flag weighted with a stone from Bennett's grave in Arlington National Cemetery. The two shared the same birthday, Oct. 25, Byrd born 1888, Bennett 1890

Benson Medal

British literary award: named after the founder A. C. Benson

---

*6th thru 8th degree may wear Red and White belt: 9th and 10th degree may wear a solid Red belt

Bensonhurst O-7741

Phone number in Ralph and Alice Kramden's Bensonhurst (Brooklyn) apartment (TV series "The Honeymooners")

Benzoo

Bengal tiger: mascot of the Cincinnati Bengals' football team

Beppo

Superman's super monkey (comic book)

Beretta .25

Automatic pistol used by James Bond for 15 years (until *Dr. No*) after which Q issues him a Walther PPK 7.65 mm, which he wears in a Berns Martin triple-draw holster, and a .38 calibre Smith and Wesson Centennial Airweight revolver. He has also used a .45 Colt and a Savage 99F rifle with a Weatherby 6 × 62 scope

Bergen, Edgar

His dummies: Charlie McCarthy, Mortimer Snerd, Effie Klinker, Podine Puffington

Berle, Milton

Uncle Miltie, Mr. Television, popular TV comedian. He debuted in movies as a baby supposedly thrown off a train but rescued by Pearl White in an episode of the serial "The Perils of Pauline" (1914)

Bernard

Sea Hag's vulture (Popeye cartoons, Thimble Theatre)

Bernard Mergendeiler

Name of Jules Feiffer's comic strip character "The Born Loser"

Bernardo

Deaf Servant of Don Diego de la Vega (Zorro) (TV series "The Mark of Zorro"): played by Gene Sheldon

Bert

Sesame Street muppet, who lives with Ernie, Bert's birthday is on July 26 (TV's "Sesame Street"): voice is that of Frank Oz

Bertha

Boob McNutt's Siberian cheesehound purchased on January 24, 1925 (Rube Goldberg's comic strip "Boob McNutt")

Bertha Cool

Woman detective in novels by A. A. Fair (Erle Stanley Gardner); she is in her 60s, weighs over 200 lbs.

Berwanger, Jay

First winner of the Heisman Trophy (1935) and first player drafted by National Football league team (Philadelphia, 1936)

Bessie, the Yaller Cow

Paul Bunyan's blue ox Babe's mate

Best Man Wins

First movie (1911) produced (by the British Horsley Brothers) in Hollywood, starring Tom Mix's future wife Victoria Forde. *The Law of the Range* (1911) is also said to be the first Hollywood-produced picture

Best Selling Novels

1975: *Ragtime* by E. L. Doctorow

1974: *Centennial* by James A. Michener

1973: *Jonathan Livingston Seagull by* Richard Bach

1972: *Jonathan Livingston Seagull* by Richard Bach

1971: *Wheels* by Arthur Hailey

1970: *Love Story* by Erich Segal

1969: *Portnoy's Complaint* by Philip Roth

1968: *Airport* by Arthur Hailey

1967: *The Arrangement* by Elia Kazan

1966: *Valley of the Dolls* by Jacqueline Susann

1965: *The Source* by James A. Michener

1964: *The Spy Who Came in from the Cold* by John Le Carré

1963: *The Shoes of the Fisherman* by Morris L. West

1962: *Ship of Fools* by Katherine Anne Porter

1961: *The Agony and the Ecstasy* by Irving Stone

1960: *Advise and Consent* by Allen Drury

1959: *Exodus* by Leon Uris

1958: *Doctor Zhivago* by Boris Pasternak

1957: *By Love Possessed* by James Gould Cozzens

1956: *Don't Go Near the Water* by William Brinkley

1955: *Marjorie Morningstar* by Herman Wouk

1954: *Not As a Stranger* by Morton Thompson

1953: *Battle Cry* by Leon Uris

1952: *The Silver Chalice* by Thomas B. Costain

1951: *From Here to Eternity* by James Jones

1950: *The Cardinal* by Henry Morton Robinson

1949: *The Egyptian* by Mika Waltari

1948: *The Big Fisherman* by Lloyd C. Douglas

1947: *The Miracle of the Bells* by Russell Janney

1946: *The King's General* by Daphne du Maurier

1945: *Forever Amber* by Kathleen Winsor
1944: *Strange Fruit* by Lillian Smith
1943: *The Robe* by Lloyd C. Douglas
1942: *The Song of Bernadette* by Franz Werfel
1941: *The Keys of the Kingdom* by A. J. Cronin
1940: *How Green Was My Valley* by Richard Llewellyn
1939: *The Grapes of Wrath* by John Steinbeck
1938: *The Yearling* by Marjorie Kinnan Rawlings
1937: *Northwest Passage* by Kenneth Roberts
1936: *Gone With the Wind* by Margaret Mitchell
1935: *Green Light* by Lloyd C. Douglas
1934: *So Red the Rose* by Stark Young
1933: *Anthony Adverse* by Hervey Allen
1932: *The Fountain* by Charles Morgan
1931: *The Good Earth* by Pearl S. Buck
1930: *Cimarron* by Edna Ferber
1929: *All Quiet on the Western Front* by Erich Maria Remarque
1928: *The Bridge of San Luis Rey* by Thornton Wilder
1927: *Elmer Gantry* by Sinclair Lewis
1926: *The Private Life of Helen of Troy* by John Erskine
1925: *Soundings* by A. Hamilton Gibbs
1924: *So Big* by Edna Ferber
1923: *Black Oxen* by Gertrude Atherton
1922: *If Winter Comes* by A. S. M. Hutchinson
1921: *Main Street* by Sinclair Lewis
1920: *The Man of the Forest* by Zane Grey
1919: *The Four Horsemen of the Apocalypse* by V. Blasco Ibañez
1918: *The U. P. Trail* by Zane Grey
1917: *Mr. Britling Sees It Through* by H. G. Wells
1916: *Seventeen* by Booth Tarkington
1915: *The Turmoil* by Booth Tarkington
1914: *The Eyes of the World* by Harold Bell Wright
1913: *Pollyanna* by Eleanor H. Porter
1912: *The Harvester* by Gene Stratton Porter
1911: *The Broad Highway* by Jeffrey Farnol
1910: *The Rosary* by Florence Barclay
1909: *The Inner Shrine* by Basil King (published anonymously)
1908: *Mr. Crewe's Career* by Winston Churchill
1907: *The Lady of the Decoration* by Frances Little
1906: *Coniston* by Winston Churchill

1905: *The Marriage of William Ashe* by Mrs. Humphrey Ward
1904: *The Crossing* by Winston Churchill
1903: *Lady Rose's Daughter* by Mrs. Humphrey Ward
1902: *The Virginian* by Owen Wister
1901: *Graustark* by George Barr McCutcheon
1900: *To Have and To Hold* by Mary Johnston
1899: *David Harum* by Edward Noyes Westcott
1898: *When Knighthood Was in Flower* by Charles Major
1897: *Quo Vadis* by Henryk Sienkiewicz
1896: *Tom Grogan* by F. Hopkinson Smith
1895: *Beside the Bonnie Brier Bush* by Ian Maclaren

Beta
Spaceship of Ranger Rod Brown (Cliff Robertson) (TV series "Rod Brown of the Rocket Rangers")

Beth
Matt Helms' wife, whom he eventually divorced (detective story series "Matt Helm" by Donald Hamilton). She received custody of their children: Matt Jr., Warren, Betsy (oldest to youngest)

Betty Boop
Doll-like cartoon character, with a face modeled after Helen Kane's, created by Max Fleischer in 1915. In movie cartoons her voice was Helen Kane's, as it was in the 1950 movie *Three Little Words* in which Debbie Reynolds played Helen Kane. The first Betty Boop talkie cartoon was *Dizzy Dishes* (1930). On radio, Mae Questel was Betty Boop's voice

Betty Jones
Private-eye Barnaby Jones' assistant and daughter-in-law (played in TV series by Lee Merriwether, Miss America, 1955)

Betty Lou
Teen Angel's girlfriend (7-Up commercials)

Betty Lou Barnes
Girlfriend of Tailspin Tommy: played in 1934 movie serial by Patricia Farr, in 1935 movie serial by Jean Rogers; in 1940 movie series by Marjorie Reynolds.

Beulah
Nickname of buzzer on radio/TV's "Truth or Consequences"

Beulah, the maid

First played on radio program "Fibber McGee and Molly" by Marlin Hurt, a white male. It later became a radio show as "The Marlin Hurt and Beulah Show" and finally "Beulah." On radio, Beulah was also played by Bob Corley, Lillian Randolph, Hattie McDaniel, and Louise Beavers. On TV Ethel Waters, Hattie McDaniel, and Louise Beavers played the part

Beulah and Beauregard

Two offspring of Borden's Elsie the cow and Elmer the bull

Beverly Hills

California city, a suburb just west of Hollywood in Los Angeles, noted as the home of the movie stars. Will Rogers was its mayor.

Bibb

The Michelin tireman in ads: in French his name is Bibendum

Bible Designed to be Read as Living Literature

Book in which James Bond keeps his Walther PPK 7.65 mm automatic; the middle pages are removed: the actual book, edited by Ernest Sutherland Bates, was published in 1936

Big band theme songs

Ray Anthony	The Man With a Horn
Louis Armstrong	When It's Sleepy Time Down South
Desi Arnaz	Babalu
Mitchell Ayres	You Go to My Head
Charlie Barnet	Cherokee, Red Skin Rumba
Blue Barron	Sometimes I'm Happy
Count Basie	One O'Clock Jump, April in Paris
Bunny Berigan	I Can't Get Started
Ben Bernie	It's a Lonesome Old Town (opening): Au Revoir—Pleasant Dreams (closing)
Will Bradley	Celery Stalks at Midnight
Les Brown	Leap Frog, Sentimental Journey
Willie Bryant	It's Over Because We're Through
Henry Busse	Hot Lips
Billy Butterfield	What's New?
Bobby Byrne	Danny Boy
Cab Calloway	Minnie the Moocher
Frankie Carle	Sunrise Serenade

Benny Carter	Melancholy Lullaby
Larry Clinton	Dipsy Doodle
Bob Crosby	Summertime
Xavier Cugat	My Shawl
Jimmy Dorsey	Contrasts
Tommy Dorsey	I'm Getting Sentimental over You
Eddie Duchin	My Twilight Dream
Sonny Duchin	Memories of You
Duke Ellington	East St. Louis Toodle-oo
	Take the "A" Train, Satin Doll
Ralph Flanagan	Singing Winds
Jackie Gleason	Melancholy Serenade
Benny Goodman	Let's Dance (opening);
	Goodbye (closing)
Glen Gray	Smoke Rings, Was I to Blame for
	Falling In Love with You?
Mal Hallett	Boston Tea Party
Lionel Hampton	Flying Home
Erskine Hawkins	Tuxedo Junction
Horace Heidt	I'll Love You in My Dreams
Fletcher Henderson	Christopher Columbus
Woody Herman	Blue Flame, Woodchopper's Ball
Richard Himber	It Isn't Fair
Earl Hines	Deep Forest
Claude Hopkins	I Would Do Anything for You
Hudson-DeLange	Eight Bars in Search
	of a Melody
Harry James	Ciribiribin
Jack Jenney	City Lights
Isham Jones	You're Just a Dream Come True
Dick Jurgens	Day Dreams Come True at Night
Sammy Kaye	Kay's Melody
Hal Kemp	How I Miss You when Summer Is
	Gone
Stan Kenton	Artistry in Rhythm
Henry King	A Blues Serenade
Wayne King	The Waltz You Saved for Me
Gene Krupa	Apurksody, Star Burst
Kay Kyser	Thinking of You
Elliot Lawrence	Heart to Heart
Ted Lewis	When My Baby Smiles at Me
Guy Lombardo	Auld Lang Syne
Johnny Long	The White Star of Sigma Nu

Vincent Lopez	Nola
Jimmy Lunceford	Jazznocracy, Uptown Blues
Freddy Martin	Bye Lo Bye Lullaby, Tonight We Love (Tchaikovsky's Piano Concerto)
Frankie Masters	Scatterbrain
Billy May	Lean Baby
Clyde McCoy	Sugar Blues
Ray McKinley	Howdy, Friends
Glenn Miller	Moonlight Serenade
Art Mooney	Sunset to Sunrise
Russ Morgan	Does Your Heart Beat for Me?
Buddy Morrow	Night Train
Red Nichols	Wailing to the Four Winds
Ray Noble	The Very Thought of You
Red Norvo	Mr. and Mrs. Swing
Tony Pastor	Blossoms
Ben Pollack	Song of the Islands
Carl Ravazza	Vieni Su
Don Redman	Chant of the Weed
Alvino Ray	Blue Rey (Opening), Nighty Night (closing)
Jan Savitt	Quaker City Jazz
Raymond Scott	Pretty Little Petticoat
Artie Shaw	Nightmare
George Shearing	Lullaby of Birdland
Bobby Sherwood	The Elks' Parade
Freddy Slack	Strange Cargo
Charlie Spivak	Star Dreams
Harold Stern	Now that It's All Over
Jack Teagarden	I've Got a Right to Sing the Blues
Claude Thornhill	Snowfall
Orrin Tucker	Drifting and Dreaming
Tommy Tucker	I Love You, Oh, How I Love You
Fred Waring	Sleep
Chick Webb	I May Be Wrong
Ted Weems	Out of the Night
Lawrence Welk	Bubbles in the Wine
Paul Whiteman	Rhapsody in Blue

Big Ben

The bell (13½ tons) in the clock tower (St. Stephen's Tower) of the Houses of Parliament in London (the name is

71

often incorrectly applied to the clock itself). It is named for Benjamin Hall, who was Chief Commissioner of Works in 1856 when the bell was cast

Big Bertha

Traditionally, a very large cannon used by the Germans to bombard Paris at a distance of over 60 miles in World War I (named for Bertha Krupp). The name is properly applied to the 42 cm howitzers used in Belgium in 1914. The Paris gun was a railroad-mounted 38/21 cm gun (1918) fired by navy, not army

Big Bird

Sesame Street's large yellow bird, whose birthday is March 20 (TV's "Sesame Street"): played by Carroll Spinney. Little Bird's birthday is December 17

Big Bopper, The

Stage name of rock 'n' roll singer J. P. Richardson (first name Jape) killed in air crash with Buddy Holly and Ritchie Valens: Biggest hit "Chantilly Lace"

Big Bunny

Hugh Hefner's all-black super-jet (DC-9): N950PB

Big 5

Theater-owning movie companies: MGM (Loew's); 20th Century-Fox; Warner Brothers; RKO; Paramount

Big Little Books

Popular small-sized (smaller and thicker than mass-market paperbacks) cartoon books (bound in paper over cardboard) that featured popular radio/movie characters of the day: Tom Mix, Jack Armstrong, etc. (produced by the Whitman Publishing Company)

Big Lucy

Nickname of the passenger ship "Lusitania"

Big Mac

Nickname of the U.S. Air Force Lockheed C5A transport, biggest airplane in the World (MAC: Military Airlift Command)

Big Mamie

Nickname of the battleship U.S.S. "Massachusetts." In 35 sea battles not a single man was lost

Big O

Basketball star Oscar Robertson (in the 1950 census his great-grandfather was declared the oldest living person in the country, age 116)

Big Red
Nickname of Man O' War (grandfather of racehorse Seabiscuit)

Big Red Cheese, The
Name given to Captain Marvel by Dr. Sivana (comic books)

Big Seven, The
Jazz band for which Pete Kelly plays cornet (movie/TV series *Pete Kelly's Blues*): on TV Pete is William Reynolds; in movie, Jack Webb

Big Six
Nickname of pitcher Christy Mathewson

Big Three, The
Colleges: Harvard, Princeton, Yale

Big Thunder A. F. B.
Air Force base where Lt. Col. Stevenson B. Canyon is stationed (cartoon strip "Steve Canyon")

Big Town
Radio and TV series about a newspaperman, Steve Wilson: also titled *Headline, Heart of the City, City Assignment*

Big Train, The
Nickname of pitcher Walter Johnson

Bijou, Muffin, and Sam
Apple family pet dogs (TV series "Apple's Way")

Bill
Kathie Merrick's collie (1946 movie *The Courage of Lassie*): Lassie is neither in the film nor mentioned

Bill Jackson
Boyfriend of Beulah, the maid (radio/TV): he had a fix-it shop. Played by Dooley Wilson and Percy Harris

Billy Batson
Captain Marvel's secret identity (see Captain Marvel: SHAZAM!)

Billy Bones
Captain Flint's first mate on the pirate ship *Walrus;* in 1934 movie *Treasure Island* played by Lionel Barrymore; in 1950 Disney version by Finlay Currie. It is Billy Bones who gets the black spot from Blind Pew

Billy Fairfield
Jack Armstrong's best friend and sidekick

Billy Jack
Karate-oriented hero (movie series starring Tom Laughlin): *Born Losers* (1967); *Billy Jack* (1971); *Trial of Billy Jack* (1974); *Billy Jack Goes to Washington* (1976)

Billy Joe McAllister
Boy who jumped off the Tallahatchee Bridge on June 3, 1953 ("Ode to Billy Joe" sung by Bobbie Gentry). In the 1976 movie *Ode to Billy Joe*, the role is played by Robby Benson and Bobbie Lee Hartley tells the story

Billy the Kid
Pseudonym of William H. Bonney (1859–1881), Brooklyn-born gunman
Played in movies by:
    Johnny Mack Brown, *Billy the Kid*, 1930
    Roy Rogers, *Billy the Kid Returns*, 1939
    Robert Taylor, *Billy the Kid*, 1941
    Jack Beutel, *The Outlaw*, 1943. Both Beutel and Jane Russell made movie debuts in this picture, completed in 1943 but not released until 1950
    Audie Murphy, *The Kid from Texas*, 1949
    Don "Red" Barry, *I Shot Billy the Kid*, 1950
    Scott Brady, *The Law Versus Billy the Kid*, 1954
    Anthony Dexter, *The Parson and the Outlaw*, 1955
    Paul Newman, *The Left Handed Gun*, 1958. Billy the Kid was actually right-handed.
    (Others were Buster Crabbe, Bob Steele, Chuck Courtney, Michael J. Pollard, Kris Kristofferson, and Geoffrey Deuel)

Bing Crosby Open
Golf tournament played on 3 golf courses at Monterey, California: Pebble Beach; Spy Glass Hill; Cypress Point

Bingo
Lou Costello's pet chimpanzee (TV series "The Abbott and Costello Show")

Bingo
Dog on box of Cracker Jacks

Binney & Smith
Company that produces Crayola Crayons (See Crayola Crayons)

Biograph Girl, The
Nickname of silent film actress Florence Lawrence

Biograph Theatre
Chicago North Side cinema 2433 Lincoln Ave. in front

of which John Dillinger (Public Enemy Number One) was shot to death by Federal agents (led by Melvin G. Purvis), July 22, 1934. The movie Dillinger had watched was *Manhattan Melodrama,* a 1934 gangster film starring Clark Gable and William Powell

Biological classification

	Mnemonic	Man
Kingdom	Kings	Animal
Phylum	Play	Chordata
Class	Chess	Mammalia
Order	On	Primates
Family	Fine	Hominidae
Genus	Grain	Homo
Species	Sand	Sapiens

Bionic Boy

Andy Sheffield (TV series "The Six Million Dollar Man"): played by Vincent Van Patten

Bionic Woman

Jaime Sommers (TV series "The Bionic Woman"): played by Lindsay Wagner. An ex-tennis pro and now a schoolteacher, she was injured in a skydiving accident and now both legs and her right arm are bionic and she has super-hearing in her right ear.

Birchwood

Elementary school which Charlie Brown, Lucy, Linus, and the other children attend. (Charles Schulz's comic strip "Peanuts")

Bird Woman

Sacajawea, Lewis and Clark's guide: a member of the Northern Shoshoni

Birdcage

Saloon owned by Miss Lilly (TV series "Lawman")

Birdie

Airboy's airplane (comic book series "Airboy"): it resembles a P-39 Airacobra, but its wings flap like a bird's

Birdie

Lee Coggins' Throckmorton P. Gildersleeve's house maid: played on radio and TV (series "The Great Gildersleeve") by Lillian Randolph

Birdman of Alcatraz

Nickname of convict Robert Stroud: played by Burt Lancaster in the movie of that name (1962). Stroud's number at Leavenworth was 17431, at Alcatraz, 594. His

first two birds (sparrows) were called Peray and Runt;
he bred canaries and became an authority on bird diseases

Birmingham, U.S.S.

U.S. Navy cruiser from which the first airplane took off.
November 14, 1910, piloted by Eugene Ely, a civilian

Birmingham Brown

Charlie Chan's assistant and chauffeur (movies): played
by Mantan Moreland

Birthdays

Monday's child is fair of face;
Tuesday's child is full grace;
Wednesday's child is full of woe;
Thursday's child has far to go;
Friday's child is loving and giving;
Saturday's child works hard for a living;
But the child that is born on the Sabbath day
Is blithe and bonny, good and gay

Births

Twins	2 babies
Triplets	3 babies
Quadruplets	4 babies
Quintuplets	5 babies
Sextuplets	6 babies
Septuplets	7 babies
Octuplets	8 babies

Birthstones and Flowers

January	Garnet
	Carnation or Snowdrop
February	Amethyst
	Violet or Primrose
March	Bloodstone or Aquamarine
	Jonquil or Daisy
April	Diamond
	Sweet Pea or Daisy
May	Emerald
	Lily of the Valley or Hawthorn
June	Pearl, Alexandrite or Moonstone Rose or Honeysuckle
July	Ruby
	Larkspur or Waterlily
August	Sardonyx or Peridot
	Gladiolus or Poppy

September	Sapphire
	Aster or Morning Glory
October	Opal or Tourmaline
	Calendula or Cosmos
November	Topaz
	Chrysanthemum
December	Zircon or Turquoise
	Narcissus or Holly

Bismarck

Germany's largest battleship in World War II: launched Feb. 14, 1939; sunk May 27, 1941, off Brest, France

Bison Bill

Buffalo Bob's "brother" who substituted for him for nearly a year when Bob Smith was incapacitated by heart trouble (TV series "Howdy Doody"): played by Ted Brown

Bizarro

Superman's not-so-identical double (comic book). He came from the square world, where everyone looks like an ugly superman or an ugly Lois Lane. He wears a button with Bizarro No. 1 on it

Black

Only color worn by country-western singer Johnny Cash during a performance: reasons stated in his song "The Man in Black," which is also the title of his autobiography

Black Arrow

Sky King's jet airplane (radio series)

Black Bart

Lone Ranger's arch rival (radio series): voice of several people, including Jay Michael

Blackbeard

Nickname of Edward Teach (died 1718). West Indies pirate; in 1952 movie *Blackbeard the Pirate,* played by Robert Newton

Black Beauty

Green Hornet's car, a Lincoln Zephyr (on TV a 1957 Lincoln Futura)

Black Bess

Black horse of British outlaw Dick Turpin

Black Betsy

Babe Ruth's 44 ounce baseball bat, made by Hillerich and Bradsby of Louisville, Kentucky (Louisville Slugger)

Black Canary
Secret identity of Dinah Drake Lance, girlfriend of the Green Arrow, who calls her Bird-Lady (comic books). Her husband Larry was killed by Aquarius. Her custom motorcycle was made for her by Superman

Black Condor, The
Secret Identity of Tom Wright (comics)

Black Eagle
Nickname of Hubert Fauntleroy Julian (Negro soldier of fortune)

Blackhawks
Comic book characters: Blackhawk (Bart Hawk), Andre, Chuck, Hendrickson, Olaf, Stanislaus, Chop Chop (Chinese cook). Debut: Military Comics #1 (August 1941)
In 1952 movie serial, *Blackhawk* (Columbia, 15 episodes):

Blackhawk—Kirk Alyn	Olaf—Don Harvey
Andre—Larry Stewart	Stan—Rick Vallin
Chuck—John Crawford	Chop Chop—Weaver Levy
Hendrickson—Frank Ellis	

Black Hole of Calcutta
146 British subjects were held prisoner overnight in a barracks cell less than 20 feet square by Siraj-ud-Dowlah, the Nawab of Bengal, June 20, 1756. Only 23 survived

Black Hood, The
Secret identity of motorcycle policeman Kip Burland comic books). His fiancee is Elizabeth Rawlings

Blackie
The Blackhawks' pet hawk (comic book series "Blackhawks")

Blackie and Tiger
President Calvin Coolidge's two pet cats

Black Jack
Nickname of General John Joseph Pershing (1860–1948)

Black Jack
Riderless horse at funeral of President John F. Kennedy

Blackjack
Horse of cowboy movie star Allan "Rocky" Lane

Black Nell
Wild Bill Hickok's horse

Black Pete
Mickey Mouse's foe (early cartoon features)

Black Rebels

Motorcycle gang (B.R.M.C.) led by Johnny (Marlon Brando) who invade the town of Wrightsville (1954 movie *The Wild One*). The rival gang is led by Chino (Lee Marvin). Johnny rides a Triumph motorcycle. The movie was banned in Great Britain for 12 years

Black Sox scandal

1919 World Series—Chicago White Sox lost to Cincinnati Reds, 5 games to 3.

Eight (White Sox) players did not play major league baseball again: Eddie Cicotte, pitcher; Happy Felsch, center field; Chick Gandil, first baseman; Joe Jackson, left field; Fred McMullin, utility player; Swede Risberg, shortstop; Buck Weaver, third base; Claude Williams, pitcher

Black Swan Hall

Virginia home of Our Gal Sunday and her British husband Lord Henry Brinthrope. Sunday was "from the little mining town of Silver Creek, Colorado"

Black Tooth

The kindest dog in the country (Soupy Sales TV show): voice by Frank Nastasi

Blackwell, Elizabeth

First woman doctor; granted degree January 23, 1849

Blacula

Black vampire whose identity is that of African Prince Manuwalde (1972 movie *Blacula* and 1972 sequel *Scream Blacula Scream*): played by William Marshall

Blair General Hospital

Where Dr. Kildare worked. In Max Brand's novel *Young Dr. Kildare*, he served his internship at Dupont General Hospital. In the 1940 movie *Dr. Kildare Goes Home*, he and Dr. Gillespie transfer to Byng State Hospital, but later return to Blair General

Blake, Robert

Roles

Our Gang: Mickey Gubitosi (his real name)
Little Beaver: Red Ryder Western movies
Mexican boy: *The Treasure of the Sierra Madre* (1948)
Perry Smith: *In Cold Blood* (1967)
Baretta: TV series "Baretta"

Blanc, Mel

Voice of Bugs Bunny, Sylvester, Tweetee Pie, Jack Benny's Maxwell, and other radio and cartoon characters

Blanch
Wife of the Wizard of Id (cartoon by Johnny Hart and Brant Parker)

Blanchette
Name of Little Red Riding Hood, who is also called Little Golden Hood in children's stories

Bleeker's Cafe
Coffee shop taken over by the Black Rebels Motorcycle Club in Wrightsville (1953 movie *The Wild One*)

Blefuscu
Nation at war with Lilliput (Swift's *Gulliver's Travels*)

Blind entertainers
Ray Charles; José Feliciano; Errol Garner; Al Hibbler; Ronnie Milsap; George Shearing; Alec Templeton; Stevie Wonder
The Greek poet Homer is said to have been blind

Blinky McQuade
Underworld secret identity of the Spider when working among criminals

Blondi
Adolf Hitler's dog

Blondie
Mrs. Dagwood Bumstead of Chic Young's cartoon strip "Blondie": first strip, Sept. 6, 1930. They were married in the strip Feb. 13, 1933. In the movie and radio series (2 films) Blondie is played by Penny Singleton, Dagwood by Arthur Lake. On radio, Blondie played by Penny Singleton, Alice White, Patricia Van Cleve (Arthur Lake's wife). In the 1954 TV series, Pamela Britton played opposite Lake. In the 1968 TV series, Will Hutchinson and Patricia Harty were Dagwood and Blondie.

Blondie movies
Starring Arthur Lake and Penny Singleton:

Blondie (1938)

Blondie Meets the Boss (1939)

Blondie Takes a Vacation (1939)

Blondie Brings Up Baby (1939)

Blondie on a Budget (1940)

Blondie Has Servant Trouble (1940)

Blondie Plays Cupid (1940)

Blondie Goes Latin (1941)

Blondie in Society (1941)

Blondie Goes to College (1942)

Blondie's Blessed Event (1942)

Blondie for Victory (1942)   *Blondie in the Dough* (1947)
It's a Great Life (1943)   *Blondie's Anniversary* (1947)
Footlight Glamour (1943)   *Blondie's Reward* (1948)
Leave It to Blondie (1945)   *Blondie's Secret* (1949)
Blondie Knows Best (1946)   *Blondie's Big Deal* (1949)
Life with Blondie (1946)   *Blondie Hits the Jackpot*
Blondie's Lucky Day (1946)   (1949)
Blondie's Big Moment (1947)   *Blondie's Hero* (1950)
Blondie's Holiday (1947)   *Beware of Blondie* (1950)

Blood and Fire

Motto of the Salvation Army (displayed on their emblem)

Bloop,Bleep, Blip

Three giant trolls who live at Magic Mountain Amusement Park in the Simi Hills, Southern California

Bloopy

Gold statuette presented by Kermit Schafer (Mr. Blooper) for the best bloopers (verbal errors on radio and TV)

Blossom

Tumbleweeds' horse (comic strip "Tumbleweeds" by Tom K. Ryan)

Bloosom

Gabby Hayes' mule (movies)

Blue

Curly's horse (1955 movie *Oklahoma!*)

Blue

Hounddog that kills himself in an attempt to track down prisoner Lucas ("Cool Hand Luke") Jackson (1967 movie *Cool Hand Luke*)

Blue and Gold

Riverdale High School school paper (Archie comics)

Blue Angels

United States Navy's flight demonstration team, based at Pensacola, Fla. They fly Skyhawk A-4Es

Bluebird

Donald Campbell's land speed vehicle. Also jet-powered motorboat: 248.62 mph in November 1958

Blue Bird Special

Boy pilot Jimmie Allen's airplane (radio's "Air Adventures of Jimmy Allen")

Bluebird Special
Malcolm Campbell's land speed vehicle (301.13 mph in 1935)

Blue Boy
Painting (1779) by Sir Thomas Gainsborough (which he painted to prove that a blue painting need not be dull): now in Huntington Library and Art Gallery. San Marino, California

Blue Boy
Prize-winning pig (movie *State Fair*)

Blue Boy
Mark McCain's horse (TV series "The Rifleman")

Blue Chip II
Boat commanded by Captain David Scott (TV series "Harbourmaster")

Blue Eagle
Symbol of NRA (National Recovery Administration). 1933–1936

Blue Fairy
Good fairy who changes Pinocchio from a puppet into a real boy

Blue Flame
Theme song of Woody Herman's orchestra

Blue, Green and Red
Rooms (or parlors) in the White House: on first floor near the South Portico

Blue Meanies
The bad guys in the Beatles' 1968 movie *Yellow Submarine*. Their chief is called His Blueness, and Max is his assistant

Blue Moon
Theme song of radio series "Hollywood Hotel": the bands performed in the fictional Orchid Room

Blue Mule
Carrol Joe Hummer's 13-speed Ford truck (1975 movie *White Line Fever*)

Blue Parrot Cafe
Cafe of Signor Ferrari (Sydney Greenstreet) (1942 movie *Casablanca*)

Blue Water
Sapphire stolen by Beau Geste

Blunderbore
Giant slain by Jack the Giant Killer

Bluto

Popeye's foe (also called Brutus)

Boardwalk

Most valuable property in the board game Monopoly. Rent charged with a hotel on it is $2,000. In the British version it's Mayfair, in France Rue de la Paix, Germany Schlossallee, Spain Paseo del Prado. See Monopoly

Boatswain

Lord Byron's Newfoundland dog (1801–1808): buried at Newstead Abbey, where his monument is larger than Byron's

Boatswain

Dog upon the whaler ship "Dolly" (Herman Melville's *Typee*)

Boatwright University

College attended by John Boy Walton (TV series "The Waltons"): played by Richard Thomas

Bob

Sheena Queen of the Jungle's mate (movie serial): played by Clayton Moore

Bob and Ray

Radio and television comedians Bob Elliot and Ray Goulding

Bobby

Bull in Schlitz Malt Liquor TV commercials

Bobby Benson

Played by Billy Halop in radio and movie serials, but originally on radio by Richard Wanamaker
Tex Mason, the ranch foreman, played by Al Hodge or Tex Ritter on radio
Harka, Indian ranchhand, played by Craig McDonnell
Windy Wales, cowboy, played by Don Knotts on radio
Diogenes Dodwaddle, played by Tex Ritter

Bobby Jeannine

Cocktail bar organist and everybody's friend in skit played by Lily Tomlin

Bobcats

Bob Crosby's band

Bobbsey Twins

Children's books by Laura Lee Hope about the adventures of Nan and Bert, 8 years old; Flossie and Freddie, 4 years old. In later stories, Nan and Bert became 12 years old, but Flossie and Freddie get to only 6, just half the older twins' age

Bobo and Glogo

Two gnomes in Upton Sinclair's novel *The Gnomobile*. Bobo is 100 years old; Glogo, his grandfather, is 1,000 years old

Bock's Car

B-29 that dropped the atomic bomb on Nagasaki, piloted by Major Charles Sweeney (August 9, 1945)

Bodega Bay

Sonoma County, Calif., seaside town, north of San Francisco, where the attack of the birds occurs (Alfred Hitchcock 1963 movie *The Birds*, which was filmed there)

Body, The

Title bestowed on actress Marie McDonald (1923–1965), a former model: real name Marie Frye

Bogart, Humphrey

Marriages: Helen Mencken, 1926–1928; Mary Phillips, 1928–1938; Mayo Methot, 1938–1945; Lauren Bacall, 1945–1957

His movies and roles;

    1930—*Broadway's Like That*, no name (10-minute feature)

    1930—*A Devil with Women*, Tom Standish

    1930—*Up the River*, Steve†

    1930—*Body and Soul*, Jim Watson

    1931—*Bad Sister*, Valentine Corliss

    1931—*Women of All Nations*, Stone

    1931—*A Holy Terror*, Steve Nash

    1932—*Love Affair*, Jim Leonard

    1932—*Big City Blues*, Adkins

    1932—*Three on a Match*, The Mug

    1934—*Midnight*, Garboni

    1936—*The Petrified Forest*, Duke Mantee

    1936—*Bullets or Ballots*, Nick "Bugs" Fenner

    1936—*Two Against the World*, Sherry Scott

    1936—*China Clipper*, Hap Stuart

    1936—*Isle of Fury*, Val Stevens

    1937—*Black Legion*, Frank Taylor

    1937—*The Great OMalley*, John Phillips

    1937—*Marked Woman*, David Graham

---

†Spencer Tracy's film debut

1937—*Kid Galahad*, Turkey Morgan
1937—*San Quentin*, Joe "Red" Kennedy
1937—*Dead End*, Baby Face Martin*
1937—*Stand-In*, Douglas Quintain
1938—*Swing Your Lady*, Ed Hatch
1938—*Crime School*, Mark Braden
1938—*Men are such Fools*, Harry Galleon
1938—*The Amazing Dr. Clitterhouse*, Rocks Valentine
1938—*Racket Busters*, Pete Martin
1938—*Angels with Dirty Faces*, James Frazier
1939—*King of the Underworld*, Joe Gurney
1939—*The Oklahoma Kid*, Whip McCord
1939—*Dark Victory*, Michael O'Leary
1939—*You Can't Get Away with Murder*, Frank Wilson
1939—*The Roaring Twenties*, George Hally
1939—*The Return of Doctor X*, Marshall Quesne
1939—*Invisible Stripes*, Chuck Martin
1940—*Virginia City*, John Murrell
1940—*It All Came True*, Grasselli (Chips Maguire)
1940—*Brother Orchid*, Jack Buck
1940—*They Drive by Night*, Paul Fabrini
1941—*High Sierra*, Roy Earle alias Roy Collins*
1941—*The Wagons Roll at Night*, Nick Coster
1941—*The Maltese Falcon*, Sam Spade*‡
1942—*All Through the Night*, Gloves Donahue
1942—*The Big Shot*, Duke Berne
1942—*Across the Pacific*, Rick Leland
1943—*Casablanca*, Rick Blaine*
1943—*Action in the North Atlantic*, Joe Rossi
1943—*Thank Your Lucky Stars*, Humphrey Bogart (as himself)
1943—*Sahara*, Sergeant Joe Gunn
1944—*Passage to Marseille*, Matrac
1944—*To Have and Have Not*, Harry Morgan
1945—*Conflict*, Richard Mason
1946—*Two Guys from Milwaukee*, Humphrey Bogart (as himself)
1946—*The Big Sleep*, Philip Marlowe

---

‡Sydney Greenstreet's film debut
*Leading roles in *Dead End*, *High Sierra*, *Maltese Falcon*, and *Casablanca* all first offered to George Raft, who turned them down.

1947—*Dead Reckoning*, Rip Murdock
1947—*The Two Mrs. Carrolls*, Geoffrey Carroll
1947—*Dark Passage*, Vincent Parry alias Alan Lynell
1948—*The Treasure of the Sierra Madre*, Fred C. Dobbs
1948—*Key Largo*, Frank McCloud
1949—*Knock on Any Door*, Andrew Morton
1949—*Tokyo Joe*, Joe Barrett
1950—*Chain Lightning*, Matt Brennan
1950—*In a Lonely Place*, Dixon Steele
1950—*Deadline U.S.A.*, Ed Hutchinson
1951—*The Enforcer*, Martin Ferguson
1951—*Sirocco*, Harry Smith
1951—*The African Queen*, Charlie Allnut (Oscar: best actor)
1953—*Battle Circus*, Major Jed Webbe
1954—*Beat the Devil*, Billy Dannreuther
1954—*The Caine Mutiny*, Captain Queeg
1954—*Sabrina*, Linus Larrabee
1954—*The Barefoot Contessa*, Harry Dawes
1955—*We're No Angels*, Joseph
1955—*The Left Hand of God*, Jim Carmody
1955—*The Desperate Hours*, Glenn Griffin
1956—*The Harder They Fall*, Eddie Willis

In the 1946 movie *Never Say Goodbye*, Errol Flynn did an imitation of Bogart that was excellent: it was Bogart's voice actually on the sound track

Bogataj, Vinko
Yugoslavian ski jumper shown on introduction to ABC television's "Wide World of Sports." He is shown going off the side of the ski jump at Oberdorf, West Germany in 1970, he was not hurt.

Bogey-men
Evil men who attempt to invade Toy Land (1934 Laurel and Hardy movie *Babes in Toyland*)

Bold Ones, The
Rotating weekly TV series (1969–1972).
The various programs were: The Doctors, (E. G. Marshall, David Hartman, John Saxon); The Lawyers (Joseph Campanella, Burl Ives, James Farentino); The Senator (Hal Holbrook); Police Drama (Leslie Neilsen, Hari Rhodes)

Bomba

The Jungle Boy (movie series "Bomba"): played by Johnny Sheffield.
Series from the novels of Roy Rockwood
Movies:
Bomba, The Jungle Boy (1949)
Bomba on Panther Island (1949)
The Lost Volcano (1950)
Bomba and the Hidden City (1950)
The Lion Hunters (1951)
Bomba and the Elephant Stampede (1951)
African Treasure (1952)
Bomba and the Jungle Girl (1952)
Safari Drums (1953)
The Golden Idol (1954)
Killer Leopard (1954)
Lord of the Jungle (1955)

Bonanza

TV series. Original cast: Ben Cartwright (Lorne Green); Joe Cartwright (Michael Landon); Hoss (Eric) Cartwright (Dan Blocker); Adam Cartwright (Pernell Roberts) Theme song by David Rose. Series ran 1959 to 1973. After 6 seasons, Adam went off to school in Europe, which permitted Pernell Roberts to leave the series. (Johnny Stephens played Adam as a child.) Joe was the only left-handed member of the family. Dan Blocker died in 1972 after 13 seasons. Mitch Vogel played Jamie; David Canary was Candy

Bonds, Bobby

Only rookie to hit a home run with bases filled in his first major league game (3rd time at bat), June 25, 1968, against the Dodgers. Bill Duggleby was the only other man to do so, in 1898. Bobby Bonds' brother Robert plays professional football; his sister Rosie was an Olympic sprinter.

Bones

Nickname (probably short for "Sawbones," traditional appelation for a surgeon) used by Captain Kirk for Dr. Leonard McCoy (TV series *Star Trek*): played by De-Forest Kelley. His daughter is Joanna

Bongo

Unicycling bear (cartoon); his nemesis is a bear named Lumpjaw

Bonhomme Richard

Captain John Paul Jones' ship, a French Indiaman 14 years old, the "Duras," renamed in honor of Benjamin Franklin, who wrote Poor Richard's almanacs

Bonnie and Clyde

Bank robbers Bonnie Parker and Clyde Barrow; killers of 14 people: played in Arthur Penn's 1967 movie by Warren Beatty and Faye Dunaway. The story had been filmed before, notably by Fritz Lang in 1951 and by William Witney in 1958 (with Dorothy Provine as Bonnie)

Bonnie Blue Butler

Baby girl born to Scarlett O'Hara and Rhett Butler (1939 movie *Gone with the Wind*): played by Cammie King

Bonny Braids

Daughter of Dick Tracy and Tess Trueheart, born in 1951 (comic strip)

Bonzo

Chimpanzee that co-starred with Ronald Reagen (1951 movie *Bedtime for Bonzo*). In the TV serial "M*A*S*H" the film is shown often to the 4077th MASH unit. Bonzo was played by Peggy

Boo Boo

Yogi Bear's little bear sidekick (TV cartoon): voice is by Don Messick

Book 'Em

Closing line of Steve McGarrett (TV series "Hawaii Five-O")

Booker T. and the M.G.'s

(M.G. stands for Memphis Group) Donald "Duck" Dunn, Steve Cropper, Al Jackson, Booker T. Jones

Boola Boola

Yale University school song

Boone City

Setting of 1946 movie *The Best Years of Our Lives*: baseball team is the Beavers

Boopadoop

Blondie's maiden name (comic strip "Blondie" by Chic Young). She had been a fan dancer before marrying Dagwood Bumstead on Feb. 13, 1933

Boop-a-Doop Girl

Nickname of Helen Kane. Her theme song: "I Wanna Be Loved By You"

Booth, Edwin (Thomas)

John Wilkes Booth's actor brother (1833-1893). He has been elected to the Hall of Fame of Great Americans

Booth, William

Known as General Booth (1829–1912); founded the Salvation Army (1878, founded in 1865 as the Christian Revival Association or Christian Mission, and still earlier known as East London Revival Society)

Boots

Stationhouse dog (TV series "Emergency")

Borden, Lizzie

Alleged murderer (August 4, 1892) of her step-mother, Sarah A. Morse, and father, Andrew Jackson Borden, at 92 Second St., Fall River, Mass. Tried, she was acquitted. Portrayed by Elizabeth Montgomery in 1975 TV movie *The Legend of Lizzie Borden*

"Lizzie Borden took an axe
And gave her mother forty whacks.
When she saw what she had done
She gave her father forty-one."

Borg-Warner Trophy

Award given for winning the Indianapolis 500-mile auto race

Boris and Natasha

Boris Badenov and Natasha Nogoodnik (sometimes Natasha Fatal), arch-enemies of Bullwinkle and Rocky (cartoon series); voices: Boris (Paul Frees), Natasha (June Foray)

Boroughs of the City of New York

Bronx (Bronx County)
Brooklyn (Kings County)
Manhattan (New York County)
Queens (Queens County)
Richmond (Richmond County: Staten Island)
They become Greater New York January 1, 1898

Boston Blackie

Private eye created by Jack Boyle: on radio and in movies played by Chester Morris (in 1923 there were two movies starring William Russell). Replaced on radio by Richard Kollmar; on TV played by Kent Taylor. (His sidekick on radio was Shorty, in movies it was the Runt.) Mary was the helpful female on radio and TV.

His credo: "Enemy to those who make him an enemy, friend to those who have no friend"

Movies (all with Chester Morris):
Meet Boston Blackie (1941)
Confessions of Boston Blackie (1941)
Alias Boston Blackie (1942)
Boston Blackie Goes Hollywood (1942)
After Midnight With Boston Blackie (1943)
One Mysterious Night (1944)
Boston Blackie Booked On Suspicion (1945)
Boston Blackie's Rendezvous (1945)
A Close Call for Boston Blackie (1946)
The Phantom Thief (1946)
Boston Blackie and the Law (1946)
Trapped by Boston Blackie (1948)
Boston Blackie's Chinese Venture (1949)

Boston Casualty
Boston, Massachusetts, firm for which Thomas Banacek does investigative work (TV series "Banacek")

Boston Strong Boy
Nickname of heavyweight boxing champion John L. Sullivan

Boston Tea Party
British ships raided (December 16, 1773) at Griffin's Wharf: "Beaver," "Dartmouth," "Eleanor"

Boswell Sisters
Singing group: Connee (originally Connie), Vet, Martha

Boulder Dam
Former name of Hoover Dam, on the Colorado River. Built 1936, it created Lake Mead. Originally Hoover Dam, it was named Boulder Dam, and in 1947 again became Hoover Dam

Bounty, H.M.S.
British ship upon which Fletcher Christian led the famous mutiny against Lieutenant (later Captain) William Bligh, 1789

Bounty Hunter, The
Rerun title of TV series "Wanted—Dead or Alive"

Bounty trilogy
Novels based on fact, by Charles Nordhoff and James Norman Hall: *Mutiny on the Bounty* (1932); *Men Against the Sea* (1934); *Pitcairn's Island* (1934). Hall

was a member of the 94th Aero Squadron (Hat-in-the-Ring) in World War I

Bourbon and Water

Detective Shell Scott's favorite drink

Bowery Boys

Acting group of teenagers originally belonging to the Dead End Kids who, led by Bobby Jordan and Leo Gorcey, joined Monogram Pictures for a series to be called "East Side Kids," Billy Benedict, Stanley Clements, Bennie Bartlett, and David Gorcey joined this group, and later Huntz Hall and Gabriel Dell left Universal to come in with them.

Leo Gorcey played Slip (or Terence Aloysius Mahoney). Huntz Hall was Sach (Horace Debussy Jones), Billy Benedict was Whitey, Bobby Jordon was Bobby, David Gorcey was Chuck, and Gabe Dell played the part of Gabe Moreno

The Bowery Boys pictures were made from 1940 to 1953 In 1956-57 a regrouping put Stanley Clements, Huntz Hall, David Gorcey, and Eddie LeRoy together, as, respectively, Duke Stanislaus Kovilesky, Horace Debussy Jones, Chuck Anderson, and Blinky

Bowl games, College football

Bowl	City	State
American Bowl	Tampa	Florida
Amos Alonzo Stagg Bowl	Phoenix City	Alabama
Astro-Bluebonnet Bowl	Houston	Texas
Blue-Gray Bowl	Montgomery	Alabama
Boardwalk Bowl	Atlantic City	New Jersey
Camellia Bowl	Sacramento	California
Cotton Bowl	Dallas	Texas
Fiesta Bowl	Tempe	Arizona
Gator Bowl	Jacksonville	Florida
Grantland Rice Bowl	Baton Rouge	Louisiana
Hula Bowl	Honolulu	Hawaii
Knute Rockne Bowl	Atlantic City	New Jersey
Liberty Bowl	Memphis	Tennessee
Lions American Bowl	Tampa	Florida

Ohio Shrine Bowl	Columbus	Ohio
Orange Bowl	Miami	Florida
Pasadena Bowl	Pasadena	California
Peach Bowl	Atlanta	Georgia
Pelican Bowl	New Orleans	Louisiana
Pioneer Bowl	Wichita Falls	Texas
Rose Bowl	Pasadena	California
Senior Bowl	Mobile	Alabama
Shrine Classic (East/West)	San Francisco	California
Shrine Game (North/South)	Miami	Florida
Sugar Bowl	New Orleans	Louisiana
Sun Bowl	El Paso	Texas
Tangerine Bowl	Orlando	Florida

Bowser

Mr. Magoo's dog (cartoons)

Box No. 5

Box seat in the Paris Opera House haunted by the Phantom because he claims it as his (1908 novel *Phantom of the Opera* by Gaston Leroux)

Box 13

Port Office box address of detective George Valentine (radio series "Let George Do It" starring Bob Bailey)

Box 204

Salt Lake City post office box address of Sonny Pruitt (Claude Akins) (TV series "Movin' On")

Boxer

The horse in George Orwell's *Animal Farm*

Box H Ranch

Cattle ranch near Medicine Bow, Wyoming, where the Virginian is foreman (1929 movie *The Virginian*). In Owen Wister's 1904 novel, the ranch is in Montana

Boy

Bradley family's pet dog (TV series "Petticoat Junction")

Boy

Pete's mutt (comic strip "Pete the Tramp" by C. D. Russell)

Boy

Only son of Tarzan and Jane in Johnny Weissmuller/Maureen O'Sullivan Tarzan movies: played by Johnny Sheffield. On TV the boy is named Jai: played by Manuel Padilla, Jr. In the Burroughs novels Tarzan's son is Korak

92

Boy Commandos

Young crimefighters (comic book series created by Joe Simon and Jack Kirby), overseen by Captain Rip Carter. They include Alfy Twidgett (English). Andre (French, originally Pierre Chavard), Jan Haasen (Dutch), Brooklyn (American). Debut: Detective Comics #64, June 1942

Boys Club of America

Motto: "Building boys is better than mending men"

Boy Scouts

Cub Scouts: age 8-10

Boy Scouts: age 11-13

Explorer Scouts: age 14 and above

Boys' Ranch

Comic book characters (Harvey comics): Angel, Clay Duncan, Dandy Dolan, Wabash, Wee Willie Weehawken

Boys Town

Founded, near Omaha, Nebraska, December 1, 1917, by Monsignor Edward J. Flanagan (see Father Flanagan)

Motto: "There is no such thing as a bad boy"

Spencer Tracy's Oscar (1938) for his role as Father Flanagan in Loew's *Boys Town* is kept at Boys Town

Boz

Pseudonym of Charles Dickens

Bozo

Adams' 500-pound pet grizzly bear (1975 movie *The Life and Times of Grizzly Adams*). In the TV/movie series the part is played by Ben

Bozo

Popular clown of the 1950s on TV and Capitol Records; created by Larry Harmon: played by Frank Avruch.

B.P.O.E.

Benevolent and Protective Order of Elks

Bradley's

Favorite tobacconist of Sherlock Holmes and Dr. Watson, on Oxford Street in London

Brady Bunch

TV series

Michael Paul (architect)—Robert Reed

Carol Ann—Florence Henderson

Alice (housekeeper)—Ann B. Davis

Greg—Barry Williams

Marcia—Maureen McCormack

Peter—Christopher Knight
Jan—Eve Plumb
Bobby—Michael Lookinland
Cindy—Susan Olsen
Mrs. Brady's maiden name was Tyler, Martin in her first marriage

Brainiac 5
Secret identity of Querl Dox; born on the planet Colu, his brain functions at the 12th level (comic books)

Bramford
Apartment building where Andrew John is born (Ira Levin's novel *Rosemary's Baby*). The building was named after Bram Stoker, the creator of Dracula

Braun, Eva
Adolf Hitler's mistress: suicide with Hitler April 30, 1945

Breadfruit trees
Cargo of H.M.S. "Bounty" at time of mutiny, 1789

Bremen Town Musicians
Dog, cat, donkey, and cock (Grimms' story)

Brenda Starr, Reporter
Heroine of the comic strip "Brenda Starr, Reporter" by Dale Messick: debut June 30, 1940. Played in movie serials by Joan Woodbury (1945); 13 episodes and on TV by Jill St. John. Her boyfriend (from 1940) was Basil St. John, whom she married in November 1975

Brennan, Walter
Only actor to win the Academy Award for best supporting actor 3 times:
Come and Get It (1936)
Kentucky (1938)
The Westerner (1940)

Brer Fox
Slung Brer Rabbit right in de briar-patch (*Uncle Remus* stories of Joel Chandler Harris)
In 1946 Disney movie *Song of the South*, voice was James Baskett's (Brer Rabbit was Johnny Lee; Brer Bear, Nicodemus Stuart)

Brian's song
Movie for TV (11 awards) about former Chicago Bears running back Gale Sayers (played by Billy Dee Williams) and his teammate Brian Piccolo (played by James Caan) who died of cancer in 1970

Bridal Veil Mountain

Land left to the three Bolt brothers if 100 women stay unmarried in Seattle for one year (TV series "Here Come the Brides")

Bride of Frankenstein

1935 James Whale movie starring Boris Karloff as the monster and Colin Clive as Doctor Frankenstein. Elsa Lanchester played the monster's bride but the Bride of Frankenstein (Doctor Frankenstein, that is) was played by Valerie Hobson

Bridge of San San Luis Rey, The

Novel (1927; Pulitzer Prize 1928) by Thornton Wilder. The five killed when the bridge fell (July 20, 1714) were Esteban, Uncle Pio, Marquesa de Montemayor, Pepita, Jaime, Brother Juniper, a Franciscan, investigated why these particular five were chosen to die in this way

Bridgeport

Bear who lives with Pogo in the Okefenokee Swamp (Walt Kelly's comic strip "Pogo")

Brigadier General

Rank held by actor James Stewart and Charles Lindbergh in the U.S. Air Force Reserve

Brigadoon

Mythical Scottish town that appears for a single day every one hundred years (musical play, 1947, and movie 1954 by Alan Jay Lerner and Frederick Loewe)

Brigham

William Cody's (Buffalo Bill's) horse

Britannia

Yacht of the British Royal family

Britt Reid

Name of the Green Hornet. Reid publishes the *Daily Sentinel* (see Green Hornet)

Broadway Joe

Nickname of New York Jets quarterback Joe Namath

Brobdingnag

The land of the giants (Jonathan Swift's *Gulliver's Travels*)

Brockton Bomber

Nickname of heavyweight champion Rocky Marciano (Rocco Francis Marchegiano)

Broderick and Elizabeth

Two bulldogs of The Captain and Tennille, appearing with them on TV

Brodie, Steve

Claimed to have jumped off the Brooklyn Bridge on a bet, and lived: July 23, 1886. He re-enacted the scene in a play, *On the Bowery,* opening in 1894. There were no witnesses to the 132.5 foot jump.

His reply, when asked to jump again: "I done it oncet."

—in 1933 movie *The Bowery* portrayed by George Raft

Broke My Heart in Two

By the Two-Tones: song announced by disc-jockey Darby Dawn on radio station 2-2-2 (Listerine ad on TV circa 1974)

Broken Bow

Cattle ranch of Steve Adam (Straight Arrow's real identity)

Brom Bones

Nickname of Abraham Van Brunt, Ichabod Crane's rival for the hand of Katrina (Irving's "The Legend of Sleepy Hollow")

Bronco Billy

Early western film hero, played by Gilbert M. Anderson (Max Aronson) (1882-1971) who starred in the first western, *The Great Train Robbery* (1903, 11 minutes long, filmed in Dove, New Jersey). Anderson and George K. Spoor founded Essanay Studios, named from their initials

Broncos Auto Repairing

Garage where Arthur Fonzarelli (The Fonz) works (TV series "Happy Days"). Originally it was Herbs Auto Repairs, but Herb sells to Otto in one episode

Bronson, Charles

Only member of both the Magnificent Seven (1960) and the Dirty Dozen (1967). His movie debut: *You're in the Navy Now* (1951), in which Lee Marvin's movie career also began

Brontë sisters

	Pen Name	Principal Novel
Charlotte	Currer Bell	*Jane Eyre*
Emily	Ellis Bell	*Wuthering Heights*
Anne	Acton Bell	*Agnes Grey*

Brookfield

The school at which Mr. Chips (Arthur Chipping) taught Latin (James Hilton's novel *Goodbye, Mr. Chips*)

Broom Hilda

1,500-year-old witch, created by Russell Myers in a cartoon series. Other characters: Gaylord, the intellectual buzzard; Irwin, shy and shaggy troll; the Grelber, master of insult; Olivia, Irwin's girlfriend; Earl, the bat

Brother Can You Spare a Dime

Theme song of the Depression: written in 1932 by Jay Gorney, lyrics by E. Y. Harburg

Brother Juniper

Cartoon clown, of the Franciscan Order: created and drawn by Father Justin McCarthy. He coaches the Rinky Dinks football team

Brother Sebastian

Cartoon monk created and drawn by Chon Day

Brothers Karamazov

Dmitri, Ivan, Alyosha, Smerdyakov (illegitimate): novel by Feodor Dostoevsky (1880)

Brown

Pet dog of Dave Blasingame (TV series "The Westerner")

Brown, Don

First person to cross the Golden Gate Bridge when it opened May 27, 1937

Brown, Johnny Mack

Cowboy star (1904-1974) of the movies. Member of football's collegiate Hall of Fame (1927 All-American for Alabama) and captain of his team in 1926 Rose Bowl. His horse was Remo

Brown, Roy

Canadian pilot who claimed the victory over the Red Baron, Manfred von Richthofen, April 21, 1918

Brown Beauty

Reputed name of borrowed horse Paul Revere rode when he warned the countryside of the approach of the British

Browns, The

Country and Western singing group: Bonnie, Jim Ed, Maxine

Bruce

The three mechanical sharks constructed for the movie *Jaws*

Bruno
Bear who played Gentle Ben (TV series "Gentle Ben")

Bruno
Augustus Mutt's dog (comic strip "Mutt and Jeff")

Bruno
Judge Roy Bean's pet bear in Langtry, Texas

Bruno
Cinderella's dog (Walt Disney cartoon feature movie)

Brutus
The ugly dachshund: Great Dane who thinks he is a dachshund (Disney feature movie *The Ugly Dachshund*): the other dachshunds are Tokey, Norma, Pesky, and Heidi

Brutus
Invisible German shepherd of Doctor Drury (1940 movie *The Invisible Man Returns*): Brutus kills Robert Griffin/alias Martin Field, the Invisible Man

Brutus
Another name for Popeye's antagonist Bluto

Brutus Thornapple
Unlucky soul who constantly experiences life's unhappy side (comic strip "The Born Loser")

Bryant, Jimmy
Sang for Richard Beymer (Tony) in movie *West Side Story*

BRyant 9-2828
Detective Nero Wolfe's phone number at his brownstone house on West 35th Street, New York City. Other phone numbers of Wolfe's were PRoctor 5-5000 and Pennsylvania 3-1212

Bryant Park
Locale of TV series "My Three Sons"

Bryant Park Bank
New York financial organization that presented Charles Lindbergh with their check, dated June 17, 1927, for $25,000, for flying solo, non-stop, New York to Paris. The prize was put up by Raymond Orteig, owner of the Brevoort and Lafayette hotels in New York in 1919

Bryant's Gap
Place near the town of Colby where the Lone Ranger, his brother Captain Daniel Reid, and four other Texas Rangers were ambushed by Butch Cavendish and the Hole-in-the-Wall gang. Only John Reid, thus "the lone Ranger," survived. Shot in the shoulder, he was nursed

back to health by Tonto. The dead Rangers were Captain
Dan Reid, Ben Cooper, Joe Brent, and Jack Stacey. They
were betrayed by a man named Collins, shot by Cavendish, and who later (first TV episode) dies in a fall

Bubbles

Wife of Boner (comic strip "Boner's Ark")

Bucephalus

Horse of Alexander the Great: given to him by his father,
Philip II, and died in India at the age of 30

Buchanan, James

Only bachelor United States president. His fiancee committed suicide when he was 28; his niece Harriet Lane
acted as his hostess when he was president

(James) Buchanan High

Bensonhurst, Brooklyn, school in which Gabe Kotter
teaches (TV series "Welcome Back, Kotter"). Among his
sweathogs (slow achievers) are Vinnie Barbarino, Frederick "Boom Boom" Washington, Juan Epstein, and Arnold
Horshack

Buck

Horse of Ben Cartwright (Lorne Green) (TV series
"Bonanza")

Buck

Hero dog (Jack London's *The Call of the Wild*), a St.
Bernard

Buck

Pet dog of the Gump family (comic strip "The Gumps")

Buckner, General Simon Bolivar

Civil War general who fought for both the Union and the
Confederacy. He was a pallbearer for both President
Ulysses S. Grant and General Robert E. Lee

Buck Rogers

Classic spaceman hero, created (1928) by Philip Francis
Nowlan in a story, "Armageddon 2419 A.D.," for *Amazing Stories* magazine. His real name is Anthony Rogers;
he fell asleep in 1929 and awoke in the 25th century.
Written by Nowlan and drawn by Dick Calkins, a comic
strip began appearing on January 7, 1929 (same day as
first "Tarzan" strip). His companions are Wilma Deering
and Dr. Huer. Buck Rogers played on radio by Matt
Crowley, Curtis Arnall, Carl Frank, John Larkin; on TV
by Kem Dibbs; in 1939 movie serial by Larry "Buster"
Crabbe (who also played Flash Gordon

Buck Rogers Spaceships (Toys)

	No.
Flash Blast Attack Ship	TS310Z
Super Dreadnought	SD51X
Fighting Destroyer	FD69Z
Pursuit Ship	PS91ZX
Battle Cruiser	BC77Y
Martian Police Ship	MP83Z

Buckshot

Horse of Wild Bill Hickok (TV series "Wild Bill Hickok")

Buckwheat, Stymie, and Farina

Three Negro boys in the "Our Gang" movie series. Buck-wheat (Billy) Thomas appeared in 89 of the 132 talkies made, Stymie (Matthew) Beard in 33, and Farina (Allen Clayton Hoskins), the first of the group, in 20. Sunshine Sammy Morrison, who appeared in the earliest "Our Gang" films in the mid-twenties, did not appear in talkies. Stymie appeared in the 1938 movie *Jezebel*

Bucky Barnes

Captain America's partner (comic books) They met as U.S. Army recruits at Camp Lehigh. In 1968 Rick Jones became Captain America's partner

Bucky Beaver

Animal character in Ipana toothpaste commercials and ads

Bud Barclay

Tom Swift, Jr.'s best friend

Budd

Colonel Lemuel Q. Stoopnagle's sidekick: Budd was Wilbur Budd Hulick (radio)

Buddha

Sacred name of Siddhartha Gautama

Buddy

First Seeing Eye dog in America (1928), brought to the U.S. from Switzerland by owner Morris Frank

Buddy Sorrell

One of three writers of the Alan Brady Show, along with Sally Rogers (Rose Marie) and Rob Petrie (Dick Van Dyke) (TV series "The Dick Van Dyke Show") Buddy's first name is Maurice. Buddy's wife's nickname is Pickles (her maiden name was Conway): played in one episode by Joan Shawlee. Buddy has a German Shepherd named Larry

Buddy Wade

Buck Rogers' young sidekick (1939 movie serial *Buck Rogers*): played by Jackie Moran. Buddy Deering was Wilma's younger brother in the comic strip

Buena Vista Lake

Large resort lake in the center of Disneyworld (near Orlando, Florida)

Buffalo Bill

Nickname of William Frederick Cody, given to him by E.Z.C. Judson movies

Buffalo nickel

U.S. 5 cent piece from 1913 through 1938: designed by James Earle Fraser, sculptor of Indian statue "End of the Trail"

The buffalo is modeled after Black Diamond, a bison in the Bronx Park Zoo, New York; it appears on the reverse of the coin

The Indian head (on the obverse) is a combination made from photographs of 3 visitors to President Theodore Roosevelt: Iron Tail, a Sioux; Big Tree, a Kiowa; Two Moons, a Cheyenne

Bugaloos

Saturday morning TV show. The Bugaloos are a 4 piece band of singing insects living in the Tranquility Forest: Harmony (Wayne Laryea); Courage (John Philpott); Joy (Caroline Ellis); I.Q. (John McIndoe). The evil witch Benita Bizarre is played by Martha Raye. Her helpers are Woofer and Tweeter

Bugs Bunny

Warner Brothers movie cartoon character: "Ah . . . what's up, Doc?": voice by Mel Blanc (who is allergic to carrots). Bugs Bunny was created by Bob Clampett after seeing Clark Gable munching a carrot in the 1934 movie *It Happened One Night*. First Bugs Bunny cartoon: *A Wild Hare* (1940). Oscar for best short subject (1958) for *Knighty Knight Bugs*. Other claimants to creating Bugs Bunny are Tex Avery and Chuck Jones

Bug Tussell

Country town, Cass County, where oil was discovered, permitting the Clampett family to migrate to Beverly Hills (TV series "The Beverly Hillbillies")

Bull Martin

One of G8's Battle Aces (comic book series). He flies a Spad with #7 on its side

Bulldog Drummond

Detective (Captain Hugh Drummond of the British Army) created (1920) by Herman Cyril McNeile ("Sapper"): later books written by Gerard Fairlie

Movies:

Bulldog Drummond (1922), Carlyle Blackwell
Bulldog Drummond (1929), Ronald Colman
Temple Tower (1930), Kenneth MacKenna
The Return of Bulldog Drummond (1934), Ralph Richardson
Bulldog Drummond Strikes Back (1934), Ronald Colman
Bulldog Jack (1935), Atholl Fleming
Bulldog Drummond at Bay (1937), John Lodge
Bulldog Drummond Comes Back (1937), John Howard
Bulldog Drummond Escapes (1937), Ray Milland
Bulldog Drummond's Revenge (1937), John Howard
Bulldog Drummond's Peril (1938), John Howard
Arrest Bulldog Drummond (1938), John Howard
Bulldog Drummond in Africa (1938), John Howard
Bulldog Drummond's Secret Police (1939), John Howard
Bulldog Drummond's Bride (1939), John Howard
Bulldog Drummond at Bay (1947), Ron Randell
The Challenge (1948), Tom Conway
Thirteen Lead Soldiers (1948), Tom Conway
Calling Bulldog Drummond (1951), Walter Pidgeon
Deadlier Than the Male (1967), Richard Johnson
Some Girls Do (1971), Richard Johnson

Bullet

Roy Rogers' wonder dog, a German shepherd

Bulletgirl

Secret identity of Susan Kent, Bulletman's partner

Bulletman

Secret identity of Jim Barr, crimefighter (comic book series "Bulletman"). Debut: Nickel Comics #1, May 17, 1940 (only comic book to sell for five cents)

Bullitt

Movie starring Steve McQueen as Police Lieutenant Frank Bullitt: San Francisco automobile chase scene in-

volved a green Ford Mustang (390 G.T.) (Bullitt's) and a
black Dodge Charger (440 Magnum) (bad guys)

Bullseye
White dog of Bill Sykes (1968 movie *Oliver* based on
Charles Dickens' *Oliver Twist*)

Bulova Watch Company
Sponsor of the first television commercial July 1, 1941, at a
cost of $9.00

Bunin, Hope and Morey
Puppeteers on "Lucky Pup" show and many other features (TV)

Bunting Blue
Secret code name of British spy Geoffrey Richter-Doug-
las (1971 movie *Zeppelin*)

Buntline Special
Long-barreled pistol used by Wyatt Earp, made for him
by Ned Buntline (pseudonym of Edward Zane Carroll
Judson)

Burke and Walsh
Traveling circus to which Corky belongs, with his ele-
phant Bimbo. The circus is headed by Tim Champion
(TV series "Circus Boy")

Burma-Shave
Roadside advertisements appearing (1925–1963) on small
boards spaced so they could be read sequentially by
motorists driving by:
A peach / looks good / with lots of fuzz / but man's
no peach / and never was / Burma-Shave
Does your husband / misbehave / grunt and grumble /
rant and rave? / shoot the brute some / Burma-Shave
Don't take a curve / at 60 per / we hate to lose / a
customer / Burma-Shave
Every shaver / now can snore / six more minutes /
than before / by using / Burma-Shave
He played / a sax / had no B.O. / but his whiskers
scratched / so she let him go / Burma-Shave
Henry the Eighth / Prince of Friskers / lost five wives /
but kept / his whiskers / Burma-Shave
Listen, birds / those signs cost / money / so roost a while
but / don't get funny / Burma-Shave
My man / won't shave / sez Hazel Huz / but I should
worry / Dora's does / Burma-Shave

Past schoolhouses / take it slow / let the little / shavers / grow / Burma-Shave

Rip a fender / off your car / send it in / for a half-pound jar / Burma-Shave

Begun on Minnesota Highway 65. Only four states never had the signs (out of 48) New Mexico, Arizona, Massachusetts, Nevada

Burnette, Smiley (Lester Alvin)

Sidekick of Gene Autry (and Roy Rogers and Charles Starrett). He played Mr. Floyd in the TV series "Petticoat Junction"

Burpelson

U.S. Air Force base (843rd Bomb Wing) commanded by General Jack D. Ripper (1963 movie *Dr. Strangelove*) Group Captain Lionel Mandrake calls President Muffley on a telephone (Burpelson 3–9180); the charge is 55¢ and he needs 20¢ from a Coca-Cola machine which Colonel Bat Guano shoots open

Burr, Raymond

Canadian actor (born 1917) noted for two successful TV series: "Perry Mason" (1957–1966), "Ironside" (1967–1975). He was earlier familiar in the movies as a heavy or, for example, as the prosecuting attorney in *A Place in the Sun* (1951) or the narrator in *Godzilla* (1954)

Bush and Burritt Streets

San Francisco corner, above the Stockton Street tunnel, where Sam Spade's partner Miles Archer was shot (4 times in the back) and killed by Brigid O'Shaughnessy with a .38 eight shot Webley Fosbery automatic (Dashiell Hammett's *The Maltese Falcon*). In the 1941 movie, the corner is Bush and Stockton, and the weapon is an (eight) shot Webley-Forsby .45 automatic

Bush, Guy

Pitcher off whom Babe Ruth hit home runs 713 and 714 on May 25, 1935, in Pittsburgh

Busted Flush

Private houseboat of detective Travis McGee, docked at Fort Lauderdale: he won the boat in a Palm Beach poker game (detective novels)

Buster

Edith Ann's dog (Lily Tomlin skits)

Buster

Joseph Francis Keaton's nickname, given to him by magician Harry Houdini when Keaton (then a child) fell down a flight of stairs

Buster Brown

Comic strip character created (1902) by R. F. Outcault, a fancy-dressed boy who lives in a shoe with his dog Tige. Among the many products named for him were Buster Brown Shoes. His sister is Mary Jane

Butch Cassidy

Pseudonym of western outlaw George (or Robert) Le-Roy Parker (1867–1911), leader of the Hole-in-the-Wall Gang or the Wild Bunch. In the 1969 movie *Butch Cassidy and the Sundance Kid,* played by Paul Newman

Butch Cavendish

Leader of the Hole-in-the-Wall gang that ambushed the Texas Rangers (Lone Ranger and Green Hornet radio series): on radio played by Jay Michael; on TV, by Glenn Strange

Butcher, The

Detective Bucher (his only name): series created by Stuart Jason

Butch's Place

Favorite hangout (movie *The Best Years of Our Lives*). Proprietor: piano-playing Butch Engle (played by Hoagy Carmichel)

Buttercup

Family cow in Louisa May Alcott's *Little Men*

Buttercup

Toots and Casper's baby (comic strip "Toots and Casper")

Butterfly

Tom Swift's speedy monoplane

Buttermilk

Dale Evans' horse: stuffed, Buttermilk appears with Trigger at the Roy Rogers museum

Butterworth, Hatch and Noel

Law firm for which George Baxter works (TV series "Hazel")

Button

Thomas Paine's horse

Buttons

Chimpanzee of Mike Reynolds (TV series "Me and the Chimp")

Buttons

Clown played by James Stewart, who is eluding the law (1952 movie *The Greatest Show on Earth*)

Buttram, Pat

Gene Autry's sidekick on radio and in some movies of the late 40's and early 50's. He was also the Sage of Winston County, Alabama, on radio's "National Barn Dance." On TV he played Mr. Haney on the TV series *Greenacres*

Buz Murdock

One of automobilists in TV's "Route 66" (replaced by Line Case): played by George Maharis

Buzz Buzzard

Woody Woodpecker's nemesis

Bwana Devil

First full-length 3D color movie, released November 27, 1952: it starred Robert Stack and was written and directed by Arch Oboler

Byrd, Richard E.

A Navy captain, he was first to fly over the North Pole (1926): pilot Floyd Bennett; both won Congressional Medals of Honor and Byrd was promoted to Commander. First to fly over the South Pole (1929): pilot Bernt Balchen; Byrd was promoted to Rear Admiral. He was the last person to bid Charles Lindbergh farewell as he began his trans-Atlantic flight (May 1927) and he himself, with Bert Acosta, Lt. George O. Noville, and Bernt Balchen, flew from Roosevelt Field in New York to the sea off Ver-sur-Mer; France, in June 1927, a month after Lindbergh's flight, in a Fokker powered by 3 Wright motors

C

C12563
  License number of converted police wagon used by Robert Ironside (TV series "Ironside")

C.A.R.E.
  Cooperative for American Relief Everywhere (originally, Cooperative for American Remittances to Europe)

C. Crow
  Sign above the door to Crow's treehouse (cartoon strip "The Fox and the Crow") : the C. stands for Crawford

C M D F
  Combined Miniature Deterrent Forces: U.S. government organization that shrank the submarine "Proteus" so it could enter the bloodstream of Doctor Benes to eliminate a blood clot on his brain (1966 movie *Fantastic Voyage*)

C T W
  Children's Television Workshop: PBS production unit that presents "Sesame Street" and "The Electric Company"

CUB1
  License number of automobile of Miss Trudy Scrumptious (Sally Ann Howe) (1968 movie *Chitty Chitty Bang Bang*)

CQD
  International distress telegraph signal: come-quick-danger (used until 1911) before SOS

CX-4
  Hop Harrigan's airplane call sign (radio series)

Cabinet Offices
  United States: Secretary of State; Secretary of the Treasury; Secretary of Defense (was War); Attorney General;

(formerly, Postmaster General; Secretary of the Navy); Secretary of the Interior; Secretary of Agriculture; Secretary of Commerce; Secretary of Labor; Secretary of Health, Education and Welfare; Secretary of Housing and Urban Development; Secretary of Transportation; Secretary of Energy

Cable car routes
Current San Francisco routes:
California Line (Route 61, between Market and Van Ness)
Powell-Hyde Line (Route 60, between Market and Aquatic Park)
Powell-Mason Line (Route 59, between Market and the Bay-Taylor turntable)
Only mobile U.S. national monument

Cadbury
The Richie family butler (Richie Rich comic books)

Cadet Happy
Sidekick of Commander Buzz Corey (TV series "Space Patrol"): played by Lyn Osborn

Cadets
Football team of U.S. Military Academy at West Point (Army)

Cadillac Ranch
Stanley Marsh III's 13,000-acre ranch outside of Amarillo, Texas, where he buries Cadillac automobiles with the rear half of the car sticking out of the ground

Caduceus
Symbol of the medical profession: a snake (or two snakes) entwined on a rod

Caesar
Derek Flint's watchdog (1966 movie *Our Man Flint*)

Caesar's wife
Sid Caesar's, that is: on TV ("Your Show of Shows") played by Imogene Coca, Janet Blair, Nanette Fabray, Gisele MacKenzie

Cafe Tambourine
Cairo, Egypt, club that is detective Ken Thurston's favorite spot (radio series "A Man Called X")

Cahill, Frank "Windy"
First man Billy the Kid shot and killed, in the Adkin Saloon, Camp Grant, Arizona, August 17, 1877. Billy was 17.

Calamity Jane

Nickname of Martha Jane Canary Burke: said to have married 12 times. She died August 2, 1903, 27 years to the day after Wild Bill Hickok, said to be her lover, was killed. Doris Day played her in the 1953 musical movie *Calamity Jane*. She has been played, among others, by Jean Arthur, Frances Farmer, Yvonne de Carlo, Evelyn Ankers, Jane Russell, and Abby Dalton

Calamity Jane

Nickname of golfer Bobby Jones' favorite putter, given to him by Jim Maiden. It was named for the famed Western sharpshooter

Calder, Alexander

American artist (1898–1977), famous for inventing the mobile. He custom-painted a Braniff Airlines plane

Calico

Gabby Hayes' horse (movies)

California

William "Hopalong" Cassidy's sidekick Jack Carlson: played by Andy Clyde

California Big Four

Built the Central Pacific Railroad: Charles Crocker, Sacramento drygoods merchant; Mark Hopkins, Sacramento hardware dealer, partner of Collis Potter Huntington; and Leland Stanford, Sacramento wholesale grocer

Call Me Bwana

Bob Hope/Anita Ekberg movie for which an advertisement on the side of a building (actually Anita Ekberg's mouth) serves as escape route for Krilencu, but he is shot by James Bond's friend Kerim, *From Russia With Love*. In the novel, the mouth was Marilyn Monroe's

Calpurnia

Third wife of Julius Caesar.
First wife, Cornelia; second wife, Pompeia

Calverton

Town near the Miller farm (Capitol City is 50 miles away) (TV series "Lassie")

Calvin Calaveras

Puppet frog (Bobby Goldsboro TV show) voice of Peter Cullen

Calvin Coolidge High

New York school at which Miss Sylvia Barrett teaches English in room 322 (room 304 in the novel by Bel Kaufman) (1967 movie *Up the Down Staircase*)

Calypso

Jacques-Yves Cousteau's research ship

Camel

One hump: native to Africa and the Near East (dromedary)

Two humps: native to Central Asia

Camel Cigarettes

Times Square "Smoking Man" advertisement sign: blew smoke rings.

The smoke-blowing Penguin sign Harpo Marx gets involved with in the 1950 movie *Love Happy* advertises Kools

Camel cigarette package

Illustration includes: 1 camel, 2 pyramids, 3 palm trees, a sultan's palace (on the back)

Cameo

Brief appearance by a well-known actor in a movie: word coined by Mike Todd for his 1956 movie *Around the World in 80 Days* in which there were 42 cameo appearances

Camp Fire Girls

Blue Birds, ages 7-10

Camp Fire Girls, ages 10-15

Horizon Club Girls, ages 15-18

Camp Fire Girls' Law

"Worship God, seek beauty, give service, pursue knowledge, be trustworthy, hold on to health, glorify work, be happy"

Camp Fremont

One of two U.S. Army posts on which M/Sgt. Ernie Bilko was stationed; near Grove City, California, the town newspaper being the *Grove City Globe* (TV series "You'll Never Get Rich"). See Fort Baxter

Camp Grace

U.S. Army basic training camp where Dobie Gillis and Maynard G. Krebs were inducted (TV series "The Many Loves of Dobie Gillis")

Camp Granada

Boys' camp from which Allan Sherman writes home in his 1962 hit song "Hello Muddah, Hello Faddah" (album,

"My Son, the Folksinger"). Some of the boys there: Leonard Skinner (who got ptomaine poisoning), Jeffery Hardy (who got lost), Joe Spivey (who got poison ivy)

Camp Henderson

U.S. Marine military post where Private Gomer Pyle is stationed (TV series "Gomer Pyle, U.S.M.C.")

Camp Swampy

Military post commanded by Gen. Amos T. Halftrack at which Beetle Bailey and Sgt. Orville Snorkle are stationed (cartoon strip "Beetle Bailey" by Mort Walker)

Campuses

University of California: Berkeley, Davis, Irvine, Los Angeles, Riverside, San Diego, San Francisco, Santa Barbara, Santa Cruz

Canada

Province or Territory	Capital
Alberta	Edmonton
British Columbia	Victoria
Manitoba	Winnipeg
New Brunswick	Fredericton
New foundland (includes) Labrador)	St. John's
Northwest Territories (includes district of Franklin, Keewatin, and Mackenzie)	Yellowknife
Nova Scotia	Halifax
Ontario	Toronto
Prince Edward Island	Charlottetown
Quebec	Quebec
Saskatchewan	Regina
Yukon Territory	Whitehorse

Canadian Football League

Eastern Conference

Ottawa Rough Riders
Toronto Argonauts
Montreal Alouettes
Hamilton Tiger-Cats

Western Conference

Edmonton Eskimos
Saskatchewan Roughriders
British Columbia Lions
Calgary Stampeders
Winnipeg Blue Bombers

Can Can

Twentieth Century-Fox movie Nikita Khruschchev watched being filmed in Hollywood in 1960; he thought it was disgusting. (Watching a film being made was suggested since Khruschchev was not allowed to visit Disneyland, because of security)

Can Do

Motto of the U.S. Navy's Seabees

Candy, Charlie and Enoch

The Marquis chimpanzees (TV series "The Hathaways")

Candy

Real name of horse ridden by Hugh O'Brian (TV series "The Life and Legend of Wyatt Earp")

Cannon, Joseph Gurney

U.S. politician, first person whose face appeared on a *Time* magazine cover: Vol. 1, No. 1, March 3, 1923

Cannonball

Train owned by C & FW Railroad Company, with engine No. 8 (TV series "Petticoat Junction")

Cannonball Express

Casey Jones' regular train on the Illinois Central, engine No. 382 (4-6-0). He was killed April 30, 1900, as relief engineer on another train running from Memphis to Canton, Mississippi

Canon

The collected works of Sherlock Homes by Sir Arthur Conan Doyle: semi-humorous usage adopted by the Baker Street Irregulars and other Sherlock Holmes societies, the canon being, generally, the accepted text of some sacred book

Canton, Ohio

Location of pro football's Hall of Fame; William McKinley, 25th president, is buried in Canton

Cape Canaveral

Former name of Cape Kennedy. Cape Kennedy is also the former name of Cape Canaveral. (Cape Canaveral became Cape Kennedy in 1963, and in 1973 it was changed back to Cape Canaveral.)

Cape of Good Hope

Often thought to be the tip of South Africa; actually Cape Agulhas is, 100 miles east and south of the Cape of Good Hope, 29 minutes of longitude further south. Cape

112

of Good Hope was originally named the Cape of Storms (Cabo Tormentoso) by Bartholomew Diaz in 1488

Cape Horn
Tip of South America, southernmost continental point except for Antarctica, 55 degrees 59 minutes south latitude

Capitals, national

Country	Capital
Afghanistan	Kabul
Albania	Tirana
Algeria	Algiers
Andorra	Andorra la Vella
Angola	Luanda
Antigua	St. John's
Argentina	Buenos Aires
Australia	Canberra
Austria	Vienna
Bahamas	Nassau
Bahrain	Manama
Bangladesh	Dacca
Barbados	Bridgetown
Belgium	Brussels
Bermuda	Hamilton
Bhutan	Thimphu
Bolivia	Sucre (La Paz: seat of government)
Botswana	Gaborone
Brazil	Brasilia
British Honduras	Belmopan
British Solomon Islands	Honiara
British Virgin Islands	Roadtown
Brunei	Bandar Seri Begawan
Bulgaria	Sofia
Burma	Rangoon
Burundi	Bujumbura
Cambodia	Phnom Pnh
Cameroon	Yaoundé
Canada	Ottawa
Cape Verde Islands	Praia
Cayman Islands	Georgetown
Central African Republic	Bangui

Country	Capital
Ceylon (now Sri Lanka)	Colombo
Chad	Fort-Lamy
Chile	Santiago
China, People's Republic of	Peking
China, Republic of (Taiwan)	Taipei
Colombia	Bogota
Comoro Islands	Moroni
Congo, Democratic Republic of (now Zaire)	Kinshasa
Congo, People's Republic of	Brazzaville
Costa Rica	San José
Cuba	Havana
Cyprus	Nicosia
Czechoslovakia	Prague
Dahomey	Porto-Novo, Cotonou
Denmark	Copenhagen
Dominica	Roseau
Dominican Republic	Santo Domingo
Dutch Guiana (now Surinam)	Paramaribo
Ecuador	Quito
Egypt	Cairo
El Salvador	San Salvador
Equatorial Guinea	Santa Isabel
Ethiopia	Addis Ababa
Faeroe Islands	Torshavn
Falkland Islands	Stanley
Fiji	Suva
Finland	Helsinki
France	Paris
French Guiana	Cayenne
French Polynesia	Papeete
Gabon	Libreville
Gambia	Bathurst
Germany, West (BRD)	Bonn
Germany, East (DDR)	East Berlin
Ghana	Accra
Gilbert and Ellice Islands	Tarawa
Greece	Athens
Greenland	Godthaab
Grenada	St. George's
Guadeloupe	Basse Terre

Country	Capital
Guatemala	Guatemala
Guernsey	St. Peter Port
Guinea	Conakry
Guyana	Georgetown
Haiti	Port-au-Prince
Honduras	Tegucigalpa
Hong Kong	Victoria
Hungary	Budapest
Iceland	Reykjavik
India	New Delhi
Indonesia	Jakarta
Iran	Tehran
Iraq	Baghdad
Ireland	Dublin
Isle of Man	Douglas
Israel	Jerusalem
Italy	Rome
Ivory Coast	Abidjan
Jamaica	Kingston
Japan	Tokyo
Jersey	St. Helier
Jordan	Amman
Kenya	Nairobi
Korea, North	Pyongyang
Korea, South	Seoul
Kuwait	Kuwait
Laos	Vientiane, Luang Prabang (royal capital)
Lebanon	Beirut
Lesotho	Maseru
Liberia	Monrovia
Libya	Tripoli, Benghazi
Liechtenstein	Vaduz
Luxembourg	Luxembourg
Macao	Macao
Malagasy Republic	Tananarive
Malawi	Zomba
Malaysia	Kuala Lumpur
Maldives	Male
Mali	Bamako

Country	Capital
Malta	Valletta
Martinique	Fort-de-France
Mauritania	Nouakchott
Mauritius	Port Louis
Mexico	Mexico City
Monaco	Monaco
Mongolia	Ulan Bator
Montserrat	Plymouth
Morocco	Rabat
Mozambique	Lourenco Marques
Namibia (South-West Africa)	Windhoek
Nauru	(No capital)
Nepal	Katmandu
Netherlands	Amsterdam
Netherland Antilles	Willemstad
New Caldeonia	Noumea
New Hebrides	Vila
New Zealand	Wellington
Nicaragua	Managua
Niger	Niamey
Nigeria	Lagos
Northern Ireland	Belfast
Norway	Oslo
Oman	Muscat
Orkney Islands	Kirkwall
Pakistan	Islamabad
Panama	Panama
Papu-New Guinea	Port Moresby
Paraguay	Asuncion
Peru	Lima
Philippines	Quezon City
Pitcairn Island	Adamstown
Poland	Warsaw
Portugal	Lisbon
Portuguese Guinea	Bissau
Portuguese Timor	Dili
Qatar	Doha
Reunion	Saint-Denis
Rhodesia	Salisbury
Romania	Bucharest
Rwanda	Kigali

Country	Capital
St. Helena	Jamestown
St. Kitts-Nevis	Basseterre
St. Lucia	Castries
St. Pierre et Miquelon	St. Pierre
St. Vincent	Kingstown
San Marino	San Marino
São Tomé Principe	São Tomé
Saudi Arabia	Riyadh
Scotland	Edinburgh
Senegal	Dakar
Seychelles	Victoria
Siam (now Thailand)	Bangkok
Sierra Leone	Freetown
Sikkim	Gangtok
Singapore	Singapore
Somalia	Mogadishu
South Africa, Republic of	Pretoria (Administrative), Cape Town (Legislative)
Southern and Antarctic Lands	Port-aux-Francais
South-West Africa (now Namibia)	Windhoek
Spain	Madrid
Spanish Sahara	El Aaiún
Sir Lanka	Colombo
Sudan	Khartoum
Surinam (Dutch Guiana)	Paramaribo
Swaziland	Mbabane
Sweden	Stockholm
Switzerland	Bern
Syria	Damascus
Taiwan	Taipei
Tanzania	Dar es Salaam
Thailand	Bangkok
Tibet	Lhasa
Togo	Lomé
Tonga	Nukualofa
Trinidad and Tobago	Port of Spain
Tunisia	Tunis
Turkey	Ankara
Turks and Caicos Islands	Grand Turk
Uganda	Kampala

Capital	State
Union of Soviet Socialist Republics	Moscow
United Arab Emirates	Abu Dhabi
United Kingdom	London
United States	Washington, D.C.
Upper Volta	Ouagadougou
Uruguay	Montevideo
Vatican City, State of	Vatican City
Venezuela	Caracas
Vietnam, North	Hanoi
Vietnam, South	Saigon
Wallis et Futuna Islands	Mata-Uta
Western Samoa	Apia
Yemen, People's Democratic Republic of	Aden, Medina as-Shaab
Yemen Arab Republic	Sana
Yugoslavia	Belgrade
Zaire	Kinshasa
Zambia	Lusaka

Capitals, U.S. states and possessions

Agana	Guam
Albany	New York
Annapolis	Maryland
Atlanta	Georgia
Augusta	Maine
Austin	Texas
Balboa Heights	Canal Zone
Baton Rouge	Louisiana (parishes)
Bismark	North Dakota
Boise	Idaho
Boston	Massachusetts (townships)
Carson City	Nevada
Charleston	West Virginia
Charlotte Amalie	Virgin Islands
Cheyenne	Wyoming
Columbia	South Carolina
Columbus	Ohio
Concord	New Hampshire
Denver	Colorado
Des Moines	Iowa
Dover	Delaware

Frankfort	Kentucky*
Harrisburg	Pennsylvania*
Hartford	Connecticut
Helena	Montana
Honolulu	Hawaii
Indianapolis	Indiana
Jackson	Mississippi
Jefferson City	Missouri
Juneau	Alaska (Divisions)
Lansing	Michigan
Lincoln	Nebraska
Little Rock	Arkansas
Madison	Wisconsin
Montgomery	Alabama
Montpelier	Vermont
Nashville	Tennessee
Oklahoma City	Oklahoma
Olympia	Washington
Pago Pago	American Samoa
Phoenix	Arizona
Pierre	South Dakota
Providence	Rhode Island
Raleigh	North Carolina
Richmond	Virginia*
Sacramento	California
Salem	Oregon
Salt Lake City	Utah
San Juan	Puerto Rico
Santa Fe	New Mexico
Springfield	Illinois
St. Paul	Minnesota
Tallahassee	Florida
Topeka	Kansas
Trenton	New Jersey

Capitol Oil Company
Bodega Bay gas station attacked by the birds, indirectly causing it to explode (1963 movie *The Birds*)

Capone, Al
Chicago gangster (1899–1947)
His business card read: "Alphonse Capone, Second Hand

---

*Officially a commonwealth

Furniture Dealer, 2222 S. Wabash." He was given his scar by Frank Galluccio in a barroom fight in his youth. In the movies played by:

Wallace Beery (as Louis Scorpio) *The Secret Six* (1931)

Paul Muni (as Tony Camonte) *Scarface* (1932)

Barry Sullivan *The Gangster* (1947)

Rod Steiger *Al Capone* (1959)

Neville Brand *The Scarface Mob* (1962): pilot for "Untouchables" series on TV

Neville Brand *The George Raft Story* (1961)

Jason Robards, Jr., *St. Valentine's Day Massacre* (1967)

Ben Gazzara *Capone* (1975)

Captain, The
Horse (1961 cartoon feature movie *101 Dalmatians*)

Captain Africa
Superhero in 15 episodes of the 1955 Columbia serial *Adventures of Captain Africa*: played by John Hart

Captain Ahab
Captain of the whaler "Pequod" (Herman Melville's *Moby Dick*). Lost his right leg to the white whale and replaced it with one of whalebone. In movies played by John Barrymore (1926—*The Sea Beast*, 1930—*Moby Dick*) and Gregory Peck (1956—*Moby Dick*)

Captain America
Nickname of Wyatt (Peter Fonda) (movie *Easy Rider*): license plate of his motorcycle California 644755

Captain America
Secret identity of (originally) Steve Rogers (comic book series). Created by Jack Kirby and Joe Simon. Debut: *Captain America Comics* #1 (March 1941). As Rogers, his sidekick was Bucky Barnes. Later, secret identity of District Attorney Grant Gardner (played by Dick Purcell in 1941 movie serial), whose sidekicks were Golden Girl, Rick Jones, The Falcon. Captain America carries a shield, taught at Lee High School

Captain Andy (Hawks)
Captain and owner of the "Cotton Blossom" (Edna Ferber's *Show Boat*)

Captain (Roderick) Anthony
Captain of the "Ferndale" (Joseph Conrad's *Chance*)

Captain (Wallace Burton) Binghamton
Captain of torpedo boat Squadron 19 (TV series "Mc-Hale's Navy"): played by Joe Flynn. Mr. McHale's crew call him Leadbottom

Captain Block
Commander of New York's 53rd Precinct (TV series "Car 54, Where Are You?"): played by Paul Reed

Captain (Peter) Blood
Freebooter captain, originally a doctor, of the ship "Avenger." From Rafael Sabatini's novels *Captain Blood, Captain Blood Returns, The Further Adventures of Captain Blood.*
Movies: *Captain Blood* Errol Flynn (1935)
Fortunes of Captain Blood Louis Hayward (1950)
Captain Blood Jean Marais (1960)
Son of Captain Blood Sean Flynn (Errol Flynn's son) (1962)

Captain (John) Braddock
Chief racket buster of San Francisco Police Department (TV series "Racket Squad"): played by Reed Hadley

Captain Brunel
Captain of the British passenger ship "Juggernaut" (1974 movie *Juggernaut*): played by Omar Sharif

Captain Cold
The Flash's chief nemesis (comic books)

Captain Crawford
Captain of H.M.S. "Defiant" (Frank Tilsley's *Mutiny*): played by Alec Guinness in movie (*Damn the Defiant*)

Captain Crook
Bad guy in McDonald Land (McDonald's Hamburgers commercials)

Captain (C.G.) Culpeper
Chief of Santa Rosita police (movie *It's a Mad, Mad, Mad, Mad World*): played by Spencer Tracy

Captain Daniel Reid
Texas Ranger John Reid's older brother who, with five other Texas Rangers, was ambushed by Butch Cavendish and his Hole-in-the-Wall gang at Bryant's Gap. Parts of Captain Reid's vest were made into the Lone Ranger's mask. Daniel Reid's son was Dan Reid, his grandson Henry Reid and great grandson was Britt Reid, who be-

came The Green Hornet. On the first TV episode, played by Tristram Coffin (who also played Captain Tom Rynning on TV series "26 Men")

Captain De Vriess

Captain of the Minesweeper "Caine," who is replaced by Lt. Commander Philip Francis Queeg (1954 movie *The Caine Mutiny*): played by Tom Tully

Captain (Roger) Dorn

Companion of detective Peter Quill (radio series "Peter Quill"): played by Ken Griffin

Captain Easy

Comic strip character created by Roy Crane in cartoon "*Wash Tubbs.*" His real identity was mentioned but once, that of William Lee

Captain Englehorn

Captain of the ship "Venture" which brought King Kong to New York: played in 1933 movie by Frank Reicher

Captain Flagg and Sergeant Quirt

Two American soldiers in France during World War I, played in 1927 movie *What Price Glory?* and in sequels *The Cockeyed World* and *Hot Pepper* (also on radio series) by Victor McLaglen and Edmund Lowe

Captain Flint

Pirate captain of the "Walrus" who buried the treasure on Treasure Island. His first mate was Billy Bones; his quartermaster was Long John Silver (Robert L. Stevenson's *Treasure Island*)

Captain Flint

Long John Silver's parrot, named for his old captain: "Pieces of eight, pieces of eight"

Captain Freedom

Secret identity of Don Wright, newspaper publisher (comic book character)

Captain (Michael) Gallant

Foreign Legion officer: played by Buster Crabbe. His boy sidekick, Cuffy Sanders, is played by Buster's son Cullen Crabbe. (TV series "Foreign Legionnaire")

Captain (Adam) Greer

Police officer directly in charge of the Mod Squad (TV series "Mod Squad"): played by Tige Andrew, whose real first name is Tiger

Captain (Daniel) Gregg

Ghost haunting (in a friendly way) Gull Cottage and Mrs.

Muir (Hope Lange) (1947 movie and later TV series "The Ghost and Mrs. Muir"): played in movie by Rex Harrison and on TV by Edward Mulhare

Captain Gustav Schroeder
5'4" commander of the "St. Louis," which carried 937 Jewish refugees from Hamburg, Germany, on May 13, 1939 (portrayed in 1977 movie *Voyage of the Damned* by Max Von Sydow)

Captain Harmon
Captain of the Rio Lines passenger ship "Queen of Brazil" on which Scat Sweeney and Hot Lips Barton and stowaways (1947 Hope-Crosby movie *Road to Rio*): played by Stanley Andrews

Captain (Arthur) Hastings
Hercule Poirot's assistant and narrator of his stories: Poirot calls him "mon ami"

Captain Henry
Captain of the "Maxwell House Show Boat" (radio series): played by Charles Winninger and then Frank McIntire

Captain (John) Herrick
Owner of the tugboat "Cheryl Ann" (TV series "Waterfront"): played by Preston Foster

Captain (Grey) Holden
Skipper of riverboat "Enterprise" (TV series "Riverboat"): played by Darren McGavin

Captain Hook
Villain, captain of pirate ship the "Jolly Roger" (James M. Barrie's *Peter Pan*): his first name is James

Captain Hook's Crew
Aboard the "Jolly Roger" Smee, Cecco, Bill Jones, Cookson, Gentleman Starkey, Noodler, Robt. Mullins, Alf Mason, Skylights (James M. Barrie's *Peter Pan*)

Captain Howdy
Regan MacNeil's imaginary playmate, who is actually the evil demon that possesses her (novel/movie *The Exorcist*): voice of the devil is that of Mercedes McCambridge

Captain Huff 'n' Puff
Captain Horatio K. Huffenpuff of the boat "The Leakin' Lena" (TV puppet show "Time for Beany")

Captain Jacobi

Master of the ship "La Paloma" which brought the Maltese Falcon from Hong Kong to San Francisco (Dashiell Hammett's *The Maltese Falcon*): in 1941 movie played by Walter Huston

Captain John Carter

Confederate Army officer of Virginia who, entering an Arizona cave to escape from a band of Indians, is transported to the planet Mars where he spends the next ten years (Martian novels of Edgar Rice Burroughs)

Captain Kinross

Commander of destroyer H.M.S. "Torrin" (1942 movie *In Which We Serve*): played by Noel Coward

Captain (James T.) Kirk

Commander of the starship "Enterprise," service number SC 937-0176 CEC (TV series "Star Trek"): played by William Shatner. The "T" stands for Tiberius. His quarters are on deck 5. He is Iowa born.

Captain Klutz!

Secret identity of Ringo Fonebone, who rides his Klutz-scooter. The police chief in his adventures is Chief O'Freenbean (created by Don Martin)

Captain (Wolf) Larsen

Captain of the schooner "Ghost" (Jack London's *The Sea Wolf*) In movies played by:

(1913) *The Sea Wolf*, Hobart Bosworth; (1920) *The Sea Wolf*, Noah Beery; (1925) *The Sea Wolf*, Ralph Ince; (1930) *The Sea Wolf*, Milton Sills; (1941) *The Sea Wolf*, Edward G. Robinson; (1958) *Wolf Larsen*, Barry Sullivan; (1975) *Wolf of the Seven Seas*, Chuck Connors

Captain Lesgate

Hired killer, alias C. A. Swan, Adams, and Wilson, who instead of killing is killed by Mrs. Wendice (1954 movie *Dial M for Murder*): played by Anthony Dawson. The killing takes place on a Saturday night, September 26, and the key is hidden on the fifth step

Captain Lindemann

Captain of the German battleship "Bismarck" when it was sunk May 27, 1941. Admiral Lutjens was the highest ranking officer on board.

Captain Marlow
Character in and narrator of Joseph Conrad's *Lord Jim, Youth, Chance, Heart of Darkness*

Captain Marvel
Secret identity of Billy Batson. Created by Ed Herren. Debut: *Whiz Comics* #2, February 1940; #1 was never issued; see Captain Thunder; *Captain Marvel Adventures,* 1941 (see SHAZAM) He is "the world's mightiest mortal" and at one time held the record for highest comic book circulation (2 million copies per issue). In 1941 movie serial *The Adventures of Captain Marvel* played by Tom Tyler (Billy Batson; Frank Coghlan, Jr.). On the Saturday morning TV series *SHAZAM!* played by Jackson Bostwick and John Davey (Billy Batson: Michael Gray). Actor Fred McMurray was used as the model for the face of the comic book Captain Marvel

Captain Marvel, Jr.
"World's Mightiest Boy": secret identity of Freddie Freeman. "Captain Marvel" is the secret word that turns Freddy Freeman into Captain Marvel, Jr., and back again. Debut: Whiz Comics No. 25, December 1941. Freddie is a crippled newsboy (crutch under left arm) who sells the *Daily Gazette.* As Captain Marvel, Jr., he wears a blue costume, lightning on chest, red cape

Captain Matt Holbrook
Police officer played by Robert Taylor (TV series "The Detectives")

Captain Midnight
Secret identity of Captain Jim "Red" Albright, chief of the Secret Squadron (radio series): played by Ed Prentiss (later by Bill Bouchey and Paul Barnes). Created by Robert Murit and Wilfred Moore, he made his debut on WGN radio (Chicago) September 30, 1940. First appearance in comic book: Funnies Comics #57, July 1941. In 1941 movie serial played by David O'Brien and on TV by Richard Webb (Sid Melton as Ikky Mudd). On radio he became Jet Jackson when sponsor changed

Captain Midnight's Secret Squadron
SS-1, Captain Midnight; SS-2, Chuck Ramsey; SS-3, Joyce Ryan (originally Patsy Donoran); SS-4, Ichabod "Ikky" Mudd, the mechanic; SS-11 Kelly (pilot) Senior officer,

Major Steel. After World War II, SS was changed to SQ. Ikky's favorite expression: "Jumpin' Jupiter"

Captain Morton

Mr. Roberts' commanding officer (movie *Mr. Roberts*): played in 1955 movie by James Cagney, in TV series by Richard X. Slattery, and in 1964 movie *Ensign Pulver* by Burl Ives

Captain (Mike) Murphy

Commander of Sealab 2020 (TV cartoon series)

Captain Nazi

Captain Marvel's foe during World War II (comic books). Debut: Master Comics #21 December 1941

Captain Nemo

Captain of the submarine "Nautilus" (Jules Verne's *Twenty Thousand Leagues Under the Sea*): in Latin the name means "nobody" (ne homo), but he is really Prince Dakkar of Bundelkund. He also appears in *The Mysterious Island*. In movies he has been played by James Mason, Herbert Com, Omar Sharif, Robert Ryan, and in a 1951 movie serial by Leonard Penn

Captain Nice

Secret identity of Carter Nash (TV series "Captain Nice")

Captain (Wilton) Paramenter

Commander of the U.S. cavalry post Fort Courage (TV series "F Troop"): played by Ken Berry

Captain Peter "Wrongway" Peachfuzz

Owner and captain of the ship U.S.S. "Pennsyltucky," and a friend of Rocky and Bullwinkle (TV cartoon series)

Captain Phil "Sam" Samson

Los Angeles police captain of Central Homicide Division, Detective Shell Scott's best friend

Captain (Christopher) Pike

First commander of the starship "Enterprise": first called Captain April, then Captain Water, and then Pike, and played by Jeff Hunter. James T. Kirk, played by William Shatner, was the second (TV series "Star Trek"). Pike commanded "Enterprise" 11 years, 4 months, 5 days, then spent his remaining years on the planet Talos IV, which has a gravity of .9 that of Earth. His crew in the pilot "The Menagerie" (originally titled "The Cage" and finally shown in two parts November 17 and 24, 1966): First Officer (Majel Barrett), Navigator José Tyler (Peter Duryea), Doctor Philip Boyce (John Hoyt); Yeoman J. M. Colt (Laurel Godwin), Mr. Spock (Leonard Nimoy)

Captain (Philip Francis) Queeg
Captain (by rank Lieutenant Commander) of U.S.S. "Caine" (Herman Wouk's *The Caine Mutiny*): played in 1954 movie by Humphrey Bogart and on the stage and on TV by Lloyd Nolan

Captain Quick
Pirate who can't eat a Marathon candy bar fast (he looks like Long John Silver) (1974 TV commercial)

Captain Ronald Tracey
Commander of the star ship "Exeter"—NCC 1706 (TV series "Star Trek"): played by Morgan Woodward

Captain Sam Scabbard
U.S. Army officer stationed at Camp Swampy ("Beetle Bailey" cartoon by Mort Walker)

Captain Smollett
Captain of the "Hispanola" (Robert Louis Stevenson's *Treasure Island*)

Captain Sparks
Fighter pilot with whom Little Orphan Annie flew (radio serial)

Captain Stacy
Captain of Columbia Airlines flight 409, a B-747 that is involved in a midair collision with a Beech Baron (1975 movie *Airport 1975*): played by Efrem Zimbalist, Jr.

Captain Stanley
Commander of Los Angeles fire station 51 (TV series "Emergency!"): played by Michael Norell

Captain Herr Thiele
Captain of the "Vera" (Katherine Anne Porter's *Ship of Fools*): played in 1965 movie by Charles Korvin

Captain 3-D
Superhero who appeared in Harvey Comics in 1953. Created by Joe Simon and Jack Kirby, he was the only superhero to appear in a 3-D comic book

Captain Thunder
Captain Marvel's original name in Thrill Comics No 1, which was never released. Captain Marvel first appeared in Whiz No. 2

Captain (Adam) Troy
Captain of the yacht "Tiki" (TV series "Adventures in Paradise"): played by Gardner McKay

Captain Van Straaten

Captain of the ship "The Flying Dutchman," condemned to wander forever on the oceans of the world

Captain (Edward Fairfax "Starry") Vere

Commanding officer of H.M.S. "Indomitable" upon which Billy Budd was foretopman (Herman Melville's *Billy Budd, Foretopman*)

Captain Video

Commander of the space ship "Galaxie," on TV played by Richard Coogan and Al Hodge, in 1951 movie serial played by Judd Holdren

Captain Von Tepp

Arch-enemy of Blackhawk, responsible for the death of Blackhawk's brother and sister (comic books)

Capulet

Juliet's family name (Shakespeare's *Romeo and Juliet*)

Car 54

Police officers Gunther Toody (Joe E. Ross) and Francis Muldoon's (Fred Gwynne) police car (TV series "Car 54, Where Are You?"); the car was out of New York's 53rd Precinct.

Caraway, Hattie (Ophelia Wyatt)

First woman elected to the U.S. Senate January 12, 1932. She was appointed in 1931 to fill the Arkansas seat left vacant by the death of her husband, and then elected (and reelected in 1938)

Carfax Abbey

Count Dracula's 20-acre English residence near London (1931 movie *Dracula*)

Cardinals

Nickname of St. Louis National League (baseball), St. Louis NFC (football), and Stanford University (football) teams. The Stanford team, originally organized by Herbert Hoover (later to be president of the United States) when he was a freshman, played in the first Rose Bowl game (1902)

Carlisle

Government Indian college in Pennsylvania for which Jim Thorpe played football on teams coached by Glenn "Pop" Warner

Carl Kolchak

The Night Stalker (TV series *The Night Stalker*); played by Darren McGavin

Carl Smith
    Young man whom Elaine Robinson marries in Santa
    Barbara as Benjamin Braddock looks on (1967 movie
    The Graduate): played by Brian Avery
Carla Britton Wolfe
    Detective Nero Wolfe's adopted daughter (she's also
    called Anna)
Carlton
    Always invisible doorman of Rhoda's apartment house
    (TV series "Rhoda"): voice is that of the show's producer,
    Lorenzo Music
Carlton Arms
    Apartment building in which Margie Albright and her
    father Vern Albright live in apartment 10A. Their neigh-
    bor is Clarissa Odettes. The landlord is Mr. Patterson,
    and the elevator operator is Charlie. (TV series "My
    Little Margie")
Carmichael
    Jack Benny's polar bear which he kept in his basement. It
    was sent to him as Christmas present (radio series "The
    Jack Benny Program"): voice of Mel Blanc. To this day
    no one knows for sure if he ate the gas man
Caroline
    Air Force One's (A.F. 26000) nickname under President
    John F. Kennedy: named for his daughter
Carpathia
    British ship that first answered the SOS of the "Titanic":
    picked up 705 survivors. The "Carpathia" was 70 miles
    away, the "Californian" only 8 miles away, but no radio
    officer was on duty on the "Californian" and "Titanic's"
    distress signal was missed
Carpenters, The
    Singing team: Karen, Richard (sister and brother)
Carry on
    British movie series: *Carry on Sergeant*, 1958; *Carry on
    Nurse*, 1959; *Carry on Constable*, 1960; *Carry on Teach-
    er*, 1961; *Carry on Regardless*, 1961; *Carry on Admiral*,
    1961; *Carry on Cruising*, 1962; *Carry on T.V.*, 1963; *Car-
    ry on Venus*, 1964; *Carry on Spying*, 1965; *Carry on
    Cleo*, 1965; *Carry on Cabby*, 1967; *Carry on Jack; Carry
    on Cowboy; Carry on Screaming; Carry on Doctor;
    Carry on Up the Khyber; Carry on Camping*, 1972;
    Carry on Again Doctor; Carry on at Your Convenience

Carson, Johnny
Host of television's "Tonight Show" since Oct. 1, 1962. Ed McMahon is the program's announcer. Doc Severinsen (who replaced Skitch Henderson) is the orchestra leader. Carson MC'd the game shows "Who Do You Trust," "Earn Your Vacation," and "The Johnny Carson Show"

Cartier-Burton Diamond
69.42-carat white diamond which Richard Burton bought for his wife Elizabeth Taylor in March 1969 for an unknown amount (estimated at more than $1,000,000)

Cartoon Museum
Located in Orlando, Florida; opened in 1975. The Museum of Cartoon Art in Greenwich, Connecticut, opened in 1974

Cartwrights
Family living on Nevada ranch (TV series "Bonanza")
Wives of Ben Cartwright: Elizabeth Stoddard, mother of Adam, married in Boston: played by Geraldine Brooks; Inger Borstrum, mother of Eric (Hoss): played by Inga Swenson; Marie, mother of Joe, married in New Orleans (from a previous marriage Marie had a son named Clay who is Joe's half-brother): played by Felicia Farr
Ben's brother Will is played by Guy Williams

Carvel
Andy Hardy's hometown, population 25,000. Andy attended Carvel High School

Casa Loma Orchestra
Glen Gray's orchestra

Casey Jones
Folksong hero, based on accounts of John Luther Jones, railroad man. Song written by his fireman, Wallace Sanders. Casey Jones' picture appeared on a 1950 U.S. postage stamp honoring railroad engineers

Casper
The friendly ghost (TV/comic book series): created by Joe Oriola and Sy Reit. Debut in 1946 movie cartoon "The Friendly Ghost." Voice: Mae Questel

Casper
The Apollo 16 command module: named for Casper the Friendly Ghost, cartoon character painted on the module

130

Caspar Milquetoast
Epitome of "The Timid Soul"; created by cartoonist H. T. Webster

Catfish Row
Negro living quarters in Charleston, South Carolina (Du-Bose Heyward's *Porgy* and *Porgy and Bess*)

Catwoman
One of Batman's foes (real name: Selina Kyle): on TV played by Julie Newmar and Eartha Kitt. Originally played by Lee Merriweather

Cavern, The
Nightclub at 10 Matthew Street, in Liverpool, England, where the Beatles were discovered by Brian Epstein, 1961. A plaque indicates they played there 292 times. Cilla Black was a hatcheck girl there

Cavorite
Antigravity substance that allows Mr. Cavor's sphere to leave the earth's surface and land on the moon (H.G. Wells' *The First Men in the Moon*, 1901)

Caw-Caw
Jungle Jim's pet crow (movie series "Jungle Jim")

Cecil
The seasick sea serpent, Beanie's friend (hand puppets on TV) Voice of Stan Freberg

Cedar Falls
Town in which radio series "Story of Mary Marlin" is set

Cedars Hospital
Medical facility in the town of Springfield (TV serial "The Guiding Light")

Cei-U
(pronounced Say You) Badhnisian magic words that give Johnny Thunder the power to have all his wishes come true for the next hour (comic books)

Cell 2455
San Quentin death row cell of convicted murderer, Caryl Chessman. *Cell 2455, Death Row*, title of his autobiography

Centaur Pendragon
Rudolph Valentino's pet Irish wolfhound

Centerville
Town in which radio/TV series "The Aldrich Family" is set. Henry Aldrich attends Centerville High

Centillion

One followed by 600 zeros (British) or 303 zeros (American)

Centipede, H.M.S.

First British tank model built during World War I. The designation as a ship was meant to conceal what was essentially a new weapon, first used in 1916

Central City

American town where Barry Allen (The Flash) is a police scientist and super-crimefighter (comic book series). The Spirit also fights crime in Central City. It is also the home of the Fantastic Four

Century Studios

Motion picture company owned by Mr. Bracken (TV series "Bracken's World")

Cerberus

Three-headed dog guarding the gates of Hell (Greek mythology). As one of his labors, Hercules had to bring Cerberus up from Hades

Cermak, Anton J.

Chicago mayor killed by assassin Giuseppe Zangara Feb. 15, 1933, in Miami, Fla. (Bay Front Park), in his attempt to shoot President-elect Franklin D. Roosevelt; Zangara's aim was deflected by Mrs. W. Cross, who yanked at his arm

Certainty, Security and Celerity

Motto of the United States Post Office

Cesare

Dr. Caligari's somnambulist (1920 movie *The Cabinet of Dr. Caligari*): played by Conrad Veidt

Cha Cha Champ of Hong Kong

1958 title held by the late Kung Fu expert Bruce Lee

Challenger

Mickey Thompson's land speed dragster

Chalo

Village where the humans live, located 30 miles south of Ape City (TV series "Planet of the Apes")

Chamberlain, Wilt

Nicknames: The Stilt, The Big Dipper. Full name: Wilton Norman Chamberlain. Scored 100 points in a single basketball game the night of March 2, 1962, for the Philadelphia Warriors against New York Knicks at Hershey, Pa. Final score: Philadelphia 169; New York

147. Previous record: 78, also set by Chamberlain. Always wears a rubber band on his right wrist.

Chambers, Marilyn
One-time Ivory soap-box girl who starred in X-rated movie *Behind the Green Door*

Chameleon Boy
Member of the Legion of Super Heroes (comic book character): born on the planet Durla, has the ability to alter his shape (true name: Reep Daggle). His pet: Protyll of the planet Antares

Champion
Gene Autry's horse, the "World's Wonder-Horse," star of "The Adventures of Champion" (TV series). Actually there were 3 different horses, the first Champion had been Tom Mix's Tony, Jr., another named Lindy was born the day (May 21, 1927) Lindbergh completed his New York-Paris solo flight

Champion
Djuna's old black Scottie dog (Ellery Queen, Jr., mystery novel series)

Chan Clan, The
Kids (TV cartoon series "The Amazing Chan" and "Chan Clan"): Allen, Flip, Henry, Moon, Nancy, Scooter, Stanley, Susie, Tom: voice of Charlie Chan is Keye Luke's

Chandu the Magician
Secret identity of Frank Chandler (radio series): played on radio by Jason Robards, Sr., Gayne Whitman, Howard Hoffman, Tom Collins; in 1932 movie by Edmund Lowe; in 1934 movie serial by Bela Lugosi

Chaney, Lon
"The man of a thousand faces," son of deaf mutes. His son Creighton Chaney afterward played as Lon Chaney, Jr. In 1957 film biography *Man of a Thousand Faces*, James Cagney played the original Chaney

Chang and Eng
Original Siamese twins (surname Bunker): born in Siam, May 11, 1811, died 1874 (in pictures of the brothers Eng is on the left, Chang is on the right). They married sisters in April 1843; Chang was father of 10 children, Eng of 12. Chang died first

Chapman, Raymond
Cleveland Indians' shortstop who was struck by a pitched ball in a game against the New York Yankees, August 16,

1920. Carl Mays threw the pitch that hit Chapman in the head. He died the following day, the only man in major league baseball to have been killed while playing

Charlemane

Lion puppet (TV series "The Morning Show")

Charles

Buffalo that runs amuck on stage (1975 movie *Funny Lady*)

Charles Atlas

Pseudonym of Angelo Siciliano, "world's most perfectly developed man": once a "97-pound weakling." He took his name from the Atlas Hotel in Rockaway, Long Island, where presumably, the original sand-kicking incident occurred.

Charleston Club

Nightclub where Pinky Pinkham (Dorothy Provine) worked (TV series "The Roaring Twenties")

Charley

Mr. Magoo's Chinese cook (cartoon)

Charley

Dinosaur Fred Flintstone works with picking up boulders at the Rockhead and Quarry Construction Company

Charley

William Clarke Quantrill's horse

Charley

John Steinbeck's French poodle (*Travels With Charley*)

Charlie

Tuna in Star-Kist Tuna TV ads (as his little fish friend says, "But Charlie, they don't want tunas with good taste, they want tunas that taste good"): voice is Herschel Bernardi's

Charlie

Herman Munster's twin brother (TV series "The Munsters"): both brothers played by Fred Gwynne

Charlie

Oriental cook aboard the ship "Venture" (1933 movie *King Kong* and 1934 movie *Son of Kong*): played by Victor Wong

Charlie Chan

Chinese detective on Honolulu police force created by Earl Derr Biggers, but never played in movies by a Chinese

On radio first played by Cy Kendall, later by Walter Connolly, Ed Begley, Santos Ortega. Ralph Camargo once played him with a Spanish accent

In movies (46 feature pictures) played by George Kuwa (1926) and Kamiyama Sojin (1928), both Japanese, E. L. Park, (1929); Warner Oland (1931–1937); Sidney Toler (1938–1947); Roland Winters (1947–1952)

On TV played by J. Carroll Naish (1957–1958) and in a TV movie, *Happiness Is a Warm Clue,* by Ross Martin

Sons played by Keye Luke, Victor Sen Yung, Benson Fong, Layne Tom, Jr., Edwin Luke, James Hong

First serialized in *Saturday Evening Post* 1925 (*The House Without a Key*)

Novels: *The House Without a Key* (1925)
　　　　The Chinese Parrot (1926)
　　　　Behind That Curtain (1928)
　　　　The Black Camel (1929)
　　　　Charlie Chan Carries On (1930)
　　　　Keeper of the Keys (1932)—only novel not made into a movie; it was a Broadway play

Charlie Chicken
　Andy Panda's friend (comic book)

Charlie Chicken's cousins
　He baby-sits for them (comic books): Herman, Sherman, Shiloh

Charlie McCarthy
　Edgar Bergen's principal dummy: carved by Charlie Mack, a woodcarver

Charlie O
　Charles O. Finley's mascot mule (Oakland A's baseball team): died 1976 aged 20

Charlie Weaver
　Character played by Cliff Arquette (radio)

Charlie Wong's Ice Cream Parlor
　Soda shop (31 Celestial Flavors) where the Central High School gang including Dobie and Maynard hangs out, TV series "The Many Loves of Dobie Gillis": played by John Lee

Chastity
　Daughter of Cher and Sonny Bono, born March 4, 1969. Title of 1969 movie written by Bono in which Cher starred

Chatsworth Osborne, Jr.
   Rich, snobby teenager, Dobie Gillis' rival (TV series "The Many Loves of Dobie Gillis") : originally played by Steve Franken

Chattanooga Choo Choo
   Glen Miller record on RCA Victor label; first solid gold record awarded, (February 10, 1942) for sales of 1,200,- 000 (The first million-seller record was "Dardanella/I'm Forever Blowing Bubbles" by Ben Selvin—Victor Records 1919)

Chauncey
   Cougar (b. 1964-d. 1975) in Lincoln/Mercury TV advertising (Ford Motor Co.)

Checkerboard Square
   St. Louis address to which to send Ralston boxtops for a return premium

Checkers
   Richard M. Nixon's dog (during his 1952 campaign for the vice-presidency)

Check Mate King 2
   Code radio name for headquarters run by Lieutenant Hanley. White Rook is the code name of the patrol headed by Sergeant Saunders (TV series "Combat")

Chee-Chee
   Doctor Dolittle's pet chimp

Cheetah, The
   Wonder Woman's arch-enemy (her identity is that of Priscilla Rich)

Cher Ami
   World War I carrier pigeon that helped save the Lost Battalion (of the 77th Division), in the battle of the Argonne, October 1918 (she is enshrined in the Smithsonian Institution)

Cherokee
   Theme song of Charlie Barnet's band

Cherub monk
   Brother Dominick, who makes 500 copies of an assignment by using a Xerox copier: played on TV commercial by Jack Eagle (who also played Mr. Cholesterol)

Cheryl Ann
   Tugboat owned by Captain John Herrick moored in San Pedro harbor (TV series "Waterfront")

Chespeake and Ohio
Railroad for which John Henry worked

Cheshire Cat
Smiling, disappearing cat in *Alice in Wonderland:* voice of Sterling Holloway in Walt Disney animated movie (1951)

Chessie
Cat used in Chesapeake and Ohio Railroad advertising; motto: "Sleep like a kitten"

Chester A. Riley
Hero of radio/TV/movie *The Life of Riley:* on radio played by Jackie Gleason (7 weeks only), Lionel Stander, William Bendix; on TV (1949) by Jackie Gleason, (1953–1958) William Bendix; in 1949 movie *The Life of Riley* by William Bendix

Chesty Pagett
The Marine Corps' mascot bulldog. Earlier mascot was Sgt.-Major Jiggs

Cheta (Cheeta)
Tarzan's pet chimpanzee (movies): first appeared in first Weissmuler movie, *Tarzan the Ape Man*, 1932. In the novels the chimpanzee was named Nkima

Chevrolet brothers
Automobile makers: Gaston, Louis

Chewbacca
100-year-old, 8 foot Wookie in 1977 movie *Star Wars:* played by Peter Mayhew

Chicago 7, The
Found innocent of inciting riots during the 1968 Democratic National Convention: Rennie Davis, David Dellinger, John Froines, Tom Hayden, Abbie Hoffman, Jerry Rubin, Lee Weiner

Chi Chi
London Zoo's giant panda (see *An-An*)

Chi Chi Club
Night club on TV series "Laugh-In": the dancing and joking take place in the Boom Boom Room.

Chicago Examiner
Newspaper for which Hildy Johnson is a reporter (play/movie *The Front Page*)

Chick Carter
Boy detective, Nick Carter's adopted son (radio series): played by Billy Lipton and Leon Janney. In 1946 movie serial, played by Lyle Talbot

Chicken
Single word that infuriates Jim Stark (James Dean) (1955 movie *Rebel Without a Cause*)

CHickering 4-5099
Shepherd Henderson's phone number (1958 movie *Bell, Book and Candle*). In the play by John Van Druten, it is MUrray Hill 6-4476

Chief (G.R.) Brandon
Police chief (Dick Tracy comic strip); retired 1946 and opened Law and Order Seed Store. Played on radio by Howard Smith

Chief Cash U. Nutt
Fireman Smokey Stover's boss (comic strip)

Chief O'Hara
Mickey Mouse's hometown police chief

Chief O'Hara
Gotham City's police chief (TV series "Batman"): played by Stafford Repp

Chief Parker
Police chief of Smallville: played by Robert Williams in short-lived series "The Adventures of Superboy"

Chief Superintendent Bagshott
Scotland Yard detective friend of British intelligence agent Tommy Hambledon (created by Manning Coles)

Chief Thunderthud
Character on TV children's show "Howdy Doody Time": played by Bill Lecornec

Chili
Favorite food of detectives Columbo and Robert Ironside (TV series)

Chim
Pet chimpanzee of Sheena, Queen of the Jungle (TV series)

Chim Chim
Pet monkey (TV cartoon series "Speed Racer")

Chinese calendar, animal designations

Year of the . . .	Lunar	Gregorian
Tiger	4672	1974
Hare (Rabbit)	4673	1975

Dragon	4674	1976
Snake (Serpent)	4675	1977
Horse	4676	1978
Sheep (Goat)	4677	1979
Monkey	4678	1980
Rooster	4679	1981
Dog	4680	1982
Pig (Boar)	4681	1983
Rat	4682	1984
Ox	4683	1985

Chinese Love
 Play written by Republican Senator Everett Dirksen, who also wrote 5 novels and over 100 other works.

Chingachgook
 Hawkeye's companion, father of Uncas (James Fenimore Cooper's *The Last of the Mohicans*)

Chip 'n' Dale
 Two cartoon chipmunks (Walt Disney cartoons). Chip has a black nose, Dale a pink nose and is not too smart. They live in State Park, U.S.A. Clarisse is their girlfriend

Chipmunks
 (Recording voices—speeded up—of David Seville records): Alvin; Simon; Theodore. On Liberty Records (Simon wears glasses)

Chipper
 Barry Lockridge's little dog (TV series "Land of the Giants")

Chips
 First United States sentry dog sent overseas during World War II: awarded Silver Star and Purple Heart

Chisholm Trail
 San Antonio, Texas, to Abilene, Kansas: sometimes spelled Chisum Trail. Named for Jesse Chisholm, part Cherokee cattle trader, who opened the route (across the Indian Territory) some time before 1967, when Abilene became a shipping point for cattle

Chito Jose Gonzales Bustomino Rafferty
 Cowboy star Tim Holt's sidekick: played by Richard Martin

Choo Choo
 The Chan Clan's dog (TV cartoon): voice of Don Messick

Chopper
Dog friend of Yakky Doodle (cartoon character): voice of Vance Colvig

Chopper One
Registration number of the West California Police Department (W.C.P.D.) on side of helicopter is N40MC; on the bottom of the helicopter it is N2098 (TV series "Chopper One")

Chopsticks
Theme music of radio series "Stoopnagle and Budd"

Christina
World's second largest yacht, belonging to Aristotle Onassis

Christopher Columbus
Theme song of Fletcher Henderson's orchestra

Christopher Robin
Winnie the Pooh's human friend: name of A. A. Milne's son, subject of some of the poems in *When We Were Very Young*

Chronos
The Atom's arch-enemy (secret identity is that of David Clinton)

Chub
Horse of Hoss Cartwright (Dan Blocker) (TV series "Bonanza")

Chubby Checker
Pseudonym of Ernest Evans ("Mr. Twist"). He attended South Philadelphia High School with Frankie Avalon and Fabian. He married Catherine Lodders, Miss World of 1962. His pseudonym was given him by Mrs. Dick Clark as a play on the name of Antoine "Fats" Domino. "The Twist" is the all-time best-selling rock 'n' roll record. It was tops in 1962, as a Chubby Checker recording, though written and recorded in 1960 by Hank Ballard (and the Midnighters). Checkers also had the top 1963 record: "Limbo Rock."

Chuck Parker
Ensign played by Tim Conway (TV series "McHale's Navy"): his middle name is Beaumont

Chucky Margolis
Boy (played by Brett Hudson) who lives in a house basement; his friend is named Allen (Hudson Brothers comedy routine). The graffiti on the building reads "Chucky Loves Cindy" (Cindy Schwartz)

Chumly
Walrus sidekick of the penguin Tennessee Tuxedo (TV cartoon series "Tennessee Tuxedo and His Tales")

Church, Ellen
First airline stewardess, a registered nurse; flew for United Airlines. Her first flight was on May 15, 1930.

Churchy La Femme
Turtle who lives with Pogo in the Okefenokee Swamp (comic strip "Pogo")

Cicero
Pseudonym of World War II spy Elyesa Bazna: played by James Mason in 1952 movie *Five Fingers*

Cincinnatus
Ulysses S. Grant's horse

Cinders
Jones family dog (TV series "Casey Jones")

Cindy Bear
Yogi Bear's girlfriend (cartoons): voice of Julie Bennett

Circe
Errol Flynn's yacht (the boat was used in the 1948 Orson Welles movie *The Lady from Shanghai*)

Circle H
Girl's summer ranch attended by Annette and other girl Mouseketeers: managed by Miss Adams. The Circle H is near the Triple R, where Spin and Marty are boarders (TV series "Mickey Mouse Club")

Circus Day
Every Thursday on TV's "Mickey Mouse Club":

Performers	*Mouseketeer*
Weight Lifters	Cubby and Karen
Clown	Roy
Lion Tamer (Fearless Clyde	Tommy
Lion	Jay Jay
Trapeze Artist (Hyer and Hyer)	Cheryl
Sword Swallower	Bobby
Fire-Eater	Dennis
Dancers	Annette, Darleen Doreen
Bearded Lady (Kurly Q)	Sharon
Ring Master	Jimmie

Circus Hall of Fame

Located at Sarasota, Florida

Ciribiribin

Theme song of Harry James' orchestra

Cisco Kid

"The Robin Hood of the Old West" created from a character in an O. Henry story, "The Caballero's Way" (1907). First played in movies by Herbert Stanley Dunn in 1923 film *The Caballero's Way* and in some 100 one-reelers, as well as the 1919 two-reeler *The Border Terror*. Played on radio by Jackson Beck and Jack Mather; on TV by Duncan Renaldo (a Romanian who served 8 months in prison as an illegal alien and was pardoned by President F. D. Roosevelt). His sidekick is Pancho (see Pancho); his horse is Diablo. A Cisco Kid comic strip was begun January 15, 1951, by José-Luis Salinas

Movies:

In Old Arizona (1929) Warner Baxter
The Cisco Kid (1931) Warner Baxter
The Return of the Cisco Kid (1939) Warner Baxter
The Cisco Kid and the Lady (1939) Cesar Romero
Viva Cisco Kid (1940) Cesar Romero
Lucky Cisco Kid (1940) Cesar Romero
The Gay Caballero (1940) Cesar Romero
Romance of the Rio Grande (1941) Cesar Romero
Ride On, Vaquero (1941) Cesar Romero
The Cisco Kid Returns (1945) Duncan Renaldo
The Cisco Kid in Old New Mexico (1945) Duncan Renaldo
South of the Rio Grande (1945) Duncan Renaldo
The Gay Cavalier (1946) Gilbert Roland
South of Monterey (1946) Gilbert Roland
Beauty and the Bandit (1946) Gilbert Roland
Riding the California Trail (1947) Gilbert Roland
Robin Hood of Monterey (1947) Gilbert Roland
King of Bandits (1947) Gilbert Roland
The Valiant Hombre (1949) Duncan Renaldo
The Gay Amigo (1949) Duncan Renaldo
The Daring Caballero (1949) Duncan Renaldo
Satan's Cradle (1949) Duncan Renaldo
The Girl from San Lorenzo (1950) Duncan Renaldo

Cissie Sommerly

Billy Batson's girlfriend (Captain Marvel comics)

Citation
First thoroughbred racehorse to win a million dollars

Citizen Kane
Charles Foster Kane, publisher of the newspaper *Inquirer* (movie *Citizen Kane*): played by Orson Welles and Buddy Swan, age 8. The movie premiered at RKO Palace Theatre, New York, May 1, 1941

City Slickers, The
Spike Jones' band

Clagmire, U. S. S.
Aircraft carrier (Hank Ketcham's comic strip "Half-Hitch"): commanded by Captain Carrick

Claire de Lune
Song played on the Benedict family organ by Uncle Brawley (Chill Wills) throughout the 1956 movie *Giant*. Theme song of radio series "The Story of Mary Marlin"

Claire Brooks
Detective George Valentine's private secretary (radio series "Let George Do It"): played by Virginia Gregg. He calls her Brooksie

Clampetts
Family name of the Beverly Hillbillies (TV series)

Clan, The
Frank Sinatra; Sammy Davis, Jr.; Peter Lawford; Dean Martin; Joey Bishop. Other members: Shirley MacLaine, Tony Curtis, Jimmy Van Heusen, Sammy Cahn, Irving Paul Lazar, Harry Kurnitz

Clara Cluck
Hen in Walt Disney cartoons: voice of Florence Gill

Clarabell (Hornblow)
Red-haired clown ("Howdy Doody" TV show): played by Bob Keeshan, who later was Captain Kangaroo. Clarabell did not talk, used a horn (right for no, left for yes) and carried a seltzer bottle

Clarabelle
Cow in Walt Disney cartoons, girlfriend of Horace Horsecollar

Claremore
Small-town railroad stop (1955 movie *Oklahoma!*)

Clarence
Cross-eyed lion (TV series "Daktari" and 1965 movie *Clarence the Cross-Eyed Lion*) Played by Freddie the Freeloader

Clarence
Detective Harry Orwell's automobile mechanic (TV series "Harry O"): played by Hal Williams

Clarence and Terrance
Ventriloquist Jerry Morgan's two dummies, each of which carries the blueprints of the secret weapon Layfayette XV27 (1954 Danny Kaye movie *Knock on Wood*)

Clark, Dick
Host (TV series "American Bandstand" which originated in Philadelphia). The show's original host was Bob Horn.

Clark, Jim
Scottish automobile racer (killed in 1968 crash) who won 7 Grand Prix races in 1963: Belgium, Netherlands, France, Great Britain, Italy, Mexico, South Africa

Clark Academy
School in town of Clarksville attended by Kit Walker (the 21st Phantom). After graduation he went on to Harrison University (*The Phantom*)

Claw, The
Enemy of Mighty Mouse and Daredevil (comic book cartoons). In movies Mighty Mouse's enemy is Oil Can Harry

Cleaver
Family name of Beaver (TV series "Leave It To Beaver"): Theodore (Beaver) played by Jerry Mathers, Wally by Tony Dow, Ward, the father, by Hugh Beaumont, June, the mother, by Barbara Billingsley. Eddie Haskell was played by Ken Osmond (he called Beaver "Squirt" and Clarence "Lumpy") Rutherford, Jr., by Frank Bank. Beaver's teacher was Miss Landers. The Cleaver home at 428 Mapleton, Mayfield, was the same house later used by Marcus Welby on TV

Clemens University
College attended by Lynn Belvedere (1949 movie *Mr. Belvedere Goes To College*)

Cleo
Goldfish (cartoon feature movie *Pinocchio*): voice of Mel Blanc

Cleo
Basset hound of Socrates "Soc" Miller (TV series "The People's Choice," starring Jackie Cooper): voice of Mary Jane Croft

144

Cleo and Caesar
Early stage names of Cher and Sonny Bono (Cherilyn La Pierre Sarkisier and Salvatore Philip Bono), who were divorced in July 1975

Cleopatra
Addams' family giant man-eating plant (TV series "The Addams Family")

Clermont
Robert Fulton's steamboat, 1807

Clerow
Commedian Flip Wilson's first name (he has 9 sisters and 8 brothers)

Climb Mt. Niitaka
Japanese code signal to begin the attack on Pearl Harbor December 7, 1941

Clinton's Folly
The Erie Canal: so called for New York's Governor De-Witt Clinton

Clio
Statuette awarded annually (since 1960) for best TV commercial. In Greek mythology, Clio was the muse of history or of playing the lyre

Clipper
Sky King's nephew, played on radio by Jack Bivens, on TV by Ron Haggerty

Clipper
Jacqueline Kennedy's German shepherd, born in 1962: given to her by Joseph Kennedy

Cloninger, Tony
Cincinnati Reds pitcher who on July 3, 1966, hit two grand-slam home runs in one game. He also broke the record for most RBIs for pitchers in a single game (9)

Clyde
Ahab the Arab's camel (novelty song by Ray Stevens)

Clyde Barrow Gang
Clyde Barrow, Bonnie Parker, Buck Barrow, Blanche Barrow, W. D. Jones (in movie *Bonnie and Clyde* he was named C. W. Moss)

Clydesdale
Breed of the horses (eight to the hitch) that pull the St. Louis (Anheuser Busch) float in the Rose Tournament Parade and the Budweiser Beer Wagon in TV commer-

cials: stabled in St. Louis or at Busch Clydesdale Hamlet, Merrimack, New Hampshire

Clyde Van Dusen
Horse that won the 1929 Kentucky Derby, trained by Clyde Van Dusen

Coach Cleats
Archie Andrews' coach at Riverdale High (comic strip series "Archie")

Cobalt Club
Exclusive New York City club to which Lamont Cranston and Police Commissioner Ralph Weston belong ("The Shadow" series)

Cobb, Ty (Tyrus Raymond)
Detroit Tigers outfielder, considered by many to have been baseball's greatest player; first man elected to Baseball's Hall of Fame. He was American League batting champion for 12 seasons. When he retired he held 90 individual records. His records include: Stolen bases—892; Most hits—4,191; Most singles—3,052; Most triples—297; Extra-base hits—1,139; Total bases—5,863; Runs scored —2,244; Games—3,033; At bat—11,429; Lifetime batting average—.367

Coca-Cola
Invented by Dr. John S. Pemberton of Atlanta, Georgia, in 1886. First sold at Jacobs Pharmacy May 8, 1886

Cochise
Chiricahua Apache Indian chief, usually sympathetically portrayed in the movies. Played by Jeff Chandler in 3 movies: *Broken Arrow* (1950), *Battle at Apache Pass* (1952), *Taza, Son of Cochise* (1953), and by Antonio Moreno (*Valley of the Sun*, 1942), Miguel Inclan (*Fort Apache*, 1948), Chief Yowlachie (*The Last Outpost*, 1951), John Hodiak (*Conquest of Cochise*, 1953), Michael Keep (*40 Guns to Apache Pass*, 1967). Michael Ansara played Cochise in the TV series "Broken Arrow"

Cochise
Horse of Joe Cartwright (Michael Landon) (TV series "Bonanza")

Coco
Nick Barkley's horse (TV series "The Big Valley")

Cocoanut Grove
Boston, Massachusettes nightclub that burned the night of November 28, 1942, killing 481 people, including movie

star Buck Jones who made it safely outside but went back to help others out. In Buck Jones' last movie, *Dawn on the Great Divide,* he sings "Rock of Ages" over an open grave and in the first scene waves goodbye to the audience

Coconino County
Arizona county in which Krazy Kat, Ignatz Mouse, and Offisa Pupp live

Cody, Iron-Eyes
Cherokee Indian actor, notable for his "one tear" ecology spot on TV

Colada
Sword of El Cid (Rodrigo Diaz de Bivar)

College Football

Big Eight Conference
  Colorado Buffaloes
  Iowa State Cyclones
  Kansas Jayhawks
  Kansas State Wildcats

  Missouri Tigers
  Nebraska Cornhuskers
  Oklahoma Sooners
  Oklahoma State Cowboys
Big Ten Conference
  Illinois Fighting Illini
  Indiana Fighting Hoosiers
  Iowa Hawkeyes
  Michigan Wolverines
  Michigan State Spartans
  Minnesota Gophers

  Northwest Wildcats
  Ohio State Buckeyes
  Purdue Boilermakers
  Wisconsin Badgers

Pacific Eight
  California Golden Bears
  Oregon Ducks
  Oregon State Beavers
  Southern California
    Trojans
  Stanford Cardinals
  UCLA Bruins
  Washington Huskies
  Washington State Cougars
Ivy League
  Brown Bruins
  Columbia Lions
  Cornell Big Red
  Dartmouth Big Green
  Harvard Crimson
  Pennsylvania Red
    and Blue
  Yale Bulldogs
  Princeton Tigers

College Football Hall of Fame
Located at Rutgers University, New Brunswick, New Jersey

Collier's Magazine
April 10, 1937, issue contained two short stories: "Stage to Lordsburg" by Ernest Haycox (made into the 1939 movie *Stagecoach* starring John Wayne) and "Bringing Up

Baby" by Hagar Wilde (made into a 1938 movie starring Cary Grant and Katharine Hepburn)

Collinwood

Haunted Maine mansion (TV series "Dark Shadows" and 1970 movie *House of Dark Shadows*)

Colo

First gorilla born in captivity, December, 1956, at the Columbus, Ohio, Zoo. Her mother was Christiana, her father Baron

Colonel Bogey March

Title of the "March from the River Kwai," recorded by Mitch Miller (1957) from movie *Bridge on the River Kwai* from Pierre Boulle novel *The Bridge over the River Kwai*

Colonel J(ohn) T. Hall

Post commander under whom Sergeant Ernie Bilko (Phil Silvers) served (TV series "You'll Never Get Rich"): played by Paul Ford. His wife, Nell, was played by Hope Sansberry

Colonel Lemuel Q. Stoopnagle

Comic figure, Budd's partner: played by F. Chase Taylor (radio)

Colonel March

New Scotland Yard official in charge of the Department of Queer Complaints: played by Boris Karloff in British TV series (1953–57) based on the stories of Carter Dickson pseudonym of John Dickson Carr

Colonel Owen Thursday (Lt.)

Commander of Fort Apache (1948 movie *Fort Apache*): played by Henry Fonda

Colonel (Hugh) Pickering

Professor Henry Higgins' friend (1964 movie *My Fair Lady*): played by Wilfrid Hyde-White. In Shaw's play *Pygmalion,* the part was first played by Dallas Cairns; in the 1938 movie Scott Sunderland played the role

Colonel Robert Hogan

U.S. Army officer in charge of the prisoners in Stalag 13 (TV series "Hogan's Heroes"): played by Bob Crane

Colonel Saito

Commandant of the Japanese prison camp (1957 movie *The Bridge on the River Kwai*): played by Sessue Hayakawa

Colonel Sebastian Moran
Professor Moriarty's partner: "The second most danger-ous man in London" ("The Adventure of the Empty House" by A. Conan Doyle)

Colonel Steve Austin
The "Six Million Dollar Man," a cyborg or bionic man(TV series starring Lee Majors): from Martin Caidan novel *Cyborg*

Colonies
Thirteen original (in order of adoption of Constitution):
Delaware, Dec. 7, 1787
Pennsylvania, Dec. 12, 1787
New Jersey, Dec. 18, 1787
Georgia, Jan. 2, 1788
Connecticut, Jan. 9, 1788
Massachusetts, Feb. 6, 1788
Maryland, April 28, 1788
South Carolina, May 23, 1788
New Hampshire, June 21, 1788
(the 9th and ratifying state)
Virginia, June 25, 1788
New York, July 26, 1788
North Carolina, Nov. 21, 1789
Rhode Island, May 29, 1790

Colorado Boulevard
Street on which "The Little Old Lady from Pasadena" (1964 hit song by Jan & Dean) is the terror, racing her car

"Colored" Seas
Black (Europe), Red (Asia and Africa), White (Europe), Yellow (Asia)

Colossal Man
Colonel Glen Manning, after he was exposed to atomic radiation (1957 movie *The Amazing Colossal Man*): played by Glenn Langan

Columbia
Apollo 11 command module; landing module was "Eagle"

Columbia
First United States ship (a fur trading ship) to complete a trip around the world (1787–1790) under command of Robert Gray (originally sailed under John Kendrick; who traded places with Gray of *Lady Washington*). Full-sized replica of this ship sails on Rivers of America, Disneyland

Columbia
Airline company whose Flight 409 to Los Angeles (Red Eye Special), a Boeing 747, is in midair collision with a Beech Baron N9750Y (pilot called himself N232Z) (1975 movie *Airport* 1975)

Columbia
Double-decker carousel, located at Marriott's Great America Amusement Park, San Jose, California: largest carousel in the world

Columbiad
Spaceship (Jules Verne's *From the Earth to the Moon*)

Columbo
Detective lieutenant for the Los Angeles Police Department: played by Peter Falk. First name, Philip;* wife's name, Mildred;* drives a 403 Peugeot; wears but one raincoat; favorite food, chili; favorite soft drink, cream soda. Played on Broadway by Thomas Mitchell (1962). Bing Crosby was first offered the TV role

Columbus
U.S.S. Enterprise's shuttlecraft, NCC 1701/2 (the other one "Galileo") (TV series "Star Trek")

Comanche
Horse of Captain Miles W. Keogh, which was lone survivor of General George Custer's command at the battle of the Little Big Horn

Come On-a My House
1951 hit record by Rosemary Clooney; lyrics by William Saroyan. Song's co-author was Saroyan's cousin, Ross Bagdasarian, who later became David Seville of Alvin and the Chipmunks

Comet
Supergirl's super horse (comic books)

Comet I
World's first commercial jet airliner, 1952

"Come with Me to the Casbah"
Phrase attributed to Charles Boyer in the 1938 film *Algiers:* in reality it was never said in the film

Comic strips and cartoon features
Creator or current artist follows the dash; date is first appearance
Abbie an' Slats—Al Capp (July 7, 1937)

---

*Author's Speculation

Abie the Agent—Harry Hershfield (Feb. 2, 1914)

Adamson—Oscar Jacobsson (1920)

Ain't It a Grand and Glorious Feelin'?—Clare Briggs

Alley Oop—V. T. Hamlin

Alphonse and Gaston—F. Opper (1902)

And Her Name Was Maud—F. Opper (May 23, 1926)

Apartment 3G—Alex Kortzky (May 8, 1961)

Archie—Bob Montana (Dec. 1941 comic book; 1947)

Barnaby—Crockett Johnson (April 1942)

Barney Google—Billy de Beck (1916)

Barney Google and Snuffy Smith—Fred Lasswell (1942)

B. C.—Johnny Hart (February 17, 1958)

Beetle Bailey—Mort Walker (Sept. 3, 1950)

Believe It or Not?—Robert Ripley (1918)

Betty—Russ Westover (1914)

Big Ben Bolt—Eliot Caplin (1949)

Big George—Virgil Partch

Blondie—Chic Young (Sept. 15, 1930)

Bobby Sox—Marty Links

Bobby Thatcher-George Storm (August 1927)

Boner's Ark—Addison (Mort Walker) (March 11, 1968)

Boob McNutt—Rube Goldberg (May 1915)

Boots and Her Buddies—Edgar Martin (February 18, 1924)

Brenda Starr—Dalia (Dale) Messick (June 30, 1940)

Brick Bradford—William Ritt and Clarence Giray (August 21, 1933)

Bridge—Clare Briggs

Bringing Up Father—George McManus (1913)

Broom Hilda—Russ Myers (1970)

Bruce Gentry—Ray Bailey (March 25, 1945)

Buck Rogers—John Dille, Dick Calkins, and Phil Nowlan (Jan. 7, 1929)

Bungle Family—Harry Tuthill (1918)

Buster Brown—R. F. Outcault (May 4, 1902)

Buz Sawyer—Roy Crane (Nov. 2, 1943)

Captain Easy—Roy Crane (July 30, 1933)

Casey Ruggles—Warren Tuft (May 22, 1949)

Casper Milquetoast—Clare Briggs (see Timid Soul)

Cicero's Cat—Bud Fisher (December 3, 1933)

Connie—Frank Godwin (1927)

Count Screwloose of Tooloose—Milt Gross (Feb. 17, 1929)

Crisis series—Gluyas Williams
Dan Dunn—Norman Marsh (October 16, 1933)
Dave's Delicatessen—Milt Gross (June 1931)
Dennis the Menace—Hank Ketcham (March 12, 1951)
Desperate Desmond—Harry Hershfield (March 11, 1910)
Dickie Dare—Milton Caniff (1934)
Dick Tracy—Chester Gould (Oct. 4, 1931)
Dingbat Family—George Herriman (June 20, 1910)
Dinglehoofer and His Dog—Adolph Harold H. Knerr
Donald Duck—Walt Disney (Aug. 30, 1936); earlier
   (1928) in movies
Dondi—Gus Edson and Irsin Hasen (September 25, 1959)
Doonesbury—G. B. Trudeau (Oct. 26, 1970)
Dowagers—Helen Hokinson
Eek and Meek—Howie Schneider (1965)
Ella Cinders—Charlie Plumb and Bill Conselman (June
1, 1925)
Elmer—A. C. Fera (May 6, 1916)
Emmy Lou—Marty Links
Fatty Felix—Walt McDougall
Favorite Indoor Sports—T. A. Dorgan
Felix the Cat—Pat Sullivan (August 14, 1923)
Ferd'nand—Mik (H. Dahl Mikkelsen) (1937)
Flappers—John Held, Jr.
Flash Gordon—Alex Raymond (Jan. 7, 1934)
Fliegende Blätter illustrations—Wilhelm Busch (called "fa-
   ther" of comic strip)
Flying Jenny—Russell Keaton (1939)
Foxy Grandpa—Bunny (Charles E. Schultze) (Jan. 7,
   1900)
Freckles and His Friends—Merrill Blosser (1915)
Fred Basset—Alex Graham (July 9, 1963)
Fritzi Ritz—Ernie Bushmiller (Oct. 9, 1922)
Gasoline Alley—Frank King (Nov. 24, 1918)
G I. Joe—David Breger (June 17, 1942)
Gordo—Gus Arriola (Nov. 24, 1941)
Gumps, The—Sidney Smith (Feb. 12, 1917)
Hägar the Horrible—Dick Browne (Feb. 1973)
Hairbreadth Harry—C. W. Kahles (1906)
Half Hitch—Hank Ketcham (Feb. 1970)
Happy Hooligan—F. B. Opper (March 26, 1900)
Harold Teen—Carl Ed (May 4, 1919)
Hazel—Ted Key

Heart of Juliet Jones—Stan Drake (March 1953)

Henry—Carl Anderson (March 19, 1932)

Hi and Lois—Mort Walker and Dik Browne (Oct. 1954)

Hubert—Dick Wingert (1942)

Inventions—Rube Goldberg

It Might Have Been Worse—T. E. Powers

It's a Great Life if You Don't Weaken—Gene Byrnes

Joe and Asbestos—Ken Kling (1925)

Joe Palooka—Ham Fisher (Jan. 1, 1931)

Katzenjammer Kids—Rudolph Dirks; also later H. H. Knerr (Dec. 12, 1897)

Keeping Up with the Joneses—Steve Dowling (March 9, 1960)

Kelly—Jack Moore

Krazy Kat—George Herriman (June 20, 1910)

Li'l Abner—Al Capp (Aug. 20, 1934)

Little Annie Rooney—Brandon Walsh (January 10, 1929)

Little Eve—Lolita

Little Iodine—Jimmy Hatlo (1943)

Little Jimmy—James Swinnerton (Feb. 14, 1904)

Little King—Otto Soglow (Sept. 9, 1934)

Little Lulu—Marge (Marjorie Henderson Buell) (June 1935)

Little Nemo—Winsor McCay (Oct. 15, 1905)

Little Orphan Annie—Harold Gray (Aug. 5, 1924)

Long Sam—Al Capp (May 31, 1954)

Mandrake the Magician—Lee Falk and Phil Davis (June 11, 1934)

Mark Trail—Ed Dodd (1946)

Mary Worth—Allen Saunders and Dale Conner (1932)

Metropolitan Movies—Denys Wortman

Mickey Mouse—Walt Disney (Sept. 16, 1934)

Mighty Mouse—Paul Terry (1945)

Miss Peach—Mell Lazarus (Feb. 4, 1957)

Mr. Breger—Dave Breger (October 19, 1942)

Mr. and Mrs.—Clare Briggs (April 14, 1919)

Moon Mullins—Frank Willard (June 19, 1923)

Mutt and Jeff—Bud Fisher (Nov. 15, 1907)

Napoleon—Clifford McBride (May 5, 1919)

Nebbs—Sol Hess and W. A. Carlson (May 22, 1923)

Newlyweds, The—George McManus (1904)

Oaky Doaks—Ralph Briggs Fuller (1935)

Our Boarding House—William Freyse (1923)

Out Our Way—J. R. Williams (Nov. 22, 1921)
Peanuts—Charles Schulz (Oct. 2, 1950)
Peter Rabbitt—Harrison Cady (Aug. 15, 1920)
Pete the Tramp—C. C. Russell (January 10, 1032)
Phantom, The—Lee Falk (Feb. 17, 1936)
Pogo—Walt Kelly (1948)
Polly and Her Pals—Cliff Sterrett (Dec. 4, 1912)
Popeye—Elzie Segar (Jan. 17, 1929, in Thimble Theatre)
Prince Valiant—Hal Foster (Feb. 13, 1937)
Redeye—Gordon Bess (September 11, 1967)
Red Ryder—Fred Harman (Nov. 6, 1938)
Rex Morgan, M.D.—Bradley and Edgington (May 10, 1948)
Rick O'Shay—Stan Lynde (April 27, 1958)
Rusty Riley—Frank Godwin (January 26, 1948)
Sad Sack—George Baker (1942)
Short Ribs—Frank O'Neal November 17, 1958)
Skippy—Percy Crosby (1920)
Small Fry—William Stieg
Smilin' Jack—Zack Mosley (Oct. 1, 1933)
Smitty—Walter Berndt (Nov. 27, 1922)
Smokey Stover—Bill Holman (March 10, 1935)
Steve Canyon—Milton Caniff (Jan. 13, 1947)
Steve Roper—Saunders and Overgard (1953)
Strange As It Seems—Elsie Hix
Superman—Jerry Siegel and Joe Shuster (Jan. 16, 1939)
Sweetie Pie—Seltzer
Tarzan—Harold Foster (Jan. 7, 1929)
Terry & The Pirates—Milton Caniff (Oct. 22, 1934)
That's What They All Say—T. A. Dorgan
They'll Do It Every Time—Jimmy Hatlo (Feb. 5, 1929)
Thrill That Comes Once in a Lifetime—H. T. Webster
Tillie the Toiler—Russ Westover (Jan. 1921)
Timid Soul—H. T. Webster (May 1924)
Toonerville Folks—Fontaine Fox (1915), later called Toonerville Trolley
Toots and Casper—Jimmy Murphy (July 8, 1919)
Tumbleweeds—Tom K. Ryan (Sept. 1965)
Us Moderns—Fred Neher
Wash Tubbs—Roy Crane (April 21, 1924)
Wee Pals—Morrie Turner (1964)
When a Feller Needs a Friend—Clare Briggs (1912)

Winnie Winkle—M. M. Branner (Sept. 20, 1920)
Wizard of Id—Parker and Hart (Nov. 9, 1964)
Woody Woodpecker—Walter Lantz
Yellow Kid—R. F. Outcault (May 5, 1895)
Simultaneous debuts: "Tarzan" and "Buck Rogers" on
Jan. 7, 1929; "Jungle Jim" and "Flash Gordon" on Jan.
7, 1934

Commandant (Wilhelm) Klink
Commander of Stalag 13 (TV series "Hogan's Heroes"):
played by Werner Klemperer. His brother is named
Wolfgang

Commander Buzz Corey
Hero of TV series "Space Patrol": played by Ed Kemmer. Cadet Happy, his assistant, was played by Lyn Osborn.

Commander Caractacus Pott
Driver of the car "Chitty-Chitty-Bang-Bang" (children's
story by Ian Fleming): played by Dick Van Dyke in
1968 movie

Commander J(ohn) J(ustin) Adams
Captain of the space cruiser C57D, sent to the planet
Altair IV in search of the space ship "Bellerophon" (1956
movie *Forbidden Planet*): played by Leslie Nielsen

Commander Whitehead
Reserved and bearded British gentleman who prefers
Schweppes for "Schweppervescence" for his mix (TV
commercial)

Commando Cubs
Juvenile crime fighters. Leader: Ace Browning; Members:
Spud O'Shea, Horace Cosgrove II, Whizzer Malarkey,
Pokey Jones (Typical stereotyped Negro in 1940s, 1950s
comics). Debut in Thrilling Comics, July 1943

Commerce Bank of Beverly Hills
Mr. Milburn Drysdale's bank in which the Clampets have
$50,000,000 deposited (TV series "The Beverly Hillbillies")

Commissioner Cary
Captain Video's boss (TV series "Captain Video")

Commissioner (James W.) Gordon
Police commissioner of Gotham City (TV series "Batman"); played by Neil Hamilton (TV series) and Lyle
Talbot (1949 movie serial *Batman and Robin*)

Commissioner Stanley Kirkpatrick
Police friend of Richard Wentworth, who is actually The Spider (movie series by Grant Stockbridge). In 1938 movie serial played by Forbes Murray; in 1941 movie serial by Joe Girard

Commissioner Weston
Police commissioner (radio series "The Shadow"); played by Santos Ortega among others. His assistant was Inspector Cardona

Commodore Brand Decker
Captain of the starship "Constellation" NCC1017 (first starship built): played by William Windom (TV series "Star Trek")

Commodore Nutt
George W. Morrison, best man to General Tom Thumb (Charles Sherwood Stratton) at his wedding to Lavinia Warren (Mercy Lavinia Bump) in 1863. Tom Thumb was 36 inches tall, and Commodore Nutt 29 inches tall

Company A
Camp Swampy's company consisting of privates Beetle Bailey, "Killer" Diller, Zero, Plato, Rocky, Cosmo, Julius "Mother" (comic strip "Beetle Bailey")

Company B
Sgt. Ernie Bilko's motor pool company (24th Division) at Fort Baxter (TV series "You'll Never Get Rich"). Also Army company to which the Boogie Woogie Bugle Boy belongs, in pop song recorded by the Andrews Sisters ("Boogie Woogie Bugle Boy of Company B") and introduced in 1941 movie *Buck Privates*. Also, Fort Apache Company that adopts Rusty and Rinty (TV series "The Adventures of Rin-Tin-Tin")

Compliments of Mason's Funeral Parlor
Advertisement inscribed on the hand fans used in the hot court room (1961 movie *Inherit the Wind*)

Conan
Barbarian Cimmerian warrior who later becomes a king: created by Robert E. Howard. Debut *Weird Tales* magazine, December 1932; later a comic book series adapted by Roy Thomas

Concorde
England and France's joint supersonic airliner (SST)

Conelrad

Control of Electromagnetic Radiation (640 and 1240 AM on radio dial): now obsolete civil defense measure

Confederate States

State	Date of Secession	Readmitted to Union
South Carolina	Dec. 20, 1860	June 25, 1868
Mississippi	Jan. 9, 1861	Feb. 23, 1870
Florida	Jan. 10, 1861	June 25, 1868
Alabama	Jan. 11, 1861	June 25, 1868
Georgia	Jan. 19, 1861	(1) June 25, 1868 (2) July 15, 1870
Louisiana	Jan. 26, 1861	June 25, 1868
Texas	Feb. 1, 1861	March 30, 1870
Virginia	April 17, 1861	Jan. 26, 1870
Tennessee	May 6, 1861	July 24, 1866
Arkansas	May 7, 1861	June 22, 1868
North Carolina	May 20, 1861	June 25, 1868

North Carolina lost most soldiers in the Civil War

Congressional Medal of Honor

Authorized by joint resolution of Congress, July 12, 1862 First awarded to the six Union soldiers who hijacked the Confederate locomotive "The General": James J. Andrews, who led the raid, was a civilian and did not get the medal Awarded to both General Arthur MacArthur and General Douglas MacArthur (father and son). Won twice by Marine General Smedley D. Butler. Won by two president's sons: Webb Hayes and Theodore Roosevelt, Jr.

Connie

Terry Lee's oriental valet; his full name is George Webster Confucius (comic strip "Terry and the Pirates")

Conniption

Western ghost town: setting of Stan Lynde's comic strip "Rick O'Shay." Rick O'Shay is the town marshal

Connolly, James B.

First athlete to win a gold medal in the modern day Olympics, at Athens in 1896. He won it in the hop, skip, and jump (triple jump) events.

Connors, Chuck

American actor (real name: Kevin Joseph Connor) in movies and TV (series: Branded, The Rifleman, Cowboy in Africa, Thrill Seekers). He pinch-hit once for Brooklyn

157

Dodgers (1949) and was first baseman in 66 games of the 1951 season with the Chicago Cubs. He played basketball in the BAA 1946–1948.

Conquistador
Pablito's horse (Walt Disney movie *The Littlest Outlaw*)

Conrad, William
Played Marshal Matt Dillon (radio's "Gunsmoke")
Played Cannon, private eye (TV series)
Narrator of TV series, "The Fugitive"

Conrad Birdie
Rock'n'roll star (1963 movie *Bye Bye Birdie*): played by Jesse Pearson. He visits the small town of Sweet Apple, Ohio

Consolidated Kitchenware
Company for which Vic Gook worked, at Plant No. 14 (radio series "Vic and Sade")

Constance Adams
Dr. John Watson's first wife. They were married Monday, November 1, 1866. She called him James. She died of diphtheria (Sherlock Holmes stories by Arthur Conan Doyle)

Constantinople
Former name for Istanbul (Turkey): officially changed March 28, 1930, to name used as early as 1453

Contest
On radio's "Truth or Consequences" for the March of Dimes. Entries, accompanied by contribution, finished a statement in 25 words or less on why to support the March of Dimes. Ralph Edwards as MC, and clues were given by the mystery celebrities

Clue	*Celebrity*
Miss Hush	Clara Bow (1946)
Mr. Hush	Jack Dempsey (1947)
The Walking Man	Jack Benny (1948)

Continental Professional Football League (1968)
Pacific Division
Sacramento (Capitols)
Seattle (Rangers)
Spokane (Shockers)
Orange County (Ramblers)
Atlantic Division
Michigan (Arrows)

Norfolk (Neptunes)
Ohio Valley (Ironmen)
Alabama (Hawks)
Charleston (Rockets)
Orlando (Panthers)
Central Division
Omaha (Mustangs)
Chicago (Owls)
Arkansas (Diamonds)
Quad Cities (Raiders)
Oklahoma City (Plainsmen)
Indianapolis (Capitols)

Continents

Africa, Antarctica, Asia, Australia, Europe, North America, South America

CONTROL

International spy agency in conflict with the evil agency KAOS. Headed by Harold Clark, the "Chief" (first name, Thaddeus); played by Edward Platt. His agents include 86, Maxwell Smart (played by Don Adams); 99, Mrs. Smart (played by Barbara Feldon, who had won $64,000 as a Shakespeare expert on the TV show "The $64,000 Question"); 13, played by David Ketchum; 43, who hides in mail boxes, trash cans, etc., and is obviously half the man Agent 86 is (played by Monroe Arnold); Hymie, a human-like robot (played by Dick Gautier); Larrabee (played by Robert Karvelas), Harrington, Foster, and K-13, Fang, the dog-agent (TV series "Get Smart")

Conway and Twitty

Loretta Hager's two pet goldfish (TV series "Mary Hartman, Mary Hartman")

Cookie

Dagwood and Blondie's daughter, born 1941

Cookie Bear

Comedy bear (TV's "Andy Williams Show"): played by Janos Prohaska

Cookie Monster

Muppet who craves cookies; birthday on November 2 (TV series "Sesame Street'): voice of Frank Oz

Cooper, Chuck

First black to play basketball in the NBA (1950) for Boston Celtics

Cootie
Plastic animal put together by rolling numbers on a die
No. 1 = Body and Tail
No. 2 = Head
No. 3 = Ears (2)
No. 4 = Eyes (2)
No 5 = Tongue
No. 6 = Leg (6)

Copa Club
Nightclub where Danny Williams is employed as an entertainer (TV series "Make Room for Daddy")

Copasetic
Word meaning everything is okay, great, groovy: coined by Bill "Bojangles" Robinson

Copenhagen
Duke of Wellington's horse

Copperfin
Submarine commanded by Captain Cassidy played by Cary Grant (1944 movie *Destination Tokyo*)

Copyright
Good for 28 years with renewal for 28 years (U.S. statute). Foreign copyright usually runs for 50 years after the author's death

Cora
Mr. Dithers' wife ("Blondie" series)

Cora
Owner of Cora's General Store and proponent of Maxwell House Coffee (TV commercials): played by Margaret Hamilton

Coral Key Park
Marine preserve where Ranger Porter Ricks and his two sons Bud and Sandy live with their pet dolphin Flipper (TV series *Flipper*)

Corky
Circus boy (TV series "Circus Boy"): played by Mickey Braddock later Mickey Dolenz of the Monkees. Corky's mother and father, the "Flying Falcons," were killed in a fall from the trapeze

Corky, Rowdy, Ching Ching
Three dogs owned by Shirley Temple as a child: a scottie, a cocker spaniel, and a pekingese

160

Cornbelt Trust Company
Boone City bank where Al Stephenson works as vice president of small loans at $12,000 a year salary (1946 movie *The Best Years of Our Lives*)

Cornelius, Don
Host of TV show "Soul Train"

Corporal (Randolph) Agarn
Not-too-bright soldier of F Troop, Fort Courage (TV series "F Troop"): played by Larry Storch

Corporal Henshaw
Assistant to M/Sgt Ernie Bilko (TV series "You'll Never Get Rich"): played by Allan Melvin

Corporal Rocco Barbella
M/Sgt Ernie Bilko's assistant (TV series "You'll Never Get Rich"): played by Harvey Lembeck

Corvette
Automobile in which Tod Stiles (Martin Milner) and Buz Murdock (George Maharis) or Linc Case (Glenn Corbett) tour the country (TV series "Route 66")

Cosby Kids, The
Bill Cosby's cartoon gang: Fat Albert, Russell (Bill's brother), Dumb Donald, Rudy, Mushmouth, Weird Harold, Bucky. They are the "Buck Buck" champions of the world

Cosmic Boy
True name is Rokk Krinn, born on the planet Braal, member of the Legion of Super-Heroes (comic book character)

Cosmo B. Topper
Central character of Thorne Smith's novel *Topper:* played on radio and in movies by Roland Young (3 pictures); played on TV by Leo G. Carroll. On TV his wife Henrietta played by Lee Patrick, in movies by Billie Burke, on radio by Hope Emerson. See George and Marion Kerby

Cosmopolitan
Magazine primarily for women, first to feature a nude male (Burt Reynolds) in a centerfold, under editorship of Helen Gurley Brown. Reynolds posed free for April 1972 number (Vol. 172, No. 4), his picture appearing on pages 186-188; price $1.00

Costello, Lou
Chubby actor (1906–1959), member of the comedy team of Abbott and Costello: real name Louis Francis Cristillo. He made one picture without Abbott: *The 30-Foot Bride of Candy Rock*

Cotton Blossom
Floating theater, a sternwheeler, registered in St. Louis run by Captain Andy Hawks and his wife Parthenia (Edna Ferber's *Show Boat*). In the 1929 movie the showboat was the "Cotton Palace"

Countdown
"10-9-8-7-6-5-4-3-2-1-Now": used in the 1929 Fritz Lang movie *Frau Im Mond* (Woman in the Moon): First known use with respect to launching a rocket. In the film after each number the words "seconds to go" was repeated, i.e., 6 seconds to go, 5 seconds to go, etc.

Counterclockwise
Widdershins, the direction contrary to the proper motion and having ritual significance. Direction in which the cylindrical door of the Martian spacecraft unscrews (1953 movie *War of the Worlds*). It is the direction water goes down the drain in the Northern Hemisphere; in the Southern Hemisphere it drains clockwise: called the Coriolis Effect

Counterspy
David Harding, head of fictional U.S. organization (radio): played by Don MacLaughlin, TV by Don Megowan

Countess Marya Zaleska
Count Dracula's daughter (1936 movie *Dracula's Daughter*): played by Gloria Holden

Count Fleet
1943 Kentucky Derby winner. His sire, Reigh count, won the Derby in 1928. Count Turf, the son of Count Fleet, won the Derby in 1951

Country Music Hall of Fame
First three members elected (1961): Jimmy Rodgers, Hank Williams, Fred Rose. The Hall of Fame is maintained in Nashville, Tennessee

Country and Western Artists
Nicknames:
Jim Reeves, Gentleman Jim
Sonny James, The Southern Gentleman
Jimmy Rodgers, The Singing Brakeman

Hank Williams, Luke, the Drifter
Eddy Arnold, Tennessee Plowboy
Merle Haggard, Okie from Muskogee
Ray Price, Cherokee Cowboy
Roy Rogers, King of the Cowboys
Roy Acuff, The Smokey Mountain Boy (King of Country Music)
Faron Young, The Singing Sheriff
Bill Anderson, Whispering Bill
Ernest Tubb, The Texas Troubadour
Hank Snow, The Singing Ranger
Charlie Rich, The Silver Fox
Chet Atkins, Mr. Guitar, The Country Gentleman

Country and western bands

Lead Artist	Group
Roy Acuff	Smokey Mountain Boys
Bill Anderson	Po' Boys
Eddy Arnold	Tennessee Plowboys
Johnny Cash*	Tennessee Three
Tom Cash*	Tomcats
Danny Davis	Nashville Brass
Jack Green	Jolly Green Giants
Merle Haggard	Strangers
Tom T. Hall	Storytellers
Ferlin Husky	Hushpuppies
Wanda Jackson	Party Times
Waylon Jennings	Waylors
Pee Wee King	Golden West Cowboys
Loretta Lynn	Coal Miners
Bill Monroe	Blue Grass Boys
Roy Orbison	Candymen
Buck Owens	Buckaroos/Bakersfield Brass
Ray Price	Cherokee Cowboys
Charlie Pride	Pridesmen
Jim Reeves	The Blue Boys
Hank Thompson	Brazos Valley Boys
Ernest Tubb	Texas Troubadours
Conway Twitty	Twitty Birds
Porter Wagoner	Wagonmasters
Hank Williams	Drifting Cowboys
Hank Williams, Jr.	Cheatin' Hearts

*Brothers

Bob Wills	Texas Playboys
Faron Young	Deputies

County General Hospital
Hospital in which Ben Casey works (TV series "Ben Casey"). 56 West—Neurosurgical Ward

Courser
Captain Stormalong's ship, biggest ship ever built (American folklore)

Cousin Itt
Short, very hairy relative of the Addamses, who jabbers rather than talks (TV series "The Addams Family"): played by Felix Silla

Coventry
English town through which Lady Godiva made her famous ride

Cowboy Bob
Dennis the Menace's favorite TV hero

Cowboys, The
TV series based on 1972 John Wayne movie *The Cowboys:* Jimmy (Sean Kelly); Weedy Fimps (Clay O'Brien); Homer (Kerry MacLane); Hardy (Mitch Brown); Slim (Robert Carradine); Cimarron (A. Martinez); Steve (Clint Howard)

Cozy Rest Hotel
Hotel in the town of Dobie owned by Amos Q. Snood (Dobie was the town near Tom Mix's TM Bar Ranch on radio)

Crabbe, Clarence Linden "Buster"
American athlete, winner of 400-meter swim in 1932 Los Angeles Olympics (only U.S. victory in men's swimming) Played in movie serials: Buck Rogers, Captain Silver, Flash Gordon, Mighty Thunda, Red Barry, Tarzan
He and Johnny Weissmuller appeared together in 1950 Jungle Jim movie *Captive Girl*. On TV he played Captain Gallant

Crabby Appleton
Villain who is brought to justice by Tom Terrific and his dog Manfred (Captain Kangaroo's TV cartoon series)

Crab Key
Island retreat of Dr. (Julius) No (James Bond adventure "Dr. No" by Ian Fleming)

Crabtree Corners
Hometown of comic strip characters Abbie and Slats

Crandall, Del

Catcher in the National League whose signature was on the bat used by Hank Aaron to hit record-breaking home run number 715

Craps

First roll of the dice resulting in a 2, 3, or 12

Crayola Crayons

Colors in the 64 crayon box (made by Binney and Smith):

Carnation Pink	Olive Green
Salmon	Pine Green
Lavender	Forest Green
Thistle	Blue-Green
Orchid	Green-Blue
Periwinkle	Turquoise Blue
Blue-Violet	Aquamarine
Violet (Purple)	Sky Blue
Plum	Navy Blue
Magenta	Cornflower
Red	Cadet Blue
Maroon	Midnight Blue
Violet-Red	Blue
Red-Violet	Blue-Gray
Mulberry	Violet-Blue
Brick Red	Raw Sienna
Orange-Red	Sepia
Red-Orange	Bittersweet
Melon	Raw Umber
Orange	Brown
Burnt Orange	Tan
Yellow-Orange	Burnt Sienna
Apricot	Mahogany
Peach	Indian Red
Maize	Copper
Goldenrod	Silver
Orange-Yellow	Gold
Lemon Yellow	Gray
Yellow	White
Yellow-Green	Black
Green-Yellow	
Spring Green	
Sea Green	
Green	

Crazy Rabbit
  Rabbit that loves Trix breakfast cereal (General Mills TV commercial): voice of Russel Horten

Creasey, John
  Mystery story writer (1908-1973), who wrote 560 books under 28 pseudonyms. Some of these pseudonyms were:

Gordon Ashe	Colin Hughes
M. E. Cooke	Kyle Hunt
Norman Deane	Abel Mann
Robert Caine Frazer	Peter Manton
Patrick Gill	J. J. Marric
Michael Halliday	Richard Martin
Charles Hogarth	Anthony Morton
Brian Hope	Jeremy York

Creature from the Black Lagoon
  1954 3D horror film in which Ricou Browning played the monstrous gillman. Sequels were *Revenge of the Creature* (1955) and *The Creature Walks Among Us* (1956). The original picture was the movie which Richard Sherman took the Girl (Marilyn Monroe) to see in the 1955 movie *The Seven-Year Itch* (she felt sorry for the monster)

Creedence Clearwater Revival (C.C.R.)
  Rock 'n' roll group: John Fogerty, Tom Fogerty, Doug Clifford, Stuart Cook. Originally called The Blue Velvets, then The Golliwogs. Recorded for Fantasy Records

Crime Doctor
  Dr. Benjamin Ordway (radio series, 1940 and after, by Max Marcin): played by Ray Collins, House Jameson, Everett Sloane, and John McIntire.
  Dr. Robert Ordway (movie series of 10 pictures, 1943-49): played by Warner Baxter

Crime Doctor
  Movies (starring Warner Baxter):
  Crime Doctor (1943)
  Crime Doctor's Strangest Case (1943)
  Shadows in the Night (1944)
  Crime Doctor's Courage (1945)
  Crime Doctor's Warning (1945)
  Crime Doctor's Man Hunt (1946)
  Just Before Dawn (1946)
  The Millerson Case (1947)

Crime Doctor's Gamble (1947)
Crime Doctor's Diary (1949)

Crime Fighters

Heroes who single-handedly fight the mob, Mafia, syndicate, etc. (see also Detectives of Fiction)

Name	Hero	Author
Arrow	Frank Arrow	Walter Deptula
Assassin, The	Briganti	Peter McCurtin
Avenger, The	Richard Henry Benson	Kenneth Robeson
Baroness, The	Penelope St. John-Orsini	Paul Kenyon
Black Samurai	Robert Sand	Marc Olden
Blood	Mark Blood	Allan Morgan
Bronson	Bronson	Philip Rawls
Butcher, The	Butcher	Stuart Jason
Cage	Huntington Cage and twin brother	Alan Riefe
Crown	John Crown	Terry Harknett
Dakota	Dakota	Gilbert Ralston
Death Merchant	Richard Camellion	Joseph Rosenberger
Decoy	Nick Merlotti	Jim Deane
Destroyer, The	Remo Williams	Richard Sapir and Warren Murphy
Enforcer, The	Alex Jason	Andrew Sugar
Executioner, The	Mack Bolan	Don Pendleton
Expeditor	John Eagle	Paul Edwards
Handyman	Jefferson Boone	John Messmann
Iceman	Henry Highland West	Joseph Nazel
Keller	Keller	Nelson De Mille
Killinger	Jedediah Killinger III	P. K. Palmer
Liquidator, The	Jake Brand	R. L. Brent
Lone Wolf, The	David Williams	Mike Barry
Malko	Prince Malko Linge	Gerard De Villiers
Marksman, The	Philip Magellan	Frank Scarpetta
Mind Masters, The	Britte St. Vincent	John F. Rossmann
Murder Master	King	Joseph Rosenberger
Narc	John Bolt	Robert Hawkes

Peacemaker	Barrington Hewes-Bradford	Adam Hamilton
Penetrator, The	Mark Hardin	Lionel Derrick
Pro, The	Dave Bolt	Richard Curtis
Revenger, The	Ben Martin	Jon Messmann
Ryker	Joe Ryker	Nelson De Mille
Secret Mission	Phil Sherman	Don Smith
Shannon	Shannon	Jake Quinn
Sharpshooter, The	Johnny Rock	Bruno Rossi
Smuggler, The	Eric Saveman	Paul Petersen
Soldato	Johnny Marini	Al Conroy
Stark	John Stark	Joseph Hedges
Stryker	Colin Stryker	William Crawford
Triphammer	Dale Shand	Douglas Enefer

Crimestoppers

Dick Tracy textbook on crimefighting: shown in the first panel of a Dick Tracy cartoon strip

Cripple Creek Barroom

1898 silent film directed by W. K. L. Dickson, Edison Picture Company. Ballantines—Scotch Whiskey is advertised on the barroom door; a clock reads 4:07. Many consider this film to be the first Western movie (see Great Train Robbery)

Croatoan

Last message of the Lost Colony of Roanoke Island, Virginia, 1587–91. It was carved on a doorpost but no trace was found of the 140 colonists.

Crockett, Davy

Hero of Walt Disney's 3-part television movie starring Fess Parker (1954–55):
Davy Crockett, Indian Fighter
Davy Crockett Goes to Congress
Davy Crockett at the Alamo

Crooked Little Finger

Distinguishing feature of the invaders discovered by David Vincent (TV series "The Invaders")

Crooner

Word coined by Louis Sobel for singer Tommy Lyman

Crooper, Illinois

Fictional town, 40 miles from Peoria, that was the locale of the radio serial "Vic and Sade," who lived on Virginia Ave.

Crows

Birds that attacked the children at the Bodega Bay school (1963 movie *The Birds*). A group of crows is technically called a murder

Cruiserline Ventiports

Portholes (usually 3) on each side of the Buick Automobile radiator cover

Cruncher

Mischievous but friendly park bear in TV series "Sierra": Played by an 8-year-old bear named Murgatroyd

Cuckoo Song

Laurel and Hardy's theme song

Cuddles

Nickname of actor S. Z. Sakall (real name Szoke Szakall). He is accidentally credited as S. K. Sakall in 1942 movie *Casablanca* in which he plays the waiter Carl

Cumberland Road

First federal highway, 600 miles from Cumberland, Maryland, to Vandalia, Illinois (1840)

CURE

Crimefighting secret government agency for which Remo Williams works (novel series "The Destroyer")

Curlew

Doctor Dolittle's boat on which he and his animals sailed to Spidermonkey Island. (The boat sank before they got there. In the 1967 movie the boat is the "Flounder")

Curley

George A. Custer's Crow scout who survived the Battle of the Little Big Horn (June 25, 1876), only man of the Brigade to survive

Curly

Pet caterpillar that Pinky Thompson kept in a shoebox; it danced to Pinky's harmonic rendition of "Yes Sir, That's My Baby" (1944 movie *Once upon a Time*). Originally in Norman Corwin's radio play "My Client Curly"

Currie

Detective Philo Vance's valet (novel series by S.S. Van Dine)

Curse of Capistrano

Title of story by Johnston McCulley from which the Zorro movies sprang

Curtis Cup
Awarded to the winners in women's British-American amateur golf competition

Curtiss
Company producing Baby Ruth and Butterfinger candy bars. Baby Ruth was named for President Cleveland's daughter

Cutty Sark
19th-century American clipper ship that established a speed record on a run from China to England: last of the tea clippers

Cyclops
One-eyed giant of Greek mythology and legend. The king of the Cyclopes, Polyphemus, was blinded and fooled by Odysseus. In early myth, there are three: Arges, Brontes, Steropes

Cyclops
Leader of the X men, secret identity of Scott Walker (Marvel Comics)

Cynthia
Marilyn Monroe's automobile in Union Oil Commercials

Cyril
J. Thaddeus Toad's horse and companion (Kenneth Grahame's *The Wind in the Willows*)

Cy Young Award
Given to year's most outstanding major league pitcher, honouring Denton "Cy" Young, whose 511 wins between 1890 and 1911 stands nearly 100 games ahead of his nearest rival, Walter Johnson

D

D. B. Cooper

Pseudonym of successful skyjacker who parachuted from airliner somewhere between Seattle and Reno on a Portland to Seattle Northwest 727 flight with $200,000 November 24, 1971

D.C.

Name of the Siamese cat whose code name is Informant X-14 (Walt Disney's 1965 movie *That Darn Cat*)

D-Day Invasion beaches

Operation Overlord (June 6, 1944) in Normandy, France
American: Omaha, Utah
British/Canadian: Sword, Juno, Gold
"Mickey Mouse" was invasion password

D.J.

Nickname of villain Dishonest John, who wore the typical all-black outfit and stovepipe hat of villains (TV puppet series "Time For Beany")

DMS-18

Naval designator of minesweeper "Caine": 1954 movie *The Caine Mutiny*. In Herman Wouk's novel it is DMS-22

Dab-Dab

Dr. Dolittle's pet duck

Daddy Bigbucks

Little Annie Fanny's rich guardian (see Little Annie Fanny)

Daddy (Oliver) Warbucks

Little Orphan Annie's rich guardian

Daffy Duck

Warner Brothers cartoon drake, created by Bob Clampett; his voice is that of Mel Blanc. Debut: "Porky's Duck Hunt" (1937)

Dafoe, Alan Roy
Doctor who delivered the Dionne quintuplets. Movie biography 1936 *The Country Doctor:* played by Jean Hersholt

Dagora
Space monster (Japanese movie, 1965)

Dagwood Bumstead
Blondie's husband: he works for Mr. Dithers

Daily Blurb
Newspaper for which Andy Panda and Charlie Chicken work as reporters (comic book)

Daily Planet
Newspaper in the city of Metropolis for which Clark Kent (Superman), Jimmy Olsen, Lois Lane, and Perry White worked (originally it was called the *Daily Star*). On TV the offices are on the 18th floor of what is in reality the Los Angeles City Hall (which is the same building destroyed by the Martians in the 1953 movie *War of the Worlds*)

Daily Sentinel
Newspaper published by Britt Reid (The Green Hornet)

Daisy
Dagwood and Blondie's dog. She has 5 puppies, one named Elmer

Daisy
Trade name of popular air rifle, "the" BB gun: "It's a Daisy"

Daisy Duck
Donald Duck's girlfriend. In her debut (1937 *Don Donald*) she was called Donna Duck

Daisy Duck's nieces
April, May, and June

Daisy Hill Puppy Farm
Animal shelter where Snoopy (Charles Schulz cartoons) was born; his original owner was Lila

Daisy June
Girlfriend of Clem Kadiddlehopper (Red Skelton): played on radio by Harriet Hilliard and Lurene Tuttle

Daisy Mae
Li'l Abner's wife, maiden name, Scraggs: in stage musical played by Edie Adams, on radio by Laurette Fillbrandt

Daisy Moses

Granny's full name (TV series "The Beverly Hillbillies")

Dale Arden

Flash Gordon's girlfriend: played in 1936 and 1938 movie serials Jean Rogers, in 1940 movie serial by Carol Hughes; on TV by Irene Champlin

Daleks

Evil robots from the planet Skaro, enemies of Dr. Who (British TV series "Dr. Who" and 1965 movie *Dr. Who and The Daleks* and 1966 movie *Daleks–Invasion Earth 2150AD*)

Dan August

Detective played in TV series by Burt Reynolds; in the pilot played by Christopher George

Dan Briggs

Original chief agent (TV series "Mission Impossible"): played by Stephen Hill

Dan Briggs

Police officer in TV series "Felony Squad" played by Ben Alexander

Dancer's Image

Race horse, owned by Peter Fuller, that won the 1968 Kentucky Derby but was disqualified when drugs (pain-killer) were found in his system

Daniel

Caine's half-brother (TV series "Kung Fu"): Caine is in search of him, in each episode. Played by Tim McIntire. His wife is Delonia, played by Lois Nettleton; his son is Zeke, played by John Blythe Barrymore

Dan'l

The celebrated jumping frog of Calaveras county (owned by Bret Harte in 1944 movie *The Adventures of Mark Twain* taken from Mark Twain's story)

Danny

Jeremiah Kincaid's pet black sheep, named him after the famous harrness horse Dan Patch (1948 Walt Disney movie *So Dear to My Heart*)

Danny O'Day

Jimmy Nelson's wise-cracking dummy. They began as gas station attendant-salesman on TV's "Texaco Star Theater" (1948–58). Farfel, the Nestle's dog, is another of Nelson's puppets.

173

Dan Patch

Harness horse, a pacer, that never lost a race: foaled in 1896.

Dan Reid

Nephew of Ranger John Reid (The Lone Ranger). Dan's grandson is Britt Reid (The Green Hornet). His father and mother were Captain Dan and Linda Reid. His white horse is Victor. Dan played on radio by Ernie Stanley, James Lipton, Dick Beals; on TV by Chuck Courtney

Dapper Dan

Brother of Dressy Bessy (girls' toy doll)

Danny Boy

Danny Thomas' theme song

Dapple

Sancho Panza's donkey (Cervantes' *Don Quixote*)

Dare, Virginia

First white child of English parents (William and Eleanor White Dare) born in the New World, Roanoke Island 1587

Daredevil

Secret identity of Bart Hill, comic book hero created by Don Rico and Jack Binder (Debut in Silver Streak comics 6 September 1940.)

Darling

Family name of children who were Peter's friends (James M. Barrie's *Peter Pan*): John, Michael, Wendy

Darrin Stevens

Samantha's husband (TV series "Bewitched"): played by Dick York (1964–1968) and Dick Sargent 1969–1971)

Davenport 2020

Phone number of San Francisco police department where detective Tom Polhaus can be reached (1941 movie *The Maltese Falcon*)

Dave's Dream

U.S. Air Force B29 that dropped the atomic bomb over Bikini lagoon, June 30, 1946. On the side of the bomb was glued a pinup of Rita Hayworth

David

First name of Attorney Wilson in Mark Twain's 1894 novel *The Tragedy of Pudd'nhead Wilson*

David and Goliath

Tom Sawyer's answer to the question by the Sunday school teacher to name the first two apostles (in the 1938 movie *The Adventures of Tom Sawyer,* he answers Adam and Eve)

David Blum Award
Broadway award for the year's most promising actor

Davidson's Pet Shop
San Francisco store where Melanie Daniels meets Mitch Brenner (1963 movie *The Birds*) The time on the wall 3:15; Alfred Hitchock is seen leaving the shop with two white poodles

David St. John
A pseudonym of E. Howard Hunt, Watergate principal, as mystery novel writer

Davie
President Wilson's airedale

Davis, Benjamin Oliver Jr.
First black general in the United States Air Force (October 1954;, the son of the first black general in the United States Army (1940) Benjamin Oliver Davis

Davis, Sammy, Jr.
Black (and Jewish) variety star. As a boy called Silent Sam, the Dancing Midget. A member of the team known as the Will Mastin Trio. His first number one record was "The Candy Man" (from movie *Willie Wonka and the Chocolate Factory*). Singer of theme for TV series "Baretta". His autobiography: *Yes I Can* (from the story of the little locomotive in the Andes)

Davis Cup
Trophy awarded since 1900 to the country whose team wins the International Lawn Tennis Championship: named for Dwight Davis, Secretary of War and Governor General of Philippines

Dawes, William
Rode along with Paul Revere and Samuel Prescott in warning the colonists of the British advance on Concord (April 18, 1775)

Dawg
Family dog of Hi and Lois Flagston (comic strip "Hi and Lois")

Dawn
Pop singer Tony Orlando's two female singing companions, Thelma Hopkins and Joyce Vincent Wilson

Dawson High

Los Angeles high school attended by Jim Stark and the other rebellious kids, located at University and 10th and founded in 1891 (1955 movie *Rebel Without a Cause*): actually filmed at Santa Monica High

Day

Family of Clarence Day, depicted by him in several books, including *Life with Father*, 1935: later popular on stage, in movies, on TV. Father was played, respectively, by Howard Lindsay, William Powell, and Leon Ames

Day of Infamy

December 7, 1941, when Pearl Harbor was attacked: so called by President F. D. Roosevelt in his speech to Congress calling for a war declaration

De Marco Sisters

Singing group: Lily, Mary, Ann

De Salvo, Albert

Self-confessed "Boston Strangler": portrayed in 1968 movie by Tony Curtis

Dead End Kids

Acting group originally appearing in *Dead End* on the stage (1935) and in the motion picture (1937): Billy Halop (Tommy): Huntz Hall (Dippy); Bobby Jordan (Angel); Leo Gorcey (Spit); Gabriel Dell (T.B.)

Bernard Punsley (Milty) joined the group in the movie

The Dead End Kids broke up in 1939, the Bowery Boys going to Monogram, the Little Tough Guys to Universal

Dead Man's hand

Black aces and eights, poker hand held by Wild Bill Hickok when shot and killed by Jack McCall, Deadwood, Dakota Territory, August 2, 1876. Ace of diamonds and clubs, eight of spades and clubs, queen of hearts: in the 1939 movie *Stagecoach* Luke Plummer holds this hand (deuce of spades is fifth card)

Dean, James

American movie star (1931–1955): real name: James Byron. His movies: *Sailor Beware*, 1951 (3 lines); *Fixed Bayonets*, 1951; *Has Anybody Seen My Gal?* 1952; *East of Eden*, 1955; *Rebel Without a Cause*, 1955; *Giant*, 1956. In *Has Anybody Seen My Gal?* his only line (to Charles Coburn was: "Hey, Gramps, I'll have a choc malt, heavy on the choc, plenty of milk, four spoons of malt, two scoops of vanilla ice cream, one mixed with the rest and one floating." Two Oscar nominations: for *East of Eden* and *Giant*. Won a Tony and the Daniel Blum Award for his performance in 1954 Broadway presentation of Gide's *The Immoralist* Biographical movie: *The James Dean Story* (1957) using Dean film clips and narrated by Martin Gabel

Dean Brothers
Baseball pitchers with St. Louis Cardinals: Paul (Daffy) and Jerome Herman or sometimes Jay Hanna (Dizzy)

Dear friends and gentle hearts
Words on a scrap of paper found in the effects of composer Stephen Foster at his death in a charity ward of Bellevue Hospital, New York, in 1864

Death Valley
Area in eastern California set aside as a national monument and containing the lowest point in the United States, 276 ft. below sea level. Gomez and Morticia Addams went there for their honeymoon

Death Valley Days
Hosts on TV series: The Old Ranger (Stanley Andrews), Ronald Reagan, Dale Robertson, Robert Taylor

Death Valley Scotty
Nickname of Western prospector Walter Scott; his home, built for him by rich friends, is in the northern part of Death Valley National Monument

Decathlon
Olympic Event:

100-meter dash	110-meter hurdles
Long jump	Discus throw
16-pound shot put	Pole vault
High jump	Javelin throw
400-meter dash	1500-meter run

December 25, 1900
Birth date of Humphrey Bogart according to Warner Brothers publicists, with the implication that anyone born on Christmas Day can't be a real villain (Bogart's actual birth date was January 23, 1899). Warner Brothers also changed James Cagney's birthday from July 14, 1899, to July 14, 1904

Deck 5
Sleeping quarters of Captain Kirk, Mr. Spock. Dr. McCoy, and Mr. Scott aboard the U.S.S. "Enterprise" (TV series "Star Trek")

Decree 720, Paragraph 6, Subhead 3
"It is forbidden for any genie to cast a love spell over her master": the chief Hadji's rule forbidding Jeannie from marrying Major Tony Nelson (TV series "I Dream of Jeannie") : if she uses a spell she will lose her powers

Deep Forest
Theme song of Earl Hines' band

Dei Gratia
British vessel, commanded by Captain David Morehouse, that found the abandoned ship "Mary Celeste" adrift in the Atlantic Ocean, December 4, 1872

Deimos and Phobos
The two moons of Mars

Deirdre Dutton
Obnoxious reporter portrayed by Lily Tomlin

Delaware
The first state of the United States (first state to ratify the Constitution, December 7, 1787)

Del Florias Tailor Shop
Cover store-entrance to U.N.C.L.E. headquarters in New York City (TV series "The Man from U.N.C.L.E.")

Dell Books
An illustration in the keyhole of their Keyhole series (1950s) indicated a certain type of fiction: Eye, Dell Mystery; Heart, Dell Romance; Ship, Dell Adventure; Skeleton Cow Head, Dell Western

Delos
Amusement Park of the future consisting of three separate areas: Medieval World; Roman World; West World (1973 movie *West World*) : visitors pay $1000 a day

Delta 9
Deadly nerve gas sprayed from Pussy Galore's airplanes over Fort Knox (1964 movie *Goldfinger*)

Deltiologist
One who collects picture postcards

Dennis the Menace
Son of Alice and Henry Mitchell, about six or seven years old. His girlfriend is Margaret. His favorite drink is root beer, his favorite sandwich peanut butter. He has a dog named Ruff, carries a slingshot in his back pocket, and annoys Mr. Wilson (and charms Mrs. Wilson). Debut in comic strip by Hank Ketchum March 12, 1951. (On March 17, 1951, in England, David Law began another

Dennis the Menace strip.) On TV played by Jay North. Inspiration for the character was Ketchum's own son Dennis

Dennis Worth, Jr.
Mary Worth's first grandchild (comic strip by Allen Saunders)

Denny
Bulldog Drummond's butler

Deputy Barney Oliver Fife
Deputy of Mayberry's Sheriff Andy Taylor. Barney was allowed to carry only a single bullet with him and that was in his shirt pocket (TV series "The Andy Griffith Show"): played by Don Knotts

Derek
Mandrake the Magician's twin brother

Derek
Flint's first name (James Coburn) (1966 movie *Our Man Flint*)

Desert Fox, The
Nickname of German general Erwin Rommel (1891–1944); portrayed by James Mason in 1951 movie *The Desert Fox* and 1953 movie *The Desert Rats*

Desire
Streetcar route in the city of New Orleans; hence *A Streetcar Named Desire,* Pulitzer Prize winning play by Tennessee Williams

Desmond
Valet, a former safecracker, of detective Rip Kirby (comic book series "Rip Kirby")

Destroyer, The
Ex-cop Remo Williams from Newark, N.J., who was framed for murder (novel series by Richard Sapir and Warren Murphy). His secret identity is Remo Cabell, Number 91

Detectives of fiction

Character	Author
Arsène Lupin	Maurice Leblanc
Asey Mayo	Phoebe Atwood Taylor
Average Jones	Samuel Hopkins Adams
Barney Cook	Harvey O'Higgins
Bertha Cool	A. A. Fair (Erle Stanley Gardner)
Boston Blackie	Jack Boyle

Bulldog Drummond	Herman Cyril McNeile ("Snapper")
Charlie Chan	Earl Derr Biggers
Colonel March	John Dickson Carr
Craig Kennedy	Arthur B. Reeve
Deputy Parr	Frederick Irving Anderson
Derek Flint	Jack Pearl
Dick Tracy	Chester Gould
Doc Savage	Kenneth Robeson
Dr. Gideon Fell	John Dickson Carr
Dr. Palfrey	John Creasey
Drake	Dan J. Marlowe
Ellery Queen	Ellery Queen (Frederic Dannay and Manfred Lee)
(Sir) Henry Merrivale	John Dickson Carr
Hercule Poirot	Agatha Christie
Inspector Javert	Victor Hugo
Inspector Maigret	Georges Simenon (Georges Sim)
James Bond	Ian Fleming
Jane Marple	Agatha Christie
John J. Malone	Craig Rice
John Putnam Thatcher	Emma Lathen
Lew Archer	Ross Macdonald
Mack Bolan	Don Pendleton
Martin Kane	Ted Hediger
Matt Helm	Donald Hamilton
Max Carrados	Ernest Bramah
Michael Lanyard (The Lone Wolf)	Louis Joseph Vance
Michael Shayne	Brett Halliday (Davis Dresser)
Mike Hammer	Mickey Spillane
Mike Waring (The Falcon)	Michael Arlen
Mr. Moto	John Phillips Marquand
Mr. & Mrs. North (Jerry and Pamela North)	Richard and Frances Lockridge
Mr. Pinderton	David Frome
(Inspector) Napoleon Bonaparte	Arthur Upfield
Nero Wolfe	Rex Stout
Nick Carter	John Russell Coryell

Nick Charles	Dashiell Hammett
Parker Pyne	Agatha Christie
Perry Mason	Erle Stanley Gardner
Pete Chambers	Henry Kane
Peter Gunn	Henry Kane
Peter Styles	Judson Philips
Peter Wimsey (Lord Peter Death Bredon Wimsey)	Dorothy Sayers
Philip Marlowe	Raymond Chandler
Philip Trent	E.C. Bentley
Philo Vance	S. S. Van Dine (Willard Huntington Wright)
Reggie Fortune	Henry Christopher Bailey
Remo Williams (The Destroyer)	Richard Sapir and Warren Murphy
Richard Henry Benson (the Avenger)	Kenneth Robeson
Rick Holman	Carter Brown
Sam Durell	Edward S. Aarons
Sam Spade	Dashiell Hammett
Scott Jordan	Harold Q. Masur
Sergeant Cuff	Wilkie Collins
Shell Scott	Richard S. Prather
Sherlock Holmes	Arthur Conan Doyle
Simon Templar (The Saint)	Leslie Charteris
Sir Henry Merrivale	John Dickson Carr
Superintendent (Henry) Wilson	G.D.H. & M.I. Cole
Thatcher Colt	Anthony Abbott
Thinking Machine (Prof. S.F.X. Van Dusen)	Jacques Futrelle
The Toff	John Creasey
Tommy Hambledon	Manning Coles
Travis McGee	John D. MacDonald
Uncle Abner	Melville Davisson Post
Virgil Tibbs	John Ball

(See also Crimefighters)

Detective Tom Smith

Western detective of the 1870s (TV series "Whispering Smith" 1959–61): played by Audie Murphy

Devil

The Phantom's pet wolf (comic strip)

Devil's Hole Gang
 Western outlaw gang of Jed "Kid" Curry and Hannibal
 Heyes; gang members were Wheat (Earl Holliman),
 Kyle (Dennis Fimple), and Lobo (Read Morgan) (TV
 series "Alias Smith and Jones")

Devils Tower
 America's first national monument, so designated in 1906
 by President Theodore Roosevelt. In Wyoming near
 America's first national park, Yellowstone

Dewey Defeats Truman
 Election night headline of the Chicago *Tribune* 1948:
 actually Truman defeated Dewey

Dexter L. Baxter
 Hubert's boss (comic strip "Hubert")

Diablo
 Cisco Kid's horse

Diablo
 Small Western town, setting of TV series "Annie Oakley"

Diamond
 Sir Isaac Newton's spaniel

Diamond Jim
 Nickname of New York financier James Buchanan Brady
 (1857–1917): played in movies especially by Edward Arnold (1935 *Diamond Jim*; 1940 *Lillian Russell*)

Diamond Lil
 Play (1928) by Mae West, adapted by her as the movie
 She Done Him Wrong (1933) in which she played Lady
 Lou

Diana Palmer
 The Phantom's girlfriend (comic book/strip by Lee Falk)

Dick Marino
 Name of the little MTM kitten on logo on TV's Mary
 Tyler Moore productions

Dick Tracy
 Comic strip detective created (1931) by Chester Gould
 (originally the strip was called "Plain/Clothes Tracy"),
 later on radio and TV and in movie serials. First appeared
 in Detroit *Mirror* Sunday, October 4, 1931. Tracy is a
 34-year-old, hatchet-faced tough guy with a snap-brim hat.
 His sidekick is Sam Catchem or Pat Patton. He married
 Tess Trueheart on December 24, 1949; their adopted son
 is Junior. On radio Tracy was played by Ned Wever, Matt

Crowley, and Barry Thomson; on TV by Ralph Byrd; in 1960 TV cartoon series, his voice was Ralph Byrd or Everett Sloane

Dick Tracy movies: *Dick Tracy, Detective* (1945), Morgan Conway; *Dick Tracy Meets Gruesome* (1947), Ralph Byrd; *Dick Tracy Versus Cueball* (1946), Morgan Conway; *Dick Tracy's Dilemma* (1947) Ralph Byrd *Dick Tracy* (1937) Ralph Byrd in 15 episode serial; *Dick Tracy Returns* (1938) Ralph Byrd; *Dick Tracy's G-Men* (1939) Ralph Byrd; *Dick Tracy vs. Crime, Inc.* (1941) Ralph Byrd

Dick West

The Range Rider's partner (TV series): played by Dick Jones

Dick Weston

Name under which Roy Rogers (real name Leonard Slye) was billed in two early films: *Wild Horse Rodeo* (1937) and *The Old Barn Dance* (1938)

Diet Smith

Wealhy inventor of many of Dick Tracy's gadgets, including his two-way wrist radio.

Dig 'Em

Cartoon frog advertising Kellogg's Sugar Smacks: voice of Len Dressler

Digger O'Dell

The Friendly Undertaker, a character in "The Life of Riley." played by John Brown on radio: "You're looking fine, Riley, very natural"

Dilithium Crystals

Anti-matter fuel that powers the U.S.S. "Enterprise" (TV series "Star Trek")

Dillinger, John

America's first Public Enemy Number One; bank robber (1902–1934) killed in Chicago by FBI men. He is buried in Crown Point, Indiana, in the same cemetery as President Benjamin Harrison

DiMaggio, Joe

Hit safely in 56 consecutive games for New York Yankees, beginning May 15 and ending July 17, 1941: stopped by Al Smith and Jim Bagby of Cleveland Indians after beating Willie Keeler's record of 44 games, set in 1897 with the Baltimore Orioles. DiMaggio began a 16-

game streak the day after his record-breaker ended. While with the San Francisco Seals he hit safely in 61 consecutive games. He appeared in the 1937 movie *Manhattan Merry-Go-Round* and was for a time married to Marilyn Monroe. He made TV commercials for Mr. Coffee, coffee-making machines. On radio "The Joe DiMaggio Show" opened in 1949

DiMaggio brothers
Baseball players: Vincent Paul (born 1912), Joseph Paul (born 1914), Dominic Paul (born 1918). All played for the San Francisco Seals; all were major leaguers

Dinah
Alice's pet cat (Lewis Carroll's *Alice in Wonderland*)

Dinah
Mule of Stan Laurel and Oliver Hardy (1937 movie *Way Out West* and 1938 movie *Swiss Miss*)

Ding-a-Ling
Hokey Wolf's small buddy (Hanna-Barbera cartoon): voice of Doug Young

Dingbat
Nickname used by Archie Bunker (Carroll O'Connor) for his wife Edith (Jean Stapleton) (TV series "All in the Family"). Her maiden name is Baines

Ding Chow
Chinese cook aboard the U.S.S. "Clagmire" (comic strip "Half Hitch")

Dinny
Alley Oop's pet dinosaur

Dino
The Flintstones' dinosaur pet (TV cartoon series): voice of Chips Spam, Dino is actually a snorkasauras

Dino, Desi, and Billy
1965 rock group including Dino Martin (Dean Martin's son), Desi Arnaz (Desi Arnaz's son), and Billy Hinsche. Bill Howard (Dorothy Lamour's son) managed the group's publishing company

Dino's
Restaurant located next to 77 Sunset Strip where "Kookie" (Edd Byrnes) parked cars (TV series "77 Sunset Strip")

Dinty Moore's Tavern
Jiggs' favorite hangout (comic strip "Bringing Up Father")

Diogenes Club
Reserved London club to which Mycroft Holmes (Sherlock Holmes' clever brother) belonged. Talking was allowed only in the Strangers Room

Dionne Quintuplets
Born May 28, 1934, to Oliva and Elzire Dionne of Callander, Ontario: Annette, Cecile, Emilie, Marie, Yvonne. Doctor Alan Roy Dafoe delivered the babies: total weight 13½ pounds. They appeared in the 1936 movies *Five of a Kind, Country Doctor,* and *Reunion.* The only lefthander is Marie.

Dipsy Doodle
Theme song of Larry Clinton's orchestra

Dirty Dozen, The
Movie (1967) directed by Robert Aldrich. The dozen were: Victor Franko (John Cassavetes); Joseph Wladislaw (Charles Bronson); Robert Jefferson (Jim Brown); Archer Maggott (Telly Savalas); Vernon Pinkley (Donald Sutherland); Samson Posey (Clint Walker); Pedro Jimenez (Trini Lopez); Milo Vladek (Tom Busby); Glenn Gilpin (Ben Carruthers); Roscoe Lever (Stuart Cooper); Seth Sawyer (Colin Maitland); Tassos Bravos (Al Mancini). Lopez sings "The Bramble Song" in the movie. Bronson also appeared as one of the Magnificent Seven

Dirty Harry
San Francisco plainclothes policeman (Harry Francis Callahan) who uses a .44 Colt Magnum (played in movies by Clint Eastwood; role originally to be played by Frank Sinatra, who hurt his wrist and was unable to play it)

Disco Tech
Alma mater of Bruce Wayne (Batman) (TV series "Batman")

Discovery-1
Jupiter spaceship (1968 movie *2001: A Space Odyssey*): commanded by Commander Bowman (Keir Dullea) and controlled by the computer HAL 9000

Disney, Walt
Motion-picture cartoon producer (1901–1960). First Oscar for 1931/32 short subject "Flowers and Trees," Worldwide 700 plus awards. Won 31 Oscars, 8 consecutively.

Disneyland
Located in Anaheim, California: Adventureland, Fantasyland; Frontierland; Tomorrowland. Opened July 17, 1955; millionth visitor 7 weeks later. Ron Ziegler and H. R. Haldeman had both worked there. On Nikita Khruschchev's 1960 visit to the United States, he was refused a tour of Disneyland because he could not be guaranteed security; instead he visited the set (Twentieth Century-Fox) where *Can-Can* was being filmed and was not favorably impressed.

Disneyworld
Located near Orlando, Florida. Location of Space Mountain: site covers 43 square miles, opened October 1, 1971

District Attorney John F. X. Markham
New York City friend of detective Philo Vance who likes to get him involved in hard-to-solve cases (S.S. Van Dine novels)

Dithers
Family name of Dagwood Bumstead's boss (Julius Caesar) and his wife (Cora)

Ditto
Hi and Lois Flagston's son (comic strip). Dot is his twin sister, Chip his older brother, Trixie his baby sister

Division of Correction Road Prison 36
Southern prison camp where Lucas "Cool Hand Luke" Jackson and Clarence "Dragline" Slidell are prisoners (1967 movie *Cool Hand Luke*)

Division 6
Location of the Olympic S.W.A.T. team (TV series "S.W.A.T.")

Dixie
Composed by Daniel Decatur Emmett 1859 and popular in the Confederacy. President Lincoln asked that it be played when he received news of Lee's surrender April 9, 1865

Dixie Cup
Contained Meadow Gold ice cream (1930–1954); lid had pictures of Hollywood movie stars, sports figures, singers. Send in 12 (or 6 or 24) lids for a colored picture of a Dixie Cup star

Doberman Gang
Doberman Pinscher dogs named: Bonnie, Clyde, Baby Face Nelson, John Dillinger, Pretty Boy Floyd, and Ma

Barker (*The Doberman Gang* (1972) and 1973 sequel *The Darling Dobermans*)

Dobie Gillis

Teenage boy who falls in love rather easily: created by Max Shulman in his novel *The Many Loves of Dobie Gillis* (1951). Played in 1953 movie *The Affairs of Dobie Gillis* by Bobby Van; on TV series "The Many Loves of Dobie Gillis" by Dwayne Hickman. On TV his sidekick is Maynard G. Krebs; he's in love with Thalia Menninger

Doby, Lawrence Eugene (Larry)

First Negro player in American League (outfielder with Cleveland Indians) 1947. Doby, Jackie Robinson, Roy Campanella, and Don Newcombe were the first blacks to play in an All-Star game (July 12, 1949)

Doc Adams

Doctor Galen Adams of Dodge City and coroner of Ford County (radio/TV series "Gunsmoke"): played on radio by Howard McNear, on TV by Milburn Stone

Doc (Benjamin) Elliot

New York City's Bellevue Hospital physician who left to practice on the open road in his camper (TV series "Doc Elliot"): played by James Franciscus

Doc Gamble

Visitor at 79 Wistful Vista (radio's "Fibber McGee and Molly"): played by Arthur Q. Bryan

Doc H. Quarts

Pharmacist friend of Captain Marvel. His store is in the building that also houses radio station WHIZ

Doc Savage

Clark Savage, Jr., pulp magazine hero of the 1930s, created by Kenneth Robeson, pen name of Lester Dent and others (published by Street and Smith). Known as The Man of Bronze, and played by Ron Ely in 1975 movie *The Man of Bronze*. Doc Savage and The Shadow were the creations of Henry Ralston of Street and Smith. Two of 181 Doc Savage novels were not published under the Robeson pseudonym; *The Man of Bronze* by Kenneth Roberts and *The Derelict of Skull Shoal* by Lester Dent

Doc Savage's crew

Brigadier General Theodore Marley Brooks (Ham); Professor William Harper Littlejohn; Lieutenant Colonel Andrew Blodgett Mayfair (Monk): Colonel John Renwick (Renny); Major Thomas J. Roberts (Long Tom), played in 1975 movie *The Man of Bronze,* respectively, by Darrel Zwerling, Eldon Quick, Michael Miller, William Lucking, Paul Gleason

Dr. A

Pseudonym of prolific writer Isaac Asimov (*The Sensuous Dirty Old Man*)

Doctor Alcazar

Clairvoyant and extraordinary sleuth created by Philip MacDonald

Dr. Alex Stone

Donna Stone's husband (TV series "The Donna Reed Show"). The children are Jeff and Mary

Doctor Axel

Phsyician who delivered Kit Walker, the present Phantom (21st in the family line) (Lee Falk's "The Phantom")

Doctor Ben Casey

Neurosurgeon (TV series): played by Vincent Edwards. Dr. Zorba (Sam Jaffe) is his superior at County General Hospital. "Man, woman, birth, death, infinity" is Dr. Zorba's line

Doctor Benes

Patient whose bloodstream is invaded by the miniaturized submarine "Proteus" to eliminate a bloodclot (novel and 1966 movie *Fantastic Voyage*)

Doctor (Josiah) Boone

Drunken physician played in 1939 movie *Stagecoach* by Thomas Mitchell (Oscar for best supporting actor) and in 1966 version by Bing Crosby

Doctor (Kelly) Brackett, M.D., F.A.C.S.

Rampart General Hospital doctor who works closely with the paramedic team (TV series "Emergency"): played by Robert Fuller

Doctor (Morton) Chegley

Doctor for whom Julia (Diahann Carroll) works (TV series "Julia"): played by Lloyd·Nolan

Doctor Christian

Paul Christian, M.D., of Rivers End, Minn., played by Jean Hersholt (movies and radio): in TV series the principal character was his nephew Mark Christian, played by MacDonald Carey, Dr. Christian movies:
Meet Dr. Christian (1939)
The Courageous Dr. Christian (1940)

Dr. Christian Meets the Women (1940)
Remedy for Riches (1940)
Melody for Three (1941)
They Meet Again (1941)

Doctor Cobra
Villain who supposedly killed Denny Colt by throwing chemicals on him (comic book series "The Spirit")

Dr. David Q. Dawson
Friend and associate of Baker St's Basil. Both live in Sherlock Holmes' cellar at 221B Baker Street, London. Basil is the Sherlock Holmes of the Mouse World and Dawson is his Watson (Basil series by Eve Titus)

Doctor Dolittle
Doctor John Dolittle, M.D., who lives in English town of Puddleby-on-the-Marsh. His Pets: Dab Dab, duck; Gub Gub, baby pig; Jip, dog; Too Too, owl; Polynesia, parrot; Chee Chee, monkey. Tommy Stubbins is the boy who lives with him and is narrator of his stories. The stories were written by Hugh Lofting (1886–1948). Dr. Dolittle was played in 1967 movie *Dr. Dolittle* by Rex Harrison

Dr. Doom
Arch-enemy of the Fantastic Four (comic book series)

Doctor Fate
Secret identity of Crime fighter Kent Nelson (comic books). Debut: More Fun Comics #55, May 1940. He is a Salem, Mass., archeologist and a member of the Justice Society of America. His girlfriend is Inza Cramer (Frank Merriwell's was Inza Burrage) Created by Garner Fox

Doctor (Gideon) Fell
Detective created by John Dickson Carr

Dr. Frank Chandler
Secret identity of Chandu the Magician (see Chandu)

Doctor (Victor) Frankenstein
Creator of the Monster that came to be known as "The Frankenstein Monster": from Mary Wollstonecraft Shelley's novel *Frankenstein* (1816). In the 1931 movie, directed by James Whale, Colin Clive played Dr. Henry Frankenstein and Boris Karloff, made up by Jack Pierce, was the Monster.

Doctor Frank Griffin
Brother of Jack Griffin, the Invisible Man (1940 movie The *Invisible Man Returns*)

Doctor Fu Manchu

Oriental villain created by Sax Rohmer (Arthur Sarsfield Ward) in 14 novels (1913–1957), the first being *The Insidious Dr. Fu Manchu* (1913): played in movies by Warner Oland, Boris Karloff, Henry Brandon, and Christopher Lee. On radio the role was originated by Arthur Hughes and later played by John C. Daly and Harold Haber. On TV a pilot starred John Carradine, but the series starred Glenn Gordon

Doctor Gillespie

Mentor of Dr. Kildare, Leonard Gillespie, M.D., played by Lionel Barrymore (movies and radio). After 1942, Dr. Gillespie was the central character of the series
On TV Raymond Massey and Gary Merrill played the part

Dr. Gillespie movie series

Movies:

> *Calling Dr. Gillespie* (1942)
> *Dr. Gillespie's New Assistant* (1943)
> *Dr. Gillespie's Criminal Case* (1943)
> *Three Men in White* (1944)
> *Between Two Women* (1944)
> *Dark Delusion* (1947)

Dr. Goldfoot

Horror movie spoofs starring Vincent Price: *Dr. Goldfoot and the Bikini Machine* (1965), *Dr. Goldfoot and the Girl Bombs* (1966)

Doctor Herbert Lee

Adventurer Terry Lee's father (played in 1940 movie serial *Terry and the Pirates* by J. Paul Jones)

Doctor Horton

Scientist who created the Human Torch who is actually a humanoid (comic books)

Dr. Huer

Buck Roger's sidekick (radio and comic strip): played on radio by Edgar Stehli, on TV by Harry Sothern, and in 1939 movie serial by C. Montague Shaw

Doctor I.Q.

Lew Valentine, Jimmy McClain, Stanley Vainrib (radio Quizmaster): program sponsored by Mars candy bars

Doctor (Sean) Jamison

Children's doctor in Hawaii (TV series "The Little People"): played by Brian Keith. His daughter Anne played by Shelley Fabares, is also Dr. Jamison

Dr. Jekyll
Henry Jekyll, the "good" side (Robert Louis Stevenson's *Dr. Jekyll and Mr. Hyde*)

Dr. Jekyll and Mr. Hyde movies

		Actor
1908		
1910	(*The Duality of Man*)	
1910	(Danish)	Alwin Neuss
1912		James Cruze
1913		
1913		King Baggot
1920	(*Der Januskopf*)	Conrad Veidt
1920		Sheldon Lewis
1920		John Barrymore
1932		Fredric March
1941		Spencer Tracy
1961	(*House of Fright*)	Paul Massie
1971	(*I, Monster*)	Christopher Lee
1972	(*Dr. Jekyll and Sister Hyde*)	Ralph Bates & Martine Beswick

Doctor Joe Early
Rampart General Hospital doctor who works closely with the paramedic team (TV series "Emergency"): played by Bobby Troup, husband of Julie London (Dixie McCall, nurse on the show) and composer of such pop tunes as "Girl Talk" and "Route 66"

Doctor Joe (Aloysius) Gannon
Played by Chad Everett (TV series "Medical Center"): in pilot played by Richard Bradford

Doctor John Chapman
Replaced Doc Adams for a few episodes of TV's "Gunsmoke": played by Pat Hingle

Doctor Jules Bedford
MD. played by Danny Thomas (TV series "The Practice")

Doctor Kildare
James Kildare, first played by Joel McCrea (*Interns Can't Take Money*) and then by Lew Ayres (movies); Lew Ayres (radio), and Richard Chamberlain and Mark Jenkins (TV). Dr. Kildare worked at Blair General Hospital;

191

his father, Stephen, was town doctor in Dartford. Character created by Max Brand

Movies:

Interns Can't Take Money (1937) Joel McCrae
Young Dr. Kildare (1938)
Calling Dr. Kildare (1939)
The Secret of Dr. Kildare (1939)
Dr. Kildare's Strangest Case (1940)
Dr. Kildare Goes Home (1940)
Dr. Kildare's Crisis (1940)
The People vs. Dr. Kildare (1941)
Dr. Kildare's Wedding Day (1941)
Dr. Kildare's Victory (1942)

Doctor (Steven) Kiley
Dr. Marcus Welby's assistant (TV series "Marcus Welby, M.D."): played by James Brolin

Doctor Konrad Styner
Los Angeles medical doctor (TV series "Medic"): played by Richard Boone (1954–1956)

Doctor Lyndon Parker
London detective Solar Pons' "Doctor Watson" and narrator of his tales which parallel those of Sherlock Holmes (series by August Derleth)

Dr. Mabuse
Evil German scientist-criminal who hypnotizes his victims, in Fritz Lang films from novel by Norbert Jacques

Doctor McKinley Thompson
Psychiatrist (TV series "Breaking Point"): played by Paul Richards

Doctor Mid-Nite
Secret identity of Dr. Charles McNider a blind surgeon and member of the Justice Society of America: created by Charles Reizenstein and Stan Asch. Debut in National All-American Comics #25, April 1941

Doctor (Edward) Morbius
Ruler of the planet Altair IV, creator of Robby the Robot and father of Altaira (1956 movie *Forbidden Planet*). He came to the planet in the space ship "Bellerophon," which left Earth on the 7th of Sextor 2351

Doctor (Julius) No
Villainous opponent of James Bond (Ian Fleming's *Dr. No*): played in movie by Joseph Wiseman

Doctor Octopus

Identity of Doctor Otto Octavius, arch-enemy of Spider-man, who calls him Doc Ock (comic books)

Doctor (Benjamin) Ordway

Psychiatrist ex-criminal referred to on radio and in movies as The Crime Doctor (see Crime Doctor). His name is Robert Ordway in the movies

Doctor Pauli

Captain Video's arch-enemy: played on TV by Hal Conklin

Doctor Paul Lochner

Head doctor at University Medical Center: (TV series "Medical Center"): played by James Daly

Dr. Pepper

Soft drink invented by chemist R. S. Lazenby of Waco, Texas, in 1885 in the Old Corner Drug Store

Doctor Peter Brady

The Invisible Man in the television series (1958–1959). The name of the actor was never revealed

Doctor Peter Goldstone

Physician (TV series "The Interns"): played by Broderick Crawford

Doctor Petrie

Companion of Scotland Yard's Sir Dennis Nayland Smith and narrator of the novels (Fu Manchu novel and movie series): first name in movies variously John, Jack, Walter. Played on radio by Bob White and on TV by Clark Howat

Dr. Praetorius

Scientist who worked with Dr. Frankenstein to create a mate for his monster (1935 movie *The Bridge of Frankenstein*): played by Ernest Thesiger

Doctor Randall "Red" Adams

Assistant doctor to Dr. Gillespie in several Dr. Gillespie movies: played by Van Johnson

Doctor Richard Kimble

Fugitive, a pediatrician (TV series "The Fugitive"): played by David Janssen. For five seasons he avoided Lieutenant Gerard, who was seeking him for supposedly strangling his wife, Helen Regan Kimble. The Kimbles lived on Westover Way in Stafford, Indiana. The one-armed man was caught in the final episode August 29, 1967

Doctor Robert Hartley
Chicago psychologist, played on TV series by Bob Newhart

Doctor (Michael) Rossi
Doctor (TV series "Peyton Place") : played by Ed Nelson

Dr. Seuss
Pseudonym of children's author Theodor Seuss Geisel

Doctor Simon Locke
Police Surgeon in Canadian TV series "Police Surgeon": played by Sam Groom

Doctor Simon Sparrow
Resident doctor at London's St. Swithian's Hospital (played by Dirk Bogarde) in the British "Doctor" series:
Doctor in the House (1954)
Doctor at Sea (1956)
Doctor at Large (1957)
Doctor in Love (1962: played by Michael Craig)'
Doctor in Distress (1964)

Doctor (Thaddeus Bodog) Sivana
World's wickedest scientist "Captain Marvel" 's enemy (comic books). He comes from the planet Venus

Doctor Stanislaus Alexander Palfrey
Head of the secret organization Z5 (created by John Creasey)

Doctor Strangelove
"Or, How I learned To Stop Worrying and Love the Bomb" (subtitle of movie). The part of Dr. Strangelove, as well as President Merkin Muffly and Group Captain Lionel Mandrake, was played by Peter Sellers. Sellers almost had a fourth role, that of Major T. J. "King" Kong, played in the movie by Slim Pickens

Doctor Ted Steffen
Physicians on the TV series "The Doctors and the Nurses": played by Joseph Campanella

Doctor Theodore Bassett
Physician played by Wendell Corey (TV series "The Eleventh Hour")

Doctor Watson
John H(amish) Watson, Sherlock Holmes' assistant and narrator of the Holmes stories. The two adventures by Holmes himself are those of the Lion's Mane and the Blanched Soldier. In the movies played by many actors, notably by Nigel Bruce (to Basil Rathbone's Holmes).

Reginald Owen and Peter Cushing played both Watson and Holmes in movies. On radio played by Leigh Lovel, Nigel Bruce, Eric Snowden, Alfred Shirley, Ian Martin.

Doctor (Marcus) Welby
General practitioner (TV series "Marcus Welby, M.D."): played by Robert Young

Dr. X
Dr. Xavier, played by Lionel Atwill in 1932 movie *Dr. X* and by Humphrey Bogart in 1939 movie *The Return of Dr. X*

Doctor (Hans) Zarkoff
Flash Gordon's companion: played in 3 movie serials by Frank Shannon; on radio by Maurice Franklin, on TV by Joe Nash

Doctor (David) Zorba
Senior to Dr. Ben Casey (TV series "Ben Casey"): played by Sam Jaffe

Dodd, Jimmie
Host of the Mickey Mouse Club (TV and in the movies occasionally as one of the Three Mesquiteers)

Dodge Aspen
Automobile commercials on television showing Rex Harrison in the setting of *My Fair Lady*. The commercials were produced by Mervin LeRoy circa 1975-1976

Dodge brothers
Automobile makers; Horace, John

Dodge City
Setting for TV series "Gunsmoke"

Dodge City
Name of the base camp in Viet Cong territory commanded by Special Forces Colonel Kirby (1968 movie *The Green Berets*)

Dodge Girls
Blonde advertising spokeswomen for Dodge automobiles and trucks (1966-1971); The Dodge Rebellion (1966-1968), Conny Van Dyke, Pamela Austin; The Dodge Fever (1968-1970), brunette Joan Anita Parker; The Dodge Material (1970-1971), Cheryl Lynn Miller. They all wore white cowboy hats

Dodge House
Most popular hotel in Dodge City (TV series "Gunsmoke")

Dodge Trophy Company
   Manufacturers of the Oscar, Emmys, and Rose Bowl trophies

Does the Spearmint Lose Its Flavor on the Bedpost Ovenight?
   Title of song composed by Billy Rose in 1924: he claimed it was the first commercial jingle written. The song made the pop charts in 1961, recorded by Lonnie Donegan as "Does Your Chewing Gum Lose Its Flavor?"

Dog
   Lieutenant Columbo's basset hound

Dogs
   Classification of the American Kennel Club:
   Working Dogs
   Sporting Dogs
   Nonsporting Dogs
   Hounds
   Terriers
   Toys

Dogpatch
   Li'l Abner's hometown, apparently somewhere in Kentucky mountains

Doiby Dickles
   The original Green Lantern's sidekick, who drove a taxicab nicknamed Gertrude (comic books)

Doll Girl
   Secret identity of Martha Roberts, girlfriend of Doll Man. Created by Will Eisner. Debut: Doll Man #37, December 1951.

Doll Man
   Secret identity of Darrell Dane, member of D.C. Comics Freedom Fighters (Doll Man and Hit comics), Debut Quality Comics 27, December 1939

Dolly
   Old whaling ship that brought the crew to the island of Nukuheva. The whaler "Julia" rescues Tommo (Melville) and Karakoee from the island (Herman Melville's *Typee*)

Dollar
   Richie Rich's dog (Harvey Comics)

Dollar Bill
   Number 1 (standing for one dollar) on its face 4 times

and on its reverse 4 times. The word "one" is written twice on the face and 6 times on the back. Total: Word, 8 times; Number, 8 times

Dolly Dimples
Celeste Geyer, one-time circus fat lady: 550 lbs. She eventually went on a diet and dropped her weight to 123 pounds

Dolly sisters
Twins, Yancsi and Roszika Dolly in silent films. Later Rosie and Jennie Netcher

Don Winslow
Winslow of the Navy (comic strip by Lt. Cdr. Frank V. Martinek, and then radio): played on radio by Bob Guilbert, Raymond Edward Johnson, John Gibson. Radio theme: "Columbia, The Gem of the Ocean." In movies played by Don Terry (*Don Wilson of the Navy*, 1942, and *Don Wilson of the Coast Guard*, 1943), on radio: "I consecrate my life to peace and to the protection of all my countrymen wherever they may be. My battle against Scorpia represents the battle between Good and Evil. Never will I enter into any jingoistic proposition, but will devote my entire life to protecting my country. The whole purpose of my life is that of promoting peace—not war, I will work in the interests of peace and will promote the fulfillment of all things that are clean, wholesome, and upright. Join me not alone in observing this creed, but likewise be patriotic. Love your country, its flag, and all the things for which it stands. Follow the advice of your parents and superiors and help someone every day."

Donald Duck
Belligerent duck, wearing sailor suit, in Walt Disney cartoons. Voice: Clarence Nash. Debut: "The Little Wise Hen," a Silly Symphony. First "starring" cartoon: "Orphan's Benefit" (1936). Donald's birthday, March 13; his girlfriend, Daisy Duck. Comic strip debut August 30, 1936. First drawn by Art Babbitt and Dick Huebner; in comic books by Al Taliaferro and Carl Barks.
Nephews: Huey, Dewey, Louie, first appeared in 1938 movie cartoon "Donald's Nephews," in which Donald's sister Dumbella gives him custody of the three. In comic strips (beignning October 17, 1937), Bella Duck leaves the three with Donald.

Donald Lam

Partner of woman detective Mrs. Bertha Cool, narrator of their novels (series by Erle Stanley Gardner as A. A. Fair)

Don Alejandro Vega

Zorro's father, who is not aware of his son's secret identity

Dondi

Orphaned Italian boy, created by Gus Edson and Irwin Hasen. His dog is Queenie. Debut in comic strip September 25, 1955. Played in 1962 movie *Dondi* by David Cory

Doodyville

Texas home of Howdy Doody and his friends (TV). Phineas T. Bluster is mayor

Dopey

One of the Seven Dwarfs (1937 Disney movie *Snow White and the Seven Dwarfs*). He supposedly never makes a sound yet when he discovers Snow White sleeping he lets out a loud yell. He is the only one of the seven without a beard

Dorothy Gale

Kansas girl who dreams of going to the land of Oz with her dog Toto: played in 1939 movie by Judy Garland (Shirley Temple had also been considered for the part). In an earlier movie version played (1925) by Dorothy Dwan. In 1962 animated movie, *Journey Back to Oz*, Dorothy's voice was that of Liza Minnelli, daughter of Judy Garland. In the Broadway musical adaptation, *The Wiz*, played by Stephanie Mills

Doubleday, Abner

Alleged inventor of baseball, who attended West Point and as captain of artillery at Fort Sumter on April 12, 1861, fired the first Union shot of the Civil War. He is said to have laid out the first baseball diamond on farmer Phinney's lot

Double Q

Boss of Secret Squirrel and his sidekick Morocco Mole (TV cartoon "Secret Squirrel")

Double R Bar

Roy Rogers' and Dale Evans' ranch (near Mineral City (radio/TV). The real ranch is located in Apple Valley, California

Douglas, John Sholto

Marquis of Queensberry who, in the 1860s, introduced the basic ring rules and regulations of boxing

Douglas D. S. T.

Airplane flown by Tailspin Tommy (cartoon strip "Tailspin Tommy" by Hal Forrest)

Dover

Race horse that Eliza Doolittle roots for at Ascot (play/movie *My Fair Lady*). She cries, "Come on, Dover, move your bloomin' asss"

Dow-Jones

Index of N.Y. Stock Exchange market level, comprising prices of 30 high-ranking industrial stocks, added and multiplied by a variable factor based on total shares

Downing Street

10—Home of British Prime Minister
11—Home of Chancellor of the Exchequer
12—Home of Government Chief Whip

Downingtown

Small town terrorized by the Blob (1958 movie *The Blob*)

Dozier, William

Executive producer and narrator of the Batman TV series: married to Ann Rutherford

Dracula

Classic vampire of fiction, from Bram Stoker's 1897 novel *Dracula*. Vampire movies made before 1931's *Dracula* included 1912 *Vampyr* (Danish) and *Nosferatu* (1923, German, starring Max Schreck: most prints destroyed after copyright infringement suit by Stoker's widow). *Dracula, The Un-Dead*, made by Universal in 1931, directed by Tod Browning, starred Bela Lugosi (born Bela Blasko in Lugos, Hungary, 1882; died 1956), who had played Count Dracula in a 1927 Broadway play written by Hamilton Deane and John Balderston from Stoker's novel (in the play Edward Van Sloan played Dr. Van Helsing and Herbert Bunston was Dr. Seward as in the movie; Dorothy Peterson played Lucy Harker); Lon Chaney, Sr., had been offered the movie role, but died before filming started.

Dracula

Maiden name of Lily Munster, who's 157 years old (TV series "The Munsters"): played by Yvonne DeCarlo

Dracula movies

Nosferatu (German) (1923)
Dracula (1931)
Dracula's Daughters (1936)
Son of Dracula (1943)
Return of the Vampire (1944)
House of Dracula (1945)
The House of Frankenstein (1945)
Abbott and Costello Meet Frankenstein (1948)
Blood of Dracula (1957)
The Horror of Dracula (1957)
The Return of Dracula (1958)
The Curse of Dracula (1959)
Brides of Dracula (1960)
Kiss of the Vampire (1963)
Billy the Kid Meets Dracula (1965)
Dracula Prince of Darkness (1965)
Dracula Has Risen from the Grave (1968)
Taste the Blood of Dracula (1969)
Count Dracula (1970)
Countess Dracula (1970)
Dracula Must Be Destroyed
Scars of Dracula (1970)
Lake of Dracula (1971—Japanese)
Dracula A.D. 1972 (1971)
Dracula Is Dead and Well and Living in London (1972)
Blacula (1972)
The Satanic Rites of Dracula (1973)
Dracula Has Risen from the Dead (1974)
Son of Dracula (1974)
Dracula (1973: for TV)

Dragline

Nickname of prisoner Clarence Slidell who befriends Cool Hand Luke (1967 movie *Cool Hand Luke*) For this role George Kennedy won an Oscar as best supporting actor

Dragnet

Sergeant Joe Friday played by Jack Webb (radio and TV). Mark VII Production: only the hands of James Drake are seen

Radio:

Ben Romero played by Barton Yarborough
Ed Jacobs played by Barney Phillips

First TV series:

Frank Smith played by Ben Alexander

Ed Jacobs played by Barney Phillips

Second TV series:

Bill Gannon played by Harry Morgan

Theme music written by Walter Schumann; hit record by Ray Anthony

As part of wrap-up: "The story you have just seen is true. Only the names have been changed to protect the innocent."

Dragon Lady

Lai Choi San, Terry's foe ("Terry and the Pirates"). Debut in comic strip December 16, 1934. On radio played by Agnes Moorehead, Marion Sweet, Adelaide Klein; on TV by Gloria Saunders; in 1940 movie serial by Sheila Darcy. Her name means "Mountain of Wealth"

Dreadnought, H.M.S.

First heavy battleship in British Navy, launched 1906: 11-inch armor, ten 12-inch guns

Britain's first nuclear submarine

For a time, even until after World War I, "dreadnought" was a synonym for all heavily armed, heavily armored battleships

Dreyfus, Alfred

French military officer, convicted unjustly. Inmate of Devil's Island Penal Colony (1895). In 1937 movie *The Life of Emile Zola* played by Joseph Schildkraut, in 1950 movie *J'accuse* by Jose Ferrer

Drifters, The

Rock 'n' roll singing group. Among the lead singers were: Clyde McPhatter, Bobby Hendricks, Ben E. King, Rudy Lewis

Drink Ginger Ale

Neon sign outside the window and across the street from Sam Spade's office in San Francisco; the San Francisco—Oakland Bay Bridge can also be seen (1941 movie *The Maltese Falcon*)

Droodles

Simplified, abstract drawings; created by Roger Price

Droopy Dog

Slow, not too sharp beagle in MGM cartoons. Debut in "Dumb-Hounded" (1943)

DRUNKY

Dean Martin's California automobile license plate on his Stutz Blackhawk

Duae tabulae rasae in quibus nihil scriptum est

"Two blank tablets on which nothing is written," translated as "Two minds without a single thought": motto created by Al Kilgore for the Sons of the Desert, the Stan Laurel and Oliver Hardy fan club

Dubious Achievements Awards

Award conferred annually upon the year's biggest fiascos or humorous events (presented by *Esquire* magazine)

Duchess

Cat who, with her three kittens, befriends an alley cat named O'Malley (Walt Disney's 1969 movie *The Aristocats*): voice of Eva Gabor

Duchess Gloriana XII

Ruler of the tiny nation of Grand Fenwick (Leonard Wibberley's "Mouse" novel series)

Duchess, The

Red Ryder's aunt, housekeeper of Painted Valley Ranch, home of Red Ryder and Little Beaver. Played in TV series by Elizabeth Slifer; in 1940 movie serial by Maude Pierce Allen

Duckburg

City, founded by Cornelius Coot, where Donald Duck and his nephews, Scrooge McDuck, Daisy, etc., live. Town is on site of Fort Duckburg on the Tulebug River. The McDuck Building was built in 1936

Duck Soup

1933 Marx Brothers comedy

Groucho: Rufus T. Firefly

Harpo: Pinkie

Chico: Chicolini

Zeppo: Bob Rolland

Also the title of 1927 Laurel and Hardy film and 1942 Edgar Kennedy comedy

Dudley

Sheep dog (TV series "The Rich Little Show")

Dudley Do-Right

Canadian Mounted Policeman who is like his name (comics): voice of Russ Coughlin and Bill Scott. His commander is Inspector Fenwick; his girlfriend is Nell. The name of his horse is Horse

Dudley Nightshade

Crusader Rabbit's foe (TV cartoon series)

Duesenberg brothers

Automobile builders: August and Frederick S.

Duffy's Tavern

"Where the elite meet to eat": locale of radio series (beginning April 1941), starring Ed Gardner as Archie the Bartender. Duffy is never heard or seen. Miss Duffy: originally played by Shirley Booth (Gardner's wife). 1945 Paramount movie *Duffy's Tavern* was showcase for studio stars

Duets

Rock and Roll singers: (1950–1970s)

Mickey and Sylvia (Mickey Baker and Sylvia Vanderpool)

Johnnie and Joe (Johnnie Richardson and Joe Rivers)

Shirley and Lee (Shirley Pixley and Leonard Lee)

Paul and Paula (Ray Hildebrand and Jill Jackson)

Loggins and Messina (Kenny Loggins, Jim Messina)

Ike and Tina (Ike and Tina Turner)

Dick and DeeDee (Dick St. John and DeeDee Sperling)

Sonny and Cher (Sonny and Cher Bono)

Skip and Flip (Clyde Batton and Gary Paxton)

Peter and Gordon (Peter Asher and Gordon Waller)

Sam and Dave (Sam Moore and Dave Prater)

Marvin and Johnny (Marvin Phillips and Joe Josea)

Don and Juan (Roland Trone and Claude Johnson)

Patience and Prudence (Patience and Prudence McIntyre)

Jan and Arnie (later Jan and Dean) (Jan Berry and Dean Torrence)

Billy and Lillie (Billy Ford and Lillie Bryant)

Santo and Johnny (Santo and Johnny Farina)

Simon and Garfunkel (Paul Simon and Art Garfunkel)

Chad and Jeremy (Chad Stuart and Jeremy Clyde)

Dale and Grace (Dale Houston and Grace Broussard)

Robert and Johnny (Robert Carr and Johnny Mitchell)

Seals and Croft (James Seals and Dash Croft)

Captain and Tennille (Daryl Dragon and Toni Tennille)

Duke

Nickname of actor John Wayne (Marion Michael Morrison), taken from a pet airedale Duke he had as a small boy. Also the name of Wayne's horse in numerous movies

Duke
Tim Holt's horse

Duke
Kelly's dog (comic strip "Kelly" by Jack Moore)

Duke
Penrod's dog (Booth Tarkington's *Penrod*)

Duke
Pet hound dog of Jed Clampett (TV series "The Beverly Hillbillies")

Duke
Penguin on board Boner's Ark (comic strip "Boner's Ark")

Duke
Tom Mix's Great Dane, which appeared in a number of films with Tom and his horse Tony

Duke, Patty
Actress in TV/Movies. As a child she won $32,000 on the TV quiz show "The $64,000 Challenge" In TV series "The Patty Duke Show" she played look-alike cousins Patty and Cathy Lane. Won Oscar for 1962 movie *The Miracle Worker* in which she played the child Helen Keller, after originating the role on the stage

Duke and Cacao
Agent James T. West's two horses, kept in a special railroad car (TV series "Wild Wild West")

Duke and Duchess
Two friendly dolphins (1969 movie *Hello Down There*)

Duke and Turk
The family dogs (Johann Rudolf Wyss's novel *Swiss Family Robinson*)

Duke of Wellington
Arthur Wellesley (1769-1852), defeated Napoleon at Waterloo, Belgium, June 18, 1815

Duluth
U.S. amphibious transport, last ship launched at the 164-year-old Brooklyn Navy Yard: christened by Mrs. Bruce Solomonson, daughter of Vice President Humphrey.

Dumbo
Flying elephant (Disney cartoon feature picture)

Dum-Dum
Gorilla aboard Boner's Ark (comic strip "Boner's Ark")

Dumont, Margaret
Appeared with Marx Brothers in 7 films:
The Cocoanuts (1929) Mrs. Potter
Animal Crackers (1930) Mrs. Rittenhouse
Duck Soup (1933) Mrs. Teasdale
A Night at the Opera (1935) Mrs. Claypool
A Day at the Races (1937) Mrs. Emily Upjohn
At the Circus (1938) Mrs. Dukesbury
The Big Store (1941) Martha Phelps
She also appeared in many other pictures, among them
with W. C. Fields in 1941 movie *"Never Give a Sucker an
Even Break"* as Mrs. Ovlietta Hemoglobin

Dunbar 3-1232
Home phone number of Judge Bradley J. Stevens and his
wife Joan (TV series "I Married Joan")

Duncan, Lee
Original owner and trainer of Rin-Tin-Tin

Durham, North Carolina
Locale of the wartime 1942 Rose Bowl Game, between
Oregon State (20) and Duke (16): only Rose Bowl
game not played in Pasadena, California

Dusty
Henry's white dog ("Henry" cartoon by Carl Anderson)

Duty—Honor—Country
Motto of West Point

Dynamite
Wild stallion that Spin and Marty try to capture (Mickey
Mouse Club Spin and Marty episodes)

E

8

Number of warm-up pitches allowed a relief pitcher coming into a baseball game

8 Ball

B17 on which Clark Gable flew missions in Europe as a tail gunner during World War II

8 Remsen Drive

Brooklyn, New York, home address of the Lane family (TV series "The Patty Duke Show")

8:18

Time traditionally shown on clocks displayed in catalogues and windows; not the time that Abraham Lincoln died, as is commonly thought (he died at 7:22 a.m.)

11

Raquel Welch's roller derby number (1972 movie *Kansas City Bomber*)

11

Shots fired from Lucas McCain's .44-40 Winchester rifle in standard opening of TV series "The Rifleman"

11

Number of lawsuits filed against Carl Denham for the damage caused by King Kong (1933 movie *Son of Kong*). A grand jury indictment was also brought against him.

11

Players on a cricket, soccer, or football team, or (in 1976 movie *Rollerball*) on a rollerball team

18

Football jersey worn by Sally (Mrs. McMillan) (TV

series "McMillan and Wife"). The number is that of Gene Washington of the San Francisco 49'ers

18

Players on an Australian football team

80

Victories credited to "The Red Baron." Manfred von Richtofen, World War I German ace: highest total of any flier in that war

87

"Fourscore and seven," the number of years mentioned in the opening of Abraham Lincoln's Gettysburg Address (November 19, 1863): reference is to 1776

87th Precinct

New York police precinct in which Detective Steve Carella works (novel/story series by Ed McBain)

88

Keys (black and white) on a piano

88

Number of consecutive basketball games won by UCLA Bruins. Jan 24, 1971, to Jan. 29, 1974

804 Devon Lane

Los Angeles home address of Debbie and Jim Thompson (TV series "The Debbie Reynolds Show")

822 Sycamore Road

Hillsdale, California, home address of the Nelson family (TV series "The Adventures of Ozzie and Harriet" and later "Ozzie's Girls"). 1847 Rogers Road was their home address on radio

835 Chartres

New Orleans home address of blind detective Mike Longstreet (TV series "Longstreet")

1164 Morning Glory Circle

Westport, Connecticut, home address of Samantha and Darrin Stevens (TV series "Bewitched")

1841 and 1881

Only two years in which the U.S. had 3 Presidents:
1841:
    Martin Van Buren (until March 3)
    William Henry Harrison (died April 4, one month after inauguration)
    John Tyler (April 6–March 3, 1845)
1881:
    Rutherford Birchard Hayes (until March 3)

James Abram Garfield (March 4—shot July 2—died September 19)

Chester Alan Arthur (September 19–March 3, 1885)

1847 Rogers Road

Home address of the Nelson family (radio's "The Adventures of Ozzie and Harriet"): their sponsors were International Silver Company, makers of 1847 Rogers Silver

802,701 A.D.

Year arrived at by the Time Traveler (H. G. Wells' *The Time Machine*). In 1960 movie the Time Traveler arrives on October 12; he returns to his own time January 5, 1900

8,000,000

Stories in New York, as stated on TV series "Naked City": "There are 8 million stories in the Naked City. Probably an echo of title of an O. Henry book of stories about New York, *The Four Million* (1906), which is in turn a play on the "400," who are supposed to control New York society

E Pluribus Unum

Motto ("Out of many, one") on Great Seal of the United States: adopted June 20, 1782. The national motto is "In God We Trust"

Eagle

Apollo 11 lunar module: "The Eagle has landed"; command module was "Columbia"

Eagle

Tattoo on the hand of the cowboy in television's Marlboro cigarette commercials (see Winfield, Darrell)

Eagle Rock, Iowa

Town (population 4006) that gave up smoking for 30 days in exchange for $25 million dollars (1971 movie starring Dick Van Dyke, *Cold Turkey*)

Eagle Scout

Highest grade in the Boy Scouts. The only president to have become an Eagle Scout was Gerald Ford

Earp, Wyatt

Wyatt Berry Stapp Earp (1848-1929), western gunfighter: played in movies, among others, by:

Walter Huston *Law and Order* (1932)

Randolph Scott *Frontier Marshal* (1939)

Henry Fonda *My Darling Clementine* (1946)

Joel McCrea *Wichita* (1955)

Burt Lancaster *Gunfight at the OK Corral* (1957)

James Stewart *Cheyenne Autumn* (1964)
Guy Madison *Duel at Rio Bravo* (1965)
James Garner *Hour of the Gun* (1967)

Earp brothers

Morgan, James, Wyatt, Virgil and Warren (half brother): Virgil and Morgan were wounded at the O.K. Corral

Earth Day

April 22, 1970: a single day set aside for peaceful demonstration (an estimated 20 million people participated) on the problems of overpopulation, pollution, slums, racial disturbance, ecology, etc.

East Side Kids

A group formed from the original Dead End Kids to work at Monogram: Danny (Bobby Jordan); Skid (Gabe Dell); Ethelbert "Muggs" McGinnis (Leo Gorcey); Glimpy (Huntz Hall); Scruno (Sunshine Sammy Morrison). See *Bowery Boys*

Eastwood, Clint

His Italian western movies ("Spaghetti Westerns" or "Dollar Films") *A Fistful of Dollars*, 1964; *For a Few Dollars More*, 1966; *The Good, The Bad and the Ugly*, 1967 (*Hang 'Em High* was made in the U.S.). They were Italian/West German/Spanish movies, starring an American, filmed in Spain, based on Japanese stories. Directed by Sergio Leone. For *A Fistful of Dollars* (originally titled *The Magnificent Stranger*, Eastwood received $15,000. Only in *Hang 'Em High* (1968) did he have a full name, Jed Cooper; in *Fistful* he was Joe, in *Good, Bad, Ugly* he was Blondie

Easy Aces

Radio series starring Goodman and Jane Ace; briefly (1949) on TV

Easy Company

Sergeant Frank Rock's Army company (comic book series "Sgt Rock")

Easy Rider

Movie (1969) about two motorcycle travelers in search of America: Wyatt or Captain America (Peter Fonda), Billy (Dennis Hopper, who also directed)

Ebbets Field

Home park, in Flatbush, of the Brooklyn Dodgers. Actor John Forsythe was once the public address announcer

Eben Adams

Artist who painted the picture of Jennie (1949 movie *Portrait of Jennie*): played by Joseph Cotten. The picture was actually painted by Robert Brackman

Eberle Brothers

Radio's singing brothers, Bob and Ray, both singers with big bands. Ray changed the spelling of his last name to Eberly

Ebony Express

Nickname for track star Jesse Owens

Ebony White

The Spirit's black sidekick, an ex-taxicab driver (comic book series "The Spirit")

Echo 1

First United States communications (TV) satellite (Telstar 1 was first United States communications satellite to amplify radio/TV signals)

Eclipse

Arabian stallion brought to England in the early 1700s. Approximately 90% of all thoroughbred horses are descended from Eclipse

ECOMCON

Emergency Communications Control: secret military group located near El Paso, Texas, composed of 100 officers and 3,600 enlisted men, created to overthrow the government of the United States and to be led by General James Mattoon Scott (1964 movie *Seven Days in May*)

Eddy, Mary Baker

Founder of Christian Science; author of *Science and Health, with Key to the Scriptures* (1875); organized First Church of Christ. Scientist (Mother Church), Boston (1892)

Ederle, Gertrude

First woman to swim, using the crawl stroke, the English Channel, Aug. 6, 1926: time was 14 hours, 13 minutes

Edgar

Annual award of the Mystery Writers of America for the year's best mystery novel, named for Edgar Allen Poe. The British equivalent is the Gold Dagger Award

Edie Hart

Peter Gunn's girlfriend (TV series "Peter Gunn"): played by Lola Albright. In 1967 TV movie *Gunn*, played by Laura Devon

Edison

Caractacus Potts' shaggy pet dog (1968 movie *Chitty Chitty Bang Bang*)

Edith Ann

Precocious 5½ year old girl in a large rocking chair who expounds the latest gossip, climaxing with "and that's the truth" and giving a raspberry (created by Lily Tomlin). Her dog is called Buster and her boyfriend is Junior Philips

Edmond Dantes

The Count of Monte Cristo (the elder Alexandre Dumas' *The Count of Monte Cristo*)

Ed Norton

Ralph Kramden's upstairs neighbor who works in the New York sewers: played by Art Carney

Edsel

Automobile named after Henry Ford's son Edsel Bryant Ford produced 1957 to 1959 (the 1960 model—only 3,000—was produced in 1959). Models: Corsair, Citation, Pacer, Ranger

Edward Bear

Winnie-the-Pooh's real name (children's stories by A. A. Milne)

Edward Jackson E. Brown

Ed Brown's full name (TV series "Chico and the Man")

Edwards, Cliff

Known as Ukulele Ike: as Jiminy Cricket sang "When You Wish upon a Star" (cartoon movie *Pinocchio*). In westerns, played Charles Starrett's sidekick Harmony

Eeyore

Winnie-the-Pooh's donkey friend who likes to eat thistles

Effie Klinker

One of Edgar Bergen's dummies

Effie Perine

Sam Spade's secretary (on radio played by Lurene Tuttle: 1941 movie *The Maltese Falcon* played by Lee Patrick; in 1931 movie by Una Merkel. Her younger sister is Buffy. In the Hammett novel, she lives on 9th Avenue in San Francisco. In the 1975 movie *The Black Bird*, Lee Patrick again plays the part

Efram

Fearless Fosdick's fearless dog (comic strip "L'il Abner")

Eggberta
Twin sister of Eggbert, the embryonic imp; she is a medium

Egypt
Ulysses S. Grant's saddle horse

Eighth Wonder of the World
Billing of Kong as theatrical act (1933 movie *King Kong*)

Eisenhower Trophy
Awarded annually to the world's best amateur golf team

El Dago
Frank Sinatra's first private aircraft, a twin-engine Martin (1950s)

Eleanor
Nickname of 1973 Yellow Mustang (1975 movie *Gone in 60 Seconds*). In this movie 93 automobiles were wrecked

Electric Theater
Supposedly the first motion picture theater, located at 262 South Main Street, Los Angeles; opened April 12, 1902

Elementary, My Dear Watson
Line never said by Sherlock Holmes in any of Conan-Doyle's stories

El Fey Club
Texas Guinan's New York speakeasy, where she greeted customers with "Hello, Suckers"

El Goofo
A nickname of New York Yankees' pitcher Vernon Gomez

El Toro
Kit Carson's partner (TV series "The Adventures of Kit Carson"); played by Don Diamond

Election Day
First Tuesday after the first Monday in November (national)

Elephants
African: large flapping ears; Asian: smaller ears, rounder head

Eliot, T. S.
Poet Thomas Stearns Eliot (1885–1965), born in St. Louis, Mo., lived in England

Elizabeth
Fred Sanford's deceased wife (TV series "Sanford and Son")

Elizabeth

Christine's pet tomcat (1948 movie *I Remember Mama*)

El Kabong

Secret identity of Quickdraw McGraw; his guitar is his Kabonger (TV cartoon series)

Ella Phant

Soupy Sales' girlfriend who lives in a trunk (she is never seen)

Ellery Queen

Pseudonym of Frederick Dannay and Manfred Bennington Lee, who wrote the Ellery Queen detective novels. Ellery lives at 212A West 87th Street, New York City, with his father, Inspector Richard Queen. Nikki Porter is his assistant.

Played on radio by Hugh Marlowe, Larry Dobkin, Carleton Young, and Sidney Smith; on TV by Lee Bowman, Hugh Marlowe, George Nader, Lee Philips, Peter Lawford, Jim Hutton, and Richard Hart.

Movies:

The Spanish Cape Mystery (1935) Donald Cook
The Mandarin Mystery (1936) Eddie Quillan
Ellery Queen, Master Detective (1940) Ralph Bellamy
Ellery Queen's Penthouse Mystery (1941) Ralph Bellamy
Ellery Queen and the Murder Ring (1941) Ralph Bellamy
Ellery Queen and the Perfect Crime (1941) Ralph Bellamy
Enemy Agents Meet Ellery Queen (1942) William Gargan
A Close Call for Ellery Queen (1942) William Gargan
A Desperate Chance for Ellery Queen (1942) William Gargan
Ellery Queen—Don't Look Behind You (1971) Peter Lawford (Harry Morgan as Inspector Queen; TV movie)
Ellery Queen (1975) Jim Hutton (movie and series for TV)

Ellis, William Webb

Student at Rugby who, in a game in 1853, took the ball in his arms and ran with it, thus establishing the first rugby game. At Rugby there is a stone commemorating his feat: "This stone commemorates the exploit of William Webb Ellis, who with fine disregard for the rules of football as played in his time, first took the ball in his arms and ran with it, thus originating the distinctive feature of the Rugby game."

Elm Street
The main street in Peyton Place, Maine (Grace Metalious' novel/TV series/movie)

Elmer
Original name of puppet Howdy Doody

Elmer
Borden's Milk's bull, who gave his name to Elmer's Glue (or vice versa). His mate is Elsie; their son is Beauregard

Elmer
One of five of Daisy's puppies, apparently the only one to have a name (comic strip "Blondie")

Elmer
Pigeon fed by Walter Mitty (1947 movie *The Secret Life of Walter Mitty*)

Elmer J. Fudd
Naive pig with red shoes who gets conned by Bugs Bunny: "I'm gonna kill dat cwazy wabbot" (Warner Brothers cartoons): voice of Mel Blanc. Debut: *A Wild Hare* (1940)

Elmer the Moose
One of Paul Bunyan's three dogs (terrier)

Elmer Sneezeweed
Dummy of Max Terhune (cowboy ventriloquist in movies). Earlier, in vaudeville, Terhune had called the dummy Skully Null

Elmo
Elsie the cow's calf (Borden's Milk)

Elm Ridge
Hometown of Joe Gannon (TV series "Medical Center")

Elmwood
Town that is the locale of the radio serial "Pepper Young's Family"

Eloi
The people enslaved by the Morlocks (H. G. Wells' *The Time Machine*). Weena, the girl who befriends the Time Traveler, is one of the Eloi (1960 movie *The Time Machine*): played by Yvette Mimieux

Elongated Man
Secret identity of super-hero Ralph Dibny. The magic substance Gingold gives him his magic powers (comic book series). His wife is Sue Dearborn Dibny

El Rancho

Night club where Susan Alexander worked after leaving her husband, Charles Foster Kane (1941 movie *Citizen Kane*)

Elsa

African lioness born February 1, 1956, whose story is told in Joy Adamson's book Born Free (made into a 1966 movie). For her role Elsa was the winner of the 1967 and 1975 TV PATSY. Follow-up volumes by Joy Adamson telling about Elsa were *Forever Free* and *Living Free*

Elsie

Borden cow, born in 1932 at Elm Hill Farms in Brookfield, Massachusetts. Her true name is "You'll Do Lobelia." Weighing 975, she has appeared in a number of movies (see Buttercup). In commercials her voice is that of actress Hope Emerson.

Elsie Beebe

Nickname of radio program *Life Can Be Beautiful*: from initials of the words

Elsie Brand

Secretary of detectives Donald Lam and Bertha Cool (A. A. Fair's detective series)

Elwood

The Old Pro's clumsy football player (Falstaff Beer TV cartoon commercial)

Emerald City

Home of the Wizard of Oz

Emerald Planet

Home planet of Starman (Japanese science-fiction-film character)

Emi and Yumi Ito

Two six-inch-high princesses protected by Mothra (1961 movie *Mothra*)

Emil Trueheart

Tess Trueheart's father, who is shot and killed by robbers just after Tess and Dick Tracy announce their engagement. Tess is then kidnapped by the killers. Because of this Dick Tracy decides to become a plainclothes policeman (comic strip, 1931)

Emily Marie

Little Orphan Annie's doll (before she met Daddy Warbucks)

Emmy

Statuette awarded annually for outstanding TV programs, actors, and technicians (personalization of Immy, for image orthicon, the television camera tube)

Emperor Jones

Nickname of 1920s champion golfer Bobby Jones: from the then-popular Eugene O'Neill play *The Emperor Jones*

Emperor Ming

Ming, the Merciless. Emperor of the Universe, ruler of the planet Mongo (Flash Gordon's foe): played in movie serials by Charles Middleton, on radio by Bruno Wick

Emperor Norton

"Emperor of the United States and Protector of Mexico": self-proclaimed title of Joshua A. Norton (1819–1880), San Francisco rice merchant and local "character"

Empire State Building

102-story New York skyscraper completed in 1931 and for many years the world's tallest building. Built on the site of the old Waldorf-Astoria Hotel, it cost $54 million. On July 28, 1945, a B-25 bomber crashed into the building between the 78th and 79th floors; 14 people were killed.

Empty Arms Hotel

Country hotel where Roy Clark is clerk (TV series "Hee Haw")

Encyclopedia Brown

Ten-year-old detective Leroy Brown, whose father is chief of police of the town of Idaville.

Brown Detective Agency

13 Rover Avenue

"No Case Too Small"

His charge is 25¢ a day plus expenses (Donald J. Sobol's Encyclopedia Brown books)

Eudurance

Sir Ernest Shackleton's ship (1914–1916) on which he, with a crew of 27, survived for over five months in the Antarctic; the ship sank but the men survived

Enforcer, The

Frank Nitti, the strong-arm of Al Capone's mob, taking over for him while Capone was in prison: in TV series "The Untouchables," played by Bruce Gordon

Englebert Humperdinck

Pseudonym of singer Gerry Dorsey (the original Englebert Humperdinck wrote the opera *Hansel and Gretel*)

Engine 1401

Southern Railways locomotive (4-6-2) that drew the train bearing the body of Franklin D. Roosevelt from Warm Springs, Ga., to Washington, D.C., April 3, 1945. The engine is now on display in the Smithsonian Institution

Enola Gay

The B-29 (Army Air Force serial number 44-86292) that dropped the atomic bomb on Hiroshima, Aug. 6 1945, piloted by Colonel Paul Tibbets, Jr., and named for his mother, Enola Gay Haggard. Bomb dropped at 31,600 feet, 8:15:17 a.m., exploded 8:16 a.m. The plane is now in the Smithsonian Institution. Original target was ancient Kyoto

Ensign Charles Beaumont Parker

Lt. Commander Quinton McHale's second-in-command (TV series "McHale's Navy"): played by Tim Conway

Ensign Chekov

Crew member of the U.S.S. "Enterprise." His full name is Pavel Andreievich Chekov (TV series "Star Trek"): played by Walter Koenig

Ensign Pulver

Role played by Jack Lemmon in 1955 movie *Mister Roberts*, for which he won an Academy Award as best supporting actor. Played by Robert Walker in 1964 sequel "Ensign Pulver." On TV series "Mr. Roberts" by Steve Harmon. On stage, played by John Forsythe, Tyrone Power, Jackie Cooper, Charlton Heston, Richard Carlson, Howard Keel, Farley Granger, Robert Sterling and David Wayne

Enterprise

First U.S. shuttle craft, 122 feet long, commissioned September 18, 1976. At commissioning 7 members of Star Trek TV cast were present and Air Force band played the Star Trek theme

Enterprise

Riverboat captained by Grey Holden (TV series "Riverboat")

Enterprise, U.S.S.

Federation's United Star Ship, Constitution class, on a five-year mission (TV series "Star Trek"): commanded by Captain James T. Kirk. Crew members 430. Ship is 947 feet long, 417 feet wide, gross weight 190,000 tons

Enterprise, U.S.S.
    First atomic aircraft carrier, commissioned 1961
Entertainment Hall of Fame
    First ten members (elected 1974)
        Tennessee Williams
        Charlie Chaplin
        Katharine Hepburn
        Irving Berlin
        Judy Garland
        Lawrence Olivier
        George Gershwin
        D. W. Griffith
        Eugene O'Neill
        George Bernard Shaw
Epic
    Tumbleweeds' horse (comic strip)
Epitaphs
    Clark Gable: "Back to silents"
    William Shakespeare: "Good friend, for Jesus' sake forbear to dig the dust enclosed here! Blessed be the man that spares these stones, and cursed be he that moves my bones"
    Reverend Martin Luther King, Jr.: "Free at last, free at last, thank God Almighty I'm free at last"
    George Bernard Shaw: "I knew if I stayed around long enough, something like this would happen"
Epstein, Brian
    The Beatles' second manager until his death, August 27, 1967. Also was manager of Gerry and the Pacemakers; Billy J. Kramer and the DaKotas; Bee Gees; Foremosts; Cilla Black. Autobiography: *A Cellar Full of Noise*. He was succeeded as the Beatles' manager by Alan Klein. The first manager was Allan Williams
Eric
    Code name of Detective Matthew (Matt) Helm
Ericsson, Leif
    Son of Eric the Red; discoverer of Vinland (America)
Eric Stoner
    Name of the Cincinnati Kid (1965 movie *Cincinnati Kid*)
Eric (or Enrique) Claudin
    Name of the Phantom (movie *Phantom of the Opera*)

Ernestine
  Telephone operator in Beautiful Downtown Burbank, played by Lily Tomlin (one ringy-dingy, two ringy-dingy, etc.). "Is this the party to whom I am speaking?"

Ernie
  Sesame Street muppet, who lives with Bert. Ernie's birthday is January 28 (TV children's series "Sesame Street"): voice of Jim Henson

Ernst Stavro Blofeld
  Word's super criminal, arch-enemy of James Bond, sometimes seen with his pet white cat.
  You Only Live Twice (1967), played by Donald Pleasance
  On Her Majesty's Secret Service (1969), played by Telly Savalas
  Diamonds Are Forever (1971), played by Charles Gray

Eroica
  Beethoven's Third Symphony, on Premier Records, performed by Symphonette Philharmonic Orchestra conducted by Claudio Gaselli: record on the record player at the Bates house (1900 movie *Psycho*) Beethoven dedicated the work to Napoleon

Erskine's Commercial Photography Studio
  Studio where Phyllis Lindstrom works as an assistant to a photographer (TV series "Phyllis")

Eshlimar, Billie Jean Jones
  The wife of singer Hank Wiliams when he died, January 1, 1953. She was also the wife of singer Johnny Horton when he died, November 5, 1960. Introduced to Williams by singer Faron Young. Others married to two country/western singers: Bonnie Campbell to Buck Owens and Merle Haggard; Mac Davis' ex-wife married Glen Campbell; Duane Eddy's ex-wife married Waylon Jennings

Esmeralda
  Captain Nemo's pet seal (1954 movie *20,000 Leagues Under the Sea*)

Esmeralda
  Cicero's cat, Cicero being the son of Augustus Mutt of Mutt and Jeff

Esmeralda
  Gypsy girl who befriends Quasimodo in *The Hunchback of Notre Dame*. In the four movie versions played by

Theda Bara (1917), Patsy Ruth Miller (1923), Maureen O'Hara (1939), Gina Lollobrigida (1957)

Esquire Cleaners

612 Whitney Blvd., Los Angeles, location of the FBI cover location that Herbert A. Philbrick used as a contact (TV series "I Led Three Lives")

Essanay

Early film company (1909), named from the initials of its founders, G. M. Anderson (Broncho Billy, or Max Aronson) and G. K. Spoor. Chaplin's studio in 1915–1916, Essanay closed in 1918

Estrellita

Theme song of radio series "Valiant Lady"

Ethel

Matt Helm's answering service girl (TV series "Matt Helm")

Ethel Maye Potter

Ethel Mertz's maiden name (TV series "I Love Lucy")

Eton

James Bond's school (Ian Fleming's novel *You Only Live Twice*), also of Lord Peter Wimsey (Dorothy Sayers' novels), and many other characters, fictional and real

Etta Candy

Wonder Woman's fat little friend, who is always devouring candy. She is a student at Holliday College (comic books)

Euclid

Father of Geometry

Euclid Avenue and East 105th Street

Cleveland, Ohio, intersection where the first traffic light in the United States was installed August 5, 1914

Eugene the Jeep

Swee' Pea's pet animal (Popeye cartoon); favorite food: $5.00 orchids

Evanston Elementary

Illinois school in which Wally Cox and Marlon Brando attended the same fourth-grade class

Evel

Nickname of daredevil stunt rider Robert Craig Knievel: played in 1974 movie *Evel Knievel* by George Hamilton

Everlasting Gobstopper

One of Willy Wonka's many inventions, a candy that can be sucked forever (1971 movie *Willy Wonka and the Chocolate Factory*)

Everly Brothers
Singing duet: Don, Phil
Everybody Loves Somebody
Dean Martin's theme song
Everytown
British setting of the H. G. Wells novel/1934 movie *The Shape of Things to Come*, set in the year 2036
Excalibur
King Arthur's sword: obtained either by pulling it out of a stone or from the Lady of the Lake. Arthur could not be wounded as long as he wore the scabbard. The sword is also called Caliburn. When Sir Bedivere threw the sword back into the water, it signaled the barge to come to carry the dying Arthur to Avalon
Excursion boats
Canopied launches that take people through Adventureland (Disneyland): named for the world's waterways— "Magdalena Maiden," "Irrawaddy Maiden," "Congo Queen," "Suwannee Lady," "Orinoco Adventuress," "Zambezi Miss," "Yangtze Lotus," "Nile Princess," "Ucayali Una," "Mekong Maiden," "Hondo Hattie," "Ganges Gal," "Kissimmee Kate," "Amazon Belle"
Executioner, The
Mack Bolan (novel series by Don Pendleton). He is out to destroy the Mafia.
Executive Order No. 9066
Order signed by President Franklin D. Roosevelt, resulting in Japanese-Americans being incarcerated in camps in the West; 112,000 people were encamped by February 19, 1942
Exotica Beauty Company
Building that sinks into the ground, run by the evil organization, Galaxy (1966 movie *Our Man Flint*)
Explorer 1
United States first satellite, launched Jan. 31, 1958; it stayed up until March 31, 1970
"Ex Scientia Tridens"
From Knowledge, Sea power: motto of United States Naval Academy at Annapolis
Extremities
50 states:
North—Point Barrow, Alaska
South—South Cape, Hawaii

East—West Quoddy Head, Maine*
West—Cape Wrangell on Attu, Alaska
Highest—Mount McKinley, Alaska
Lowest—Death Valley, California
Center—near Castle Rock, South Dakota
48 states:
North—Northwesternmost point in Minnesota
South—Key West, Florida
East—West Quoddy Head, Maine
West—Cape Alava, Washington
Highest—Mount Whitney, California
Lowest—Death Valley, California
Center—near Lebanon, Kansas
(39°50° north latitude; 98°35° west longitude)

Eyes and Ears of the World, The
Paramount News' motto

---

*The 180th meridian divides part of the Aleutians, putting
some of the islands in the eastern hemisphere, and making the
most eastern part of the United States actually to the west

F

4

Players on a polo team; bridges of Toko-ri (James Michener novel)

4

Number of biplanes that attack King Kong on top of the Empire State Building in the 1933 movie (in many posters and stills up to 8 planes are shown, drawn in by an artist)

4

Number of shots fired at opening of credits on TV series "I Spy"

4:00 A.M.

Time that Susie and her boyfriend woke up in the 1957 song by the Everly Brothers "Wake Up Little Susie (song was actually banned in Boston)

4 Alpha 1

Call sign of Lt. Trench (TV series "Harry O")

4 chaplains

Clergymen who perished aboard the transport U.S.S. "Dorchester" after giving up their life jackets to other soldiers, February 3, 1943: Rabbi Alexander D. Goode, Father John P. Washington, Reverend George L. Fox, Reverend Clark V. Poling

4 C's of a Diamond

To denote the value of a diamond: 1) Cut; 2) Carat; 3) Clarity; 4) Color. (Cost could be a factor.)

4 Dimensions

Length; width; depth; time

4 Evangelists
Writers of the Gospels in the New Testament: Matthew, Mark, Luke, John

4 feet 8½ inches
Standard railroad-track gauge used in the United States. It approximates the width of the Roman chariot wheels

4 Freedoms
Incorporated in speech by Franklin D. Roosevelt in January 6, 1941, message to Congress: Freedom of speech and expression; Freedom of religion; Freedom from want; Freedom from fear everywhere in the world

4 Horsemen of the Apocalypse

	Color of horse
Conquest (War)	White
Famine	Black
Pestilence (Slaughter)	Red
Death	Pale Green

Title of 1918 novel by Vicente Blasco Ibañez, made (1922) into a Valentino movie, and again in 1962

4 Horsemen of Notre Dame
Football backfield from 1922 to Rose Bowl game of 1925: Harry Stuhldreher (156 pounds) quarterback; Don Miller (164 pounds) halfback; Jim Crowley (166 pounds) halfback; Elmer Layden (163 pounds) fullback

4 humors
Black bile, yellow bile, phlegm, blood

4H Club
Motto: "We learn to do by doing"
The four H's: Head, Heart, Hands, Health

4H Club Pledge
I pledge:
My Head to clearer thinking
My Heart to greater loyalty
My Hands to larger service, and
My Health to better living, for
My Club, My Community and My Country

4 Largest Islands
Greenland (839,800 sq. mi.); New Guinea (305,577 sq. mi.); Borneo (280,107 sq. mi.); Madagascar (230,035 sq. mi.). (Australia, almost 3 million sq. mi., is a continent).

4 to 2

Final score of baseball game in which the Mighty Casey struck out, causing no joy in Mudville (Ernest L. Thayer's "Casey at the Bat")

4U-13-41

New York State license plate number of Bruno Richard Hauptmann, kidnapper of the Lindbergh baby (March 2, 1932). His number was taken down by a New York City filling-station attendant alerted by police to take note of anybody buying gas with gold notes (see A7397664A)

4 Whitehall Place

Address of the headquarters of the London Metropolitan Police Department. The building was built in 1829 and, because the street behind it was called Scotland Yard Lane, it began to be called Scotland Yard, hence the name of the London Police Department. A newer headquarters was built years later, hence New Scotland Yard

5

Members of a basketball team

5

Minimum number of victories over enemy aircraft to become an ace. America's first ace (May 31, 1918) was Lt. Douglas Campbell

5

Number of seconds in which tape will self-destruct (TV series "Mission Impossible"): voice on tape is Bob Johnson's. Sometimes it is 10 seconds

Five Able 44

Call sign of unit to which San Francisco policeman Bert D'Angelo belongs (TV series "Bert D'Angelo Superstar")

Five Books of Moses

First five books of the Old Testament: Genesis, Exodus, Leviticus, Numbers, Deuteronomy. These constitute the Torah (Law) of Jewish religion and are called the Pentateuch (the five rolls or scrolls)

5¢

Lucy Van Pelt's fee for psychiatric advice ("Peanuts" comic strip): inflation later raised her rates to 10¢

5¢

Fare on the Staten Island Ferry (Battery to St. George)

5 Civilized Tribes

Cherokees, Choctaws, Chickasaws, Creeks, Seminoles

5 Finders of Willie Wonka's Golden Tickets

Augustus Gloop (Michael Bollner); Veruca Salt (Julie Dawn Cole); Violet Beauregarde (Denise Nickerson); Mike Teevee (Paris Themmen); Charley Bucket (Peter Dstrum) (1971 movie *Willie Wonka and the Chocolate Factory*)

Five Little Peppers and How They Grew

Novel (1881) by Margaret Sidney (pseudonym of Harriett Mulford Stone Lothrop)

The five Pepper children were Ben, Phronsie, Polly, Joel, Davie

5 Nations

Indian tribes also known as the Iroquois League: Seneca, Mohawk, Oneida, Onondaga, Cayuga

5 O'Clock Charlie

North Korean pilot who flies a sputtering aircraft in attempts to bomb the 4077th MASH unit but always manages to miss (TV series "M*A*S*H")

Five Pennies

Ernest Loring "Red" Nichols' band. Title of 1959 movie in which Danny Kaye portrayed Red Nichols

Five Points

Town, locale of radio/TV series "The Guiding Light"

5 Rivers of Hades

In Greek mythology:

Acheron, river of woe

Cocytus, river of lamentation

Lethe, river of oblivion

Phlegethon, river of fire

Styx, river of hate

Five W's

Who . . . What . . . When . . . Where . . . Why

5 years

Length of mission of the U.S.S. "Enterprise": "To explore strange new worlds; to seek out new life and new civilizations; to boldly go where no man has gone before" (TV series "Star Trek")

5 years

Age at which a filly becomes a mare

14

Lines in a sonnet

14

Number on the collar of the uniform of Captain Dreyfus (Jose Ferrer) (1958 movie *I Accuse*)

14 Farraway Street

London home address of Belgian detective Hercule Poirot (Agatha Christie detective series)

14 Maple Street

Mayberry, North Carolina, home address of Andy Taylor, his son Opie, and his Aunt Bee (TV series "Mayberry R.F.D."/"Andy Griffith Show")

15

Members of a hurling team

15 Medals

Awarded to Audie Murphy, most decorated American soldier in World War II (Neville Brand the actor was the fourth most decorated)

40

In the Bible:
It rained for 40 days and 40 nights.
Moses was on the mount 40 days and 40 nights.
Israel spent 40 years in the wilderness.
Elijah spent 40 days and 40 nights in the wilderness.
Jonah gave Nineveh 40 days to repent.
Christ's sojourn in the wilderness was 40 days.
(Lent is also 40 days long)

40

Distance in feet between stakes in horseshoes

40

Office number of Spade & Archer Private Investigators (1941 movie *The Maltese Falcon*)

40

Teeth of a male horse (female horses have 36)

—40°

Temperature at which the Farenheit and Centigrade (Celsius) scales coincide

Fortymile Creek

Location of Alaskan gold discovery (1886)

41

Age of Delta Dawn, who lives in the town of Brownsville ("Delta Dawn," country and western song)

46

Height in inches of actor Michael Dunn (1935–1973), co-star of 1965 movie *Ship of Fools* (in which he played Glocken)

46 River Road

Home address in the town of Spring City of the Webster family (radio series "Those Websters")

48

Freckles on puppet Howdy Doody's face (stood for the 48 states in the 1950s) (TV chidren's series "Howdy Doody Time")

49 West 10th Street

Manhattan address (apartment 5B) of Paul and Corie Bratter (TV series "Barefoot in the Park")

50

Number of white pianos played by 50 girls in "The Words Are in My Heart" sequence in Busby Berkeley's movie *Gold Diggers of 1935*

50

Eggs eaten by Lucas Jackson in one hour (1967 movie *Cool Hand Luke*)

51

Number on engine of Von Ryan's Express (1965 movie *Von Ryan's Express*)

51

Years that J. Edgar Hoover (1895–1972) served as Assistant Director (1921–1924) and Director (1924–1972) of the F.B.I. He served under 9 Presidents (8 as Director): Warren G. Harding through Richard M. Nixon

51-50

Final score of basketball game at 1972 Munich Olympics (September 9) between the U.S. and the U.S.S.R. The Russians broke U.S. win streak of 63 games that began in 1936 Olympics. The final basket was scored for the Russians by Alexander Belov. Final decision on game was not given until January 18, 1973. Technical representative of F.I.B.A. was Mr. Bigot

52-20

Unemployed GI's after World War II, entitled to $20 a week for 52 weeks

53

Number painted on the side of Herbie the Volkswagen (movies *The Love Bug* and *Herbie Rides Again*). California license is OFP857

53rd Precinct

Police station out of which policeman Anthony Baretta works (TV series "Baretta")

53 1/3

Width in yards of a football field (160 feet)

55

Number on football jersey worn by Karen Angelo (TV series "Karen")

56

Number of curls Shirley Temple wore in her hair as a child star. They were set by her mother who thus made sure of the exact number

56

Signers of the American Declaration of Independence. On the Bicentennial $2 bill, 42 of the signers are shown on the bill's reverse. One of the signers is depicted as a Negro

57

Advertised varieties of Heinz products (actually hundreds). Established in 1869. The joke arose that Mr. Heinz had 58 products but he died and took one with him

58

Consecutive shutout innings pitched by Don Drysdale. Los Angeles Dodgers (May 14-June 8, 1968)

59

Elapsed time of a 15-round boxing match:
3-minute rounds = + 45 minutes
1 minute between = + 14 minutes
                    ——————————
                    59 minutes

467

People who worked for Charles Foster Kane at his newspaper, the *New York Inquirer:* inscribed on the trophy they presented to him (1941 movie *Citizen Kane*)

473FEM

License plate number of the Snoop Sisters antique automobile (TV series "The Snoop Sisters")

500

Sheets of paper in a ream

500

Hats worn by Bartholomew Cubbins (book by Dr. Seuss, pen name of Theodor Geisel)

505 East 50th Street

New York City home address of the Williams family, apartment 542 (TV series "Make Room for Daddy")

511

Games won as a pitcher by Cy Young, 1890–1911. Young pitched 751 complete games in the major leagues

518 Crestview Drive

Beverly Hills home address of the Clampett family (TV series "The Beverly Hillbillies")

558 DeKoven St.

Address of Mrs. Catherine O'Leary's barn. The October 8-9, 1871 Chicago fire began when her cow kicked over a kerosene lantern here: the Chicago Fire Academy is now located at this address. Some accounts say Mrs. O'Leary's neighbor Peg Leg Sullivan was to blame

1400 McDoogal Street

San Francisco home address of Julie and Dave Willis (TV series "Love on a Rooftop")

1428 Maple

Greenpoint home address of Spanky (Our Gang series): shown in one episode

1438 North Beachwood

Address of the Monkees' pad (TV series "The Monkees")

$1500

Amount of money each player is given at the start of a session of Monopoly: 2 $500; 2 $100; 2 $50; 6 $20; 5 $10; 5 $5; 5 $1

1564

Year Galileo and Shakespeare were born, year Michelangelo died

4004 B.C.

Sunday, October 23, 9:30 a.m. the time of the Creation, calculated by Archbishop James Ussher of Armagh, Ireland, and contemporaries (about 1650)

4077th

Mobile Army Surgical Hospital unit (TV series "M*A*S*H"): inspiration was actual 8055th MASH unit in Korea

4,280

Buffaloes killed by William Cody (Buffalo Bill) in 18 months

4802 Fifth Avenue

Address of Fred Rogers (TV series "Mr. Rogers' Neighborhood")

4863 Valley Lawn Drive

Los Angeles home address of Lucille Carter (TV series "Here's Lucy")

5000

Number of fans who watched Casey strike out (poem "Casey at the Bat"): "10,000 eyes were on him . . ."

$5,000

Bounty on Clark Gable, dead or alive, offered to any German flier during World War II by Herman Goering

5050th Quartermaster Trucking Company

Unit of World War II's Red Ball Express (3rd Army) featured on TV series "Roll Out!"

5135 Kensington Avenue

St. Louis address of the Smith family (1944 movie *Meet Me in St. Louis*). The house was built on the same street as Andy Hardy's house on the MGM lot

5446 Elizabeth Avenue

St. Louis home address of major league catcher Joe Garagiola when he was a young boy

5447 Elizabeth Avenue

St. Louis home address of major league catcher Lawrence "Yogi" Berra when he was a young boy, across the street from Joe Garagiola's house. Their fathers worked together at the Laclede Christy Clay Products Company

40,671

Number of flies killed by General William Dean while he was a prisoner in North Korea (the count gave him something to do, which kept his sanity)

40886

Mobster Al Capone's prison number at Atlanta Federal Prison

45472

Prison number of former middleweight boxer Rubin "Hurricane" Carter at Rahway State Prison, New Jersey

47237

Michele's uniform number when a prisoner in Devil's Island Penal Colony (1929 movie *Condemned*)

57348

Michael "Beau" Geste's service number in the French Foreign Legion. He enlisted under the name of Michael Jones (1939 movie *Beau Geste*)

421-7596

San Francisco home phone number of Detective Lieutenant Frank Bullitt (1968 movie *Bullitt*)

555

Neutral and official exchange established by phone companies and after used for fictitious numbers

555-1079

Home phone number of Fred Sanford (TV series "Sanford and Son")

555-2368

Home phone number of Jaime Sommers (TV series "The Bionic Woman")

555-2368

Detective Jim Rockford's telephone number in his house trailer (TV series "Rockford Files")

555-3743

Phone number of Thaddeus, Control's chief (TV series "Get Smart")

555-4144

Detective Lew Archer's office telephone number (TV series "Archer")

555-6161

Brady family phone number (TV series "The Brady Bunch")

555-6644

Home phone number of Joe Mannix (TV series "Mannix")

555-6772

Captain Dobey's phone number (TV series "Starsky and Hutch")

555-7862

Mary Richards' home phone number (TV series "The Mary Tyler Moore Show")

$5,000,000

Price United States paid Spain for Florida, 1819

$5,368,709.12

One cent doubled every day for 30 days:

1st day - $.01   3rd day - $.04

2nd day - $.02   4th day - $.08

  5th day - 0.16, and so on to 30 days

$15,000,000

Price of Louisiana Territory, bought from Napoleon of France by President Jefferson (1803), averaging 2¢ an acre

53310761

Elvis Presley's Army serial number (March 1958-March 1960)

F-AMPJ

Letters on the side of the airplane that takes Ilsa Lund Laszlo and Victor Laszlo out of Casablanca (1942 movie *Casablanca*)

FFA Motto

(Future Farmers of America)

"Learning to do,

Doing to Learn,

Earning to Live,

Living to serve."

F.O.E.

Fraternal Order of Eagles, "The Fighting Fraternity" (founded 1898)

F.P.

Signature used by George Metesky (The Mad Bomber) who bombed a number of New York City's Consolidated Edison Company facilities and other buildings during the 1940s and 1950s. He signed his warning letters with F.P., which he later said stood for "fair play."

Fah Lo Suee

Doctor Fu Manchu's daughter (in 1932 movie *The Mask of Fu Manchu,* played by Myrna Loy and in the 1940 movie *Drums of Fu Manchu* by Gloria Franklin)

Fahrenheit 451

"The temperature at which book paper catches fire, and burns"; novel (1953) by Ray Bradbury

Movie (1966) with Oskar Werner; directed by Francois Truffaut. No titles were on the screen; all credits were oral

Fairbanks, Douglas

Acrobatic handsome leading man (1883–1939) of silent movies. Married Mary Pickford; founder United Artists

233

Studio. In 1917 a mountain peak in Yosemite National Park was named in his honor

Fala

President Franklin D. Roosevelt's Scottie dog (Medworth was his other dog). Full name; Murray of Fallahill

Falcon, The

Nickname of Mike Waring (radio/TV series "The Falcon"): played on TV by Charles McGraw, on radio by James Megham, Les Damon, Berry Kroeger, Les Tremayne, George Petrie

Movie serial detective played by George Sanders (Gay Lawrence) and Tom Conway (Tom Lawrence), who were brothers, and John Calvert. The movies were a spin-off of "The Saint" series.

Based on Michael Arlen's 1940 *Gay Falcon,* in which the Falcon's name is Gay Stanhope Falcon, whose real identity is Gay Lawrence. Pseudonyms: Colonel Rock, Spencer Pott

Falconhurst

Maxwell family plantation (Kyle Onstott's *Mandingo* novels)

Falcons

The Air Force Academy's football team

Faline

Bambi's cousin and mate, doe of Ena and sister of Gobo (Felix Salten's novel *Bambi*)

Family Barber Shop

Where Charlie Brown's father works as a barber ("Peanuts" comic strip)

Fang

Phyllis Diller's husband in her comedy routines

Fang

Control's canine (Agent K-13) (TV series "Get Smart")

Fanny

Boat at Hampton Roads, Virginia, from which John LaMountain, Union aeronaut, ascended in a balloon, August 3, 1861: "Fanny" thus may be called the first aircraft carrier

Fantastic Four, The

Crime fighters Mr. Fantastic (Mr. Reed Richards); Human Torch (Johnny Storm); The Thing (Ben Grimm); Invisible Girl (Sue Storm Richards) in comic book series created by Stan Lee and Jack Kirby. First appearance:

Fantastic Four #1, November 1961. Also in TV cartoon series, voices are Reed Richards (Gerald Mohr), Sue Richards (Jo Ann Pflug), Johnny Storm (Jack Flounders), Ben (Paul Frees)

Fantasticar

The Fantastic Four's flying vehicle

Farewell to Arms, A

Novel (1929) by Ernest Hemingway, made (1933) into a movie starring Gary Cooper and Helen Hayes. The movie had two endings: in one Helen Hayes dies, in the other she lives; former for European release, latter for American release

Farmer in the Dell, The

(children's nursery rhyme)
Heigh-ho, the derry-oh
The Farmer takes a wife
The wife takes the child
The child takes the nurse
The nurse takes the dog
The dog takes the cat
The cat takes the rat
The rat takes the cheese
The cheese stands alone

Farrow, Mia

Actress, daughter of actress Maureen O'Sullivan and director writer John Farrow (who won Oscar for script of *Around the World in 80 Days*). Ex-wife of Frank Sinatra; later married André Previn. Her picture appeared on the cover of the first issue of People Magazine (March 4, 1974)

Fat Albert

Nickname for the Boeing 737 jet airliner (from a character in "The Cosby Kids"): fuselage as wide as B707

Father Brown

Catholic priest, of St. Francis Xavier's Church, Camberwell, England (amateur detective created—1911—by Gilbert Keith Chesterton in short stories). Modeled after Father John O'Connor, a friend of Chesterton's, Father Brown has no first name, though in "The Eye of Apollo" he is given the initial "J" and in "The Sign of the Broken Sword" he is referred to as "Paul." Played on radio by Karl Swenson, and in movies by Walter Connolly (1934 movie *Father Brown, Detective*) and Alec Guinness (1954 movie *Father Brown, Detective*)

Father Chuck O'Malley

Young parish priest of St. Dominic's (1944 Academy Award best picture *Going My Way*): played by Bing Crosby (Oscar for best actor). He appeared in the sequel, the 1945 movie *The Bells of St. Mary's*. On TV, played by Gene Kelly in 1962 series

Father Nature

Tobacco planter on El Producto cigar TV commercials

Fat Man

Name given A-bomb (plutonium) dropped on Nagasaki: named for Winston Churchill. It was 10'8" long and 5' in diameter

Fat Man, The

Nickname of Brad Runyon (radio series "The Fat Man," created by Dashiell Hammett): played by J. Scott Smart (in movies as well). The character is based on Hammett's magazine detective The Continental Op

Fatima (of the Seven Veils)

Ahab the Arab's lover (novelty song by Ray Stevens, "Ahab the Arab")

Faust, Frederick Schiller

American writer (1892–1944), especially for pulp magazines and of Western novels under the pen name Max Brand: killed in Italy at age 52 serving as a war correspondent. Creator of, among others, Dr. Kildare and author of *Destry Rides Again*

Fay and Evey

Ma Perkins' daughters (radio show)

Fearless Fosdick

Cartoon detective who closely resembles Dick Tracy, appearing in the "Li'l Abner" comic strip by Al Capp. His adventures are in a comic strip by Lester Gooch, which has as its greatest fan Li'l Abner. (This all occurs within the Li'l Abner strip. Fosdick marries Prudence Pimpleton and, since he must do what his hero does, Li'l Abner marries Daisy Mae. Fosdick wakes up to discover it was all a dream. Li'l Abner wakes up to find it wasn't and that he is really married) His face was supposedly designed after that of actor Jack Holt

Fears, Bobby Lee

Black ex-convict with whom ex-Georgia governor Lester Maddox performed in a singing duet on stage at Mr. P's Supper Club in Sanford, Florida, May 1977. Fears had been Maddox's dishwasher

Federal Holidays

New Years Day (January 1)
Washington's Birthday (third Monday in February)
Memorial Day (last Monday in May)
Independence Day (July 4)
Labor Day (first Monday in September)
Columbus Day (second Monday in October)
Veterans Day (November 11 or fourth Monday in October)
Thanksgiving Day (fourth Thursday in November)
Christmas (December 25)

Federal penitentiaries

Atlanta, Georgia; Leavenworth, Kansas; Lewisburg, Pennsylvania; McNeil Island, Washington; Marion, Illinois; Terre Haute, Indiana

Federation Cup

Women's parallel to the Davis Cup: national-team championship

Feliciano, Jose

Blind guitarist, singer and song writer who performs the theme song for TV series "Chico and the Man"

Felix the Cat

Newspaper syndicated cartoon character, drawn by Pat Sullivan. His girlfriend is Phyllis. The first image transmitted on TV (experimental) in the 1920s was that of Felix

Felix Leiter

James Bond's American CIA contact (James Bond novels by Ian Fleming). In movies played by R. K. Van Nutter (*Thunderball*), Cec Linder (*Goldfinger*), David Hedison (*Live and Let Die*), Jack Lord (*Dr. No*), Norman Burton (*Diamonds are Forever*)

Feminum

Rare metal found only on Paradise Island (TV series "Wonder Woman"): Wonder Woman's bracelets are made from this material

Fencing
Three weapons: foil, épée, saber

Ferdinand
Flower-smelling bull in Munro Leaf's book (1936) and later in 1938 movie cartoon for which Disney won an Oscar

Ferdinand
Austrian archduke Francis Ferdinand (1863–1914), nephew of Emperor Francis Joseph of Austria-Hungary, and heir to the throne on the deaths of Rudolph, the crown prince (suicide with Marie Vetsera in 1889), and his father Charles Louis. On June 28, 1914, in Sarajevo, Bosnia, in Serbia, Ferdinand and his wife, Sophie Chotek, Duchess of Hohenberg, were assassinated by Gavrilo Prinzip (or Princip) as they rode in a 1912 Graf und Stift automobile. The unrelieved crisis that resulted ended in mobilization, ultimatum, and within weeks the outbreak of World War I

Ferdinand Magellan
President Franklin D. Roosevelt's private railroad car

Ferndale
Captain Roderick Anthony's ship (Joseph Conrad's *Chance*)

Fernwood, Ohio
Hometown of Mary Hartman (TV series "Mary Hartman, Mary Hartman")

Fibber McGee and Molly
Radio comedy starring Jim Jordan as Fibber and Marian (Driscoll) Jordan as Molly. Fibber's closet at 79 Wistful Vista and such visitors as Mayor LaTrivia, Throckmorton P. Gildersleeve, and Doc Gamble kept the show on the air from 1935 until 1952, originally from Peoria, Ill. Before Fibber McGee and Molly, the Jordans had a radio series (1925) called "The Smith Family." Movies: *This Way Please* (1938), *Look Who's Laughing, Here We Go, Heavenly Days* (1944). In 1959 TV series, played by Bob Sweeney and Cathy Lewis

Fido
20-foot python which starred with Ormi Hawley in the 1914 film *The Eternal Sacrifice*

Fields, W. C.
Actor, juggler, and humorist (1879–1946): real name, William Claude Dukinfield

238

Fiery Furnace
Cast into the furnace (Daniel 3) were Daniel's brothers: Shadrach (Hannaniah), Meshach (Mishael), Abednego (Azariah)

Fifth Dimension, The
Original members of the singing group: Bill Davis Jr.; Florence LaRue; Lamonte McLemore; Marilyn McCoo; Ron Townson. Davis and McCoo left the group in 1976

Figaro
The Barber of Seville (play by Beaumarchais; operas by Mozart, Rossini, Paisiello)

Figaro
Gepetto's cat (feature cartoon movie Pinocchio)

Fillmore
Name of rock 'n' roll auditoriums run by Bill Graham in late 1960's-early 1970's: Fillmore West in San Francisco. Fillmore East in New York City

Fillmore Jr High School
School attended by Marcia Brady (TV series "The Brady Bunch")

Fire Chief, The
Nickname of Ed Wynn (real name, Isaiah Edwin Leopold) on the Texaco radio show

Firefly
Horse owned and ridden by Rudolph Valentino in the 1926 movie *Son of the Sheik*

Fireman John Gage
One of the two paramedic firemen (TV series "Emergency") : played by Randolph Mantooth

Fireman Roy DeSoto
One of the two paramedic firemen (TV series "Emergency") : played by Kelvin Tighe

First Artists Production Company
Film company founded in 1969 by Paul Newman, Barbra Streisand, and Sidney Poitier (Steve McQueen and Dustin Hoffman joined later)

First Brooklyn Savings Bank
Banking institution, located at 285 Prospect Park West, robbed in the 1976 movie *Dog Day Afternoon*

First Gentleman of the Screen
Nickname of actor George Arliss

First Lady of Radio
   Nickname originated by Time Magazine in 1939 for Kate Smith
First Lady of the Screen
   Nickname of actress Norma Shearer
First Lady of the Theatre
   Nickname of Actress Helen Hayes

First Names

Last	First	Actor	TV/Movie
Addams	Morticia	Carolyn Jones	The Addams
	Gomez	John Astin	Family
Archer	Lew	Brian Keith	Archer
Banacek	Thomas	George Peppard	Banacek
Banyon	Miles	Robert Forster	Banyon
Baretta	Tony	Robert Blake	Baretta
Boggs	Frank	Robert Culp	Hickey and Boggs
Brenner	Roy (father)	Edward Binns	Brenner
	Ernie (son)	James Broderick	
Bronkov	Alexander	Jack Palance	Bronk
Bronson	Jim	Michael Parks	Then Came Bronson
Brooks	Constance (Connie)	Eve Arden	Our Miss Brooks
Bullitt	Frank	Steve McQueen	Bullitt (movie)
Burke	Amos	Gene Barry	Burke's Law
Cade	Sam	Glenn Ford	Cade's County
Cain	Nicholas	Mark Richman	Cain's Hundred
Cannon	Frank	William Conrad	Cannon
Carter	Andrew	Larry Novis	Hogan's Heroes
Columbo	Philip*	Peter Falk	Columbo
Deeds	Longfellow	Gary Cooper	Mr. Deeds Goes to Town (movie)
Dolittle	John	Rex Harrison	Dr. Dolittle (movie)
Drummond	Hugh	Various	Bulldog Drummond
Elliott	Benjamin	James Franciscus	Doc Elliott
Faraday	Steve (son)	James Naughton	Faraday and Co.
	Frank (father)	Dan Dailey	
Flack	Humphrey	Alan Mowbray	Coloney Flack

240

		Willard Waterman	The Great
Gilder-sleeve	Throck-morton P.		Gildersleeve
Harper	Lew**	Paul Newman	Harper (movie)
Hawk	John	Burt Reynolds	Hawk
Hawkins	Billy Jim	James Stewart	Hawkins
Hennessy	Charles "Chick"	Jackie Cooper	Hennessy
Hickey	Al	Bill Cosby	Hickey and Boggs
Hogan	Robert	Bob Crane	Hogan's Heroes
Ironside	Robert	Raymond Burr	Ironside
Jones	Abraham Lincoln	James Whitmore	The Law and Mr. Jones
Judd	Clinton	Carl Betz	Judd for the Defense
Klute	John	Donald Sutherland	Klute (movie)
Kojak	Theo	Telly Savalas	Kojak
Kolchak	Carl	Darren McGavin	Night Stalker
Lancer	Murdoch	Andrew Duggan	Lancer
Madigan	Dan	Richard Widmark	Madigan
McCloud	Sam	Dennis Weaver	McCloud
McCoy	Amos (father)	Walter Brennan	The Real McCoys
	Luke (son)	Richard Crenna	
McHale	Quinton	Ernest Borgnine	McHale's Navy
McMillan	Stuart	Rock Hudson	McMillan and wife
	Sally	Susan St. James	
McQ	Lon	John Wayne	McQ (movie)
Mannix	Joe	Mike Connors	Mannix
Markham	Roy	Ray Milland	Markham
Munsters	Herman	Fred Gwynne	The Munsters
	Lily	Yvonne DeCarlo	
Newkirk	Peter	Richard Dawson	Hogan's Heroes
Norby	Pearson	David Wayne	Norby
Novak	John	James Franciscus	Mr. Novak
Peepers	Robinson	Wally Cox	Our Miss Brooks, Mr. Peepers
Petrocelli	Tony	Barry Newman	Petrocelli

*Author's Speculation
**Actually the same character as Lew Archer, the name being changed to Harper since Paul Newman has had such good luck with "H" movies (see "H" movies)

Roberts	Douglas	Roger Smith	Mr. Roberts (TV)
Rockford	James	James Garner	The Rockford Files
Sanford	Fred (father)	Redd Foxx	Sanford and Son
	Lamont (son)	Demond Wilson	
Schultz	Hans	John Banner	Hogan's Heroes
Shaft	John	Richard Rountree	Shaft
Smart	Maxwell	Don Adams	Get Smart!
Smith	Eugene	Fess Parker	Mr. Smith ... (TV)
	Jefferson	James Stewart	Mr. Smith Goes to Washington (movie)
Snoop	Ernesta	Helen Hayes	The Snoop Sisters
	Gwen	Mildred Natwick	
Tenafly	Harry	James McEachin	Tenafly
Toma	Dave	Tony Musante	Toma
Topper	Cosmo	Leo G. Carroll	Topper
		Roland Young	Topper (movies)
Valdez	Bob	Burt Lancaster	Valdez is Coming (movie)

First recorded message

"Mary had a little lamb": by Thomas Edison, 1877. His assistant, Mrs. Harriet Atwood, played the piano, thus becoming the first recording artist

First telegraph message

"What hath God wrought": Samuel F. B. Morse, May 1844

First telephone message

"Mr. Watson, come here, I want you": by Alexander Graham Bell, (March 10, 1876) to his assistant Thomas Augustus Watson

First transoceanic cable message

"Europe and America are united by telegraph. Glory to God in the highest and on earth peace and good will towards men": August 16, 1858

Fischer Quintuplets

Born September 14, 1963, in Aberdeen, South Dakota to Andrew and Mary Fischer: Jimmie, Cathy, Margie, Mary Ann, Maggie

Fisher

Company that produces the bodies for General Motors automobiles: "Body by Fisher"

Fisher, Eddie

Popular ballad singer of the 1950s noted for marrying Hollywood's more glamorous stars. Wives: Debbie Reynolds (1955–1959); Elizabeth Taylor (1959–1964); Connie Stevens (1968–1969). He was one of Michael Todd's three Best Men when he married Elizabeth Taylor; the other two were Michael Todd, Jr., and Cantinflas

Fisherman I and II

Zane Grey's private schooners

Fisherman's Ring, The

The Pope's ring

Fitzgerald, Barry

Irish character actor: winner of 1944 Oscar for supporting actor as Father Fitzgibbon in *Going My Way*. Fitzgerald was also nominated for best actor for the same role, the only time this has happened in the history of the Academy Awards

Flag

Jody Baxter's fame fawn (Marjorie Kinnan Rawlings' *The Yearling*)

Flambeau

Father Brown's French private detective friend, formerly a master criminal (Father Brown stories by G. K. Chesterton). He lives in Lucknow Mansions, Hampstead, England

Flamingo

Las Vegas hotel built at a cost of $6 million by gangster Benjamin "Bugsy" Siegel, opened on December 26, 1946. It was the first hotel built on the famous Las Vegas Strip. "Flamingo" was Bugsy's nickname for his girlfriend Virginia Hill

Flanagan, Father Edward Joseph

Founder of Boys Town, near Omaha, Nebraska. In 1935 movie *Boy's Town* and 1941 movie *Men of Boy's Town*, portrayed by Spencer Tracy

Flanakins

Horse Ralph Neves rode at Bay Meadows, California, May 8, 1936, when the horse fell over another horse. The P.A. system announced that Neves was dead but he woke up in the hospital with no injuries. Flanakins died of his injuries

Flash, The

Original comic strip series: secret identity of Jay Garrick, of Keystone City, in the Golden Age of comics: 1940s

Second comic strip series: secret identity of Barry Allen of Central City: first appearance in DC Showcase Comics #4, October 1956

Flash's Foe

(modern day version):

Villian	Identity
Captain Boomerang	Digger Harkness
Mr. Element (Dr. Alchemy)	Al Desmond
The Trickster	James Jesse
The Weather Wizard	Mark Mardon
The Mirror Master	Samuel J. Scudder
The Pied Piper	Thomas Peterson
The Top	Roscoe Dillon
Heat Wave	Mick Rory
(comic books)	

Flash Gordon

Hero of comic strip by Alex Raymond, first appearing Sunday, January 7, 1934

Movie serials beginning in 1936, featured:

Flash Gordon—Buster Crabbe

Dr. Zarkov—Frank Shannon

Dale Arden—Jean Rogers (Carol Hughes, 1940)

Princess Aura—Priscilla Lawson (Shirley Deane, 1940)

Emperor Ming—Charles Middleton

Movies (serials):

Flash Gordon, 13 episodes (1936)

Flash Gordon's Trip to Mars, 15 episodes (1938)

Flash Gordon Conquers the Universe, 12 episodes (1940)

Serials into movies:

Flash Gordon became *Perils from the Planet Mongo* and *Spaceship to the Unknown*

Flash Gordon Conquers the Universe became *Purple Death in Outer Space*

Flash Gordon's Trip to Mars became *The Deadly Ray From Mars*

Flatt and Scruggs

Earl Scruggs and Lester Flatt

Performed the theme song for the TV programs "Petticoat Junction" and "The Beverly Hillbillies": Jerry Scoggins was the vocalist. They also played "Foggy Mountain Breakdown," the sound-track theme song of the movie *Bonnie and Clyde*. When they split up, Flatt founded Nashville Grass, Scruggs The Five-String Banjo

Flattop
One of Dick Tracy's antagonists (1942). Full name: Flattop Jones

Fleming, Ian
Creator of the James Bond adventure novels, author of *Chitty Chitty Bang Bang* and TV series "The Man from U.N.C.L.E."

Flicka
Ken McLaughlin's horse on the Goose Bar Ranch (TV series "My Friend Flicka")

Flight 1203
Tragic flight in the 1960 hit song "Ebony Eyes" by the Everly Brothers

Flight of the Bumblebee
The Green Hornet's theme song, performed for TV series by Al Hirt. The music is Rimsky-Korsakov's

Flintstones
Fred J., Wilma, Pebbles, who live in town of Bedrock (TV cartoon series): created by Hanna-Barbera. Wilma's maiden name is Flagghoople, Voices: Fred, Alan Reed; Wilma, Jean Vanderpyl)

Flip
Happy Hooligan's pet dog (comic strip "Happy Hooligan")

Flipper
Talented and friendly dolphin (TV series "Flipper"). Winner of 1965, 1966, 1967 TV PATSY award

Flipper, Henry
First black officer to be graduated from West Point, June 15, 1877

Flo (Florrie)
Andy Capp's wife (comic strip). They call each other Pet

Florence Nightingale Pledge
Oath taken by nurses just entering their profession—much like the Hippocratic Oath

Florida Evans
   Maude's (Beatrice Arthur) black house maid (Esther Rolle) until she got her own TV series "Good Times"

Flounder, The
   Ship on which Dr. Dolittle and his crew sailed (movies). In the novels it's "Curfew"

Flower
   Skunk (1942 cartoon feature movie *Bambi*)

Floyd
   Astro-chimp companion of Lt. Robin Crusoe (Dick Van Dyke) 1966 movie *Lt. Robin Crusoe, U.S.N.*

Floyd and Lloyd
   The two sons of Oswald the Rabbit (comic book cartoons)

Flubber
   Magic substance invented by Professor Ned Brainard (1961 movie *The Absent Minded Professor*

Fluffy
   Brady Family's pet cat (TV series "The Brady Bunch")

Flush
   The Barretts' red cocker spaniel (Rudolph Besier's *The Barretts of Wimpole Street*)

Flyer
   Wright Brothers' 1903 airplane

Flying Crown Ranch
   Sky King's home, where he lives with his niece Penny and nephew Clipper, near the town of Grover. The crown has 5 points

Flying Dutchman
   Ship condemned to wander the oceans forever, commanded by Captain Vanderdecken or Van Straaten

Flying Fickle Finger of Fate
   Award given out by Dick Martin and Dan Rowan for the current week's fiasco or embarrassing news story (TV series "Laugh-In")

Flying Finn
   Paavo Nurmi, Olympic track and field star, who won 7 gold and 3 silver medals in the 1920–1924–1928 Olympics

Flying Fish
   The A-1, first successful U.S. hydroplane, build by Glenn Curtiss, 1911

Flying Laboratory, The

Amelia Earhart's Lockheed Electra in which she and navigator Fred Noonan disappeared in the Pacific. 1937

Flying Needle

Buck Rogers' airplane

Flying Nun, The

Sister Bertrille (TV series): played by Sally Field. Sister Bertrille's name was Elsie Ethrington

Flying Red Horse

Trademark of Mobil Gasoline

Fly Me Girls

Stewardesses who fly and advertise for National Airlines, each National Airlines airplane being named for a stewardess: "I'm Susy, fly me"

Fly Movies

Horror movies about a half-human half-fly: *The Fly* (1958); *The Return of the Fly* (1959); *The Curse of the Fly* (1965)

Flynn and Blake

Two Mudville players on base when the Mighty Casey struck out, Flynn on third, Blake on first ("Casey at the Bat" by Ernest L. Thayer)

Flynn–de Havilland movies

Movies in which Errol Flynn and Olivia de Havilland appeared together: *Captain Blood* (1935); *The Charge of the Light Brigade* (1936); *The Adventures of Robin Hood* (1938); *Four's a Crowd* (1939); *Dodge City* (1939); *The Private Lives of Elizabeth and Essex* (1939); *Santa Fe Trail* (1940); *They Died with Their Boots On* (1941); *Thank Your Lucky Stars* (1943)

Fontaine, Joan

Actress, 1941 Oscar winner for role of Lina in *Suspicion:* sister of actress Olivia de Havilland (real name Joan de Havilland), both born in Tokyo, Japan. Fontaine was their mother's maiden name. When Joan won the Oscar, she defeated her sister, who was nominated for her role in *Hold Back the Dawn*

Fontane Sisters

Singing group: Geri, Bea, Marge

Fonzie

Nickname of very cool high school dropout Arthur Fonzarelli: played by Henry Winkler (TV series "Happy

247

Days") He is also called The Fonz, and refers to square people as "Nurds"

Foodini
Puppet on "Lucky Pup" show (TV)

Football Hall of Fame
Museum for professional football, located at Canton, Ohio

Football Jersey numbers
Conventional usage:

1–19	Quarter backs
20–29	Halfbacks
30–39	Fullbacks
40–49	Halfbacks
50–59	Centers and Linebackers
60–69	Guards
70–79	Tackles
80–89	Ends and Flankers

Forbes Field
Pittsburgh baseball stadium (1909–1970) where no one ever pitched a no-hit game. Since the Pirates moved to Three Rivers Stadium in 1970, the record seems secure

Ford
1934 4-door automobile in which Bonnie Parker and Clyde Barrow met their deaths May 23, 1934. 187 bullet holes were found in the car. In the 1967 movie *Bonnie and Clyde,* the car was painted yellow

Ford, Robert
"The dirty little coward" who shot and killed Jesse James, April 3, 1882, at St. Joseph, Mo. In 1939 movie *Jesse James,* played by John Carradine; in 1949 movie *I Shot Jesse James,* by John Ireland. On a February 1953 episode of "You Are There" on TV titled "The Capture of Jesse James," Ford was played by James Dean

Forio
Horse with broken leg, shot by Marnie Edgar (1964 Alfred Hitchcock film *Marnie*)

Forsyte Saga, The
Novel, trilogy by John Galsworthy (1867–1933): *The Man of Property* (1906), *In Chancery* (1920), *To Let* (1921). The trilogy called *A Modern Comedy* (1924–1928) and several "interlude" novels complete the long family history. The first book is the basis of the 1949 movie with Errol Flynn and Greer Garson *That Forsyte*

Woman. The success of the series as a public TV multi-week production led to expansion of producing novels as episodic TV series sketching over many weeks

Fort Abraham Lincoln

The fort in Dakota Territory from which George Armstrong Custer departed May 17, 1876, with the Seventh Cavalry on his way to the Little Big Horn. The military band played "Garry Owen," the regimental march (adopted in 1867), while the troops were in the fort and "The Girl I Left Behind Me" as the troops were leaving

Fort Apache

Military post in Arizona Territory (TV series "Rin-Tin-Tin"). Also title of 1948 John Ford movie starring John Wayne

Fort Baxter

U.S. Army post in the town of Roseville, Kansas, where M/Sgt. Ernest ("Ernie") G. Bilko is stationed (TV series "You'll Never Get Rich"). See Camp Fremont

Fort Benlin

1864 frontier cavalry fort where Major Amos Charles Dundee is posted (1965 movie *Major Dundee*)

Fort Courage

Military post (TV series "F Troop"): commanded by Captain Parmenter. Fort is named for General Sam Courage

Fort Frazzle

Post commanded by Major Minor where Klondike Kat is stationed, Savoir Fare, a mouse, being their nemesis (TV cartoon)

Fort Lehigh

U.S. Army post where Steve Rogers (Captain America) and Bucky Barnes met during World War II

Fort Linton

U.S. 9th Cavalry post to which First Sergeant Braxton Rutledge of D Troop is posted (1960 movie *Sergeant Rutledge*)

Fort Lowell

Frontier 5th cavalry post commanded by Captain Adams (TV series "Boots and Saddles")

Fort McHenry

Fort on Baltimore Harbor bombarded by the British, Sept. 13-14, 1814. Francis Scott Key was inspired to write a poem that later became "The Star Spangled Banner" as he watched from the British ship "The Minden." The banner Key described had 15 stripes and 15 stars (Vermont and Kentucky had joined the Union); Congress reverted to 13 stripes in 1818

Fortress of Solitude
Secret hideaway in the Arctic of Doc Savage, built by his father

Fortress of Solitude
Arctic hideaway where Superman keeps his mementoes, memorabilia, and the bottle city of Kandor: located on Blue Peak Mountain

Fort Sam Clemens
Replica of frontier fort located in Adventureland at Disneyworld near Orlando, Florida

Fort Sumter
Union fort located in Charleston Harbor, South Carolina, fired upon by Southern troops, April 12, 1861, to begin the Civil War. First shot was fired by 75-year-old Edmund Ruffin; response was fired from the fort by Abner Doubleday

Fort Wilderness
Fort on Tom Sawyer Island ("Adventureland" section of Disneyland). Flies the 15-stripe flag flown at Fort McHenry (see above)

Fort Zinderneuf
French Foreign Legion in Morocco where Beau and John Geste were stationed. Their brother Digby was stationed at Fort Tokotu (1926 and 1939 movies *Beau Geste*)

Fortuna
Mr. Lucky's gambling yacht (TV series "Mr. Lucky")

Foss, Joe J.
U.S. Air Force officer, Medal of Honor winner; shot down 26 Japanese planes during World War II. Governor of South Dakota (1955-1959); first Commissioner of the American Football League (1959); host of TV series "The Outdoorsman"

Foster School for Girls
All girls' school inherited and run by John Forsythe (TV series "The John Forsythe Show")

Foul Fellows Club
Lodge to which the Big Bad Wolf (Zeke) belongs (comic strip "Li'l Bad Wolf")

Foundation Trilogy, The
Science fiction novels by Isaac Asimov: *Foundation* (1951); *Foundation and Empire* (1952); *Second Foundation* (1953)

Four-in-One
NBC's rotating weekly series (1970–1971). The original four programs were: McCloud, San Francisco International, The Psychiatrist, and Night Gallery
(McCloud later became a part of NBC's Sunday Mystery Movie)

"Four" Sisters movies
Four Daughters (1938), *Four Wives* (1939), *Four Mothers* (1941), starring as Ann, Thea, and Kay Lemp, the Lane sisters, Priscilla, Lola, and Rosemary, with Gale Page (who was not a real sister) as Emma Lemp

Four Star Playhouse
Television anthology series (1952–1956) produced by Four Star Productions. Original stars were Dick Powell, Rosalind Russell, Joel McCrea, and Charles Boyer; other hosts were David Niven and Ida Lupino

Fourth Musketeer, The
Gascon nobleman, D'Artagnan (Alexandre Dumas' *The Three Musketeers*). He joins Athos, Porthos, and Aramis in many adventures, and is actually the hero

Fox, The
Adventures of radio actor who plays detective, starring Red Skelton in 3 MGM movies: *Whistling in the Dark* (1941), *Whistling in Dixie* (1942), *Whistling in Brooklyn* (1943). *Whistling in the Dark,* same story, same title, had starred Ernest Treux in 1933

Fox and the Crow
Comic book characters. Their first names are Fauntleroy and Crawford respectively. They are also Columbia Pictures cartoon Characters. Debut: *The Fox and the Grapes* (1941). Fox and Crow (Renard et Corbeau) were the characters in one of La Fontaine's best-known fables

FOXXXX
Redd Foxx's California automobile license plate

Foxy Loxy
Ate Turkey Lurkey, Goosey Loosey, Ducky Lucky, Henny Penny, and Chicken Little

Fraka
   The Phantom's trained falcon, who helps deliver messages (comic strip "The Phantom")

Francis
   Talking mule (movie series), created by David Stern. Voice: Chill Wills, Winner of first PATSY award (1951) With Donald O'Connor as Peter Stirling:
   Francis, (1949)
   Francis Goes to the Races, (1951)
   Francis Goes to West Point, (1952)
   Francis Covers the Big Town, (1953)
   Francis Joins the WACS, (1954)
   Francis in the Navy, (1955) (also in film were the young actors Martin Milner, David Janssen, Clint Eastwood)
   With Mickey Rooney (voice, Paul Frees):
   Francis in the Haunted House, (1956)

Frank Smith
   Sgt. Joe Friday's TV partner ("Dragnet"): played by Ben Alexander

Frankenstein
   Novel (1816) by Mary Wollstonecraft Shelley, the wife of Percy Bysshe Shelley. The full title is *Frankenstein: or, The Modern Prometheus.* Victor Frankenstein (in the 1931 movie his first name became Henry) is the scientist who revivifies the composite of corpses, NOT the monster

Frankenstein Movies

Year	Movie	Monster	Dr. Frankenstein or Mad Doctor
1910	*Frankenstein*	Charles Ogle	
1915	*Life Without Soul*	Percy D. Standing	
1931	*Frankenstein*	Boris Karloff*	Colin Clive
1935	*Bride of Frankenstein*	Boris Karloff	Colin Clive
1939	*Son of Frankenstein*	Boris Karloff	Basil Rathbone
1942	*Ghost of Frankenstein*	Lon Chaney Jr.	Sir Cedric Hardwicke (Ludwig Frankenstein)

*Bela Lugosi reportedly turned down the role because the make-up obscured his features.

Year	Title	Monster	Doctor
1943	*Frankenstein Meets the Wolf Man*	Bela Lugosi	None
1944	*House of Frankenstein*	Glenn Strange	Boris Karloff
1945	*House of Dracula*	Glenn Strange	None
1948	*Abbott and Costello Meet Frankenstein*	Glenn Strange	None
1957	*Curse of Frankenstein*	Christopher Lee	Peter Cushing
1957	*I Was A Teenage Frankenstein*	Gary Conway	Whit Bissell
1958	*Revenge of Frankenstein*	Michael Gwynne	Peter Cushing
1958	*Frankenstein 1970*	Mike Lane	Boris Karloff
1958	*Frankenstein's Daughter*	Sandra Knight	None
1964	*Evil of Frankenstein, The*	Kiwi Kingston	Peter Cushing
1966	*Jesse James Meets Frankenstein's Daughter*	Cal Bolder	
1966	*Frankenstein Conquers the World* (Japanese)		
1966	*Frankenstein Meets the Space Monster*		Robert Feilly
1967	*Frankenstein Created Woman*	Susan Denberg	Peter Cushing
1969	*Frankenstein on Campus*		Robin Ward
1969	*Frankenstein Must Be Destroyed*	Freddie Jones	Peter Cushing
1970	*Horror of Frankenstein, The*	David Prowse	Ralph Bates
1971	*Frankenstein's Bloody Terror* (Spanish)		
1971	*Dracula vs. Frankenstein* (or *Blood of Frankenstein*)	John Bloom	

1973	*Frankenstein* *(The True Story)* (TV movie)	Leonard Whiting	Michael Sarrazin
1973	*Frankenstein and the Monster from Hell*	David Prowse	Peter Cushing
1973	*Frankenstein* (TV movie)	Bo Svenson	Robert Foxworth
1975	*Flesh of Frankenstein* (an Andy Warhol pornographic film)		
1975	*Young Frankenstein*	Peter Boyle	Gene Wilder

Frankie and Johnny

Woman and her philandering man, respectively, in folk song

Franklin

Son of Mr. Reed Richards (Mr. Fantastic) and Sue (Storm) Richards (Invisible Girl) (comic series "The Fantastic Four")

Franklin, Benjamin

His portrait appeared on the first U.S. postage stamp, a 5¢ red brown, issued July 1, 1847. A 10¢ black, with portrait of George Washington, was issued simultaneously

"Frankly, my dear I don't give a damn"

Last line said by Rhett Butler (Clark Gable) in the 1939 movie *Gone With the Wind*. In the Margaret Mitchell novel the line read "My dear, I don't give a damn." However it was not the last line of the movie: "After all, tomorrow is another day" said by Scarlett O'Hara (Vivien Leigh) was the last line in both novel and movie

Frank Fuller

Gunslinger who is arriving at Hadleyville on the noon train to kill Marshal Will Kane (1952 movie *High Noon*): played by Ian McDonald

Frank Merriwell

Yale University star athlete and student, created by Burt L. Standish (Gilbert Patten) in *Tip Top Weekly* (1896) and the hero par excellence of the cheap "dime novel" of the early 20th century. His girlfriend was Inza Burrage. Played on radio by Lawson Zerbe; in movie serial *The Adventures of Frank Merriwell* (Universal; 12 episodes, 1936) by Don Briggs

Franks, Bobby

Victim of murder by Nathan F. Leopold, Jr. and Richard A. Loeb, both reported in the press to be the idle sons of retired millionaires. Their intended victim was William Deutsch, heir to the Sears, Roebuck estate. The name the two signed to the ransom note sent to the Franks was George Johnson. Clarence Darrow was Leopold and Loeb's lawyer. From the novel (and later play) by Meyer Levin, *Compulsion*, a 1959 movie, was made telling the story in fictional form, Leopold, Jr. at age 18 was the youngest person to graduate from the University of Chicago with a B.Ph

Frazier
19 year old ex-circus lion who sired 35 cubs in 16 months at Lion County, Los Angeles

Fred
Super Chicken's lion partner (Walter Lantz comics)

Fred
Husband of Mickie Finn, the banjo player (TV series "Mickie Finn's")

Fred
Tony Baretta's pet white 20-year-old Australian cockatoo (TV series "Baretta"): played by a cockatoo named Lala trained by Ray Berwick

Freed, Alan
D. J. who is credited with coining phrase "Rock 'n' Roll." Called himself Moondog. With Rocky Graziano starred in 1957 movie *Mr. Rock and Roll*. Broadcast over Cleveland radio station WJW (1952), then moved To New York's WINS in 1955. In *Transatlantic Merry-go-round* (1934), the Boswell Sisters sang a song called "Rock and Roll," and in 1948 an obscure group, Billy Mathews and the Balladeers, recorded a song "Rock and Roll." But the term applied to the musical fact is apparently due to Freed.

Freedonia
Republic of which Rufus T. Firefly (Groucho Marx) is president. Freedonia is at war with Sylvania (1933 movie *Duck Soup*). Sylvania is also the setting of the 1929 movie *The Love Parade*

Fremont
Mr. Wilson's pet dog (TV series "Dennis the Menace")

Fresh Air Taxicab Company of America Incorpolated
Amos 'n' Andy's cab company. On TV Amos drives a 1948 DeSoto

Friar Tuck
Plump religious member of Robin Hood's band; played by

Eugene Pallette (1938 movie *The Adventures of Robin Hood*) and Edgar Buchanan (1946 movie *The Bandit of Sherwood Forest*), among many others in Robin Hood pictures

Friendship

Theme song of radio series "My Friend Irma"

Friendship 7

Capsule in which Colonel John Glenn became the first American to orbit the earth (February 20, 1962). John Glenn won $25,000 on the TV quiz show *Name That Tune* prior to becoming an astronaut. He later became a senator from Ohio (1974)

Fritz

Dr. Frankenstein's crippled assistant (1931 movie *Frankenstein*): played by Dwight Frye

Fritz

William S. Hart's pinto horse (movies): lived to be 31

Fritz Brenner

Nero Wolfe's Swiss chef at the old brownstone house on West 35th Street, Manhattan (Nero Wolfe novels by Rex Stout)

Fritzie Ritz

Comic strip (1922) by Larry Whitington, later by Ernie Bushmiller: later the strip was titled "Fritzie Ritz and Nancy" and finally "Nancy," when Fritzie's little niece took over the general interest. Fritzie's boyfriend is Phil Fumble; Nancy's is Sluggo

Fritz the Cat

First X-rated animated cartoon movie (1970), created by Robert Crumb. *The Nine Lives of Fritz the Cat* (1974) was a sequel

Froggie the Gremlin

Wise-cracking frog (radio's "Buster Brown Show"): played by Ed McConnell

Frog Millhouse

Gene Autry's sidekick: played in movies by Lester "Smiley" Burnette

Front Street

Dodge City street on which Marshal Matt Dillon's office and the Long Branch saloon are located (TV series "Gunsmoke")

Frostbite Falls

Hometown, in Koochiching County, Minnesota, of Rocket J. Squirrel and Bullwinkle J. Moose (TV cartoon series)

Frosty

"The Snowman" (comic book character). "Frosty the Snowman" was a 1952 Gene Autry hit

Frye, Johnny

First Pony Express rider, though the honor is often claimed for Johnson William "Billy" Richardson. He departed St. Joseph, Mo., April 3, 1860, at exactly 7:15 p.m. Eastbound from San Francisco rode James Randall. William Hamilton was the last of 30 men to carry the mail on the westward trip, arriving after midnight on the morning of April 14, 1860. Time: 1 hour less than 10 days

Fugi

The Osmond Brothers pet dog (Saturday morning TV cartoon show): voice of Paul Frees

Fulton's Folly

Robert Fulton's double sidewheel steamboat "Clermont": first demonstrated 1807

Fu Manchu

Oriental villain in Sax Rohmer novels: always *Doctor* Fu Manchu

Funeral March of a Marionette

Theme song of the Alfred Hitchcock's TV series "Alfred Hitchcock Presents"

Funiculi, Funicula

Theme song of radio's "Lorenzo Jones"

Fun with Music Day

Every Monday on the Mickey Mouse Club. Featured were the six ports of the world. Shown were China, France, Hawaii, India, Ireland and Spain (TV's "Mickey Mouse Club")

Fury

Black stallion owned by Joey Clark on the Broken Wheel Ranch (TV series "Fury"): Fury is played by the horse Gypsy

Futurama

General Motor's exhibition at the New York World's Fair, 1939 (showed what America would look like in the year 1960)

G

GBK

Radio station that features children's talent contests in the town of Greenpoint (*Our Gang* series)

G8 and His Battle Aces

Comic book series about a Spad-flying World War I pilot. His aces were Bull Martin and Nippy Weston

GG-300

District of Columbia automobile license plate of the 1963 Blue Lincoln Continental in which President Kennedy was shot. The car was chauffeured by William R. Greer on the fatal day. (It is one of a fleet of 3 special built cars)

G.I. Jane

United States Army WAC

G.I. Joe

United States Army soldier: World War II

G.I. Joe

World War II carrier pigeon that saved the lives of over 1,000 British soldiers by delivering a message, enabling a rescue: Italy, October 18, 1943

G.O.P.

Grand Old Party (Republican)

Gabilan

Jody's pony (John Steinbeck's *The Red Pony*)

Gable, Clark

His wives: Josephine Dillon, 1924–1930; Rhea Langham, 1930–1939; Carole Lombard, 1939–1942; Silvia Hawkes, 1949–1952; Kay Spreckels, 1955–1960

Gable-Crawford movies

Films in which Clark Gable and Joan Crawford appeared together:

Dance Fools Dance (1931)
Laughing Sinners (1931)
Possessed (1931)
Dancing Lady (1933)
Forsaking All Others (1934)
Chained (1934)
Love on the Run (1936)
Strange Cargo (1940)

"Gable's back and Garson's got him"

Film advertisement for the 1945 Clark Gable and Greer Garson movie *Adventure* (another slogan that emerged was *Gable's the guy who put the arson in Garson*)

Gabor sisters

Zsa Zsa; Magda; Eva (Mother: Jolie)

Gabor, Zsa Zsa

Her husbands: Burhan Belge; Conrad Hilton; George Sanders; Herbert L. Hutner; Joshua Cosden, Jr.

Gaedel, Edward Carl

Midget (1925–1961) who pinch-hit for the St. Louis Browns in a game against Detroit in 1951. He stood 43 inches tall, weighed 65 lb.; uniform number 1/8. Batting for Frank Saucier, he walked, was replaced by Jim Delsing, the regular outfielder, who ran for him; he never batted again in the major leagues. Ed Hurley, the plate umpire, permitted him to bat when Zack Taylor, Browns' manager, showed him a contract signed by Gaedel. The Detroit pitcher was Bob Cain

Gagarin, Yuri A.

First man in space, on board Russian Vostok 1, April 12, 1961, for 1 hour 48 minutes

Galahad Glen

Home of Crusader Rabbit (TV cartoon series)

Gala Poochie Pup

Rootie Kazootie's pet dog (TV puppet show)

Galaxie, The

Captain Video's space ship (TV series)

Galaxy

Evil organization in the 1966 movie *Our Man Flint* starring James Coburn.

Galella, Ron
New York photographer who hounded Jacqueline Kennedy Onassis for a number of years. A judge ruled that Galella couldn't approach Jacqueline and her children closer than 100 yards.

Galileo
U.S.S. "Enterprise" shuttle craft, NCC1701/7 (TV series "Star Trek")

Gallery
Men's magazine published by attorney F. Lee Bailey. First issue November, 1972

Galloping Ghost
Nickname for football player Harold "Red" Grange of University of Illinois

Galloping Gourmet
Afternoon television program starring Graham Kerr, celebrated international cooking expert

Gallstones
Singing trio, two guys and a girl featured in Dick Tracy comic strip.

Gammera
Giant prehistoric monster (Japanese movie)

Gangsters
Nickname:

> Arizona Barker—Ma
> Al Capone—Scarface
> Vincent Coll—Mad Dog
> Jack Diamond (John T. Noland) Legs
> Arthur Flegenheimer—Dutch Schultz
> Charles Floyd—Pretty Boy
> Alvin Karpis (Abin Karpowicz) Old Creepy
> George Kelly—Machine Gun
> George Nelson (Lester Gillis) Baby Face
> Earl Weiss—Hymie

Garbo Laughs!
M-G-M advertisement for the 1939 Greta Garbo movie *Ninotchka,* her first comedy

Garbo Talks
M-G-M advertisement for the 1930 Greta Garbo movie *Anna Christie,* her first talkie.

Garco
Robot that appeared in several 1950's TV programs, including Walt Disney's *Mars and Beyond*

Gardner, Ava
Her real name: Lucy Johnson
Her husbands: Mickey Rooney, 1942–1943; Artie Shaw,
1945–1947; Frank Sinatra, 1951–57

Gargoyle
Ex-Sing Sing convict and muscleman for The Bishop
(radio series "The Bishop and the Gargoyle"): played by
Milton Herman and Ken Lynch

Garland, Judy
American actress and singer (1922–1969), real name
Frances Gumm, famous as Dorothy in 1939 movie *The
Wizard of Oz*. Married 4 times: David Rose (1941–1943),
Vincente Minelli (1945–1950), Sid Luft (1952–1955),
Mark Herron (1955–1960); mother of Liza Minelli

Garland—Rooney movies
Judy Garland and Mickey Rooney appeared together in:
Thoroughbred's Don't Cry (1937)
Love Finds Andy Hardy (1938)
Babes in Arms (1939)
Andy Hardy Meets Debutante (1940)
Strike up the Band (1940)
Life Begins for Andy Hardy (1941)
Babes on Broadway (1941)
Girl Crazy (1943)
Thousands Cheer (1943)
Words and Music (1948)

Garrett, Pat
Sheriff who shot and killed Billy the Kid (July 14, 1881);
later became a Texas Ranger. Killed in a dispute with a
tenant

Garson, Greer
When accepting her Oscar for Best Actress of 1942 (Mrs.
Miniver) she gave an acceptance speech which lasted
over 30 minutes, henceforth acceptance speeches were
limited to a much shorter period.

Gashouse Gang
St. Louis Cardinals of the early 1930's: Frank Frisch,
manager Outstanding players: Pepper Martin, third base;
Ducky Medwick, outfield; Rip Collins, first base; Leo
Durocher, short-stop; Bill Delancy, catcher; Tex Carleton,
pitcher; Dizzy Dean, pitcher; Paul Dean, pitcher. In the
1955 movie *Strategic Air Command*, Lt. Col. Robert

"Dutch" Holland (James Stewart) had been a third baseman for the St. Louis Cardinals.

Gateman, Goodbury and Graves
Morticians for which Herman Munster (Fred Gwynne) works. Mr. Gateman played by John Carradine (TV series *The Munsters*)

Gay, George
U.S. Navy ensign who became the sole survivor of Torpedo Squadron 8 (30 men) at the Battle of Midway (June 3-6, 1942). After being shot down he watched the battle from his life raft.

Gaylord
The intellectual buzzard friend of Broom-Hilda the Witch (cartoon series *Broom-Hilda* by Russell Myers)

Gazoo
Fred and Barney's little friend from the planet Zetox, who is always trying to perform good deeds. (TV series *The Flintstones*) Voice of Harvey Korman

Gehrig, Lou
Member, behind Babe Ruth, of Yankees' Murderers' Row; hit the most grand-slam home runs in major league career, 23. Played in 2,130 consecutive baseball games (1925–1939): replaced Wally Pipp at first base (June 1, 1925) and was replaced by Babe Dahlgren (May 2, 1939). Portrayed in 1942 movie *Pride of the Yankees* by Gary Cooper, played as a boy by Douglas Croft. The same day Gehrig benched himself (April 30, 1939) the New York's World Fair opened in Flushing, Meadow, Long Island. In the movie, the role of Babe Ruth was played by Babe Ruth

Gehrig's Disease
Name applied (as in AMA *Journal*) to amyotrophic lateral sclerosis, the disease that killed Lou Gehrig June 2, 1941, at age 37

GEN II
Automobile license plate of Chitty Chitty Bang Bang, a magical Paragan Panther automobile (Ian Fleming's novel *Chitty-Chitty-Bang-Bang*). GEN II was supposed to mean Gentle, yet in the movie the license plate reads GEN 11

Gene Autry
Town in Southern Oklahoma on the AT & SF Railroad

line named after the cowboy movie star. Berwyn had been the town's previous name. (See Autry, Gene)

General, The
President John Tyler's horse

General, The
Confederate locomotive engine belonging to Georgia's Western and Atlantic railroad hijacked by 20 Union soldiers during the Civil War: see *Texas, The*. Led by James J. Andrews. Andrews portrayed in 1956 movie by Fess Parker.
Theme of 1926 silent film starring Buster Keaton as Johnnie Gray

General Amos T. Halftrack
One-Star Commander of Camp Swampy in Mort Walker's Beetle Bailey comics

General Burkhalter
Commandant Klink's superior officer, played by Leon Askin (TV series *Hogan's Heroes*)

General Frank Savage
Commander of the 8th Air Force Bombardment Group—stationed in Britain in the novel/movie/TV series *12 O'Clock High*. Played in 1950 movie by Gregory Peck. Played in TV series by Robert Lansing.

General Insurance Company
Organization for which Jim Anderson (Robert Young) works on TV series *Father Knows Best*.

General Sherman
Sequoia, largest living thing in the world; it stands 272 feet, 4 inches tall (Sequoia National Park, California)

General Tom Thumb
Nickname of Charles S. Stratton. He stood 36 inches tall and worked for P. T. Barnum. Weighed 9 lbs., 2 ounces at birth.

Genoa City
Locale of TV daytime serial "The Young and the Restless". The series' theme song became a hit, *Nadia's Theme*, by Barry DeVorzon, in 1976.

Genoa Maru
Japanese ship featured in the 1942 movie *Across the Pacific* starring Humphrey Bogart.

Gentle Ben
650 lb. bear (TV movie series). Played by Bruno who won the 1968 TV and movie PATSY

Gentleman from Virginia
Nickname of film star Randolph Scott

Gentle on My Mind
Glen Campbell's television theme song. (Composed by John Hartford)

Gentleman Jim
Nickname of boxer James J. Corbett. His brother Joe Corbett pitched for the Baltimore Orioles in the 1890s. His autobiography is entitled *The Roar of the Crowd*.

Geoffrey
The Toys "Я" Us giraffe; GiGi, Mother; Baby Gee, Baby

George
Family pet alligator in the Walt Disney 1967 movie *The Happiest Millionaire*

George
Lee Liberace's (Wladziu Valentino) brother. Liberace's legal name is now one word. Lee is a nickname.

George and Marge
Union Oil Gasoline's husband and wife customers (TV ads)

George and Marion Kerby
Ghosts who are friends of Cosmo Topper (TV, radio, movies) from Thorne Smith's *Topper*. Their dog was named Neal (in novel the dog was called Oscar) TV: George (Robert Sterling) *"the most sporting spirit"* Marion (Anne Jeffreys) *"the ghostest with the mostest"* On radio: Paul Mann and Frances Chaney 1937 movie *Topper* by Cary Grant and Constance Bennett. In novel and movie they were killed in car accident in TV series by an avalanche on their fifth wedding anniversary

George Eliot
Pen name of Mary Ann Evans

George O'Brien
Man for whom listeners are requested to cast a vote for in order to get poor old Charley off the M.T.A. (Metropolitan Transit Authority) 1960 hit *M.T.A.* by the Kingston Trio

George Russell
Davy Crockett's (Fess Parker) sidekick who wrote ballads about Davy. Russell is played by Buddy Ebsen (Walt Disney's 1954–55 Davy Crockett movie series)

Georges
  Belgian detective Hercule Poirot's valet

George Wilson
  Mayor of Metropolis on the TV series *The Adventures of Superman.*

Georgia Peach, The
  Nickname of baseball player Ty Cobb, lifetime batting average .367, highest in baseball

Georgie
  Statuette awarded by the AGVA (*American Guild of Variety Arts*) to performers of the year for their live performances. Named for George M. Cohan.

Gepetto
  Pinocchio's creator and "father" (a woodcarver). Voice of Christian Rub in 1940 movie

Geranium
  Judy Canova's housemaid (played by Ruby Dandridge) on the radio series *The Judy Canova Show*

Gerald McBoing Boing
  Cartoon boy (movie cartoon and TV show "The Boing Boing Show") Debut 1951, voice of Marvin Miller

Geraldine Jones
  Character in female costume played by Flip Wilson (TV show): "What you sees is what you get." Her boyfriend is Killer

Gerber Baby, The
  Said, in error, to be a portrait of Humphrey Bogart when he was a baby (Gerber Baby Foods). He actually was the Mellins Baby Food baby. The portrait was painted by his mother, Maude Humphrey Bogart "The Original Maude Humphrey Baby" The Real Gerber Baby is Ann Turner Cook whose picture Gerber began using in 1928. Dorothy Hope Smith did the drawing (Mitzi Gaynor's real name is Francesca Mitzi Gerber)

Germaine
  The only female in the 1940 James Cagney movie *The Fighting 69th.* Germaine, who won Best Animal Actor of the year, is a mule. (The award was presented to her by Humphrey Bogart)

Germania
  New name of Berlin which Adolf Hitler chose and planned to use when the new city was finished. Germania was to be designed by architect Albert Speer.

Geronimo

(1829-1909) Apache Indian chief. His Indian name was Goyathlay (*One Who Yawns*)

Gertie Lade

Perry Mason's blonde office receptionist (Erle Stanley Gardener's Perry Mason series) Played on TV by Connie Cezon and Brett Somers

Gertie

The Dinosaur (actually a Brontosaurus) comic strip by Winsor McCoy in 1913. "Gertie the Dinosaur" (1909) was one of the earliest animated movies. "Humorous Phases of Funny Phases" (1906) made by Thomas Edison with drawings by James Stuart Blackton was the first cartoon on film.

Gertrude

Pocket Books' kangaroo trademark, named by artist Frank Liberman after his mother-in-law

Gertrude

Pet duck accompanying the 19th Century expedition in the 1959 movie *Journey To The Center of the Earth*

Ghidrah

Three-headed monster that Godzilla, Rodan, and Mothra team up to stop (Japanese movie, 1965)

Ghosts

Spirits appearing to Ebenezer Scrooge (Charles Dickens' *A Christmas Carol*): Marley's ghost. The Ghost of Christmas Past. The Ghost of Christmas Present. The Ghost of Christmas to Come

Gibson, Hoot

Cowboy actor, real name Edward Richard, called *Champion Cowboy of the World*. He claimed to have been Hollywood's first stuntman.

Gibson Girl

Created by professional artist Charles Dana Gibson in 1912. The original Gibson Girl was Irene Langhorne, his wife. She was the sister of Nancy Langhorne (Lady Astor). (Nickname given to hand-cranked rescue radios) The first model was Jobyna Howland

Gibson, Josh

Negro player for the Homestead Grays of the Negro League. He hit 84 home runs in one season and hit over 800 home runs in his career. He is the only person ever to hit a home run out of Yankee Stadium (Exhibition game)

Gidget

Nickname of Frances Lawrence. In novels by Frederick Kohner.

Movies:

Gidget (1959) Sandra Dee

Gidget Goes Hawaiian (1961) Deborah Walley

Gidget Goes to Rome (1963) Cindy Carol

Gidget Grows Up (1970) Karen Valentine (TV movie)

Gidget Gets Married (1972) Monie Ellis (TV movie)

Gidget (TV series) Sally Field

Gidney and Cloid

Moon men who come to earth in various episodes of *The Rocky and Bullwinkle Show*

Gifts of the Magi

Gold, Frankincense, Myrrh (Luke 2:11)

Gigantis

Fire monster (Japanese movie. *Gigantis, the Fire Monster*, 1959)

Gilbert

Goofy's nephew (Disney cartoon), he wears a mortarboard cap

Gilbreth, Frank Bunker

Renowned efficiency expert in American industry. Portrayed in 1950 movie *Cheaper by the Dozen* by Clifton Webb. His wife Lillian, portrayed in the movie by Myrna Loy, became a renowned lecturer and the recipient of numerous degrees. She is also portrayed by Myrna Loy in the sequel movie of her life *Belles On Their Toes*. (1952)

Gillis

Chester A. Riley's best buddy (played by Tom D'Andrea) His wife is Honeybee (Joan Blondell)

Gill-Man

Monster in 1954 3D movie *The Creature From The Black Lagoon* (played in movies by Ricou Browning) and sequels *Revenge of the Creature* (1955) by Ben Chapman and *The Creature Walks Among Us* (1956) by Don Megowan. *The Creature from the Black Lagoon* is the movie in which Tom Ewell takes Marilyn Monroe to in the 1955 movie *The Seven Year Itch*

Gimme Shelter
   1970 Rolling Stone's movie about their concert at the Altamont Speedway, California (see Hunter, Meredith)

Gin, Sherry and Martini
   Mr. and Mrs. North's (Jerry and Pam) three pet cats (novel/T.V. series)

Gin-Gin
   Jeannie's (Barbara Eden) genie dog that likes to turn invisible at times (TV series *I Dream of Jeannie*)

Gingol 1
   Substance that gave Ralph Dibny the magic power to become the Elongated man (comic books)

Gipp, George (Gipper)
   Played for Notre Dame (#66) 1917–1920. Died of pneumonia in 1920 at age 25. In a 1928 game against Army, Knute Rockne was supposed to have told his team that Gipper said, "Sometime when the boys are up against it and the pressure's really on Notre Dame, tell them to win one for the Gipper." Rockne told team Gipp had said this on his death bed. Notre Dame won 12–6. Portrayed in 1940 movie *Knute Rockne-All American* by Ronald Reagan. Gipper's family filed a lawsuit and had the famous line deleted from the TV airing of the film. Gipp once ran, in full uniform, 100 yards in 10.2 seconds. At the time of his death he had a contract to play baseball for the *Chicago Cubs*

Girl Commandos
   Comic book answer to the Boy Commandos Leader: Pat Parker (nurse).
   Members: Tanya, Mei-Ling, Ellen (Harvey Comic Books).

Girl from Albany
   Play being presented at the Geary Theatre in San Francisco for which Joel Cairo (Peter Lorre) has a ticket for Wednesday the 18th at 8:30 p.m. (price $3.30 Row 8, seat 15) in the 1941 movie *The Maltese Falcon*. Title of play is fictitious.

Girl Hunters, The
   1964 movie in which detective Mike Hammer is played by his author, Mickey Spillane. Hammer returns after seven years as a drunken bum.

Girl Scouts
  Five Points:
  Cleanliness, Sunshine, Food, Rest and Exercise

Gish Sisters, The
  Actresses, notably in silent movies: Lillian, Dorothy. Real name: De Guiche (Lillian's autobiography: *The Movies, Mr. Griffith & Me*)

Gitchee Gumee
  River by which Hiawatha lives. (Longfellow's poem *Hiawatha*)

Give Service
  Camp Fire Girl's Slogan

Gladstone Gander
  Donald Duck's wavy haired lucky cousin who detests work (cartoon). Debut January 1948

Gladys
  Pet seal in 1969 movie *Hello Down There*

Gladys
  Pete's (Harry Morgan) wife on TV series *December Bride*. Gladys was never seen* but in the TV series *Pete and Gladys*, she is played by Cara Williams

Gladys Ormphby
  Purse-swinging old maid played by Ruth Buzzi, who is always slugging the dirty old man played by Arte Johnson (TV series "Laugh In")

Gleason, Jackie
  "The Great One." His TV personalities: The bachelor, Charley Bratton the loudmouth, Pedro the Mexican, Joe the bartender, Ralph Kramden, the Poor Soul, Reginald Van Gleason III, Rudy the repairman, Stanley R. Soog (announcer of Mother Fletcher's products), Fenwick Babbit. Gleason also played Chester Riley in 1949 TV series "Life of Riley" and on radio (7 weeks). Host of 1961 TV quiz show "You're In the Picture" and on radio (7 weeks)

Glencairn
  Tramp Steamer on which John Wayne is a crew member in 1940 movie *The Long Voyage Home*. The movie's theme song is *Harbor Lights*

Glendale
  Town location of radio series *Hilltop House*.

---

*In one episode she was seen, but wearing a gorilla costume

Glens Falls

Town, locale of radio serial "Big Sister". Ruth Evans Wayne was Big Sister

Glinda

The good witch of the North (*The Wizard of Oz*): played in 1939 movie by Billie Burke. Singing voice dubbed by Lorraine Bridges voice of Rise Stevens in 1962 cartoon Journey Back to Oz

Global Airways

Airline company whose Boeing 707, Flight 502, flown by Captain Hank O'Hara (Charlton Heston) is hijacked. (1972 movie *Skyjacked*, title changed to *Sky Terror* for TV). By coincidence another TV movie was made in 1975 titled *Flight 502* about the events onboard a Boeing 747. Robert Stack played the pilot. Walter Pidgeon played a passenger in both movies

Gloria

Felix Ungar's wife whom he divorced. In TV series, "The Odd Couple" they remarry after 5 years of divorce (played by Janis Hansen).

Gloria Scott Case

Sherlock Holmes first case as a detective (*"His Last Bow"* being the final case). The first published case was *A Study in Scarlet* (1887) and the last published case was *Shoscombe Old Place* (1927).

Gloryosky!

Little Annie Rooney's favorite expression (comic strip *Little Annie Rooney*).

Gnomobile, The

Walt Disney movie based on the Gnice Gnew Gnarrative with Gnonsense, but Gnothing Gnaughty book, by Upton Sinclair, who wrote the 1936 story for his granddaughter. In the 1967 movie *Gnome-Mobile*, the car was driven by D. J. Mulrooney (Walter Brennan)

Goat

Low man in marks in West Point graduating class

Gobo

Bambi's cousin

God/Jesus

Role played in movies:

Jesus—Monsieur Normand—*The Life of Christ*—1914
Jesus—Robert Henderson Bland—*From the Manger to the Cross*—1914

Jesus—Howard Gaye—*Intolerance*—1916
Jesus—H.B. Warner—*King of Kings*—1927
Jesus—Cameron Mitchell—*The Robe*—1953
God (voice)—Donald Hayne—*The Ten Commandments*—1956
Jesus—Claude Heater—*Ben Hur*—1959
Jesus—Jeffrey Hunter—*King of Kings*—1961
Jesus—Max Von Sydow—*The Greatest Story Ever Told*—1965
Jesus/Judas—John Drew Barrymore—*Pontius Pilate*—1966
God (voice)—John Huston—*The Bible*—1966
Jesus—Robert Elfstrom—*Gospel Road*—1973
Jesus—Victor Garber—*Godspell*—1973
Jesus—Ted Neeley—*Jesus Christ, Superstar*—1973

God Bless America

Written by Irving Berlin (Israel Baline), 1918 throwing it into a trunk until 20 years later. His profits from the song were donated to the Boy and Girl Scouts. Miss Kate Smith was originally given exclusive rights to sing the song. She first sang it Armistice Day 1938. Sung by Kate Smith in 1943 movie *This is the Army*

God Bless Captain Vere

Billy Budd's last words before being hung (Herman Melville's *"Billy Budd"*)

God Bless Our Home

Sampler (or picture) Jesse James was adjusting on the wall of his house in St. Joseph, Missouri when shot by Robert Ford who received $10,000 for his deed.

God Save the King (or Queen)

National anthem of Great Britain. Played at end of every performance in movie theaters

Godfather, The

Don Vito Corleone (novel by Mario Puzo): played in 1971 movie by Marlon Brando. In Godfather II, he's Michael Corleone (Al Pacino)

Godfrey Daniels

W.C. Fields' most popular exclamation, others "mother of pearl," "Oh drat!"

Godzilla

Radioactive, fire breathing 164 foot high Tyrannosaurus Rex (Japanese movies, 1956 and subsequent years): voice of narrator in English dubbing in original movie was Raymond Burr's; Burr also played a reporter. Created by Tnoshira Honda and Eiji Tsuburuya. Godzilla was originally called Gojira in 1954 movie named after a workman at the Toho Studios.

Movies:

Godzilla, King of the Monsters (1955)
Return of Godzilla (1955)
King Kong vs. Godzilla (1963)
Godzilla vs. The Thing (1964)
Godzilla vs. the Sea Monster (1966)
Son of Godzilla (1969)
Godzilla vs. the Smog Monster (1971)
Godzilla vs. Megalon (1973)

(In the 1966 movie *Monster Zero*, Godzilla makes an appearance.)

His picture has appeared on the cover *of Newsweek Magazine*

Golbasto Momaren Evlame Gurdilo Shefin Mully Ully Gue

The most mighty Emperor of Lilliput, the land of Little People (Jonathan Swift's *Gulliver's Travels*)

Goldbergs, The

Dramatic-comedy series written by Gertrude Berg, radio series from 1929:

Gertrude Berg—Molly
James R. Waters—Jake
Menasha Skulnik—Uncle David
Roslyn Siber—Rosalie
Alfred Ryder, Everett Sloane—Sammy
lived at 17 South Jackson

TV series:

Gertrude Berg—Molly
Philip Loeb—Jake (Actor committed suicide after being black listed during McCarthy witch hunt)
Eli Mintz—Uncle David
Arlene McQuade—Rosalie
Larry Robinson—Sammy
Lived at 1083 E. Tremont Ave., Bronx, N.Y. Apt 3B

On Broadway *Molly and Me* (1943); 1950 Movie *The Goldbergs:* starred Gertrude Berg

Gold Cup

Awarded annually to winner of unlimited hydroplane championship. Guy Lombardo won the cup in 1946. In his speedboat Tempo VI he has won The Gold Cup, President's Cup and National Sweeps three times, breaking several world's records

Gold Dagger
Award given annually by the British Crime Writer's Association to the best mystery novel

Gold Diggers
Series of musical movies, stemming from Avery Hopwood's 1919 play *The Gold Diggers:*
Gold Diggers (1923)
Gold Diggers of Broadway (1929)
Gold Diggers of 1933 (1933), part of which is shown in the movie-show sequence of *Bonnie and Clyde* (1967)
Gold Diggers of 1935 (1935)
Gold Diggers in Paris (1938)
Painting the Clouds with Sunshine (1951) followed the original story line

Golddiggers
Dancing group on *The Dean Martin Show* (TV series)

Gold Dust Twins
Goldy and Dusty, two little boys on label of Gold Dust products: slogan "Let the twins do your work" (also a radio program) on radio by Harvey Hindermyer and Earl Tuckerman

Golden Bear
Nickname of golfer Jack Nicklaus

Golden Dreams
The nude calendar photograph of Marilyn Monroe taken by photographer Tom Kelly, May 27, 1949, which Hugh Hefner used in the first issue of Playboy Magazine.

Golden Gate Casino
San Francisco saloon owned by Cash Conover (Doug McClure) on TV series *Barbary Coast*.

Golden Hinde, The
Sir Francis Drake's ship, originally the "Pelican": circumnavigated globe 1577-1580. Drake is portrayed in numerous movies/TV by Terrace Morgan

Golden Knights
U.S. Army's precision parachute team

Goldenrod
The Summers brothers' land speed record automobile: 409.227 mph. Nov. 12, 1965. Bonneville, Utah

Golden Secret
Jack Armstrong's Uncle Jim Fairfield's dirigible

Goldie

Hoot Gibson's golden Palomino which he rode in his western movies

Gold Medal

Award given to Jiminy Cricket by the Blue Fairy after Pinocchio became a real boy—The medal read *"Official Conscience/18Kt."*

Gold Record award

45 RPM's: million copies sold

33 RPM's (LP's): million dollars in sales (includes tapes and cassettes) Columbia Records developed the 33rpm (Lp invented by Peter Goldmark in 1918) RCA Victor developed the 45rpm

Goldwynisms

Statements or sayings attributed to producer Samuel Goldwyn. Example: "A verbal contract isn't worth the paper it is written on"

Goldy

Jonathan G. (Goldy) Locke, the Falcon's chauffeur (in movies played by Allen Jenkin, Don Barclay, Cliff Edward, Ed Brophy, Vince Barnett)

Golem

Clay statue that comes to life. He loses his life though when the Star of David is removed from his chest (played by Paul Wegener in the 1920 movie "Der Golem"

Golf Hall of Fame

Located at Pinehurst, North Carolina. Dedicated by President Ford, April 7, 1974

First members elected were:

1. Bobby Jones
2. Francis Ouimet
3. Walter Hagen
4. Gene Sarazen

Golf's Big Four

United States Open, Masters, P.G.A., British Open

The Grand Slam of Bobby Jones (1930), an amateur player, included the British Amateur, the British Open (291), the U.S. Amateur, the U.S. Open (287). In the British Amateur final, he beat Roger Wethered 7 and 6; in the U.S. Amateur final, he defeated Gene Homans 8 and 7

Golf Clubs

Woods
No. 1:Driver
No. 2:Brassie
No. 3:Spoon
No. 4:Baffy/Cleek

Irons
No. 1:Driving iron/Cleek
No. 2:Midiron
No. 3:Mid mashie
No. 4:Mashie iron
No. 5:Mashie
No. 6:Spade mashie
No. 7:Mashie niblick
No. 8:Pitching niblick/Lofter
No. 9:Niblick
No. 10:Wedge/Sand wedge
— Putter

Six iron was club used by astronaut Alan Shepard to hit three golf balls on the moon February 6, 1971.

Only 14 clubs are allowed in tournament play: the No. 10 iron is usually omitted

Gone with the Wind

A Story of the Old South

Novel (1936; Pulitzer Prize, 1937) by Margaret Mitchell; sold about 1,500,000 copies in its first year.

The original book weighed three pounds, 1037 pages, sold for $3.00 *"Tomorrow is Another Day"* is book's original title. Title *Gone with the Wind* came from Ernest Dowson's poem "Cynara", thirteenth line "I have forgot much Cynara! Gone with the Wind"

Premiered at Lowe's Grand Theatre in Atlanta December 15, 1939. The Governor proclaimed the day a state holiday. In 1967 the movie was re-released with 70mm widescreen and stereophonic sound

Premiered on TV Sunday-Monday Nights November 7-8, 1976

The movie ran 219 minutes and won ten oscars. George Cukor, the original director was replaced by Victor Fleming.

Scarlett's original name in novel was to have been Pansy. Scarlett's father calls her Katie.

Considered for the role of Scarlett were: Bette Davis (who turned the role down), Jean Arthur, Loretta Young, Lucille Ball, Joan Crawford, Marcella Martin, Norma Shearer, Paulette Goddard, Miriam Hopkins, Susan Hayward, Lana Turner, Joan Bennett, Mary Anderson, Joan

Fontaine, Alicia Rhett, Tallulah Bankhead, Catherine Campbell and Katherine Hepburn
Considered for Rhett were: Ronald Colman, Basil Rathbone, Errol Flynn and Gary Cooper
Six actors who appeared in the movie later starred in their own TV series.
Thomas Mitchell (O. Henry Playhouse)
Cliff Edwards (Ukuele Ike)
Hattie McDaniel (Beulah)
Victor Jory (Manhunt)
Ward Bond (Wagon Train)
George Reeves (Superman)
Eddie Rochester, Rand Brooks and others appeared on TV but did not star
Movie roles (Oscar, best picture, 1939):
  Scarlett O'Hara, by Viven Leigh (Oscar)
  Rhett Butler (A visitor from Charleston), Clark Gable
  Ashley Wilkes, Leslie Howard
  Melanie Hamilton, Olivia de Havilland
  Mammy, Hattie McDaniel (Oscar)

Goodrich, B.F.
Benjamin Franklin Goodrich (1841-1888), Ohio rubber manufacturer "We're the guys without the blimp"

Good, the Bad and the Ugly, The
1968 Italian Western filmed in Spain
The Good—the man with no name (Clint Eastwood)
The Bad—Sentenza (Lee Van Cleef)
The Ugly—Tuco Benedicto Pacifico Juan Maria Ramirez (Eli Wallach), role originally offered to Charles Bronson

Good Grief!
Charlie Brown's favorite expression (Charles Schulz *Peanuts*)

Gooding, Gladys
Played for the New York Rangers. New York Knicks and Brooklyn Dodgers in a single season (as organist)

Good to the Last Drop
Slogan of Maxwell House coffee. Theodore Roosevelt created the saying as a guest at a dinner party while being served coffee. The coffee company picked up on the statement, making it their slogan. The Maxwell House, located in Nashville, Tenn., was built in 1859, destroyed in 1961

Goodyear Blimps

Names	*Stationed*
Columbia II	Longbeach, Calif.
America	Houston, Texas
Mayflower III	Miami, Florida
Europa	Rome, Italy

Goody Two-Shoes

Children's story, published 1765 by John Newbery and said to have been written by Oliver Goldsmith, about a very poor little girl and her excitement over having a *pair* of shoes

Goofy

Silly friend of Mickey Mouse. Premiered in 1932 Disney Cartoon *Mickey's Revue*. Voice of Pinto Colvig. His nephew is named Gilbert. (Goofy was originally called Dippy Dawg)

Googol

One followed by 100 zeroes: word credited to the mathematician Edward Kasner's 9-year-old nephew Milton Sirotta. Introduced in 1940 book "Mathematics and the Imagination" Mathematic name for a googol is ten duotrigintillion. A googolplex is $10^{10^{100}}$

Goo Goo

Radio comedian Joe Penner's duck *Wanna buy a duck?* Voice of Mel Blanc

Gook

Last name of Victor Rodney and Sade, and their son Rush (radio series Vic and Sade)

Gookie

Special humorous look given off by Harpo Marx usually getting a number of guffaws. The expression is borrowed from a man Harpo knew in his youth who was nicknamed Gookie

Gopher wood

Used to build Noah's Ark (Genesis 6:14)

Gordian Knot

Tied by Gordius, king of Phrygia, and cut by Alexander the Great (rather than untie it). He fulfilled the prophecy that whoever undid the knot would rule the East. Alexander portrayed in 1956 movie *Alexander the Great* by Richard Burton

277

Gordon Hathaway

Madison Avenue character played by Louis Nye on TV's The Steve Allen Show *Hi-Ho Stevearino.*

Gordon Tracy

Dick Tracy's brother. In 1937 movie serial played by both Richard Beach and Carleton Young

Gorgeous George

Nickname of blond 1950's wrestler who wore his hair in rollers. Born George Raymond Wagner, (1915-1964) Before he entered the ring Chanel #10 had to be sprayed

Gorgon

Character played by prominent attorney Melvin Belli on TV series *Star Trek,* episode "And the Children Shall Lead"

Gorgons

Daughters of Phorcys and Ceto in Greek mythology:
Stheno, the mighty
Euryale, the wide-wandering
Medusa, the cunning one, also called The Gorgon, the sight of whom petrified mortals—literally

Gorilla

Played by Walter Pidgeon (in disguise) in the 1931 movie *The Gorilla.* In 1939 movie *The Gorilla* by Art Miles, in 1938 Laurel and Hardy movie *Swiss Miss* by Charles Gamora

Gorman Elementary

Chicago school where Emily Hartley (Suzanne Pleshette) teaches (TV series *The Bob Newhart Show*)

Gorman, Margaret (Miss Washington, D.C.)

First Miss America, 1921: blue-eyed blond, 5'1", 30-25-32, 108 lbs., 16 years old. King Neptune (His Oceanic Majesty) was the only judge. He was Maxim Hudson, the inventor of smokeless gunpowder

Gort

Klaatu's (Michael Rennie) 8-foot robot (1951 movie *The Day the Earth Stood Still*). Played by Lock Martin (J. Lockard Martin) the 7'7" doorman at Grauman's Chinese Theatre. He was so weak he couldn't pick up Patricia Neal

Gosde, Nathuram

37 year old who assassinated Mohandas Karamchand Gandhi January 30, 1948 in New Delhi

Gotham Bus Company
Transit company for which Ralph Kramden (Jackie Gleason) works as a driver on the Madison Avenue line. His boss is Mr. Marshall, the president is Mr. Monahan. (TV series *The Honeymooners*) The bus company's address is 225 River Street

Gotham City
Hometown of Batman and Robin, 14 miles from the Bat Cave.
Nickname for New York City

Gotham City Trust and Savings Bank
Bank through which John Beresford Tipton awards his million dollar checks, delivered by Michael Anthony (TV series, *The Millionaire*)

Gowdy, Harry (Hawk)
First major league baseball player to enlist in U.S. Armed Forces in World War I, June 2, 1917. He became a sergeant.

Grable, Betty
Most popular pinup girl of World War II (closely followed by Rita Hayworth) Ruth Elizabeth Grable, nicknamed "the legs" (insured for $250,000) Husbands: Jackie Coogan (1937–40); Harry James (1943–65)
She is the movie star Stosh "Animal" (Robert Strauss) kept dreaming about in 1953 movie *Stalag 17*

Graceland
Name of Elvis Presley's 14 acre East Memphis estate bought in 1957. The address is 3764 Elvis Presley Blvd.

Graduate, The
Benjamin Braddock (Charles Webb's novel *The Graduate*): played in 1967 movie by Dustin Hoffman (Robert Redford turned the role down)

Graf Spee
German pocket battleship and raider blown up and scuttled by her own crew, December 1939, outside Montevideo harbor. In the first major naval engagement of World War II. "Spee" had sought refuge there from the Royal Navy's "Achilles," "Ajax," and "Exeter". Her commander Captain Hans Langsdorff committed suicide

Grafton's General Mercantile Co.
Sundries and Saloon
Small Wyoming town bar in which Shane kills gunfighter

California Jack Wilson (Jack Palance) (Will is the bartender) 1953 movie *Shane*. Movie was filmed in Jackson Hole, Wyoming

Graf und Stift
Automobile, 1912 model, in which Archduke Ferdinand and his wife Sophie were riding when they were assassinated June 28, 1914, by Gavrilo Prinzip. The automobile became known as the car with a curse, since more than a dozen people have been killed by it or while riding in it

Graf Zeppelin
First lighter-than-air airship to fly around the world, completed trip in 21 days (1929). The Graf Zeppelin II was the sister ship of the Hindenburg

Graham, Barbara
First female executed in the state of California December 3, 1953. Portrayed in 1958 movie *I Want to Live* by Susan Hayward

Grail Knight
Sir Galahad, sinless son, in Arthurian legend, of Sir Lancelot and Elaine, daughter of King Pelles. In German literature and Wagnerian opera, the Grail Knight is Parsifal

Gramercy Five
Artie Shaw's quintet

Grampa Jones
Nickname first given to country singer Louis Jones when he was 23 years old, and he is yet to be a real life grandfather

Grand Fenwick
Tiny country (15¾ sq. miles) in the French Alps founded by Sir Roger Fenwick in 1430 that declares war on the United States (Leonard Wibberley's *The Mouse That Roared*)

Grand Canyon Disaster
Midair collision of a TWA Super Constellation and a United DC-7 over the Grand Canyon, June 30, 1956. It was the first midair collision between two passenger aircraft. 128 people died. The wreck was removed from the Canyon when the legal suit was finally settled in 1976. The result of this crash was a vastly improved air traffic control system

Grand Old Man of Football, The
(See Amos Stagg)

Grand Ole Opry
Founded by the "Solemn Ole Judge" George Hay. Originating on November 28, 1925 on radio station WSM

Grand Pooh-Bah
Headman of the Loyal Order of the Water Buffaloes, fraternity of Fred Flintstone and Barney Rubble (TV cartoon series)

Grand Slam of Tennis
U.S., winning, of the British, French and Australian Opens

Grand Turk
Ship shown on the bottles of Old Spice cologne

Grane
Siegfried's horse (German mythology)

Graney, Jack
First sports announcer that had been a baseball player, also first player to wear a uniform number and also the first American league batter to face Babe Ruth who was then a pitcher.

Granny
The talking piano (radio series "The Buster Brown Show")

Grant, Joe
Gunfighter who in January, 1880 came to Fort Sumner, New Mexico to challenge Billy the Kid in a gunfight. It was in Hargroove's saloon where Billy asked to see the man's Colt thus putting the empty chamber to be fired next. When the duo eventually had their showdown, Grant's gun clicked on an empty chamber while Billy's didn't, thus killing Grant.

Grant, U.S.
Ulysses Simpson Grant (1822-1885), 18th president of the United States (1869-1877)
Portrayed in movies:
Abraham Lincoln (1930) Fred Warren
They Died with Their Boots On (1942) Joseph Crehan
Silver River (1948) Joseph Crehan
How the West Was Won (1962) Harry Morgan
TV series *Wild, Wild West*—James Gregory

Grant Avenue Grammar School
Mayfield elementary school attended by Theodore Cleaver on TV series *Leave It To Beaver*

Grant's Tomb
137 Amsterdam Avenue, Manhattan location of Harry Grant's (Gabe Dell) bar (TV series *The Corner Bar*)

Grapefruit
Yoko Ono's (wife of ex-Beatle John Ono Lennon) book, released in 1971

Grasshopper
Master Po's name for young Caine (TV series "Kung Fu") Caine called "Po Old man"

Grauman's Chinese Theater
Movie theater on Hollywood Boulevard (6925 Hollywood Blvd.) outside which stars have left footprints and other marks in wet cement since Norma Talmadge began the tradition in 1927. Built by Sid "Little Sunshine" Grauman in 1927. Over 150 signatures written in cement (with hands and feet prints). Sonja Henie has her skate marks, William S. Hart has his 2 six-guns, Bob Hope and Jimmy Durante their noses, Joe E. Brown, his mouth, Betty Grable, her right leg, Roy Rogers, his six-gun, Trigger's two front hoofs, Tony's front hoof print. And Star Wars' C3PO, R2D2 and Darth Vader. Opened May 18, 1927, first of Fox chain, cost $1,000,000, seats 2,200. The first film shown was the debut of Cecil B. DeMille's *King of Kings* at $2.00 a seat

Gravely, Jr., Samuel L.
First black U.S. Admiral promoted April 27, 1971.

Graves, Leonard
Narrated TV series "Victory at Sea" (26 episodes)

Graves, Peter
Actor in TV and movies, especially "Mission Impossible" on TV as Phelps; real name Peter Arness, brother of actor James Arness

Gray Ghost
Cowboy Jack Holt's horse in movies

Gray, Pete
One-armed (left only) outfielder (real name: Peter Wyshner) who played for the St. Louis Browns in 1945 and batted .218. He was MVP in Southern Association in 1944 where he hit .333 stealing 68 bases

Great Britain, India, Nepal
Three nations whose flags were set atop Mt. Everest, May 28, 1953, on its first ascent by Edmund Hillary and Tenzing Norkay; the UN emblem was also included

"Great Caesar's Ghost"

Perry White's (editor of the Daily Planet newspaper) favorite expression (TV series *Superman*)

Great Gildersleeve, The

Throckmorton P. Gildersleeve, character originally in radio's "Fibber McGee and Molly" and later with his own show: played by Hal Peary and Willard Waterman (radio and TV). He was water commissioner of Summerfield

Great Imposter, The

Ferdinand Waldo Demara, Jr., alias: Ben W. Jones, Assistant Warden; Brother John Payne, Trappist monk; Dr. Cecil Boyce Hamann; Dr. Joseph C. Cyr. surgeon; Dr. Robert Linton French; Martin Godgart, latin teacher, Dr. James Lore—assistant at Boy's school. In the 1960 movie *The Hypnotic Eye* Demara played nine roles. As Dr. Cyr he successfully operated on 19 South Korean soldiers in a single night aboard the Canadian destroyer HMCS Cayuga, after the incident he was called The Miracle Doctor. Portrayed in 1960 movie *The Great Imposter* by Tony Curtis

Great Lakes

H-O-M-E-S
Huron
Ontario
Michigan
Erie
Superior (largest body of fresh water in the world)

Great Profile, The

The nickname of actor John Barrymore (1882–1942). He was portrayed in the 1958 movie, *Too Much, Too Soon* by Errol Flynn

Great Seal, The

Adopted September 16, 1789 (both sides are shown on reverse of one-dollar bill): 13 stars, 13 stripes, 13 clouds, 13 arrows, 13 laurel leaves, 13 berries, 13 feathers in left wing, 13 feathers in right wing, 13 feathers in tail, 13 rows in pyramid, 13 letters each in the mottoes (*E pluribus unum and Annuit coeptis*)

Great Stone Face

Nickname of Joseph "Buster" Keaton

Great Train Robbery, The

Considered by many to have been the first Western movie (1903) Edison produced by Edwin S. Porter with G. M.

"Bronco" Billy Anderson, filmed in New Jersey. However in 1898 the Edison Company produced a short film titled Cripple Creek Barroom directed by W. K. L. Dickson—which many contend to be the first western.

Great White Fleet, The
American battleship fleet, painted white, circumnavigated the world in 1908 (December 16, 1907, to February 22, 1909), stopping in many foreign ports and covering 46,000 miles: "Connecticut" (flagship), "Georgia," "Illinois," "Kansas," "Kearsarge," "Kentucky," "Louisiana," "Minnesota," "Missouri," "Nebraska," "New Jersey," "Ohio," "Rhode Island," "Vermont," "Virginia," "Wisconsin"

Greek alphabet
Alpha, Beta, Gamma, Delta, Epsilon, Zeta, Eta, Theta, Iota, Kappa, Lambda, Mu, Nu, Xi, Omicron Pi Rho, Sigma, Tau, Upsilon, Phi, Chi, Psi, Omega

Greek orders
Architectural: Ionic, Doric, Corinthian

Green
Color of Mr. Spock's blood due to its copper base (T-negative Vulcan blood) (TV series "Star Trek")

Color of The Thing's blood (1951 movie)

Color of Ichabod Crane's eyes

Color of dress Scarlet O'Hara made from the drapes at Tara

Color of the streetcar named Desire

Green Arrow, The
Secret identity of Oliver Queen (comic book series) his sidekick is Speedy. Debut *More Fun Comics #73* (November 1941)

Green Hornet, The
Secret identity of Britt Reid, great-grand-nephew of the Lone Ranger

Created by Fran Striker and George Trendle

Originated on Detroit radio station WXYZ

Debut Harvey Comics December 1940

Radio: Al Hodge, Donovan Faust, Bob Hall, Jack McCarthy

Movie serials:
Gordon Jones—The Green Hornet (1939)
Warren Hall—The Green Hornet Strikes Again (1940)
Family Tree

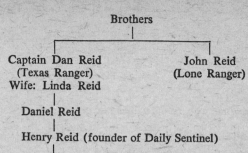

Brothers

Captain Dan Reid (Texas Ranger) Wife: Linda Reid — John Reid (Lone Ranger)

Daniel Reid

Henry Reid (founder of Daily Sentinel)

Britt Reid (The Green Hornet)

The Green Hornet is the great-grand-nephew of the Lone Ranger

Green Lama

Secret identity of super-hero Jethro Dumont—He became a super-swami when he chanted *Om Mani Padmi Om!* (Prize Comics 1940's) played on radio by Paul Frees

Green Lantern, The

Secret identity of Alan Scott (Golden Age) debut *All American Comics* #16 (July 1940)

His original creed: "And I shall shed my light over the dark things for the dark things cannot stand light. The light of the Green Lantern"

Modern Day (second version). Identity of test pilot Hal Jordon becomes one of the many Green Lanterns when Abin Sur died passing his trip on to him. Debut Showcase Comics #22 (October 1959)

His oath: "In brightest day, in blackest night, no evil shall escape my sight. Let those who worship evil's might, beware my power—Green Lantern's light"

Green Monster, The

Art Arfons' jet-powered car, held speed record 1964–1965

Green Monster, The

Nickname for Boston's Fenway Park's left-field fence, 315' from home plate, 37' high with 23' screen on top equalling a 60' green wall

Greenpoint

Fictitious town in which Our Gang lives and plays (MGM *Our Gang* series, later The Little Rascals)

Grelber

The Master of insult. He lives in a hollow log. On the log is a sign reading, "Free Insults" (Cartoon series *Broom-Hilda* by Russell Myers)

Grendel

Monster slain by Beowulf

Grey Cup

Awarded annually to the winners of the Canadian Football League

Greyhound Hall of Fame

Located in Abilene, Kansas

Grimes, Burleigh

Last pitcher to legally throw the spitball, which was banned in 1920. Grimes retired from baseball in 1934

Grimm Brothers

Linguists and compilers of children's fairy tales: Jacob Ludwig (1785–1863), Wilhelm Karl (1786–1859) portrayed in 1962 movie Wonderful World of Grimm by Karl Boehm and Laurence Harvey

Grimus

McDonald-Land character who loves Milk Shakes (McDonald Hamburgers)

Grimy Gulch

Western town where Tumbleweeds and the gang live. Their favorite saloon is the Nugget. (cartoon *Tumbleweeds*)

Grinch

Green-skinned Dr. Seuss creature who steals Christmas (TV program narrated by Boris Karloff)

Grinder Switch

Minnie Pearl's hometown (in her comedy routines) her newspaper is the Grinder Switch Gazette

Grindl

The housemaid played by Imogene Coca (TV series *Your Show of Shows*)

Grok

A term used in science fiction circles as a term meaning: complete, unequivocal, understanding and comprehension. (Robert A. Heinlein's "Stranger in a Strange Land") A favorite Trekkie expression is "I grok Spock"

Groucho Marx

Stage name of Julius Marx, the brother with the mustache —named for Groucho Monk, a comic strip character

Debuted in movies at age 33
Autobiography: *"Groucho and Me"*
His movie roles:
  Humorisk, 1920
  The Cocoanuts, 1929, Mr. Hammer
  Animal Crackers, 1930, Captain Geoffrey T. Spaulding
  Monkey Business, 1931, no name
  Horse Feathers, 1932, Professor Quincey Adams Wagstaff
  Duck Soup, 1933, Rufus T. Firefly
  A Night at the Opera, 1935, Otis B. Driftwood
  A Day at the Races, 1937, Dr. Hugo Z. Hackenbush
  Room Service, 1938, Gordon Miller
  At the Circus, 1939, J. Cheever Loophole
  Go West, 1940, S. Quentin Quayle
  The Big Store, 1941, Wolf J. Flywheel
  A Night in Casablanca, 1946, Ronald Kornblow
  Copacabana, 1947, Lionel Q. Devereaux
  Love Happy, 1949, Sam Grunion
  Double Dynamite, 1951, Emil J. Kech
  The Story of Mankind, 1957, Peter Minuit
Host of TV quiz show *You Bet Your Life,* Groucho Marx and William "Bud" Abbott were both born October 2, 1895

Grover
  Sesame street muppet whose birthday is on October 14, (TV's *Sesame Street*)

Grover
  Stan Freberg's puppet, also Orville the moon creature

Grover's Corners
  U.S. town in Thornton Wilder's play *Our Town*

Grovers Mill
  Wilmuth farm in New Jersey, fictional landing place of Martians (Orson Welles' radio broadcast "War of the Worlds," October 30, 1938): in the H. G. Wells novel the landing place was Horsell Common, near Woking, Surrey, England. In 1953 movie they land in Corona, California

Grumman F5F Skyrocket
  The Blackhawks' first plane (comic book series "Blackhawk"), later they flew a Lockheed XF90

G-String Murders, The
Mystery novel credited to Gypsy Rose Lee. Actually written by Craig Rice (Georgiana Ann Randolph)

Gub-Gub
Doctor Dolittle's baby pig

Guess Where II
Civilian version (C-87A) of the B24-Liberator. Custom-tailored for President Franklin D. Roosevelt's use during World War II. First unofficial presidential airplane (Serial number 124159) piloted by Major Henry T. Myers. (The Guess Where I was General Harold L. George's C84 (DC-3B)

Guest Book
Popular gimmick on Carol Burnett TV show, signed by weekly guests at close of show. First to sign (1967) was Jim Nabors

Guiteau, Charles J.
Assassin of James Garfield. As he shot the president, Guiteau shouted, "I am a stalwart and now Arthur is president."

Guinevere
King Arthur's wife and Sir Lancelot's lover
Played in movies:
  King of the Round Table (1953) Ava Gardner
  Sword of Lancelot (1963) Jean Wallace
  Camelot (1967) Vanessa Redgrave

Gulf of Tonkin
North Vietnam PT boats reported to have attacked destroyers U.S.S. "Maddox" and "C. Turner Joy," August 25, 1964
The "C. Turner Joy" fired the last official U.S. shot of the Vietnam war

Gull Cottage
Schooner Bay, Maine house haunted by Captain Gregg and inhabited by Mrs. Muir (TV series "The Ghost and Mrs. Muir")

Gull Island
Destination of aviatrix Toni Carter (Rosalind Russell) as solo pilot on a secret mission for the U.S. Government, 1943 movie *Flight For Freedom*. Amelia Earhart's destination was Howland Island. 2 miles long, ½ mile wide

Gulliver's Travels

Novel (originally published 1726) by Jonathan Swift. The lands and people Lemuel Gulliver visited were:

Lilliput, a nation of 6-inch-high people

Blefuscu, a country of 6-inch-high people at war with Lilliput

Brobdingnag, a nation of 60-foot-tall giants

Laputa, a flying island inhabited by forgetful, scientific quacks

Glubdubdrib, a land of magicians and sorcerers

Luggnag, an island where the inhabitants, the Struldbrugs, live forever

Houyhnhnms, a nation where rational, intelligent horses rule over human-ike Yahoos

Balnibarbi, the land of inventors and projectors; capital: Lagado

GUM

Moscow's largest department store

Gosudarstvennoye Universalniy Magazin

Gumby

Little bendable plastic man that appeared 3 dimensional —his human friend was Bobby Nicolson—Many Gumby toys have been sold. His horse was named Pokey (TV cartoon and plastic toy)

Gumps, The

Comic strip (1917–1959) by Sydney Smith and then Gus Edson: Min. (Minerva) Andy (Andrew), Chester, Uncle Bim, Tilda the maid. On radio:

Min—Dorothy Denver, Agnes Moorehead

Andy—Jack Boyle, Wilmer Walter

Chester—Charles Flynn Jr.—Jackie Kelk

Gun Club of Baltimore

Organization which sponsored sending the Columbiad to the Moon in Jules Verne's *From the Earth to the Moon*. The club also organized to change the earth's surface in the sequel novel *The Purchase of the North Pole*

Gunga Ram

Indian elephant boy played by Nino Marcel (TV series "Andy's Gang")

Gungnir

Odin's spear

Guns

Used by various fictitious characters:

Nick Carter (Killmaster)	9mm Luger
Shell Scott	.38 Colt Special
Dirty Harry	Colt .44 Magnum (Model 29)
Michael Shayne	Harvey's Banker's Special .32
Emma Peel	Italian Beretta 7.65
Lewis Archer	.38 special .38 automatic
Lone Ranger	2—Colt 45's
John Steed	Walther 7.65
Napoleon Solo	Luger Special "S"
Joe Mannix	.38 Smith & Wesson/.45
Paladin	Colt .44
The Shadow	2—.45 Automatics
Matt Helm	Cold Woodsman .22/Snubnosed .38
April Dancer	.32 Caliber Purse
John Drake (Secret Agent)	.25 Beretta
Steve McGarrett	.32 Police
Dick Tracy	.38 Police
Drake	9mm Smith & Wesson automatic in Bianchi belt holster
Alexander Scott	.357 Magnum
Kelly Robinson	.38 automatic and .32 Tennis Racquet
Philip Marlowe	Luger Colt Smith & Wesson .38 special

Gunsmoke

Longest running TV Western

"The first man they look for, and the last they want to meet"

Radio series (April 26, 1952):

Matt Dillon, played by William Conrad

Chester Wesley Proudfoot, Parley Baer

Kitty Russell, Georgia Ellis

Doc Galen Adams, Howard McNear

Narrated by Roy Rowan, George Walsh

In the original audition show (1949) Howard Culver played Marshal Mark Dillon

TV series (September 10, 1955—September 1, 1975):
  Matt Dillon, played by James Arness
  Chester Goode, Dennis Weaver (Replaced by Festus)
  Kitty Russell, Amanda Blake
  Doc Galen Adams, Milburn Stone
  Festus Haggin, Ken Curtis
  Narrated by George Walsh
First TV episode was introduced by John Wayne who was first offered the role—In the first eight years Matt shot down Arvo Ojala (not seen) at program's introduction. Ojala was replaced by Fred McDougall and Ted Jordon Ken Curtis sang with the Tommy Dorsey and Shep Fields bands, also with Sons of the Pioneers. He starred in 1951 movie serial Don Daredevil Rides Again
Matt Dillon's horse is Buck played by Marshal. TV series retitled "Gun Law" in Great Britain

Gus
Elderly fire chief to whom Beaver Cleaver befriended (TV series *Leave It To Beaver*) played by Bert Mustin

Gus Goose
Grandma Duck's hired hand and nephew (cartoon) debut TV cartoon *Donald's Cousin Gus*

Gutenberg Bible
First book set in print (1450–1455) There are only 49 known Gutenberg Bibles in the world

Guthrie, Janet
First woman to race in the Indy 500 (1977)

Gwen
Miss Marple's red-headed maid (Detective series by Agatha Christie)

Gwendoline
13-year-old daughter of Mrs. Violet Wells Norton whom her mother claimed in a 1937 court case to be the daughter of Clark Gable. Instead, Mrs. Norton was found guilty of using the U.S. mails to defraud.

Gypsy Moth IV
53-foot sailboat in which 65 year old Sir Francis Chichester sailed around the world in 9 months (August 28, 1966 to May 18, 1967). For this feat he was knighted

Gyro Gearloose
Donald Duck's inventor friend who has his friend the light bulb called Helper always with him (Disney cartoon)

H

$100,000 infield
Philadelphia Athletics' infield (managed by Connie Mack) 1911–1914; John Phelan "Stuffy" McInnis, 1B; Edward Trowbridge Collins, 2B; John Joseph Barry, SS; John Franklin "Home Run" Baker, 3B

H A L 9000
Computer of spaceship "Discovery-1" (1968 movie *2001: A Space Odyssey*). Became operational at the Hall Plant, Urbana, Illinois January 12, 1997. Hal's voice is that of Douglas Rain. HAL-Heuristic and Algorithmic (two learning systems) HAL is IBM stepped down one letter

H Movies
Of Paul Newman: *Helen Morgan Story, The*, 1957: *Hustler, The* 1961; *Hemingway's Adventures of a Young Man*, 1962; *Hud*. 1963; *Harper*, 1966; *Hombre*, 1967; *Hall of Mirrors*, 1969 (original title of movie WUSA)

H.M.S. Pinafore
Operetta by W. S. Gilbert and Arthur Sullivan: subtitle —*The Lass that Loved a Sailor*

Habeas Corpus
Lt. Colonel Andrew Blodgett Mayfair's (Monk) pet pig. (Monk is a member of Doc Savage's crew)

Hadji
Master of genies, over Jeannie (Barbara Eden), Hadji is played by Abraham Safaer. (TV series "I Dream of Jeannie")

Hadleyville
Western town of which Will Kane (Gary Cooper) was

marshal, his deputy, Harvey Pell played by Lloyd Bridges
(1952 movie *High Noon*)

Haight and Ashbury
San Francisco street intersection that was considered the
center of the Hippie (flower children) community

Hail to the Chief
Official song of the President. Words by Sir Walter Scott
(*The Lady of the Lake*, Canto II)

Hair Bear Bunch, The
TV cartoon series: Bubi, Hair, Square

Half Moon, The
Henry Hudson's ship (1609)

Hall Closet
Fibber McGee's overflowing, overstuffed hallway closet
first introduced in their skit on March 5, 1940, when Molly
went looking for a dictionary to look up the word (sic)
anahiliated. Been part of the show ever since. Radio's
Fibber McGee and Molly

Hall of Fame
Gallery of busts or commemorative tablets "of Great
Americans" (New York University, Washington Heights).
Elections to the Hall of Fame occur every 3 years. First
member: George Washington

Halley's Comet
Recurring, highly visible comet; it has been traced to
240 B.C. It is named for Sir Edmund Halley (1656–
1742), astronomer royal, who calculated its 76-year
period and predicted its return in 1758. It appeared the
year of Mark Twain's birth (1835) and also the year of his
death (1910). Also Italian Astronomer G. V. Schiaparelli
(1835–1910)
In comic strip Gordo's bus is named El Cometa Halley

Ham
Chimpanzee, first United States animal to orbit, Jan. 31,
1961

Hamburglar
Bad guy in McDonaldland (McDonald's Hamburger ads)

Hamelin
Town in Germany from which the Pied Piper chased
the mice.
In 1957 movie *Pied Piper of Hamelin* the piper is played
by Van Johnson (Originally broadcast as TV special)

Hamilcar

Carthaginian general, father of Hannibal. In 1960 movie *Hannibal*, Hannibal is portrayed by Victor Mature

Hamilton Building

On Broadway, between third and fourth streets. Location of Sheldon Scott, Investigations (Shell Scott series by Richard S. Prather)

Hamilton High School

Learning facility of which Stu Erwin (Stu Erwin) is the principal (TV series *The Stu Erwin Show*)

Hamlet

Sarah Bernhardt's dog

Hancock, John

Boston merchant: first signer of the Declaration of Independence, only one to actually sign on July 4, 1776

Hand of God, The

Sculpture by Auguste Rodin, at Metropolitan Museum of Art, New York

Handsome Dan

The Yale football team's mascot bulldog

Handy, William C.

Father of the Blues, (1873–1958): "St. Louis Blues," etc. 1958 movie biography titled *St. Louis Blues*

Hanging Judge, The

Isaac Parker, who sentenced 79 men to be hanged (see Parker, Isaac)

Hanks

Country music fame: Hank Locklin; Hank Snow; Hank Thompson; Hank Williams; Hank Williams, Jr.; Hank Cochran

Hanley, Barbara

The little girl who inspired the Barbie Doll, designed by her mother and manufactured by Jack Ryan, Zsa Zsa Gabor's sixth husband

Hannibal

Missouri town in which Mark Twain grew up, 1839–1853. (He was born in Florida, Missouri, in 1835). Birth place of Cliff Edwards

Hannibal

Israel Boone's (Darby Hinton) pet goose on the TV series Daniel Boone

Hannibal

Ben Calhoun's (Dale Robertson) horse in 1966 TV western "Iron Horse"

Hannibal 8 (Twin-8)

Six wheeled automobile of Professor Fate (Jack Lemmon) (1965 movie *The Great Race*). The car uses Firestone tires, #5 in the race. Six different cars were built for the movie

Hans and Fritz

The Katzenjammer Kids. Hans, the blond, and Fritz, the one with the dark brush cut, appeared first in 1897, drawn by Rudolph Dirks, later by Harold Knerr. During World War I, the strip was retitled "The Captain and the Kids" and the strip ran under both titles simultaneously (see Katzenjammer Kids)

Hanson, John

Maryland political leader (1721–1783), first "president of the United States Congress assembled" (Nov. 1781–Nov. 1781) under the Articles of Confederation and sometimes therefore considered first President of the United States: he presided, however, over the Congress, not over the United States

Hansons

Family in TV series "Mama," adapted from 1948 movie *I Remember Mama*: lived on Steiner Street, San Francisco; in movie on Larkin Street

Happiness Boys, The

Early radio vocal duo: Ernie Hare, Billy Jones. On October 21, 1921 they introduced the first radio theme song

Happy and Walter

Health and exercise enthusiast Jack LaLanne's two white dogs that appear with LaLanne on his daily TV exercise show

HAppydate 270

Phone number of Happydale Sanitarium, headed by Mr. Witherspoon (Edward Everette Horton) (1944 movie *Arsenic and Old Lace*)

Happy Homemaker Show

Sue Ann's (Betty White) television program on Minneapolis station WJM (TV series *Mary Tyler Moore Show*)

Happy Hooker, The

Nickname of Xaviera Hollander, used as title of her best-selling autobiography

Happy Hotpoint
    3-inch pixie that advertised Hotpoint appliances on TV's
    Ozzie and Harriet Show. Played by 17 year old Mary Ty-
    ler Moore
Happy McMann
    Martin Kane's aide (radio series "Martin Kane, Private
    Eye"): played by Walter Kinsella
Happy Tooth
    Animated character who advertised Colgate Dental
    Cream on TV commercials
Happy Trails
    Theme song of Roy Rogers (Leonard Slye) and Dale
    Evans (Frances Octavia Smith) (when sponsored by
    Dodge automobiles). Before Dodge, it was "Smiles Are
    Made Out of Sunshine" and later "It's Roundup Time on
    the Double R Bar"
Happy Warrior
    Nickname of Alfred E. Smith (1873–1944), four-time
    governor of New York State and 1928 Democratic can-
    didate for President: noted for his brown derby hat. Por-
    trayed in 1960 movie *Sunrise at Campobello* by Alan
    Bunce
Hardy Boys, The
    Stories written (first in "The Tower Treasure") by Frank-
    lin W. Dixon about 18 year old Frank and 17 year old
    Joe, sons of detective Fenton and Laura Hardy
    On TV series Frank played by Parker Stevensen, Joe by
    Shaun Cassidy (brother of David Cassidy)
    On TV series on *The Mickey Mouse Club* Tim Considine
    played Frank; Tommy Kirk played Joe
Hardy, Carroll
    The only player to have ever pinch-hit for Ted Williams
    (1960)
Harlem Globetrotters
    Comical group of basketball players founded by Abe Sa-
    perstein on January 27, 1927, in Chicago
    The team was previously known as the Savoy Big Five
    because they played ball at the Savoy Ballroom.
    The original members were:
    Walter "Toots" Wright
    Byron "Fats" Long
    Willie "Kid" Oliver
    Andy Washington

Al "Runt" Pullins
(Wilt Chamberlain later played with them for a short time)
Only three white men have played for the Globetrotters: Abe Saperstein, Bunny Levitt and Bob Karstens
In 10,000 games (as of March 6, 1970) they had won 9,678 (see: Saperstein, Abe)

Harlow, Jean
Hollywood actress born Harlean Carpentier in 1911. The name Harlow is actually her mother's maiden name. Marriages: Charles McGrew (1927–1931), Paul Bern (1932, widowed), Hal Rossen (1933–1935) Died June 7, 1937. In 1965 two biographical movies were made both titled *Harlow*. Portrayed by Carroll Baker and Carol Lynley (see Saratoga)
She was the first female movie star to appear on the cover of Life Magazine

Harlow—Gable Movies
Jean Harlow and Clark Gable appeared together in (MGM):

The Secret Six*	(1931)
Red Dust	(1932)
Hold Your Man	(1933)
China Seas	(1935)
Wife Vs. Secretary	(1936)
Saratoga	(1937)

(See Saratoga)
Together they made 6 movies, the first ironically titled *The Secret Six*

Harmonia Gardens
New York City's huge beer parlor of 1890's where Dolly Levi (Barbra Streisand) makes her appearance—Louis Armstrong leads the house band. 1969 movie musical *Hello Dolly*

Harmony
Charles Starrett's sidekick, cowboy character played by Cliff Edwards

Harper
(See Lew Archer)

Harper Valley P.T.A.
Country and western song recorded by Jeannie C. Riley:

---

*Debut film of Ralph Bellamy

Mrs. Johnson, miniskirted mother who attacks the P.T.A. P.T.A. members: Bobby Taylor, Mr. Baker, Widow Jones, Mr. Harper, Shirley Thompson. Composed by Tom T. Hall

Harrah's South Lodge

Lake Tahoe hotel from which Frank Sinatra, Jr., was kidnapped Sunday December 8, 1963. The men involved in the kidnapping were: Barry W. Keenan (23), Joseph Clyde Amsler (23) and John W. Irwin (42). The ransom was $240,000

Harrison, William Henry

Nicknamed Tippecanoe, President of the United States (1841, died one month after inauguration) and grandfather of President Benjamin Harrison: oldest (68) president at inauguration. His father signed the Declaration of Independence

Harry and Blanche Morton

George Burns and Gracie Allen's next door neighbors on their television show. Harry played by Hal March, Bob Sweeney, Fred Clark and finally Larry Keating. Blanche played by Bea Benaderet

Harry Lime

The third man (Graham Green's *The Third Man*): played in the 1949 Carol Reed-directed movie by Orson Welles; radio by Orson Welles; TV by Michael Rennie

Harry Palmer

British spy played by Michael Caine in 3 English movies adapted from Len Deighton novels:

The Ipcress File (1965)

Funeral in Berlin (1966)

Billion Dollar Brain (1967)

Harry S Truman Memorial High

Webster Grove, Missouri (near St. Louis) High School (built in 1934) at which Lucas Tanner (David Hartman) is an English teacher and baseball coach. The school paper is the Truman High Trumpet. Prior to Truman's death the school was named Webster Groves High School. (TV series "Lucas Tanner") His late wife Ellie had also been a teacher there

Hartford

Admiral D. G. Farrugut's flagship at New Orleans and at Mobile Bay

Hartford, Hereford and Hampshire

3 British towns that Eliza Doolittle is taught to enunciate

by Professor Higgins in order to teach her not to drop her H's. *"In Hartford, Hereford and Hampshire, hurricanes hardly ever happen.* (play/movie *My Fair Lady*)

Hartline, Mary

Blonde leader of the Circus band (TV series "Super Circus" 1949)

Hartmann, Erich

World War II German fighter pilot: all-time ace of aces, with 352 confirmed victories on the Russian front

Hartville

Home town of barber Bill Davidson (played by Arthur Hughes) radio series *Just Plain Bill*

Harvard University

Ivy League college founded in 1636

Graduates who became U.S. Presidents: John Adams, John Quincy Adams, Theodore Roosevelt, Rutherford B. Hayes, Franklin D. Roosevelt, and John F. Kennedy

In fiction, school attended by detective Philo Vance

Harvey

Invisible 6′3½″ pooka, friend of Elwood P. Dowd (play by Mary C. Chase) (See Pooka)

Harvey Girls

Susan Bradley (Judy Garland)

Alma (Virginia O'Brien)

Deborah (Cyd Charisse)

1946 MGM movie *The Harvey Girls*

Harvey's Banker's Special

Detective Michael Shayne's .32 caliber pistol

Hatchet, The

Carry Nation's newspaper dedicated to her fight against alcohol

Hatfields and McCoys

Famous feuding hillbilly families (Pike County, Kentucky, 1880's to 1890's) Hatfield lived in Mingo County, W. Virginia. McCoys in Pike County, Kentucky. They were separated by the Tug River. Feud finally ended by an interfamily marriage March 21, 1891 after 150 family members had been killed

Hat-in-the-Ring

Nickname of the 94th Aero Pursuit Squadron of Allied Forces in France during World War I, to which Eddie Rickenbacker and author James Norman Hall were flyers

Hathaway, Anne

Wife of William Shakespeare. They were married in November 1582. Children:

Susannah, born May 1583

Hamnet and Judith (twins), born January 1585

Hauptmann, Bruno Richard

German immigrant carpenter who kidnapped and murdered (1932) Charles Lindbergh's 20-month-old son. He was tried (1935) at Flemington, New Jersey, convicted, and electrocuted (April 3, 1936)

Hawaiian Islands

Eight largest: Hawaii, Kahoolawe, Kauai, Lanai, Maui, Molokai. Niihau, Oahu

Hawaiian Village Hotel

Setting where Cricket Blake (Connie Stevens) is a singer (TV series *Hawaiian Eye*)

Hawkeye

Natty Bumppo, the trapper (James Fenimore Cooper's *Last of the Mohicans* and other Leatherstocking novels) In 1957 TV series by John Hart. In movies:

1922—(silent)—James Gordon

1932—Harry Carey

1936—Randolph Scott

1952—Jon Hall

Hawkgirl

Shiera Saunders (Carter Hall's girlfriend)—Debut Flash Comics #24 Shayera (second version)

Hawkman

Secret identity of Carter Hall, Katar Hol (second version) (comic book series). Debut Flash Comics #1 (January 1940)

Hayes, George "Gabby"

(1885–1969) Played the sidekicks of Gene Autry, Hopalong Cassidy (as Windy Halliday), Roy Rogers, John Wayne, Bill Elliott, Randolph Scott. Gabby called his beard whiskers

Hayworth, Rita

Actress (real name Marguerite Carmen Cansino)

Her husbands: Edward Judson, 1937-1943; Orson Wells, 1943-1947; Aly Khan, 1949-1951; Dick Haymes, 1953-1955; James Hill, 1958-1961. She sang with Xavier Cugat's orchestra

Hazel
　　Priscilla's mother (cartoon "Priscilla's Pop" by Al Vermeer)

Hazel
　　Switchboard operator for Shell Scott, private eye (Richard S. Prather novel series)

Hazel Burke
　　Maid of the Baxter family including their little boy Harold "Sport." Cartoon strip by Ted Key, originally in the *Saturday Evening Post* (TV series *Hazel* starred Shirley Booth)

He ain't heavy, he's my brother
　　Inscription on statue at Boys Town, Nebraska (statue of a boy carrying his younger brother on his shoulders) Title of popular song by the Hollies, on which Elton John plays the piano

Head
　　1969 movie starring the Monkees (their only movie)

Hearts
　　The shape of Lolita's sunglasses (played by Sue Lyon in the 1962 movie Lolita)

Heavenly Messenger 7013
　　Angel played by Edward Everett Horton in 1941 movie *Here Comes Mr. Jordan* and 1947 sequel *Down to Earth*

Heavyweight Boxing Champions
　　1882-1892 John L. (Lawrence) Sullivan
　　　　(Sullivan was the last bare-knuckle champion)
　　1892-1897 James J. Corbett, by decision, 21 rounds
　　1897-1899 Robert Fitzsimmons, by KO, 14 (Australian)
　　1899-1905 James J. Jeffries, by KO, 11
　　1905-1906 Marvin Hart, by KO, 11
　　　　(Defeated Jack Root)
　　1906-1908 Tommy Burns (Noah Brusso by decision, 20 (Canadian)
　　1908-1915 Jack Johnson, by KO, 14
　　1915-1919 Jess Willard, by KO, 26
　　1919-1926 Jack Dempsey, by KO, 3
　　1926-1928 Gene Tunney, by decision, 10
　　1930-1932 Max Schmeling, on foul, 4 (German)
　　　　(Defeated Jack Sharkey)
　　1932-1933 Jack Sharkey (Joseph Zukauskas), by decision, 15

1933-1934 Primo Carnera, by KO, 6 (Italian)
1934-1935 Max Baer, by KO, 11
1935-1937 James J. Braddock, by decision, 15
1937-1949 Joe Louis, (Joseph Lewis Barrow)
    (Louis defended his title 25 times)
1949-1951 Ezzard Charles, by decision, 15
    (Defeated Joe Walcott)
1951-1952 Joe Walcott (Arnold Raymond Cream), by
KO, 7
1952-1956 Rocky Marciano (Rocco Marchegiano), by
KO, 13 (Undefeated)
1956-1959 Floyd Patterson, by KO, 5
    (Defeated Archie Moore)
1959-1960 Ingemar Johansson, by KO, 3 (Swedish)
1960-1962 Floyd Patterson, by KO, 5 (Regained title)
1962-1964, Sonny Liston (Charles Liston), by KO, 1
1964-1967 Cassius Clay (Mohammad Ali), by KO, 7
1970-1973 Joe Frazier, by KO, 5 (defeated Jimmy Ellis)
1973-1974 George Foreman, by KO, 2
1974-   Muhammad Ali, by KO, 8 (Regained title)
Champions who retired undefeated: James J. Jeffries,
Gene Tunney, Joe Louis, Rocky Marciano. Joe Louis
came out of retirement and was defeated by Ezzard
Charles

Movie Portrayals	Actor	Fighter
The Great John L. (1945)	Greg McClure	John L. Sullivan
Gentleman Jim (1942)	Ward Bond	John L. Sullivan
Gentlemen Jim (1942)	Errol Flynn	James J. Corbett
The Great White Hope (1970)	James Earl Jones	Jack Johnson
The Joe Louis Story (1953)	Coley Wallace	Joe Louis
Requiem for a Heavyweight (1962)	Cassius Clay	Cassius Clay

Max Baer, Jack Dempsey, Jess Willard and James J.
Jeffries all appeared in 1933 movie The Lady and the
Prizefighter
Robert Fitzsimmons and Jack Johnson are buried within
200 feet of each other at Chicago's Graceland Cemetery
Robert Fitzsimmons was the middleweight champion
(1891-1897) and light-heavyweight champion (1903-
1905)
Gene Tunney was the light-heavyweight champion in 1923

Olympic champions were: Floyd Patterson, (middle-weight); Muhammad Ali (Light heavyweight); Joe Frazier and George Foreman

Muhammed Ali had nicknamed Patterson, the rabbit; Liston, the bear; Frazier, the turtle

Heckle and Jeckle

Two magpies in movie cartoons (Terrytoon) Created by Paul Terry. Debut: The Talking Magpies (1946)

Hedorah

The Smog Monster (1971 Japanese movie *Godzilla vs the Smog Monster*)

Hee Haw

TV featuring country and western music and humor

Main characters: Roy Clark, Buck Owens, Buckaroos, Grandpa Jones, Cathy Baker, Archie Campbell, Jenifer Bishop, Susan Raye, Jeannine Riley, Lulu Roman, Junior Samples, Stringbean (David Akeman), Sunshine, Gordie Tapp, Shep Wooley, Minnie Pearl, Mary Ann Gordon, The Hagger Twins, Barbi Benton, Don Halon, Beauregard Jr. and Buddy the Wonder Dog

Hegira

The flight of Mohammed from Mecca to Medina. September 13 622 (Moslem calendar begins with this date)

Heidi

Heidi by Johanna Spyri. Published 1880. *Heidi Grows Up* by Charles Tritten (Johanna Spyri's translator)

Movies: 1937—Shirley Temple
        1953 (Swiss) Elsbeth Sigmund*
        1968 (Austrian-German) Eva Maria Singhammer

Heidi

President Eisenhower's weimaraner dog

Heidi Doody

Howdy Doody's sister (TV series *Howdy Doody*)

Heidi Game

Football game (Nov. 17, 1968) between the New York Jets and the Oakland Raiders. The movie *Heidi* pre-empted the last two minutes of the game, New York ahead 32-29. In 2 minutes Oakland scored twice, to win 43-32.

---

*Sigmund played the role in a sequel, *Heidi and Peter* (1955)

Heisman Trophy
Awarded to most outstanding college footbell player of
the year (first awarded in 1935 to Jay Berwanger of
Chicago). Notre Dame players have won the most. Given
by the Downtown Athletic Club of New York.

Helen of Troy
"The face that launched a thousand ships" (Marlowe);
her eloping with Paris of Troy caused her husband
Menelaus to gather the Greeks and attack Troy in the
Trojan War. *Movie Portrayals: The Face That Launched a
Thousand Ships* (1953) Hedy Lamarr, *The Story of Man-
kind* (1957) Dani Crayne, *Doctor Faustus* (1967) Eliza-
beth Taylor

Helga (later Hilda)
Commandant Klink's private secretary at Stalag 13
(played by Cynthia Lynn in TV series *Hogan's Heroes*).
She was later replaced by Hilda (Sigrid Valdis)

Helga
Wife of Hagar the Horrible. Honi is their daughter
(comic strip *Hagar the Horrible*).

Henderson
Town locale (TV serial "Search for Tomorrow")

Hendersons
Family for which Beulah worked (radio/TV "Beulah")

Henery Hawk
Chicken hawk friend of Ollie the Owl. Voice of Mel
Blanc in *Merry Melody/Looney Tunes*

Henrietta
Ship bought by Phileas Fogg for $60,000 that gets him
from New York to Liverpool (Jules Verne's *Around the
World in 80 Days*) In the 1956 movie the ship's captain
was played by Jack Oakie

Henrietta
Henry the speechless boy's girlfriend (*Henry* comic strip)

Henry
Amos Burke's valet (TV series "Burke's Law")

Henry
Ringo Kid's (John Wayne) first name (1939 movie *Stagecoach*) (In the short story it was Malpais Bill)

Henry Aldrich
Played in movies by Jackie Cooper and James Lydon.
Played on radio and on Broadway by Ezra Stone. Also on

304

radio by Normal Tokar, Raymond Ives, Dickie Jones and Bobby Ellis

Henry Cool

Deceased husband of detective Bertha Cool (series by Erle Stanley Gardner as A.A. Fair)

Henry Fleming

Young soldier of the 304th New York Regiment, Army of the Potomac in Civil War (Stephen Crane's *The Red Badge of Courage*). Played in 1951 movie by Audie Murphy, in 1976 tv movie by Richard Thomas

Henry Tremblechin

Little Iodine's father (comic strip). His boss is Mr. J. P. Bigdome, Henry's wife is Effie

Henson, Matthew Alexander

Negro (1886-1955) who accompanied Admiral Robert Peary in 1909 journey to the North Pole. Henson reached the Pole first. Four Eskimos also reached the Pole with them: Ooqueah, Ootah, Egingwah, Seegloo

Herald, The

Newspaper originally sold by Billy Batson (Captain Marvel)

Herb and Tootsie (Harriet) Woodley

Dagwood and Blondie Bumstead's neighbors. In movies played by Emory Parnell and Isabel Withers

Herbert

Frank McBride's (Eddie Albert) pet plant (TV series *Switch*)

Herbert Philbrick

Private citizen, high level member of the Communist party, and counterspy for the FBI, played by Richard Carlson (TV series "I Led 3 Lives")

Herbert, Master/Sergeant Tony

Korean War's most decorated GI

Herbie

Good Humor ice cream salesman played by Flip Wilson

Herbie

The Love Bug, a Volkswagen (Disney movies *The Love Bug, Herbie Rides Again* and *Herbie Goes to Monte Carlo*). Number 53 was painted on the side of the car. Herbie was named after Tennessee's (Buddy Hackett) uncle

Hercule Poirot

5'4" Belgian detective created by Agatha Christine appearing in 38 books. First in *The Mysterious Affair at Styles* (1920) Madame Christie's first novel. His partner is Captain Arthur Hasting. Curtain written in 1940 (completed 1975) was Hercule Poirot's last adventure being a wheel-chair-ridden old man.

Played on radio by Harold Huber, in movies by:

Austin Trevor "Lord Edgware Dies" (1934)

Tony Randall "The Alphabet Murders" (1966)

Albert Finney "Murder on the Orient Express" (1975)

Retired from the Belgian police department in 1904. His brother is named Achille, he is Catholic, played on stage in Alibi in 1928 by Charles Laughton

Here Come da' Judge

Laugh-in sketch featuring Pigmeat Markham as da judge, sketch later used by Sammy Davis Jr. (In one of the *Our Gang* comedies Buckwheat announced *"Here comes the Judge"*)

Pontiac even came out with an automobile da' Judge (1960's)

Here Come the Clowns

Theme song of the *Ringling Brothers—Barnum and Bailey Circus Greatest Show On Earth*

Here lie the broken bones of L. B. Jefferies

Inscription on the cast of Mr. Jefferies (James Stewart) broken left leg (1954 movie *Rear Window*)

Here's Johnny

Johnny Carson's theme, played by Carl "Doc" Severinsen's orchestra on the television series *The Tonight Show* Written by Paul Anka for which he gets $30,000 a year

Herman

The duck (voice by Clarence Nash) (radio "Burns and Allen Show")

Hermitage, The

Home of President Andrew Jackson located in Nashville, Tennessee.

Hero

The Phantom's horse (comic strip). The first Phantom's horse was named Thunder

Hero

British sailor on the packages of Player Cigarettes

Hess, Dean E.

World War II and Korean War clergyman (colonel) who became a fighter pilot played in 1957 movie *Battle Hymn* by Rock Hudson. He was a minister in the Christian Church

Heth, Joice

P. T. Barnum's fake 161-year-old Negro woman for whom it was claimed that she was a former slave of George Washington

Hey Boy

Paladin's Chinese servant at the Hotel Carlton in San Francisco, played by Kam Tong, on radio by Ben Wright) TV/radio series *Have Gun–Will Travel*

Hey Girl

Hey Boy's girlfriend and female servant to Paladin. Played on radio by Virginia Gregg and on TV by Lisa Lu

Hialeah

First race track to use the photofinish (1936)

Hickenloopers

Charles and Doris' not-too-bright family featured on TV's *Your Show of Shows* starring Sid Caesar and Imogene Coca

Hilgemeir, Jr. Edward

Contestant on TV quiz show (July 1958) *Dotto*. He revealed to the New York District Attorney that players were being given the answers in advance thus beginning one of the nation's biggest scandals, *The Quiz Show Scandal*

Higgins

Name of Baby Snook's family (radio)
Baby Snooks—Fanny Brice
Daddy (Lancelot)—Hanley Stafford
Mommy (Vera)—Arlene Harris/Lalive Brownell
Her brother Robespierre—Leone Ledoux

Higgins

Pet dog (TV series "Petticoat Junction") Winner of 1966 TV PATSY second member of the Animal Hall of Fame. Played Benji in 1975 movie *Benji*

High Tower

Detective agency for which Tenafly works

High Lama

250-year-old founder and ruler of the ageless paradise of *Shangri-La*. Father Perrault founded it in 1713 in the Valley of the Blue Moon and is himself the High Lama who hasn't aged in over 200 years. (In 1937 movie *Lost*

Horizon played by Sam Jaffe 1973 movie by Charles Boyer)

Hi Hat
Racehorse ridden by Harpo winning the final race in the Marx Brothers 1937 movie *A Day at the Races*

Hildegard Hamhocker
Only girl (single) in town of Grimy Gulch (cartoon *Tumbleweeds*) by Tom K. Ryan

Hildegard Withers
Amateur sleuth who assists N.Y.C. Police Inspector Oscar Piper, created by Stuart Palmer. In movies played by:
Edna May Oliver, Eve Arden, Helen Broderick, Zasu Pitts

Hill, Virginia
Girlfriend of gangster Ben "Bugsy" Siegel. She had a small part in the 1941 movie *Ball of Fire*. Portrayed by Dyan Cannon in the 1974 TV movie *The Virginia Hill Story*. Benjamin "Bugsy" Siegel was killed June 20, 1947 in her Beverly Hills home.

Hillbillie Bears
TV cartoon: voices Paw Bear (Henry Corden), Maw Bear (Jean Vander Pyl), Floral (Jean Vander Pyl), Shag (Don Messick)

Hilltop House
Radio serial: "Dedicated to the women of America. The story of a woman who must choose between love and the career of raising other women's children." Program later called The Story of Bess Johnson

Him and Her
President Lyndon B. Johnson's two beagles, both born June 27, 1963

Hindenburg
Zeppelin commanded by Ernst Lehmann that exploded at Lakehurst, New Jersey, May 6, 1937: 36 died out of 97 people on board, call sign DEKKA
Herb Morrison a news reporter, witnessed (as he was broadcasting) the landing. He broke down in tears as he described the crash over Chicago's WLS radio, thus becoming the first recorded news broadcast

Hindu Trinity
Brahma, The Creator
Shiva, The Destroyer and Restorer
Vishnu, The Savior

Hippocrates
    Father of medicine, Greek physician of 4th and 5th century B.C.
    Portrayed in 1957 movie *The Story of Mankind* by Charles Coburn

His Master's Voice
    Slogan of RCA Victor, symbolized by the terrier Nipper listening to an old phonograph (see Nipper)

Hispaniola
    Captain Smollett's 200-ton ship (Robert Louis Stevenson's *Treasure island*)

Hispano—Suiza
    Greta Garbo's automobile in the 1932 movie *Grand Hotel*

Hitchcock, Alfred
    Motion picture director, since 1925, he has made a cameo appearance in more than 30 of the 50 movies he has directed. Before each episode of his TV series ("Alfred Hitchcock Presents") he greeted viewers with "Good e-ve-ning." He has never won an Oscar for Best Director
    Some of his cameo appearances:
    The Lodger (1927—twice)—man wearing a cap who is leaning against an iron railing, one of the bystanders also at a desk in a newsroom.
    Murder (1929)—Man on the street
    Blackmail (1929)—Man reading a book in subway, being bothered by a small boy.
    The 39 Steps (1935)—The man passing in the street.
    Young and Innocent (1937)—Man who is a photographer outside the courthouse
    The Lady Vanishes (1938)—Man in a railway station
    Rebecca (1940)—Man passing by telephone booth (George Sanders in booth)*
    Foreign Correspondent (1940)—Man walking along the sidewalk
    Mr. and Mrs. Smith (1941)—Man who walks past Robert Montgomery on street
    Saboteur (1942)—Man standing in front of a newsstand
    Shadow of a Doubt (1943)—Man playing cards onboard a train
    Lifeboat (1944)—The man in the *Before* and *After* newspaper ad for Reducing One's Weight (The Reduco Cor-

---

*Scene did not appear in film

poration) read by Gus (William Bendix)

Spellbound (1945)—The man carrying a violin coming out of an elevator

Notorious (1946)—The man at a party drinking champagne

The Paradine Case (1947)—The man carrying a cello case

Rope (1948)—Man crossing a street

Under Capricorn (1949)—The man listening to a speech/ Man on the stairs of the Government House

Stage Fright (1950)—The man who turns around to look at Jane Wyman on a street

Strangers on a Train (1951)—The man boarding a train carrying a base fiddle

I Confess (1953)—Man walking across the top of a flight of stairs

Dial "M" for Murder (1954)—The man in the class reunion photograph

Rear Window (1954)—Man winding a clock

To Catch a Thief (1955)—The man who is seated next to Cary Grant on a bus

The Trouble with Harry (1956)—Man walking along in front of exhibition

The Man Who Knew Too Much (1956)—The man who is seen from the bank watching Arab acrobats

The Wrong Man (1957)—Man who narrates the movie's prologue

Vertigo (1958)—Man crossing a street

North by Northwest (1959)—The man who misses a bus

Psycho (1960)—The man wearing a cowboy hat outside of an office

The Birds (1963)—The man leaving a pet shop with two white poodles

Marnie (1964) The man strolling through the hotel corridor

Torn Curtain (1966)—The man sitting in a hotel lobby with baby on his lap

Topaz (1969)—Man in a wheelchair at the airport

Frenzy (1970)—The man listening to a speech

Family Plot (1976) The man whose shadow can be seen through a door window talking to another man.

Hitchcock, Patricia

Alfred Hitchcock's daughter, who appeared in three of

Alfred Hitchcock's movies:
(1950) *Stage Fright*
(1951) *Strangers on a Train*
(1960) *Psycho*

Hi There! and Dear John

Graffiti painted on the two H-Bombs within the B-52 SAC plane. Major T. J. "King" Kong (Slim Pickens) manually frees *Hi There!* and rides it down to Russian earth. 1964 movie *Dr. Strangelove*. In the novel by Peter George the bombs are Hi There! and Lolita

Hitler, Adolf

Time Magazine's "Man of the Year for 1938"
Movie Portrayals:
The Story of Mankind (1957) Bobby Watson
Hitler (1962) Richard Basehart
Is Paris Burning? (1966) Billy Frick
Hitler: The Last Ten Days (1973) Alec Guinness

Hitless Wonders, The

1906 Chicago White Sox baseball team, who won the American League pennant (and the World Series against the Chicago Cubs) with a team batting average of only .230, no regular team member batting as high as .280

Ho Ho Song

Red Buttons' (real name: Arron Chwatt) theme on TV

Hobart Arms

Home of detective Philip Marlowe on Franklin St., near Kenmore, Los Angeles

Hoboken Four, The

Singing group with which Frank Sinatra first sang. They made a famous appearance on Major Bowes' Amateur Hour September 8, 1935
The Hoboken Four: James Petrozelli, Patty Principi, Fred Tamburro, Frank Sinatra
Prior to Sinatra joining the group they were known as the Three Flashes

Hockey Hall of Fame

The Canadian museum is located at Toronto, Canada; the American is at Eveleth, Minnesota

Hodge

Dr. Samuel Johnson's cat

Hodgson, Peter

The inventor of silly putty.

Holden Caulfield
Hero of J. D. (Jerome David) Salinger's *The Catcher in the Rye*

Hole-in-the-Wall Gang
Butch Cavendish's gang: ambushed the Lone Ranger and his fellow Texas Rangers
Also name of Butch Cassidy's outlaw gang of the 1890's (A/K/A The Wild Bunch) Most noted members were:
Butch Cassidy (Robert Leroy Parker)
The Sundance Kid (Harry Longbaugh)
Kid Curry (Harvey Logan)

Holiday Inn
Movie (1942) from which came the song "White Christmas" (by Irving Berlin). The song was recorded on Decca Records 18429A by Bing Crosby with the Ken Darby Singers and John Scott Trotter's orchestra. On the "B" side was "God Rest ye Merry Gentlemen"
Holiday Inn was remade in 1954 as *White Christmas* starring Bing Crosby

Holliday, John Henry
Known as "Doc" Holliday: a dentist he took part with the Earp brothers in the O.K. Corral shootout in Tombstone, Arizona Oct. 26, 1881. He died of tuberculosis in Colorado in 1897 (See Earp, Wyatt)
Movie Portrayals:
Law and Order (1931) Harry Carey, Jr.
Frontier Marshal (1939) Cesar Romero
My Darling Clementine (1946) Victor Mature
Gunfight at the OK Corral (1957) Kirk Douglas
Cheyenne Autumn (1964) Arthur Kennedy
Hour of the Gun (1967) Jason Robards, Jr.

Holloway, Sterling
Hollywood character actor and voice of numerous cartoon characters. He was the first Hollywood actor drafted in the U.S. Army during W.W.II (James Garner was the first man drafted in the Korean War from the state of Oklahoma)

HOLLYWOODLAND
Original word of white sign overlooking Hollywood on Mt. Lee built to advertise a real estate development. Years later the last 4 letters were taken down. It was from the last letter that Peg Entwistle, a young actress, jumped to her death in 1932.

Hollywood Ten

Witnesses who invoked the 5th Amendment before the House Committee on Un-American Activities hearings (1947) to investigate alleged Communist activity. The ten were fired by their studios, fined, and sentenced to a year in jail. They and others accused of radical sympathies were not given work in Hollywood for more than a decade. They were: Alvah Bessie, Herbert Biberman, Lester Cole, Edward Dymtryk (served only two months, only one to confess to being a communist), Ring Lardner, Jr., John Howard Lawson, Albert Maltz, Samuel Ornitz, Adrian Scott, Dalton Trumbo (who won an Oscar in 1957 for *The Brave One* under the pseudonym of Robert Rich). Actors Larry Parks' and John Garfield's careers were ruined. The Hollywood Ten was actor Robert Vaughn's dissertation for his Ph.D.

Holmby Hills Rat Pack

Group of party makers who gathered at the home of Humphrey Bogart and Lauren Bacall. Their motto *"Never Rat on a Rat"*

Members: (Among others)

Judy Garland	Frank Sinatra
Nathaniel Benchley	David Niven
Sid Luft	Mike Romanoff
Jimmy Van Heussen	John Houston
Harry Kurnitz	Irving Paul Lazar

(Group existed prior to Sinatra's own *Rat Pack*)

Holey Moley!

Favorite expression of Captain Marvel (comic book series)

Homer

Wednesday Addams' (Lisa Loring) pet Black Widow spider (TV series The Addams Family)

Homer

Father of poetry, reputed blind author of the *Iliad* and *Odyssey*

Homer and Jethro

Homer Haynes and Kenneth Burns. Country's most successful comedy singing team. Both their birthdays were on July 27

Homer Brown

Henry Aldrich's friend, always reading the book *"How to Win the Love of a Good Woman"* (radio series "The Al-

313

drich Family"): played by Jackie Kelk, TV by Jackie Kelk, Robert Barry; movies, Charles Smith

Honest Abe
Son of Li'l Abner and Daisy Mae (comic strip)

Honey Fitz
John F. Kennedy's presidential yacht. The name is a nickname of his grandfather, John F. Fitzgerald, one-time mayor of Boston

Honeymoon
Daughter of Moonmaid and Junior (Dick Tracy comic strip)

Honeymooners, The
Domestic skit appearing regularly on TV series "The Jackie Gleason Show": Alice Kramden (Audrey Meadows, Sheila MacRae): Ralph Kramden (Jackie Gleason); Ed Norton (Art Carney); Trixie Norton (Joyce Randolph, Jane Kean). The sketches first appeared on "Cavalcade of Stars," with Pert Kelton playing Alice. The Kramdens were married in 1951. Ralph's closing lines *"Baby you're the greatest"*

Honeywell and Todd
Investment Counseling firm for which Vern Albright (Charles Farrel) Margie's father, worked (TV series "My Little Margie") Mr. George Honeywell was played by Clarence Kolb

Hong Kong Phooey
Secret identity of police station janitor Henry Pooch (TV cartoon series *Hong Kong Phooey*)

Honky Tonk
1941 Clark Gable movie being played at the Hickam post theater on Pearl Harbor day, December 7, 1941

Honolulu
City, state capital, on the island of Oahu, Hawaii

Honor Thompson
Woman (Geraldine Brooks) who shot Chief Robert Ironside, paralyzing him and putting him in a wheelchair (TV series "Ironside") She owned a metal art shop in Sausalito called The Forge

Hood, H.M.S.
British battle cruiser of World War II: sunk by the German battleship "Bismarck," May 24, 1941, off Iceland

Hooray for Captain Spaulding

Theme song of Groucho Marx's TV game show *"You Bet Your Life"*

Captain Spaulding being a character he played in the 1930 film "Animal Crackers"

Hooterville

Town setting of TV series *"Petticoat Junction"* and *"Green Acres."* The town newspaper is the Hooterville World Guardian

Hop Harrigan

America's Ace of the Airways (radio serial)

Originally a comic book hero. In 1946 movie serial played by William Bakewell, on radio by Chester Stratton and Albert Aley. His comic book fan clubs were called the All American Flying Club

Hop Sing

Chinese cook of the Cartwrights (TV series "Bonanza") played by Victor Sen Yung

Hopalong Cassidy

Cowboy hero William Cassidy of novels written by Clarence E. Mulford

In 66 movies, played by William Boyd. His horse: Topper
Sidekicks (movies):

"Clarence" California Carson (played by Andy Clyde)
Lucky Jenkins (Russell Hayden; real name: Pate Lucid)
Rand Brooks
Windy Halliday (George "Gabby" Hayes)
Johnny Nelson (James Ellison), Brad King
Breezy Travers (Jay Kirby)
Speedy McGinnis (Britt Wood)
Jimmy Rogers (Jimmy Rogers)

Sidekick (TV): Red Connors (Edgar Buchanan) radio: California (Andy Clyde)

Drawn in comic strip by Dan Spiegle

Prior to choosing William Boyd to play the role James Gleason and David Niven were considered

While with Hopalong Cassidy George Hayes called himself "Windy" Hayes, but due to a copyright he had to change his name to Gabby when he changed studios

Hope

Min and Chester Gump's pet cat (comic strip *"The Gumps"*)

Hope

Only thing that remained in Pandora's box after she opened it

Hope, U.S.S.

American hospital ship, established by the Health Opportunity for People Everywhere. Launched September 22, 1960 from San Francisco. Previously the U.S. Naval hospital ship was the U.S.S. Consolation. Prior to that she was called Maine Walrus

Hope Memorial Hospital

Setting for TV daytime serial *The Doctors*

Hopkins, Oceanus

Only child born aboard the "Mayflower" at sea (1620); parents were Stephen and Elizabeth Hopkins

Hopper, William

Played private investigator Paul Drake (TV series "Perry Mason"). Hopper is the son of gossip columnist Hedda Hopper

Hoppy

The Rubble's sabretooth cat. Voice of Don Messick (TV cartoon series *The Flintstones*)

Hoppy

Bunny who becomes Captain Marvel Bunny, the world's mightiest bunny when he says the magic word "SHA-ZAM" (comic book series)

Hoppy, Gene and Me

Song recorded in 1974 by Roy Rogers about Hopalong Cassidy, Gene Autry and himself

Horace and Jasper

Two British thugs who attempt to kidnap (dognap?) all of the 101 Dalmatians (1961 cartoon movie *101 Dalmatians*)

Horace Horsecollar

The horse in early Mickey Mouse cartoons, debut in a Silly Symphony cartoon

Horatio Hornblower

Went from midshipman to Lord of the Admiralty [novel series by C. S. (Cecil Scott) Forester (1899–1966)] Played in 1951 movie *Captain Horatio Hornblower* by Gregory Peck.

Hornblower Saga, The

(chronological order of events)   Date novel published
Mr. Midshipman Hornblower (June 1974-
    May 1800)   1950

Lieutenant Hornblower (May 1800-March 1803)   1952
Hornblower and the Hotspur (Apr 1803-July 1805)   1962
Hornblower and the Atropos (Oct 1805-Jan 1808)   1953
Beat to Quarters (first book written)
  (or The Happy Return) (June 1808–April 1810)   1937
Ship of the Line (May 1810-Oct 1810)   1938
Flying Colours (Nov 1810-June 1811)   1938
Commodore Hornblower (May 1812-Oct 1812)   1945
Lord Hornblower (Oct 1813-May 1814)   1946
Admiral Hornblower in the West Indies
  (May 1821-Oct 1823)   1958
Hornblower During the Crisis

Hornet, U.S.S.
Aircraft carrier from which Lt. Colonel James Doolittle led the attack of 16 B-25's on Tokyo: called "Shangri-La" by President Franklin D. Roosevelt. The ship's captain was Marc "Pete" Mitscher. In 1944 movie *Seconds Over Tokyo* Doolittle was portrayed by Spencer Tracy

Horrible Hill; Transylvania
Home of Milton the Monster (voice of Bob McFadden) TV cartoon series Milton the Monster

Horse
The name of Dudley Do-Right's mounted steed (TV cartoon)

Horseshoe Ranch
Cowboy movie star William S. Hart's Los Angeles County ranch. His brand was WS

Horse's Neck
Chief of the Kyute Indian tribe in comic strip Rick O'Shay

Horton
Dr. Seuss' egg-hatching elephant

Hotdog
Dennis Mitchell's cat (comic strip *Dennis the Menace*)

Hot Dog
Jughead Jones' pet dog (*Archie* comics)

Hot Dog
Term coined by Sports columnist Tad Dorgan in this 1905 cartoon *Hot Dog*—the food *hot dogs* had been previously referred to as dachshund sausages

Hot Springs

Town in New Mexico renamed Truth or Consequences as publicity for the radio game show "Truth or Consequences"

Hotel Carlton

Paladin's home in San Francisco (TV series "Have Gun Will Travel") His room number is 314. It was outside the Carlton Hotel in Cannes where Brigitte Bardot was supposedly "discovered"

Hotel de Cocoanut

Florida hotel run by Mr. Hammer (Groucho Marx) in the first Marx Brothers film—*The Cocoanuts* (1929)

Hotel Theresa

New York City hotel featured in 1969 movie *Topaz*

Hot Lips

Major Margaret Houlihan, head nurse of the 4077th MASH Unit in 1970 movie M*A*S*H played by Sally Kellerman; in TV series played by Loretta Swit

Hot Rod

Fonzie's (Arthur Fonzarelli) favorite magazine. He usually carries a copy with him

Houdini, Harry

Stage name of Ehrich Weiss (1874–1926), American magician, escape artist, investigator of psychic phenomena, portrayed in 1953 movie *Houdini* by Tony Curtis, in 1976 TV movie *The Great Houdinis* by Paul Michael Glaser.
He gave Joseph Keaton his nickname of Buster. He died Halloween (Oct. 31. 1926)

Hotsy Totsy Club

Jack *"Legs"* Diamond's New York nightclub on Broadway (circa 1920's)

Hotsy Totsy Orchestra

Lawrence Welk's band in the 1930's

Hourman

Secret identity of chemist Rex Tyler who discovered Miraclo, which gives him his super powers for one hour (Comic books)

Housatonic

Union vessel that on February 17, 1864 became the first vessel to be sunk by a submarine. Sunk by Confederate sub *The David*

House of Frankenstein

1944 movie featuring the following monsters:

318

The Frankenstein Monster (Glenn Strange)
The Wolf Man (Lon Chaney Jr.)
Dracula (John Carradine)
They again appeared in the 1945 sequel *House of Dracula*

House of Wax, The
Second full-length 3-D movie in color: starred Vincent Price

House that Ruth Built, The
Yankee Stadium, Bronx, New York: opened 1923, in the first game played there Babe Ruth hit a home run

Howard Johnson
Restaurant in the space station in Stanley Kubrick's 1968 movie *2001: A Space Odyssey*. The hotel in the space station was the Hilton

How Can I Leave You?
Theme song of radio series Stella Dallas

How Little We Know
Song sung by Marie (Lauren Bacall: her movie debut) in Gerard's Cafe while Cricket (Hoagy Carmichael) plays the piano (1945 movie *To Have and Have Not*) Her singing voice was dubbed by 14 year old Andy Williams

How to Win the Love of a Good Woman
The book that Henry Aldrich's friend Homer was always reading

Howdy Doody Time
TV series for children debut December 27, 1947 until 1960: Buffalo Bob Smith, Howdy Doody (the puppet star). Clarabelle the clown (Bob Keeshan), Chief Thunderthud ("Kowabonga"), Dilly Dally, Dan Jose Buster, Flub-A-Dub, John T. Fadoozle, Phineas T. Bluster (Mayor of Doodyville). Princess Summerfallwinterspring, Chief Thunderchicken, Cornelius J. Cobb, Captain Scuttlebutt, Oil Well Willy, Heidi Doody (Howdy's sister), Double Doody (Howdy's twin brother), Mr. X, Ugly Sam, Hector Hamhock Bluster. Howdy Doody was created by puppeteer Rufus C. Rose. Howdy and his twin brother Double Doody were born on December 27, 1941. Bob Smith was Howdy's voice.
In 1976 an unsuccessful attempt was made to bring the series back with Howdy having real hair.
"Say kids what time is it?
"It's Howdy Doody Time"

The theme song was sung to the tune of Ta-Ra-Ra-Boom-de-a

Howe, Julia Ward

American poet (1819-1910), wrote the words of "The Battle Hymn of the Republic" to replace those of "John Brown's Body"

Hubbell, Carl

New York Giants' southpaw pitcher; nicknamed the Meal Ticket, King Carl struck out in succession in the 1934 All Star game: Babe Ruth, Lou Gehrig, Gimmy Foxx, Al Simmons, Joe Cronin July 10, 1934, New York Polo Grounds. After Cronin, Bill Dickey got a single, then he struck out Lefty Gomez. The first 5 men he struck out, plus Hubbell are members of Baseball's Hall of Fame
Carl's catcher was Gabby Hartnett

Huckleberry Finn

Created by Mark Twain in 1884 sequel to Tom Sawyer. Played in films *"The Adventures of Huckleberry Finn"*:
Mickey Rooney (1939)
Eddie Hodges (1960)
Lewis Sargent (1920)
Jeff East (1974)

Huckleberry Hound

Hanna-Barbera's first TV cartoon character which debuted in 1959. His favorite song is Clementine. Voice of Daws Butler

Hudson

Automobile models:
Commodore, Hornet, Pacemaker, and Wasp

Hudson Brothers

Singing and comedy group Mark, Brett and Bill

Hudson High

Jack Armstrong's school (radio series)

Hudson High Fight Song

Song of Jack Armstrong's alma mater, sung on radio by the Norsemen:
"Wave the flag for Hudson High, boys,
Show them how we stand!
Ever shall our team be champion
Known throughout the land!
Rah Rah Boola Boola Boola Boola"

Hudson University

College that Dick Grayson (Robin) attends as Bruce Wayne's (Batman's) ward.

Hughes, Sarah

U.S. District judge who swore in Lyndon Johnson the day John F. Kennedy was assassinated. Only woman ever to administer the presidential oath

Hugin and Munin

Two ravens that sit on the shoulders of Odin; they represent thought and memory

Hugo

One award for the year's best science-fiction writing. Another award is the Nebula. Named in honor of Hugo Gernsback. First presented in 1953 at the 11th World S.F. Convention in Philadelphia. First awarded to Alfred Bester for *The Demolished Man*

Hugo

Nickname for Nick Carter's stiletto (Nick Carter—Killmaster series)

Hulk

Huge green-skinned giant. Secret identity of Doctor Robert Bruce Banner. His lone friend is Rick Jones (comic book). Debut May 1962. Played in 1977 TV movie *The Hulk* by Bill Bixby (Lou Ferrigno as the creature)

Hull House

Settlement house in Chicago founded by Jane Addams and Ellen Gates Starr (1889)

Human Body

Parts of the body that have only three letters; arm, ear, eye, gum, jaw, leg, lip, rib, toe

Human Bomb, The

Roy Lincoln, appeared in Police Comics (comics) He swallowed the secret formula 27QRX which changes him into The Human Bomb

Human Torch

(1940's original version)
An android (named Jim Hammond) created by Professor Horton. His sidekick is Toro. Debut Marvel Mystery Comics #1, November 1939, created by Carl Burgos
Member of All-Winners Squad. To burst into flame he states "Flame on." (modern day version)

Human psyche

Theory of Signmund Freud: Ego, Id, Superego. Freud was portrayed by Alan Arkin in the 1976 movie *The Seven Per Cent Solution*

Human senses (traditional)

Hearing, sight, smell, taste, touch

Humorisk

Marx Brothers' first film (1926 silent short subject). No copies seem to exist today.

Humphrey Agnew

Last passenger to board Flight 420, Hawaii to San Francisco (Ernest K. Gann's *The High and the Mighty*): in the 1954 movie played by Sidney Blackmer

Humphrey Higsbye

Glasses-wearing, Jimmy Nelson dummy

Humphrey Pennyworth

Joe Palooka's fat friend who drove a bicycle with house on it (comic strip)

Hundred Acre Woods

Home of Winnie-the-Pooh and Tigger Too, also WOL the owl

Hungerdunger, Hungerdunger, Hungerdunger and McCormick

Captain Geoffrey T. Spaulding's (Groucho Marx) lawyers as indicated when he dictates a letter to Horatio Jamison (Zeppo) (1930 movie "Animal Crackers")

Hunny

Winnie-the-Pooh's favorite food

Hunter, Meredith

18-year-old Black man stabbed to death by members of the Hell's Angels motorcycle gang at the Altamont Speedway rock festival, December 6, 1969. *The Rolling Stones*, the featured group, had paid the Hell's Angels $500 worth of beer to protect the stage. During the stabbing the Stones were singing one of their hit songs *"Under My Thumb."* Shown in the movie *Gimme Shelter*

Hunter's Civic Biology

Textbook from which John Scopes read "We have now learned that animal forms may be arranged so as to begin with the simple one-celled-forms and culminate with a group which includes man himself" to his class. For this he was tried and fined $100

Hurricanes

First to be named after girls (1952-54) by the weather bureau: The first list included:

Alice	Hazel	Orpha	Vicky
Barbara	Irene	Patsy	Wallis
Carol	Jill	Queen	
Dolly	Katherine	Rachel	
Edna	Lucy	Susie	
Florence	Mabel	Tina	
Gilda	Norma	Una	

A decision inspired by George Stewart in his novel *"Storm"*

Hurricanes

Ralph Kramden's (Jackie Gleason) and Ed Norton's (Art Carney) bowling team (TV series *The Honeymooners*)

Huw

Adult narrator of the 1941 movie *How Green was my Valley* (Irving Pichel). Roddy McDowall plays Huw as a child

Huxley

College of which Professor Quincey Adams Wagstaff (Groucho Marx) is president. Their arch rival is Darwin. (1932 movie *"Horse Feathers"*). They won their last football game in 1888

Hymie

CONTROL's Robot (TV series "Get Smart"): played by Dick Gautier

He was Agent 86's best man at his wedding to Agent 99

Hynkel

Dictator of Tomania (patterned after Hitler) played by Charlie Chaplin. Napaloni, dictator of Bacteria (patterned after Mussolini) played by Jack Oakie.

(1940 movie *"The Great Dictator"*)

Hynkel's insignia ✗✗

Napaloni's insignia ♦♦

I

IBAC
Villain (Captain Marvel comic strip adventures): gets his powers from (initials):
Ivan the Terrible
Borgia the Poisoner
Attila the Hun
Caligula, the Emperor
His real name is Stinky Printwhistle

ICE
Intelligence Coordination and Exploitation. In Matt Helm novels Organization for Intelligence and Counter-Espionage headed by MacDonald "Mac"

INS
Independent News Service for which Carl Kolchak (Darren McGavin) is a reporter. His editor is Tony Vincenzo (Simon Oakland) (TV series *"The Night Stalker"*)
INS was also a real news service (International News Service). Bought out by United Press in 1958; afterwards UP became UPI

I Am Woman
Helen Reddy's theme song (TV show)

I Believe in Music
Country singer Mac Davis' theme song (TV series *"The Mac Davis Show"*)

I Can't Get Started
Theme song of Bunny Berigan's orchestra

I, Claudius
1937 movie starring Charles Laughton, Merle Oberon,

Flora Robson and Emlyn Williams which was never completed

I got a warrant right here, Sheriff
Sole line of George Plimpton in movie *Rio Lobo*, spoken to John Wayne. Line originally read, "This here's your warrant, mister," but it was changed at the last minute by director Howard Hawks

I Love a Mystery
Radio adventure (debut January 16, 1934) of Jack Packard; Doc Long, a Texan; Reggie York, an Englishman, who ran the A-1 Detective Agency, "just off Hollywood Boulevard and one flight up": "No job too tough, no mystery too baffling"
Radio cast:
Jack: Michael Raffeto, Russell Thurson
Doc: Barton Yarborough, Jim Boles
Reggie: Walter Patterson, Tony Randall

Ibis the Invincible
Prince Amente with magic powers, born in Egypt 4000 years ago . . . Awoke in 1940
Debut: Whiz Comics #2 Feb 1940

Ibistick
Ibis the Invincible's magic wand (comic book series "Ibis")

Ice Cream Blonde
Nickname of actress Thelma Todd

Ichabod Mudd (Ikky)
Captain Midnight's mechanic (radio series)
Radio:
Hugh Studebaker, Sherman Marks, Art Hern; TV: Sid Melton
In comics also known as Sgt. Twilight

Ida
Queen of the Ants (*B.C.*) comic strip by Johnny Hart

Idaho
Only state in the U.S. over which no foreign flag has ever flown

Ideal Novelty and Toy Company
Manufacturer which produced the first Shirley Temple dolls in 1934

Ides of March
March 15th, day Julius Caesar was assassinated (44 B.C.)

"Beware the Ides of March" was said to Caesar by his wife Calpurnia 16 nights before his death

If I Didn't Care
Ink Spots' theme song

If the job's too tough, you've got a job for me
Detective George Valentine's (Bob Bailey) advertisement motto (Radio's *Let George Do It*)

Igloo
Admiral Byrd's fox terrier that accompanied his master to both the Arctic and Antarctic

Ignatz
Pet Monkey aboard the ship "Venture" (movie *King Kong*)

Ignatz Mouse
Krazy Kat's friend who is always throwing bricks. Ignatz's sons are Moshie, Milton and Irving. Krazy Kat debuted in 1916 cartoon Krazy Kat and the Ignatz. The two debuted in comic strip The Family Upstairs. On TV Krazy Kat's voice is that of Penny Phillips
Ignatz's voice on TV cartoons by Paul Frees
When Krazy Kat gets hit by a brick he exclaims "Li'l 'Ainjil"

Igor
Grandpa's (Al Lewis) pet bat (TV series "The Munsters")

Igor (Ygor)
Dr. Frankenstein's assistant (movie series). In the 1931 movie *Frankenstein* Dwight Frye plays a cripple named Fritz; in the 1939 *Son of Frankenstein*, Bela Lugosi plays Ygor, the mad shepherd twisted by an abortive hanging, who takes care of the unconscious Monster. In movie *Ghost of Frankenstein* Ygor's brain was transplanted into the monster. Played by Marty Feldman in 1974 movie *Young Frankenstein*

Igor
Professor Henry Jarrod's (Vincent Price) henchman played by Charles Bronson in the 1953 movie *House of Wax*

"I guess that'll hold the little bastards"
Line supposedly said by Uncle Don, (Don Carney) M.C. of his own children's radio show at the end of a program in which he thought the mike was off

I Kid You Not!
Favorite expression of late night TV host Jack Paar, title

of his autobiography. Line was used by Captain Queeg (Humphrey Bogart) in the movie *The Caine Mutiny*

I Know A Man
Witty little conundrum said by Cary Grant to Shirley Temple in 1947 movie *"The Bachelor and the Bobby-soxer"*

I Know A Man,
What man?
Man with a power,
What power?
The Power of Voodoo!
Who do?
You do!
Do what?
Know a man!
What man?
Man with a power!
What power?
ETC.

Ile de France
Passenger ship that rescued survivors of the Andrea Doria. Actor Gardner McKay one of its passengers shot many rescue pictures

I'll Be Seeing You
Liberace's theme song

Illustrated Man, The
1969 movie from novel by Ray Bradbury. Carl (Rod Steiger) is the Illustrated Man
The 3 tales told are:
1. *The Long Rains*
2. *The Last Night of the World*
3. *The Veldt*

Illustrated Press
Newspaper edited by Steve Wilson (TV series "Big Town")

Illya Nickovetch Kuryakin
Agent for U.N.C.L.E. (played by David McCallum) sidekick of agent Napoleon Solo (Robert Vaughn) (TV series *The Man From U.N.C.L.E.*)

Illyria
Fictitious European country that is the setting of the 1934 Lubitsch musical movie *"The Merry Widow"*

I Love Lucy
One of television's most successful comedy shows Debut October 15, 1951 (CBS) (1951-1956) originally a radio program. Top television series 1952-55 and 1956-57. Starred Lucille Ball as Lucy Ricardo and Desi Arnaz as Ricky Ricardo. Married 1940, Lucy and Desi formed the Desilu Television Company* as husband and wife which went on to produce many top television series. Series also starred:
Vivian Vance as Ethel Mertz** and William Frawley as Fred Mertz**. The Ricardo's son, Little Ricky, supposedly joined the series at his birth in 1953 but was actually played by Richard Keith. Lucy and Desi were divorced in 1960.

Il Trovatore
New York Opera Company presentation which the Marx Brothers add chaos to in the 1935 movie *A Night at the Opera*

I Made a Fool of Myself Over John Foster Dulles
Song sung by Carol Burnett on television in the mid 1950's.

I'm A Fugitive from a Georgia Chain Gang
Story written by Robert Burn after he escaped from an actual Georgia chain gang, appeared in True Detective Magazine made into a movie in 1932, *I Am a Fugitive From a Chain Gang* starring Paul Muni.

I'm Getting Sentimental Over You
Theme song of Tommy Dorsey's orchestra

IMF Agents
Impossible Mission Force: James Phelps and his Mission Impossible crew (TV series "Mission Impossible") starring Steven Hill (as Dan Briggs) and later Peter Graves (as James Phelps)

Imhook (Abraham Lincoln Imhook)
Kodiak's (Clint Walker) old Eskimo sidekick (Abner Biberman) (TV series *Kodiak*)

Im-ho-tep
3000 year old mummy in the 1932 movie starring Boris Karloff, *The Mummy*

---

*Built upon the old RKO studio
**The first choices for Ethel and Fred were Bea Benaderet and Gale Gordon

Imperial Potentate

Highest position held in the Ancient Arabic Order of Nobles of the Mystic Shrine (Shriners)

I'm So Glad We Had This Time Together

Carol Burnett's closing theme on her TV series

Imperial Wizard

Title of leader of the Ku Klux Klan (leader of the original KKK—1865-1877—was the Grand Cyclops) First organized in Pulaski, Tenn. in 1865

In A Tradition of Quality

Slogan of Selznick Pictures

In Canis Corpore Transmuto

Magic Borgia spell that transforms Wilby Daniels (Tommy Kirk) into the old English Sheep Dog (1959 movie *The Shaggy Dog*)

In God We Trust

Motto of the United States, adopted July 30, 1856; first appeared on U.S. coins, 1864

In Hoc Vinces Signo

In This Sign I Conquer. Motto on pack of Pall Mall Cigarettes

In This Style 10/6

Sign on the Mad Hatter's hat (as originally illustrated by Sir John Tenniel in Lewis Carroll's *Alice's Adventures in Wonderland*)

Incitatus

Caligula's horse. The Roman emperor is said to have wanted to bestow the rank of Consul upon this, his favorite steed

Incredible Journey, The

Pet animals in the novel (1961) by Sheila Burnford; Luath, bull terrier; Tao, Siamese cat; Bodger, retriever (played by Rink, Syn Cat and Muffey in 1963 movie)

Incredible Shrinking Man, The

Scott Carey, who keeps growing smaller each day (1957 movie by Richard Matheson): played by Grant Williams

Independence, The

Harry S. Truman's DC-6 Presidential Airplane

Indian Love Call

Title of movie in TV release and of song in it (by Rudolf Friml. Otto Harbach, and Oscar Hammerstein II) sung by Jeanette MacDonald and Nelson Eddy (1936 movie

Rose Marie) Song Jeanette MacDonald sang at Jean Harlow's funeral

Indianapolis 500

"Gentlemen, start your engines": 200-lap Decoration Day race since 1911 (won then by Ray Harroun in a Marmon Wasp at 74.59 mph. Winners traditionally drink milk in the winner's circle. Eddie Rickenbacker once owned the speedway

Indianapolis, U.S.S.

U.S. Navy cruiser that transported the two A bombs from the U.S. to Saipan to be dropped on Japan. The ship was sunk on its return trip by the Japanese submarine I-58 July 30, 1945.

India Queen

Ship which Walter Mitty dreams that he is Captain of (James Thurber's movie version *The Secret Life of Walter Mitty*)

Indomitable, H.M.S.

Ship upon which Billy Budd was the foretopman (novel by Herman Melville). In 1962 movie *Billy Budd*, Budd is played by Terence Stamp

Information Please

Radio quiz program (1938-1952)

M.C.: Clifton Fadiman

Original panelists:

Clifton Fadiman (replaced by Oscar Levant when he became M.C.)

John Kieran

Franklin Pierce Adams (F.P.A.)

Ingrid

Blind insurance investigator Mike Longstreet's (James Franciscus) deceased wife. TV series *Longstreet*

Ink Spots

Original members: Ivory (Deek) Watson (tenor), Orville (Hoppy) Jones (bass), Charlie Fuqua (baritone), Slim Green (tenor), Billy Kenny joined the group in 1934
If I Didn't Care was their theme song

Inka Dinka Doo

Jimmy Durante's theme song, first appearing in 1933 movie *Joe Palooka*

Inky and Dinky

Nephews of Felix the Cat (comic books)

Icky and Tut

Sidekicks of Jet Jackson (TV series "Jet Jackson, Flying Commando")

Inn of the Eight Happinesses

Mission-hotel founded by Gladys Aylward (biographical novel movie *The Inn of the Sixth Happiness*). The title of the story is from an ancient Chinese wish for the five happinesses: tranquility, virtue, position, wealth, and a peaceful death in old age (the sixth happiness must be found by everyone within himself). Gladys Alyward was portrayed in 1958 movie by Ingrid Bergman

Inoki, Antonio

Japanese wrestler who Muhammad Ali "fought" in Tokyo June 26, 1976. After 15 rounds the match was declared a draw. Ali made $6,000,000

Inspector Andrew Elliot

Scotland Yard policeman who is ex-school mate and friend of detective Dr. Gideon Fell

Inspector Andrews

Scotland Yard policeman friend of detective Bulldog Drummond

Inspector Blake

Played by Hayden Stevenson in 1927 *"Blake of Scotland Yard"* and 1929 *"Ace of Scotland Yard"* with Crauford Kent. 1937 movie serial (15 episodes) played by Herbert Rawlison

Inspector Bucket

First important British detective in fiction. Appeared as Scotland Yard policeman in Charles Dickens' *Bleak House* (1852)

Inspector Jacques Clouseau

French detective of great ineptness (movies *The Pink Panther* 1964, and *A Shot in the Dark*, 1964): played by Peter Sellers. In *Inspector Clouseau* (1968) Alan Arkin played the role. In 1974, *The Return of the Pink Panther* by Peter Sellers and again by Sellers in 1976, *The Pink Panther Strikes Again*

Inspector (L. T.) Cramer

Head of New York City's homicide bureau and acquaintance of sleuth Nero Wolfe, his assistant is Sgt. Purley Stebbins

Inspector Crane

Police detective acquaintance of Michael Lanyard (The

331

Lone Wolf) in Lone Wolf movies. Played by:
Thurston Hall, William Davidson, William Frawley

Inspector Faraday
Policeman on "Boston Blackie" series (radio/TV) Movies:
Richard Lane, TV: Frank Orth

Inspector Fenwick
Dudley Do-right's boss Ray K. Fenwick in the Canadian
Mounted Police (comics). Voice of Paul Frees

Inspector Fernack
New York City's Chief Police Inspector friend of The
Saint. Played in movies by Jonathan Hale

Inspector Fix
Scotland Yard detective who hounds Phileas Fogg
around the world under the impression that he is a bank
robber (Jules Verne's *Around the World in 80 Days*): in
the 1956 movie played by Robert Newton. Played by
Orson Welles (as Dick Fix) in 1946 musical play

Inspector Fox
Detective created by Ngaio Marsh

Inspector Ganimard
Chief-Inspector of French police immediate superior of
master criminal turned detective, Arsene Lupin (created
by Maurice Leblanc)

Inspector Gerard (Lieutenant)
Pursuer of Dr. Richard Kimble (TV series "The Fugitive"): played by Barry Morse. Gerard's wife is Marie
(Barbara Rush)

Inspector (George) Gideon
Chief Inspector of Scotland Yard, played in 1959 movie
Gideon of Scotland Yard by Jack Hawkins

Inspector Greenwood
Scotland Yard Inspector of Police, friend of amateur
detective, Father Brown (G. K. Chesterton's *"Father
Brown"*)

Inspector (William) Henderson
Police detective in Metropolis (TV series "Superman" by
Robert Shayne)

Inspector Japp
Scotland Yard C.I.D. man and friend of Hercule Poirot.
Played in 1966 movie *The Alphabet Murders* by Maurice
Denham

Inspector Javert
Policeman who tracks down Jean Valjean (Victor Hugo's

Les Miserables). In 1935 movie by Charles Laughton, in 1952 movie by Robert Newton

Inspector Lestrade
Scotland Yard detective who seeks the aid of Sherlock Holmes. Radio: Gale Gordon and others. TV: Archie Duncan and others. Movies: Dennis Hoey and others

Inspector (Jules) Maigret
Chief of detectives in novels by Georges Simenon. Played by Jean Gabin in 1958 movie *Inspector Maigret,* also by Charles Laughton in 1950 movie *The Man on the Eiffel Tower*

Inspector Mark Saber
TV series *"Mark Saber Mystery Theater"* starring Tom Conway. His partner is Sergeant Maloney, (James Burke). In 1957, series became *Uncovered* starring Donald Gray as Saber and his sidekick Barney O'Keefe by Michael Balfour

Inspector Murchison
Sir Charles Murchison, Chief Inspector of Scotland Yard, friend of Oriental Secret Agent, Mr. Moto. The motto on his desk is "Softly Softly Catchee Monkey" played in movies by Lester Matthews

Inspector Napoleon Bonaparte
Australian, half-aborigine detective whose nickname is Bony. Created by Arthur Upfield. First novel *The Barrakee Mystery** (1928)

Inspector (Colonel) Neilson
Scotland Yard friend of Bulldog Drummond

Inspector Queen
Richard Queen, a New York City police officer, father of Ellery Queen (novels of Frederic Dannay and Manfred B. Lee writing as Ellery Queen)
Radio: Santos Ortega, Bill Smith
Movies: Charley Grapewin, Guy Usher, Wade Boteler
TV: Harry Morgan, David Wayne

Inspector Steve Keller
Lieutenant Mike Stone's (Karl Malden) sidekick played by Michael Douglas, son of actor Kirk Douglas (TV series *The Streets of San Francisco*)

Inspector Sugg
Scotland Yard friend of detective Lord Peter Wimsey

---

*American title *The Lure of the Bush*

Inspector (Claud Eustace) Teal

Chief Inspector of Scotland Yard. He competes with detective Simon Templar (The Saint) in solving outstanding crimes. On radio—John Brown, movies—Gordon McLeod and Charles Victor (Leslie Charteris *"The Saint"*) TV: Winsley Pithey, Norman Pitt, Ivor Dean

International Institute of Four-Square Evangelism

Religious organization founded by Aimee Semple McPherson in Los Angeles in the early 1920's. She built the Angelus Temple which included a $75,000 radio studio. Faye Dunaway portrayed Aimee McPherson in the 1976 TV movie *The Disappearance of Aimee*

Intertect Unlimited

Computer agency for which Joe Mannix worked before he opened his own private detective agency (TV series "Mannix"). His boss was Lou Wickersham (played by Joseph Campanella)

In the Hall of the Mountain King

Tune that Hans Beckert (Peter Lorre) whistles in the 1931 movie *"M"* prior to committing his murders

Intolerance

Epic motion picture (1916) by David Wark Griffith that told four stories simultaneously: Jesus played by Howard Gaye

The Modern Story (capital and labor)

The Babylonian Story (the fall of Babylon)

The French Story (the massacre of the Huguenots)

The Judean Story (the story of Christ)

Between episodes Lillian Gish appeared rocking a cradle in reference to Walt Whitman's "Out of the cradle endlessly rocking"

Intrepid

Apollo 12 lunar module: command module "Yankee Clipper"

Intrepid

Federation Starship manned by a crew of 400 Vulcans. The ship was destroyed by a giant Amoeba (TV series "Star Trek") The Intrepid was actually destroyed in two different Star Trek episodes, an oversight

Inverted Jenny

(C3A Curtis Jenny biplane) First U.S. Airmail 24¢ stamp. A sheet of 100 stamps were produced with the airplane flying upsidedown (38262 registration number is on the aircraft). A single stamp has sold for $36,000

Invisible Man

Jack Griffin name of *The Invisible Man* in H. G. Wells' novel: in 1933 movie played by Claude Rains. In later *"Invisible Man"* movies, played by Vincent Price, Jon Hall, and Arthur Franz, the name became Geoffrey Radcliffe, Frank Raymond, Robert Griffin, and Tommy Nelson. *"The Invisible Man's Revenge"* (1944), Robert Griffin (Jon Hall)

TV series Daniel Westin (David McCallum) The Invisible Man. Played by Arthur Franz in 1951 movie *Abbott and Costello Meet the Invisible Man*. Voice of Vincent Price at end of 1948 movie *Abbott and Costello Meet Frankenstein*

Invoco legem magiciarum

Mandrake the Magician's magic chant *"I invoke the law of magic"*

Iowa State Fair

Annual festival festured in the 3 times made movie *State Fair* 1933, 1945, 1962. Iowa (River City) is also the setting for the movie *The Music Man*

I.Q. (Intelligence Quotient)

(Lewis M.) Terman's classification:

Above-140 Genius	80-90—Dull
120-140—Very Superior	70-80—Borderline
110-120—Superior	50-70—Moron
90-110—Average	25-50—Imbecile
Below 25—Idiot	

Irene

The steamship that brought the Statue of Liberty from Roven, France to New York June 1885. The statue was in 214 crates

Irene Adler

Detective Sherlock Holmes' lover. An opera singer (contralto) born in New Jersey. (Speculation has it that out of the relationship came a baby, possibly twins, additional speculation has it that one of the babies was none other than the sleuth Nero Wolfe). She married Godfrey Norton in St. Monica's Church on Edgware Road. She lived in Briony Lodge, St. John's Wood, London. Died in 1903.

Iron Butterfly, The
Nickname of actress Jeanette MacDonald; also name of popular rock group

Iron Curtain
Invisible barrier between the free world and the communist countries. Coined by Winston Churchill

Iron Mike
Automatic baseball pitching machine

Iron Mike
Epithet applied to Jack Dempsey's right hand

Ironman One
Apollo space capsule on which retrofire fails (1969 movie *Marooned*)

Ironside
Chief Robert T. Ironside of the San Francisco police department confined to a wheelchair since being paralyzed after being shot by Honor Thompson: using a .30 Springfield rifle. He was shot on Commissioner Randall's Glen Ellen chicken farm. Confined to St. Mary's Hospital in Sonoma; he works in the field from a specially fitted van (TV series "Ironside"): played by Raymond Burr

Irving G. Thalberg Memorial Award
Presentation at the Academy Awards to a person who is noted for their consistent high quality within the film industry. The receiver of the award is chosen by the Academy's Board of Governors

Irwin
Broom Hilda's shaggy Troll friend. Olivia the Troll is Irwin's girlfriend (cartoon series *"Broom Hilda"* by Russell Myers)

Ishi
Lone survivor of a Yana tribe, the Yahi, he stumbled into Oroville, California, in 1911, his first contact with white people

Ish Kabibble
Novelty singer with Kay Kyser's Kollege of Musical Knowledge. His real name being Mervyn A. Bogue

Ishmael
Narrator in Herman Melville's *Moby Dick,* lone survivor of the Pequod. Played by Richard Basehart in 1956 movie *Moby Dick*

336

Isis

Sacred secret identity of teacher Andrea Thomas (JoAnna Cameron) (Saturday morning TV series)

I Talk To The Trees

One of two songs sung by Clint Eastwood in 1969 movie *"Paint Your Wagon"* The other was "I Shall See Eliza"

It Girl, The

Clara Bow (1905-1965), movie actress who appeared in the 1927 movie *It*

Itasca, U.S.S.

Coast Guard cutter that last had communications with Amelia Earhart, July 3, 1937

It's All in the Game

Hit song, words by Carl Sigman, recorded (1951, 1958) by Tommy Edwards (1963) by Cliff Edwards, based on a melody written (1912) by Charles G. Dawes, later U.S. Vice President under Coolidge. As vice president, Dawes won the 1925 Nobel Peace Prize

It's a Mad, Mad, Mad, Mad World

Comedy spectacular movie (1963) produced and directed by Stanley Kramer. The goal was to find $350,000 in buried money left by Smiler Grogan (Jimmy Durante)

Cast	Role
Spencer Tracy	Captain C. G. Culpeper
Milton Berle	J. Russell Finch
Sid Caesar	Melville Crump
Buddy Hackett	Benjy Benjamin
Ethel Merman	Mrs. Marcus
Dorothy Provine	Emmeline Finch
Edie Adams	Monica Crump
Mickey Rooney	Ding Bell
Phil Silvers	Otto Meyer
Dick Shawn	Sylvester Marcus
Jonathan Winters	Lennie Pike
Terry-Thomas	Lt. Col. J. Algernon Hawthorne
Jim Backus	Tyler Fitzgerald

Cameo appearances were made by: Eddie "Rochester" Anderson, Peter Falk, Leo Gorcey, William Demarest, Alan Carney, Andy Devine, Madlyn Rhue, Stan Freberg, Norman Fell, Nicholas Georgiade, Stanley Clements, Allen Jenkins, Tom Kennedy, Roy Engle, Paul Birch, Paul Ford, Charles McGraw, Ben Blue, Carl Reiner, Charles

337

Lane, Jesse White, Bobo Lewis, Harry Lauter, Eddie Ryder, Don C. Harvey, Zasu Pitts, Sterling Holloway, Moe Howard, Larry Fine, Joe DeRita (of The Three Stooges), Barrie Chase, Edward Everett Horton, Buster Keaton, Don Knotts, Joe E. Brown, Marvin Kaplan, Arnold Stang, Lloyd Corrigan, Selma Diamond (voice only), Louise Glenn (voice only), Ben Lessy, Mike Mazurki, Nick Stewart, Sammee Tong, Doodles Weaver, Jerry Lewis, Jack Benny, Dale Van Sickel, Roy Roberts, Barbara Pepper, Cliff Norton, Chick Chandler

I Spy

TV series starring Robert Culp, as Kelly Robinson, a Californian Phi Beta Kappa from Temple University, and Bill Cosby, as Alexander Scott of Pennsylvania. They are spies for a U.S. agency headed by Mr. Donald Mars

It's Not Unusual

Tom Jones (Thomas Woodward) theme song, recorded in 1967

Ivan

Cat in 1946 Disney movie cartoon version of Prokofiev's "Peter and the Wolf"

Ivan Ivanovitch

Ethnic nickname applied to the average Russian

Ivan Shark

Arch-enemy of Captain Midnight played on radio, by Boris Aplon. In 1942 movie serial: by James Craven. His henchman is Gardo, his daughter, Fury

I've Got a Right to Sing the Blues

Theme song of Jack Teagarden's orchestra

Ivy College

Institute of higher learning of which William Todhunter Hall was president. Played on radio and TV by Ronald Colman. Benita Hume, Colman's actual wife, played his wife Vicky. (Series *Halls of Ivy*)

Ivy League

Group of old, established Eastern colleges: so-called in athletic competition

College	*Location*	*Date Founded*	*Football Nickname*
Brown	Providence, R.I.	1764	Bruins
Columbia	New York, N.Y.	1754	Lions
Cornell	Ithaca, N.Y.	1865	Big Red
Dartmouth	Hanover, N.H.	1769	Big Green

Harvard	Cambridge, Mass.	1636	Crimson
Pennsylvania	Philadelphia, Pa.	1740	Red and Blue
Princeton*	Princeton, N.J.	1746	Tigers
Yale**	New Haven, Conn.	1701	Bulldogs

Ivy Town

Town where *The Atom* (Al Pratt) lives (comic books)

I Wanna Be Your Man

Only song written and recorded by the *Beatles* which was also performed by the *Rolling Stones*. Composed for the Stones by Lennon-McCartney

I Want To Be Alone

Line said by Greta Garbo to John Barrymore in *Grand Hotel*. 1932 movie

I Want You

World War I Army recruiting poster showing Uncle Sam pointing his finger at the viewer—designed by James Montgomery Flagg who drew himself as Uncle Sam. It was the most popular U.S. poster ever made with over 5 million copies printed

Iwo Jima

American flag was raised (Feb. 23, 1945) during World War II on Mount Suribachi by U.S. Marines: John H. Bradley, Michael Strank, Harlon H. Block, Franklin R. Sousley, Rene A. Gagnon, Ira H. Hayes***
The Pulitzer Prize winning photo was taken by Joe Rosenthal. In the 1949 John Wayne movie *Sands of Iwo Jima*, Gagnon, Hayes and Bradley portray themselves. When John Wayne placed his hand prints at Grauman's Chinese Theatre the sand used in the cement was brought from Iwo Jima. A 78-foot bronze reproduction of the scene by Felix de Weldon, overlooking Washington D.C., stands outside Arlington National Cemetery, Virginia.

---

*Known as Old Nassau
**Known as Old Eli
***A movie, *The Outsider* was made (1961) about Ira Hayes, starring Tony Curtis. A song was recorded by Johnny Cash, "Ballad of Ira Hayes" from a poem by Peter LaForge.

Lee Marvin portrayed Hayes on TV's Sunday Showcase (March 27 1960) titled *The American*

J

J

Joan Garrity, author of the best-seller *The Sensuous Woman*

J2G063

Amos Burke's (Gene Barry) license number of his Rolls Royce. (TV series "Amos Burke"/"Burke's Law")

J & B Rare Scotch

Justerini and Brooks

J. C. Penney

James Cash Penney, American businessman, retailer

J. J.

Nickname of Jennifer Jo Drinkwater (Julie Sommers) in TV series *"The Governor and J.J."*

J. J.

Outspoken, hip James Evans Jr. (Jimmie Walker) (TV series *"Good Times"*). Favorite expression *Dy-no-mite!*

JO 58269

Kansas automobile license plate: (The plate came off of a wrecked De Soto.) on the stolen 1949 Chevrolet driven by Richard Hickock and Perry Smith the night that the pair killed the Clutter family of Holcomb, Kansas November 15, 1959. In the 1967 movie *In Cold Blood* the killers were portrayed by Scott Wilson and Robert Blake respectively

J. R.

Parking lot attendant (Robert Logan) who replaced Kookie (Edd Byrnes) on TV series *"77 Sunset Strip"*

J. W.

Little fat sheriff who sells Dodge automobiles (TV com-

mercials): played by Joe Higgins (He's a general in Air
Force Reserves)
"You're in a heap of trouble, boy!" He and Carrol
O'Connor both played blacksmiths on the TV series *The
Rifleman*

J. Fred Muggs
Chimpanzee on Dave Garroway's "Today Show" (TV)

J. Worthington Foulfellow
Sly fox (Disney feature cartoon movie *Pinocchio*) who
tries to lead Pinocchio astray. His partner is Gideon the
cat. The voice of Foulfellow is Walter Catlett's

Jabbar, Kareem Abdul-
Name adopted by 7'2" basketball player Lew Alcindor
as a practicing Muslim

Jabez Stone
New England farmer who sells his soul to the Devil and is
defended by Daniel Webster (Stephen Vincent Benet's
"The Devil and Daniel Webster"): played (in *All That
Money Can Buy*) by James Craig

Jack
Ingall's family dog (TV series *Little House on the Prairie*)

Jack
The young lad (Jackie Coogan) who is adopted by Charlie
Chaplin in 1921 movie *"The Kid"*

Jack
Sailor boy on Cracker Jacks box

Jack and the Beanstalk
1952 Abbott and Costello movie which began in black
and white and ended in color. *The Wizard of Oz* made in
1939, also began in black and white, changed to color,
but ended in black and white

Jack Armstrong
The All-American Boy, he attended Hudson High. Spon-
sored on radio by Wheaties—the Breakfast of Champions
—with Uncle Jim, Billy and Betty Fairfield
Played on radio: St. John Terrell, Jim Ameche, Stanley
Harris, Charles Flynn, Michael Rye
Movie serial (1947) by John Hart

Jack Armstrong's Training Rules
1. Get plenty of sleep, fresh air and exercise
2. Make a friend of soap and water because dirt breeds
germs and germs can make people sickly and weak
3. For sound nourishment and keen flavor, eat this

341

"Breakfast of Champions"—a big bowlful of Wheaties, with plenty of milk or cream and some kind of fruit
(The rules were on the boxes of Wheaties and given orally by the radio announcer)

Jack Benny High
School in Waukegan, Illinois, Jack Benny's home town. The school nickname is the 39er's

Jack Griffin
Name of "The Invisible Man" in H. G. Wells' novel in 1933 movie played by Claude Rains. In later "Invisible Man" movies, played by Vincent Price, Jon Hall, and Arthur Franz, the name became Geoffrey Radcliffe. Frank Raymond, Robert Griffin, and Tommy Nelson (see Invisible Man)

Jackie Paper
Puff, the Magic Dragon's human friend (song by Peter, Paul, and Mary)

Jack Kennedy
Was the victim of a murder in the very first issue of Action Comics No. 1, June, 1938. He was killed by Bea Carroll a singer at the Hilow Night Club, who was brought to justice by Superman

Jacko
The reversible dog, one of Paul Bunyan's three dogs

Jackson
Name comedian Phil Harris always called Jack Benny on radio

Jackson High
Boone City high school where Homer Parrish (Harold Russell) was quarterback before joining the Navy (1946 movie *The Best Years of Our Lives*)

Jackson Island
Where Huckleberry Finn meets up with Miss Watson's runaway slave Jim, both then traveling on the Mississippi River (Mark Twain's *The Adventures of Huckleberry Finn*)

Jackson, Shoeless Joe
See Shoeless Joe Jackson

Jacksons, The
Singing group: Maron, Tito, Jackie, Jermaine, Michael, Randy. The group was "discovered" by Diana Ross

342

Jack the Ripper
1888 London murderer of five prostitutes. He was never apprehended.
Victims:
Mary Anne "Polly" Nichols (August 31, 1888)
"Dark" Annie Chapman (September 8, 1888)
Elizabeth "Long Liz" Stride (September 30, 1888)
Catherine Eddowes (September 30, 1888)
"Black Mary" Jane Kelly (November 9, 1888)

Jack Tar
Nickname for a common sailor in the days of sailing ships, especially a British sailor: the name is either from "tarpaulin" or from the tar used on ropes that rubbed off on hands and clothing

Jacob
The Brown's family dog in 1944 movie *"National Velvet"*

Jacob Marley
Ebenezer Scrooge's dead partner (Charles Dickens' *A Christmas Carol*): his ghost haunts Scrooge with clanking chains and other weird sounds. He died Christmas eve

Jaime Summer
Bionic Catalog 87312. First bionic woman, Steve Austin's ex-girlfriend and fiancee, she was injured while sky diving (she is played by Lindsay Wagner). She dies after her body rejects her bionic transplants but is brought back to life for subsequent series *The Bionic Woman*. (TV series *The Six Million Dollar Man* and *The Bionic Woman*)

Jake Axminster
Private detective of the 1930's played by Wayne Rogers in the TV series *"City of Angels"*

James
Son of Will Sonnett (Walter Brennan) whom he searched for in each episode. Played by Jason Evers. TV series *"Guns of Will Sonnett"*

James Bond
Hero (secret agent) of novels written by Ian Fleming (1908-1964). Bond (C.M.G., R.N.V.R.) is a British secret agent in an organization headed by M. A gourmet, single and a womanizer, he married Teresa Draco, who is killed soon after, though retaining a solid affection for Miss Moneypenny, M's secretary—The name James Bond was borrowed from an ornithology book "Birds of the

343

West Indies" by James Bond, one of Fleming's favorite books

Casino Royale (1954)

Diamonds Are Forever (1956) ·

Doctor No (1958)

For Your Eyes Only (1959)

From Russia, with Love (1957) One of JFK's books on his list of ten favorites

Goldfinger (1959)

Live and Let Die (1955)

The Man with the Golden Gun (1965)

Moonraker (1955) The screen rights are owned by actor John Payne

Octopussy (1966)

On Her Majesty's Secret Service (1963)

The Spy Who Loved Me (1962)

Thunderball (1961)

You Only Live Twice (1964)

Colonel Sun (1968) by Robert Markham (Kingsley Amis)

Movies (name of actor playing Bond in parentheses):

Movie	Theme song performer
Dr. No, 1963 (Sean Connery)	John Barry
From Russia with Love, 1964 (Sean Connery)	Matt Monroe
Goldfinger, 1965 (Sean Connery)	Shirley Bassey
Thunderball, 1965 (Sean Connery)	Tom Jones
You Only Live Twice, 1967 (Sean Connery)	Nancy Sinatra
Casino Royale, 1967 (David Niven)	Herb Alpert and the Tijuana Brass
On Her Majesty's Secret Service, 1970 (George Lazenby)	John Barry
Diamonds Are Forever, 1971 (Sean Connery)	Shirley Bassey
Live and Let Die, 1973 (Roger Moore)	Paul and Linda McCartney
The Man with the Golden Gun, 1974 (Roger Moore)	Lulu
The Spy Who Loved Me, 1977 (Roger Moore)	Carly Simon

Ian Fleming pictured Hoagy Carmichael as his image of Bond. James Bond was first played by Barry Nelson on an episode of the TV series *Climax* titled *Casino Royale,* October 21, 1954

Jamestown, Va.

Ships, under Christopher Newport, brought settlers to Jamestown (1607): "Sarah Constant," "Discovery," "Godspeed"

Jamison

The Lone Wolf's butler. Played in movies by Eric Blore and Alan Mowbray

Jane

Andy Hardy's wife (Patricia Breslin) They marry in the 1958 film *Andy Hardy Comes Home*. Their first child is Andy Jr. (played by Teddy Rooney, Mickey Rooney's real son)

Jane Angelica Thrift

Wrangler Jane's (Melody Patterson) full name (TV series "F Troop")

Jane Mast

Pseudonym under which Mae West wrote her first (1926) play *Sex*

Jane Porter

Tarzan's mate: in the 1932 *Tarzan the Ape Man* (the first Weissmuller picture) she is played by Maureen O'Sullivan and named Jane Parker. She and her father are from Baltimore

Jano Poporopolus

Greek depositor whose name bank teller, Sandy Duncan had trouble pronouncing on TV. United California Bank commercials. In frustration she asks him if she could call him Nick (seen in Western U.S.)

January 1

Universal birthday for a horse born that year

January 1, 2001

The first day of the 21st century

Japanese Monsters

In movies:

Doroga—Gigantic Jellyfish

Ebirah—Gigantic Shrimp

Gammera—Huge Turtle

Gappa—Large Lizard

Godzilla—164 foot high Tyrannosaurus Rex

Goke—Vampire
Gorath—Huge Reptile
Gyaos—Fox
Hedorah—Smog Monster
Mantanga—Spreading Fungus
Mothra—Giant Moth
Rodan—Giant Pterodactyl
Varan—Large Bat
Viras—Giant Squid

Jaq and Gus
Mice (Walt Disney's cartoon movie *Cinderella*) voices of James McDonald

Jasper
Gregg family's pet dog (TV series "Bachelor Father")

Jay, John
American diplomat (1745-1829), first chief justice of the Supreme Court (1789-1795), first (acting) secretary of state under the Constitution (1789-1790), author of some *Federalist* papers

Jazz Age, The
The 1920's: title coined by F. (Francis) Scott Fitzgerald (*Tales of the Jazz Age*, 1922)
In the 1959 movie *Beloved Infidel* Gregory Peck portrays Fitzgerald and Deborah Kerr portrays Sheila Graham

Jazz Singer, The
First "talkie" movie, debut October 6, 1927 Warner's Theater on Broadway, Warner Brothers: starring Al Jolson, played on Broadway by George Jessel.
The Jazz Singer's name is Jack Robin, in first talkie Jolson says, "Wait a minute, wait a minute, you ain't heard nothing yet". Movie remade in 1953 with Danny Thomas as the Jazz Singer. The quiz show *Split Second* used the same stage on which the 1927 movie was filmed

J. Bolling Bumstead
Dagwood Bumstead's millionaire father, who disowned him (Chic Young's *Blondie*)

J. C. Dithers
Dagwood Bumstead's boss Julius Caesar Dithers (See Mr. J. C. Dithers)

Jean
Paul Bunyan's son

Jean Hersholt Humanitarian Award

Presentation at the Academy Awards to a person within the film industry noted for their humanitarian practices. The receiver of the award is chosen by the Academy's Board of Governors. It was actor Jean Hersholt who founded the Motion Picture Relief Fund

Jeeves

Butler of Bertie Wooster in P. G. (Pelham Grenville) Wodehouse novels, played in 1936 movie *Thank You, Jeeves* by Arthur Treacher. (Both P. G. Wodehouse and Arthur Treacher died in 1975)

Jefferson City Junior High

School at which Robinson J. Peepers (Wally Cox) taught science (TV series "Mr. Peepers"). He eventually weds Nancy Remington (Pat Benoit), the school nurse

Jefferson High

School at which Mr. Novak (James Franciscus) taught (TV series "Mr. Novak") Albert Vane, (Dean Jagger) is the principal

Jefferson High

School that the gang attends (TV series "Happy Days") The school newspaper is the Jefferson Crier

Jefferson Public School

Fort Wayne, Indiana school which George Taylor (Charlton Heston) attended in his youth (1968 movie *Planet of the Apes*)

Jeffords, Tom J.

Ex-civil-war Captain who, unarmed, went through Indian country to make peace with the Apache Chief Cochise. He later became the Indian agent. Jeffords was portrayed in the 1950 movie *Broken Arrow* by James Stewart and on TV series by John Lupton. Cochise was played in 3 movies by Jeff Chandler, on television series by Michael Ansara

Jellystone Park

Home of Yogi Bear (TV cartoon) headed by Ranger John Smith

Jennie

The mule of Jane Gibson (the Pig Woman) who discovered the bodies in the Hall-Mills murder case of the 1920's: every trivial thing in this case became subject for headlines

Jennifer

Cary Grant's daughter, born to him and Dyan Cannon February 26, 1966 when Cary was 62 years old

Jennifer

Professor Julius Kelp's (Jerry Lewis) pet Mynah Bird (1963 movie *"The Nutty Professor"*)

Jerry

Cartoon mouse (of "Tom and Jerry" series) who was Gene Kelly's dancing partner in *Anchors Aweigh*. Jerry was King of Pomerania (1945) (See Tom and Jerry)

Jersey Lily

Judge Roy Bean's saloon, named for actress Lilly Langtry, in Langtry, Texas, where he was "the law west of the Pecos". The sign was misspelled by a Swede named Oscar. Bean saw Lilly Langtry only once at San Antonio in 1888. Lilly Langtry was portrayed in movies: *The Westener* (1939) Lilian Bond, *Life and Times of Judge Roy Bean* (1972) Ava Gardner

Jessie Garon

Elvis Arron Presley's twin brother who died at birth January 8, 1935

Jesus wept

Shortest verse in the Bible (John 11:35)

Jet Jackson

Hero of TV series "Jet Jackson, Flying Commando": played by Richard Webb. New title of Captain Midnight series with Ovaltine as sponsor

Jetman

Television cartoon series for which Richard Hollister (Richard Benjamin) works as a cartoonist (TV series *He and She*)

Jet Pilot

Race horse that announcer Clem McCarthy said was the winner of the 1947 Preakness before realizing his mistake. The actual winner was *Faultless* which *"Mister Horse Racing"* then announced.

Jets and Sharks

Two rival gangs in movie *West Side Story* (Best Picture, 1961 Academy Awards)
Leader of the Jets—Riff Lorton played by Russ Tamblyn
Leader of the Sharks—Bernardo: played by George Chakiris

Jim

Miss Watson's Negro slave who accompanies Huckleberry Finn down the Mississippi on a raft. They met on Jackson Island

Jim Bell

Sky King's foreman (radio series)

Jim Blane

The old, retired Texas Ranger that managed the Lone Ranger's silver mine (He knows the Lone Ranger's identity) played on TV by Ralph Littlefield. In comic books the silver mine was named the Lost Lode and was found by Tonto

Jim Hawkins

Boy hero of Robert Louis Stevenson's *Treasure Island*. Played in 1934 movie by Jackie Cooper, in 1950 movie by Bobby Driscoll 1972 by Kim Bluefield. Two earlier versions had girls playing the role, in 1920 by Shirley Mason

Jiminy Cricket

Pinocchio's cricket friend (Disney cartoon feature movie): voice of Cliff Edwards

Jimmy the Greek

Nickname of Las Vegas odds-maker James Snyder (original name, before 1939: Dimitrios Synodinos)

Jimmy and Jane Webb

Tom Mix's wards (radio series). George Gobel was one of several actors to play Jimmy

Jimmy Olsen

(James Bartholomew) Office boy for the *Daily Planet* ("Superman")

Radio: Jackie Kelk; TV: Jack Larson. Debut: Superman Comics #13, November 1941. In comics also known as Elastic Lad and Mr. Action.

His birthday is on November 29th. Played in 1948 and 1950 movie serials by Tommy Bond

Jingles Jones

Wild Bill Hickok's partner (radio/TV series "Wild Bill Hickok"): played by Andy Devine (Jeremiah Schwartz) His horse is Joker "Hey Wild Bill, wait for me"

Jip

Doctor Dolittle's dog

Jno

Signature of John R. Neil, artist of L. Frank Baum's Oz

Books. He did all but the first book which was drawn by
W. W. Denslow

Joad

Name of migrant Okie family (John Steinbeck's *The Grapes of Wrath*)

Joanna

Doctor Leonard McCoy's daughter from his previous marriage (TV series *Star Trek*)

Jock

Scottish terrier in *Lady and the Tramp* (Disney cartoon feature movie)

Jockey's Hall of Fame

Located in Detroit, Michigan

Joe

German Shepherd starring in Saturday morning TV series *Run, Joe, Run*. Played by Heinrich of Midvale

Joe Btfsplk

The World's Worst Jinx, walks around with a cloud over his head (Al Capp's *Li'l Abner* cartoon)

Joe Corntassel

Orphan Annie's boyfriend, radio: voice of Mel Torme and Allan Baruck

Joe the Monster

Villain in Ian Fleming's *Chitty-Chitty-Bang-Bang*. His gang: Man-Mountain Fink, Soapy Sam, Blood-Money Banks

Joe Palooka

Champion boxer, created in comic strip by Ham Fisher— His manager is Knobby Walsh. Married Anne Howe in 1949. On radio; Teddy Bergman, (Alan Reed), Norman Gottschalk, Karl Swenson

Played in movies by Joe Kirkwood, Jr., Stu Erwin (1934 movie *Joe Palooka*)

Joe Shlabotnik

Charlie Brown's favorite baseball player (*Peanuts*)

Joey

Circus clown (Noah Beery, Jr.) who watches over Corky (TV series "Circus Boy") Joey's ful name was Alexander Phillip Perkins

Joey

Dennis the Menace's younger friend (Hank Ketcham's comic strip)

Joey Chill

Shot and killed Mr. Thomas Wayne, father of Bruce Wayne (Batman). Batman revealed his identity to him prior to Chill's death.

At the sight of her husband being shot Martha Wayne, his mother, died of a heart attack, the night of June 7, 1924.

Bruce Wayne then dedicates himself to fighting crime and revenging his parents' deaths. This is very similar to *Tim Tyler's Luck*. In the serial Tim's father Professor Tyler is killed by Spider Webb, he then dedicates himself to fight crime. Same with the Red Ryder, Spiderman, Dick Tracy and others who lost relatives to crime

Joey Starrett

Small Wyoming farm boy (Brandon De Wilde) who worships the ex-gunfighter *Shane* (Alan Ladd) 1953 movie *"Shane."* In the 1966 TV series *"Shane"* Joey was played by Chris Shea. "Shane, Come back, Come back Shane"

Joey Stivic

Archie Bunker's grandson, Joseph Michael Stivic (TV series *All in the Family*) played by the twins Justin and Jason Draeger

Jonathan Rebel

Puppet dog on the Bobby Goldsboro TV series

John

Loretta Young's announcer (TV show "The Loretta Young Show")

John and Alice Clayton

Lord and Lady Greystoke. Tarzan's father and mother

John Birch Society

Named after United States missionary and intelligence officer killed (1945) by Chinese Communists; founded by Robert Welch, retired candy manufacturer, December 9, 1958

John Brown's Body

Tune to which Julia Ward Howe's words for "Battle Hymn of the Republic" are sung

John Bull

Personification of the British people

John Carter

Adventures of the Confederate Captain, John Carter on the planet Mars (Barsoom) Martian series created by Edgar Rice Burroughs debut novel "A Princess of Mars." Became a comic strip by John Burroughs, Edgar's son, debut on December 7, 1941

John Charles Muckinfuss

Character on radio's Fred Allen Show. Name was created for its effect on the audience

John Doe

The plaintiff in a court case—The defendant being Richard Roe (British legal system)

John Fitch

World War 2 liberty ship, that was launched 24 days after the keel was laid.

John Henry

"The Steel Driving Man" Worked for the Chesapeake and Ohio Railroad. Polly Anne was his woman. Died when he competed against Captain Tommy's steam drill in laying the most track

John J. Malone

Detective in Craig Rice stories: played by Frank Lovejoy on radio

John Reid

Texas Ranger who became the Lone Ranger (Since he never officially resigned, is he A.W.O.L.?)

Johnny

Señor Wences' hand puppet. Appeared in 1947 movie *Mother Wore Tights*

Johnny

John Roventini the 47", 49 lb. Philip Morris page boy: "Call for Philip Morris" (sometimes played by Freddy Douglas). He began at the Hotel New Yorker, became head bellboy at the Beverly Hills Hotel. The musical theme in the background was Ferde Grofe's *Grand Canyon Suite*, "On the Trail"

Johnny Appleseed

Nickname of John Chapman, 1774-1845, who planted apple seeds throughout the Ohio Valley

Johnny Corkscrew

Pet name of the cutlass of Smee, Captain Hook's first mate (James M. Barrie's *Peter Pan*)

Johnny Jupiter

Spaceman puppet friend of store clerk Ernest P. Duckweather (played by Wright King) on TV show (1953-1954)

Johnny Thunderbolt

Secret identity of John L. Thunder born at 7 a.m. on the 7th of July, 1917. When he says the magic Badhnisian word Cei-u (Say You) everything he wishes comes true (comic books)

Johnson-Allyson Movies

Films starring Van Johnson and June Allyson:

Two Girls and a Sailor (1944)
Till the Clouds Roll By (1946)
High Barbaree (1947)
The Bride Goes Wild (1948)
Too Young to Kiss (1951)
Remains to Be Seen (1953)

Johnny Yuma

"The Rebel" in TV series: starred Nick Adams, who was studying to become a journalist

Johnson, Andrew

President of the United States after Lincoln's assassination (1865): also called Tennessee Johnson. Quarreling with the more severe wing of the Republican Party over Reconstruction tactics, he was impeached by the House of Representatives on March 4, 1868, on 11 counts, and was acquitted when the Senate failed by one vote to reach a ⅔ majority for conviction on the first 3 counts. He is buried with a copy of the U.S. Constitution

Johnson, Lyndon B.

President of the United States after Kennedy's assassination (1963). His wife, Claudia Alta Taylor Johnson, was called Lady Bird. His children (married names): Lynda Bird Robb and Lucy (Luci) Baines Nugent

Johnson Smith & Co.

Detroit, Michigan company that advertised a full page in expensive novelty items—in many comic books of 1930s-1940s. A popular item was *Throw Your Voice* by buying for 10¢ *The Ventrillo*. Other items—live Chameleon, electric telegraph—World Mike, Magnetic Pups Motto: *"We're in Business for Fun"*

John Sunlight

Only villain to appear in two Doc Savage novels:

Fortress of Solitude (1938)
The Devil Genghis (1938)

Join the Army and See the Navy
Travelogue which Harpo carries on his back in the 1933 movie *Duck Soup*

JoJo
The dog-faced boy, exhibited in the United States in 1885. Real name: Theodore Peteroff

Joker
Jingles Jones' (Andy Devine) horse (radio/TV series *Wild Bill Hickok*)

Joker, The
Batman's green-haired arch-enemy who originally worked for and robbed the Monarch Playing Card Company. His original and other identity is that of The Red Hood

Jolly Green Giant
Large character who helps sell Green Giant vegetable products. His only words are *"Ho-Ho-Ho"*. Voice of Herschel Bernardi. Also nickname of Sikorsky Army Helicopter HH-3E

Jolly Roger
Pirate flag of white skull and crossbones in a black field

Jolly Roger
Captain Hook's pirate ship (James M. Barrie's *Peter Pan*)

Jon, Gee
First person to be executed in a gas chamber. Nevada State Prison at Carson City February 8, 1924.

Jonathan Livingston Seagull
Best-selling novel by Richard Bach, in 1973 movie voice of James Franciscus, scored by Neil Diamond

Jones, Buck
(1889-1942) Charles Gebhart (Jones) Western movie star, began as extra and stunt man. Fox hired him as a threat to Tom Mix. Died as a result of injuries sustained in the Coconut Grove fire in Boston of Nov. 38, 1942 where he was the guest of honor (played *The Red Rider** in 1934 movie serial)

Jones, John Luther
Casey Jones's real name (see Casey Jones)

Jones, John Paul
America's Revolutionary War hero famous for stating *"I have not yet begun to fight"* became a Russian Admiral (1788) after the war, Kontradmiral Pavel Ivanovich Jones

---

*Not to be confused with Red Ryder

Jordon, Ted

The actor who portrayed the cowboy who drew first yet was supposedly shot by Marshal Matt Dillon (James Arness) at the opening sequence of TV series *Gunsmoke,* yet viewers never saw him. (See *Gunsmoke*)

Jor-El and Lara

Superman's real parents (Originally Jor-L and Lora in comics) who died when the planet Krypton was destroyed. In 1948 movie serial *Superman* played by Nelson Leigh and Luana Walters. On first TV episode of "Superman" titled *Superman On Earth* (1951) played by Robert Rockwell and Aline Towne. In 1978 movie *Superman* played by Marlon Brando and Susannah York

Jorgensen, George Jr.

Christine Jorgensen's name before sex-change operation in Copenhagen, 1951. Christine took her first name from that of surgeon who treated her, Dr. Christian Hamburger. Portrayed by John Hansen in 1970 movie *The Christine Jorgensen Story*

Jose Bluster

Phineas T. Bluster's good guy, twin-brother (TV series *Howdy Doody*)

Jose Jimenez

Mexican-Spanish comic: played by Bill Dana ("My name Jose Jimenez") Jose Jimenez was Danny Williams elevator operator on TV series *Make Room for Daddy*

Josephine

Widow of Alexandre, Vicomte de Beauharnais, who became Napoleon's first wife six years his senior (married 1796, divorced 1809). He then married (1810) Princess Marie Louise of Austria. "Josephine" was Napoleon's last word. Portrayed in 1954 movie *Desiree* by Merle Oberon and in 1957 movie *The Story of Mankind* by Marie Windsor

Josephine

Late actress/author Jacqueline Susann's pet French poodle which she wrote about in her first best seller *Every Night Josephine!* She also wrote a short story about her next poodle, *Along Came Joe.*

Josephine

Female plumber in TV Comet cleanser commercials; played by Jane Withers

Josephine Ford
  Ford tri-plane piloted by Commander Richard E. Byrd and co-piloted by Floyd Bennett when they were the first to fly over North Pole, May 9, 1926. They began and landed at Kings Bay, Spitzbergen. Named after Edsel Ford's daughter Josephine

Josh Randall
  The bounty hunter (TV series "Wanted—Dead or Alive") : played by Steve McQueen. He called his 30-40 carbine "Mare's Laig" The horse he rode was actually named Ringo

Josiah Kessel College
  Learning Institute where Professor James Howard (Jimmy Stewart) teaches anthropology (TV series *The Jimmy Stewart Show*)

Jot 'Em Down Store
  In Pine Ridge, Arkansas, location of radio/TV series "Lum and Abner" Lum Edwards (Chester Lauck) and Abner Peabody (Norris Goff)
  Abner's wife is Elizabeth, his daughter is Pearl. Their telephone signal is three long rings

Journey Back to Oz
  1962 animated cartoon—Voices:
    Dorothy—Liza Minnelli
    Wicked Witch of the West—Ethel Merman
    The Good Witch—Rise Stevens
    Tin Man—Danny Thomas
    Scarecrow—Mickey Rooney
    Cowardly Lion—Milton Berle
    Woodenhead, the horse—Herschel Bernardi
    Crow—Mel Blanc
    Mombi, the bad witch—Ethel Merman
    Signpost—Jack E. Leonard

J. P. Bigdome
  Little Iodine's father's boss (Little Iodine cartoon)

J. Thaddeus Toad
  Mr. Toad's of Toad Hall, full name, Kenneth Grahame's *The Wind in the Willows*

Juanita
  Theme song of radio series *The Romance of Helen Trent*

Jubalaires
  Singing group on radio's *Amos 'n' Andy*

356

Judge Bradley J. Stevens

Joan Stevens' (Joan Davis) husband played by Jim Backus on TV series *I Married Joan*

Judge (James) Hardy

Andy Hardy's father: for most of the series played by Lewis Stone (in the first picture, *A Family Affair*, Lionel Barrymore was Judge Hardy), Mrs. Hardy was played by Spring Byington and Fay Holden

Judy

Chimpanzee (TV series "Daktari"). Winner of 1967 movie and 1967 TV PATSY

Judy, Judy, Judy

Never said by Cary Grant in any movie: used by imitators as characteristic Grant exclamation

Judy Splinters

Shirley Dinsdale's dummy (radio/TV)

Juffure, Gambia

African village home of Kunta Kinte (Alex Haley's *Roots*)

Jughead Jones

Archie Andrews' sidekick Forsythe P. Jones (comics). He wears a shirt with an "S" on it and a bottle cap shaped hat. In comics he became super hero Captain Hero. Played on radio by Cameron Andrews and Harlan Stone, Jr., on TV by Derrel Maury

Julius

Family dog of the Boyle family (TV cartoon series *Wait Till Your Father Gets Home*)

Julius

Jeff's twin brother ("Mutt and Jeff" comic strip) Ima is Mutt's brother

July 1, 21 B.C.

Birth date of Jeannie in Pompeii, TV series *I Dream of Jeannie*

July 2

Middle day of the year, 182 days prior, 182 days to go (non leap year)

July 4

U.S. Independence Day, day on which ex-presidents Thomas Jefferson and John Adams (1826, 50th anniversary of Declaration of Independence) and James Monroe (1831) died. Stephen Collins Foster, popular song writer, was born the day Adams and Jefferson died, and

George M. Cohan claimed July 4, 1878, as his birth date (actually July 3). President Calvin Coolidge's birthday (1872). Horatio Hornblower's birthday (1776) Lou Gehrig Day at Yankee Stadium (1939)

July 4, 1776

The lone inscription of the tablet held by the Statue of Liberty

Jumbo

Broadway musical produced by Billy Rose. Rehearsals took six months, possibly the most expensive Broadway production. *Jumbo the Elephant,* the show's star's real name, was Big Rosie

Jumbo Jets

American manufactured:
Boeing 747, Douglas DC-10, Lockheed L-1011, Lockheed C-5A

June 6

Date Damien (Harvey Stephens) was born at 6:00 a.m. (666) in 1976 movie *The Omen.* Also date of events in 1974 movie *The Front Page*

June 16, 1904

Setting in Dublin of James Joyce's novel *Ulysses,* spanning 19 hours in over 700 pages. About two men; Leopold Bloom and Stephen Dedalus.

June Bug

Glenn Curtiss' first airplane, winner of the Aeronautical Trophy, 1908

June Taylor Dancers

Dancers on Jackie Gleason's TV show. Gleason's third wife is the sister of June Taylor

Juneau

ARCO tanker that was the first ship to take on oil from the Alaskan Pipeline at Valdez, Alaska August 1, 1977

Juneau, U.S.S.

United States cruiser on which the five Sullivan brothers lost their lives. Nov. 13, 1942, off Guadalcanal during the American landings. Sunk by Japanese sub I-26. Their hometown was Waterloo, Iowa. Portrayed in 1944 movie *The Sullivans:*

Sullivan	As an Adult	As a Child
Frank	John Campbell	Marvin Davis
George (oldest)	James Cardwell	Buddy Swan
Matt	John Alvin	John Calkins

| Joe | George Offerman, Jr. | Billy Cummings |
| Al (youngest) | Edward Ryan | Booby Driscoll |

Jungle Book, The

Children's story by Rudyard Kipling (1894 and 1895)
1967 animated cartoon movie voices:
- Baloo the Bear—(Phil Harris)
- Bagheera, Black Panther—(Sebastian Cabot)
- Shere Khan—Tiger (George Sanders)
- Kaa, the Snake—(Sterling Holloway)
- Mowgli—(Bruce Reitherman)
- King Louis of the Apes—(Louis Prima)

Jungle Jim (Bradley)

Created by Alex Raymond in comics debut Sunday January 7, 1934 in the same issue as the debut of the comic strip Flash Gordon. Movie series (1948) played by Johnny Weissmuller: Caw-Caw, pet crow; Skipper, his son; Tamba, pet chimp; Kaseem, native companion
On radio: Matt Crowley; in 1937 movie serial: Grant Withers

Jungle Twins, The

Tono and Kono (created by Edgar Rice Burroughs)

Junior

Chester A. Riley's son (radio/TV "Life of Riley")
Radio: Tommy Cook, Jack Grimes, Scotty Beckett, Conrad Binyon
TV: Wesley Morgan

Junior

Dick and Tess Tracy's adopted son. Junior's wife is Moon Maid, his daughter his Honey Moon
Played in 1937 movie serial by Lee Van Atta
Played in 1938 movie serial by Jerry Tucker

Junior

Horse on which Glen Campbell is mounted on the cover of his record album *Rhinestone Cowboy*

Junior Phillips

Edith Ann's (Lily Tomlin) six year old boyfriend

Junior Woodchucks

Organization to which Donald Duck's nephews, Huey, Dewey, and Louie belong. The head man is the High Mogul.
Their oaths:
DDB oath: Don't ditch a buddy

ABC oath: We solemnly swear to be A-Able bodied, B-bold, C-Courageous

Junkville

Bucky Bug and June Bug's home (Walt Disney cartoon characters). Bucky and June were married in comic strip on March 11, 1934

Jupiter

Central Pacific wood-burning locomotive No. 60 that met the Union Pacific coal-burning locomotive No. 119 at Promontory, Utah, May 10, 1869

Jupiter II

The Robinson's spaceship. Departed Earth on October 16, 1997. (TV series *Lost in Space*). Their original destination was Alpha Centauri

Justice, Inc.

Evil-fighting organization led by The Avenger (Richard Henry Benson): headquarters on Bleek Street, Manhattan (novel series created by Kenneth Robeson). Members of the organization: Fergus MacMaudie, Cole Wilson, Algernon Heathcote Smith (Smitty), Nellie Gray, Josh Newton (Joshua Elijah H. Newton), Rosabel Newton

Justice League of America

Comic book series featured:

1940's—called Justice Society of America:

Atom, Flash, Batman, Hawkman, Superman, Dr. Midnite, Mr. Terrific, Wonder Woman, Green Lantern, Johnny Thunder, Black Canary, Dr. Fate, Hourman, Red Tornado, Sandman, Spectre, Starman, Wildcat (note that the first 10 heroes have a progression from 4 letters through 13 letters in their names) (All-Star comics/All American Comics)

(Modern Day)—Justice League of America

Atom, Flash, Batman, Hawkman, Superman, J'onn J'Onzz, Green Arrow, Wonder Woman, Green Lantern, Aquaman, Elongated Man, Black Canary, Red Tornado (similar progression)

Honorary Members:

Sargon the Sorcerer, Phantom Stranger

Justice through Strength and Courage

Motto of the Captain Midnight's Secret Squadron

Justinian, H.M.S.

First British Naval ship that Horatio Hornblower was assigned to (age 17). Commanded by Captain Keene (C. S. Forester's Hornblower series)

K

K2

    Mt. Godwin-Austen or Dapsang, 28,250 feet, second highest mountain in the world: in Himalayas (Karako-rams) First climbed July 31, 1954

KGC

    Gotham City radio station. Hot Rod Harry is the D.J.

K H A Q Q

    Amelia Earhart's call sign on her last flight, July 3, 1937. In the 1976 TV movie *Amelia Earhart* was portrayed by Susan Clark (Kim Diamond as a girl)

K H W B B

    Call sign of Toni Carter's Lockheed Electra NR16056 (Played by Rosalind Russell, 1943 movie *Flight for Freedom,* based on Amelia Earhart's life)

KL 17811

    Banacek's mobile radio call sign in his 1973 Fleetwood Cadillac (TV series *Banacek*)

KL5-9988

    Phone number of Laverne and Shirley (TV series *Laverne and Shirley*)

KLAS

    Las Vegas Television Station that Howard Hughes bought so he could watch late-night movies

KMA 367

    Frequency 1, radio channel of one-Adam 12 (KMA 361 is their emergency channel), TV series "Adam-12"

KMD9990

    Doctor Elliot's (James Franciscus) radio call numbers located in his pickup truck (the letters are displayed on his camper) TV series *Doc Elliot*

KMG 365

Radio call sign of the para-medical truck unit. (TV series *Emergency*)

KORN

Chicken-shack radio station, featuring D.J. Charlie Farquharson (Don Harron) on TV show *Hee Haw*

KRML

Carmel, California radio station for which Dave Garland (Clint Eastwood) is the evening disc jockey (1971 movie *Play Misty for Me*)

KXIU

Phoenix, Arizona television station (Channel 2) where Dick Preston (Dick Van Dyke) hosts a talk show, television series *The New Dick Van Dyke Show*

Kaa

Python (Rudyard Kipling's *The Jungle Book*) in cartoons voice of Sterling Holloway

Kabar

Rudolph Valentino's pet Doberman

Kala

The ape of the Kerchak tribe that adopted and raised the baby Tarzan

Kala Nag

Toomai's (played by Sabu) pet elephant (played by Irawatha) 1937 movie *Elephant Boy*

Kal-El

Superman's name on the planet of his birth, Krypton

Kamikaze

The Divine Wind: name adopted by Japanese World War II suicide pilots

Kandor

Kryptonian city shrunk into a bottle by the evil villian Brainiac. It is kept in Superman's Fortress of Solitude

Kaneewah Fury!

Straight Arrow's war whoop, said to his horse Fury

Kanga

Kangaroo friend of Winnie-the-Pooh. Her baby is named Roo. Voice of Barbara Luddy on TV.

Kansas City Star

Newspaper for which both Ernest Hemingway (as a re-

porter) and Walt Disney (as an artist) worked. Hemingway and Disney had both been ambulance drivers.
Title of 1965 hit record by Roger Miller

KAOS
Evil organization (TV series "Get Smart")

Karas, Anton
Zither player (only his hands appear) who plays theme song and a waltz (1949 movie *The Third Man*)

Kara Zor-el
Supergirl's name on her planet of birth, Krypton. She lived in Argo City. She adopted the secret identity on Earth of Linda Lee Danvers. She is Superman's cousin (comic book series *Supergirl*)

Karen
Title of two different television series: *Karen* starring Debbie Watson began as one of three comedy series under the title *90 Bristol Court* lasted only the 1964 season. *Karen* starring Karen Valentine began in the 1975 season

Katie
Emmett Dalton's first horse, once belonged to Jesse James

Kato
The Green Hornet's valet (TV series "The Green Hornet") played by Bruce Lee. In the radio series earlier, Kato, played by several actors, is said to have changed from Japanese to Filipino when World War II broke out. On radio: Raymond Toyo, Rollon Parker, Mickey Tolon Movie serials: Keye Luke

Kato
Inspector Clousseau's valet. *A Shot In The Dark* etc. played by Burt Kwouk

Katzenjammer Kids
Comic strip begun (December 12, 1897) by Rudolph Dirks and continued (from 1912) by Harold Knerr. Also known by the names "Hans and Fritz" (Dirks) and "The Captain and the Kids" (since World War I). Hans is blond, Fritz has black hair. The two uncles are The Captain and The Inspector (a truant officer)

Kaw-Liga
Cigar-store wooden Indian (song written by Hank Williams and Fred Rose)

Kayo
Moon Mullin's brother

363

Kearsarge, U.S.S.

Only U.S. battleship not named after a state. The screw sloop "Kearsarge" sank the Confederate raider "Alabama" in 1864. When the "Kearsarge" was lost in the West Indies in 1894, the name was given, because of popular demand, to one of the new battleships

Keeling, U.S.S.

Commander George Krause's destroyer (C.S. Forester's *The Good Shepherd*)

Keep On Truckin'

Mr. Crumb's favorite expression (comic strip by Robert Crumb)

Keep Your Eye on the Sparrow

Theme song of TV series *Baretta* sung by Sammy Davis Jr. Singer Ethel Waters autobiography is titled *His Eye Is On the Sparrow*

Keeshan, Bob

Played Clarabell the clown ("Howdy Doody Show") and Captain Kangaroo

Kehoe's Drug Store

Where Jean Harlow was "discovered" by a Hollywood director. She was standing out in front looking for a dime to buy a soda, so the legend goes.

Kelcy's Bar

Archie Bunker's favorite hangout (TV series "All in the Family"), Kelcy played by Bob Hastings. On the window of the bar the spelling is Kelcy's while in the TV credits it's spelled Kelsy's

Kelly, Grace

Won Best Actress Oscar for *The Country Girl* in 1954. She met Monaco's Prince Rainier while in that country filming *To Catch a Thief*. In 1956 they were married. She appeared in only 11 movies. She recorded a number one record in 1956, *True Love* with Bing Crosby. Her picture appeared on the cover of the last edition of Collier's magazine January 4, 1957

Kelly School

Elementary school of which Miss Peach is a teacher. Mr. J. W. Grimmis is the principal and Miss Peach's class consists of: Freddy (Foster), Ira (Brown), Francine, Marcia (Mason), Arthur (Strimm), Linda, Walter, Stuart, Sheila, Lester, Miss Crystal—fellow teacher, Mr. Musselman—Gym teacher, Tweetie—Arthur's pet parakeet (cartoon *Miss Peach* by Mell)

Kelso

Race horse named Horse of the Year 1960 through 1964.

Kemmler, William

On August 6, 1890 became the first person to be executed in the electric chair. That same day Denton True "Cy" Young appeared in his first major league baseball game.

Kemo Sabe

Meaning "trusty scout": said of the Lone Ranger by Tonto. Kemo Sabe was named by James Jewell, the show's producer. It was the name of his father's boys camp (Kee-Mo-Sah-Bee). Tonto gave the Lone Ranger that name when as boys the Lone Ranger nursed Tonto back to life

Kemp Morgan

The world's greatest oil well driller (American folklore)

Ken

Identity of radio's "A Man Called X" (detective played by Herbert Marshall)

Ken Thurston

Barbie the doll's boyfriend doll

Kennedy children

The family of Joseph (1888-1969) and Rose Fitzgerald Kennedy:

Joseph, Jr., killed (1944) in World War II

Jack (John) (1917-1963), President of the United States, 1961-1963: assassinated

Rosemary, mentally retarded

Kathleen, killed (1948) in plane crash

Eunice, married R. Sargent Shriver (1953-   )

Patricia, married Peter Lawford (1954-1967)

Robert (1925-1968), Attorney General of the United States (1961-1963) and United States Senator from New York (1965-1968); assassinated

Jean, married Stephen Smith

Edward, United States Senator from Massachusetts (1962-   )

Kennedy, John Fitzgerald

(1917-1963), youngest man elected President of the United States, 43 years old when elected in 1960 (Theodore Roosevelt was the youngest inaugurated, 42 years, 10 months, 18 days, when sworn in Sept. 14, 1901)

His children: Caroline (born 1957), John (born 1960),

Patrick (born 1963; died soon after birth). While president his secret service code names were:

Lancer—The President
Lace—The First Lady
Lyric—Caroline
Lark—John Jr.

Kent Allard

Secret identity of The Shadow, though he uses the guise of Lamont Cranston. The real Lamont Cranston, a world explorer, has given Allard permission to use his name (pulp magazine series "The Shadow")

Kents

Martha (was Mary) and Jonathan (or John) adopted infant Kal-El April 10, 1926. The Kents ran a general store in Smallville, Illinois; their wedding anniversary is October 21. Clark is Martha's maiden name. In George Lowther's novel *Superman* the Clark's first names are Sarah and Eben, those names were used on the TV series. 1948 movie *Superman* Eben (Edward Cassidy), Martha (Virginia Carroll), TV series Eben (Tom Fadden), Sarah (Frances Morris)

Kentucky Derby

Annual horse race at Churchill Downs, Louisville, Kentucky (run on the first Saturday in May). First winner (1876): Aristides

Kermit T. Frog

Puppet frog reporter, middle name, The. Voice of creator Jim Henson (TV series "Sesame Street")

Kewpie

Brutus Thornapple's pet dog (comic strip *The Born Loser*)

Kewpie Doll

Baby doll with pointed curl on its head. Given out as a prize in early carnivals, fairs, etc. Created from a drawing first published in 1909 by Rose O'Neill

Keystone Kops

They worked for Keystone Pictures
Original members:
Slim Summerville, Mack Riley, Edgar Kennedy, Bobby Dunn. Hank Mann, Georgie Jeske, Charlie Avery

Khartoum

$600,000 race horse that is beheaded in Mario Puzo's "The Godfather" (The head used was an actual horse's head)

Kid Flash
  Flash's (second version) nephew and sidekick, Wally West
Kid Galahad
  Nickname of fighter Ward Guisenberry
  In novel by Francis Wallace
  In movies played by Wayne Morris (1937) and by Elvis
  Presley (1962)
Kid Shelleen/Tim Strawn
  Lee Marvin's dual role as goodbad twins (movie *Cat
  Ballou*): won Oscar as best actor 1965
Kienast Quintuplets
  Born Feb. 24, 1970: Ted; Gordon; Abigail; Sara; Amy
Kigmy
  Animal glad to have aggressions taken out on it ("Li'l
  Abner" comic strip)
Kiko
  Friendly white gorilla in the 1933 movie *Son of Kong*
KILLER
  Flip Wilson's California automobile license plate of his
  $40,000 Rolls Royce
Killer
  Geraldine's (Flip Wilson) boyfriend
Killer Kane
  Buck Roger's arch-enemy (1939 movie serial *Buck Rog-
  ers*)
  Radio: Bill Shelley, Dan Ocko, Arthur Vinton
  Movie Serial: Anthony Warde. His girlfriend is Ardala
Kilroy Was Here
  Graffiti used by American G.I.'s written on many Euro-
  pean buildings, fences, etc. during World War II
  1947 movie *Kilroy Was Here*—Jackie Cooper
  Kilroy was supposedly an inspection Sergeant who after
  checking something wrote on it *Kilroy Was Here*
Kim
  Kimball O'Hara, Irish orphan in Lahore, India (Rudyard
  Kipling's *Kim*): played in 1950 movie by Dean Stockwell
Kimba
  The white lion (TV cartoon). Voice of Billie Lou Watt
Kin Lung
  Singapore-bound ship on which Captain Alan Gaskell
  (Clark Gable) is skipper (1935 movie *China Seas*)
Kimota
  Magic word which changes young Micky Moran into

Marvelman, the Mightiest Man in the Universe (British comic book version of Captain Marvel)

King

Horse, short for Blaze King (TV series "National Velvet"). Ridden by Velvet Brown. In the 1944 movie the horse was called The Pie, as he was in Enid Bagnold's 1935 novel (short for The Piebald)

King

Alaskan husky used as dog-team leader by Sergeant Preston of the Yukon

King and Queen of Hollywood

Title given to Clark Gable and Myrna Loy through a contest run by Ed Sullivan on his radio show (1938)

King Arthur Carousel

Merry-Go-Round in *Fantasyland, Disneyland* with 72 horses on it

King, Billie Jean

Top U.S. women's tennis player, victor over former Wimbledon and Forest Hills winner Bobby Riggs in straight sets, 6-4, 6-3, 6-3, in the Houston Astrodome, Sept. 20, 1973. She is the sister of San Francisco Giants' pitcher Randy Moffitt

King Blozo

King of Nazilia (cartoon "Thimble Theatre")

King Cheops

Greek form of the Egyptian name Khufu, the pharaoh who built Egypt's largest pyramid (at Giza)

King of the Cowboys

Roy Rogers' title

King Creole

Title of 1958 movie made from Harold Robbins' *A Stone for Danny Fisher:* Elvis Presley played the role of Danny Finnell

King Edward Hotel

Hotel at which police detective Anthony "Tony" Baretta resides. He pays $90 a month rent. (TV series *Baretta*)

King Kala

Ruler of the Shark Men on the planet Mongo. Played by Duke York Jr. (1936 *Flash Gordon* movie serial)

King Khufu

The real identity of The Hawkman (Carter Hall's secret identity) Khufu was killed by Hath-Set but was reincarnated as Carter Hall (*The Hawkman* comic books)

King Kong

Giant gorilla brought from Skull Island by Carl Denham (Robert Armstrong) and John Driscoll (Bruce Cabot) to New York on Captain Englehorn's ship "Venture." Ann Darrow (Fay Wray) is later kidnapped by Kong. Kong climbs the Empire State building and is shot down by airplanes.

The 1933 movie, from a story by Edgar Wallace and Merian C. Cooper, was directed by Cooper and Ernest B. Schoedsack. The animation of the ape monster was by Willis O'Brien

The monster ape's dimensions were supposedly:

Height, 50 ft.	Nose, 2 ft.
Reach, 75 ft.	Ear, 1 ft. long
Arm, 23 ft.	Eye, 10 in. long
Leg, 15 ft.	Chest, 60 ft.
Face, 7 ft.	Molar, 14 in. round, 4 in. high

King Kong Movies:
King Kong (1933)
Son of Kong (1933)
King Kong vs. Godzilla (1963)
King Kong Escapes (1968)
King Kong (1976)

King Lear's daughters

Goneril, wife of Duke of Albany
Regan, wife of Duke of Cornwall
Cordelia, the youngest daughter, wife of King of France

King Leonardo Lion

King of all Bongo Congo (comic strip). His advisor is Odie Colodie

King Mong Kut

King of Siam in
1946 movie *Anna and the King of Siam*
  (Rex Harrison)
Stage Play *Anna and the King of Siam*
  (Yul Brynner)
1956 movie *The King and I**
  (Yul Brynner)
1972 TV series (short series)

---

*For which Yul Brynner won an Oscar for Best Actor (1956)

Anna and the King
(Yul Brynner)

King Shahdov
Ruler of the Kingdom Estrovia, played by Charlie Chaplin (1957 movie *A King in New York*)

King Sisters
Singers: Donna, Alyce, Louise, Maxine, Yvonne, Marilyn

King Solomon's Ring
Magic ring worn by Solomon that enabled him to understand the animals and gave him power over all things

King Timahoe
President Nixon's Irish setter

King Vultan
Ruler of the Hawkmen who dwell in the Sky City. Played by John Lipson (*Flash Gordon* movie serials)

Kingdoms of Nature
Animal. Vegetable. Mineral. (Generally used as opening question of a Twenty Question game)

Kingfish
George Stevens' title on *Amos 'n' Andy* (he was top man of The Mystic Knights of the Sea Lodge). Radio; Freeman Gosden, TV: Tim Moore. His wife is Sapphire, played on radio and TV by Ernesta Wade. In the 1930 movie *Check and Double Check* the Kingfish played by Russell Power. Nickname of Louisiana governor Huey P. Long

Kingsbury
Television newscaster Howard K. Smith's middle name. He underlines the *K*

Kingston Trio
Group established in 1958. Original members: Bob Shane; Dave Guard (replaced by John Stewart); Nick Reynolds

Kippered Herring
Barrels in which Harpo, Zeppo, Chico and Groucho (left to right) stow away on board ship—they sing *Sweet Adeline* while in the barrels. 1931 movie *Monkey Business*

Kirk Douglas Award
Harvard Lampoon's annual award to the year's worst actor

Kissy Suzuki
Japanese girl who James Bond (Sean Connery), under the guise of Mr. Fisher, marries in 1967 movie *You Only Live Twice*. Kissy, played by Mie Hama (also see Teresa [Tracy] Draco)

Kit Carson Rifle
Trophy awarded to the winner of the annual Arizona va. New Mexico University football game.

Kit Kat Club
1931 Berlin nightclub setting where Sally Bowles (Liza Minnelli) sings (1972 movie *Cabaret*)

Kitten and Tom
President John F. Kennedy's two pet cats

Kitty
Girlfriend (Mae Clarke) who gets half a grapefruit shoved in her face by Tom Powers (James Cagney) (movie *The Public Enemy*, 1931). A grapefruit was once thrown out of an airplane to Brooklyn Dodger manager Wilbert Robinson, who was expecting a baseball. It landed on his head knocking him out

Kitty
The Rubble's pet sabre-tooth tiger (cartoon *The Flintstones*)

Kiwi, The
An 1871 Schooner (TV series "The Wackiest Ship In the Army") commanded by Major Simon Butcher (Jack Warden)

Klaatu
Man (Michael Rennie) who came from outer space with his 8-foot robot, Gort. He traveled 250 million miles in 5 months to arrive on Earth. He is 78 years old. While on Earth he takes up the identity of Mr. Carpenter and boards at a house at 1412 Harvard St., Washington D.C. He was wounded and stayed at the Walter Reed Hospital, Room 309, under Doctor White. (1951 movie *The Day the Earth Stood Still*)

Klaatu Borada Nikto
Words that stop the huge robot Gort from destroying the earth as he has been programmed to do (1951 movie *The Day the Earth Stood Still*): said by Mrs. Helen Benson (Patricia Neal)

Klarion

The Kelly Elementary School's newspaper (comic strip *Miss Peach*)

Klinger

Soldier who wears female clothes in hopes of getting a discharge from the Army. First name, Maxwell: played by Jamie Farr (TV series *"M*A*S*H"*)

Klingons

Enemies of the Federation (TV series *Star Trek*)

Knievel, Robert Craig

Daredevil motorcycle stunt rider, known as Evel Knievel: suffered many crashes and broken bones

Knighthood

Orders (9) of Great Britain (highest to lowest):

Garter (royalty or peerage), KG

Thistle (Scottish nobles), KT

St. Patrick (Irish nobles), KP

Bath (3 classes), GCB, KCB, CB

Star of India (3 classes), GCSI, KCSI, CSI

St. Michael and St. George (3 classes), GCMG, KCMG, CMG

Indian Empire (3 classes), GCIE, KCIE, CIE

Victorian Order (5 classes; open to women)

British Empire (5 classes; open to women)

(Baronets rank just below Knights of the Bath; Knights Bachelor are not members of any order)

On June 11, 1923 Benito Mussolini received The Order of Knight Grand Cross of the Order of the Bath from Britain's King George V. In C.S. Forester's novels Horatio Hornblower became a Knight of the Most Honorable Order of the Bath

Knights of the Round Table

The Round Table was given to Arthur by Leodegraunce, his father-in-law, whose men filled 100 seats; Merlin seated 28 more, Arthur 2, and 20 were left for worthy knights. The Siege Perilous, next to Arthur, was the death of any who sat in it except the Grail Knight.

King Arthur's retainers and hunchmen who sat at a smaller Round Table with him were: Sir Lancelot; Sir Galahad; Sir Gawain; Sir Percivale; Sir Kay; Sir Tor; Sir Gareth; Sir Tristram; Sir Palomides; Sir Lamorack; Sir Modred; Sir Mark; Sir Acolon; Sir Bors; Sir Floll; Sir Lionel

In comics Prince Valiant becomes one of these knights

Knobby Walsh
> Joe Palooka's trainer and manager (comic strip "Joe Palooka"). In a Monogram movie series, played by Leon Erroll and James Gleason. In 1934 movie *Joe Palooka* by Jimmy Durante, on radio by Frank Readick

Knox, William J.
> In 1913 became the first bowler to bowl a 300 game in an A.B.C. Championship contest.

Kojak
> Theo (Theodore) Kojak, New York City detective, (TV series "Kojak"): played by Aristotle "Telly" Savalas. To cut down smoking, he sucks Tootsie Roll pops. Telly Savalas' racehorse is named Telly's Pop

KoKo
> Clown drawn "Out of the Inkwell" (movie cartoons) by Max Fleischer. Debut in 1917 cartoon "Out of the Inkwell" On 1961 TV serial voice of Larry Storch
> Max Fleischer's son Richard was the director of the movies *20,000 Leagues Under the Sea* (1954) and *Dr. Dolittle*

KoKo
> Rex Allen's movie horse.

Kokura
> Japanese City—number two on the priority list to drop the Atomic bomb on August 9, 1945. Because of bad weather the next target Nagasaki was chosen instead

Kolin Kelly
> Owner of brickyard where Ingnatz Mouse gets his bricks to throw at Krazy Kay. (comic strip *Krazy Kat*)

Kollege of Musical Knowledge
> Radio quiz show M.C.'d by Kay Kyser answering correct questions with *"That's wrong, you're right!"* and wrong guesses with *"That's right, you're wrong."*

Kolu
> Jungle Jim's native companion (comics). Kaseem in movies/TV

Kon-Tiki
> Thor Heyerdahl's balsawood raft, sailed from Lima, Peru, to Tuamotu Islands (1947). Title of 1951 documentary movie

Konigin Luise
> German patrol boat pursued by the "African Queen" on the Ulanga River (*The African Queen* by C. S. Forester) In the 1951 movie the boat is called the Louisa

Kookie

Parking lot attendant for Dino's Restaurant (TV series "77 Sunset Strip"): played by Edd Byrnes (Edward Brietenburger). Kookie's full name is Gerald Lloyd Kookson III. He and Connie Stevens had a hit record in 1959 titled *Kookie, Kookie, Lend Me Your Comb*. J. R. Hale (Robert Francis Logan) later replaced Kookie on series

Kor

Kingdom of the 2000 year old African sorceress "She" (Ayesha or "She Who Must Be Obeyed") in H. Rider Haggard's novel *She*. She rules the Amahaggars

Movies:

In 1935 by Helen Gahagan, in 1956 and 1964 sequel by Ursula Andress

Korak

Tarzan and Jane's son in the 1920 movie *The Son of Tarzan*. Played by Gordon Griffith as a boy and by Kamuela Serle as a man—Serle was killed by an elephant named Tantor in filming the movie

Kornfield Kounty

Setting of TV series "Hee Haw"

Krells

Super-intelligent creatures that live below the surface of the planet Altair IV (1956 movie *Forbidden Planet*)

Krepysh

Race horse belonging to Czar Nicholas of Russia, the horse was executed in front of a firing squad

Krypto

Superboy's superdog, "dog of steel"

Krypton

Superman's planet of birth in the city of Kandor (the capital city is Kryptonopolis). The planet blew apart on June 16

Kryptonite

Metal that affects Superman's powers, colors green, blue, red, white and gold, green being the only one to kill Superman

Kukla, Fran, and Ollie

Burr Tillstrom, puppeteer,
Fran, Fran Allison
Announcer: Hugh Downs
Puppets on the TV show: Kukla; Ollie; (Oliver J. Dragon)

Madame Oglepuss; Beulah the Witch; "Dumb" Cecil Bill; Windbag Colonel Crackie; Dolores Dragon; Mercedes; Fletcher Rabbit; Ollie's Niece, Ophelia

Kwai Chang Caine

Chinese-American lad who becomes a Shaolin Priest. Played by Ramdemas Pera as a boy, by Keith Carradine* as a youth; by David Carradine as a man (TV series *Kung Fu*)

---

*Sang and composed the 1975 Academy Award winning song *I'm Easy* from the movie *Nashville*

L

L90
Police unit commanded by Sergeant MacDonald (Mac, played by William Boyett) (TV series "Adam 12") Also uses L20

L. B. J.
Initials common to all members of President Johnson's family:

Lyndon	Baines	Johnson
Lady	Bird	Johnson (Claudia Alta)
Lucy	Baines	Johnson (Nugent)
Lynda	Bird	Johnson (Robb)

L. L.
Most common initials of Superman's friends and arch enemies:

Friends	*Foes*
Lois Lane	Lorraine Lewis
Lana Lang	Lex Luthor
Lori Lemaris	
Lightning Lad	
Luma Lynai	
Linda Lee	

LSD
Lysergic acid diethylamide. First synthesized by Albert Hofman April 7, 1943

L.S./M.F.T.
Lucky Strike/Means Fine Tobacco, (later) Lucky Strike/Means Filter Tips

LZ36

German World War I Zeppelin featured in the 1971 movie *Zeppelin*

La Belle Aurore

Paris saloon where Rick Blaine (Bogart) and Ilse Lund (Bergman) meet for the last time before Casablanca. Sam was pianist there. 1942 movie *Casablanca*

La Cucaracha

(The Cockroach) Theme song of Mexican bandit Doroteo Arango (Francisco "Pancho" Villa)

Lacy Carpet Cleaning

Company that supplied their door as the first stage at the Hollywood Bowl (1919)

La Paloma

Ship that brought the Maltese Falcon from Hong Kong to San Francisco (Dashiell Hammett's *The Maltese Falcon*). The ship burns at its San Francisco pier. In novel arrived 8:25 a.m., in movie 5:35

Ladadog

Nash family dog (TV series "Please Don't Eat the Daises") In 1960 movie the dog is named Hobo

Laddie Boy

President Harding's airedale. Laddie Buck, his half brother was owned by President Coolidge who changed his name to Paul Pry

Ladd-Lake Movies

Films starring Alan Ladd and Veronica Lake:
This Gun for Hire (1942)
The Glass Key (1942)
Star Spangled Rhythm (1942)
Duffy's Tavern (1945)
Variety Girl (1947)
The Blue Dahlia (1946)
Saigon (1948)

Lady Be Good

World War II 9th A.F. 376th Bomb group B24 (tail number 124301) that landed in Libyan Desert after crew bailed out: plane crashed April 4, 1943. First spotted from the air November 9, 1953 by geologist Ronald MacLean. All bodies were found except for gunner Sgt. Vernon L. Moore. The pilot was Lt. William J. Hatton, the plane was enroute from Soluch to Naples

Lady in Black, The
Woman who annually placed flowers (mid 40's*-1954) on the grave of silent movie star Rudolph Valentino. For years she was a mystery—finally identified as Ditra Flame, (Ditra Helena Mefford). She would deliver 13 roses, one dozen red, one white every August 23rd.

Lady with the Lamp
Florence Nightingale (1820-1910), English nurse in Crimean War; first woman to receive Order of Merit (1907)

Lafayette Street
House no. 1381. St. Joseph house address where Thomas Howard (Jesse James) was shot and killed by Robert Ford, April 3, 1882. His rent was $14 a month

Laika
"Barker": first dog to orbit Earth, in Russian Sputnik II, November 1957

Lake of the Woods
Lake between Minnesota and Canada, contains the most northerly point of the 48 contiguous states

Lakeport
Hometown of the Bobbsey Twins (Children's books)

Lakeview
Locale of TV serial "How to Survive a Marriage"

Lambert
The sheepish lion of 1952 Disney cartoon movie

Lamont Cranston
Real identity of The Shadow. But compare *Kent Allard*

Lamont, Texas
Hometown of the Wheeler family (TV series *The Texas Wheelers*

Lampoon
Harvard University's satirical school newspaper

Lampwick
The bad boy who leads Pinocchio astray. Because of his badness he turns into a donkey.

Lana Lang
Superboy's girlfriend when he lived and grew up in Smallville (comic book series "Superboy"). Played by Bunny Henning on TV series *The Adventures of Superboy*. In comics she is also known as Insect Queen

---

*Possibly earlier but not recorded

Lancelot Link

Chimpanzee that belongs to APE (Agency to Prevent Evil) (TV series "Lancelot Link"). CHUMP (Criminal Headquarters for Underworld Master Plan) is the evil organization with which APE is in constant battle. Commander Darwin is the head of APE, Baron Von Butcher of CHUMP

Land of Nod

Country east of Eden where Cain lived after killing Abel

Landon, Michael

Actor (real name, Eugene Orowitz) who was Little Joe in TV series "Bonanza" and Charles Ingalls in "Little House on the Prairie"

In movies, played the Werewolf in 1957 *I Was a Teenage Werewolf* and Dave Dawson, the albino, in 1958 *God's Little Acre*

Lane Sisters

Actresses (real name Mullican): Lola, Rosemary, Priscilla: appeared together (with Gail Page) in *Four Daughters* (1938), *Four Wives* (1940), *Four Mothers* (1941). They sang with Fred Waring's Orchestra

Lange Cup

Trophy awarded for the sport of professional skiing.

Langley, U.S.S.

First United States aircraft carrier, commissioned March 20, 1922 (ex coal carrier "Jupiter", sister ship of the "Collier Cyclops," famous mystery ship lost in the Bermuda Triangle)

Lang Memorial

Hospital that Dr. Marcus Welby (Robert Young) attends (TV series "Marcus Welby, M.D.")

Laramie

Town setting for the TV series *Lawman*

Larsen, Don

New York Yankee pitcher who on October 8, 1956, pitched the only perfect game in World Series history. It was at Yankee Stadium against the Brooklyn Dodgers, not one of whose batters reached first base. Final score: New York 2, Brooklyn 0. Larsen made only 97 pitches and struck out 7, including the last batter, Dale Mitchell, who batted for Larsen's opposing pitcher, Sal Maglie

Laser

Light Amplification by Stimulated Emission of Radiation

Lash La Rue

Movie cowboy Al La Rue who uses a 15-foot bullwhip as his primary weapon. His horse is named Rush

Lassie

Collie first appearing in Eric Knight's novel *Lassie Come Home*. Rudd Weatherwax is her trainer and owner. Played by his dog Pal in 1943 movie *Lassie Come Home*, (the dog lived to be 19 years old). Pal, Jr., played Lassie on the various television series. On radio Lassie's barking was by Earl Keen.

Lassie was eliminated from competing for the PATSY Award as she had already won too many. All the Lassies have been male. First animal named to Animal Hall of Fame (1969)

Last Chance Saloon

Rough bar in the Western town of Bottleneck of which James Stewart plays the sheriff (1939 movie *Destry Rides Again*)

Last of the Red Hot Mamas

Nickname of singer Sophie Tucker (1884-1966). *My Time Is Your Time*, title of autobiograhpy. First woman roasted by the Friars Club

Last Names

Last	First	Series	Actor
Parker	Nakia	Nakia	Robert Forster
Findlay	Maude	Maude	Beatrice Arthur
Morganstern (Gerard)	Rhoda	Rhoda	Valerie Harper
Stiles	Willard	(Movie)	Bruce Davison
Bannon	Hud	(Movie) "Hud"	Paul Newman
McCoy	Shamus	(Movie) Shamus	Burt Reynolds
Lindstrom	Phyllis	Phyllis	Cloris Leachman
DeFazio and Feeney	LaVern and Shirley	LaVerne and Shirley	Penny Marshall and Cindy Williams

Tarleton	Tammy	Tammy	Debbie Watson (TV) Debbie Reynolds (Movie) Sandra Dee (Movie)
Baker	Julia	Julia	Diahann Carroll
Archer	Lew	Archer	Brian Keith
Peterson	Irma	My Friend Irma	Marie Wilson
Collins	Bob	Love That Bob	Bob Cummings

Bob & Carol & Ted & Alice (TV)
  Bob Sanders (Robert Urich)
  Carol Sanders (Anne Archer)
  Ted Henderson (David Spielberg)
  Alice Henderson (Anita Gillette)
Bridget Loves Bernie (TV)
  Bridget Fitzgerald (Meredith Baxter)
  Bernie Steinberg (David Birney)

Last Songs

Songs on the charts at the time of the deaths of the artists who sang them:

I'll Never Get Out of this World Alive—Hank Williams

It Doesn't Matter Anymore—Buddy Holly

Hang Up My Rock and Roll Shoes/What Am I Living For—Chuck Willis

Three Steps to Heaven—Eddie Cochran

Las Vegas Nightclubs

Robbed by Danny Ocean (Frank Sinatra) and his band of eleven hoods:

Sahara, Riviera, Desert Inn, Sands and Flamingo. 1960 movie *Oceans 11*. It was at the Sands where Sinatra married Mia Farrow on July 19, 1966

Latin

Subject taught by Mr. Chips (James Hilton's *Goodbye Mr. Chips*)

Laugh-In

Original cast (1968) included: Dan Rowan, Dick Martin, Judy Carne, Arte Johnson, Jo Anne Worley, Henry Gibson,

Ruth Buzzi, Garry Owens. Goldie Hawn joined in mid-season

Laughing Water
Bride of Hiawatha (*Hiawatha's Wedding Feast* by Henry Wadsworth Longfellow)

Laura Keene
Liberty ship on which Charles *"Lucky"* Luciano was deported from the U.S. to Italy February 10, 1946.

Laurel Records
Record Company for which Vince Everett (Elvis Presley) records (1957 movie *Jailhouse Rock*)

Lawrence
The Hartford Insurance Elk, used as their trademark, appears in their TV commercials. Trained by Steve Martin

Lawrence, D. H.
David Herbert Lawrence (1885-1930), English novelist and poet: *Sons and Lovers* (1913), *Lady Chatterley's Lover* (1928)

Lawrence, (Captain) James
U. S. naval officer who said "Don't give up the ship," when he fell mortally wounded aboard the "Chesapeake" fighting the "Shannon," June 1, 1813

Lawrence of Arabia
Thomas Edward Lawrence (1888-1935), alias T. E. Shaw, alias Aircraftman Ross. English scholar, soldier, diplomat, and secret agent. Autobiography: *Seven Pillars of Wisdom*. Portrayed by Peter O'Toole in 1962 movie *Lawrence of Arabia*

Laws
Murphy's Law: "Whatever can be done wrong, eventually will be (at the worst possible time)"

Parkinson's Law: "Work expands so as to fill the time available for its completion"

Gresham's Law: "Bad money will drive good money out of circulation"

Worth's Law: "When something fails to work and you demonstrate it for a repairman, it works better than ever, as if it never failed to work at all"

Peter Principle: "In a hierarchy, every employee tends to rise to his level of incompetence"

Spinoza's Law: If facts conflict with a theory either the theory must be changed or the facts

Lawton Street School
San Francisco elementary school attended by the 7 children of the school bus hijacked by the killer Scorpio (1971 movie *Dirty Harry*)

Lazarus
The man Jesus Christ raised from the dead. Portrayed by Michael Gwynn in 1962 movie *Barabbas*

Lazarus and Bummer
Emperor Norton's two dogs

Leap Frog
Theme song of Les Brown's orchestra

Leapin' Lizards
Little Orphan Annie's favorite expression

Leatherstocking
Natty Bumppo, hero of novels by James Fenimore Cooper. In the order in which they are supposed to have occurred, they are
The Deerslayer (1841)
The Last of the Mohicans (1826)
The Pathfinder (1840)
The Pioneers (1823)
The Prairie (1827)
Natty Bumppo is also called Deerslayer, Hawkeye, Trapper, and Pathfinder, as well as Leatherstocking

Lear, William
Industrialist-inventor who invented the autopilot, 8-track stereo car tapes, and builder of the Lear Jet

Lee
Charlie Chan's number one son, "Gee Pop". In novels Henry is Charlie Chan's eldest son. First appeared in 1935 movie *Charlie Chan in Paris* played in movies by: Keye Luke, Victor Sen Yung, Benson Fong. On radio: Leon Janney; TV: James Hong

Lee, Bruce
Martial arts champion. Played Kato on TV series *The Green Hornet*. He was the cha-cha champ of Hong Kong in 1958. He died in 1973 at the age of 32. Appeared in numerous Martial Arts movies.

Lee Smith
Name on Bank Americard in the TV commercial with the little man leading an orchestra. No. on the card: 4019 123 456 789.

Leeds, Lila
 Actress in whose home actor Robert Mitchum was arrested for possession of marijuana on August 31, 1948. Her address was 8443 Ridpath Drive, Los Angeles (Laurel Canyon)

Left handed U.S. Presidents
 James A. Garfield, Harry S. Truman, Gerald Ford

Left or Right

Right	Eye over which Edgar Bergen's dummy Charlie McCarthy wears a monocle.
Left	Eye over which Rooster Cogburn (John Wayne) wears an eye patch 1969 movie *True Grit*
Left	Eye over which Richard Widmark wears a patch (1966 movie *Alvarez Kelly*)
Left	Side of face John Boy (Richard Thomas) has a mole (*The Waltons*)
Left	Ear painter Vincent Van Gogh cut off a part of
Right	Actor Jack Elam's wandering eye
Left	Hand replaced by a hook of Captain James Hook (Peter Pan)
Right	Deputy Chester Goode's (Dennis Weaver) stiff leg (TV series *Gunsmoke*)
Left	John J. MacReedy (Spencer Tracy) injured arm which he keeps in his pocket (1954 movie *Bad Day at Black Rock*)
Left	Armstrong's foot that became man's first footprint on the moon
Left	Sammy Davis Jr.'s glass eye
Right	Peter Falk's glass eye
Right	Maxwell Smart's shoe phone
Left	Wiley Post's eye patch
Left	Captain Ahab's peg leg (made of ivory)
Left	Hand in which Charlie Chaplin carried his cane
Right	Dr. Strangelove's crippled hand which makes the Nazi salute
Left	Long John Silver's missing leg
Left	Art Carney's deaf ear on which he wears a hearing aid
Right	Hand on which German women wear their wedding rings
Left	Side of a horse on which a rider mounts
Left	Side of a skirt that the zipper is on

Left   Eye over which Commander Klink wears his
        monocle

Legend of Sleepy Hollow, The
Story by Washington Irving in *The Sketch Book* (*of Geoffrey Crayon*) (1819-20): The headless horseman, said to be the ghost of a Hessian soldier who lost his head by a cannonball in the Revolutionary War, was impersonated by Brom Bones who thus scared schoolmaster Ichabod Crane out of the village and won the hand of Katrina Van Tassel

Legs
Insects, 6 legs; Spider, 8 legs; Octopus, 8 legs; Squid, 10 legs; Lobster, 8 legs

Legs, The
Nickname of actress Betty Grable

Lehigh University
College attended by both Dagwood and Blondie in 1942 movie *Blondie Goes to College*

Lemac
Title conferred upon a contestant that could answer 5 questions in a row correctly, radio's *The Bob Hawk Show*, whose sponsor was Camel cigarettes. Lemac is Camel spelled backwards.

Lemuel Gulliver
Hero of Jonathan Swift's *Gulliver's Travels*, played by Kerwin Mathews in 1960 movie *The Three Worlds of Gulliver*

Lemuel Q Stoopnagle
Col. Stoopnagle of "Col. Stoopnagle and Budd"

Lena the Hyena
Ugliest woman in lower Slobbovia (comic strip series "Li'l Abner")

Lenin, Nikolai
Pseudonym of Vladimir Ilyich Ulyanov (1870-1924), leader (1917) of Bolshevik (Communist) revolution in Russia: also called V. I. Lenin

Leningrad
Formerly St. Petersburg (1703-1914) and Petrograd (1914-1924). Founded by Peter the Great in 1703, it was the Russians capital until after the 1917 Revolution. The first bomb dropped on Leningrad by the Germans in WWII killed the only elephant in the city's zoo

Lennie and George
Characters in John Steinbeck's *Of Mice and Men:* George tells Lennie "all about the rabbits." Lennie Small and George Milton. Played in 1939 movie by Lon Chaney, Jr. and Burgess Meredith

Lennon Sisters
Singers: Diane, Peggy, Janet, Kathy

Lenore
Mandrake the Magician's younger sister.

Lenore Case
"Casey"—Britt Reid's (*Green Hornet*) secretary. Radio: Lee Allman, movie serials: Anne Nagel

Leo
The MGM lion (trademark) portrayed by three lions: Slats, Jackie and Tanner (in color). He first roared July 31, 1928 for debut of movie *White Shadows of the South Seas.* The roar was heard via a phonograph record since it was a silent movie

Leopard Lodge
Fraternal organization. Leopard Lodge #196 to which Mr. Howard Cunningham (Tom Bosley) belongs (TV series *Happy Days*)

Leper Colony
B-17 belonging to the 918th Bomber Group to which the misfits were assigned (1949 movie *Twelve O'Clock High*)

Leper Colony
SAC B-52 that flew beyond the Fail Safe point in novel *Dr. Strangelove.* Movie—Piloted by Major T. E. "King" Kong (Slim Pickens)

Lepidopterist
A collector of butterflies or moths

Leprechaun
Advertises Lucky Charms breakfast cereal. Voice of Arthur Anderson (General Mills TV commercial)

Leroy (Forrester)
Throckmorton P. Gildersleeve's little nephew. On radio (Walter Tetley). TV (Ronald Keith) "Where is that boy?"

Leroy Fedders
Fernwood High School basketball coach who drowned in a bowl of Mary Hartman's chicken soup (helped by Seconals and Jack Daniels) (TV series *Mary Hartman, Mary Hartman*)

Loretta Haggers sang *That Old Black Magic* at his funeral.

Leslie Special

White automobile driven by Leslie Gallant III (Tony Curtis) (movie *The Great Race*) Car #1. Built by the Weber Carriage Co.

Lester

Willie Tyler's dummy (TV's "Laugh-In")

Lester

Family in Erskine Caldwell's *Tobacco Road:* Jeeter Lester is the poor-white father. Dramatized by Jack Kirkland, it ran on Broadway for 3,182 performances (1933-1941). In 1941 movie by Charley Grapewin

Lester Mainwaring

Fictitious name—used as a code at Lincoln Airport—calling security policeman, used over public address system (Arthur Hailey's "Airport")

Let Me Be Your Friend

Theme song of TV series *Doc*

Letterman

Cartoon character who returns words to their original meaning after the villain Spellbinder distorts them.
"Faster than a rolling O. Stronger than silent E, able to leap capital T in a single bound. It's a word, it's a plan, it's Letterman"
PBS television *The Electric Company*

Let's Dance

Theme song of Benny Goodman's orchestra. In 1955 movie *The Benny Goodman Story* he was portrayed by Steve Allen

Levant, U.S.S.

Corvette upon which Philip Nolan died (Edward Everett Hale's "The Man Without A Country")

Lew Archer

109 W8340
Detective in Ross Macdonald's novels
Lew Archer (Lewis A. Archer), born 1913
Previously a Long Beach Policeman
Movie *Harper* starring Paul Newman is from Ross Macdonald's Lew Archer novel *The Moving Accident*
The name was changed because of Newman's luck with movies beginning with an "H"

TV series *Archer* starring Brian Keith lasted 6 episodes was cancelled after 2nd show (1975)

Newman plays Harper in 1975 movie *The Drowning Pool*. All of MacDonald's Archer novels begin title with "The"

1974 TV movie starred Peter Graves "The Underground Man"

Lewis and Clark
Captain Meriwether Lewis and Lieutenant William Clark who led expedition from St. Louis to Pacific Ocean and back (1804-1806). Lewis was first governor of the Lousiana Territory, committed suicide in 1809. Portrayed in 1955 movie *The Far Horizons*, Lewis by Fred Mac-Murray, Clark by Charlton Heston

Lewis, Jerry
American comedian, actor, and director (real name: Joseph Levitch). Since 1951 has raised over $100 million for Muscular Dystrophy

"The _____" character movies: *The Stooge*, 1953; *The Caddy*, 1953; *The Delicate Delinquent*, 1957; *The Sad Sack*, 1958; *The Geisha Boy*, 1958; *The Bellboy*, 1960; *The Errand Boy*, 1961; *The Ladies Man*, 1961; *The Nutty Professor*, 1963; *The Patsy*, 1964; *The Disorderly Orderly*, 1964; *The Big Mouth*, 1967

Lewis's partner until 1956 was Dean Martin. Martin and Lewis hadn't seen each other in 20 years until Frank Sinatra surprised Lewis September 5, 1976 at one of Lewis' telethons in Las Vegas by bringing Martin on stage, thus ending the feud.

Lewis, Shari
Ventriloquist. Her puppets: Lamb Chop, Charlie Horse, Baby, Hush Puppy

Leviathan
World War I U.S. troop carrier converted from Germany's largest passenger ship the *Vaterland*. Humphrey Bogart was assigned to this ship during the war

Lewis, Tommy
Alabama fullback who came off the sideline bench to tackle Dick Moegle of Rice in the 1954 Cotton Bowl. Referee Cliff Shaw gave Rice the touchdown

Lex Luthor
Superman's arch-enemy, one time Superboy's best friend.

In 1950 movie serial *Atom Man vs Superman* played by Lyle Talbot (Talbot's real name is Lyle Hollywood)

Lexington
George Washington's saddle horse

Lexington, U.S.S.
Carrier lost in the Battle of the Coral Sea (May 1942) Admiral Frederick Sherman's black cocker spaniel Admiral Wags was on board. Both were saved.

Liberal Arts
Trivium: Grammar, Logic, Rhetoric
Quadrivium: Arithmetic, Geometry, Astronomy, Music

Liberty
President Gerald Ford's golden retriever dog

Liberty
John Hancock's schooner

Liberty Bell
Cracked when it was first rung for the death march of Chief Justice John Marshal. July 8, 1835. On the bell *Pennsylvania* is misspelled

Liberty, Intelligence, Our Nation's Safety
Motto of the Lions Club

Liberty Island
Location of the Statue of Liberty in New York harbor (formerly Bedloe's Island). Named Liberty Island July 23, 1956

Liberty Lake
Large lake at the 1939 New York World's Fair

Liberty Magazine
Founded in 1924. Gave reading time for all articles

Liberty, U.S.S.
United States ship attacked near Sinai Peninsula by Israeli planes and PT boats during Six Day War (June 8, 1967): 34 killed, 75 wounded

Liddell, Alice
Ten year old girl that was Lewis Carroll's inspiration for Alice in *Alice's Adventure's in Wonderland* and *Through the Looking Glass*

Lido, The
Joseph Valachi's Greenwich Village Nightclub. (He was portrayed by Charles Bronson in 1972 movie *The Valachi Papers*)

Lieutenant Abrams
San Francisco Police detective friend of Mr. Nick and

Nora Charles (*The Thin Man* movie series) played by Sam Levene

Lieutenant Ben Guthrie
San Francisco police officer (inspector) in radio series/TV series and 1958 movie *The Line Up*. Played by Bill Johnstone on radio, by Warner Anderson on TV and in the movie

Lieutenant Colonel
Permanent rank held by George Armstrong Custer when killed at the Little Big Horn (1876)

Lieutenant Colonel Henry Braymore Blake
Commander of the 4077th *MASH* unit, until discharged in 1952, after which he was shot down and killed in an airplane (played by McLean Stevenson) TV series "M*A*S*H"

Lt. Colonel L. Nicholson
(Played by Alec Guinness) Commander of the captured British soldiers who built the bridge over the River Kwai for their Japanese captors, Feb.-May 1943. Guinness won an Oscar for Best Actor (1957), the movie won the Academy Award for Best Film 1957. (1957 movie *Bridge On the River Kwai*)

Lieutenant Commander Montgomery Scott "Scotty"
Chief Engineer aboard the starship U.S.S. Enterprise. His service number is SE-197-514. Played on TV series *Star Trek* by James Doohan

Lieutenant Elroy Carpenter
Captain Binghamton's assistant, played by Bob Hastings, TV series *McHale's Navy*

Lieutenant Flap
Black lieutenant (cartoon series "Beetle Bailey")

Lieutenant (Sonny) Fuzz
Young lieutenant (cartoon series "Beetle Bailey")

Lieutenant George Kirby
New York detective played by George Raft on 1953 TV series *I'm the Law*.

Lieutenant (Dan) "Hondo" Harrelson
Head of the Olympic S.W.A.T. Unit (Steve Forrest)* TV series S.W.A.T

Lieutenant Jacoby
Peter Gunn's police friend (assigned to 13th precinct (on

---

*Younger brother of Dana Andrews

TV played by Herschel Bernardi). In 1967 movie *Gunn* by Edward Asner

Lieutenant (Walt) Levinson
5th Precince police acquaintance of private detective Richard Diamond (on radio played by Ed Begley)

Lieutenant Manuel "Manny" Quinn
San Diego policeman (Henry Darrow). Friend of Harry (David Janssen). TV series "Harry O"

Lieutenant Matt Reardon
Police officer (Charles Cioffi) who is officer Christie Love's (Teresa Graves) supervisor (TV series *Get Christie Love*)

Lieutenant Quint
Los Angeles City Police Officer (Clifton James) at wits with Detective Jake Axminster (Wayne Rogers) TV series *City of Angels*

Lieutenant Pinkerton
Madame Butterfly's lover, an American Navy officer (opera by Giacomo Puccini, 1904-1905). In 1932 movie *Madame Butterfly* by Cary Grant

Lieutenant Rip Masters
Commander of Fort Apache played by Jim Brown (TV series *Rin-Tin-Tin*)

Lieutenant (Edward) Ryker
Police officer who keeps his eye on his junior police officers Terry, Mike and Chris (TV series *The Rookies*) played by Gerald S. O'Loughlin

Lieutenant (K.C.) Trench
Private detective Harry Orwell's Santa Monica police acquaintance (Anthony Zerbe) TV series *Harry O*

Lieutenant Uhura
Communications Officer on board the *Starship Enterprise*. Played by Nichelle Nichols. In Swahili Uhura means freedom

Lieutenant Val Wangsgard
Police officer who broke in Pete Malloy when he was a rookie (TV series *Adam-12*)

Life Savers candy
Order of colors in five-flavor roll: Yellow, Red, Orange, Green, White, Red, Yellow, Green, White, Red, Orange. Company that sponsored the 250 foot parachute jump in 1939 New York World's Fair

Light Horse Harry
General Richard Henry Lee (1756-1818). American cavalry officer in the Revolutionary War, father of General Robert E. Lee

Lightnin'
Janitor Willie Jefferson of Amos 'n' Andy's Mystic Knights of the Sea Lodge
Radio: Freeman Gosden
TV: Nick O' Demus

Lightning Lad
Native of the planet Winath (true name: Garth Ranzz) he creates lightning in fight against evil: charter member of the Legion of Super-Heroes (comic books)

Li'l Abner
Hero of comic strip by Al Capp, begun August 12, 1935. He and his father and mother, Pappy and Mammy Yokum, live in Dogpatch, somewhere in the Appalachian mountains. Li'l Abner marries Daisy Mae Scraggs. Abner is 19 years old. Li'l Abner was played in the movies by Buster Keaton (1940: *Li'l Abner or Trouble Chaser*), in 1959 musical film by Peter Palmer, who also played the part in the New York stage musical, and on radio by John Hodiak

Lil' Bad Wolf
Son of the Big Bad Wolf, (Ezekiel "Zeke"), he is the friend of the *Three Little Pigs* (comic books)

Li'l Folks
Comic strip about children drawn by "Sparky" (Charles Schulz). This strip came just before Schulz's *Peanut* strip (1947-1949)

Lilliput
Land of the small people (Swift's *Gulliver's Travels*) (see Blefuscu)

Linc Case
One of the automobilists in TV's "Route 66" (replaced by Buz Murdock): played by Glenn Corbett

Lincoln Highway
First coast-to-coast paved road in the United States (New York to California), opened in 1913

Lincoln International
Fictitious Chicago Airport of Arthur Hailey's *Airport*

Lincoln Island

Name of "The Mysterious Island" in the novel (1870) by Jules Verne.

Lincoln Memorial

Classical building (architect Henry Bacon, 1922) west of The Mall, Washington, D.C., with monumental statue of seated Lincoln by Daniel Chester French: first appeared on reverse of Lincoln penny in 1959

Lincoln, Robert Todd

Eldest son of Abraham Lincoln. He was present immediately after his father was assassinated (1865), also after Garfield's assassination in 1881 and also when McKinley was shot to death in 1901.

Lindbergh, Charles

Made solo flight, May 20-21, 1927, in Ryan monoplane, "The Spirit of St. Louis," from Roosevelt Field. Long Island, New York, to Le Bourget Air Field, Paris, France, 33 hours, 30 minutes. Left New York 7:52 a.m., arrived Paris 5:24 p.m. (N.Y. time). Nicknamed Slim, Lucky Lindy. The dance Lindy Hop named in his honor. Awarded Medal of Honor; won the 1954 Pulitzer Prize for autobiography *The Spirit of Saint Louis*

Portrayed in 1957 movie *The Spirit of Saint Louis* by Jimmy Stewart

Lipton Tea Girl, The

Mary (radio commercials)

Lisa Marie

Elvis Presley's custom Convair 880 jet (cost $1.2 million) named for his daughter

Little Annie Fanny

Very sexy heroine appearing in comic strip adventure, debut October 1962 appearing in Playboy Magazine. Created by Harvey Kurtzman and Will Elder. Sugardaddy Bigbucks is her adopted daddy. Solly Brass is her agent, Wanda Homefree is her girlfriend.

Little Annie Rooney

Cartoon strip by Brandon Walsh debut January 10, 1929. Played by Mary Pickford in 1925. She's 12 years old. Her dog is Zero

Little Audrey

Playful little girl, whose boyfriend is Melvin (Little Audrey in Harvey Comic books). In cartoons voice of Mae Questel

Paramount Pictures Cartoon character
Debut: *The Lost Dream* (1949)

Little Beaver
Navajo Indian sidekick of Red Ryder. His father is Chief Beaver. Played on radio by Tommy Cook and Henry Blair. In movies by Tommy Cook, Bobby Blake and Don Kay Reynolds. On TV by Lovis Letteri

Little Bend, Texas
Home town of the Maverick Brothers (TV series *Maverick*)

Little Black Sambo
Black Jumbo was his father, Black Mumbo his mother

Little Boy
Code name for the 10,000 lb. atomic bomb (uranium 235) dropped on Hiroshima. Originally named the Thin Man after F.D.R.

Little Boys
Made of "frogs and snails and puppy dog tails"

Little Brown Jug
Trophy awarded to the winner of the annual Minnesota-Michigan football game

Little Caesar
Caesar Enrico Bandello, central Chicago gangster role (1930 movie *Little Caesar*): played by Edward G. Robinson

Little Church of the Flower
Hollywood church from where Father Divine broadcast, also where a number of celebrities were married including Lew Ayres to Ginger Rogers

Little Corporal
Nickname of Napoleon Bonaparte, who was 5 ft. 6 in. tall
Movie portrayals:
    Desiree (1954) Marlon Brando
    The Story of Mankind (1955) Dennis Hopper
    Waterloo (1971) Rod Steiger

Little Egypt
Pseudonym of Catherine Devine, who danced at the Chicago World's Fair in 1893. Portrayed in 1936 movie *The Great Ziegfeld* by Miss Morocco

Littlefeather, Sacheen
Woman (real name Maria Cruz) who announced at the 1972 Academy Awards that Marlon Brando would not

accept his Oscar for the Best Actor Award for his role in *The Godfather*. She had previously won an MGM Miss Vampire Contest for the movie *House of Dark Shadows*

Little girls
Made of "sugar and spice and everything nice"

Little Green Sprout
The Jolly Green Giant's little helper (advertisement)

Little Jinx
Mischievous little girl who is forever tormenting her father. Greg is her boyfriend (Archie comics)

Little John
One of Robin Hood's men, (John Little) belonging to his Band of Merry Men. Played in 1922 silent film *Robin Hood* by Alan Hale. Played in 1946 movie *The Bandit of Sherwood Forest* by Ray Teal. Played in 1938 movie *The Adventures of Robin Hood* by Alan Hale. Played in 1950 movie *Rogues of Sherwood Forest* by Alan Hale

Little League World Series
Played at the home of Little League baseball, Williamsport, Pa. Founded in 1939. Taiwan was the winningest country (5 times) until banned

Little Lord Fauntleroy
Character from the story by Frances Hodgson Burnett. Heir to the Earl of Dorincourt. Played in 1936 movie by Freddie Bartholomew. Played in 1921 movie by Mary Pickford

Little Lulu
Girlfriend of Tubby, her father is George G. Moppet (comic strip *Little Lulu*) her friends are Iggy and Annie Magee, Kathy Crowe, Gloria Darling, Alvin Jones

Little Mermaid, The
Statue by Edward Ericksen at the water's edge in Copenhagen Harbor, depicting the heroine of one of Hans Christian Andersen's stories

Little Nellie
James Bond's autogiro equipped with weapons. (1967 movie *You Only Live Twice*)

Little Nemo
Small King who spends a great amount of his time in Slumberland. Created by Winsor McKay (comic strip)

Little Old Winemaker
Italian Swiss Colony character who was featured on TV

commercials. Played by Ludwig Stossel, voice of Jim
Backus. Title of Dean Martin hit song

Little Orphan Annie
Ageless, pupilless little girl created by Harold Gray, debut
in New York Daily News, August 5, 1924. Her dog is
named Sandy. Her adopted parents were Mr. and Mrs.
Silo. On radio Orphan Annie was played by Shirley Bell
and Janice Gilbert. Played in 1932 movie by Mitzi Green

Little People
Little armless/legless wooden dolls of Fisher-Price toys:
Patty, Daddy, Mommy, Pee Wee, Butch, Penny, Fido
(the dog)

Little Rascals, The
Named "Our Gang" after MGM bought the rights from
Hal Roach in 1938

Little Red-haired Girl
Girl Charlie Brown is in love with (Charles "Sparky"
Schulz says that he will never draw her)

Little Richard
Pseudonym of rock 'n' roll singer Richard Penniman,
born December 25, 1935

Little Theater off Times Square
Fictitious setting for the radio series *First Nighter*

Littleton, U.S.A.
Fictitious setting of stories on radio soap opera *Aunt
Jenny*

Little Tough Guys
Group formed from Dead End Kids to work at Universal.
It included Huntz Hall, Gabriel Dell, Billy Halop, and
Bernard Punsley

Little Tramp, The
A nickname of Charles Chaplin. Chaplin's 1964 autobiography *My Autobiography*

Little Tyke
Big Spike's son (bulldogs) comic books

Littleville
Tailspin Tommy's hometown—Three Point Airport is
where he learned to fly

Little White Dove
Running Bear's little Indian maiden (song "Running
Bear" by Johnny Preston) Song written by J. P. Richardson (The Big Bopper) whose voice is in the background
as one of the whooping Indians

Little Wise Guys
Crime-fighting kids: Meatball, Scarecrow, Pee Wee, Jock (comic book series): their mentor is Daredevil

Lizard, The
Secret identity of Dr. Curtis Connors, arch-enemy of Spiderman (comic books)

Liz Cooper
Wife of George Cooper, radio series *My Favorite Husband* starring Lucille Ball and Richard Denning

Lizzy
Douglas "Wrong Way" Corrigan's airplane: also known as "The Flying Crate" NX9243, 9 year old Curtis Robin. Corrigan helped build Lindbergh's *Spirit of St. Louis* in San Diego. He pulled the chalks from the plane's wheels on Lindbergh's first test flight. He received his nickname in an incident when he crossed the Atlantic intentionally, landing in Ireland on July 18, 1938. He claimed he flew the wrong way because he was never given approval for the flight. His destination was supposedly San Diego

Llanview
Locale of TV serial "One Life to Live." The Banner is the town newspaper

Llanwelly
Welsh village where Sir John Talbot (Claude Rains) and his son Larry, who is in reality *The Wolf Man*, (played by Lon Chaney Jr.) live in their castle. 1941 movie *The Wolf Man*

Llewellyn
John L. Lewis' middle name

Lobo
The trained dog with Horace Heidt's band

Lobo
Call sign of Army patrol in Norman Mailer's *The Naked and the Dead* (1958 movie)

Lockard, Joe
The radar operator at Pearl Harbor who spotted the approaching Japanese planes but was told to ignore it, December 7, 1941. Lt. Kermit Tyler told Lockard "Well, don't worry about it"

Lockheed XF90
Plane flown by the Blackhawks, after they flew the Grumman F5F (comic book series "Blackhawk")

Lockspur High School
Where Andrea Thomas (*Secret Identity of Isis*) teaches. TV series *Isis* starring JoAnna Cameron

Loco
Horse ridden by Pancho (Cisco Kid's partner)

Loew's Grand Theater
Atlanta, Georgia movie house where *Gone With the Wind* premiered December 15, 1939.

Loki
Thor's brother and arch-enemy (comic books)

Lois Lane
Superman's girlfriend who works as a reporter for the "Daily Planet" Debut Action Comics #1 (June 1938)
Radio: Joan Alexander, Movies: Noel Neill, TV: Noel Neill, Phyllis Coates. TV Animated series: voice of Joan Alexander. Her sister Lucy is Jimmy Olsen's girlfriend

Lollipops
Tootsie Roll pops, substitute for cigarettes adopted by Lt. Kojak (Telly Savalas) (TV series *Kojak*). When he does smoke it is usually Sherman cigarettes

Lombard, Carole
Real name Jane Alice Peters. Married to William Powell (1931-1933). Married to Clark Gable (1939-1942). "The first woman to be killed in action in the defense of her country in its war against the Axis power"—Inscription upon medal awarded posthumously to Carole Lombard by the President of the United States. She was killed in a TWA DC-3 while on a government bond drive January 16, 1942, the plane hit Table Mountain near Las Vegas. At the time of her death, Gable was filming *Somewhere I'll Find You*. In January, 1944, Irene Dunne broke a bottle of champagne across the bow of the Liberty Ship S.S. Carole Lombard. TV host Mike Douglas was later assigned to this vessel while in the Navy. Portrayed in the 1976 movie *Gable and Lombard* by Jill Clayburgh

Lombardi Trophy
Given to the winning team of the Super Bowl

Lombard Street
San Francisco, California street called the most crooked street in the world (turns 8 times within one block)

Lombardo brothers
Guy (Gaetano) (leader of the "Royal Canadians," who play "the sweetest music this side of heaven"): Carmen

(whose flute training gave his saxophone playing a distinctive sound); Lebert (trumpet), Victor (saxophone) Their sister Rose Marie sang with the orchestra

Lon, Alice

Lawrence Welk's Champagne Lady (TV). Lois Best was the first official Lady

London Bridge

Re-erected at Lake Havasu City, Arizona (bought in 1969)

Londonderry Air

Tune to which the words of "Danny Boy" are sung. Theme song of radio series *The O'Neills*

Lone Eagle, The

Nickname of Charles Lindbergh

Lone Ranger

Secret identity of Texas Ranger John Reid (born 1850) Created by Fran Striker and George W. Trendle. Debut WXYZ Detroit radio January 30, 1933. Narrated by Fred Foy

His horse is named Silver

His sidekick is an Indian named Tonto, whose horse is named Scout (or earlier, White Feller or Paint)

Radio, played by George Seaton (Stennius), Jack Deeds, Earle Graser, Brace Beemer. (Jim Jewell, the program director played him a few times)

Movies serials played by Robert Livingston, Lee Powell

TV, played by Clayton Moore, John Hart. Debut ABC-TV September 15, 1949

Movies: Clayton Moore

On Stage: Earle Graser

Comic strip begun in 1938 by Fran Striker, Artist: Ed Kressley

TV cartoon series (1966) voice of Michael Rye

1938 novel by Fran Striker *The Masked Rider of the Plains*

George Seaton, the original Lone Ranger later became a screen writer, director and producer. He directed the movies *Miracle on 34th Street* and *Airport*

Origin:

While out riding with his brother Captain Dan Reid and four other Texas Rangers, The Six Rangers were all ambushed by Butch Cavendish and his Hole-in-the-Wall gang at Bryant's Gap. The sole survivor was John Reid, who with the help of an Indian named Tonto was brought back to life. His mask was made from his dead brother's vest. When Reid asked Tonto if his brother was still alive Tonto replied that all the others were dead and that he was the Lone Ranger now.

The radio program to which the Rosenberg family was listening to when arrested by the F.B.I.

In 1933 movie serial *The Lone Ranger* the Lone Ranger's name was Allen King (Lee Powell). In 1944 movie serial *The Lone Ranger Rides Again* his name is Bill Andrews (Bob Livingston). On TV he wore blue shirt and pants, red kerchief, black mask and white hat

Lonesome Luke

Character played by Harold Lloyd in a number of silent movies

Lone Wolf, The

Nickname of Michael Lanyard created by Louis J. Vance
Movies:

H. B. Warner (silents), Jack Holt (silents), Bert Lytell (silents), Warren William (8), Gerald Mohr (3), Ron Randall (1), Francis Lederer (1), Melvyn Douglas (1)
TV: Louis Hayward

Lonesome George

Nickname adopted by George Gobel (TV)

Long Branch

Dodge City saloon owned by Miss Kitty Russell (Amanda Blake) (TV series "Gunsmoke") located on Front Street

Long Count, The

Occurred in the Jack Dempsey-Gene Tunney heavyweight championship fight, Sep. 22, 1927, at Soldier Field, Chicago. Tunney, on the canvas for thirteen seconds in the seventh round, went on to win the 10-round decision (Referee Dave Barry began counting only when Dempsey had gone to a neutral corner, as the rules required). That very afternoon Babe Ruth hit his 56th home run of the season to tie his previous record (He would hit 60 that year). Also that afternoon Lou Gehrig broke Ruth's record of 170 rbi's by driving in two runs giving Gehrig 172

Longhorn Ranch

Mrs. Kate Andersen's (Diana Douglas) ranch, in Spanish Wells, N.M. where the young cowboys lived. (TV series *The Cowboys*)

Long John Silver
Peg-legged pirate, right leg only (Robert Louis Stevenson's *Treasure Island*): formerly Captain Flint's quartermaster
Movies
  1934-Wallace Berry
  1950-Robert Newton
  1954-Robert Newton (*Long John Silver*)
  1972-Orson Welles (*Long John Silver*)
  TV-Robert Newton

Long Tom
Captain Hook's ship's cannon (James M. Barrie's *Peter Pan*)

Looks, The
Nickname of actress Lauren Bacall

Looney Tunes
Cartoon series by Warner Brothers (together with "Merrie Melodies"): "That's All, Folks"

Lord Greystoke
John Clayton, title of both Tarzan and his father. Name Marlon Brando signs on hotel registers

Lord Haw-Haw
Nickname of William Joyce (1906-1946) Irish-American who broadcast for Germans during World War II: he was tried, convicted of treason, and hanged

Lord Henry Brinthrope
England's richest and most handsome lord who married an orphan girl named Sunday. Radio series *Our Gal Sunday* (see Silver Creek)

Lord Nelson
The Martin family's dog (TV series *The Doris Day Show*)

Lord of San Simeon
William Randolph Hearst (1863-1951). California newspaper publisher who built palace-like estate at San Simeon

Lord of the Rings Trilogy
(LOTR) Written by J. R. R. Tolkein (John Ronald Reuel)
  Part I   *Fellowship of the Ring* (1954)
  Part II   *The Two Towers* (1954)
  Part III *The Return of the King* (1955)
The trilogy contains approximately ½ million words

Lordsburg
 Destination after leaving Tonto of the Overland Stage in John Ford's 1939 movie *Stagecoach*. In 1966 version Dryfork to Cheyenne

Lorelei Kilbourne
 Steve Wilson's society editor and girlfriend (radio TV series "Big Town"): played on radio by Claire Trevor, Ona Munson, and Fran Carlon

Los Angeles
 (ZR-3) German built American dirigible launched October 15, 1924, decommissioned in 1932 at Lakehurst, New Jersey.

Los Angeles, U.S.S.
 Nuclear submarine that President Carter rode on May 27, 1977.

Los Angeles Star
 Newspaper with headline "KILLER KNOWN" in the 1941 movie *High Sierra*.

Los Angeles Sun
 Newspaper for which Tim O'Hara (Bill Bixby) works (TV series *My Favorite Martian*)

Lost Boys
 Orphaned boys of Never-Never Land in *Peter Pan*
 Tootles, Nibs, and The Twins
 James M. Barrie's *Peter Pan*

Lost Horizon
 Novel (1933) by James Hilton: the first paperback book issued by Pocket Books (1939), cost 25¢. 1937 and 1973 movies

Lothar
 Mandrake the Magician's giant partner (comics) Radio: Juano Hernandez
 1939 Movie serial: Al Kikume
 TV: Woody Strode (former Rams football player)

Lou Wickersham
 Mannix's former boss at Intertect (TV series "Mannix"): played by Joseph Campanella

Louie
 Ed Brown's (Jack Albertson) garbageman (Scatman Crothers)
 TV series *Chico and the Man*

Louie's Sweet Shop
 Bowery Boys' hangout run by Louis Xavier Dumbrowsky

(played by Bernard Gorcey, Leo Gorcey's father). Louie's wife is Sarah (Jody Gilbert). Bernard Gorcey played the original role of Isaac Cohen in the play *Abie's Irish Rose*

Louis XIV candelabra (or candelabrum)

Liberace's constant companion (placed on his piano)

Louisiana, U.S.S.

Ship upon which Theodore Roosevelt sailed to Panama and Puerto Rico making him the first U.S. President to visit a foreign country while in office

Louisville Lip

Nickname of boxer Cassius Clay (Muhammad Ali), noted for his volubility "float like a butterfly—sting like a bee"

LOVE AND HATE

Words tattooed on the knuckles of fanatic preacher Harry Powell (Robert Mitchum). *Love* is on his right hand, *Hate* is on his left. 1955 movie *Night of the Hunter* (Only movie directed by Charles Laughton)

Love for Three Oranges

March from score by Prokofiev, theme song of radio series *The FBI in Peace and War*

Love in Bloom

Jack Benny's theme song: originally sung by Bing Crosby in *She Loves Me Not* (1934)

"Love is never having to say you're sorry"

Line said by Jenny Cavilleri (Ali McGraw) to Oliver Barrett IV (Ryan O'Neal) in movie *Love Story*. Line was again used by Judy Maxwell (Barbara Streisand) to Howard Bannister (Ryan O'Neal) in movie *Whats Up Doc* (he remarks *"That's the dumbest thing I've ever heard"*)

Love Nest

Theme song of George Burns and Gracie Allen. George Burns became the oldest winner of an Oscar for his best support role in 1975 movie *The Sunshine Boys*. His autobiography is titled *Living It Up* (or: *They Still Love Me In Altoona*)

Love Nest

Theme song of radio series *Ethel and Albert*

Love Story

Novel (1970) by Erich Segal (when the movie made from it was shown on TV, nearly 72 million people watched, the largest audience ever for one TV show till that time)

Lovelace, Linda
Female star of X-rated movie *Deep Throat*

Low, Juliette Gordon
Founded the Girl Scouts (originally Girl Guides) in the United States, March 12, 1912

Loweezy
Snuffy Smith's wife (comic strip *Barney Google*)

Loyal Order of Benevolent Zebras
Fraternal organization of which Mel Blanc was a member on radio's *The Mel Blanc Show*. The secret password was *Ugga ugga boo—Ugga boo boo ugga*

Lubanski, Ed
Bowled two consecutive 300-point games at Miami's Bowling Palace, June 22, 1959

Luce, Henry Robinson
American publisher (1898-1967), founder of *Time* (1923), *Fortune* (1930), and *Life* (1936) magazines

Lucifer
Cinderella's stepmother's cat (Disney cartoon movie)

Lucifer Ornamental Yokum
Pappy Yokum's full name (comic strip *Li'l Abner*)

Lucille
B. B. King's (Riley B. King) red electric Gibson guitar (B.B. = Blues Boy)

Lucille McGillicuddy
Lucy Ricardo's maiden name (TV series "I Love Lucy")

Lucky
The *National Enquirer's* dog

Lucky Charms
Breakfast cereal that comes in the shapes of:
Hearts, Moons, Stars, Clovers, Diamonds

Lucky Day
Theme song of radio/television program *Your Hit Parade*

Lucky Lady II
First round-the-world nonstop airplane flight (1949): B-50 Superfortress (refueled four times)

Lucky Linda
Triple A Airline's sole airplane, piloted by Timothy "Spud" Barrett (Tim Conway) TV series *The Tim Conway Show*

Lucky Pup
  The puppet show (puppeteers: Hope and Morey Bunin)
  Featured puppets: Lucky Pup, Pinhead, Foodini
Lucky Smith
  Detective in series on radio: played by former heavy-
  weight champion Max Baer
Lucky Liz
  Lockheed Lodestar aircraft that exploded in midair
  March 22, 1958 killing movie producer Mike Todd and 3
  other passengers, thus leaving Elizabeth Taylor a widow.
  The other 3 men aboard were Art Cohn, pilot Bill Jenner
  and co-pilot Tom Barclay
Lucy
  Guitar of Albert King (blues singer)
Lucy
  Goose (Walt Disney's cartoon movie feature *101 Dal-
  matians*)
Lucy
  Elephant led to safety across the Alps to Switzerland by a
  British soldier (movie 1969 *Hannibal Brooks*)
Lucy Lane
  Lois Lane's younger sister (comic books)
Ludwig Von Fossil
  Nutty Scientist played on TV's Texaco Star Theater by
  Milton Berle
Luke
  Roscoe "Fatty" Arbuckle's dog, who appeared with him
  in a number of Mack Sennett comedies
Luke the Drifter
  Nickname of country singer Hiram "Hank" Williams
Lulu
  Cartoon elephant that you are asked to draw for Art In-
  struction School, Inc. (Magazine Ads)
Lulubelle
  Sergeant Joe Gunn's (Humphrey Bogart) M-3 Army
  tank, serial number W-304512 (1943 movie *Sahara*)
Lulubelle
  Bongo the Bear's girlfriend (see Bongo)
Lumpjay
  Bear in Walt Disney's 1946 movie *Song of the South*
Lunar Schooner
  Space Mouse's rocket ship. Mice live on the planet

Rhodentia while cats live on the planet *Felina* (cartoon comics)

Luno

Winged stallion of Mighty Mouse cartoons (comic book TV series)

Lupus, Peter

Actor who played Willie Armitage in TV series "Mission Impossible". He was winner of titles Mr. Indianapolis, Mr. Indiana, Mr. Hercules, Mr. International Health. He appeared on the cover of the record album *Muscle Beach Party* holding Annette on his shoulders

Lurch

Butler of the Addams family (TV series "The Addams Family"): played by Ted Cassidy "You rang?"

Lusitania

Cunard liner, torpedoed and sunk May 7, 1915 by U20 submarine off Old Head of Kinsale, Ireland, in a voyage from New York. Some 1,198 lives were lost. Her call letters were MSU. Alfred Vanderbilt and novelist Justus Forman perished

Lycanthropy

Ability to change form, from that of a human to that of a wolf (Werewolf)

Lydia, H.M.S.

Captain Horatio Hornblower's 36 gun frigate (C.S. Forester's novel series) After the Lydia he received command of the 74 gun H.M.S. Sutherland (formerly the Dutch Eendract)

Lydia the Tattooed Lady

Favorite song sung by Groucho Marx, first sung in the 1939 movie *At the Circus*

Lynch, Charles

Commanded Virginia volunteer regiment during the Revolutionary War. Head of court to punish lawbreakers, hence Lynch's Law (to hang)

Lynn, Loretta

Very popular Country and Western singer, was married at age 15 and a grandmother at 29. Her musical and written autobiography is *Coal Miner's Daughter*. Her sister is singer Crystal Gayle

M

M

Admiral Sir Miles Messervy, K.C.M.G., James Bond's supervisor in His Majesty's Secret Service. Played in movies by Bernard Lee

M

Author of the best-selling book *The Sensuous Man*

M2-F3

NASA experimental aircraft in which Colonel Steve Austin (Lee Majors) crashed at Edwards A.F.B. (TV series "The Six Million Dollar Man")

MA 5-1190

(Madison-exchange) Perry Mason's (Raymond Burr) phone number at his office (TV series)

M*A*S*H

Mobile Army Surgical Hospital: title of 1970 movie starring Donald Sutherland, Elliott Gould, and Sally Kellerman, and subject of 1952 *Battle Circus* starring Humphrey Bogart and June Allyson

The TV series features Alan Alda

MBE

Medal awarded to the rock group *The Beatles* by Queen Elizabeth June 12, 1965. (Members of the Order of the British Empire)

M D Twins

Cute girls on packages of MD Tissues. Their names are Maisy and Daisy

M G

Morris Garage. British maker of automobiles.

M-G-M

Metro-Goldwyn-Mayer: Metro being Marcus Loew's early film company; Goldwyn being Samuel Goldwyn; Mayer being Louis B. Mayer

M-G-M's lion is called Leo

The company motto, *Ars Gratia Artis* ("Art for Art's Sake"), appears in the circular band framing the lion's head

MGP-1A

Spaceship piloted by an astronaut (Paul Mantee) which lands on Mars (1964 movie *Robinson Crusoe on Mars*)

M & M Enterprises

Business headed by Lt. Milo Minderbinder (M&M) (Jon Voight) throughout the European Theatre during World War II (1970 movie/novel *Catch-22*)

MV

Secret identification signal of the French fleet, discovered and used by Captain Horatio Hornblower (1951 movie *Captain Horatio Hornblower* starring Gregory Peck)

Ma Barker

Kate Barker, born (1872) Arizona Donnie Clark in Springfield, Mo.; she married George Barker, who died in 1932; an outlaw, she was reputed head of gang which included her boys (sons) Arthur, Fred, Herman, Lloyd. Arthur was killed trying to escape from Alcatraz, Fred was slain with his mother in an FBI shootout in Florida in 1935, Herman committed suicide, and Lloyd was killed by his wife: In the 1970 movie *Bloody Mama* Kate was portrayed by Shelley Winters

Ma and Pa Kettle

Movie series in which principal roles were played by Marjorie Main and Percy Kilbride as a pair of rustics

Originally in *The Egg and I*, 1947 (in which Marilyn Monroe made her screen debut as an extra)

Ma and Pa Kettle, 1949

Ma and Pa Kettle Go to Town, 1950

Ma and Pa Kettle at the Fair, 1952

Ma and Pa Kettle Go on Vacation, 1953

Ma and Pa Kettle Back on the Farm, 1954

Ma and Pa Kettle at Home, 1954

Ma and Pa Kettle at Waikiki, 1955

The Kettles in the Ozarks, 1956 (Pa did not appear)

The Kettles on Old MacDonald's Farm (Parker Fennelly as Pa), 1957

13 children, Tom, the oldest, played by Richard Long

Ma Perkins

Ran a lumberyard in Rushville Center (radio series, 1933-1960)

Daughters: Fay, Evey, Radio: Virginia Payne. Her husband John played by Gilbert Faust

Mabel

Rocky King's (Roscoe Karns) wife whom viewers never saw (TV series *Rocky King, Detective*)

Mac

The 97-pound weakling who gets sand kicked in his face prior to taking the Charles Atlas course in physique-building

Macaroni

Caroline Kennedy's pony. Also name Yankee Doodle gave to his feather after he stuck it in his hat. John-John's pony was named Leprechaun

MacDonald

Matt Helm's boss

McDonalds

Hamburger chain originally begun in 1948 in San Bernadino by Maurice "Mac" and Richard (brother) McDonald. The largest restaurant is on Guam

McDonald's Big Mac

Jingle:

"Two all beef patties, special sauce, lettuce, cheese, pickles, onions and a sesame seed bun" (one version states "on," instead of "and")

MacDougal

Philip Boynton's frog (TV series "Our Miss Brooks")

McDougals' Cave

Cave where Tom Sawyer and Huck Finn found an iron box filled with gold coins. (Mark Twain's *Adventures of Tom Sawyer*)

Macedonia

Ship commanded by Captain Death Larsen, the only man Wolf Larsen fears, his brother (Jack London's *The Sea-Wolf*)

MacGuffin

That thing that is sought after in each Alfred Hitchcock film

Mach Five, The
Speed Racer's white racing car (TV cartoon)

Mack Bolan
Detective created by Don Pendleton

MacLaine, Shirley
Actress; sister of actor Warren Beatty

Mac Murdie Drugstore
Pharmacy on Waverly Place, New York, cover for the Avenger's Laboratory (Pulp magazine, *Avenger's* by Kenneth Robeson)

MacNeill, Don
Host of "The Breakfast Club" (radio series). MacNeill also was host of "Tea Time at Morrell's," one afternoon a week

Macy's (R. H. Macy) Rowland Hussey Macy
New York-based department store; main store was setting for the movie *Miracle on 34th Street*
Stuart Scheftel, the grandson of R. H. Macy, created *Sports Illustrated* magazine, husband of actress Geraldine Fitzgerald

Mad Hatter
Secret identity of Batman's foe Jervis Tetch (played by David Wayne) (TV series *Batman*)

Mad Hatter's tea party
Attended by the Hatter, the March Hare, Dormouse, Alice (Lewis Carroll's *Alice's Adventures in Wonderland*)

Mad Monk, The
Epithet applied to Rasputin (1871-1916). Russian monk at the court of Czar Nicholas II. Movie portrayals:
Rasputin and the Empress (1932) Lionel Barrymore
Nights of Rasputin (1960) John Drew Barrymore
Rasputin and the Mad Monk (1966) Christopher Lee
Nicholas and Alexandra (1971) Tom Baker

Mad Russian, The
Radio comedian Bert Gordon (radio series "The Eddie Cantor Show") "How do you d-o-o?"

Madame Queen
Andrew H. Brown's girlfriend ("Amos 'n' Andy"): played on radio by Harriet Widmer

Madge
Wife of Caspar Milquetoast (comic strip *The Timid Soul* by H. T. Webster)

410

Madge
   Manicurist in Palmolive dishwashing liquid TV commercials played by actress Jan Miner
   In France she's Francoise
   In Germany Tilly and in Finland Marissa
   She works at the Salon East Beauty Parlor

Madison High
   School at which Miss Brooks teaches (TV series "Our Miss Brooks")

Mafia
   Word intentionally deleted from the Mario Puzo 1972 movie "The Godfather" (but appears in the 1974 sequel "Godfather II") *Morte Alla Francia Italia Anela* (Death to the French is Italy's cry)

Mafia
   Name of white poodle given to Marilyn Monroe by Frank Sinatra

Maggie
   Jiggs' wife (comic strip "Bringing Up Father") played on radio by Agnes Moorehead, her daughter is Nora

Magic Castle Club
   Exclusive Hollywood magician's club where Anthony Blake (Bill Bixby) both performs and lives. (TV series *The Magician*)

Magnificent Seven, The
   1960 movie following 1954 Japanese *The Seven Samurai* (directed by Akira Kurosawa and starring Toshiro Mifune). The seven were played by Charles Bronson (Bernardo), Yul Brynner (Chris), James Coburn (Britt), Horst Buchholz (Chico), Steve McQueen (Vin), Robert Vaughn (Lee), Brad Dexter (Harry)
   Sequels: *Return of the Seven* (1966); *Guns of the Magnificent Seven* (1969); *The Magnificent Seven Rides Again* (1972). The casts varied in each film
   In movies *Westworld* and *Futureworld* Yul Brynner plays the robot Chris from *The Magnificent Seven*
   The movie's theme song was performed by Leonard Bernstein. It became a hit record by Al Caiola and the theme was used on TV on Marlboro Cigarette commercials

Maharishi Mahesh Yogi
   The Beatles' guru, other followers were Mia Farrow, Donovan, Mick Jagger and the Beach Boys

411

Mahatma Kane Jeeves
>Pseudonym under which W. C. Fields wrote the story and screenplay *The Bank Dick* in 1940

Maid Marian
>Marian Fitz Walter, Robin Hood's companion
>Played in movies:
>*The Adventures of Robin Hood* (1938) Olivia de Havilland; *Robin and Marion* (1976) Audrey Hepburn

Maid of Orleans
>One appellation of 19-year-old Joan of Arc
>Portrayed in movies:
>*Joan of Arc* (1948) Ingrid Bergman;
>*Joan of Arc* (1957) Jean Seberg
>*The Story of Mankind* (1957) Hedy Lamarr

Main Street
>Novel (1920) by Sinclair Lewis. The street characterizes the small-town narrowness of Gopher Prairie, Minnesota

Maine, U.S.S.
>First U.S. battleship (actually a battle cruiser), launched Nov. 18, 1890, sank after explosion in Havana Harbor, Feb. 15, 1898, with 250 killed

Maintain the Right
>Official slogan of the Royal Canadian Mounted Police

Maisie
>Starring Ann Sothern as Maisie Ravier in nine movies (1939-1946) (originally meant for Jean Harlow)
>On radio series by Ann Sothern

Major
>Old horse turned into a coachman for Cinderella's carriage (Walt Disney's cartoon feature movie)

Major Amos Barnaby Hoople
>Main character in Gene Ahern's comic strip *Our Boarding House*. Played on radio by Arthur Q. Bryan, his wife Martha by Patsy Moran. His brother is Jake, his nephew, Alvin

Major Greenbrass
>U.S. Army officer at Camp Swampy in *Beetle Bailey* cartoon strip by Mort Walker

Major James T. West
>Secret Agent under President U. S. Grant. Played by Robert Conrad. His partner is Artemus Gordon played by Ross Martin (TV series *Wild Wild West*). West became a Major at the age of 23

Major Minor

Canadian Mountie Klondike Kats' superior officer at Fort Frazzle (TV cartoon *Klondike Kat*)

Major Seth Adams

Wagonmaster (TV series "Wagon Train"): originally played by Ward Bond. After Bond's death Chris Hale (John McIntire) became the wagonmaster. Ward Bond previously played a wagonmaster in the 1950 John Ford movie *Wagonmaster*. The last episode of the TV series November 23, 1960 was directed by John Ford, John Wayne appeared as Gernal Sherman

Major Tony Nelson

Astronaut who is Jeannie's "Master" (played by Larry Hagman) (Jeannie played by Barbara Eden) (TV series *I Dream of Jeannie*). When series began, Nelson was a Captain

Major William Martin

"The Man Who Never Was": fictitious World War II British (Royal Marines) courier. His real identity was known only to his father. On April 30, 1942 his body was launched from the British sub Seraph off the coast of Spain (*Operation Mincemeat*)

Making Our Dreams Come True

Theme song of TV series "Laverne and Shirley." Sung by Cyndi Greco

Malcolm X

Name adopted by Malcolm Little (1925-1965), black nationalist, founder of Organization of Afro-American Unity. His autobiography was told to and taken down by Alex Haley

Maltese Falcon

16th Century gift given to King Charles V of Spain by the Knights Templar of Malta (Charles never received the gift). 1941 movie *The Maltese Falcon*

Man in Black, The

Host of radio program *Suspense* portrayed by Joe Kearns

Man in the Hathaway Shirt

Baron George Wrangell, who wore a patch over his right eye

Man on the Street

Skit on Steve Allen's "Tonight Show" (TV), in which were interviewed: Don Knotts, Louis Nye, Tom Poston, Bill Dana, Gabe Dell, Dayton Allen

Man O'War

Race horse (1917-1947) defeated only once in 20 starts (by Upset, 1919). Among the horses he sired was War Admiral. He was owned by Samuel D. Riddle

The Man with a Horn

Theme song of Ray Anthony's orchestra

Manassa Mauler

Nickname (coined by Damon Runyon) of Jack Dempsey, world heavyweight champion 1919-1926; he was born in Manassa, Colorado, in 1895. Jack Dempsey was the best man at John J. Sirica's marriage. Sirica had been a sparring partner for welter-weight champion Jack Britton

Mandrake the Magician

(Comic strip by Lee Falk & Phil Davis) Lothar his side kick, Princess Narda his girlfriend

Radio: Raymond Edward Johnson

Movies (serial):

Warren Hull (1939)

TV: Coe Norton

Manhattan Project

Code name for development of the A-Bomb

Manhattan Serenade

Theme song of radio series *Easy Aces*

Manhunter

Secret identity of Dan Richards (comic book series) and secret identity of Paul Kirk (comic book series)

Manhunter

Adventures of Dave Barrett (Ken Howard) (TV series *Manhunter*)

Mann, Carl

Owner of the Deadwood, South Dakota, saloon in which Wild Bill Hickok was shot and killed by Jack McCall on August 2, 1876. McCall's gun was a .45 Colt. Sitting at the table were Carl Mann, Charlie Rich, Doc Pierce and Captain Frank Massey (who was wounded by the same bullet that killed Hickok). Hickok normally always sat facing the swinging doors—but in this game he had his back to the doors. The name of the saloon, owned by Mann and Jerry Lewis, is variously given as No. 6, No. 66, No. 10, according to Frank J. Walstach; others give the name as Bella Donna Saloon and Nuttall and Mann's Number Ten Saloon. See Dead Man's Hand

Manners

The 6 inch high Kleenex Napkin butler played by Dick Cutting (TV commercials)

Man of a Thousand Faces

Name given to Lon Chaney, Sr., master of disguises. He was born on April Fools Day, 1883, to deaf and dumb parents, died in 1930. His film biography was portrayed in 1957 movie: *The Man of a Thousand Faces* by James Cagney. In the movie, Lon Chaney, Jr. (Creighton Tull Chaney) was played by Roger Smith, Robert Lyden, Dennis Rush, Richie Sorensen (at various ages)

Mannix

TV series about a private eye. Joe Mannix was played by Mike Connors

Manon Bell

Trophy awarded to the winner of the annual Wabash-DePauw football game

Manor Farm

Farm on which the animals live (George Orwell's *Animal Farm*). In the 1955 cartoon movie Maurice Denham is the voice of all the animals

Mansfield, Jayne

Born Vera Jane Palmer in 1933. Her figure was 40-21-35. She claimed to have an I.Q. of 163. Her picture has appeared on the cover of over 500 magazines. Died in a car accident June 29, 1967, her head being decapitated. Pink was her favorite color, the color of her home and car. Her Hollywood home was called The Pink Palace
Husbands:
Paul Mansfield (1950-1957)
Mickey Hargitay (1958-1964) Hungarian refugee and Mr. Universe, Matt Clinber (1964-1966)
She was *Playboy* magazine's playmate of the month for February, 1955

Mansion on the Hill

Song according to legend that Hank Williams composed for music publisher Fred Rose in 20 minutes in his office to prove that, indeed, he wrote his own songs—upon their first meeting

Mantell, Thomas F.

Air Force captain who crashed in his P51 (NG3869) near Godman A.F.B. Kentucky, January 7, 1948 while chasing a U.F.O.

Mantle, Mickey

New York Yankee switch-hitting outfielder, credited with hitting (batting left-handed) the longest home run, 565 feet: off Chuck Stobbs of the Washington Senators in Griffith Stadium, April 1953. It hit a sign 460 feet from home plate, 565 feet was estimated. Played in most games as a Yankee (2,400). Mantle, Roger Maris and Yogi Berra appeared in the 1962 movie *That Touch of Mink*

Mantz, Paul

Stunt pilot killed July 8, 1965 at age 62 when the "Phoenix" crashed in making the movie *The Flight of the Phoenix;* he had been a stunt pilot in the 1927 movie *Wings.* He was known as the Honeymoon Pilot, as he flew couples (such as Artie Shaw and Lana Turner) from Los Angeles to Las Vegas or Reno so they could get married. The call number of his red Vega was NC48M nicknamed Nellie the Goon. In the 1976 TV movie *Amelia Earhart* he was portrayed by Stephen Macht

Manufacturer's Trust (Bankers Trust Company)

Banking firm that was in possession of the questions and answers asked on the TV quiz show *The $64,000 Question*

Man With Nobody's Face, The

Said of Earl Drake the Detective (novel series by Dan J. Marlowe)

Man-Woman-Birth-Death-Infinity

Opening lines of TV series *Ben Casey* (said by Sam Jaffe)

Man You Love To Hate, The

Title conferred on actor Erich von Stroheim

Maranville, Walter "Rabbit"

Played in only two World Series; 1914 for Boston Braves and in 1928 with St. Louis Cardinals. In both series he came to bat 13 times, getting 4 hits, thus batting .308 in both series

Marathon Candy Bar Characters

Marathon John introduces these characters to a Marathon Bar: Quick Carl, Quick Claude, Quick Kirk, and Captain Quick. Marathon John played by Patrick Wayne, son of John Wayne

Marcella

Little girl who plays with Raggedy Ann and Raggedy Andy dolls in Johnny Gruelle's Children Books

March Sisters

In Louisa May Alcott's *Little Women:* Amy, Beth, Jo, Meg

They called their mother Marmee

1933 movie: Amy (Joan Bennett; Beth (Jean Parker); Jo (Katherine Hepburn); Meg (Frances Dee)

1949 movie: Amy (Elizabeth Taylor); Beth (Margaret O'Brien); Jo (June Allyson); Meg (Janet Leigh)

Louisa May Alcott was the first woman to register to vote in the state of Connecticut

March 21

Beginning of astrological year

March Hare

Insane rabbit that attended the Mad Hatter's tea party. Voice of Jerry Colonna, 1951 movie *Alice in Wonderland*

March of Dimes

Campaign of the National Foundation for Infantile Paralysis to raise money for children stricken with polio. The foundation was founded by Franklin D. Roosevelt

March of the Ancestors

From Gilbert and Sullivan's Ruddigore theme of radio series *Shelock Holmes*

Marciano, Rocky

World heavyweight champion (Rocco Marchegiano) 1952-1956, called the Brockton Bomber, won all his 49 professional bouts, 43 by KOs; defended his title six times; killed in a plane crash in Iowa, Aug. 31, 1969, one day prior to his 46th birthday. He had once tried out as a catcher with the Chicago Cubs. One month prior to his death a NRC315 computer was programmed to determine who would win a movie fight between Marciano and Muhammad Ali. The result was that Marciano knocked Ali out in the thirteenth round. (When the film was shown in England, Ali was the winner)

Marcus

James Dean's male siamese cat, given to him by Elizabeth Taylor

Marengo

Napoleon Bonparte's horse

Mare's Laig

Pet name for Josh Randall's (Steve McQueen) 30-40 sawed-off carbine (TV series "Wanted—Dead or Alive")

Margaret

Ed Brown's (Jack Albertson) deceased wife (TV series *Chico and the Man*)

Margaret Wade

Dennis the Menace's girlfriend. Played on TV by Jeannie Russell

Margo Lane

Girlfriend of the Shadow (Lamont Cranston). On radio: Gertrude Werner, Marjorie Anderson, Agnes Moorehead, Grace Matthews, Lesley Woods. In 1940 movie serial *The Shadow* by Veda Ann Borg

Marge

Sister that Sid is calling over the phone, but ends up talking to his nephew instead, *"Fine Thank You, Fine,"* comedy routine from album *Inside Shelly Berman*

Maria

Captain Horatio Hornblower's wife whom he married in April, 1803. They had 3 children, two dying of smallpox (C. S. Forester's *Horatio Hornblower* series)

Maria

The wind. The rain is *Tess,* the fire's *Job.* Lerner-Loewe song *They Call The Wind Maria.* 1969 musical *Paint Your Wagon*—sun by Harve Presnell

Maria

A girl (played by Brigitte Helm) who is abducted and has a robot made in her image in 1926 German film *Metropolis*

Marie Samuels

Name that Marion Crane (Janet Leigh) signed on the motel register at the Bates Motel (1960 movie *Psycho*). The signature just above hers was for Michael Scott dated 4/18

Marine Hymm

Song played by Professor Kelp's (Jerry Lewis) pocket watch each time he opens the lid (1963 movie *The Nutty Professor*)

Mariner's rule of thumb

"Red sky at night, sailor's delight,
Red sky in morning, sailor take warning"

Marineland of the Pacific

Museum where Mike Nelson (Lloyd Bridges) works. TV series *Sea Hunt*

Markey, Gene

Hollywood writer/producer who has been married to Joan Bennett (1932-1937), Hedy Lamarr (1939-1940) and Myrna Loy (1946-1950)

Markie

Persistent little boy who demands his Maypo for breakfast, *I want my Maypo* (1960's TV commercial)

Marko (Vukcic)

Detective Nero Wolfe's twin brother (they were born in Trenton, New Jersey, 1892 or 1893). He established Rusterman's Restaurant in New York City, died and left it to Nero

Mark Trail

Guardian of the forests—Protector of Wildlife Champion of man and nature (comic strip and radio) on radio played by Matt Crowley, Statts Cotsworth, John Larkin

Mark Twain

Pseudonym of Samuel Langhorne Clemens (1835-1910), American writer, who took the name from the cry of the leadsman sounding the depth of the river, Sam Clemens having been a Mississippi River pilot 1859-1861. Mark twain meant a depth of two fathoms or 12 feet

Mark Twain

Disneyland's 1850 three-deck stern-wheeler steamboat on the ½ mile long Rivers of America. The two riverboats at Disneyworld are the Richard F. Irvine and Admiral Joe Fowller

Marlin

The Kennedys' 52-foot cruiser

Marmon Wasp

Car (Number 32) driven (1911) by Ray Harroun in winning the first Indianapolis 500 race. It was the first single seat racer and first to use a rear-view mirror

Marriages

Entertainment:

John Agar—Shirley Temple

Eddie Albert—Margo (Marie Margarita Guadelupe Castilla)

Steve Allen—Jayne Meadows

Woody Allen—Louise Lasser
Desi Arnaz—Lucille Ball
John Astin—Patti Duke
Lew Ayres—Lola Lane
Lew Ayres—Diana Hall
Burt Bacharach—Angie Dickinson
Lex Barker—Arlene Dahl
Lex Barker—Lana Turner
John Barrymore—Dolores Costello
Wallace Beery—Gloria Swanson
Edward Begley—Martha Raye
Jack Benny—Mary Livingstone
Ernest Borgnine—Ethel Merman
George Brent—Ann Sheridan
Charles Bronson—Jill Ireland
Mel Brooks—Anne Bancroft
George Burns—Gracie Allen
Jack Carson—Lola Albright
Jack Cassidy—Shirley Jones
Charles Chaplin—Paulette Goddard
John Conte—Marilyn Maxwell
Jackie Coogan—Betty Grable
Joseph Cotten—Patricia Medina
Xavier Cugat—Abbe Lane
Xavier Cugat—Charo
Tony Curtis—Janet Leigh
Bobby Darin—Sandra Dee
Ossie Davis—Ruby Dee
Sammy Davis, Jr.—May Britt
Troy Donahue—Susanne Pleshette
Paul Douglas—Jan Sterling
William Dozier—Ann Rutherford
Howard Duff—Ida Lupino
Leo Durocher—Laraine Day
Douglas Fairbanks—Mary Pickford
Douglas Fairbanks, Jr.—Joan Crawford
Jose Ferrer—Rosemary Clooney
Mel Ferrer—Audry Hepburn
Eddie Fisher—Debbie Reynolds
Eddie Fisher—Elizabeth Taylor
Henry Fonda—Margaret Sullavan
Glenn Ford—Eleanor Powell
Anthony Franciosa—Shelly Winters

Martin Gabel—Arlene Francis
Elliott Gould—Barbra Streisand
Farley Granger—Shelley Winters
Stewart Granger—Jean Simmons
Phil Harris—Alice Faye
Jack Haley, Jr.—Liza Minelli
Rex Harrison—Lilli Palmer
Moss Hart—Kitty Carlisle
Dick Haymes—Joanne Dru
Dick Haymes—Rita Hayworth
Lyle "Skitch" Henderson—Faye Emerson
John Hodiak—Anne Baxter
Howard Hughes—Jean Peters
John Huston—Evelyn Keyes
John Ireland—Joanne Dru
Harry James—Betty Grable
Al Jolson—Ruby Keeler
George Jones—Tammy Wynette
Spike Jones—Helen Grayco
Buster Keaton—Natalie Talmadge
Ernie Kovaks—Edie Adams
Fernando Lamas—Arlene Dahl
Fernando Lamas—Esther Williams
Martin Landau—Barbara Bain
Charles Laughton—Elsa Lanchester
Steve Lawrence—Eydie Gorme
John Lennon—Yoko Ono
Allen Ludden—Betty White
Fred MacMurray—June Havor
Joel McCrea—Frances Dee
Steve McQueen—Ali MacGraw
Guy Madison—Gail Russell
Lee Majors—Farrah Fawcett
Tony Martin—Alice Faye
Tony Martin—Cyd Charisse
Burgess Meredith—Paulette Goddard
Vincente Minnelli—Judy Garland
George Montgomery—Dinah Shore
Audie Murphy—Wanda Hendrix
Paul Newman—Joanne Woodward
Clifford Odets—Luise Rainer
Laurence Olivier—Vivien Leigh
John Payne—Gloria De Haven

Carlo Ponti—Sophia Loren
Dick Powell—Joan Blondell
Dick Powell—June Allyson
William Powell—Carole Lombard
Prince Rainier—Grace Kelly
Aldo Ray—Jeff Donnell
Ronald Reagan—Jane Wyman
Rob Reiner—Penny Marshall
Jason Robards, Jr.—Lauren Bacall
Roy Rogers—Dale Evans
Gilbert Roland—Constance Bennett
Billy Rose—Martha Raye
Billy Rose—Fanny Brice
Elliott Roosevelt—Faye Emerson
Tommy Sands—Nancy Sinatra
Raymond Scott—Dorothy Collins
Gordon Scott—Vera Miles
David O. Selznick—Jennifer Jones
Artie Shaw—Evelyn Keyes
Artie Shaw—Ava Gardner
Artie Shaw—Lana Turner
Artie Shaw—Kathleen Winsor
Roger Smith—Ann-Margret Olson
Rod Steiger—Claire Bloom
Robert Sterling—Ann Sothern
Craig Stevens—Alexis Smith
Dean Stockwell—Millie Perkins
Robert Taylor—Barbara Stanwyck
Mike Todd—Joan Blondell
Franchot Tone—Joan Crawford
Rip Torn—Geraldine Page
Robert Wagner—Natalie Wood (twice)
Robert Walker—Jennifer Jones
Hal B. Wallis—Martha Hyer (twice)
Johnny Weissmuller—Lupe Velez
Orson Welles—Rita Hayworth
William Wyler—Margaret Sullavan
Gig Young—Elizabeth Montgomery
Florenz Ziegfeld—Billie Burke
(other multiple marriages are mentioned throughout the book)

Marryin' Sam

Married Li'l Abner to Daisy Mae. His fee was $1.35. The

marriage took place in 1952. Played by Stubby Kaye in 1959 movie *Lil' Abner*

Marseillaise, La

French national anthem, words by Claude Joseph Rouget de Lisle: originally titled "War Song of the Army of the Rhine" ("Chant de Guerre de l'Armée du Rhin")

Marshal Mort Dooley

Elwood law man (Ben Gage) who has a gunfight with Bret Maverick (James Garner) in the Maverick spoof of *Gunsmoke*. (The town saloon was the Weepin' Willow Saloon) (TV series "Maverick")

Marshall, James Wilson

Pioneer (1810-1885) who discovered gold at Sutter's Mill, Coloma, California, Jan. 24, 1848. Portrayed in 1962 movie *How the West was Won* by Craig Duncan

Martha

James Cagney's private yacht

Martian Manhunter

Secret identity of Jonn J'onzz (Detective comic books)

Martin Beck

Chief of Stockholm Homicide Squad (detective series by Maj Sjowall and Per Wahloo)

Martin J. Scheilman, Esq.

Mad magazine's libel lawyer

Martin Kane

Detective created for radio by Ted Hediger: played on radio by William Gargan and on TV by Gargan, Lee Tracy, Lloyd Nolan and Mark Stevens

Martinez

Ferryboat sunk in San Francisco harbor; the schooner "Ghost" Captain Wolf Larsen picked up survivor Humphrey Van Weyden (Jack London's *The Sea Wolf*)

Marvel Family

(Comic book series) Captain Marvel (Billy Batson); Captain Marvel, Jr. (Freddy Freeman); Mary Marvel (Mary Batson); Uncle Marvel (Dudley Batson); Baby Marvel, Freckles Marvel, Hoppy the Marvel Bunny

Marx Brothers

Sons of Sam and Minnie Schoenberg Marx (she was sister of Al Shean of Gallegher and Shean, famous vaudeville team). With their mother and aunt, they billed themselves as the six musical mascots; later the brothers called themselves the Four Nightingales. Charles A.

(Gus) Mager's comic strip *Mager's Monks* provided the nicknames for the brothers. Harpo's autobiography is titled *Harpo Speaks*. Although Harpo never spoke a line in the movies he did whistle and laugh

    Chico (Leonard, 1891-1961)

    Harpo (Adolph, afterwards Arthur, 1893-1964)

    Groucho (Julius, born 1895-1977)

    Zeppo (Herbert, born 1901)

    Gummo (Milton, not part of the comedy team, -1977)

Groucho's roles are listed separately, under his name

Mary

The Lipton Tea Girl (radio)

Mary Ann

B17 (serial number 05564) flown in 1943 movie *Air Force*, Captain Mike Quincannon *"Irish"* (pilot)—John Ridgley. The number ten was painted on the side

Mary Bromfield

Mary Marvel's adopted name, given her when she was separated at birth from her twin brother, Billy Batson (Captain Marvel). See *Marvel Family*. She debuted in Captain Marvel Comics #18 (Dec. 1940). She was raised on the Bromfield Estate

Mary Celeste

Ship that left Boston for Genoa in November 1872, found abandoned in Atlantic four weeks later, all sails set and the crew completely disappeared

Mary Had A Little Lamb

Children's song written by Sarah Josepha Hall in 1830. She was editor of *Godey's Lady's Book*. She had persuaded Abraham Lincoln to designate Thanksgiving Day as a National Holiday

Mary Jane

Little blonde-headed girl who has a little mouse friend named Sniffles. In order to become his size she chants:

"Now I shut my eyes real tight,

Then I wish with all my might,

Magic words of Poof, Poof, Piffles,

Make me just as small as Sniffles" (comic book)

Maryland, My Maryland

Song played as horses are paraded before the running of the Preakness in May each year

Mary Morstan

Doctor John H. Watson's second wife. They married May

1, 1889 in Camberwell (Sir Arthur Conan Doyle's Sherlock Holmes)

Mary Nestor
Girlfriend (eventually wife) of Tom Swift, mother of Tom Swift, Jr.

Mary Poppins
Nanny to Jane and Michael Banks (1964 movie *Mary Poppins*) created in novel by P. L. Travers (Pamela L. Travers)

Mary's Florist
Store that is to the left (as you look at it) of Goodwin's Variety Store (TV Crest Toothpaste commercials with Arthur O'Connell)

Mary Shumway
Mary Hartman's (Louise Lasser) maiden name (TV's *Mary Hartman, Mary Hartman*)

Mary Wesley
Boston Blackie's girlfriend (radio-TV)
Radio: Lesley Woods, Jan Miner
TV: Lois Collier

Mascots
Military academy football teams:
Army, Mule; Navy, Goat; Air Force, Falcon
The first Navy goat was El Cid. In 1893 he first attended the fourth annual Army-Navy game

Mason-Dixon Line
Boundary between Pennsulvania and Maryland, surveyed (1763-1767) by Charles Mason and Jeremiah Dixon. As the line separating the free and the slave states, it became the traditional division between North and South

Master Chen Ming Kan
Monk in charge of Shaolin Monastery, Hunan, China, where young Kwai Chang Caine becomes a Shaolin priest and master of Kung Fu (played by Philip Ahn). Caine's other masters were Master Po, Master Sun, Master Wong, Master Yuen, Master Teh, Master Shun (TV series *Kung Fu*)

Master Po
Blind monk in Shaolin Monastery, China, young Caine's master and friend (TV series *Kung Fu*); played by Keye Luke. Po called Caine Grasshopper, Caine called Po Old

Man. Po was killed by the Emperor's nephew, who was in turn slain by Caine, who then fled from China to America

Masterson, Bat
Pseudonym of William Barclay Masterson (1853-1921). U.S. marshal in frontier area, later a sports writer (portrayed on 1957-61 TV series by Gene Barry)

Mata Bond
Agent Sir James Bond's (David Niven) daughter in 1967 movie satire *Casino Royale,* she is played by Joanna Pettet

Mata Hari
Pseudonym of Gertrude Margarete Zelle, World War I spy, executed (1917) by the French (portrayed by Greta Garbo in 1932 movie *Mata Hari*)

Mata Hari
Lancelot Link's girlfriend (TV monkey series)

Match King, The
Nickname of Ivar Kreuger (1880-1932), Swedish entrepreneur and monopolist. Portrayed in 1932 movie *The Match King* by Warren William

Mathias, Bob
Only man to win the Olympic decathlon twice (1948-1952). In 1948 he was the only person ever to surpass the 7,000 point mark in the decathlon (7,139). For many years his picture was on the package of Wheaties breakfast cereal

Matilda
Beep, Beep, the Road Runner's wife (Warner Brothers cartoons)

Matt Helm
Detective (Matthew L. Helm) (novels by Donald Hamilton), he stands 6'4", weighs 200 lbs. and lives in Santa Rosa, California. He had been a Captain in the Navy. In novels he drives a Chevy pickup truck. Played on TV series by Tony Franciosa. *Death of a Citizen* is title of first Matt Helm novel

Matt Helm movies
Dean Martin starred as Matt Helm: *The Silencers,* 1966; *Murderers' Row,* 1966; *The Ambushers,* 1967; *The Wrecking Crew,* 1968

Mauch Chunk
Town in Pennsylvania renamed (1954) Jim Thorpe after the Olympic champion who had died the year before

Maude's Husbands

Chester (played by Martin Balsam), Albert, Barney, Walter Findlay (current) played by Bill Macy. TV series *Maude.* Her daughter is Carol (Adrienne Barbeau)

Mauretania

Sister ship of the "Lusitania." Lancey Howard (Edward G. Robinson) claimed to have played in a poker game lasting six days on the ship's maiden voyage (1965 movie *The Cincinnati Kid*)

Maverick

Brothers living in the frontier West (TV series "Maverick"): Bret (James Garner), Bart (Jack Kelly), Brent (Bob Colbert), Beau, their cousin (Roger Moore), Pappy Beauregard (James Garner). Each brother carried a $1,000 bill pinned inside his coat. (Jack Kelly's sister Nancy Kelly played Dorothy on the radio series *The Wizard of Oz*)

Max

Joe Palooka's adopted son

Max

Maximillian Meen. Sidekick of evil-doer Professor Fate (Jack Lemmon). Max played by Peter Falk (1965 movie *The Great Race*)

Max

The bionic dog (TV series "Bionic Woman"). Named Maximillion because he cost $1 million. He has a bionic jaw and four bionic legs

Max Brand

Pseudonym of Frederick Schiller Faust (1892-1944). Western adventure novel writer. Other pseudonyms were: Evan Evans, David Manning, George Owen Baxter

Max Carrados

Blind detective born Max Wynn created by Ernest Bramah (Smith) (1868-1942). His assistant and "eyes" is Parkinson

Maxine

Maxwell House instant coffee caterer (TV commercial, played by Vivian Vance)

Maxwell

Make of Jack Benny's antique 1924 automobile (California License PU8054). Black with blue fenders, no windshield, geraniums are growing out of the spare tire. Voice of Mel Blanc. License plates varied over the years; another was 12S9523

Maxwell Trophy
Awarded annually to the most Outstanding football player either collegiate or professional

Mayagüez, S.S.
U.S. ship captured by Cambodia on May 12, 1975. The ship was taken back by the U.S. at a cost of 38 American lives

Maycomb
Fictitious Alabama town which was the setting for the 1962 film *To Kill A Mockingbird*

May Company
Department store where Jack Benny's girlfriend Mary Livingston (Mrs. Benny) worked on Jack's radio/TV series. Jack Benny actually met his future wife in the hosiery department of the Los Angeles May Company store where she worked. Her real name is Sadie Marks. The character Mary Livingston hails from Plainfield, New Jersey. It was in the May Company store where Hedy Lamarr was arrested for shoplifting on January 28, 1966. She was found not guilty

Mayflower
Ship captained by Miles Standish that carried 102 Pilgrims from Southampton, England, to Plymouth, Massachusetts, September to November 1620: her companion ship, "Speedwell," could not make the voyage

Mayflower
Presidential yacht used by Presidents Theodore Roosevelt, William Howard Taft, Woodrow Wilson, Calvin Coolidge and Warren Harding

Mayflower
President Woodrow Wilson's private railroad car

Maynard G. Krebs
Dobie Gillis' beatnik buddy (TV series "The Many Loves of Dobie Gillis"): played by Bob Denver. He claimed his middle initial G stood for Walter. "Hi ya good buddy," "You rang," "Hi big daddy"

Mayo Brothers
Famous American surgeons at Rochester, Minn.: Charles Horace (1865-1939), William James (1861-1939), sons of William Worrall Mayo (1819-1911), American surgeon

Mayor Charles La Trivia
Caller at 79 Wistful Vista (radio's *Fibber McGee and Molly*): played by Gale Gordon, on TV by Hal Peary

Mayor McCheese

Mayor of McDonaldland (McDonald Hamburger commercials)

McCall, Jack

Shot and killed Wild Bill Hickok in the Carl Mann's Saloon, Deadwood City, Black Hills, Dakota Territory, August 2, 1876. Jack "Buffalo Curly" McCall used a .45 Colt, serial no. 2079 (five cartridges were defective). In his youth Hickok killed Jack's younger brother Andy by hitting him on the head with a hoe. Portrayed in 1936 movie *The Plainsman* by Porter Hall, in 1953 movie *Jack McCall, Desperado* by George Montgomery

McConnell, James

Top American ace of the Korean War: 16 victories. Portrayed in 1955 movie *The McConnell Story* by Alan Ladd

McDaniel, Hattie

First Negro to win an Oscar (1939), for the role of Mammy in *Gone with the Wind*

McGill

Montreal University, first to play, against Harvard, at Harvard. May 1874 or 1875, an intercollegiate football match under "Harvard rules," a mixture of rugby and soccer

McGregor

Farmer whose garden Peter Rabbit invades

McGuire Sisters

Singing group: Christine, Dorothy, Phyllis

McKean, Thomas

Delaware jurist (1734-1817), President of the Continental Congress when the Articles of Confederation were adopted (1781) on Maryland's ratification (sometimes called first President of the United States)

McMahon, Ed

Announcer of TV's Johnny Carson's "Tonight Show," previously his announcer on TV quiz show *Do You Trust Your Wife?* Circus clown in early 1950's on TV show "Big Top." One time next door neighbor to Dick Clark in Drexel Hill, Philadelphia

McMann and Tate

Advertising agency located in the Templar Building for which Darrin Stephens works as an executive. His boss is

Larry Tate (David White). Darrin is played by Dick York and Dick Sargent (TV series "Bewitched")

McNeil and Hodgson

Detective Hercule Poirot's solicitors (lawyers) series by Agatha Christie

McWhirter Brothers

(Born in London in 1925) Twin brothers who founded the Guinness Book of World Records, originally called in 1956 *The Guinness Book of Superlatives*. Norris is 20 minutes older than Ross. Both joined the British Navy in World War II, being the first time in their lives that they were separated and were reunited when the two ships they were on collided in the Malta Harbor. Ross McWhirter was killed by terrorists Nov. 27, 1975

Meadowwood

Community that protests when runway 22 is being used for aircraft departure and arrivals at Lincoln International Airport (Arthur Hailey's "Airport") (Runway 29 was closed when a jet got stuck in the snow)

Mean Machine

State Prison convict football team headed by Paul Crewe (Burt Reynolds), no. 22 as quarterback. They beat the Guardsmen 36 to 35 (1974 movie *The Longest Yard*)

Mean Mary Jean

Chrysler-Plymouth girl Judy Strangis (TV ads). She wears Jerseys No. 16, 1 and 75

Meatball

Major Gregory "Pappy" Boyington's (Robert Conrad) pet dog on TV series *Baa Baa Black Sheep*

Meathead

Archie's nickname for Michael Stivik, his son-in-law (Rob Reiner) (TV series "All in the Family"). It was the name Archie was called in high school

Medfield

College for which professor Ned Brainard (Fred MacMurray) is a teacher. He discovers Flubber, a magic rubber that flies. This allows his basketball team to win against Rutland in the movie. *The Absent-minded Professor* and his football team to win in *Son of Flubber*. College also in Disney movie *The Strongest Man in the World*

Medicare Card #1

Issued to former President Harry S. Truman

Meeseka Mooseka Mousekeer
Mouse Kartoon Time Now Is Here
Magic chant said by a mousekeeter to open the door of
the Mickey Mouse Treasure Mine—in order to announce
the day's cartoon

Megaphone Mark
Nickname of college radical Mark Slackmeyer (*Doonesbury* by Trudeau)

Megaphone Trophy
Trophy awarded to the winner of the annual Michigan-
Notre Dame football game

Megopolis
City in which Tennessee Tuxedo and his buddy Chumley
live. They reside at the Megopolis Zoo, Stanley Livingstone being the Zoo's head man, the zoo keeper is
Flunkey (TV cartoon series *Tennessee Tuxedo and his Tales*)

Mehitabel
Cat friend of Archy the cockroach, whose battle cry was
"toujours gai": she thinks she is Cleopatra/reincarnated
into a cat (created by Don Marquis). Played by Eartha
Kitt and Tammy Grimes in Broadway play *Shinbone
Alley*

Melancholy Baby
Traditional song drunks ask night club singers to sing. In
the 1954 movie *A Star is Born*, a drunk asks Judy Garland
to sing *Melancholy Baby*, the voice requesting the song is
that of Humphrey Bogart though the drunk seen was only
an extra

Melancholy Serenade
Theme song of *The Jackie Gleason Show*. Written by
Gleason (See *Tenderly*)

Melody Ranch
Home of Gene Autry (radio); became name of his real
San Fernando Valley ranch

Mel's
The 1950's drive-in at Modesto, California (movie *American Graffiti*). Also name of Phoenix, Arizona restaurant
where Alice Hyatt (Linda Lavin) works (TV series
"Alice")

Melvin
Audrey's boyfriend (comic book *Lil Audrey*)

Memphis Bell

First B17 bomber to complete 25 missions over Germany during W.W. II. Producer William Wyler made a film about this aircraft

Memphis Classic

Golf tournament in which former President Ford shot a hole in one, on the 177-yard 5th hole of the Colonial Country Club course June 8, 1977. Tournament held annually by Danny Thomas to raise money for St. Jude Children's Research Hospital in Memphis

Memphis, U.S.S.

Cruiser that brought Charles Lindbergh and his plane home from France after his famous flight (1927), arriving in U.S. June 11, 1927

Mera

Aquaman's wife (comic books)

Mermaid

Chicken of the Sea Tuna voice of Darla Hood, ex Little Rascal

Merrie Melodies

Movie cartoon series by Warner Brothers (as well as "Looney Tunes"); "That's All, Folks." Title similar to Disney's *Silly Symphonies* which came first

Merrimack

Confederate ship, renamed the "Virginia" as an ironclad, that fought "Monitor" 5 hours on March 9, 1862, at Newport News, Va.

Merry-Go-Round Broke Down, The

Theme song of Warner Brothers' *Looney Tunes* and *Merrie Melodies* cartoons

Merry Men

Robin Hood's band in Sherwood Forest. Among them: Alan-a-Dale, George-a-Green, Little John (John Little), Friar Tuck, Will Scarlet, Will Stutely, Midge (Much) the Miller's Son, David of Doncaster, Arthur-a-Bland

Mervyn Bunter

Detective Lord Peter Wimsey's valet (series by Dorothy L. Sayers). Served as Captain Wimsey's sergeant during WW I

Messala

Ben Hur's rival in the great chariot race (Lew Wallace's *Ben-Hur*). Played in movies: 1907—William S. Hart, 1926—Francis X. Bushman, 1959—Stephen Boyd

Me. 262
German twin-jet Messerschmitt aircraft that flew during World War II

Metal Men
Group of super robots created by Doctor Will Magnus. Members are: Tin, Platinum (Tina), Iron, Gold, Lead, and Mercury (D.C. comic books)

Metaluna and Zahgon
Two neighboring planets that are having an atomic war with each other (1955 movie *This Island Earth*)

Me Tarzan, You Jane
Line never said by Tarzan in any of his films.

Methuselah
Lived 969 years (Genesis 5:27). His father, Enoch, only lived 365 years

MEtropolis 6-0500
Phone number of the Daily Planet newspaper in Metropolis (TV series *Superman*)

Metropolis, Illinois
Superman's hometown on Earth (he lived in Smallville when he was Superboy until age 26). In Metropolis as Clark Kent he lived at the Standish Arms, then at 344 Clinton St. *Metropolis* is the title of the 1927 Fritz Lang film set in the year 2000

Metropolis University
College where Clark Kent graduated prior to going to work as a reporter of the Daily Planet

Metropolitan
Hotel in New York City where José Jimenez (Bill Dana) worked as a bell boy (1963 TV series *The Bill Dana Show*)

Mewsette
Sexy heroine cat of the 1962 animated cartoon *Gay Purr-ee*. Mewsette's voice is that of Judy Garland

Mexican Spitfire
Movie series starring Lupe Velez as Carmelita and Leon Errol as Uncle Matt
(*The Girl from Mexico*, 1939)
Mexican Spitfire, 1939
Mexican Spitfire Out West, 1940
Mexican Spitfire's Baby, 1941
Mexican Spitfire at Sea, 1942
Mexican Spitfire's Elephant, 1942

Mexican Spitfire Sees a Ghost, 1942
Mexican Spitfire's Blessed Event, 1943

Michael

Pet bee of The Red Bee, kept in Rick Raleigh's belt (comic book series)

Michael Anthony

The Millionaire's executive secretary who delivers the checks (TV series "The Millionaire"): played by Marvin Miller

Michael J.

Doonesbury's first name and initial (comic strip *Doonesbury* by G. B. Trudeau)

Michael Lanyard

The Lone Wolf, TV detective from a character created by Louis Joseph Vance in a 1914 novel (see Lone Wolf)

Michael Shayne

Hardboiled redheaded Miami Beach detective in novels by Brett Halliday. On radio by Jeff Chandler
On TV (debut NBC Sept. 1960) by Richard Denning
In 1940 movie *Michael Shayne Private Detective* by Lloyd Nolan
In 1941 movie *Dressed to Kill* by Lloyd Nolan, 1946 movie *Murder is My Business* by Hugh Beaumont
His secretary is Lucy Hamilton

Mickey Mouse

Most popular cartoon character ever. Created by Ub Iwerks, but credited to Walt Disney who did his voice, followed by James MacDonald. Originally drawn by Ub Iwerks, originally named Mortimer Mouse. On radio (1937) *The Mickey Mouse Theater of the Air.* His girlfriend is Minnie Mouse, his dog is Pluto. His two nephews are Ferdy and Morty (debut 1933 cartoon *Giantland*). Newspaper comic strip (daily) first appeared on January 13, 1930—Floyd Gottfredson was the ghost writer.
Debuted in 1928 Silent cartoon *Plane Crazy,* though *Plane Crazy* and *Gallopin' Goucho* (his second movie) were released after *Steamboat Willie* (see *Steamboat Willie*)
The first Mickey Mouse doll was designed by Bob Clampett
In 1938 Mussolini banned all American comics from Italy. All except Mickey Mouse.

Mickey Mouse Club

TV series (1955-1959) featuring Jimmie Dodd and the Mouseketeers (see Mouseketeers)

Each day of the week was set aside for different events:

Original Series (*1960*)	*New Mickey Mouse Club*
Monday—Fun With Music Day	How To Do Day
Tuesday—Guest Star Day	Let's Go Day
Wednesday—Anything Can Happen Day	Surprise Day
Thursday—Circus Day	Discovery Day
Friday— Talent Round-up Day	Showtime Day

Midnight

Black cat with diamond-studded collar in introduction to TV series "Mannix" and "Barnaby Jones" (Winner of 1974 TV PATSY)

Midnight

Violin-playing cat on the "Smilin' Ed Show" and "Andy's Gang". The only thing the cat says is "Nice"

Midnight

Cowboy Rowdy Yates' (Clint Eastwood) horse (TV series *Rawhide*)

Midnight Cowboy

Adventures of Joe Buck (novel by James Leo Herlihy). In 1969 movie played by Jon Voight. Buck befriends sickly Rico Rizzo (Dustin Hoffman) who he calls Ratso

Midshipmen

U.S. Naval Academy's football team

Midtown High

School that Peter Parker (Spider Man) attends. After graduation he went on to attend Eastern State University (comic books)

Midvale High School

School that Linda Lee Danvers (Supergirl) attended. She later was class advisor at New Athens Experimental School (comic book series *Supergirl*)

Midville

Town where Dondi, the war orphan lives

Midway

Naval battle of June 4-6, 1942, the three American carriers were *Enterprise, Hornet* and *Yorktown** (damaged), The four Japanese carriers sunk were *Kaga, Akagi* (flagship), *Hiryu* and *Soryu.*

Midwestern University

College attended by Jay Garrick, where during an experiment with Professor Hughes breathed in fumes which gave him the ability to become *The Flash* (comic books)

Mighty Joe Young

10 foot gorilla (also called "Mr. Joseph Young of Africa"). In 1949 movie *Mighty Joe Young* befriends Jill Young (Terry Moore) and is brought to America to appear at the nightclub *The Golder Safari.* Joe Young's favorite song is *Beautiful Dreamer.* Animation by Willis O'Brien (*King Kong* fame)

Mighty Manfred

Tom Terrific's dog (cartoon)

Mighty Mouse

Movie Terrytoons Cartoon mouse with super-powers created by Isidore Klein (Paul Terry). Debut: Super Mouse in Pandora's Box (1943). Debut in comics: Terrytoons comics 38, 1945

"Mr. Trouble never hangs around,

When he hears this might sound,

Here I come to save the day!

Which means that Mighty Mouse is on the way.

Yes sir, when there is a wrong to right

Mighty Mouse will lead the fight.

On the sea or on the land

He gets the situation well in hand."

Mighty Thor

The Thunder God, secret identity of Dr. Don Blake (comic book series. Debut "Journey Into Mystery" #83, August 1962)

Mike

Lunar computer of the 21st Century ruling the moon. Robert A. Heinleins' *The Moon is a Harsh Mistress.*

Mike and Ike

Richard Benson's (*The Avenger*) custom .22 pistol and knife (Kenneth Robeson's *The Avenger* series)

---

*On june 6 torpedoed by the Japanese submarine I-168, sunk.

Mike Fink

King of the River (played by Jeff York). Raced against Davy Crockett to New Orleans via the Ohio River. His Riverboat was the Gullywhumper, Davy's was the Bertha Mae (Walt Disney's *Davy Crockett* series)

Mike Kovac

Free-lance photographer (played by Charles Bronson) on the 1958-1960 TV series *Man With A Camera*

Mike Hammer

Detective created by Mickey Spillane (Frank Morrison Spillane), originally in *I the Jury* (1947): played by Darren McGavin on TV (Debut 1958). In his first five novels Mike Hammer killed 48 people

Movies: *I the Jury* (1953) Biff Elliott

Kiss Me Deadly (1955) Ralph Meeker

My Gun Is Quick (1957) Robert Bray

The Girl Hunters (1963) Mickey Spillane

Mickey Spillane who played his own creation in the 1963 movie originally drew comic books such as Plastic Man and others.

Mike Waring

Real name of the Falcon (see The Falcon)

Mildred

Lieutenant Columbo's wife whom viewers never see. Also name of Colonel Sherman Potter's (Harry Morgan) wife on M*A*S*H. She is also never seen

Miles Archer

Sam Spade's partner, killed in *The Maltese Falcon*. Played in 1931 movie by Walter Long, and in 1941 movie by Jerome Cowan

Military Aircraft

Designator	Name	Manufacturer
Attack Bomber:		
A1	Skyraider	Douglas
A2	Savage	North American
A3	Skywarrior	Douglas
A4	Skyhawk	Douglas
A5	Vigilante	North American
A6	Intruder	Grumman
A7	Corsair 2	Ling-Temco-Vought
A12	Shrike	Curtiss
A20	Havoc	Douglas

A26 (later B26)	Invader	Douglas
A37	Dragonfly	Cessna

Bomber:

B17	Flying Fortress*	Boeing
B18	Digby	Douglas
B24	Liberator	Consolidated Convair
B25	Mitchell	North American
B26	Marauder	Martin
B29	Fortress	Boeing
B36	Peacemaker	Convair
B45	Tornado	North American
B47	Stratojet	Boeing
B50	Superfortress	Boeing
B52	Stratofortress	Boeing
B57	Canberra	Martin
B58	Hustler	Convair
B66	Destroyer	Douglas

Cargo:

C1	Trader	Grumman
C2	Greyhound	Grumman
C4		Grumman
C5	Galaxy	Lockheed
C7	Caribou	DeHavilland
C9	Skytrain II	Douglas
C46	Commando	Curtiss-Wright
C47	Skytrain-Dakota	Douglas
C54	Skymaster	Douglas
C97	Stratocruiser	Boeing
C117	Super DC3	Douglas
C118	Liftmaster	Douglas
C119	Packet/Friendship	Fairchild-Hiller
C121	Warning Star	Lockheed
C123	Provider	Fairchild-Hiller
C124	Globemaster	McDonnell-Douglas
C130	Hercules	Lockheed
C131	Samaritan	Convair
C133	Cargomaster	Douglas

---

*The first Flying Fortress built was flown by General Curtis LeMay in the beginning years of WW2

438

C135	Stratolifter	Boeing
C137	Stratoliner	Boeing
C140	Jet Star	Lockheed
C141	Starlifter	Lockheed

Electronics:

E1	Tracer	Grumman
E2	Hawkeye	Grumman

Fighter:

F1		North American
F3	Demon	McDonnell-Douglas
F4	Phantom II	McDonnell-Douglas
F5	Freedom Fighter	Northrop
F6	Skyray	Northrop
F8	Crusader	Ling-Temco-Vought
F9	Cougar	Grumman
F10	Skynight	McDonnell-Douglas
F11	Tiger	Grumman
F12		Lockheed
F14	Tomcat	Grumman
F15	Eagle	McDonnell
F18	Hornet	Northrop
P38	Lightning	Lockheed
P39	Airacobra	Bell
P40	Tomahawk	Curtiss
P43	Lancer	Republic
P47	Thunderbolt	Republic
P51	Mustang	North American
P61	Black Widow	Northrop
F80	Shooting Star	Lockheed
F84	Thunderstreak/ Thunderjet/ Thunderflash	Republic
F86	Sabre	North American
F89	Scorpion	Northrop
F100	Super Sabre	North American
F101	Voodoo	McDonnell
F102	Delta Dagger	Convair
F104	Starfighter	Lockheed
F105	Thunderchief	Republic
F106	Delta Dart	Convair
F111		General Dynamics

Refueler:

KC135	Stratotanker	Boeing

Observation:

OV1	Mohawk	Grumman
OV10	Bronco	North American

Patrol:

P2	Neptune	Lockheed
P3	Orion	Lockheed

Trainer:

T1	Sea Star	Lockheed
T2	Buckeye	North American
T28	Trojan	North American
T29	Flying Classroom	Convair
T33	Shooting Star	Lockheed
T34	Mentor	Beech
T37		Cessna
T38	Talon	Northrop
T39	Sabreliner	North American
T41	Skyhawk	Cessna
T42	Baron	Beech

Search:

S2	Tracker	Grumman
SR71	Blackbird	Lockheed

Utility:

U1	Otter	DeHavilland
U2		Lockheed
U3	Model 310	Cessna
U4	Commander 560	Aero
U6	Beaver	DeHavilland
U8	Queen Air	Beech
U9	Grand Commander	Aero
U10	Super Courier	Helio
U11	Aztec	Piper
U16	Albatross	Grumman
U17	Skywagon	Cessna
U18	Rangemaster	Navion
U19	Sentinel	
U20	Model 195	Cessna

Millard Fillmore High School

Milwaukee High School attended by Laverne and Shirley (TV series *Laverne and Shirley*).

Millionaire, The

John Beresford Tipton (TV series "The Millionaire"): Marvin Miller as Michael Anthony delivered the checks for him. Viewers never saw Tipton's face, his voice was

440

Paul Frees. Tido Fedderson, the wife of the show's producer Don Fedderson appeared in each episode, usually in a cameo role. Marvin Miller also narrated the TV series "The FBI"

Millenium Falcon

Corellian pirate starship commanded by Han Solo (Harrison Ford) 1977 movie *Star Wars*

Mills Brothers

Singing group: John, Jr. (John, Sr., after John, Jr's death in 1935); Herbert; Harry; Donald. Originally billed as Four Boys and a Guitar

Milo

Ape scientist (played by Sal Mineo) and then baby (chimpanzee) named for him, born to Zira and Cornelius, the two simian scientists (1971 movie *Escape from the Planet of the Apes*, in the series based on Pierre Boulle's *Planet of the Apes*). The baby grows up to become Caesar, leader of the revolt in the next film, *Conquest of the Planet of the Apes*

Milton

Kellogg's Pop-Tarts cartoon toaster (TV commercials, voice of William Schallert)

Milton Armitage

Smooth youth (played by Warren Beatty) who gives competition for Dobie Gillis for the attentions of Thalia Menninger on TV series *The Many Loves of Dobie Gillis*.

Milton the Monster

Lovable cartoon monster made up of: "3 drops of essence of terror
5 drops of sinister sauce
a (touch) of tenderness but not too much" (TV cartoon series)

Minden, The

English ship (flag of truce boat) aboard which Francis Scott Key wrote "The Star Spangled Banner" originally titled "Defense of Fort McHenry" (Sept. 13-14, 1814, in Baltimore Harbor). He had watched the battle for 25 hours

Minerva

Cat belonging to landlady Mrs. Maggie Davis (TV series "Our Miss Brooks") played by Orangey the cat (see Rhubarb)

Mingo

Daniel Boone's Indian companion (TV series "Daniel Boone"): played by singer Ed Ames

Ministry of Miracles

Nickname of Central Office Eight of the Metropolitan Police, headed by Sir Henry Merrivale (by John Dickson Carr)

Minnehaha

Hiawatha's wife in H. W. Longfellow's poem "Hiawatha"

Minnelli, Liza

Actress and singer (born 1946), daughter of Vincente Minnelli and Judy Garland: and named after the Gershwin song "Liza". Oscar as best actress (for Sally Bowles in *Cabaret*), 1972. She won a Tony, an Oscar and an Emmy all in the same year, 1972. She made her screen debut in the 1949 musical *In the Good Old Summertime* standing between her mother and Van Johnson in the closing scene. She was 2½ years old. The movie was directed by her father.

Minnesota Fats

Pool champ Rudolf Wanderone, Jr. (1961 movie *The Hustler*): portrayed by Jackie Gleason

Minnie

Paul Bunyan's wife, who wore a wooden leg

Minnie the Moocher

Theme song of Cab Calloway's band

Minnie Mouse

Mickey Mouse's girlfriend. Debut in 1928 cartoon *Plane Crazy*. Voice of Marcellite Garner and Thelma Boardman

Minnie's Yoo Hoo

Mickey Mouse's theme song, also theme song of TV series *The Mouse Factory*

Minnow, S.S.

Boat that ran aground approximately 300 miles southeast of Hawaii (TV series "Gilligan's Island")

Mint marks

United States coins:

	Mark
Philadelphia	None
Denver	D
San Francisco	S

(Obsolete mints and marks: New Orleans [O]. Carson City [CC])

The last coin minted in San Francisco was a penny on March 24, 1955

Minuit, Peter

Dutch governor who purchased Manhattan Island from the Indians for 60 guilders, the equivalent of $24, in beads and other geegaws (1626): portrayed by Groucho Marx in the movie *The Story of Mankind* (1957)

Minute Man

Secret identity of Private Jack Weston (comic book character)

Miranda

Andy Panda's girlfriend

Misfits, The

1961 motion picture, written by Arthur Miller, directed by John Huston, last movie for Clark Gable and Marilyn Monroe

Lead actors: Montgomery Clift (Perce Howland); Clark Gable (Gay Langland); Marilyn Monroe (Roslyn Taber); Thelma Ritter (Isabelle Steers); Eli Wallach (Guido)

The film opened on Gable's birthday (Feb. 1, 1961); he was 60. Gable's last line in the movie was "Just head for that big star, it will take us home." Gable had also appeared with Jean Harlow in her last film *Saratoga*

Mishe-Mokwa

Great bear in H. W. Longfellow's *Hiawatha*

Mishe-Nahma

Sturgeon in H. W. Longfellow's *Hiawatha*

Miss America 1941

Actress Rosemary LaPlanche (Miss California)

Miss America 1943

Actress Jean Bartel (Miss California)

Miss America 1945

Bess Myerson (Miss New York)

Miss America 1955

Actress Lee Meriwether (Miss California)

Miss America 1950

Title never awarded in the Miss American Pageant yet the annual contest has never missed a year since it began in 1921. The pageant for 1949 was held September 1949, that only allowed the winner to be Miss America for that year for three more months. Therefore, the pageant for 1951 was held September 1950, allowing Miss America

1951 to serve during 1951. Although there was a pageant in 1950, there was no Miss America 1950

Miss America 1957
Actress and Clairol girl (TV ads) Marian McKnight (Miss South Carolina)

Miss America 1959
Mary Ann Mobley (Miss Mississippi)

Miss America 1961
Nancy Fleming (Miss Michigan)

Miss America 1971
Phyllis George (Miss Texas)

Miss Beazly
Riverdale High's school cook (*Archie* cartoon series by Bob Montana)

Miss (Genevieve) Blue
Andy's secretary (radio/TV series "Amos 'n' Andy"): played by Madaline Lee, "Buzz me, Miss Blue"

Miss Burbank
Winner (1948): Debbie Reynolds (Then named Mary Frances)

Miss Buxley
Camp Swamp's General Amos Halftrack's private secretary (*Beetle Bailey*)

Miss Columbia
First airplane purchased by the United States government: from the Wright Brothers, August, 1909

Miss Congeniality
Title awarded to one contestant in the *Miss America Contest*. The contestants' votes determine who will win the title. First awarded in 1939 to Doris Coggins (Miss Mississippi)

Miss Crabtree
Our Gang's young, pretty schoolteacher in many of the early *Our Gang* comedies. Played by June Marlowe, her brother is named Jack

Miss Dallas 1926
Joan Blondell

Miss Deep Freeze
Title held by Marilyn Novak (Kim Novak) for Thor Appliances which brought her to Hollywood where she was discovered by Harry Cohn

Miss Elvira Gulch
Bicycling spinster who attempts to take Toto away from

Dorothy. In the Land of Oz she becomes the Wicked Witch. Played by Margaret Hamilton (1939 film *The Wizard of Oz*)

Miss Frances
Dr. Frances Horwich (born Frances Rappaport), host of TV series "Ding Dong School" (1952-1956)

Miss Grundy
Archie Andrew's teacher at Riverdale High (comic strip series *Archie*)

Miss Hungary
Winner (1936): Zsa Zsa Gabor. She had to give up the title when it was revealed that she wasn't even 16, the minimum age to enter

Miss Jameson
Private secretary of Billy Batson (Captain Marvel) comic books)

Miss Josephine Ford
Fokker trimotor airplane in which Lt. Commander (later Admiral) Richard E. Byrd flew over the North Pole on May 9, 1926: piloted by Floyd Bennett

Miss Kansas 1948
Vera Miles, then known as Vera Ralston. She placed third in the 1948 Miss America Contest

Miss Lemon
Belgian detective Hercule Poirot's 48-year-old confidential secretary (Agatha Christie detective series)

Miss Long Beach 1941
Title held by actress Jeanne Crain. Also runner up in the Miss America Contest

Miss (Jane) Marple
Aged female sleuth created by Agatha Christie, debut *Murder at the Vicarage* (1930). She lives in the village of St. Mary Mead—her small maid is named Gwen. Her nephew Raymond West is a writer.
Played in movies by Margaret Rutherford:
Murder, She Said (1962)
Murder at the Gallop (1963)
Murder Ahoy (1964)
Murder Most Foul (1965)
The Alphabet Murders (1966)
Made final appearance in novel *Sleeping Car Murder*

Miss Moneypenny

Secretary to M (James Bond's boss): played in movies by Lois Maxwell and Barbara Bouchet (*Casino Royale*)

Miss Nell (Fenwick)

Dudley Do-Right's girlfriend (TV cartoon series), daughter of Inspector Fenwick

Miss New Orleans

Winner (1931): Dorothy Lamour; (1957): Donna Douglas

Miss Oklahoma 1959

Title held by Anita Bryant who was runner up in 1959 Miss America Contest

Miss Pennsylvania

Actress Jane Howard, runner up in the Miss America Contest

Miss Pittsburgh

Title held by actress Shirley Jones

Miss Radial Age

Giant B. F. Goodrich girl who encourages the sale of Goodrich tires in commercials. Portrayed by Pat Christman

Miss United States

First beauty pageant, taking place in 1880 at Rehoboth Beach, Delaware. The winner was Myrtle Meriwether. The judges were Judge Harrington of Delaware's Supreme Court, Monsieur Banwart, and Thomas A. Edison

Miss U.S.A. 1974

Actress Lynda Carter (TV's *Wonder Woman*)

Miss Wonderly

One of two phoney names used by Bridgid O'Shaughnessy (Mary Astor) in 1941 movie *The Maltese Falcon*. The other phoney name was Miss Le Blanc

Miss World 1963

Catherina Lodders (of Haarlem, Holland) married Ernest Evans (Chubby Checker) December 12, 1963

Mission Impossible

TV series opening with "self-destruct" tapes and dealing with hard espionage and counterespionage. Voice of Bob Johnson. Original cast included Steven Hill, Martin Landau, Barbara Bain, Peter Lupus, Greg Morris. Replacing Hill, Landau and Bain, the latter couple leaving the show in 1970, were Peter Graves, Leonard Nimoy, Lesley

446

Warren, Lynda Day George and Barbara Anderson (debut September 17, 1966)

Missions of California
From the South to north:

1769* San Diego de Alcala (San Diego)
1798 San Luis Rey de Francia
1776* San Juan Capistrano#
1771* San Gabriel Arcangel (San Gabriel)
1797 San Fernando Rey de España (San Fernando)
1782* San Buenaventura (Ventura)
1786 Santa Barbara Virgen y Martir (Santa Barbara)
1804 Santa Ynez Virgen y Martir (Santa Inez)
1787 La Purisima Concepcion
1772* San Luis Obispo de Tolosa (San Luis Obispo)
1797 San Miguel Arcangel (San Miguel)
1771* San Antonio de Padua
1791 Nuestra Señora de la Soledad (Soledad)
1770* San Carlos Borromeo del Carmelo (Carmel)
1797 San Juan Bautista
1791 Santa Cruz
1777* Santa Clara de Asis
1797 San Jose de Guadalupe
1776* San Francisco de Asis (Mission Dolores)
1817 San Rafael Arcangel (San Rafael)
1823 San Francisco Solano (Sonoma)

Mississippi Mudcat Band
Baseball player Pepper Martin's *Gas House Gang* musical group (1930's St. Louis Cardinals)

Mississippi, U.S.S.
Commodore Matthew Calbraith Perry's flagship on his voyage (1852-1854; to open Japan's ports to American trade

Missouri, U.S.S.
Battleship upon which the Japanese signed surrender terms in Tokyo Bay, September 2, 1945, ending World War II. The American flag that flew on the mast was the same flag that flew over the Capitol building on December 7, 1941

---

*Founded by Father Junipero Serra (1713-1784)
#Each year on St. Joseph's Day (March 19) the swallows return to the mission from their winter migration in Argentina

The battleship was nicknamed the *Mighty Mo*. Her number on side was 63. Missouri also happened to be Truman's home state. The ship was brought out of mothballs for the 1976 movie *MacArthur* starring Gregory Peck as the general

Misty Girl

Victoria Barkley's horse (TV series *The Big Valley*)

Mitzi

Mighty Mouse's girlfriend (comic book/TV series). In movie cartoons, his girlfriend is Pearl Pureheart

Mix, Tom

Popular Cowboy star of the 1920's movies. Home is T-M Bar Ranch, Tony is his Wonder Horse. The Tom Mix Museum is in Dewey, Oklahoma. Radio played by: (Tom Mix never played himself on radio) Artells Dickson, Russell Thorson, Jack Holden, Curley Bradley (also played Pecos)

Publicity propaganda had it that Tom Mix was a fighter in the Spanish-American war, fought in the Philippines, took part in the Boer War, Boxer Rebellion, spending some time in Mexico. He was once a Texas Ranger, Deputy U.S. Marshall and Sheriff

Mobile Two

The 1975 television pilot movie for the television series *Mobile One*. The television station changed its call letters from KITE to KONE (Channel 1)

Moby Dick

Pet Pelican of Kate Fairchild (Stefanie Powers) (1970 movie *The Boatniks*)

Mod Squad

Three young reformed delinquents active on the police force (TV series): Julie Barnes (Peggy Lipton); Linc Hayes (Clarence Williams III); Pete Cochran (Michael Cole)

Modernaires

Singing group (radio), original members: Bill Conway, Harold Dickinson, Chuck Goldstein and Ralph Brewster

Molene

The daughter of Dick Tracy's nemesis *The Mole*

Molink

Hot line between Washington and Moscow

Molly Byrd
Head nurse of Blair General Hospital (*Doctor Kildare* movie series): played by Alma Kruger

Mombi
The evil Wizardess from the Gillikins Country in the Land of Oz. She raised Tip as a youth (*Oz* series)

Mona Lisa
Painting by Leonardo da Vinci (circa 1500). The model was the wife of an official of Florentine, Francesco Giocondo—the other title of the masterpiece is La Gioconda

Mongo
Evil planet ruled by Emperor Ming in *Flash Gordon* series. The rightful ruler of the planet is Prince Barin

Monitor
Union ironclad ship launched February 15, 1862, that fought the Confederate ship "Merrimack" ("Virginia") at Hampton Roads, Va., March 9, 1862: sank off Cape Hatteras, December 1862, but was pattern for 60 more Union ironclads before Civil War ended

Monkees, The
TV series: Micky Dolenz (formerly of TV series "Circus Boy"); Davy Jones; Mike Nesmith; Peter Tork (Halsten Thorkensen). Micky, whose real name is George Michael Dolenz, Jr.. auditioned just ahead of Henry Winkler for the role of Fonzie on TV's "Happy Days"

Monocaine
Indian drug that enables Dr. Griffin to become invisible (1933 movie *The Invisible Man*)

Monopoly
Real estate board game invented (1933) by Charles Darrow, American heating engineer. Manufactured by Parker Bros. All places named on the game board are in Atlantic City, N.J. Starting from GO (collect $200.00 salary as you pass), the squares are, in order:

	Price		Price
Mediterranean Ave.	$ 60	Kentucky Ave.	$220
Community Chest		Chance	
Baltic Ave.	$ 60	Indiana Ave.	$220
Income Tax		Illinois Ave.	$240
Reading Railroad	$200	B & O Railroad	$200
Oriental Ave.	$100	Atlantic Ave.	$260

Chance		Ventnor Ave.	$260
Vermont Ave.	$100	Water Works	$150
Connecticut Ave.	$120	Marvin Gardens	$280
Jail (a corner square)		Go To Jail (a cornersquare)	
St Charles Place	$140	Pacific Ave.	$300
Electric Company	$150	North Carolina Ave.	$300
States Ave.	$140	Community Chest	
Virginia Ave.	$160	Pennsylvania Ave.	$320
Pennsylvania Railroad	$200	Short Line Railroad	$200
St. James Place	$180	Chance	
Community Chest		Park Place	$350
Tennessee Ave.	$180	Luxury Tax	$75
New York Ave.	$200	Boardwalk	$400
Free Parking (a cornersquare)		Go	

The only street that is misspelled from that in Atlantic City is Marvin Gardens, called Marven Gardens

Monopoly (British Version)

Trade Mark 711981

Real Estate	Color	Price
Old Kent Road	Brown	£ 60
Community Chest		
Whitechapel Road	Brown	£ 60
Income Tax (Pay 200)		
Kingscross Station		£200
The Angel Islington	Light Blue	£100
Chance		
Euston Road	Light Blue	£100
Pentonville Road	Light Blue	£120
Jail		
Pall Mall	Lavender	£140
Electric Company		£150
Whitehall	Lavender	£140
Northumber Land Avenue	Lavender	£140
Marylebone Station		£200
Bow Street	Orange	£180
Community Chest		
Marlborough Street	Orange	£180
Vine Street	Orange	£200
Free Parking		
Strand	Red	£220
Chance		
Fleet Street	Red	£220

Trafalgar Square	Red	£240
Fenchurch Station		£200
Leicester Square	Yellow	£260
Coventry Street	Yellow	£260
Water Works		£150
Piccadilly	Yellow	£280
Go To Jail		
Regent Street	Green	£300
Oxford Street	Green	£300
Bond Street	Green	£320
Liverpool St. Station		£200
Chance		
Park Lane	Blue	£350
Supertax	Pay £100	
Mayfair	Blue	£400
Go	Collect £200 Salary As You Pass	

Monroe, Marilyn
American actress (1926-1962): real name, Norma Jean Baker (Mortenson). Named for actresses Norma Talmadge and Jean Harlow. It was cameraman Leon Shamroy who named her Marilyn Monroe
Her husbands: James Dougherty, 1942-1946; Joe DiMaggio, 1954 (9 months); Arthur Miller, 1956-1962
James Dougherty worked with Robert Mitchum at Lockheed
She appeared on the cover of *Life* magazine, 9 times
In 1963 Rock Hudson narrated a documentary movie.
In 1976 movie *Goodbye Norma Jean* portrayed by Misty Rowe

Monsieur Bon-Bon's Secret "Fooj"
Recipe given at end of Ian Fleming's *Chitty-Chitty-Bang-Bang*

Monster, The
Movie playing at the drive-in theater where the Flintstone and Rubble families attend in the opening segment of the TV serial *The Flintstones*
Title of actual 1925 horror film starring Lon Chaney as Dr. Ziska

Monsters of the Midway
Nickname of the 1940 Chicago Bears football team

Monster Society of Evil
Comic book series featuring Captain Nazi, Nippo, Ibac,

451

Dr. Smash, The Orange Octupus, Herkimer the Crocodile Man, headed by Mr. Mind

Monstro

The whale in which Pinocchio and Gepetto are trapped (Walt Disney's *Pinocchio*)

Montague

Romeo's family name (Shakespeare's *Romeo and Juliet*). In 1936 movie Romeo played by Leslie Howard

Monticello

Thomas Jefferson's home, near Charlottesville, Virginia: the mansion was designed by Jefferson. Shown on reverse of a nickel

Monticello

Town, location of TV serial "The Edge of Night"

Montgomery Auditorium

Montgomery, Alabama where on January 4, 1953 funeral services were held for Hiram "Hank" Williams. Red Foley sang *Peace in the Valley*, Ernest Tubb sang *Beyond the Sunset* and Roy Acuff added *I Saw the Light*

Montini, Giovanni Battista

Pope Paul VI. During the period that the Vatican is selecting who is going to be the next Pope, smoke is emitted from a certain chimney. If the smoke is black, no decision has been made; if the smoke is white, a new Pope has been selected

Monty

Abernathy's pet dog (comic strip *Mr. Abernathy* by Ralston (Bud) Jones and Frank Ridgeway)

Moo

Land ruled by King Guzzle (comic strip *Alley Oop*)

Moon Maids

Vaughn Monroe's four member female backup vocal group

Moon Plaque

Placed by crew of Apollo 11: "Here men from the planet Earth first set foot upon the Moon, July 1969, A.D. We came in peace for all mankind"

Neil A. Armstrong, Astronaut

Michael Collins, Astronaut

Edwin E. Aldrin, Jr., Astronaut

Richard Nixon, President, United States of America

Moonlight Serenade

Theme song of the Glenn Miller orchestra

In the 1954 movie *The Glenn Miller Story* James Stewart portrayed the band leader

Moons

Planet	Moon	Planet	Moon
Mercury	None	Saturn	Dione
Venus	None	(cont.)	Rhea
Earth	Moon (Luna)		Titan
Mars	Phobos		Hyperion
	Deimos		Iapetus
Jupiter	Io		Phoebe
	Europa	Uranus	Miranda
	Ganymede		Ariel
	Callisto		Umbriel
	(8 others, all numbered)		Titania
Saturn	Janus		Oberon
	Mimas	Neptune	Triton
	Enceladus		Nereid
	Tethys	Pluto	None

In his writings Jonathan Swift mentioned that Mars had two moons two centuries prior to their discovery

Moonshine
Moon Mullin's full first name (comic strip)

Moose
Midge Clump's boyfriend Marmaduke Mason (*Archie* comics)

Moptop
Brady family's pet dog on the TV cartoon series *The Brady Kids*

Morgan, J. P.
John Pierpont Morgan (1837-1913), American financier, founder of New York City's Metropolitan Club (Millionaire's Club)

Morgan, Linda
"The Miracle Girl" (14 years old) who was aboard the "Andrea Doria" (stateroom 52) when that ship collided, July 26, 1956, with the "Stockholm," and was found alive on the "Stockholm" when the ships separated and the "Andrea Doria" sank. Her father is news commentator Edward P. Morgan. The picture of the sinking of the "Andrea Doria" won the Pulitzer Prize for best photograph of 1956

Morgan, William G.
Invented volleyball at Holyoke, Massachusetts in 1895

Morgiana

Ali Baba's woman slave, who discovered and killed the 40 thieves hiding in the oil jars

Morlands

Company at 83 Grosvenor Street, W1 London that makes the special Balkan and Turkish mixture cigarettes smoked by James Bond; the cigarette has 3 gold rings

Morlocks

Dominant group of people of 802,701 A.D. (H. G. Wells' *The Time Machine*)

Morning Express

Newspaper for which Casey worked (played by Stats Cotsworth) (radio series *Casey, Crime Photographer*)

Morning Telegraph

New York newspaper on which Bat Masterson was the sports editor. Prior to this job, he was personally appointed to U.S. Marshal by President Theodore Roosevelt

Morocco Mole

Secret Squirrel's sidekick (he has a voice similar to Peter Lorre) (TV cartoon)

Morris

Finicky cat in "9-Lives" cat food advertisements (TV commercial). Morris was previously named Lucky because he was rescued from being put to sleep. Original voice of John Irwin. Winner of 1973, 1974 PATSY. Appeared as "Cat" in 1973 movie *Shamus*. He has been replaced on TV commercials by Harry the Cat

Morrissey, Mick

Jockey who, while riding in the 1953 Grand National Steeplechase on a horse named Knother, was thrown into the saddle of the favorite, Royal Student, during a collision in which Royal Student lost its rider and Morrissey was thrown from his horse. Morrissey, on Royal Student, finished last

Morro Castle, S.S.

Ward line passenger ship that burned off Asbury Park, N.J., Sept. 8, 1934, with loss of 125 lives. Captain Robert Willmott was mysteriously found dead. The ship's call letters were KGOV

Mortimer Mouse

Mickey Mouse's original name, after Disney's real pet mouse

Mortimer Snerd

Edgar Bergen's bucktoothed dummy. "Pretty stupid, huh?"

Morton Girl

Girl on front of Morton Salt packages: "When it rains, it pours." Four different girls have appeared: drawing changed in 1914, 1921, 1956, 1972

Mother

The Avengers' heavyset, wheelchair ridden boss (TV series): played by Patrick Newell "Mother Knows Best"

Mother Fletcher

Products sold by Stanley R. Soog (Jackie Gleason)

Mother Goose

Said to be nickname of Mrs. Isaac Goose of colonial Boston, but the name has been traced back to centuries before (Perrault's fairy tales of 1697 were titled *Mother Goose Stories*)

Mother Nature

Proponent of Chiffon Margarine on television commercials, played by Dena Dietrich, "It's not nice to fool Mother Nature"

Mother of Country Music

Nickname given to Maybelle Carter, mother of June Carter, Johnny Cash's second wife

Mother's

Peter Gunn's favorite nightclub. Mother was played on TV series by Hope Emerson and Minerva Urecal. In 1967 TV movie *Gunn* by Helen Traubel

Mother of Mercy, is this the end of Rico?

Last line of Caesar Enrico Bandello (Edward G. Robinson) in the 1930 movie *Little Caesar*

Mothra

Monster moth (Japanese movie, 1962)

Motown

Detroit record company, founded by Berry Gordy, Jr., in 1963. Motown recording artists include: Supremes, Four Tops, Miracles, Temptations, Marvelettes, Diana Ross, Contours, Martha and the Vandellas, Mary Wells, Marvin Gaye, Jr. Walker and the All Stars, Stevie Wonder, Gladys Knight and the Pips, Smokey Robinson. The Supremes were originally called the Primettes named after the group the Primes, who later became the Temptations

Mouse Series, The

Novels by Leonard Wibberley. The series concerns the adventures of the people of Grand Fenwick
The Mouse that Roared (1955) (1959 movie)
Beware of the Mouse (1958)
The Mouse on the Moon (1962) (1963 movie)
The Mouse on Wall Street (1969)

Mouseketeers, The

Members of the Mickey Mouse Club (TV program series debut October 3, 1955) included Cheryl, Bobbie, Annette, Karen, Cubby (Cubby is a drummer with the Carpenters), Darlene, Sharon, Tommy, Doreen (Doreen is the niece of Ben Blue), Jimmie Dodd (adult), Roy Williams (adult)—he designed the insignias of the Navy Seabees and Flying Tigers—Mouseketeer (regular member), Meesketeer (small member), Moosketeer (adult member). Adults: Big Moosketeer (Roy Williams), Musical Moosketeer (Jimmie Dodd), Roving Moosketeer (Tom Moore), Leader of Mickey Mouse Club Band (George Burns). Several mouseketeers went on to appear on other TV series:
Johnny Crawford ("The Rifleman")
Don Grady ("My Three Sons")
Bobby Burgess ("Lawrence Welk")
Paul Peterson ("Donna Reed Show")
Tim Considine ("My Three Sons")
On January 17, 1977 a "New Mickey Mouse Club" came to TV. The Mouseketeers were: Todd, Nita, Shawnte, Angel, Scott, Mindy, Kelly, Julie, Lisa and Curtis

Mousetrap, The

Play written by Agatha Christie for Queen Mary. Originally titled *Three Blind Mice,* the play now holds the world's record for the longest running play. Debut November 25, 1952—still running to date

Movietone Newsreel

Short black and white film of current events produced by Fox, begun in 1919, narrated by Marshal Foch

Movin' On Up

Theme song on the TV series "The Jeffersons"

Mowgli

Boy hero of Rudyard Kipling's *The Jungle Books* ("Little Frog"): on TV cartoon's voice of Roddy McDowall, in 1976 movie voice of Bruce Reitherman

Mozart

Robinson family pet parrot (TV series "Swiss Family Robinson")

Mr. Adams and Eve

Married show business movie-star team, Howard and Eve Adams, played by Howard Duff and Ida Lupino (1956-58 TV series)

Mr. & Mrs. Bertram Charles

Nick Charles' parents (1944 movie *The Thin Man Goes Home*) featuring William Powell and Myrna Loy as Mr. & Mrs. Nick Charles and Lucile Watson and Harry Davenport as Nick's mother and father

Mr. & Mrs. Country Western

Title conferred upon husband and wife country singers George Jones and Tammy Wynette (now divorced)

Mr. and Mrs. Richard Lancing

Real parents of Tarzan and Jane's adopted son, Boy (Johnny Sheffield). His parents were played in the 1939 movie *Tarzan Finds A Son* by Morton Lowry and Laraine Day. They both get killed in a plane crash

Mr. B

Name that Mr. Baxter's maid Hazel calls him (TV series *Hazel*)

Mr. Beasley

Mailman who delivers to Dagwood and Blondie Bumstead: played in movies by Irving Bacon, Walter Sande, Eddie Acuff, Frank Jenks. TV: Lucien Littlefield, Dick Wessel. Mr. Beasley who also a mailman on the *George Burns* and *Gracie Allen TV Show*, played by Ralph Seadan

Mr. Belvedere

Movie series starring Clifton Webb as Lynn Belvedere *Sitting Pretty* (1948), *Mr. Belvedere Goes to College* (1949), *Mr. Belvedere Rings the Bell* (1951)

Mr. Big

Foreign agents Boris and Natasha's boss in Pottsylvania (*Rocky and Bullwinkle* comics). He lives in the Krumlin

Mr. Bilbo Baggins
   50-year-old hobbit who lives in Bag End, Under Hill, Hobberton (central character of J.R.R. Tolkein's *The Hobbit*)

Mr. Blooper
   Kermit Schafer, who presents the gold statuette Bloopy to the best bloopers (verbal or other errors that are broadcast)

Mr. Blue, Mr. Green, Mr. Grey, Mr. Brown
   Assumed names of the four men who hijack a New York subway train for $1,000,000 ransom in 1973 movie *The Taking of Pelham 1-2-3*. All wore fake moustaches and glasses:
   Mr. Blue—Robert Shaw
   Mr. Green—Martin Balsam
   Mr. Grey—Hector Elizondo
   Mr. Brown—Earl Hindman

Mr. Bluebeard
   Play being presented the night of the worst theater fire in U.S. history, December 30, 1903, at Chicago's Iroquois Theater in which 602 people lost their lives. In a scene from the 1955 movie *The Seven Little Foys,* Eddie Foy was one of the acts

Mr. Bojangles
   Nickname of Luther "Bill" Robinson (1878-1949), Negro tapdancer popular in the 1920's and 1930's. In the 1936 movie *Swing Time* Fred Astaire portrayed him in the number "Bojangles of Harlem." Title of hit song by Nitty Gritty Dirt Band. Robinson was Shirley Temple's dancing partner in the movies: *The Little Colonel* (1935), *The Littlest Rebel* (1935), *Just Around the Corner* (1938), *Rebecca of Sunnybrook Farm* (1938). He once danced 100 yards backwards in 13.5 seconds

Mr. Boynton
   Biology teacher at Madison High. His pet frog was named MacDougal. Radio played by Jeff Chandler, TV played by Robert Rockwell (Series *Our Miss Brooks*)

Mr. Bumble
   Workhouse boss whom young Oliver Twist asks for more oatmeal; *"Please, sir, I want some more"* (Charles Dickens' *Oliver Twist*)

Mr. Bush
   Captain Horatio Hornblower's second-in-command on

board the H.M.S. Lydia and H.M.S. Sutherland (C. S. Forester's *Hornblower* series)

Mr. C

Name Perry Como's announcer, Frank Gallop, would call him on his TV program

Mr. Clarence McNabbem

Truant officer who chases after Tubby when he plays hookey (comic books)

Mr. Chipping

Full last name of Mr. Arthur Chips (James Hilton's *Goodbye, Mr. Chips*). Played in films: 1939 movie, Robert Donat; 1969 movie, Peter O'Toole

Mr. Coffee Nerves

Invisible evil villian who constantly upset personal situations (comic strip by Paul Arthur—actually Milton Caniff and Noel Sickles). Strip was sponsored by Postum, a coffee substitute drink. In comic books and Sunday comics

Mr. (Longfellow) Deeds

Millionaire hero "the pride of Mandrake Falls" of movie *Mr. Deeds Goes to Town* (1936): played by Gary Cooper, on TV series by Monte Markham

Mr. Dirt

Embodiment of dirty engines (Mobil Oil TV commercials): played by Ronnie Graham

Mr. District Attorney

Radio program pledge:

"And it shall be my duty as District Attorney not only to prosecute to the limit of the law all persons accused of crimes perpetrated within this county but to defend with equal vigor the rights and privileges of all its citizens." On radio played by: Dwight Weist, Raymond E. Johnson, Jay Jostyn. On TV: Jay Jostyn, David Bryan

Mr. J. C. Dithers

Dagwood Bumstead's boss (Julius Caesar Dithers). Radio: Hanley Stafford, Jonathan Hale. TV: Florenz Ames, Jim Backus. On TV Backus' wife Henny played Mrs. Cora Dithers. Owner of J. C. Dithers Construction Company

Mr. Dunahee

Customer that Joe the Bartender (Jackie Gleason) serves.

He was never seen or heard from. Joe the Bartender's favorite tune was *My Gal Sal*

Mr. Ed
Palomino talking horse of Wilbur (Alan Young) (TV series "Mr. Ed"). Voice of Allan "Rocky" Lane. Winner of 1962, 1963, 1964, 1965 TV PATSY

Mr. Foofram
Mr. Hi Flagston's boss (comic strip *Hi and Lois* by Mort Walker and Dik Browne)

Mr. (Giles) French
The British manservant (Sebastian Cabot). Valet to Bill Davis (Brian Keith) and babysitter of: Cissy (Kathy Garver), Jody (Johnnie Whitaker), Buffy (Anissa Jones) twins in series. (TV series "Family Affair")

Mr. George Whipple
Fussy supermarket manager who begs the ladies not to squeeze the Charmin (toilet paper). Played by Dick Wilson. His twin brother is Elmer. He calls his son Georgy

Mr. Goodwin
Pharmacy owner Arthur Goodwin who advises all his customers of the advantage of brushing with Crest Toothpaste. Played on TV commercials by Arthur O'Connell. The number of his drugstore is 1212

Mr. Green Jeans
Captain Kangaroo's friend, played by Hugh "Lumpy" Brannum

Mr. H. J. Overcash
Wealthy customer of Midas Muffler shops. Drives a Rolls Royce (TV commercials circa 1973-74)

Mr. H. M. Woggle-Bug, T. E.
Large friendly bug who befriends Tip in the *Oz* series.
H. M. = Highly Magnified
T. E. = Thoroughly Educated

Mr. Hooper
Owner of the soda fountain on Sesame Street. His birthday is on April 25: played by Will Lee

Mr. Hyde
Edward Hyde, the "evil" side of the split person in Robert Louis Stevenson's *Dr. Jekyll and Mr. Hyde*

Mr. Inside and Mr. Outside
Felix "Doc" Blanchard and Glenn Davis, fullback and halfback of Army (U.S. Military Academy) football teams,

1944-1946. They appeared in the 1947 movie *Spirit of West Point*. Davis married actress Terry Moore

Mr. Jinks
Cartoon cat that chases after Pixie and Dixie (mice); "I'll get you meeces," voice of Daws Butler

Mr. Johnson
The owner and landlord of the Kramden's and Norton's apartment building (TV series *The Honeymooners*)

Mr. Keen
Tracer of lost persons (radio program): played by Bennett Kilpack, Phil Clarke, and Arthur Hughes

Mr. Limpet
Man who turns into a fish (1962 movie *The Incredible Mr. Limpet*): played by Don Knotts

Mr. (Buddy) Love
Cool, suave personality that manifests itself after Professor Kelp (Jerry Lewis) drinks his magic potion. (The reverse of *Dr. Jekyll and Mr. Hyde*) (1963 movie *The Nutty Professor*)

Mr. Lucky
Nickname of Joe Adams (1943 movie *Mr. Lucky*): played by Cary Grant; on TV, the role of Lucky Santell was played by John Vivyan

Mr. (Quincy) Magoo
Near-sighted cartoon character in movies (voice by Jim Backus). Debut: UPA cartoon *Ragtime Bear* (1949), winner of two Oscars

Mr. McGregor
Owner of garden that Peter Rabbit invades

Mr. (Wilkins) Micawber
Played by W. C. Fields in 1935 movie *David Copperfield*

Mr. Moto
Japanese detective in novels by John Phillips Marquand (5 written between 1936 and 1942). In the novels he is Mr. I. A. Moto, in movies he's Kentaro Moto of the International Police. In the movies he was played by Peter Lorre
  Think Fast, Mr. Moto, 1937
  Thank You, Mr. Moto, 1938
  Mr. Moto's Gamble, 1938
  The Mysterious Mr. Moto, 1938
  Mr. Moto's Last Warning, 1939
  Mr. Moto in Danger Island, 1939

Mr. Moto Takes a Vacation, 1939

The Return of Mr. Moto, 1965, starring Henry Silva as Mr. Moto

Mr. Moto's Gamble began as a Charlie Chan movie, but when Warner Oland died, it became a Mr. Moto film. In the movie, Keye Luke plays the role of Lee Chan

Mr. MXYZPTLK
Superman's foe from the fifth dimension (get him to say his name backwards—KLTPZYXM—and he will return to the fifth dimension for 90 days). His mother is TLNDSA, his father FUZASTL. They all came from the land of ZRFFF, ruled by King BPRXZ

Mr. Parker Pyne
(J. Parker Pyne) London detective whose personal advertisement in the London Times reads *Are You Happy? If not, consult Mr. Parker Pyne, 17 Richmond Street* (created by Agatha Christie). His first name has also been referred to as Christopher

Mr. Peabody
Sherman's superintelligent genius of a dog (actually he's master of the boy Sherman), who wears a red bow tie and glasses *"Every dog should have a boy"* (TV cartoon series). Voice of Bill Scott

Mr. Peanut
Planters Peanuts' trademark, wears a monocle on his right eye

Mr. (Robinson J.) Peepers
TV series starring Wally Cox, who played a junior high school science teacher at Jefferson City Jr. High

Mr. Republican
Nickname of Robert A. Taft

Mr. Sanders
Name over the door of Winnie-the-Pooh's house (A. A. Milne's children's books)

Mr. Scratch
Name of the Devil in Stephen Vincent Benét's *The Devil and Daniel Webster*

Mr. Slate
Fred Flintstone's boss (TV cartoon series)

Mr. (Jefferson) Smith
Naive politician hero of 1939 movie *Mr. Smith Goes to Washington*: played by James Stewart: played in 1963 TV series by Fess Parker as Eugene Smith

Mr. Spock
Science officer, second in command of the starship "Enterprise." He holds the rank of Commander. Service No. S-179-276-SP (TV series "Star Trek"): played by Leonard Nimoy. He is half human and half Vulcan. His parents, Amanda and Sarek, were played by Jane Wyatt and Mark Lenard. He previously served under Captain Pike for 9 years

Mr. Stern Wheeler
Southern gentleman on TV's "Hee Haw" show who has various items blow up in his face

Mr. Stubbs
Toby Tyler's chimpanzee

Mr. Tawny
Talking tiger (Tawky Tawny) who dressed in human clothes in *Captain Marvel* comics

Mr. Terrific
TV comedy show of 1967 starring Stephen Strimpell

Mr. Terrific
Crime fighter, superhero Terry Sloane. The words *Fair Play* are on the front of his uniform. Debut, *Sensation Comics* #1, January, 1942

Mr. Veeblefester
Brutus Thornapple's boss (comic strip *The Born Loser*)

Mr. (Kit) Walker
Assumed name of the Phantom (comic strip/books)

Mr. Warmth
Nickname of comedian Don Rickles. The Merchant of Venom is another

Mr. Weatherbee
Principal of Riverdale High (*Archie* comics). Radio: Arthur Maitland

Mr. Wizard
Science explicator (Don Herbert) on TV educational series "Mr. Wizard"

Mr. Wong
(James Lee Wong) Chinese detective created by Hugh Riley: played in five movies by Boris Karloff (1938-1940) and one by Keye Luke

Mr. and Mrs. North
Pamela and Jerry, the mystery-busting pair: played on radio by Joseph Curtin and Alice Frost; played on TV by Richard Denning, Joseph Allen and Barbara Britton,

Mary Lou Taylor. In 1941 movie *Mr. and Mrs. North* played by William Post, Jr. and Gracie Allen. On Broadway by Albert Hackett and Peggy Conklin. The characters originally appeared in novels by Richard and Frances Lockridge

Mr. and Mrs. Polka

Little Dot's parents (comic book cartoon series *Little Dot*)

Mr. and Mrs. Silo

Little Orphan Annie's adoptive parents (comic strip by Harold Gray). Annie's real last name is Bottle. On radio the Silos were played by Jerry O'Mera and Henrietta Tedro

Mr. and Mrs. Wilson

Denis the Menace's neighbors, George and Martha Wilson. TV: Joseph Kearns, Gale Gordon and Martha by Sylvia Field

Mrs. Bardell

British detective Sexton Blake's landlady on Baker Street, London. (Novels by Harry Blyth)

Mrs. Beasley

Favorite doll of Buffy Davis (Anissa Jones) (TV series "Family Affair")

Mrs. Bloom

Molly Goldberg's friend across the areaway (radio/TV series "The Goldbergs")

Mrs. C

Fonzie's nickname for Mrs. Cunningham (TV's "Happy Days")

Mrs. Calabash

Said to be Jimmy Durante's first wife Maude Jean Olson, who died in 1943: his TV shows closed with his line, "Good night, Mrs. Calabash, wherever you are." For 20 years, Durante kept the identity secret. Calabash was the name of a small town outside of Chicago which Jeannie and Jimmy both fell in love with

Mrs. Davis

Constance Brook's landlady (played on radio and TV by Jane Morgan) (TV series "Our Miss Brooks"). On TV her home address is: 295 Carol Avenue

Mrs. Dibbs

Proponent of *Good Seasons Salad Dressing*. Played on TV commercial by Barbara Bel Geddes

Mrs. Emma Peel
   Government agent John Steed's (Patrick Macnee) partner (played by Diana Rigg). She lives on Primrose Hill in London and uses an Italian Beretta 7.65 pistol (TV series "The Avengers") (See Peter Peel)

Mrs. Hannah Gruen
   Nancy Drew's adopted mother. Nancy was left motherless at age 3

Mrs. (Martha) Hudson
   Sherlock Holmes' housekeeper and landlady at 221B Baker Street, London. In Rathbone-Bruce movies played by Mary Gordon and Irene Handl

Mrs. Livingston
   Tom and Eddie Corbett's housekeeper, played by Miyoshi Umeki (TV series "The Courtship of Eddie's Father")

Mrs. Muir
   Widow who inhabits Gull Cottage, haunted by the ghost of Captain Gregg (movie and TV series "The Ghost and Mrs. Muir"): played in 1947 movie by Gene Tierney and in TV series by Hope Lange (See Captain Gregg)

Mrs. O'Leary's cow
   Traditionally said to have started the Chicago fire of October 8, 1871, when it kicked over a lantern in Mrs. Molly O'Leary's barn on DeKoven Street. The fire was probably started by Mr. Patrick O'Leary smoking his pipe in the barn. Alice Brady portrayed Mrs. O'Leary in 1938 movie *In Old Chicago*

Mrs. Olson
   Proponent of Folger's Coffee (TV commercials): she apparently knows hundreds of young, married couples: played by Virginia Christine

Mrs. Pym
   Female detective created by Nigel Morland. In 1939 movie *Mrs. Pym of Scotland Yard* starred Mary Clare

Mrs. Robinson
   Lover of Benjamin Braddock (Dustin Hoffman), mother of Elaine (Katharine Ross) whom Benjamin falls in love with. Her first name is never mentioned but in the novel by Charles Webb *The Graduate* she sends a telegram signed G. L. Robinson

Mrs. Sarah Tucker
   Proponent of *Cool Whip Whipping Cream* on TV commercials. Played by Marge Redmond

Mrs. Trumball

Lucy and Ricky Ricardo's neighbor that often babysat little Ricky. Played by Elizabeth Patterson (TV series "I Love Lucy"). She lives in Apartment 3C

Mt. Ararat

Traditional landing place of Noah's Ark, in Armenia (April 15, 2348 B.C., according to Archbishop Usher)

Mt. Blanc

Highest mountain (15,771 feet) in Europe (eastern border of France)

Mt. Everest

Highest mountain (29,028 feet) in the world: Nepal-Tibet border in Asia

First conquered by Edmund Hillary and Tenzing Norkay, May 29, 1953

Mt. Idy

Ohio hometown of Charley Weaver, population 308 (role played by Cliff Arquette): its inhabitants include: Elsie Krack, Wallace Swine, Grandpa Ogg, Clara Kimball Moots, Granma Ogg, Ludlow Bean, Dr. Beemish, Goo Goo Shultz, Leonard Box, Ockluck, Byron Ogg, Grandma Heise (Richest Woman in Town), Grandpa Snider, Gomar Cool, Birdie Rodd, Melvin Box, Irma Clodd, Widow Darby, Joe Cutter, Fred and Gladys Swine (twins)

Mt. Kilimanjaro

Highest mountain in Africa, 19,340 feet, in Tanzania: now called Mt. Kibo

Mt. Nebo

Mountain from which Moses viewed the Promised Land

Mt. Olympus

Home of the gods (Greek mythology)

Mt. Pisgah

Where Moses died

Mt. Rushmore

Black Hills peak sculptured by Gutzon Borglum (1927-1941). The presidential faces are those of George Washington, Thomas Jefferson, Abraham Lincoln, Theodore Roosevelt. A mock reproduction was used in Alfred Hitchcock's 1959 movie *North By Northwest*

Mt. Sinai

Desert mountain where Moses received the Ten Commandments

Mt. Suribachi

Elevation on Iwo Jima, in the Volcano Islands, south of Japan, where the U.S. flag was raised during a fierce battle of World War II, March 15, 1945 (See Iwo Jima)

Mt. Vernon

Virginia home of George Washington, 15 miles south of Washington, D.C.

Mt. Vesuvius

Volcano on the Bay of Naples that erupted in 79 A.D. and buried the towns of Pompeii and Herculaneum

Mudville

Home town of Casey's baseball team ("Casey at the Bat," poem by Ernest L. Thayer, 1888): said to be Boston. Thayer received $5.00 for the poem. Grantline Rice wrote a sequel poem titled "Casey's Revenge"

Muhammad Ali

Religious name adopted by Cassius Marcellus Clay (born 1942), world heavyweight champion boxer, "The Louisville Lip"

Mulholland Book Shop

Boston rare book store owned by the friend of detective Thomas Banacek, Felix Mulholland, expert on practically all subjects. Located at 50 Beacon Street. Phone number 555-0716 (TV series "Banacek")

Mulligan

Milligan the detective's sidekick (radio series *Milligan and Mulligan*)

Mummy movies

The Mummy, Karloff as Im-Ho-Tep, 1932

Mummy's Boys (Wheeler & Woolsey comedy), 1935

Mummie's Dummies (3 Stooges comedy), 1938

The Mummy's Hand, Tom Tyler as Kharis, 1940

The Mummy's Tomb, Lon Chaney, Jr., as Kharis, 1942

The Mummy's Ghost, Lon Chaney, Jr., as Kharis, 1944

The Mummy's Curse, Lon Chaney, Jr., as The Mummy, 1945

Abbott and Costello Meet the Mummy, Edwin Parker as The Mummy, Kharis, 1955

The Mummy, Christopher Lee as Kharis, 1959

The Curse of the Mummy's Tomb, 1964

Wrestling Women vs. the Aztec Mummy, 1965 (Mexican)

The Mummy's Shroud, Toolsie Persand as Kah-To-Bey, 1967
Blood from the Mummy's Tomb, Valerie Leon as Tera, 1972
The only actor to have appeared in the movies *Dracula* (1931), *Frankenstein* (1931), and *The Mummy* (1932) was Edward Van Sloan

Munchkins
Little people who live in Munchkinland (*The Wizard of Oz*): played by the 128 Singer Midgets in 1939 movie. The coroner who declares the Wicked Witch of the East dead, "She's not only merely dead, she's really most sincerely dead" was played by Meinhardt Raabe who in the 1930's played Oscar the Wiener Man for Oscar Hot Dogs. The voice of the Mayor was that of Ken Darby

Murania
Underground scientific city visited by Gene Autry (1935 movie serial *The Phantom Empire,* also called, as a feature picture, *Men with Steel Faces*)

Murderer's Row
Heavy hitters of the 1927 New York Yankees: in order, the key players were Babe Ruth, Lou Gehrig, Bob Meusel, Tony Lazzeri, each with an R.B.I. over 100 (544 total). *Murderer's Row* was coined by writer Arthur Robinson

Murphy, Bridey
Virginia Tighe (Ruth Simmon was her pseudonym) under hypnosis in 1952 said that she was a girl living in Ireland in the year 1806, named Bridey Murphy (Doctor Morey Bernstein conducted the sessions)

MUrrayhill 3-5097
Telephone number that Leona Stevenson (Barbara Stanwyck) dials to reach her husband's office. Somehow the line gets mixed up and she overhears a plot to murder her. Her home address and phone number is: 43 Sutton Place, PLaza 9-2265. (1948 movie *Sorry, Wrong Number*) (Phone number in book by Allan Ullman and Lucille Fletcher is MUrrayhill 3-0093)

MUrrayhill 8-9933
Telephone number for Major Bowes at the Capitol Theatre, New York City "Original Amateur Hour" (radio)

Murray the K
Popular screaming D. J., Murray Kaufman, who during

the 1960's was one of the country's most popular disc jockeys. Worked for New York City radio station WINS

Musical Knights
Horace Heidt's band

Muskie
Deputy Dawg's little muskrat friend (TV cartoon)

Mustache Gang
Nickname of the Oakland A's baseball team

"Mustard and Custard"
Pat Aloysius Brady (Roy Roger's partner's) favorite expression

Mutiny on the Bounty
Actual mutiny on board a British naval ship, taking place on April 28, 1789. In 1808 as governor of South Wales, William Bligh again had to put down a mutiny against him. 1933 Australian movie, Lt. William Bligh (Mayne Lynton), Fletcher Christian (Errol Flynn). 1935 MGM movie: Lt. William Bligh (Charles Laughton), Fletcher Christian (Clark Gable), winner of Best Picture. 1962 MGM movie: Lt. William Bligh (Trevor Howard), Fletcher Christian (Marlon Brando), nominated for Best Picture
Three actors from the 1935 version were nominated for Best Actor: Clark Gable, Charles Laughton and Franchot Tone. Victor McLaglen winning for his performance in *The Informer*. In the 1935 version, Ray "Crash" Corrigan, David Niven and James Cagney each played extras in a single scene

Mutt and Jeff
Comic strip characters created by Bud Fisher. Augustus Mutt; Julius is Jeff's twin brother. Debut November 15, 1907

Mutley
Dick Dastardly's (voice of Paul Winchell) snickering dog (TV cartoon series "Wacky Racers"). Mutley's voice is Don Messick's

My Blue Heaven
Theme song of singer Gene Austin

My Country 'Tis of Thee
One name for "America," patriotic anthem played in waltz style

My Day
Eleanor Roosevelt's newspaper column

My Declaration of Principles
Published in the New York Inquirer:

I

I will provide the people of this city with a daily paper that will tell all the news honestly

II

I will also provide them with a fighting and tireless champion of their rights as citizens and as human beings. —
Charles Foster Kane—The Publisher

My Fair Lady
Adaptation to musical stage of George Bernard Shaw's play *Pygmalion* (1912). Eliza Doolittle, the heroine, was played by Julie Andrews in the theater; in the 1964 movie version she was played by Audrey Hepburn, whose songs were sung by Marni Nixon. 1938 movie *Pygmalion* by Wendy Hiller

My Gal Sal
Song always sung by Joe the Bartender ("Jackie Gleason" TV)

My Happiness
The song that Elvis Presley paid to record as a present for his mother, at the Sun Studio, in 1953. Two songs for $4.00—the flip side was *"That's When Your Heartaches Begin"*—because of this recording, Sam Phillips of Sun Records signed Elvis to a contract

My Little Chickadee
Only movie (1940) in which Mae West and W. C. Fields appeared together. The screenplay was written by Mae West

My Mother the Car
A 1928 Porter (in TV series): voice by Ann Sothern. The surviving members of the Crabtree family were played by Jerry Van Dyke, Maggie Pierce, Randy Whipple, and Candy Eilbacher. California license plate of Porter: PZR 317

My Old Kentucky Home
Song played as horses are paraded before the running of the Kentucky Derby in May each year. Theme song of radio series *Ma Perkins*

My Personality
What Alfalfa called his cowlick (*Our Gang* series)

470

My son

Answer to the riddle, "Brothers and sisters I have none, but this man's father is my father's son"

Mycroft Holmes

Sherlock Holmes' brother, supposed to have been even more clever than Sherlock. He is 7 years older than Sherlock; he appeared in three stories: *The Greek Interpreter, The Final Problem, The Adventure of Bruce-Partington Plans*

Mycroft is credited with writing *The Last Bow*

Peter Cushing played him and Sherlock in films: played by Christopher Lee in 1971 movie *The Private Life of Sherlock Holmes*

Mystery Ship

Airplane that was the first Thompson Trophy Race winner (1929)

Mystic Knights of the Sea

Fraternal lodge to which Amos and Andy belonged: George Stevens was the Kingfish

N

9

Weight in pounds of hammer swung by John Henry (American folk ballad)

9

The CB radio channel allocated for emergency use

9 Primrose Crescent

London address of Tara King (Linda Thorson), TV series "The Avengers"

9 to 0

Score of a forfeited baseball game (7 to 0 is a softball game)

$9.40

Dinner check presented to Otis B. Driftwood (Groucho Marx) 1935 movie *A Night At The Opera*

Nine Muses

Clio, History
Melpomene, Tragedy
Thalia, Comedy and Burlesque
Calliope, Epic Poetry
Urania, Astronomy
Euterpe, Lyric Poetry
Terpsichore, Dancing and Choral Song
Polymnia, Song and Oratory
Erato, Love Poetry

90

Distance in feet between bases in baseball

97 Pitches

Total number of pitches thrown by Don Larsen of the

New York Yankees who pitched the first and only perfect World Series game October 8, 1956

97

Weight in pounds of weakling who gets sand kicked in his face before he takes the Charles Atlas course

98.6

Normal human body temperature in degrees Fahrenheit

99 44/100%

Purity of Ivory soap

99 Rimble Road

Home address of Carter Hall who is actually the *Hawkman,* who is actually *King Khufu* reincarnated (comic books)

918th Bomber Group

B-17 squadron in the 8th Air Force (movie/TV series "12 O'Clock High")

930 Van Ness

Los Angeles home address of private eye Jake Axminster (Wayne Rogers) (TV series "City of Angels")

963 North Gilbert

Chicago address of the Evans family apartment building on TV series "Good Times"

999

Henry Ford's racing car, named after a railroad locomotive Barney Oldfield won the 1903 National Champion in the 999. In 1904 Ford built a new 999 in which he broke the world's speed record with 91.37 m.p.h.

1926 Hupmobile

Automobile shown in the forefront of the reverse side of a $10 bill

1930's—1960's

3 baseball players who played in the 1930s through 1960s in the major leagues
Early Wynn—1939-1963
Ted Williams—1939-1960
Mickey Vernon—1939-1960

1937

Date on the giant penny kept in the Trophy Room of the Bat Cave. Batman received the one cent piece in 1947 for the *Penny Plunderers Case*

1941 Mercury

Fat Albert's car that has a Cessna aircraft engine in it (Bill Cosby's character *Fat Albert*)

1977
Year in which the 1971 movie *The Omega Man* starring Charlton Heston is set

9114 South Central
Los Angeles home address of Fred G. Sanford's junk yard (TV series "Sanford and Son")

91419
Lottery number of Steve Jackson (Sidney Poitier) which won $50,000 (1975 movie *Uptown Saturday Night*)

94768
Prison number of Marsh Williams (James Stewart) in 1952 movie *Carbine Williams*

904-2133
Home phone number of Lee Ann "Pepper" Anderson (Angie Dickinson) (TV series "Police Woman")

9215143
Police identification number of Batman's arch-enemy The Penguin (TV series *Batman*)

900-242-1611
Telephone number used to reach President Carter on a national phone-in held on March 5, 1977. 42 Americans talked to the President. Joseph Willman of Sterling Heights, Mass., was the first caller

N3
Nick Carter's code name. He is senior Killmaster for AXE (*Killmaster*, detective novel series)

N772W
Registration number of the twin engine aircraft that collides into the 20th floor of a skyscraper (1977 TV movie *Flight to Holocaust*)

N975B
Registration number (call sign) of the helicopter in TV series *Whirlybirds*

N63158
Call sign of Tyler Fitzgerald's (Jim Backus) twin Beech aircraft, which Benjy Benjamin (Buddy Hackett) flies through a billboard (*The Pause that Refreshes—Drink Coca Cola*) in the 1963 movie *It's A Mad, Mad, Mad, Mad World*

N07107
Call numbers of Jenny Dare's comet airplane (cartoon strip *Flyin' Jenny*)

NAGIRROC YAWGNORW OT LIAH

Newspaper headline praising Douglas "Wrong Way" Corrigan's flight to Ireland July 17, 1938 (read the line backwards)

NAL

Call letters of Navy Lakehurst the ill-fated night that the *Hindenburg* exploded May 6, 1937. The commanding officer at Lakehurst was Commander Charles E. Rosendahl who was the navigating officer on board the *Shenandoah* when it crashed September 14, 1925. He had been the commander of the *Los Angeles*, first commander of the *Akron* and he sailed on the around-the-world maiden flight of the *Graf Zeppelin*, October 1928

NATO

North Atlantic Treaty Organization, established March 1949. Member countries at present are:

Belgium*	Luxembourg*
Canada*	Netherlands*
Denmark*	Norway*
France**	Portugal*
Greece	United Kingdom*
Iceland*	United States*
Italy*	Turkey
West Germany	

NBC-1

California automobile license plate of Sammy Davis' custom Continental

NCC 1017

Registration number of the U.S.S. Constellation. Commanded by Captain (Commodore) Matt Decker (TV series *Star Trek*)

NCC-1701

Registration number of the U.S.S. "Enterprise" (TV series "Star Trek")

NGS549672

Star from which the Overlords came, prior to arriving on Earth, in the Constellation Carina, 40 light years from Earth (Arthur C. Clarke's *Childhood's End*)

---

*Original member
**Resigned 1967

NLX-590

License number of the Chevrolet bus used by the Partridge Family on TV series

NR 16020

Registration number of Amelia Earhart's lost Lockheed Electra, bought for her by Purdue University for $50,-000

In the 1976 TV movie *Amelia Earhart*, she was portrayed by Susan Clark (Kim Diamond as a girl)

NR 16056

Registration number of Toni Carter's airplane in 1943 movie *Flight for Freedom* (based on Amelia Earhart's life)

NSMAPMAWOL

Not so much a programme, more a way of life—1960's BBC television series title

Nairobi Trio

Comic musical group created by Ernie Kovac's (gorilla band)

The tune they "played" was *Solfaggio*, composed by George Gershwin. The tune is also used in TV commercials for Colt 45 Malt Liquor

Naismith, James

Physical education teacher at Springfield College, Mass.; inventor (1891) of the game of basketball; first game played Jan. 20, 1892. It was his student Frank Mahon who gave the name "basketball" to the game

Naismith Trophy

Awarded to the year's most outstanding college basketball player

Na-Mor

Sub Mariner's name (comic books)

Son of Princess Fen and Commander McKenzie of the U.S. Navy

Nana

St. Bernard who guarded the Darling children (James Barrie's *Peter Pan*)

Nancy Drew

Children's books by Carolyn Keene. Over 50 books were written by Stratemeyer, Edward L. and later by Harriet S. Adams, his daughter.

18-year-old—Nancy lives with her widowed lawyer father Carson Drew in the small town of River Heights. Hannah

Gruen is the family housekeeper. First story in the series was *The Secret of the Old Clock* (1930).
Movie series starring Bonita Granville:
Nancy Drew, Detective (1938)
Nancy Drew—Reporter (1939)
Nancy Drew—Trouble Shooter (1939)
Nancy Drew and the Hidden Staircase (1939)
Played on TV by Pamela Sue Martin

Nancy with the Laughin' Face
Song written by Jimmy Van Heusen and comedian Phil Silvers for Nancy Sinatra (born Sandra June 8, 1940) when she was five years old; afterwards recorded by her father, Frank Sinatra. Tommy Dorsey is Nancy's godfather

Nanu
World's greatest athlete (1974 Walt Disney movie *The World's Greatest Athlete*): played by Jan-Michael Vincent

Napoleon
Country dog in Walt Disney's *The Aristocats*, 1970 movie (Napoleon's voice was that of Pat Buttram). His buddy canine is named Lafayette

Napoleon
Uncle Elby Eastman's 250-pound Irish wolfhound mongrel dog (comic strip *Napoleon* by Clifford McBride)

Napoleon
Born on the island of Corsica (1769)
Exiled to the island of Elba (1814)
Died on the island of St. Helena (1821)

Napoleon
Leader of the animals, a pig (George Orwell's *Animal Farm*)

Napoleon Brandy
Detective Lord Peter Wimsey's favorite drink. He also prefers Villary Villar Cigars

Napoleon Solo
Chief Enforcement Agent for U.N.C.L.E. Agent #11 (he is played by Robert Vaughn) (TV series *The Man from U.N.C.L.E.*)

Nardroff, Elfrida Von
Largest winner of any television quiz show. Won $200,500 on "21"

Narcissus
Tugboat operated by Annie Brennan
Played by:

1933 movie *Tugboat Annie* Marie Dressler (M-G-M had labeled her as the world's Greatest Actress)

1940 movie *Tugboat Annie Sails Again* by Marjorie Rambeau

1945 movie *Captain Tugboat Annie* by Jane Darwell

TV series by Minerva Urecal

NASCAR
National Association for Stock Car Auto Racing

Nash, Clarence
Voice of Donald Duck

Nast, Thomas
(1840-1902) American political cartoonist. His works appeared in *Harper's Weekly*. He created the symbols for the Tammany Tiger, the Democratic Donkey (*Harper's Weekly* January 15, 1870) and the Republican Elephant (*Harper's Weekly* November 7, 1874). In 1863 his drawing of a plump and jolly Santa Claus was the beginning of the fat Santa as we know him today, with red suit, wide belt and white beard

Natalie Wood Award
Harvard Lampoon's annual award to the year's worst actress

National Airways
Airline for which pilot Jimmie Allen flew (radio series *The Air Adventures of Jimmie Allen*)

National Baseball League

Eastern Division	Western Division
Chicago Cubs	Atlanta Braves
Montreal Expos	Cincinnati Reds
New York Mets	Houston Astros
Philadelphia Phillies	Los Angeles Dodgers
Pittsburgh Pirates	San Diego Padres
St. Louis Cardinals	San Francisco Giants

National Basketball Association
Atlantic Division (Eastern Conference)
Boston Celtics
Buffalo Braves
New York Knick(erbocker)s
Philadelphia 76ers
New York Nets
Central Division (Eastern Conference)
Atlanta Hawks
New Orleans Jazz

Cleveland Cavaliers
Houston Rockets
Capitol Bullets (Washington, D.C.)
San Antonio Spurs
Midwest Division (Western Conference)
Chicago Bulls
Detroit Pistons
Kansas City-Omaha Kings
Milwaukee Bucks
Denver Nuggets
Indiana Pacers (Indianapolis)
Pacific Division (Western Conference)
Golden State (San Francisco) Warriors
Los Angeles Lakers
Phoenix Suns
Portland Trail Blazers
Seattle Supersonics

National Football League

American Conference:
 Central Division
  Cincinnati Bengals
  Cleveland Browns
  Houston Oilers
  Pittsburgh Steelers

 Eastern Division
  Baltimore Colts
  Buffalo Bills
  Miami Dolphins
  New England Patriots
   (Foxboro, Mass.)
  New York Jets
 Western Division
  Denver Broncos
  Kansas City Chiefs
  Oakland Raiders
  San Diego Chargers

National Conference:
 Central Division
  Chicago Bears
  Detroit Lions
  Green Bay Packers
  Minnesota Vikings
  Tampa Bay Buccaneers
 Eastern Division
  Dallas Cowboys
  Philadelphia Eagles
  New York Giants
  St. Louis Cardinals
  Washington Redskins

 Western Division
  Atlanta Falcons
  Los Angeles Rams
  New Orleans Saints
  San Francisco 49ers
  Seattle Sea Hawks

National Hockey League

Prince of Wales Conference:
 Charles P. Adams Division
  Boston Bruins
  Buffalo Sabres

Toronto Maple Leafs
Cleveland Bruins
James Norris Division
Montreal Canadiens
Los Angeles Kings
Pittsburgh Penguins
Detroit Red Wings
Washington Capitols
Clarence Campbell Conference
Lester Patrick Division
Philadelphia Flyers
New York Islanders (Carle Place, Long Island)
Atlanta Flames
New York Rangers (Madison Square Garden)
Conn Smythe Division
Chicago Blackhawks
Vancouver Canucks
St. Louis Blues
Minnesota North Stars (Bloomington)

National Lawn Tennis Hall of Fame
Located at Newport, Rhode Island

National Museum of Racing
Horse racing Hall of Fame located at Saratoga Springs, New York

National Rodeo Hall of Fame
Located in Oklahoma City, Oklahoma

National Security Bank
Institute for which Cosmo Topper (Leo G. Carroll) works as vice-president. Mr. Schuyler (Thurston Hall) is the president (TV series *Topper*)

National Softball Hall of Fame
Located in Oklahoma City, Oklahoma

Natures
"That's Serutan spelled backwards"
Popular laxative product advertised on TV

Nautilus
Captain Nemo's submarine (Jules Verne's *20,000 Leagues under the Sea*): the world's first atomic submarine, U.S.S. "Nautilus," (SSN571) launched on January 21, 1954 (christened by Mrs. Eisenhower): first ship to cross under the North Pole from Atlantic to Pacific. Jules Verne selected the Nautilus from Robert Fulton's submarine built

in 1798. Nautilus is named after the eel "Nautilus Electrius"

Navy rank

Rank	Star	
Fleet Admiral	5	1-4-0
Admiral	4	1-3-0
Vice Admiral	3	1-2-0
Rear Admiral	2	1-1-0
Commodore	1	1-0-0 (war rank only)

Nazerman

Name on pawnshop in New York in the 1965 movie *The Pawnbroker*. The owner, Sol Nazerman, was played by Rod Steiger

Neal

St. Bernard who drank dry martinis with olive up (TV series "Topper")

Marion Kerby named him after her Uncle George: played on TV by Buck

In the 1939 movie *Topper Takes a Trip* the Kerbys own a wire terrier named Mr. Atlas (played by Skippy, who also played Asta in the *Thin Man* movies)

Neapolitan Nights

Theme song of radio series *First Nighter*

Near You

Milton Berle's ("The Thief of Bad Gags") theme song

Nearer My God to Thee

Hymn played by the band aboard the "Titanic" as it sank, April 15, 1912

Nearing, Vivienne

Contestant on TV quiz show "21" who defeated Charles Van Doren

Nebuchadnezzar

Babylonian emperor: said to have built the Hanging Gardens of Babylon

Nebula

Annual award given by Science Fiction Writers of America. First awarded in 1965 to Frank Herbert for *Dune* (see Hugo)

Nectar

Drink of the gods

Ned Beaumont

Detective in Dashiell Hammett's *The Glass Key* starring George Raft in the 1935 version and Alan Ladd in the

1942 film (in both versions the first name was changed to Ed)

Ned Buntline
Pseudonym of Edward Zane Carroll Judson (1823-1886). American writer (of over 400 books) and promoter, especially of Buffalo Bill Cody

Nefertiti and Solomon
Two dolphins who have befriended the Phantom and his female companion Diana Palmer (Lee Falk's comic book series *The Phantom*)

Nell Fenwick
Sweetheart of Dudley Do-Right, daughter of Inspector Fenwick. Voice of June Foray

Nellie
Oaky Doaks' horse (comic strip *Oaky Doaks* by Ralph Briggs Fuller)

Nellie Bly
Pseudonym of Elizabeth Cochrane, 22-year-old woman reporter sent around the world by Joseph Pulitzer's newspaper *The World*, to compete against Jules Verne's *Around the World in 80 Days*. Nellie made it in 72 days, 6 hours and 11 minutes, finishing on January 21, 1890. The name *Nellie Bly* is from a Stephen Foster song

Nellybelle
Pat Brady's jeep (TV series "Roy Rogers")

Neomarinthe Hemingwayi
Species of rosefish named in honor of author Ernest Hemingway

Nelson, Horatio
British admiral and lord (Viscount Nelson)
His commands:

Battle	Ship
Toulon, Corsica	1793 H.M.S. "Agamemnon"
Cape St. Vincent	1797 H.M.S. "Captain"
The Nile (Aboukir)	1798 H.M.S. "Vanguard"
Copenhagen	1801 H.M.S. "Elephant"
Trafalgar	1805 H.M.S. "Victory"

At the battle of the Nile, he lost an arm and his left eye

Nelson, Jimmy
His dummies: Danny O'Day; Farfel (dog), who sang the "N-E-S-T-L-E-S" song. Nestles Chocolate Company is Switzerland's largest corporation. Jimmy Nelson, Edgar

Bergen and Abe Saperstein have all attended Lake View High School in Chicago

Nerka, U.S.
Submarine of Commander "Rich" Richardson (Clark Gable) (movie *Run Silent, Run Deep*)

Nero
The gentle circus lion in TV series *Circus Boy*

Nero the Bear
One of Paul Bunyan's three dogs (the hounddog)

Nero Wolfe
Corpulent detective created (*Fer-de-Lance*, 1934) by Rex Stout; he raises orchids as a hobby. His assistant is Archie Goodwin. In the movies Wolfe was played by Edward Arnold and Walter Connolly (Archie by Lionel Stander); on radio by Santos Ortega and Sydney Greenstreet. Wolfe owns over 10,000 orchids, he weighs about 278 lbs., stands 5'8" tall and his favorite color is yellow. Movies: *Meet Nero Wolfe* (1936) Edward Arnold
League of Missing Men—Walter Connolly

Nessie
Nickname of the Loch Ness monster. Nessie appears in the 1969 movie *The Private Life of Sherlock Holmes*

Neuffer, Judy
U.S. Navy's first female pilot (flies P3's)

Neustandt
German town setting of 1961 movie *Town Without Pity*. Theme song sung by Gene Pitney

Nevada Smith
Role (his last) created by Alan Ladd (1964 movie *The Carpetbaggers*). His early years are told in 1966 movie *Nevada Smith*, starring Steve McQueen. Nevada Smith's real name is Max Sand. His father and mother, Samuel and Kaneha, were killed by three men whose life he seeks in his early years. Played in 1975 TV movie *Nevada Smith* by Cliff Potts

Never Can Say Goodbye
Popular hit song recorded by the *Jackson 5*, written by actor Clifton Davis of TV series *That's My Mama*

Never, Never Land
Peter Pan's home "second to the right and then straight on till morning" (in James Barrie's novel it is simply called Never Land)

Nevermore

The one word spoken and repeated by the Raven (Edgar Allan Poe's poem "The Raven"). In the 1963 movie *The Raven* James Junior is the bird's voice

New City

Town that John People (Paul Maxey) is mayor of, whose daughter Amanda (Pat Breslin) is secretly married to Socrates Miller (Jackie Cooper) (TV series *People's Choice*)

New Colossus, The

Poem by Emma Lazarus inscribed on the pedestal of the Statue of Liberty (the statue was dedicated July 4, 1884)

New Deal agencies

AAA, Agricultural Adjustment Administration
CCC, Civilian Conservation Corps
FDIC, Federal Deposit Insurance Corporation
FHA, Federal Housing Administration
NLRB, National Labor Relations Board
NRA, National Recovery Administration
NYA, National Youth Administration
SEC, Securities and Exchange Commission
SSA, Social Security Administration
TVA, Tennessee Valley Authority
WPA, Works Progress Administration

New England states

Maine, New Hampshire, Vermont, Massachusetts, Connecticut, Rhode Island

New Hope

Small-town setting of TV soap *A Brighter Day*

New Jersey

(BB62) Last U.S. Battleship of the line to see action. Served in World War II, Korean War, Vietnamese War

Newlywed Game

Daytime TV show hosted by Bob Eubanks. Program on TV at the Robinson's house in 1967 movie *The Graduate*. (Eubanks asked *What is your wife's most unusual habit? Answer—Not shaving her legs*)
Also program that the mayor of New York is watching in 1974 movie *The Taking of Pelham 1-2-3*

Newman-Woodward movies

Paul Newman and his wife Joanne Woodward appearing together:
The Long Hot Summer (1958); *Rally 'Round the Flag Boys* (1958); *From the Terrace* (1960); *Paris Blues*

(1961); *A New Kind of Love* (1963); *Winning* (1969); *WUSA* (1970) (originally titled *Hall of Mirrors*); *The Drowning Pool* (1975) (originally titled *Ryan's the Name*)

New North Hospital

Training facility featured in the 1962 movie *The Interns*

New Orleans, U.S.S.

U.S. cruiser under attack at Pearl Harbor, December 7, 1941 upon which Chaplain Howell M. Forgy expressed his now famous phrase (it later became a title of a World War II song) *Praise the Lord and pass the ammunition*

Newport Arms Hotel

Newport Beach, California hotel owned by Mickey Grady (Mickey Rooney) TV series *Mickey*

News on the March

Movie newsreel featuring the life of Charles Foster Kane, who died in 1941 (movie *Citizen Kane*). Narrated by William Alland

Newsview Magazine

Magazine for which Don Hollinger (Ted Bessell) works (TV series *That Girl*)

New Trier High School

Winnetka, Illinois high school attended by Rock Hudson, Ann-Margret and Charlton Heston. Where Charles Linster, a 16-year-old student, set a push-up record on October 7, 1965 with 6,006 pushups in 3 hours, 54 minutes

New Year's Eve

The day the passenger ship S.S. "Poseidon" is hit by a gigantic 90-foot tidal wave (1972 movie *The Poseidon Adventure*)

New York Chronicle

Newspaper for which Martin Lane (William Schallert) is editor (TV series *The Patty Duke Show*)

New York City's rhyming pro teams

Jets: football (NFL)
Mets: baseball (NL)
Nets: basketball (ABA)
Sets: tennis (WTT)

New York Clarion

Newspaper for which newswoman Maggie Du Bois (Natalie Wood) worked. Her racing car was number 7 in the New York-to-Paris race. (1965 movie *The Great Race*)

New York Daily Bugle
Newspaper founded in 1890 for which Peter Parker (Spiderman) works. J. Jonah Jameson is the editor (comic books/TV series)

New York Daily Herald
Newspaper with the EXTRA headline *Dawn Mourns Baby Face Martin* (1937 movie *Dead End*)

New York Gazette
Newspaper for which reporter Flannigan (Ken Swofford) works (TV series *Ellery Queen*)

New York Herald
Newspaper that sent Henry Morton Stanley to find Dr. David Livingstone in Africa. He found him November 10, 1871

New York Herald
Newspaper for which Oscar Madison is a sports writer (*The Odd Couple*)

New York Knickerbockers
First organized baseball team, 1845

New York Loons
Baseball team inherited by Rhubarb the cat (H. Allen Smith's novel *Rhubarb*). In the 1951 movie *Rhubarb* the team is the Brooklyn Dodgers

New York Record
Newspaper for which Scott Norris (Rex Reason) and Pat Garrison (Donald May) work as reporters (TV series *The Roaring Twenties*)

New York Record
Newspaper for which Nick Alexander (Nick Adams) worked as a reporter (TV series *Saints and Sinners*)

New York Times
Motto: "All the news that's fit to print"

New York Tribune
Newspaper founded by Horace Greeley, April 10, 1841

New York World
Newspaper for which Nellie Bly wrote when she went around the world in 72 days, 6 hours, 11 minutes and 14 seconds (November 14, 1889 to January 25, 1890). Newspaper also carried first crossword puzzle December 21, 1913, created by Arthur Wynne

New York World's Fair, 1939
Name of Howard Hughes' airplane (NX 18973) in which

he set a record by flying around the world, July 10-14, 1938 (91 hours, 14, min., 10 sec.)

New York World's Fair, 1939-1940
Theme center: Trylon and perisphere
Themes of other worlds fairs are:
London (1858): Crystal Palace
Paris (1897): Eiffel Tower
Brussels (1958): Atonium
Seattle (1962): Space Needle
New York (1964-65): Unisphere
(All are still standing)

New York Yankees
Team to win the most World Series titles, team to first use uniform numbers (1929), 30 pennants and 21 World Series championships. Prior to being called the *Yankees* (1913) their name was the *Highlanders*

New Zoo Review
Characters in TV series: Freddie the Frog, Henrietta the Hippo, Charlie the Owl
Hosts: Doug Momary and Emily Peden

Newsboy Legion
Crimefighting newsboys created by Joe Simon and Jack Kirby (comic book series): Big Words, Gabby, Scrapper, Tommy. They live in Central City
Their guardian (at night): Officer Jim Harper (debut *Star Spangled Comics* #7, April 1942)

Niagara
Capital of 25th century society setting on radio series *Buck Rogers in the 25th Century*

Nibbles
Elizabeth Taylor's pet chipmunk when she was a girl. She wrote a book about him, titled *Nibbles and Me*

Nicholls, Mary Anne
Jack the Ripper's first victim (London, August 31, 1888)

Nick Adams
Narrator in Ernest Hemingway short stories. James Dean to have played Nick Adams in Hemingway's TV production of *The Battler* on Playwrights '56 broadcast 10-18-55. He was replaced because of his death by Paul Newman

Nick Carter
Dime-novel detective in some 1,000 first-person novels: debut in *New York Weekly* in 1886, begun by John R.

Coryell and published by Street and Smith
Radio series *Nick Carter, Master Detective* by Lon Clark
Movies:
Nick Carter, Master Detective (1939) Walter Pidgeon
Sky Murder (1940) Walter Pidgeon
The Adventures of Nick Carter (1972 TV movie) Robert
Conrad

Nick Carter-Killmaster series
New series begun in the 1960's. Nicholas Huntington
Carter lives in an apartment 40 stories above Broadway
in N.Y.C. Code name N3—senior member Killmaster in
the AXE organization. He carries a 9mm Luger nicknamed Wilhelmina, also a stiletto nicknamed Hugo

Nickel
Coin that mobster Guido Rinaldo (George Raft) flips
throughout the 1932 movie *Scarface*. 1930's gangster
Jack "Machine Gun" McGurn would place a nickel in
the hands of his victims

Nickle Trophy
Trophy awarded to the winner of the annual North Da-
kota-North Dakota State football game

Nicknames
Cities:

Nickname	City
Alamo City	San Antonio, Texas
Big D	Dallas, Texas
Beantown	Boston, Massachusetts
Big Apple	New York City
Biggest Little City in the World	Reno, Nevada
Birthplace of American Liberty	Lexington, Massachusetts
Bison City	Buffalo, New York
Canoe City	Old Town, Maine
Celery City	Kalamazoo, Michigan
Cement City	Allentown, Pennsylvania
Chocolate Capital of the World	Hershey, Pennsylvania
City of Brotherly Love	Philadelphia, Pennsylvania
City by the Golden Gate	San Francisco, California
City of Light	Paris, France
Crescent City	New Orleans, Louisiana
Eternal City	Rome, Italy

Film Capital of the World	Hollywood, California
Gateway to the West	St. Louis, Missouri
Grass Capital of the World	Toledo, Ohio
Gulf City	Mobile, Alabama
Hub of the Universe	Boston, Massachusetts
Insurance City	Hartford, Connecticut
Mile High City	Denver, Colorado
Motor City (Motown)	Detroit, Michigan
Music City	Nashville, Tennessee
Orchid Capital	Hilo, Hawaii
Palmetto City	Charleston, South Carolina
Peanut City	Suffolk, Virginia
Pittsburgh of the South	Birmingham, Alabama
Pretzel City	Reading, Pennsylvania
Railroad City	Indianapolis, Indiana
Rubber Capital of the World	Akron, Ohio
Silk City	Paterson, New Jersey
Steel City	Pittsburgh, Pennsylvania
Twin Cities	Minneapolis-St. Paul, Minnesota
Windy City	Chicago, Illinois

States:

State	Nickname
Alabama	Cotton State / Yellowhammer State / Heart of Dixie
Alaska	The Last Frontier / Land of the Midnight Sun
Arizona	Grand Canyon State / Sunset State
Arkansas	Wonder State / Land of Opportunity
California	Golden State
Colorado	Centennial State / Silver State
Connecticut	Nutmeg State / Constitution State / Land of Steady Habits
Delaware	Blue Hen State / First State / Diamond State
Florida	Sunshine State
Georgia	Peach State / Empire State of the South
Hawaii	Aloha State / Paradise of the Pacific
Idaho	Gem State / Gem of the Mountains / Spud State / Panhandle State
Illinois	Land of Lincoln / Prairie State

Indiana	Hoosier State
Iowa	Hawkeye State
Kansas	Sunflower State / Jayhawk State / Wheat State
Kentucky	Bluegrass State
Louisiana	Creole State / Sugar State / Pelican State
Maine	Pine Tree State
Maryland	Free State / Old Line State
Massachusetts	Bay State / Old Colony State
Michigan	Wolverine State
Minnesota	North Star State / Land of 10,000 Lakes / Gopher State
Mississippi	Magnolia State
Missouri	Show-Me State
Montana	Treasure State
Nebraska	Cornhusker State / Beef State
Nevada	Sagebrush State / Silver State / Battle-Born State
New Hampshire	Granite State
New Jersey	Garden State
New Mexico	Cactus State / Land of Enchantment / Sunshine State
New York	Empire State
North Carolina	Tar Heel State / The Old North State
North Dakota	Sioux State / Flickertail State / Old Colony State
Ohio	Buckeye State
Oklahoma	Sooner State
Oregon	Beaver State
Pennsylvania	Keystone State
Rhode Island	Little Rhody
South Carolina	Palmetto State
South Dakota	Coyote State / Sunshine State
Tennessee	Volunteer State
Texas	Lone Star State
Utah	Beehive State
Vermont	Green Mountain State
Virginia	The Old Dominion / Cavalier State / Mother of Presidents
Washington	Chinook State / Evergreen State
West Virginia	Mountain State
Wisconsin	Badger State
Wyoming	Equality State

Nightmare
Horse ghost, friend of Casper the friendly ghost (comic book/TV cartoon series)

Nightmare
Theme song of Artie Shaw's orchestra

Nikki Porter
Ellery Queen's private secretary, on radio by: Marion Shorkly and Barbara Terrell
Movies by: Margaret Lindsay

Nine Lives
Novel that Paul Varjak (George Peppard) writes and has published in 1961 movie *Breakfast at Tiffanys*

Ninth Metal
The secret that gives The Hawkman his supernatural powers. The Metal defies the pull of gravity

Nip and Tuck
President Calvin Coolidge's two canaries

Nipper
Little black boy who wears a Confederate cap (comic strip *Wee Pals* by Morrie Turner)

Nipper
RCA Victor dog in the trademark "His Master's Voice." Nipper (1884-1895). Born in Bristol, England. The original painting of the dog was by his second master Francis Barraud. He first became the symbol of the Gramophone Company, then the Victor Talking Machine Company, finally RCA Victor in 1929. The phonograph shown in the picture is an Edison. For 22 years the city of Baltimore had a 15 foot statue of Nipper which they sold in 1975 for one dollar.

Nippy Weston
One of G8's battle aces

Nitto Maru No. 3
Japanese patrol boat, camouflaged as a fishing boat that spotted the U.S.S. Hornet enroute to Doolittle's raid on Tokyo. The boat radioed information ahead. The destroyer *Nashville* sank the Japanese boat.

Nixon, Marni
Soprano who sang the parts for Margaret O'Brien in 1948 movie *Big City*, for Deborah Kerr in 1956 *The King and I*, for Natalie Wood in 1961 movie *West Side Story*, and for Audrey Hepburn in 1964 movie *My Fair Lady*. Her only movie appearance was as a nun in *The*

Sound of Music. Her husband is music composer Ernest Gold, their son is rock musician Andrew Gold

Nixon, Richard Milhous
37th President of the United States, first to resign (August 9, 1974) the office. Ford was sworn in at 12:03 p.m. He married Thelma Catherine Patricia Ryan. Their children: Tricia (Patricia), married Edward Finch Cox; Julie, married David Eisenhower

Noah Bain
Head of SIA (TV series "It Takes a Thief"): played by Malachi Throne. In the 1967 TV pilot *Magnificent Thief* Bain's boss was played by Raymond Burr

Noah's Ark
300×50×30 cubits (Genesis 6:15): cubit = 18 inches. Carried eight human passengers. Noah and his wife and three sons and their wives.

Noah's sons
Ham, Shem, Japheth

Nobel Prizes
Established by will of Alfred Nobel (1833-1896). Swedish inventor of dynamite, and first given in 1901
Awarded for:
Chemistry
Economics (first awarded in 1969)
Literature
Medicine / physiology
Physics
Promotion of Peace (Awarded to Theodore Roosevelt in 1906, becoming first American to receive a Nobel Prize, and Woodrow Wilson in 1919, awarded 1920)
(The Day Alfred Nobel died (December 10, 1986) Ira Gershwin was born)
Nobel Prizes for Literature to Americans
Sinclair Lewis (1930), Eugene O'Neill (1936), Pearl S. Buck (1938), William Faulkner (1949), Ernest Hemingway (1954), John Steinbeck (1962), Saul Bellow (1976). T.S. Eliot won the 1948 prize for the British although he is American born
In 1976 all the Nobel prizes were awarded to Americans, no peace prize was given

Nola
Theme song of Vincent Lopez's orchestra

No Name City
Gold mining California town that Clint Eastwood and Lee Marvin destroy in the 1969 musical movie *Paint Your Wagon*

Noonan, Fred
Amelia Earhart's co-pilot on her last flight, June 1-July 2, 1937

Noonan and Marshall
1950's comedy team:
Tommy Noonan
Peter Marshall (M.C. of Hollywood Squares)
Pete LaCock, son of Marshall plays baseball for the Chicago Cubs

Nora
Jiggs and Maggie's daughter (comic strip "Bringing Up Father")

Normandie
French Liner that caught fire and burned at Hudson River pier in New York City February 9, 1942

Norseman
Chrysler's $100,000 experimental automobile, built by Ghia of Italy, that was on board the Andrea Doria when it sank July 26, 1956

Northfork
New Mexico Territory. Town of which Micah Torrance (Paul Fix) is marshal, town near Lucas McCain's (Chuck Connors) ranch (TV series "The Rifleman")

North Manual Trades
Fictitious high school in New York City that is the setting for Evan Hunter's novel, 1955 movie *Blackboard Jungle*

North Quay Secondary School
London school at which Mr. Thackery (Sidney Poitier) teaches (1967 movie *To Sir, With Love*)

North Star
Cornelius Vanderbilt's 256-foot yacht

North Valley League
Los Angeles youth hardball league on which Amanda (Tatum O'Neal) is a pitcher (#11) for the Bears.
TEAMS:
Yankees (Champions), Mets, Cubs, Indians, White Sox, Athletics, Bears (Chico's Bail Bonds sponsor) 1976 movie *Bad News Bears*

Northwestern

First winner of the television series *College Bowl,* begun in 1957. The losing team was Brown.

Norton, Violet

Woman who claimed that Clark Gable was the father of her child. The case went to court April 22, 1937. Mrs. Norton was later indicted for using the mails to defraud

Notary Sojac

Graffiti in Smokey Stover comic strip by Bill Holman— Usually in the last strip in the lower right corner

Nova

Mute girl that befriends the astronaut Taylor (Charlton Heston) and later the astronaut Brent (James Franciscus) in the two movies:

Planet of the Apes (1968), *Beneath the Planet of the Apes* (1970) (played by Linda Harrison)

November

Frankenstein's Monster's month of creation

Now Voyager

1942 movie starring Bette Davis and Paul Henreid, to which Hermie took Aggie and Oscy took Miriam, at the little theater on Packett Island (1971 movie *Summer of '42*)

Nubia

Wonder Woman's black sister kidnapped as a baby by the God Mars (comic books)

Number One

Captain Christopher Pike's second in Command, executive officer (played by Majel Barrett) (see Captain Pike) TV series *Star Trek*

Numbers

United States and France: 1 followed by

6 zeroes, million	36 zeroes, undecillion
9 zeroes, billion	39 zeroes, duodecillion
12 zeroes, trillion	42 zeroes, tredecillion
15 zeroes, quadrillion	45 zeroes, quattuordecillion
18 zeroes, quintillion	48 zeroes, quindecillion
21 zeroes, sextillion	51 zeroes, sexdecillion
24 zeroes, septillion	54 zeroes, septendecillion
27 zeroes, octillion	57 zeroes, octodecillion
30 zeroes, nonillion	60 zeroes, novemdecillion
33 zeroes, decillion	63 zeroes, vigintillion

In British usage, a million is 1000×1000, or 1 followed by 6 zeroes, as in American and French usage. But a billion is a million millions, or 1 followed by 12 zeroes, and a trillion is 1 followed by 18 zeroes, etc. A British quadrillion (1 followed by 24 zeroes) is equivalent to the American/French septillion Sesqui (1½). Quasqui (1¼), word invented by Merriam-Webster at the request of a town celebrating its quasquincentennial (125 years) sesquicentennial is 150 years

Numismatist
A collector of coins or medals

Nurse Jane Fuzzy Wuzzy
Uncle Wiggily's housekeeper

Nurse Judy Price
Doctor Christian's nurse (radio/movie series) played by Dorothy Lovett on film, on radio by Rosemary DeCamp, Lurene Tuttle, Helen Claire, Kathleen Fitz

Nurse June Gale
Doctor Rex Morgan's nurse who is in love with him (comic strip "Rex Morgan, M.D.")

Nurse Mary "Molly" Lamont
Blair General Hospital nurse engaged to Doctor Kildare in seven Dr. Kildare movies. Played by Laraine Day.

Nutt, Emma
On September 1, 1878 became the first female telephone operator

Nyoka (Meredith Gordon)
Name of Jungle Girl (played by Frances Gifford; in Republic movie serial (1941)
Jungle Girl ran for 15 episodes. Also played by Kay Aldridge in 1942 serial *The Perils of Nyoka* (15 episodes)

○

007

James Bond's number (Double O Seven) as a secret agent (Ian Fleming novel series): the 00 / prefix gives the agent license to kill. It is the number of seconds left until the A-bomb was to explode in Fort Knox when it was shut off (1964 movie *Goldfinger*) and the number of seconds left on the control panel when Bond destroys Spectre's rocket ship (1967 movie *You Only Live Twice*)

0A5599

Colorado license plate number of Kawalski's (Barry Newman) 1970 White Dodge Charger (1971 movie *Vanishing Point*)

1/9

Part of iceberg above the water

1/6

Moon's surface gravity in relation to Earth's

One

Buck Rogers' robot (radio series)

1-0

Score of a forfeited football game

1-0

Final score of 1st organized basketball game in which the Student Unions defeated 23rd Street, at Springfield College, Massachusetts, 1891

1 Cherry Street

Address in New York City of first presidential mansion. George Washington moved in on April 23, 1789 "George Washington Slept Here"

One O'Clock Jump

Theme song of Count Basie's orchestra

$1.98

Price on Minnie Pearl's (Sarah Ophelia Colley Cannon) hat

100

Number of 6-foot toy soldiers that Oliver Hardy had built. He mixed up the order for 600 one foot soldiers. 1934 movie *Babes in Toyland* (*The March of the Wooden Soldiers* starring Laurel and Hardy)

100

Number of years Sleeping Beauty slept

$100.00

Prize won by contestants who say the secret word held by the duck, on Groucho Marx's TV show *You Bet Your Life* (each contestant won $50.00) *It's a common word, something you see everyday* etc.

$100

Fine paid by John T. Scopes when he was found guilty, July 21, 1925, in the Scopes "Monkey" trial in Dayton, Tennessee

100 to 1

The odds on Velvets' race horse, (No. 28) *The Pie* in the Grand National Steeple Chase. (1944 movie *National Velvet*)

101

CONTROL code for shoot on recognition (TV series *Get Smart*)

101 Dalmatians

Walt Disney cartoon feature 1961 movie: The Colonel and Towser (older dogs), Pongo and Perdita (parent dogs) Pongo's voice is Rod Taylor, Perdita that of Cate Bauer

102

Floors of the Empire State Building (34th Street and 5th Avenue, New York)

102 Crestview

Los Angeles home address of Lee Ann "Pepper" Anderson (Angie Dickinson) TV series *Police Woman*

105

Elements discovered to date (1978): adopted as standard in 1968

108

Stitches on a regulation baseball

110 years
Age of former slave Miss Jane Pittman (Cicely Tyson) (1975 TV movie *The Autobiography of Miss Jane Pittman*)

110A Piccadilly
London flat address of Lord Peter Wimsey. (Detective series by Dorothy L. Sayers)

117
Number dialed on Maxwell Smart's telephone in order to use the phone as a gun. (TV series *Get Smart*)

117 Pine Street
Address of Olive Oyl's house that burnt down. Popeye and Bluto being the firemen (movie cartoon)

119 North Weatherly Street
Minneapolis home address of Mary Richards (Mary Tyler Moore) apartment D (TV series *The Mary Tyler Moore Show*)

123 Elm Drive
Home address of Porky Pig

123 Main Street
Address of Washington, D.C. CONTROL headquarters TV series *Get Smart*

123 Marshall Road
Hydsberg, New York home address of the Baxter family on TV series *Hazel*

132
Germans captured by Sgt. Alvin York in the battle of the Argonne (October 8, 1918) in World War I. York also killed 25 Germans in the same battle with his Enfield Rifle. Awarded the Medal of Honor
York insisted that Gary Cooper portray him in his movie biography in which Cooper won an Oscar for Best Actor for 1941

138
Elevation in feet of Disneyland (shown on the Railroad Station sign at entrance to Disneyland). Frontier Station is 144 feet

148 Bonnie Meadow Road
New Rochelle, New York address of the Petrie family; Rob, Laura and Richie (TV series *The Dick Van Dyke Show*)

165 Eaton Place
Address of the Bellamy family house in the TV series *Upstairs, Downstairs*

$162.39

Weekly pay of officer Virgil Tibbs of the Philadelphia Police Department (1967 movie *In the Heat of the Night*)

169

Pancakes eaten by Little Black Sambo because he was so hungry. His mother, Black Mumbo, ate 27. His father, Black Jumbo, ate 55.

185 West 73rd Street

Manhattan home address (apartment 3B) of Irma Peterson (Marie Wilson) (TV series *My Friend Irma*)

194

Lt. Columbo's (Peter Falk) automobile radio call number. (TV series *Columbo*)

1001

Apartment number in the Coronet Apartments on San Francisco's California Avenue where Brigid O'Shaughnessey, alias Miss Wonderly, alias Le Blanc lives. Played by Mary Astor in 1941 version of *The Maltese Falcon*

1101 Coast Road

Home address of detective Harry Orwell (David Janssen) in the TV series *Harry O*

1003.16

First Dow-Jones closing average over 1000 (N.Y. Stock Exchange) in history, November 14, 1972

1127 Walnut Street

Los Angeles home address of Professor Theodore Von Schwarzenhoffen, M.D., A.D., D.D.S., F.L.D., F.F.F. and F. (Billy Gilbert). Where Stan Laurel and Oliver Hardy deliver a piano (1932 movie *The Music Box*)

1137 Oak Grove St.

Cocoa Beach, Florida home address of Captain (later Major) Tony Nelson (Larry Hagman) and Jeannie (Barbara Eden) (TV series *I Dream of Jeannie*)

1163 Rexford Drive

Beverly Hills home address of Bentley Gregg (John Forsythe) in the TV series *Bachelor Father*

1803 Ridgewood Drive

Hollywood address of the Buells (TV series *The Mothers-in-Law*)

1805 Ridgewood Drive

Hollywood address of the Hubbards (TV series *The Mothers-in-Law*)

10086 Sunset Boulevard

Hollywood home address of ex-actress Norma Desmond (Gloria Swanson). Her home phone number is CRestview 5-1733 (1950 movie *Sunset Boulevard*)

10327 Oak Street

Los Angeles home address of the Everett family (TV series *Nanny and the Professor*)

13249

Amos Jones' license number (worn on his hat) for his taxi cab company *Fresh Air Taxicab Company* (radio's *Amos 'n 'Andy*)

131425

Al Mundy's (Robert Wagner) prison number at San Jobal Prison. (TV series *It Takes A Thief*)

137596

Sam Spade's license number as a private investigator (radio series "Sam Spade")

139345

Serial number of Wild Bill Hickok's Colt Revolver, "Wild Bill" engraved on the butt. Pat Garrett, the sheriff of New Mexico, once owned it after Hickok's death. It was supposedly the gun that Garrett used to kill Billy the Kid.

186,272

Speed of light in miles per second

1,000,000th Run

Scored in Major League History by Bob Watson (29 years old), Houston Astro first baseman—on May 6, 1975 against the San Francisco Giant's pitcher John Montefusco. Astro's catcher Milt May providing the home run in the 2nd inning. The first run was scored 99 years—12 days from the day, by Wes Fisler of the Philadelphia team. Tootsie Rolls awarded the Astros 1,000,000 pennies

105-36-22

Ralph Kramden's (Jackie Gleason) social security number (TV series *The Honeymooners*)

1,771,561

Number of Tribbles as deduced by Mr. Spock to have accumulated by reproduction on board the space station (TV series *Star Trek* episode *Trouble With Tribbles*)

10610918

Captain (later Major) Tony Nelson's (Larry Hagman) Air Force serial number on TV series *I Dream of Jeannie*

19125047

Clark Gable's Army Air Corps serial number. He enlisted as a private August 12, 1942, at age 41. He was discharged as a Major by Captain Ronald Reagen

1A12

Call sign of Plymouth police car driven by officers Pete Malloy (Martin Milner) and Jim Reed (Kent McCord). Their first police car had serial number 80789 license E 193742 (TV series *Adam-12*)

1D15

Bronk's (Jack Palance) radio call sign of his Cadillac. (TV series *Bronk*)

1K80

Sergeant Joe Friday's plainclothes Ford police unit (TV series *Dragnet*)

O Canada

Canadian national anthem (previously "The Maple Leaf Forever")

O. Henry

Pseudonym of William Sydney Porter (1862-1910), short story writer who created The Cisco Kid among many other characters. The "O. Henry ending" to a story incorporates an unexpected twist. He served three years in the Federal Penitentiary in Columbus, Ohio for bank fund embezzlements. There he met and became friends with outlaw Al Jennings.

O. J.

Orenthal James Simpson (Orange Juice) holds the record for rushing for a single season, 2003 yards (1973)

O.K. Corral

Site of famous gunfight just off Front St., Tombstone, Arizona, Wednesday, Oct. 26, 1881:

Virgil Earp		Frank McLaury (killed shot by Wyatt and Morgan)
Wyatt Earp	against	Tom McLaury (killed, shot by Doc Holliday)
Morgan Earp		Billy Clanton (killed, shot by Morgan)
Doc Holliday		Ike Clanton (unarmed and unhurt)

Virgil and Morgan were wounded by Billy Clanton
Doc Holliday was wounded by Frank McLaury

Wyatt Earp was unhurt
Virgil Earp was the Marshal, Wyatt was his deputy
The other two people present were Sheriff John Behan and Billy Claibourne. Although they both favored the Clantons, they stayed out of the fight hiding behind a building
On trial in November, the Earps were acquitted as law officers
Leon Uris wrote the screen play for the fictitious 1957 movie *Gunfight at the O.K. Corral*
Movie portrayal:
Wyatt Earp (Burt Lancaster)
Doc Holliday (Kirk Douglas)
Virgil Earp (John Hudson)
Morgan Earp (DeForest Kelley)
Ike Clanton (Lyle Bettger)
Billy Clanton (Dennis Hopper)
The two McLaury's were replaced by two fictitious characters

O. P. E.
SAC alert B52 recall code invented by General Jack D. Ripper (Sterling Hayden). A mixing of the initials and words *Peace on Earth or Purity of Essence* (1964 movie *Dr. Strangelove*)

Oakdale
Town location of TV serial "As the World Turns"

Object of My Affection, The
Alfalfa's favorite song. Usually sung to his girlfriend and numersou times to Darla. (*The Little Rascals*)
The song was composed by Pinky Tomlin for Miss Oklahoma (1933), Joanne Alcorn.

Oblio
Little boy who was born without a pointed head in a village of all pointed headed people (1971 cartoon movie *The Point*)

Oceans
Arctic, Atlantic, Indian, Pacific

Ocean City
Fictitious California community (founded in 1875) in which Alex Bronkov is a policeman (Jack Palance) (TV series *Bronk*)

Ocean Queen
Ship upon which Susanna Pomeroy (Gale Storm) works

as social director (TV series *The Gale Storm Show*) Filmed onboard the S.S. President Wilson

October 2, 1872
Wednesday 8:45 p.m. date on which Phileas Fogg began his trip around the globe in Jules Verne's *Around the World in 80 Days*—He returned on Saturday December 20, 1872, at 8:45 p.m. having crossed the International Date Line on his Eastward trek. He actually traveled around the world in 79 calendar days (taking 80 days to do it) spending the last day in London

Octopus
Arch-enemy of The Spider, comic books (see Spider, The)

Odd Couple, The
Oscar Madison, the good-natured sports writer and slob, and Felix Ungar, the prissy news writer, characters in 1965 play by Neil Simon: played by Walter Matthau and Art Carney. In 1967 movie played by Walter Matthau and Jack Lemmon. In TV series, played by Jack Klugman and Tony Randall, who became a commercial photographer

Oddjob
Korean with steel derby hat (movie *Goldfinger*): played by Harold Sakata

Officer (Sgt.) Ben Romero
Sgt. Friday's radio then TV partner (TV series *Dragnet*) Played by Barton Yarborough

Officer Bill Gannon
Sgt. Friday's latest TV partner (played by Harry Morgan)

Officer Chris Owens
Police officer (Bruce Fairbarn) TV series *The Rookies*

Officer (Sgt) Deacon Kay
Police officer assigned to the 6th Division team. Played by Rod Perry (TV series *S.W.A.T.*)

Officer Dominic Luca
Police officer assigned to the 6th Division team. Played by Mark Shera (TV *S.W.A.T.*)

Officer Frank Smith
Sgt. Joe Friday's partner (1952-1959) on TV's *Dragnet* series. Smith was played by Ben Alexander. His wife was Fay

Officer James Street
Police Officer assigned to the 6th Division team. Played by Robert Urich (TV's *S.W.A.T.*)

Officer Mike Danko
Police officer (Sam Melville) TV series *The Rookies*

Officer (Eve) Whitfield
San Francisco police woman, assistant to retired Chief of Detectives Robert Ironside. Eve Whitfield played by Barbara Anderson (she appeared in first 4 seasons) Replaced by Officer Fran Belding (Elizabeth Baur)

Offissa B(ull) Pupp
Policeman in "Krazy Kat" (Cartoon series by George Herriman). On TV voice of Paul Frees

Oh, Sadaharu
Japan's Home Run King, he has won 13 straight home run crowns
Plays for Yamiuri Giants, hit 714th home run Oct 11, 1976 in 8th inning against the Hanshin Tigers

Oh What a Lovely Bunch of Coconuts
Merv Griffin's theme song

Ohio
State in which 7 United States Presidents were born:
  Ulysses Simpson Grant, born 1822, Point Pleasant
  Rutherford Birchard Hayes, born 1822, Delaware, Ohio
  James Abram Garfield, born 1831, Cuyahoga County
  Benjamin Harrison, born 1833, North Bend
  William McKinley, born 1843, Niles
  William Howard Taft, born 1857, Cincinnati
  Warren Gamaliel Harding, born 1865, Morrow County
Three vice presidents from Ohio were:
Hendricks, Fairbanks and Dawes

Ojai, California
Astronaut, Colonel Steve Austin's hometown where his mother, Helen Elgin (Martha Scott), and stepfather, Jim Elgin (Ford Rainey), live (TV series *The Six Million Dollar Man*) *Ojai Valley News* is the local paper

Okefenokee Swamp
Home of:
Bumbazine (human child), Pogo—Opossum, Churchy La Femme—turtle, Dr. Howland Owl, Beauregard Bugleboy, Porky Pin, Wiley Catt, Deacon Mushrat, Simple J. Malarkey (Senator Joseph McCarthy). (Comic strip *Pogo*)

Oklahoma Kid
Nickname of cowboy Jim Kincaid (James Cagney) who is out to avenge his father's death by killing outlaw Whip

McCord (Humphrey Bogart). (1939 movie *The Oklahoma Kid*)

O.K. Oil Company
Large oil corporation which purchased Jed Clampett's land on which he discovered oil (TV series *The Beverly Hillbillies*)

Ol' Bullet
Dog (comic strip "Barney Google and Snuffy Smith")

Ol' Man River
Mississippi River: (Indian name for Father of Rivers) title of song by Jerome Kern and Oscar Hammerstein II in *Show Boat*. Song sung by: William Warfield in *Showboat* (1951), Paul Robeson in *Showboat* (1936) and Frank Sinatra in *Till the Clouds Roll By* (1946)

Old Betsy
Davy Crockett's rifle

Old Bill
Fox terrier which became the mascot of the British Navy during World War I. He was found onboard the wreckage of a German ship. He was taken on board the British battleship *SS Falmouth* and his name was changed from Fritz.

Old Blue
Tom Mix's first saddle horse in movies. (Tom once wrote that he was the best horse he ever rode)

Old Faithful
Geyser in Yellowstone National Park, Wyoming: erupts every 64.5 minutes (average)

Old Fuss and Feathers
Nickname of General Winfield Scott

Old Hickory
Nickname of President Andrew Jackson

Oldies But Goodies
Collection of 12 Rock and Roll Hits. This particular series first released in 1959. Volume One, produced by Original Sound Records 5001, contained these tunes: Side One: (Dreamy Side), *In the Still of the Night* (5 Satins), *Earth Angel* (Penguins), *Eddie My Love* (Teenqueens), *Tonite Tonite* (Mello Kings), *Heaven and Paradise* (Don Juan & Meadowlarks), *The Letter* (Medallions), Side Two: *Let the Good Times Roll* (Shirley & Lee), *Confidential* (Sonny Knight), *Stranded in the Jungle* (The Cadets), *The*

505

Way You Look Tonight (Jaguars), *Dance With Me Henry* (Etta James), *Convicted* (Oscar McLollie), (Art Laboe, a Los Angeles D.J. and owner of the company, gave his remarks on back of album cover)

Due to superstition a Volume 13 was never made, Volume 14 followed Volume 12

Old Ironsides
Nickname of the U.S.S. "Constitution" launched at Boston, September 20, 1797. (Enemy cannonballs seemed to bounce off her sides)

Old Joe
Camel Cigarettes' 2-humped camel depicted on the package

Old John Feather Merchant
Name of B25 bomber (Army 0577) piloted by Colonel Bill Smith which crashed into the 79th floor (Catholic War Relief Services office) of the Empire State building on Saturday July 28, 1945 at 9:55 a.m.

Old MacDonald
In children's nursery rhyme, had a farm (E-I-E-I-O) and on this farm he had some chicks, ducks, turkeys, pigs, cows, donkeys, sheep

Old Noll
Nickname of Oliver Cromwell. Portrayed by Richard Harris in 1970 movie Cromwell

Old North Church
Steeple from which Paul Revere is supposed to have received the signal (2 lights) for his famous ride, April 18, 1775: actually Revere was in the steeple when the signal was set and rode out toward Concord later. Now 189 Salem St., Boston

Old Oaken Bucket
Trophy awarded to the winner of the annual Indiana-Purdue football game

Old Philosopher
Comedian Eddie Lawrence *Is that's what's troubling you, Bunky?*

Old Shoe
Trophy awarded to the winner of the annual Bucknell-Temple football game

Old Ranger, The
Stanley Andrews (radio/TV series "Death Valley Days") He also played Daddy Warbucks on radio

Old Rough and Ready

Nickname of President Zachary Taylor

Old Wrangler

Tom Mix's sidekick: later on TV his pal was Sheriff Mike Shaw. On radio the Old Wrangler was played by Percy Hemus

Old Yellowstain

Nickname of Captain Philip Francis Queeg, of the Minesweeper *Caine*. The name derived from the fact that Queeg had ordered a yellow-dye marker into the water when under attack from shore batteries, rather than leave his ship there, he put the markers in the water and retreated. Some of the crew composed a song, *Yellowstain Blues* (movie 1954 *The Caine Mutiny*)

Olive Oyl

Popeye's girlfriend: sister of Castor Oyl, daughter of Cole and Nana Oyl. Voice of Mae Questel

Ollie

Glasses-wearing little owl who is the friend of Henery Hawk (comic book cartoon character)

Olsen and Johnson

Zany comedy team: John "Ole" Olsen, Harold "Chick" Johnson, popular in 1940s

Olympia, U.S.S.

Admiral Dewey's flagship

Olympic

Sister ship of the "Titanic" ship upon which Archibald Alexander Leach (Cary Grant) first came to the U.S. as a boy in July 1920. Ship upon which Charlie Chaplin returned to England in August 1921. Chaplin again went to England in 1931 this time on board the Mauretania, the sister ship of the Lusitania

Olympic Creed

"The most important thing in the Olympic Games is not to win but to take part, just as the most important thing in life is not the triumph but the struggle. The essential thing is not to have conquered but to have fought well."

Baron Pierre de Coubertin (the founder of the modern day Olympic Games 1896).

Olympic Games

	Year	Location		Year	Location
Summer					
	1976	Montreal		1928	Amsterdam

1972	Munich	1924	Paris
1968	Mexico City	1920	Antwerp
1964	Tokyo	1912	Stockholm
1960	Rome	1908	London
1956	Melbourne	1906	Athens
1952	Helsinki	1904	St. Louis
1948	London	1900	Paris
1936	Berlin	1896	Athens
1932	Los Angeles		

Winter

1976	Innsbruck, Austria
1972	Sapporo, Japan
1968	Grenoble, France
1964	Innsbruck, Austria
1960	Squaw Valley, California
1956	Cortina d'Ampezzo, Italy
1952	Oslo, Norway
1948	St. Moritz, Switzerland
1936	Garmisch-Partenkirchen, Germany
1932	Lake Placid, New York
1928	St. Moritz, Switzerland
1924	Chamonix, France

George S. Patton entered the Pentathlon in the 1912 Olympics

Errol Flynn was on The Irish Boxing team in 1928 Olympics

Cornel Wilde was on the U.S. Fencing team in 1936 Olympics

Noel Harrison was on the British Ski team in 1952 and 1956 Olympics

Four men who played Tarzan won Olympic Gold Medals (see Tarzan)

Olympic Motto:
"Citius, Altius, Fortius" originally meaning *"faster, higher, braver"*, but the current accepted version means, *"swifter, higher, stronger"*

Olympic Rings
Colors (one of which appears on every national flag in the world) of interlocking circles: Black, Blue, Red, Green, Yellow. Five rings represent the five continents

Olympic Van & Storage
Moving company used by the Jefferson family when they

508

moved from 708 Hauser Street to downtown Manhattan (Apartment 12D, on the 12th floor)

Omaha Community Playhouse
Operated by Marlon Brando's mother, Mrs. Dorothy Brando. Where Henry Fonda made his stage debut (1925) in a production of Philip Barry's *You and I*

Once in Love With Amy
Ray Bolger's theme song

Once Over Lightly
Novel written by David Niven in 1951

One-Armed Man
Killer of Dr. Richard Kimble's wife (TV series "The Fugitive") His name was Johnson, played by Bill Raisch

One-Eyed Jacks
Jack of Spades, Jack of Hearts, 1961 movie directed and starred Marlon Brando—only movie he ever directed

One Hour With You
Theme song of Radio series "The Eddie Cantor Show"

One Man's Family
Longest running American radio drama (1932-1959): *"One Man's Family* is dedicated to the mothers and fathers of the younger generation and to their bewildering offspring"

One Riot—One Ranger
Motto of the Texas Rangers, created by Ranger M. T. (Lone Wolf) Gonzaullas

Onischenko, Boris
Russian fencer who rigged his épée in the 1976 Olympics

Onoda, Lt. Hiroo
Japanese World War II lieutenant who hid on the Philippine Island jungle of Lubang until February 20, 1974 (over 29 years) not knowing the war was over

On the Good Ship Lollipop
Sung by Shirley Temple in the 1934 movie *Bright Eyes*

On the Line
Bob Considine's newspaper sports column

Oola
Alley Oop's girlfriend

Oompa Loompas
The Little men who live and work with Willy Wonka in his Chocolate Factory. (1971 movie *Willy Wonka and the Chocolate Factory*)

509

Oomph Girl, The
   Nickname of actress Ann Sheridan (Clara Lou Sheridan)
   Christened by Warner Brothers studio

Ooragnak
   Indian tribe of which Chief Thunderthud (Bill Lecornec)
   is the head man. Ooragnak spelled backwards—Kangaroo.
   (TV series *Howdy Doody*)

Opel, Robert
   Man who streaked across the stage at the Academy
   Awards Presentations at Dorothy Chandler Music Center
   Pavilion held April 2, 1974. David Niven was on stage;
   Niven remarking *"Just think, the only laugh that man will
   probably ever get is for stripping and showing his short-
   comings."*

Open America
   Washington, D.C. based citizens' lobby organization.
   Founded by Dale W. Bush (TV series *Karen*)

Open Sesame
   Secret words spoken only by Lord Peter Wimsey to open
   the inner door of his safe (detective series by Dorothy L.
   Sayers)

Open Sesame
   Magic words that opened the secret treasure cave: "Ali
   Baba and the Forty Thieves," a tale from *The Arabian
   Nights*

Operation Avalanche
   Code name during World War II of the Allied invasion of
   Italy

Operation Crossbow
   World War II Allied air attack on German V-bomb rocket
   sites

Operation Crossroads
   The dropping of an Atomic bomb in Bikini Lagoon July
   25, 1946. The carrier *Saratoga* was sunk along with other
   Naval vessels. The carrier *Independence* was damaged

Operation Detachment
   Invasion of Iwo Jima (February-March 1945)

Operation Grand-Slam
   Auric Goldfinger's code name for his break-in of Fort
   Knox to make the gold radioactive for 58 years (novel/
   movie *Goldfinger*)

Operation Overflight
Gary Powers' U-2 mission over Russia (shot down May 1, 1960)

Operation Overlord
Allied invasion of Europe, June 6, 1944 (D-Day). The Navy's action was called Operation Neptune

Operation Sea Lion
World War II projected German invasion of Great Britain (1940)

Operation Soapsuds
World War II Allied air attack on Ploesti oil field in Romania. August 1, 1943

Opertion Torch
World War II Allied landings along the coast of North Africa, begun November 8, 1942

Operation Vittles
Berlin Air Lift (June 1948-October 1949)

Or How I Flew from London to Paris in 25 Hours and 11 Minutes
Alternate title of 1965 movie *Those Magnificent Men in Their Flying Machines*

Orange Bird
Sunshine Orange Juice's bird (TV commercials). As advertised by Anita Bryant

Oranges
Top producing states: California, Florida, Texas

Orbit
Partridge family's robot dog (TV cartoon show *Partridge Family: 2200 A.D.*)

Orbit High School
School attended by Judy Jetson on TV cartoon series *The Jetsons*

Orbit Jet
Space Ranger Rocky Jones' (Richard Crane) spaceship. His followers were called Junior Spacemen (TV series *Rocky Jones, Space Ranger*)

Orca
Boat in which Brody, Hooper and Quint pursue the shark in 1975 movie *Jaws*

Oregon Trail
Pioneer route from Independence, Missouri, to Fort Vancouver, Washington, in Oregon Territory. Francis Park-

man's book (1849) was originally titled *The California and Oregon Trail*

Orient Express
Train that runs from Paris, France, to Istanbul, Turkey (June 5, 1883 to May 22, 1977). Renamed the Simplon-Orient Express when it began running through the Simplon Tunnel

Original Amateur Hour
Variety show featuring non-professional specialty acts. Radio series hosts: Major Edward Bowes, Jay C. Flippen, Ted Mack "Wheel of Fortune—Around and around she goes and where she stops nobody knows"
TV series host :Ted Mack; announcer: Dennis James

Oriole
Beulah's friend (radio/TV series "Beulah"): on radio played by Ruby Dandridge, on TV by Butterfly McQueen (real name Thelma Lincoln)

Orion
Schooner on which Clark Savage, Jr. (Doc Savage) was born November 12, 1901

Orrin Cobb
Engineer of agent Major James T. West's private train. (TV series *Wild Wild West*)

Ortega, Santos
Radio star who has appeared in the following roles:

Role	Series
Hannibal Cobb	Hannibal Cobb
Nero Wolfe	The Adventures of Nero Wolfe
Peter Salem	The Affairs of Peter Salem
Bulldog Drummond	Bulldog Drummond
Commissioner Weston	The Shadow
Roger Kilgore	Roger Kilgore, Public Defender
Charlie Chan	Charlie Chan
Oliver Drexton	Our Gal Sunday
Perry Mason	Perry Mason
Dr. Duncan Carvell	Big Sister
Inspector Queen	Ellery Queen
Captain Clayton	Joyce Jordan, Girl Interne

Phineas T. Grant	*The Man I Married*
Jack Arnold	*Myrt and Marge*
Mr. Collins	*The O'Neills*
Clint Morley	*Portia Faces Life*
Narrator	*Green Valley, USA*

and has appeared in a number of other programs

Orville

The Wright brother who first flew at Kitty Hawk, N.C., December 17, 1903. 120 feet 12 seconds. It was decided by a flip of a fifty cent piece, Orville won with heads

Osage War Drum

Trophy awarded to the winner of the annual Kansas—Missouri football game.

Osborne Brothers

Country and western group: Bob, Sonny, Benny Birchfield

Oscar

Annual award, in 23 categories, of the Acdemy of Motion Picture Arts and Sciences: Designed by Cedric Gibbons, 13½" high, 6¾ lbs. He holds a sword standing on a reel of film. Named for the uncle of Miss Margaret Herrick (she later became executive director of the Academy), after her 1931 remark "Why, it looks like my Uncle Oscar, (Oscar Pierce)." Bette Davis (who "renounces" the claim) and Sidney Skolsky have also been credited as originator; H. L. (Henry Louis) Mencken also ties the story to the Academy, but differently. During WW 2 the oscars were made of plaster. The Academy will buy back any unwanted Oscar for ten dollars. First presented at the Academy Awards Presentation at Hollywood's Roosevelt Hotel May 16, 1929. In Germany its equivalent is the Bambi, in Finland Snosiki.

Oscar

St. Bernard (Thorne Smith's *Topper*)

Oscar II

Henry Ford's peace ship of 1915

Oscar the Grouch

"Sesame Street" green muppet that lives in a garbage can, his birthday is June 1 (Voice of Carroll Spinney)

Oscar's

Washington D.C. barber shop where Clifton (Clifton Davis) works (Oscar was his father) TV series *That's My Mama*

Oscar Zoroaster Phadrig Isaac Norman Henkle Emmanuel Ambroise Diggs

The Wizard of Oz's complete name (books by L. Frank Baum)

Osgood Conklin

Principal of Madison High (radio and TV series "Our Miss Brooks"): played by Gale Gordon. His wife is Martha (TV, Paula Winslowe). His daughter is Harriet (radio/TV, Gloria McMillan)

Osmond, (Olive) Marie

Sister to the popular Osmond Brothers. Her first two hit records (1973) were *Paper Roses* and *My Little Corner of the World*, both songs which were hits for Anita Bryant in the early 1960's

Osmonds

Singing family group (oldest to youngest) Alan, Wayne, Merrill, Jay, Donny, Marie, Jimmy

Oso Safe Company

Manufacturer of Uncle Scrooge's gigantic money bin

Ostfriesland

First battleship, a captured German ship, sunk by an airplane (experiment in bombing by General William "Billy" Mitchell, July 21, 1921): the heavily armored warship sank in 21½ minutes

Oswald the Rabbit

Walt Disney's first cartoon character. Oswald the Lucky Rabbit (1928). He actually belonged to Charles Mintz who worked for Disney. Oswald later became the property of Walter Lanz

Otis B. Driftwood

Groucho Marx's role in 1935 movie *A Night at the Opera*. Fiorello was played by Chico; Tomasso by Harpo

Otto

Sgt. Snorkel's bulldog (comic strip "Beetle Bailey")

Otto

West Germany's award for the most popular actor in motion pictures, equivalent to the Oscar

Our American Cousin

English comedy (1859) by Tom Taylor, starring Laura Keene, given at Ford's Theatre, Washington D.C., the night Abraham Lincoln was shot by John Wilkes Booth (April 14, 1865). The line being said when he was shot was "I know enough to burn you inside out, you sockdologizing old mantrap"

Our Gal Sunday
Daytime radio series:
"The story that asks the question: Can this girl from a mining town in the West find happiness as the wife of a wealthy and titled Englishman?" She was born in the Colorado mining town of Cripple Creek

Our Gang
Comedy series (1922-1944) by Hal Roach and later MGM: called "The Little Rascals" in TV showings. They live in Greenpoint. Something like 200 "Our Gang" kids appeared in literally hundreds of the comedies, among them:

Carl (Alfalfa) Switzer
George (Spanky) McFarland
Billy (Buckwheat) Thomas
Darla Hood
Eugene (Porky) Lee
Baby Patsy
Matthew (Stymie) Beard
Jackie Lynn Taylor
Jean Darling
Mickey Gubitosi (Bobby Blake)
Mary Kornman
Ernie (Sunshine Sammy) Morrison
Mickey Daniels
Jackie (Toughie) Davis
Eugene (Pineapple) Jackson
Joe (Wheezer) Cobb
Johnny Downs
Allen Clayton (Farina) Hoskins
Darwood K. (Waldo) Smith
Walton (Wally) Albright, Jr.
Scotty Beckett
Jackie Cooper
Mickey McGuire (Mickey Rooney)
Jackie Condon

Ernie was also a member of the East Side Kids
Carl Switzer appeared in Elizabeth Taylor's first movie *There's One Born Every Minute* (1942)

Our Lady of Guadalupe
Patron saint of Mexico

Ovaltine
"The drink of Swiss Mountain Climbers" Sponsor of radio series *Little Orphan Annie* and *Captain Midnight* for which they sold shake-up mugs

Over and Out
A contradictory phrase used on TV and in a great many movies, when a person is terminating a radio transmission. In reality, the term does not exist, since *Over* means *This conversation is ended and I expect a response* and

Out means *This conversation is ended and no response is expected* (yet Hollywood continues to use this obvious error in their films)

Over-the-Hill Gang

Three retired Texas Rangers: Pat O'Brien, as Oren; Walter Brennan, as Nash; Edgar Buchanan, as Jason (1969 TV movie). In *The Over-the-Hill Gang Rides Again.* Chill Wills and Fred Astaire join Brennan and Buchanan

Overland Stage Line

Stagecoach company founded in 1862 by Ben Holladay. Stageline in 1939/1966 movie, *Stagecoach.* Also TV series *Stagecoach West*

Over There

First popular song played in St. Patricks Cathedral in New York City. Played at the funeral of George M. Cohan in 1941

Owens, Brick

Umpire that Babe Ruth hit with his fist after Owens threw Ruth out of the baseball game June 23, 1917 at Fenway Park during a Red Sox-Washington meeting. The lead off batter was Ray Morgan for Washington—Ruth pitched four pitches—all balls—this brought Ruth to the plate cussing out Brick till he threw him out of the game (fined $100)

Ernie Shore then came into the game and pitched a perfect game (only one of 8 on record) and the only perfect game pitched by a relief pitcher

Owens, Jesse

Broke or tied six world track records in one afternoon on May 25, 1935 at Ann Arbor, Michigan:

  100-yard dash (9.4 seconds: tied)
  Broad jump (26 feet, 8¼ inches)
  220-yard dash (20.3 seconds)
  220-yard low hurdles (22.6 seconds)

The records for the 200-meter dash and the 220-meter low hurdles were broken in the equivalent non-metric races.

Owens won 4 gold medals and set 3 Olympic records in the 1936 Berlin Olympics

OXford 8704

Phone number in the Bradbury Building of private detective Jake Axminster (Wayne Rogers). His switchboard operator is Marsha (Elaine Joyce). (TV series *City of Angels*)

Oz

Land over the rainbow made up of the Emerald City and 4 countries: Winkie Country—West (yellow), Munchkin Country—East (Blue), Quading Country—South (Red), Gillikin Country—North (Purple), (L. Frank Baum's Oz series)

Ozzie and Harriet

America's favorite young couple Ozzie Nelson (Oswald George Nelson 1907-1975) and his wife, Harriet Hilliard Nelson, who had been the vocalist with a band led by Ozzie. "The Adventures of Ozzie and Harriet" became a big radio hit, with their sons David and Ricky also members of the cast. Then the show was transferred (1952-1966) to TV. It reappeared in the 1973-74 season without the sons, and with title changed to "Ozzie's Girls". Eric "Rick" Nelson married Kristin Harmon, daughter of Michigan football great Tom Harmon. At age 13 Ozzie was the youngest Eagle Scout in the U.S. He was later a Rutgers honor student. Ozzie and Harriet were regulars on "The Red Skelton Show" on radio. The family was featured in 1952 movie *Here Come the Nelsons*

P

PATSY

Annual Award to animal performers in movies (beginning 1951) and TV (beginning 1958) by the AHA (Animal Humane Association)

Acronym for either Picture Animal Top Star of the Year *or* Performing Animal Television Star of the Year

First winner: Francis the Talking Mule, 1951—The show's first M.C. was Ronald Reagan

Also entries are made to the Animal Hall of Fame of which Lassie and Higgins (Benji) are the first two members

PBX

Private Branch Exchange (telephone switchboard)

PER540

License number of the Monkee's custom Pontiac GTO automobile (TV series *The Monkees*)

P. F. Flyers

Popular tennis shoes of the 1950s

P. F. = Posture Foundation

PTA

Parent Teachers Association. Founded in 1897 by Mrs. Phoebe Hearst and Mrs. Alice Birney

PT-73

Torpedo boat of Squadron 19 commanded by Lt. Commander Quinton McHale (Ernest Borgnine, who spent 10 years in the U.S. Navy) "McHale's Navy" (TV series)

PT-109

Lt. John F. Kennedy's torpedo boat, sunk in the Solomons

during World War II. Prior to 109 he commanded PT101, after PT109 he commanded PT59

Title of 1963 movie starring Cliff Robertson as Kennedy —President Kennedy wanted Warren Beatty to portray him in the movie

PX-37

Airplane flown by Barney Baxter (comic strip *Barney Baxter* by Frank Miller)

Pablo

The cold-blooded penguin (cartoon movie)

Pacific Coast Baseball League

One of baseball's AAA leagues (just below the major-league classification)

Teams in 1940's and 1950's:
  Hollywood Stars
  Los Angeles Angels
  Oakland Oaks
  Portland Beavers
  Sacramento Solons
  San Diego Padres
  San Francisco Seals
  Seattle Rainiers

Packard Darrin

(1941) Investigator Thomas Banacek's (George Peppard) antique automobile. Massachusetts license number 1 78344 (TV series *Banacek*)

Packy

Straight Arrow's sidekick

Packy East

Ring name under which Leslie Townes—Bob Hope— fought in his youth

Pagan Zeldschmidt

Ken Thurston's sidekick (radio series "A Man Called X"): played by Leon Belasco

Page Memorial Hospital

Medical facility where Nora Drake (played by Charlotte Holland, Joan Tompkins, Mary Jane Higby) is a nurse. (radio series *This is Nora Drake*)

Pahoo Ka-ta-wah

"Wolf who stands in water" Yancy Derringer's (Jock Mahoney) Indian companion (TV series "Yancy Derringer"): played by X. Brands

Painted Cave
Location where Steve Adams changed his identity to Straight Arrow (radio series *Straight Arrow*)

Painted Valley Ranch
Home of Red Ryder, Little Beaver, and Red's aunt the Duchess (radio series "Red Ryder"). Near the town of Rimrock, Colorado

Pal
Cowboy Tim McCoy's horse in movies

Paladin
Mercenary gun-fighter in the West of 1872 (TV series "Have Gun Will Travel"): played by Richard Boone. From his business card, reading "Have Gun Will Travel, Wire Paladin. San Francisco," the gag arose that Paladin's first name was Wire. His logo is a chess knight. Played on radio by John Dehner (debuted after the TV series)
In the 1972 TV series Hec Ramsey (starring Richard Boone) Ramsey was sheriff of New Prospect, Oklahoma. In the series Ramsey states that he was Paladin in his youth

Pale Green
Color of Scarlet O'Hara's eyes, as described by Margaret Mitchell in her novel *Gone With the Wind*

Palindromes
Sentences (or words) that can also be read the same backwards:
Madam, in Eden, I'm Adam
(*Eve's reply*): "Name No One Man"
Egad, a base tone denotes a bad age
Evil I did dwell; lewd did I live
Poor Das is a droop
Able was I ere I saw Elba
Tini saw drawer, a reward was in it
Taem, no Devil lived on meat
Ten animals I slam in a net
Otto saw pup; pup was Otto
A man, a plan, a canal—panama!
No, it is open on one position
Was it a car or a cat I saw?
Gateman sees name, garageman sees name tag
Draw pupil's lip upward
Straw? No, too stupid a fad. I put soot on warts
Pa's a sap

Won't lovers revolt now?
A dog! A panic in a pagoda
Draw no dray a yard onward
Zeus was deified, saw Suez
Draw putrid dirt upward
"Do nine men interpret?" "Nine men," I nod
I roamed under it as a tired, nude Maori
I'm a Reviver, Am I?
Was it a rat I saw?
Live not on evil
Ma is as selfless as I am

Pan American flight #101

N704PA Aircraft (Boeing 707) on which the *Beatles* arrived in the U.S. (Kennedy International) February 7, 1964 for their first American tour

Pan Am Orion

The passenger spaceship ferrying people between the earth and the moon. It docks at the moon's spaceport where there is a Howard Johnson and Hilton (1968 movie *2001: A Space Odyssey*)

Panama

Where Atlantic Ocean is west of Pacific Ocean. The Pacific side of the Panama Canal is 27 miles east of the Atlantic side. Locks lower ships to the Pacific side. The first ship to pass through the Canal was the Alex Lavalley (January 7, 1914)

Panay

450-ton U.S. gunboat sunk by Japanese airplanes December 12, 1937 in the Yangtze. Commanded by Lt. Cmdr. James J. Hughes. One sailor was killed

Pancho

Cisco Kid's partner Pan Pancho (TV series "The Cisco Kid"): played by Leo Carrillo. On radio: Louis Sogin, Harry Lang, Mel Blanc; in movies: Martin Garralaga, Chris-Pin-Martin, Leo Carrillo

Pandas

Given to United States by China (1973), kept at Washington, D.C. zoo: Ling-Ling, Hsing-Hsing

Pandemonium

Capital of Satan (John Milton's *Paradise Lost*)

Pandora

Sailing vessel which Captain William Bligh (Charles

Laughton) wrecked in his pursuit of the mutineers of the Bounty (1935 movie *Mutiny on the Bounty*)

Pansy

Mammy Yokum's (Li'l Abner's mother) first name. (Al Capp's *Li'l Abner*)

Papa

Nickname of author Ernest Hemingway, given to him by Marlene Dietrich

Papillon (Butterfly)

Nickname of Henry Charrière, prisoner in French penal colony on Devil's Island, French Guiana. Portrayed in 1974 movie *Papillon* by Steve McQueen

Papoose

Little Beaver's pony (see Little Beaver)

Paradise, S. S.

Gambling ship run by Jim Carter (Spencer Tracy) in the 1935 movie *Dante's Inferno*

Paradise Cafe

Barbary Coast Club owned by Blackie Norton (Clark Gable). It is destroyed in the 1906 earthquake (1936 movie *San Francisco*),

Paradise Island

Home of Wonder Woman and her mother: (comic books/tv). On the TV series the Island is located 30°22′N, 60°47′W

Paramount News

Motto: "The Eyes and Ears of the World"

Pard

Dog befriended by Roy Earle (Humphrey Bogart) in 1941 movie *High Sierra* played by Zero

Paret, Benny "Kid"

Former welterweight boxing champion who died after being knocked out by Emile Griffith in the 12th round of their fight March 24, 1962, at Madison Square Garden: Ruby Goldstein was the referee

Park Avenue Hillbilly

Singer Dorothy Shay's nickname. Her sole movie was *Comin' Round the Mountain* (1951)

Paris and London

The two cities of Charles Dickens' *A Tale of Two Cities*

Parker

Lone detective created by Richard Stark (Donald E. Westlake) in novel series. In the movies *Point Blank*

522

(1967) Lee Marvin appeared as Walker (the name was changed) and *The Split* (1968) Jim Brown as McClain (the name changed again)

Parker, Colonel Tom
Was Elvis Presley's manager: also was manager of Eddy Arnold and Hank Snow, Andy Griffith, Gene Austin. Earned 25% of Elvis' income

Parker, Eddie
Hollywood stunt man who doubled for Larry "Buster" Crabbe in both *Flash Gordon* and *Buck Rogers* serials

Parker, Isaac Charles
Judge for the U.S. District Court for Western Arkansas, seated at Fort Smith (1838-1896), noted as the "Hanging Judge." In his 21 years on the bench, there were 172 capital convictions in his court. He hung the first six men to face him. He hung 88 men. His hangman was George Maledon who personally hung 60 men. His area of jurisdiction was finally broken down into 72 separate courts

Parker Ranch
Located on the Island of Hawaii, is the largest privately-owned ranch in the United States

Parkinson
Blind detective Max Carrados' valet (Ernest Bramah's detective series)

Parkland Hospital
Dallas, Texas hospital where President John F. Kennedy and Governor John Connally were taken after being shot. Lee Harvey Oswald was also taken there after he was shot by Jack Ruby. Jack Ruby was taken there in 1966. Kennedy, Oswald and Ruby all died there

PArk 1000
Chicago phone number of the police department where Lt. Tom Flaherty (Thomas Jackson) can be reached. (1930 movie *Little Caesar*)

Park Sheraton Hotel
Manhattan hotel in which Gangster Albert Anastasia (Lord High Executioner) was shot to death by Vito Genovese's gang Oct. 25, 1957, while getting a haircut by barber Arthur Grasso in the hotel's barbershop

Parlaphone
Label of *British* (*E.M.I.*) Record Company for which the Beatles first began recording in England on October, 1962. (the first label they recorded for was *Polydor* a

German label when they were doing appearances in Hamburg) Their first hit on the Parlaphone label was *Love Me Do**. Prior to signing with Parlaphone, Decca Records turned them down after an audition. In the U.S. Swan, Vee Jay, MGM, ATCO, Tollie and Capitol became the U.S. distributor until the Beatles formed their own label, Apple.

Partridge Family, The
TV series: Shirley (played by Shirley Jones); Keith (David Cassidy); Laurie (Susan Dey); Danny (Danny Bonaduce); Chris (Brian Forster and Jeremy Gelbwaks); Tracy (Suzanne Crough)

Parvati
Hindu goddess which possesses 10 arms (also referred to as Doorga)

Pasha
President Richard Nixon's Yorkshire terrier

Passepartout
Phileas Fogg's French valet's first name, Jean. (Jules Verne's *Around the World in 80 Days*) Played in 1946 musical play by Larry Laurence, in 1956 movie by Cantinflas (Mario Moreno). On a TV cartoon series voice of Ross Higgins

Pat Novak
Detective (radio series "Pat Novak for Hire"): played by Jack Webb

Pat Patton
Dick Tracy's first partner, who eventually became Chief of Police. Played on radio by Walter Kinsella

Pat Ryan
Terry Lee's sidekick, played by Granville Owen in 1940 movie serial *Terry and the Pirates*

Patent
Good for 17 years (U.S. law)

Pathfinder, The
Nickname of John C. Fremont (1830-1890) whose father-in-law was Thomas Hart Benton. American Army officer, explorer, and politician. First Republican candidate for president.

---

*The drummer on "Love Me Do" was Andy White, Ringo Starr played the Tambourine

Patna
Ship abandoned by its crew before it sank (Joseph Conrad's *Lord Jim*). (The day Joseph Conrad died, August 3, 1924, Leon Uris was born)

Patrick Henry
First Liberty ship of World War II

Patton, George Smith, Jr.
American general (1885-1945) known as "Old Blood and Guts." Leader of the 3rd Army in the break-out after the Normandy landings in June 1944 in World War II
His grandfather George Smith Patton was a Brigadier General in the Civil War at age 26. His great-great-great grandfather was a Brigadier General in the Revolutionary War and later served as governor of Virginia.
George S. Patton was named the Army's first Master of the Sword in 1912
First American to enter the Olympic Pentathlon (1912) finished fifth
Patton became notorious for slapping Pvt. Paul G. Bennett at the 93d Evacuation Hospital on August 10, 1943, 8 days after he had slapped and kicked Pvt. Charles H. Kuhl in the 3d Battalion Aid Station, in each instance presumably in a rage at what he considered malingering
Subject of 1970 movie *Patton*, (winning 7 Oscars) directed by Franklin Schaffner, in which George C. Scott played the title role, winning an Oscar for Best Actor, he refused the Academy Award. He was not the first person to refuse an Oscar. In 1949 producer Walter Wanger refused one for his 1948 movie *Joan of Arc*

Paul
The friendly gorilla on PBS Television *The Electric Company* played by Jim Boyd

Paul Bunyan
American folk hero, lumberjack of tremendous size. His wife is Minnie, his son is Jean, daughter is Tennie, his Blue Ox is named Babe
His dogs: Elmer the moose—terrier; Nero the bear—hound; Jacko the reversible dog

Paul Jones
River boat upon which Mark Twain received his training as a cub pilot

Pauline Wayne
President William Howard Taft's family cow which grassed on the White House lawn

Pauling Dr. Linus Carl
American chemist (born 1901)
He is the only person to have received two Nobel Prizes outright: Chemistry (1954), Peace (1962)
Marie Curie is the only woman to have received two Nobel prizes: Physics (1903) shared with husband Pierre, and Chemistry (1911)

Pax
Blind insurance investigator Mike Longstreet's (James Franciscus) seeing-eye dog (TV series "Longstreet")

Peace
Dave Garroway's byword on TV's *Today Show*

Peace Is Our Profession
Motto of the United States Air Force Strategic Air Command (SAC)

Peacelord of the Universe
Title of astronaut Perry Rhodan, Commander of the spaceship Stardust II (see Perry Rhodan)

Peacock
Logo of NBC television network color presentations. There were a total of 11 plumes in the peacock's tail. Retired December 31, 1975

Peanut Gallery
Bleachers where the child guests sat on the Howdy Doody Show

Peanut One
Nickname of Jimmy Carter's campaign jet. By coincidence, the pilot's name was James Kenneth Carter, a United Airlines Captain

Peanuts
Characters (in Charles Schulz's cartoon strip). Debut October 2, 1950, most read comic strip in the world. They all live in Sebastopol, California. The four original members were Charlie Brown, Snoopy, Patty and Sherman
Charlie Brown, "Good grief," the put-upon
Linus, with the security blanket, Lucy's brother (1952). His blanket is made of Outing flannel
Lucy van Pelt, the militant, in love with Schroeder (1952)
Peppermint Patty Reichardt
Pig-Pen (engulfed in a cloud of dust)

Schroeder, the toy-piano player and Beethoven fanatic (1951)
Sherman "Shermy"
Snoopy, the beagle who plays at fighting the Red Baron
Violet
Woodstock, Snoopy's bird secretary (1970)
Sally (Charlie's little sister) (1959)
Franklin (Black lad) (1968)
Frieda (1961). Her cat is Faron (named after singer Faron Young)
Clara, little girl who gave Snoopy his first ball
Debut on TV December 9, 1965
A Charlie Brown Christmas
1969 movie *A Boy Named Charlie Brown*
1972 movie *Snoopy, Come Home*
Plays: *You're A Good Man, Charlie Brown* (Charlie played by Gary Burghoff, music by Rod McKuen); and *Snoopy*
Charles Schulz illustrated Art Linkletter's 1957 book *Kids Say The Darndest Things*

Pearl Bodine
Mother of Jethro (played by Bea Benaderet) (TV series *The Beverly Hillbillies*)

Pearl Harbor's battleships
In Pearl Harbor December 7, 1941:
Arizona—sunk
California—sunk (salvaged)
Maryland—damaged
Nevada—beached (salvaged)
Oklahoma—sunk
Pennsylvania—damaged
Tennessee—damaged
Utah (target ship)—sunk
West Virginia—sunk (salvaged)
When John Dillinger was in the Navy he was stationed on the U.S. Utah

Peck, Gregory
Popular American actor (Oscar for Best Actor, 1962) he once posed for men's clothing in the 1940 Montgomery Ward catalog

Peck's Bad Boy
Stories by American humorist George Wilbur Peck, molded about his son. His first work *Peck's Bad Boy and*

His Pa (1883). Played in 1921 silent film by 6-year-old Jackie Coogan

Pecos Bill

Legendary hero who dug the Rio Grande. Widow Maker is his horse. Slue Foot Sue his wife. He worked on the Cross-Eyed Ranch

Pecos Williams

One of Tom Mix's sidekicks (radio): played by Joe "Curley" Bradley

Pedro

Crazy Mexican played by Mel Blanc on radio's *The Judy Canova Show*

Pedro

Detective Sexton Blake's pet dog

Peekaboo Girl, The

Nickname of actress Veronica Lake

Peeping Tom

Tailor struck blind after peeping at the nude Lady Godiva

Peg

Chester Riley's wife (radio/TV series *Life of Riley*)
On TV: Rosemary De Camp (opposite Jackie Gleason), Marjorie Reynolds (opposite William Bendix)
On radio: Grace Coppin and Paula Winslow

Pegasus

Winged horse (Greek mythology): sprang from the blood of Medusa

Pegleg Pete

Mickey Mouse's nemesis in early cartoons; *Steamboat Willie, Gallopin' Gaucho,* etc. (his right leg has the peg on it). His sidekick is Sylvester Shyster

Peggy Fair

Joe Mannix's secretary (TV series "Mannix"): played by Gail Fisher. Her son is Toby (Marc Copage)

Peko

Pet marmoset of Dr. Fu Manchu

Pelé

Nickname of Edson Arantes do Nascimento (born 1941), Brazilian (Santos) soccer player (inside forward), called "The Black Pearl." A high-scoring, spectacular player, he became the highest paid athlete in the world before he retired from international competition in 1974. In the 1958 World Cup quarterfinals he scored the goal that beat Wales 1-0; in the semifinals he scored 3 times in defeating

France 5-2; in the finals at Stockholm his 2 goals helped defeat Sweden 5-2

Penelope
Odysseus' wife (Homer's *The Odyssey*): every night she unraveled the wedding gown she spent all day making, to the growing impatience of her many suitors. Played in 1954 movie *Ulysses* by Silvana Mangano

Penfold Hearts
Brand of golf ball used by James Bond when he played against Auric Goldfinger (1964 movie *Goldfinger*)

Penguin
Evil villian who does battle with Batman and Robin in Gotham City. His real name is Oswald Chesterfield Cobblepot. On TV played by Burgess Meredith

PEnnsylvania 6-5000
Hit instrumental by Glenn Miller: composed by Jerry Gray (real name Graziano). The phone number is that of New York's Pennsylvania Hotel (now the Statler) which people would dial for reservatiions for the Cafe Rouge in which Miller made many appearances

Pennsylvania, U.S.S.
U.S. Navy cruiser on which the first airplane landed on a ship. Piloted by Eugéne Ely landing his Curtiss bi-plane January 18, 1911 (see Birminghan, U.S.S.)

Pennsylvanians, The
Fred Waring's orchestra. First band ever to appear on TV. Fred Waring is the inventor of the Waring Blender

Penny
Sky King's niece (radio: Beryl Vaughn; TV: Gloria Winters—she married Kirby Grant who played Sky King)

Penny Black
World's first postage stamp issued in Britain in 1840.

Pentathlon
Men's: Riding, Fencing, Shooting, Swimming, Running (cross-country)
Women's: 100-meter hurdles, Shot put, High jump, Long jump, 200-meter dash

People Magazine
Publication which Glenn Howard (Gene Barry) heads—Howard Publications (TV series *Name of the Game*). This series was filmed prior to the actual Time/Life birth of *People* magazine

Peoria, Illinois
City from which Stan Laurel and Oliver Hardy came, on their trip to Mexico to capture Larceny Nell (1945 movie *The Bullfighters*). Also hometown of Fibber McGee and Molly

Pepe Le Pew
French skunk (character in Warner Brothers' cartoons). Debut in *Ordor-Abe Kitty* (1944 cartoon), voice of Mel Blanc

Pepito
Gordo's nephew (comic strip *Gordo* by Gus Arriola)

Pepper
The movie star alley-cat. One of Mack Sennett's animal actors

Pepperland
Home of the Lonelyheart Club Band (Beatles) which is attacked by the Blue Meanies (1968 cartoon feature movie *The Yellow Submarine*)

Peppermint Lounge
1960's New York nightclub where the twist fad started. The house band, Joey Dee (Joseph DiNicola) and Starliters, recorded a number of twist records including "Peppermint Twist." Located in the Knickerbocker Hotel on West 45th Street, setting of 1961 movie *Hey, Let's Twist*

NENCN-KONA
Pepsi Cola in Russian (first U.S. consumer product for sale in the U.S.S.R.). Pepsi is Hugh Hefner's favorite drink, also was Elvis Presley's
James Dean's first film appearance was in a Pepsi Cola TV commercial with Nick Adams (1950)
In 1959 Joan Crawford became a member of Pepsi Cola's board of directors (in the 1930's Joan Crawford did advertisements for Coca Cola).
Richard Nixon was once a lawyer for the company

Pepsi Twins
For Pepsi Cola: Pepsi, Pete

Pequod
Captain Ahab's whaling vessel in Herman Melville's *Moby Dick*. The actual ship used in the 1956 movie was named the *Hispanola*. In the 1930 movie version the ship was called *Shanghai Lil*

Percy Dovetonsils
Poet who wore very thick eyeglasses and drank Martinis:

played on TV by Ernie Kovacs, who created Percy

Perfect Fool, The
Stage appellation for comedian Ed Wynn

Perfect Numbers
A positive integer which is equal to the sum of its factors.
The first 5 perfect numbers:
(6), (28), (496), (8,128), (33,550,336)

Perfect Song, The
Opening theme song of Amos 'n' Andy on radio

Perils of Pauline (Hargrave)
Motion picture serial (1914) starring Pearl White. A
movie biography in which Betty Hutton played Pearl
White was made in 1947 and bore this title, too. In 1933
movie serial by Evalyn Knapp

Periwinkle, S.S.
Ship upon which Laurel and Hardy's twin brothers are
stationed. Bert (Ollie's) and Alfie (Stan's) (1936 movie
Our Relations)

Perkins, Frances
First woman to hold a cabinet post: Secretary of Labor
(1933-1945) under F. D. Roosevelt

Perry Mason
Sharp Los Angeles lawyer-detective (born in 1891) cre-
ated by Erle Stanley Gardner (1880-1970), himself a law-
yer
Radio:
CBS (October 18, 1943-1955) sponsored by Procter
and Gamble:
Perry Mason: John Larkin, Bartlett Robinson, Santos
Ortega, Donald Briggs
Della Street: Joan Alexander, Gertrude Warner, Jan
Miner
Paul Drake: Matt Crowley, Charles Webster
Lt. Tragg: Mandel Kramer, Frank Dane
Television:
Original series (1957-1966):
Perry Mason: Raymond Burr
Della Street: Barbara Hale
D. A. Hamilton Burger: William Talman
Detective Lt. Arthur Tragg: Ray Collins
Paul Drake: William Hopper
The Judge: Kenneth McDonald
Gertie: Connie Cezon

Erle Stanley Gardner appeared in the last episode *The Case of the Final Fade-Out* (May 22, 1966). It was the only episode in color. On the January 31, 1963 episode titled *The Case of the Constant Doyle* while Raymond Burr was in the hospital Bette Davis filled in playing a lawyer—she too won her case

Second series (1973, 13 weeks)
   Perry Mason: Monte Markham
   Della Street: Sharon Acker
   Hamilton Burger: Harry Guardino
   Sgt. Tragg: Dane Clark
   Paul Drake: Albert Stratton
   Gertie: Brett Somers

Perry Mason cases
   Novels by Erle Stanley Gardner, the titles all beginning "The Case of the":

Velvet Claws, 1933
Sulky Girl, 1933
Curious Bride, 1934
Howling Dog, 1934
Lucky Legs, 1934
Caretaker's Cat, 1935
Counterfeit Eye, 1935
Sleepwalker's Niece, 1936
Stuttering Bishop, 1936
Dangerous Dowager, 1937
Lame Canary, 1937
Shoplifter's Show, 1938
Substitute Face, 1938
Perjured Parrot, 1939
Rolling Bones, 1939
Baited Hook, 1940
Silent Partner, 1940
Empty Tin, 1941
Haunted Husband, 1941
Careless Kitten, 1942
Drowning Duck, 1942
Buried Clock, 1943
Drowsy Mosquito, 1943
Black-Eyed Blonde, 1944
Crooked Candle, 1944
Golddigger's Purse, 1945

Half-Wakened Wife, 1945
Borrowed Brunette, 1946
Fan-Dancer's Horse, 1947
Lazy Lover, 1947
Lonely Heiress, 1948
Vagabond Virgin, 1948
Cautious Coquette, 1949
Dubious Bridegroom, 1949
Negligent Nymph, 1950
Angry Mourner, 1951
Fiery Fingers, 1951
One-Eyed Witness, 1951
Grinning Gorilla, 1952
Moth-Eaten Mink, 1952
Green-Eyed Sister, 1953
Hesitant Hostess, 1953
Fugitive Nurse, 1954
Restless Redhead, 1954
Runaway Corpse, 1954
Glamorous Ghost, 1955
Nervous Accomplice, 1955
Sun Bather's Diary, 1955
Demure Defendant, 1956
Gilded Lily, 1956
Terrified Typist, 1956
Lucky Loser, 1957

Perry Mason was played in movies by Warren William, Donald Woods and Ricardo Cortez

Perry Rhodan

Peace lord of the Universe—The Third Power 35-year-old former Major of U.S. Spaceship Stardust (U.S. Space Force). Created in Germany by K. H. Scheer and Walter Ernsting, 1961, with hundreds of adventures published. A comic strip featuring Rhodan appeared in 1968. "Enterprise Stardust" was the first in the series of novels. *S.O.S. From Outer Space* was the first Rhodan movie. Released in the U.S. in 1968 as *Mission Stardust,* it starred Lang Jefferies as Perry Rhodan

Perry White

Clark Kent's editor at the *Daily Planet* newspaper. Winner of the Pulitzer Prize, his original name was George Taylor, editor of the *Daily Star.* Played on radio: Julian Noah, on TV: John Hamilton in 1948 and 1950 movie serials by Pierre Watkins

"Persecution and Assassination of Jean-Paul Marat as Performed by the Inmates of the Asylum of Charenton Under the Direction of the Marquis de Sade, The"

Winner of 1966 Tony Award. Title of 1967 Peter Brook movie referred to as *Marat/Sade*

Pet

Andy and Flo's nickname for each other (cartoon *Andy Capp* by Smythe)

Pet and Patty

Two horses that pulled the Ingall's family to Oklahoma in Laura Ingall Wilder's *Little House on the Prairie*

Pete

Our Gang's dog: with a ring around his left eye

Pete

Friendly butcher in Shake 'n' Bake television commercials (circa 1974-77)

Pete

The boys, Sandy and Bud Rick's pet pelican (TV series "Flipper")

Peter

Gregg family servant, played by Sammee Tong on TV series *Bachelor Father*

Peter and Aurelan Kirk

Captain James T. Kirk's parents (played by Craig Hundley and Joan Swift) (TV series *Star Trek*)

Peter Cottontail

Character created by Gene Autry in his 1955 million-selling hit record

Peter Gunn

TV detective, created by Henry Kane: played by Craig Stevens. Theme song by Henry Mancini sold over 1,000,000 records. Played by Craig Stevens in 1967 movie *Gunn*

Peter Pain

Ben Gay's arch-enemy (comic book ads)

Peter Pan

Hero of James Barrie's (1904) novel *Peter Pan*. Played on Broadway and television special by Mary Martin (1955, repeated), voice of Bobby Driscoll 1952 Walt Disney movie, 1924 silent film by Betty Bronson. In Kensington Gardens, London there is a statue of Peter Pan

The royalties of his book went to the Great Ormond Street Children's Hospital in London

Peter Pan was the name of Babe Hoey's 8-woman orchestra in the 1930's

Peter, Paul and Mary

Folk singing group: Peter Yarrow, Paul Stookey, Mary Travers

Peter Peel

Mrs. Emma Peel's (Diana Rigg) missing husband, found after years of absence in the Amazon Jungle (TV series *The Avengers*). This caused the departure of Mrs. Peel

534

from *The Avengers* and introduced Tara King. Peel's only advice to King is that Steed likes his tea stirred counterclockwise

Peter Quill

Radio detective and scientist: played by Marvin Miller

Peter Rabbit

His brothers and sisters: Flopsy, Mopsy, Cotton-tail. Created by Beatrix Potter in 1902

Peter Wimsey

Lord Peter Death Bredon Wimsey, 2d son of (and brother of) the Duke of Denver. He was born in 1890, attended Eton, lives at 110A Piccadilly in London. His father is Mortimer Gerald Bredon (15th Duke of Denver). His mother is named Dowager (Duchess of Denver), his brother is Gerald, sister is Mary

Played in movies:

    The Silent Passenger (1935) Peter Hadden

    Busman's Holiday (1940) Robert Montgomery

On PBS TV series by Ian Carmichael

Detective invented by Dorothy Sayers, beginning with *Whose Body?* (1923). Married Harriet Vane (*Gaudy Night*, a/k/a *Busman's Honeymoon*)

Pet Rocks

Fad created by Gary Dahl, making him an overnight millionaire

Petticoat Junction

Three sisters (TV series "Petticoat Junction"): Bobbie Jo, Billie Jo, Betty Jo

Petunia

Porky Pig's girlfriend

Petunia Number One

Name of Phillips 66 oil well that stands directly in front of the Capitol building in Oklahoma City. The name came from the flower bed in which the oil well was built on November 10, 1941

Pew

Blind beggar (Robert Louis Stevenson's *Treasure Island*): he gives the "Black Spot" to Billy Bones

Peyton Place

Novel (1956) written by Grace Metalious, sequel (1960) *Return to Peyton Place*, additional sequels by Roger Fuller: *Again Peyton Place, Carnival at Peyton Place, Pleasures of Peyton Place, Secrets of Peyton Place*. TV series

1964-1969—514 episodes, eventually being shown 3 times weekly

1957 movie *Peyton Place* and 1961 sequel *Return to Peyton Place*. 1977 TV movie *Murder in Peyton Place*

Her working title was *The Tree and the Blossom*, reached #4 on best selling list prior to the book's release due to advance publicity. #1 for 26 weeks—on best seller list for 2 years

Phantom, The

Masked seeker after justice, Mr. Kit Walker "The Ghost Who Walks" (comic strip by Lee Falk and Ray Moore): he is the latest of a dynasty of Phantoms, (#21) ruling the Bandari Jungle in Africa for over 400 years. The first Phantom in a line of 21 swore his oath on February 17, 1536. He was the son of Sir Christopher Standish. Kit Walker is an assumed name. Debut as comic strip February 17, 1936. Played by Tom Tyler in 1943 movie serial *The Phantom* (in the film his identity is Godfrey Prescott)

Phantom, The

Thief who steals the gem *The Pink Panther* from Princess Dala leaving behind at the scene of his crimes a white glove with the initial P on it. 1964 movie *The Pink Panther*

Phantom Girl

Secret identity of Tinya Wazzo who was born on the planet BGZTL (comic books)

Phantom Lady

Secret identity of Sandra Knight (debut *Police* Comics #1 August 1941)

Phantom of the Opera

Acid-scarred Erique (Erik) Claudin
Played in Universal movies by: Lon Chaney, 1925 (silent); Claude Rains, 1943; Herbert Lom, 1962 as Professor LePetrie. On Lux Radio Theatre (September 13, 1943) by Basil Rathbone; in 1974 movie *Phantom of Paradise* by William Finley

Pharaon

Cargo ship on which Edmond Dantès was first mate (Alexandre Dumas' *The Count of Monte Cristo*): the spelling is the French for "pharaoh"

Phelps' Department Store

Setting for the Marx Brothers 1941 movie *The Big Store*

Philadelphia Philharmonic
Orchestra conducted by Leopold Stokowski who conducted the music on the soundtrack for Walt Disney's 1940 film *Fantasia*

Philatelist
A collector of postage stamps

Philbert Desenex
Wonder Warthog's secret identity (*Underground* comics)

Phileas Fogg
Englishman who bet he could travel around the world in 80 days
(Jules Verne's *Around the World in 80 Days*)
Played in movies:
William Desmond (1923)
David Niven (1956)
1946 play by Arthur Margetson
TV cartoon series Alistar Duncan

Philip Marlowe
Private eye created by Raymond Chandler, six foot, 190 pound brown-eyed detective born in Santa Rosa, California. He lives at the Hobart Arms on Franklin St., Los Angeles. His office is in the Cahuenga Building on Hollywood Blvd. on sixth floor, phone: GLenview 7537. Played on radio by Gerald Mohr, Howard Duff and Van Heflin, on TV by Philip Carey
Movies:
Dick Powell *Murder My Sweet* (1944)
Humphrey Bogart *The Big Sleep* (1946)
Robert Montgomery *Lady in the Lake* (1947)
George Montgomery *The Brasher Doubloon* (1947)
James Garner *Marlowe* (1969)
Elliot Gould *The Long Goodbye* (1973)
Robert Mitchum *Farewell, My Lovely* (1975)

Philip Nolan
"The Man Without a Country" in story (1863) by Edward Everett Hale: played by Raymond Shannon in 1958 movie

Philo Kretch
Detective played by Soupy Sales. His villain is The Mask and the Mask's sidekick Onions Oregano (Frank Natasi) who kills people by breathing on them

Philo Vance
Affected detective in very popular novels by S. S. Van

Dine (William Wright). First novel was *The Benson Murder Case* (1926). (Debut NBC radio July 5, 1945)
Movies:
The Canary Murder Case (1929) William Powell
The Greene Murder Case (1929) William Powell
The Bishop Murder Case (1929) Basil Rathbone
The Benson Murder Case (1930) William Powell
The Scarab Murder Case (1930) Wilfrid Hyde-White
The Kennel Murder Case (1933) William Powell
The Dragon Murder Case (1934) Warren William
The Casino Murder Case (1934) Paul Lukas
The Garden Murder Case (1936) Edmund Lowe
Night of Mystery (1937) Grant Richards
The Gracie Allen Murder Case (1939) Warren William*
Calling Philo Vance (1940) James Stephenson
Philo Vance Returns (1947) William Wright
Philo Vance's Gamble (1947) Alan Curtis
Philo Vance's Secret Mission (1947) Alan Curtis
On radio played by Jackson Beck and José Ferrer

Philosopher's stone
A substance the alchemists believed could turn metal into gold

Phineas J. Whoopie
Friend and advisor to Tennesssee Tuxedo and his friend Chumley (TV cartoon series)

Phineas Pig
Porky Pig's father (comic books)

Phiz
Charles Dickens' illustrator, Hablot K. Browne

Phoebe B. Beebee
Chimpanzee mate of J. Fred Muggs (Dave Garroway's TV show "Today")

Phoenix
Fabled bird that after a period of time (a century usually) sets fire to its nest, burns itself to ashes, and then springs out of the ashes to a new life.
Name of Rudolph Valentino's yacht

Phonetic alphabet
See the entry for *Alphabet, spoken*

---

*Also starred Gracie Allen—especially written for her

Phred
B.D.'s (Running Dog) Viet Cong buddy (comic strip *Doonesbury* by G. B. Trudeau)

Phyllis
Pet pig of circus clown Felix Adler

Phyllis
Detective Michael Shayne's wife who died in 1943

Phyllis Blossom
Wife of Walt Wallet (comic strip *Gasoline Alley*)

Phyllis Clavering
Girlfriend and eventual wife of detective Captain Hugh "Bulldog" Drummond

Pi
3.14159265+ (Ludolph's number): in 1873 computed to 707 places by William Shanks; in 1961 an IBM 7090 computed pi to 100,265 places

Pianola
Statuette awarded annually to composers and lyric writers of hit songs who are chosen for the Songwriters' Hall of Fame (beginning 1970)

Pianosa
Mediterranean Island setting of the 256th Squadron (B-25's). Novel/movie *Catch 22* (created by Joseph Heller)

Picadilly, Lilly
B17 in which General Frank Savage (Gregory Peck) flies missions (1949 movie *12 O'Clock High*).

Picasso, Pablo
Only living artist who had his work displayed in the Grand Gallery of the Louvre

Piccaninnies
Tribe of redskins at war with Captain Hook's pirates (James M. Barrie's *Peter Pan*)

Piccard Brothers
Twins who made scientific explorations in stratospheric balloons and bathyscaphic diving vehicles: Auguste (1884-1962), Jean Felix (1884-1963)

Pickfair
Hollywood mansion built by Mary Pickford and Douglas Fairbanks after their marriage. A radio program originated from their home *Parties at Pickfair*

Pickrick
Ex-Georgian governor Lester Maddox's fried chicken cafe-

teria from which on July 3, 1964 he chased 3 blacks with an axe handle, 891 Hemphill Ave., across from Georgia Tech. After being governor he opened his second Pickrick in 1974 in which he serves all, selling souvenir axe handles

Pie, The

Race horse belonging to Velvet (1944 movie *National Velvet*) (Pi or Pie is short for Piebald)

In the movie Velvet Brown (Elizabeth Taylor) rode the horse to victory in the Grand Nationals

In the movie Piebald was played by King Charles, the grandson of Man O'War. On Miss Taylor's 14th birthday the studio gave her the horse

Pied Pipers

Singing group on radio: Chuck Lowry, Allen Storr, Lee Gotch, Jo Stafford and John Huddleston

Pierce Publishing Company

Thriller magazine company where Walter Mitty (Danny Kaye) works in the 1947 movie *The Secret Life of Walter Mitty* from novel by James Thurber

Pig Woman, The

Jane Gibson, chief witness in the 1926 Halls-Mills murder trial

Pigasus the Pig

Prank 1968 Presidential candidate

Piglet

Tiny pig who is Winnie-the-Pooh's friend

Pilgrim

Brig on which Richard Henry Dana sailed (August 14, 1834) to California (*Two Years Before the Mast*): his return voyage was on the "Alert," 1836)

Pilot License No. 1

Issued to Glenn Curtiss

Piltdown Man

Supposed species of prehistoric (early Pleistocene) man found in Piltdown, England, in 1911: exposed as a hoax in 1953

Pine Ridge

Arkansas town, locale of radio's *Lum and Abner*. In 1936, Waters, Ark., changed its name to Pine Ridge in tribute to the popular show and opened a real Jot 'Em Down store

Pine Valley

Town, locale of daytime serial "All My Children"

Ping and Pong

Two little penguin friends of Chilly Willy, the "cold" penguin (comic book series). Also the names of the two talking Panda Bears on the animated TV series *The Brady Kids*

Pinhead

Puppet on "Lucky Pup" show (TV)

Pink Panther

Priceless diamond owned by Princess Dala, sought by the Phantom, who is in turn sought by Inspector Clouseau (1964 movie *The Pink Panther*)

Pinkie

Portrait of Miss Sarah Moulton-Barrett (1783-1795) by Sir Thomas Lawrence. She died at age 12, the year of the portrait

Pinky

Mr. Scarlet's boy sidekick (*Wow* comic series "Mr. Scarlet")

Pinocchio

Novel (1881) by Carlo Collodi (Carlo Lorenzini). Tale of a little wooden puppet who turns into a real boy as a dream of his carver-father Geppetto. 1940 Walt Disney movie featuring Cliff Edwards as Jiminy Cricket singing *When You Wish Upon A Star* which won an Oscar for best song. Pinocchio voice of Dickie Jones. On 1957 TV musical special played by Mickey Rooney. 1961-62 marionette/cartoon series

Pinochle

Combination of Jack of Diamonds and Queen of Spades: scores 40

Pinto Ben

Title of William S. Hart film, based on poem he wrote dedicated to his horse Fritz

Pin-up girls

The two most popular of World War II: Betty Grable, Rita Hayworth

Pirate, The

The old bearded man who collected and sold kindling for a quarter a load (John Steinbeck's *Tortilla Flat*. His dogs were Enrique, Rudolph, Fluff, Pajarito, and Senor

541

Alec Thompson. Played by Frank Morgan in 1942 movie *Tortilla Flat*

Pitcairn Island

South Pacific island settled by H.M.S. "Bounty" mutineers in 1790: it was discovered by Carteret in 1767 and named for the midshipman who sighted it. This sailor, Robert Pitcairn, was the son of Major John Pitcairn, who commanded the British troops at Lexington, April 19, 1775, and is said to have given the famous order, "Disperse, ye rebels!" When the H.M.S. "Briton" visited the island in 1812, only one survivor was left—John Adams

Pitching Horseshoes

Billy Rose's newspaper column with the New York Herald Tribune (January 1947-December 1950)

Pixie and Dixie

Mice, friends of Mr. Jinks, the cat (TV cartoon). Pixie wears a bow tie, Dixie wears a vest. Voice for both is that of Don Messick

Place, Etta

Denver school teacher, companion of the Sundance Kid. She traveled with Sundance and Butch Cassidy to South America. Portrayed in 1969 movie *Butch Cassidy and the Sundance Kid* by Katharine Ross, who also portrayed Etta in 1976 TV movie *Wanted: The Sundance Woman*

Plainclothes Tracy

Original title of Chester Gould's Dick Tracy comic strip when it debuted in the Chicago Tribune—New York News Syndicate October 12, 1931

Plainfield, New Jersey

Home town of Mary Livingston in comedy routines on Jack Benny's radio show

Planets

(In order from the Sun)

Mercury

Venus

Earth

Mars

Jupiter

Saturn

Uranus (discovered by William Herschel in 1781, originally called Georgium Sidus, George's Star, after King George III)

Neptune (discovered by J. G. Galle September 23, 1846)
Pluto (discovered by Clyde Tombaugh in 1930)

Plastic Man (Plas)

Secret identity of Eel O'Brian (comic book series *Plastic Man*). Created by Jack Cole, debut *Police Comics* #1 August 1941

Platinum Record

Award for LP record selling 1,000,000 copies, grossing approximately $5,000,000 (gold record is for LP with $1,000,000 sales)

Plato

The intellectual recruit who is usually found reading (*Beetle Bailey* cartoons)

Plato

Rebel Jim Stark's (James Dean) only friend. Plato's real name is John (1955 movie *Rebel Without a Cause*) played by Sal Mineo. He kept a picture of Alan Ladd in his school locker

Play It Again, Sam

Line *not* said by Rick Blaine (Humphrey Bogart) to Sam (Dooley Wilson) in *Casablanca*. Ilsa Laszlo (Ingrid Bergman) gets him to play "As Time Goes By" by saying "Play it, Sam." Rick later says, "You played it for her, you can play it for me. . . . If she can stand it, I can; play it." 1969 Woody Allen movie *Play It Again, Sam* in which he dreams of being Humphrey Bogart. Jerry Lacy plays Bogie in the movie. *As Time Goes By* was first recorded by Rudy Vallee

Playboy

Entertainment for Men magazine founded by Hugh Marston Hefner in December 1953. The Big Bunny, which appears on every cover, was designed by Arthur Paul. Marilyn Monroe was the first playmate of the Month. Jayne Mansfield was Playmate for February 1955, Donna Mitchell was first Playmate of the Year, 1964. Gloria Johnson was the first Negro Bunny. Only the first issue referred to the Playmate as "Sweetheart of the Month." The Playboy Bunny can be found somewhere on every cover issue of *Playboy* magazine

Playboys

Pinky's (Dorothy Provine) house dance band at the Charleston Club (TV series *The Roaring Twenties*)

PLaza 5-6098
> Phone number of Fred and Ethel Mertz (TV series *I Love Lucy*)

Pleasure Island
> Location where the sly fox J. Worthington Foulfellow took Pinocchio to have fun

Pledge of the U.S. Post Office/Postal Service
> "Neither snow, nor rain, nor heat,
> Nor gloom of night stays these
> Couriers from the swift completion
> of their appointed rounds"
> Herodotus (484-425 B.C.)

PLES RING IF AN RNSER IS REQUIRD
> Sign on WOL the Owl's tree-house door (Winnie-the-Pooh's friend)

Plimpton, George
> American writer (born 1927): the Professional Amateur.
> Books: *Out of My League* (1961), *Paper Lion* (1966)
> Practiced as quarterback with Detroit Lions and Baltimore Colts
> Boxed 3 rounds with Archie Moore
> Pitched in a pre-season game in Yankee Stadium
> Played percussion in a session with the New York Philharmonic
> Performed comedy routine in Caesar's Palace, Las Vegas
> Performed as trapeze artist with circus
> Drove in an actual auto race
> Acted as guard at Buckingham Palace
> Participated in an African safari
> Rode in a steeplechase
> Acted in 1970 John Wayne movie *Rio Lobo*
> In 1968 movie *Paper Lion* Plimpton is portrayed by Alan Alda

Pluto
> Mickey Mouse's dog. Debut in Disney cartoon *The Chain Gang* (1930). In first two cartoons he was called Rover. Voice of Jim MacDonald

Pluto
> Storyteller's cat's name is Edgar Allan Poe's tale *The Black Cat*, though the black cat is unnamed

Plutonium
> Womanless planet on which Bob Hope and Bing Crosby find themselves (1962 movie *The Road to Hong Kong*)

Pocahontas Remedies
> Bottled cure-alls sold by Doctor John Pearly (Will Rogers) in his last movie (1935) *Steamboat 'Round the Bend*

Podoloff Cup
> Given to the Most Valuable Player in the National Basketball Association

Pogo
> Possum that lives in Okenfenokee swamp in Ware County, Georgia (cartoon strip by Walt Kelly, May 1949-July 20, 1975). Originally titled *Bumbazine and Albert the Alligator*, then changed to *Albert and Pogo* and finally *Pogo*

Poil
> Redheaded guest, girlfriend of Spooky, the Tuff Little Ghost (comic book series)

Point Maley
> Coast Guard cutter in Walt Disney movie *The Boatniks*

Pointer Sisters
> Popular 1970's female singing team featuring Ruth, Anita, Bonnie, June

Poison Sumac
> Rootie Kazootie's arch-enemy (TV puppet show)

Poker Hands
> (in order of value, most to least value)
> Royal Flush
> Straight Flush
> Four of a Kind
> Full House
> Flush
> Straight
> Three of a Kind
> Two Pairs
> One Pair
> High Card (no pair)

Pokey
> Gene Autry's sidekick: played by Sterling Holloway

Po-Ko
> Little Beaver's little Indian girlfriend (comic book)

Polaris
> Tom Corbett's rocket ship (TV series *Tom Corbett, Space Cadet*)

Polecats
> Twelve member Indian tribe who brew Kickapoo Joy Juice (*Li'l Abner* comic strip by Al Capp)

Polly

Jack Benny's parrot (radio). Rochester and Dennis Day taught her to talk, "Polly wants a cracker." Voice of Mel Blanc

Polly Anne

John Henry's (the steel-drivin' man) woman (folk song)

Polo Field

300 yards × 200 yards

Polygons

Sides		Sides	
3	Triangle	8	Octagon
4	Quadrilatera.	9	Nonagon
5	Pentagon	10	Decagon
6	Hexagon	12	Dodecagon
7	Heptagon		

Polynesia

Parrot that taught Doctor Dolittle to talk to the animals

Ponderosa

Ranch home of the Cartwright family, near Virginia City, Nevada (2,000 sq. miles in size) (TV series "Bonanza," reruns titled "Ponderosa")

Ponsonby Britt

Producer of TV cartoon series *The Rocky Show*. The name is fictitious. Actually produced by Jay Ward

Pontypridd

South Wales village where actor Richard Burton was born November 10, 1925. Singer Thomas Jones Woodward (Tom Jones) was born there June 7, 1940

Pony Express

Between St. Joseph, Missouri and Sacramento, California: April 3, 1860 to October 24, 1861 (lasting 18 months, 21 days). In its short existence, it carried 34,-753 pieces of mail

Pony-hoss'

Ranger John Reid's (*The Lone Ranger*) gray horse for 8 years before he found the stallion Silver in *Wild Horse Valley*

Pooka

Elwood P. Dowd's 6'3½" invisible friend. A *Pooka* is defined as: *"From old Celtic mythology, a fairy spirit in animal form, always very large, The Pooka appears here and there, now and then, to this one and that one. A be-*

*nign but mischievious creature. Very fond of rum pots,
crack pots."* Mary Chase's novel *Harvey,* 1950 movie

Pool Balls

Pocket Pool

1-Yellow	solid
2-Blue	solid
3-Red	solid
4-Purple	solid
5-Orange	solid
6-Green	solid
7-Plum	solid
8-Black	solid
9-Yellow	stripe
10-Blue	stripe
11-Red	stripe
12-Purple	stripe
13-Orange	stripe
14-Green	stripe
15-Plum	stripe
Cue Ball-White	solid

Poole

Dr. Jekyll's butler (Robert Louis Stevenson's *Dr. Jekyll
and Mr. Hyde*)

Poopdeck

Popeye the Sailor's pappy

Poopsy

Talking seagull in the comic strip *Half Hitch* by Hank
Ketcham; he talks only in lower-case letters

Poor Butterfly

Theme song of radio series *Myrt and Marge:* song played
on gramaphone in 1938 movie *Dawn Patrol*

Popeye

Cartoon sailor with gigantic triceps and small biceps who
appeared in E. C. Segar's *Thimble Theater.* His first
movie appearance was in a *Betty Boop* cartoon (1933)
titled *Popeye the Sailor.* He gets his strength from eating
spinach (originally garlic). His girlfriend is Olive Oyl, his
nemesis is Bluto. Voice of Popeye is that of Jack Mercer
and Floyd Buckley. In 1930's voice dubbed by band leader
Candy Candido. In Crystal City, Texas, there is a statue
of Popeye, since the area grows much spinach, dedicated
March 26, 1937

"I'm Popeye the Sailor Man, I am what I am and that's all that I am"

Popeye

Code name of New York detective James Doyle, played by Gene Hackman in 1971 movie *French Connection* and 1975 movie *French Connection II*. In the novel by Robin Moore, his name is Edward Egan, the policeman after whom the character is copied. The real Edward Egan appeared in the 1971 film

Popeye's Nephews

Peepeye; Pipeye; Poopeye; Pupeye

Pop Gunn

Character on radio series *Great Gunns* played by Phil Lord (not Peter Gunn's father, as the joke ran)

Pop's Choklit Shoppe

Soda fountain where Archie, Veronica, Betty, Jughead, Reggie, Moose and other Riverdale High students hang out (*Archie* comics)

Poppin' Fresh

Pillsbury's little dough boy, voice of Paul Frees
Characters in a toy line were:
Flapjack—dog
Popper—little boy
Poppie Fresh—little girl
Biscuit—cat
Bun Bun—baby
Granmommer
Granpopper

Poppy

Pillsbury's little dough girl

Pork Corners, Kansas

Hometown of Sgt. Snorkel (*Beetle Bailey* comic strip)

Porky Pig

Warner Brothers cartoon character created by Tex Avery, his voice is that of Mel Blanc (debut *Golddiggers of '49* [1936])

Porsche Spyder (550)

$7,000 sports car in which James Dean was killed, Sept. 30, 1955. He ran into Donald Turnupseed on Highway 66 near Paso Robles, California. Turnupseed was driving a Ford. Dean's passenger Roth Weutherich recovered. Written on the side of Dean's car was the number 130 and on the rear the words *Little Bastard*

Potsdam Conference

International meeting at end of World War II in Europe (July 17-August 2, 1945): attended by Harry S. Truman (U.S.); Joseph Stalin (U.S.S.R.); Winston Churchill/ Clement Atlee (U.K.)

Potted palm trees

Trees belonging to Captain Morton thrown overboard by Lt. Roberts (Thomas Heggen's *Mr. Roberts*)

Potts Twins

Commander Caractacus and Mimsie Potts' twin boy and girl: Jeremy (black-haired boy), Jemima (golden-haired girl) (Ian Fleming's *Chitty-Chitty-Bang-Bang*)

Pottsylvania

Home country of Boris and Natasha (arch-enemies of Bullwinkle and Rocky)

Powerfull Puss

Mighty Mouse's cat foe (comic book cartoon)

Powers, Francis Gary

U-2 pilot, shot down over Russia, May 1, 1960: later exchanged for Russian spy Colonel Rudolf Abel. The U-2 incident caused cancellation of a scheduled conference between President Eisenhower and Premier Khrushchev. Powers became a traffic spotter for TV station KNBC, Los Angeles, and died when his helicopter crashed August 1, 1977, while he was ferrying a cameraman, George Spears, to cover a Santa Barbara brush fire. In the 1976 TV movie *Francis Gary Powers: The True Story of the U-2 Spy Incident* he was portrayed by Lee Majors. He was shot down on Mayday; Mayday is the international word for Emergency

Powhatan

Father of Pocahontas (Pocahontas was renamed Rebecca in England). Woodrow Wilson's wife Edith claimed to be descended from Pocahontas

Prairie Stop

Deserted bus stop on Highway 41 where Roger Thornill (Cary Grant) is attacked by a bi-plane crop duster. In 1959 movie *North by Northwest*. Actually filmed in Indiana

Premier Dimitri Kissov

Soviet Leader with whom President Merkin Muffley (Peter Sellers) converses over the hot line about the runaway B52 headed for Russia (1963 movie *Dr. Strange-love*)

Pendergast Tool and Die Company

Firm for which Archie Bunker (Carroll O'Connor) works as a foreman on the loading dock (TV series *All in the Family*)

President for a Day

David Rice Atchison, President of the Senate pro tempore President Polk's term ended Sunday noon, March 4, 1849, his Vice-President George Dallas resigned President of the Senate March 2, 1849. President Zachary Taylor took his oath on March 5, 1849. Therefore, David Rice Atchison was President of the U.S. for a day

Presidential Administration Slogans

Square Deal	Theodore Roosevelt
Fair Deal	Harry S Truman
New Freedom	Woodrow Wilson
New Deal	Franklin D. Roosevelt
New Frontier	John F. Kennedy
Great Society	Lyndon B. Johnson

Presidential Oath of Office

"I do solemnly swear (or affirm) that I will faithfully execute the Office of the President of the United States, and will to the best of my ability, preserve, protect and defend the Constitution of the United States"

Presidents of the United States

		Birthplace	Brth/Death Dates
1	George Washington	Virginia	1732-1799
2	John Adams	Massachusetts	1735-1826
3	Thomas Jefferson	Virginia	1743-1826
4	James Madison	Virginia	1750/51-1836
5	James Monroe	Virginia	1758-1831
6	John Quincy Adams	Massachusetts	1767-1848
7	Andrew Jackson	South Carolina	1767-1845
8	Martin Van Buren	New York	1782-1862
9	William Henry Harrison	Virginia	1773-1841
10	John Tyler	Virginia	1790-1862
11	James Knox Polk	North Carolina	1795-1849
12	Zachary Taylor	Virginia	1784-1850
13	Millard Fillmore	New York	1800-1874
14	Franklin Pierce	New Hampshire	1804-1869

15	James Buchanan	Pennsylvania	1791-1868
16	Abraham Lincoln	Kentucky	1809-1865
17	Andrew Johnson	North Carolina	1808-1875
18	Ulysses Simpson Grant	Ohio	1822-1885
19	Rutherford Birchard Hayes	Ohio	1822-1893
20	James Abram Garfield	Ohio	1831-1881
21	Chester Alan Arthur	Vermont	1830-1886
22	Stephen Grover Cleveland	New Jersey	1837-1908
23	Benjamin Harrison	Ohio	1833-1901
24	Stephen Grover Cleveland	New Jersey	1837-1908
25	William McKinley	Ohio	1843-1901
26	Theodore Roosevelt	New York	1858-1919
27	William Howard Taft	Ohio	1857-1930
28	Thomas Woodrow Wilson	Virginia	1856-1924
29	Warren Gamaliel Harding	Ohio	1865-1923
30	John Calvin Coolidge	Vermont	1872-1933
31	Herbert Clark Hoover	Iowa	1874-1964
32	Frank Delano Roosevelt	New York	1882-1945
33	Harry S Truman	Missouri	1884-1972
34	Dwight David Eisenhower	Texas	1890-1969
35	John Fitzgerald Kennedy	Massachusetts	1917-1963
36	Lyndon Baines Johnson	Texas	1908-1973
37	Richard Milhous Nixon	California	1913-
38	Gerald Rudolph Ford	Nebraska	1913-
39	Jimmy Earl Carter	Georgia	1924-

Abraham Lincoln and Charles Darwin were both born February 12, 1809

Presidents, U.S.

Fictitious movies:

Seven Days in May (1964) Jordan Lyman (Fredric March)

Advise and Consent (1962) The President (Franchot Tone)

Dr. Strangelove (1964) Merkin Muffley (Peter Sellers)

Fail Safe (1964) The President (Henry Fonda)

Kisses for My President (1964) Leslie McCloud (Polly Bergen)

Wild in the Streets (1968) Max Frost (Chris Jones)

The Man (1972) Douglas Dilman (James Earl Jones)

The Forbin Project (1970) The President (Gordon Pinsent)

TV:

Washington: Behind Closed Doors (1977) Monckton (Jason Robards, Jr.)

Play:

Of Thee I Sing (1931) John P. Wintergreen (William Gaxton)

His vice president is Alexander Throttlebottom (Victor Moore)

Preston

Town setting of radio series *Joyce Jordon, Girl Interne*

Preston, Shirley

In April, 1967, became the first female taxicab driver in London

Price-Waterhouse & Company

Public accounting firm that certifies the Academy Award and Emmy nominations, they also total and verify the votes

Primrose Lane

Theme song of the 1971-1972 TV series *The Smith Family* starring Henry Fonda. The theme was sung by Jerry Wallace who originally recorded the song in 1959

Prince

Rudolph Valentino's pet German Shepherd

Prince Barin

Rightful ruler of the planet Mongo played by Richard Alexander and Roland Drew (*Flash Gordon* movies serials)

Prince Charming

Woke Snow White with a kiss—In the 1937 Disney movie Harry Stockwell, father of Dean Stockwell, sang the role of the prince

Prince of Wales

British ship upon which President Roosevelt and Prime Minister Churchill signed the Atlantic Charter August 14, 1941

Prince Philip

Woke Sleeping Beauty with a kiss (1959 Walt Disney cartoon movie) Voice of Bill Shirley

Prince Rainier III

Albert Alexandre Louis Pierre Grimaldi ruler of the country of Monaco. Married Hollywood movie star Grace Kelly, April 19, 1956

Prince Tallen

Ruler of Saturn in 1939 serial *Buck Rogers* (played by Philson Ahn)

Prince Valiant

Comic strip Viking hero drawn by Hal Foster debut— February 13, 1937. Played by Robert Wagner in 1954 movie *Prince Valiant*

Princess Anck-es-en-Amon

The Mummy's (Im-ho-tep) mate. She is played by Zita Johann in 1932 movie *The Mummy*

Princess Aura

Daughter of Ming the Merciless (Emperor of planet Mongo). She befriends Flash, Dale, and Dr. Zarkow (*Flash Gordon series*) Played in serial by Priscilla Lawson and Shirley Deane. In comics she was the wife of Prince Barin

Princess Aurora

Sleeping Beauty's name, also called Briar Rose (Fairy Tale)

Princess Dala

Owner of the precious diamond *The Pink Panther* which is stolen from her. (Played by Claudia Cardinale) 1964 movie *The Pink Panther*. Her pet poodle is named Amber

Princess Leia Organa

Young Senator from Alderaan (1977 movie *Star Wars*) Played by Carrie Fisher, the daughter of Debbie Reynolds and Eddie Fisher

Princess Summerfall—Winterspring

Pretty Indian maiden on TV series, originally a puppet eventually a real person *Howdy Doody Time*. Played by Judy Tyler

Princeton, U.S.

Navy gunboat on which a 12-inch gun exploded, February 28, 1844, killing the Secretary of State, Abel P. Upshur and Secretary of the Navy, Thomas W. Gilmer. Other government officials were also killed. President Tyler was on board, but unhurt

Priscilla

Pig on board Boner's Ark (comic strip *Boner's Ark*)

Private Duane Doberman

Dumb but loveable little guy played by Maurice Gosfield on TV series *You'll Never Get Rich* (The Phil Silvers Show). He also plays his sister Diane, who has a striking resemblance to Duane.

Prizefighter and the Lady, The

1933 movie starring Myrna Loy, Walter Huston, Otto Kruger, Max Baer, Jack Dempsey, Jess Willard, James J. Jefferies, Primo Carnero

Probe

Organization that sends agents throughout the world to combat crime, equipped with hidden cameras, microphones and receivers. Rotating agents are:

Hugh Lockwood (Hugh O'Brian)

Christopher Grove (Doug McClure)

Nick Bianco (Tony Franciosa)

B. C. Cameron (Burgess Meredith) is head of Probe (TV series *SEARCH*)

Producers/Directors

Middle Initials:

Cecil B. DeMille = Cecil Blount DeMille

David O. Selznick = David Oliver Selznick

Louis B. Mayer = Louis Burt Mayer

Darryl F. Zanuck = Darryl Francis Zanuck

Irving G. Thalberg = Irving Grant Thalberg

Professor Archimedes Q. Porter

Jane Porter's father. Jane Porter eventually became Mrs. John Clayton Jr., better known as Tarzan's mate, Jane. (novels)

Professor Edam

Famed mouse scientist, father of Mighty Mouse's girl-friend, Mitzi (comic book series "Mighty Mouse")

Professor (Harold) Everett

Mathematics instructor played by Richard Long. TV series "Nanny and the Professor"

Professor Farrell

Mount Jennings Observatory (Chicago) astronomer who first reported several explosions on the planet Mars. Orson Welles' *Mercury Theatre on the Air* broadcast of H. G. Wells' *The War of the Worlds* October 30, 1938 broadcast Professor Morse of Macmillan University later reports three explosions on the planet Mars

Professor Fate

Villain who drove the car Hannibal Twin 8 (1965 movie *The Great Race*): played by Jack Lemmon

Professor Flutesnoot

Chemistry teacher at Riverdale High School (*Archie* Comics)

Professor Goodie

Salesman of Aunt Jemima Waffles. Wallace the Waffle Whiffer, who needless to say loves waffles, is always a bother to the Professor

Professor Harold Hill

Better known as *The Music Man* played by Robert Preston in 1962 movie

Professor (Henry) Higgins

Phonetics expert who taught Eliza Doolittle to be a lady (G.B. Shaw's play *Pygmalion* and stage/movie musical *My Fair Lady*). Played in 1938 movie *Pygmalion* by Leslie Howard. In 1964 movie *My Fair Lady* by Rex Harrison

Professor Horton

Scientist who created the Human Torch (comic book series "The Human Torch")

Professor Howland Owl

Wizard owl who resides along with Pogo in the Okefenokee Swamp (comic strip *Pogo*)

Professor (Julius) Kelp

The Nutty Professor (played by Jerry Lewis) at A. S. University. After drinking his magic formula he turns into the cool, suave Buddy Love (1963 movie *The Nutty Professor*)

Professor Kokintz

Leading Scientist of Grand Fenwick. Played by David Kossoff in 1963 movie *The Mouse on the Moon*

Professor LeBlanc

Jack Benny's violin teacher (Played by Mel Blanc) on radio's *The Jack Benny Program*

Professor Lucifer G. (Gorgonzola) Butts

Creator of complicated and ingenious inventions in Rube Goldberg cartoons

Professor Ludwig von Drake

Scottish relative of Donald Duck and Scrooge McDuck. Voice of Paul Frees. Debut on Walt Disney's *Wonderful World of Color* (1961)

Professor Marvel

Itinerant salesman who becomes the Wizard of Oz in Dorothy's dream (L. Frank Baum's *The Wizard of Oz*)

Professor (James) Moriarty

Sherlock Holmes' arch enemy.

Professor Ned Brainard

The absentminded professor of Medfield College played by Fred MacMurray in the 1961 movie *The Absentminded Professor* and 1963 movie *Son of Flubber*. He invented a magic substance called Flubber

Professor Ohm

Cat enemy of Mighty Mouse (comic book cartoon) others are The Claw and Oil Can Harry

Professor Pierre Aronnax

Narrator of Jules Verne's novel *20,000 Leagues Under the Sea*. Played by Paul Lukas in 1954 movie

Professor Quiz

One of the earliest radio quiz programs (1936): Craig Earl was the quizmaster

Professor Reinstein

Scientist who created the secret potion that turns Steve Rogers into *Captain America*

Professor Richard Pierson

Princeton University professor who was the main character (played by Orson Wells) in his Mercury Theatre on the Air radio broadcast of H. G. Wells' *The War of the Worlds*, October 30, 1938

Professor Roy Hinkley

One of the 7 survivors of a shipwreck. Played by Russell Johnson on TV series *Gilligan's Island*

Professor Augustus S.F.X. Van Dusen

The Thinking Machine: detective created by Jacques Futrelle who perished on board the Titanic when it sank

Professor Wonmug

Inventor of the time machine that allows Alley Oop and his friends to appear in the 20th Century

Profiles In Courage

Biographical work by John F. Kennedy
The only president awarded a Pulitzer Prize, 1957

Proud Lady

Columbia's Gem of the Ocean.
Columbia Picture's logo of a woman holding a torch in her lifted right hand. She was retired in 1976 for a new

trademark after serving for over 50 years. Sixteen year old Jane Chester posed for the picture

Promontory Point

Place north of Salt Lake, Utah, where we linked the Union Pacific and Central Pacific Railroads May 10, 1869. The Golden Spike was first hit by Leland Stanford at 2:47 P.M. EST (first swing missed the spike); spike was made by Schultz, Fisher and Machling of San Francisco. The weight was 18 oz. with a 6-inch nugget attached to the head. Union Pacific locomotive was No. 119, Central Pacific locomotive was No. 60 named "Jupiter". The telegrapher sent out the single word "done" after the spike was driven. The same spike was used in Cecil B. DeMille's 1938 movie *Union Pacific*

Proteus

Nuclear-powered submarine (U91035) miniaturized so that it can travel through the bloodstream of a human patient injected in the carotid artery (Isaac Asimov's *Fantastic Voyage*)
In 1968 animated TV series the vessel is called The Voyager

Proxima Centauri

Faint star near Alpha Centauri, 4.16 light years distant; nearest star (except for the Sun) to the Earth

Prudence Pimpleton

Detective Fearless Fosdick's perennial fiancee

P's and Q's

Old English saying "Mind your P's and Q's" refers to watching one's pints and quarts. Wife's remark to husband as he went to his favorite pub

Pseudonyms

Pseudonym	Original Name
Don Adams	Donald Yarmy
Eddie Albert	Edward Albert Heimberger
Fred Allen	John Florence Sullivan
Woody Allen	Allen Stewart Koningsberg
June Allyson	Ella Geisman
Leon Ames	Leon Wycoff
Julie Andrews	Julia Elizabeth Welles
Eve Arden	Eunice Quedens
Richard Arlen	Richard Van Mattemore

557

Edward Arnold	Guenther Schneider
Jean Arthur	Gladys Georgianna Greene
Fred Astaire	Frederick Austerlitz
Mary Astor	Lucille Vasconcells Langhanke
Lauren Bacall	Betty Joan Perski
Anne Bancroft	Anne Maria Italiano
Freddie Bartholomew	Frederick Llewellyn
Tony Bennett	Antonio Benedetto
Jack Benny	Benjamin Kubelsky
Milton Berle	Milton Berlinger
Gertrude Berg	Gertrude Edelstein
Irving Berlin	Israel Baline
Robert Blake	Michael Gubitosi
Max Brand	Frederick Faust
Shirley Booth	Thelma Booth Ford
Charles Bronson	Charles Bunchinsky
Billie Burke	Ethelbert Appleton Burke
George Burns	Nathan Burnbaum
Richard Burton	Richard Walter Jenkins Jr.
Red Buttons	Aaron Chwatt
Rory Calhoun	Francis Timothy Durgin
Judy Canova	Julia Etta
Eddie Cantor	Israel Itskowitz
Jeff Chandler	Ira Grossel
Cyd Charisse	Tula Ellice Finklea
Dane Clark	Barney Zanville
Claudette Colbert	Lily Chauchoin
Mike Connors	Krekor Ohanian
Joan Crawford	Billie Cassin/Lucille LeSueur
Tony Curtis	Bernard Schwartz
Vic Damone	Vito Farinola
Bobby Darin	Robert Walden Cassotto
Jane Darwell	Pattie Woodward
Dennis Day	Eugene Dennis McNutly
Doris Day	Doris Van Kappelhoff
Laraine Day	Loraine Johnson
Yvonne De Carlo	Peggy Yvonne Middleton
Sandra Dee	Alexandra Zuck
Marlene Dietrich	Maria Magdalene von Losch
Richard Dix	Ernest Carlton Brimmer
Troy Donahue	Merle Johnson, Jr.
Diana Dors	Diana Fluck
Kirk Douglas	Issur Danielovitch Demsky

Melvyn Douglas	Melvin Hesselberg
Mike Douglas	Michael Dowd
Marie Dressler	Leila von Koerber
Bob Dylan	Robert Zimmerman
George Eliot	Mary Ann Evans
Dale Evans	Frances Octavia Smith
Douglas Fairbanks	Julius Ullman
Alice Faye	Alice Jeanne Leppert
Jose Ferrer	Jose Vincente Ferrery Centron
Barry Fitzgerald	William Joseph Shields
Rhonda Fleming	Marilyn Louis
Joan Fontaine	Joan de Havilland
Redd Foxx	John Sanford
Glen Ford	Gwyllyn Ford
Wallace Ford	Samuel Jones
Arlene Francis	Arlene Kazanjian
Connie Francis	Concetta Franconero
Kay Francis	Katharine Gibbs
Clark Gable	William Clark Gable
Greta Garbo	Greta Gustafsson
John Garfield	Julius Garfinkle
Judy Garland	Frances Gumm
James Garner	James Baumgarner
Janet Gaynor	Laura Gainor
Mitzi Gaynor	Francesca Mitzi Gerber
Gladys George	Gladys Clare
Georgia Gibbs	Freda Gibbson
Paulette Goddard	Pauline Levy
Gloria Grahame	Gloria Grahame Hallward
Stewart Granger	James Stewart
Cary Grant	Archibald Leach
Kathryn Grayson	Zelma Hendrick
Jane Greer	Bettyjane Greer
Buddy Hackett	Leonard Hacker
Alan Hale	Alan MacKahn
Ann Harding	Dorothy Gatley
Jean Harlow	Harelan Carpentier
Rex Harrison	Reginald Harrison
Laurence Harvey	Lauruska Mischa Skikne
June Haver	June Stovenour
Sterling Hayden	John Hamilton
Susan Hayward	Edythe Marrener
Rita Hayworth	Margarita Casino

Van Heflin	Emmet Evan Heflin
Audrey Hepburn	Audry Hepburn-Ruston
William Holden	William Beedle, Jr.
Billie Holiday	Eleanora Holiday
Judy Holliday	Judith Tuvim
Hedda Hooper	Elda Furry
Harry Houdini	Ehrich Weiss
Rock Hudson	Roy Scherer (Adopted by Wallace Fitzgerald, hence Roy Fitzgerald)
Jennifer Jones	Phyllis Isley
Boris Karloff	William Henry Pratt
Danny Kaye	David Daniel Kuminsky
Arthur Lake	Arthur Silverlake
Veronica Lake	Constance Ockelman
Heddy Lamarr	Hedwig Eva Maria Kiesler
Dorothy Lamour	Dorothy Kaumeyer
Elsa Lanchester	Elizabeth Sullivan
Carole Landis	Frances Ridste
Priscilla Lane	Priscilla Mullican
Mario Lanza	Alfred Arnold Cocozza
Stan Laurel	Arthur Stanley Jefferson
Piper Laurie	Rosetta Jacobs
Steve Lawrence	Sidney Leibowitz
Gypsy Rose Lee	Louise Hovick
Janet Leigh	Jeanette Morrison
Vivien Leigh	Vivian Hartley
Lenin	Vladimir I. Ulyanov
Jerry Lewis	Joseph Levitch
Margaret Lindsay	Margaret Kies
Carole Lombard	Jane Alice Peters
Jack Lord	Jack Ryan
Sophia Loren	Sofia Villani Scicolone
Myrna Loy	Myrna Williams
Bela Lugosi	Bela Blasko
Paul Lukas	Paul Lugacs
Diana Lynn	Dorlores Loehr
Shirley MacLaine	Shirley MacLean Beaty
Guy Madison	Robert Moseley
Marjorie Main	Mary Tomlinson
Karl Malden	Malden Sukilovich
Dorothy Malone	Dorothy Maloney
Jayne Mansfield	Vera Jane Palmer

560

Fredric March	Ernest Bickel
Dean Martin	Dino Crocetti
Tony Martin	Alfred Morris
Marilyn Monroe	Norma Jean Baker
Virginia Mayo	Virginia Jones
Butterfly McQueen	Thelma Lincoln
Ethel Merman	Ethel Zimmerman
Vera Miles	Vera Ralston
Ray Milland	Reginald Truscott-Jones
Ann Miller	Lucille Ann Collier
Carmen Miranda	Maria Do Carmo
	Miranda Da Cunha
Maria Montez	Maria Africa Vidal de Santo Silas
George Montgomery	George Letz
Robert Montgomery	Henry Montgomery Jr.
Terry Moore	Helen Koford
Dennis Morgan	Stanley Morner
Frank Morgan	Francis Philip Wuppermann
Henry Morgan	Henry Lerner Van Ost, Jr.
Paul Muni	Muni Weisenfreund
Kim Novak	Marilyn Pauline Novak
Jack Oakie	Lewis Offield
Merle Oberon	Estelle Merle
	O'Brien Thompson
Hugh O'Brien	Hugh J. Krampe
Margaret O'Brien	Angela O'Brien
Maureen O'Hara	Maureen Fitzsimmons
Dennis O'Keefe	Edward Flanagan
Janis Page	Donna Mae Tjaden
Pattie Page	Clara Ann Fowler
Debra Paget	Debralee Griffin
Jean Parker	Mae Green
Susan Peters	Suzanne Carnahan
Mary Pickford	Gladys Smith
Jane Powell	Suzanne Bruce
Paula Prentiss	Paula Ragusa
Robert Preston	Robert Preston Meservey
George Raft	George Ranft
Basil Rathbone	Philip St. John
	Basil Rathbone
Martha Raye	Margaret Reed
Donna Reed	Donna Mullenger

Debbie Reynolds	Mary Frances Reynolds
Marjorie Reynolds	Marjorie Goodspeed
Edward G. Robinson	Emanuel Goldenberg
Sugar Ray Robinson	Walker Smith
May Robson	Mary Robison
Ginger Rogers	Virginia McMath
Roy Rogers	Leonard Slye
Gilbert Roland	Louis Antonio Damaso Alonso
Lillian Russell	Helen Louise Leonard
Lizabeth Scott	Emma Matzo
Randolph Scott	Randolph Crane
Artie Shaw	Abraham Isaac Arshawasky
Luke Short	Frederick Glidd
Penny Singleton	Mary Ann Dorothy McNulty
Ann Sothern	Harriette Lake
Barbara Stanwyck	Ruby Stevens
Belle Starr	Myra Belle Shirley
Robert Sterling	William John Hart
Gale Storm	Josephine Owaissa Cottle
Robert Taylor	Spangler Arlington Brugh
Danny Thomas	Amos Jacobs
Arthur Treacher	Arthur Veary
Conway Twitty	Harold Jenkins
Jersey Joe Walcott	Arnold Cream
John Wayne	Marion Michael Morrison
Clifton Webb	Webb Hollenbeck
Tennessee Williams	Thomas Lanier Williams
Shelley Winters	Shirley Schrift
Stevie Wonder	Steveland Morris
Natalie Wood	Natasha Gurdin
Jane Wyman	Sarah Jane Fulks
Ed Wynn	Isaiah Edwin Leopold
Gig Young	Bryon Ellsworth Barr

Puddleburg

Hometown of Woody Woodpecker and his niece and nephew Splinter and Knothead

Puddleby-on-the-Marsh

English village in which Doctor John Dolittle lives

Pueblo, U.S.S.

Electronics surveillance ship (GER2) commanded by Commander Lloyd Bucher when captured by North Korea January 23, 1968. Bucher had been a mayor of Boy's Town in his youth. He appeared as an extra in the 1957 movie *Hellcats* since it was filmed on the submarine he was assigned to, the U.S.S. Besugo. In the 1975 T-V-play he was portrayed by Hal Holbrook

Puerto Rican Nationalists

March 1, 1954 five members of Congress were shot on the floor of the House of Representatives by three Puerto Rican Nationalists. Wounded were:

Alvin M. Bentley (Michigan Republican) (35)

Ben F. Jensen (Iowa Republican) (61)

Clifford Davis (Tenn. Democrat) (56)

George H. Fallon (Maryland Democrat) (51)

Kenneth A. Roberts (Alabama Democrat) (41)

The three Puerto Ricans arrested were:

Lolita Lebron (34), Rafael C. Miranda (25), Andres Cordero (29), all three of New York City. A fourth, Irving Flores (27) was arrested at a bus depot

Puff

Magic dragon who lived in a land called Honalee: song by Peter, Paul, and Mary

Puff

Dick and Jane's cat (primary readers)

Pulitzer Prizes

Awards in journalism, creative writing, music, and related areas, established under the will of Joseph Pulitzer (1847-1911), first made in 1917. Awarded annually in May in 18 categories. The prize is $1000 (originally $500). Carl Sandburg won the prize in two subjects; 1940 for History "Abraham Lincoln, the War Years" and in 1951 for Poetry "Complete Poems of Carl Sandburg"

Sinclair Lewis refused the prize in 1926 for *Arrowsmith* yet is credited for the prize that year

Puller, Chesty

Only marine to win 5 Navy Crosses (Lt. Gen. Lewis B. Puller)

Punchbowl Hill

Location of Charlie Chan's bungalow, where he lived in Honolulu (novels)

Punjab

Henchman of Oliver "Daddy" Warbucks (Little Orphan Annie's foster father) in Harold Gray's comic strip

Purgatory

Silent western movie star Dustin Farnum's horse in films

Purity, Body, Flavor
Words on the three rings on the label of Ballantine Beer

Purple Onion
San Francisco North Beach club where the Kingston Trio (1958), the Smothers Brothers, Pat Paulsen, and Phyllis Diller, among others, first made their appearance

Purple People Eater
Hit record written and sung by Sheb Wooley on MGM Records in 1958. One week after release it was the number one hit in the country, *One-eyed, one horn Flying Purple People Eater*. The P.P.E. finished the song by saying *"Tequila"*

Purple Pit
A. S. University's school hangout where Buddy Love (Jerry Lewis) makes his appearance as the suave, cool personality. Buddy Love is Professor Kelp's alter ego (1963 movie *The Nutty Professor*)

Pushinka
President J. F. Kennedy's Russian mongrel, given to him by Premier Khrushchev. Pushinka was an offspring of Strelka, a dog that had been in space. He was born in 1960. Pushinka's puppies by Caroline Kennedy's dog, Charlie, were *White Tip, Streaker, Butterfly* and *Blackie*

Pushmi-Pullyu
Dr. Dolittle's two-headed llama sent to him by the naturalist Straight Arrow

Pusser, Buford
6'6", 250 lb. McNairy County, Tennessee Sheriff. Killed in 1974. Played in movies *Walking Tall* (1974) by Joe Don Baker and *Walking Tall II* (1975) by Bo Svenson. At age 32 he had been stabbed 7 times and shot 8 times

Pussy Galore
Goldfinger's lesbian accomplice who runs a flying school for female pilots (1964 movie *Goldfinger*): played by Honor Blackman

Pussy Gato
Gordo's cat (comic strip *Gordo* by Gus Arriola)

Put Your Dreams Away
Frank Sinatra's theme song, sung by him at closing of radio's *Your Hit Parade*

Pyewacket
Lavendar cat supposedly a witch's familiar (1958 movie *Bell, Book and Candle*) Winner of 1959 PATSY

Pyncheon

Name of family living in the *House of the Seven Gables* (novel by Nathaniel Hawthorne). Clark Gable and Carole Lombard's ranch purchased in 1939 was nicknamed The House of the Two Gables

Pythagoras

Greek mathematical philosopher of 6th century B.C. His 4 basic elements and their qualities:

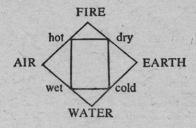

Q

Q

The Branch of His Majesty's Secret Service that is in charge of weapons and equipment distribution to its agents. Major Boothroyd (Desmond Llewelyn) is the head of Q (James Bond novels/movies). He has supplied James with all of his super gadgets

Q

Nickname of California State Prison San Quentin. Where Pete Ryan (Robert Wagner) spent 5 years. Sent there by Frank MacBride (Eddie Albert). TV series *Switch*

Q Bomb

Quadium bomb designed by Professor Alfred Kokintz stolen by the soldiers of Grand Fenwick from the United States (*The Mouse that Roared*)

Q and Z

Letters not on the telephone dial

QB VII

Novel (1970) by Leon Uris meaning Queen's Bench Number 7, the court in which the libel trial takes place. Most expensive movie ever made for TV: $2.5 million till that time

QQRXQ

Space Command code for S.O.S. sent out from the spaceship Stardust (*Perry Rhodan* series)

Quarrymen, The

First group founded 1955 by John Lennon, with Paul McCartney, before establishing the Beatles. Other names they used were Skiffle group, Johnny and the Moondogs, Moonshiners, Beat Boys, The Silver Beatles

Quasimodo

The Hunchback of Notre Dame: played in movies by Henri Krauss (1911), Glen White (1917), Lon Chaney, Sr. (1923), Charles Laughton (1939), and Anthony Quinn (1957) (from Victor Hugo's *The Hunchback of Notre Dame*)

Que Sera Sera

Doris Day's theme song from the 1956 Alfred Hitchcock movie *The Man Who Knew Too Much* (Hitchcock had previously filmed the movie in 1934). Doris Day also sang the song in the 1960 movie *Please Don't Eat the Daisies* and the 1965 movie *The Glass Bottom Boat*. It became her TV theme song

Queen Anne's Revenge

Blackbeard's pirate ship

Queen Conch

Harry Morgan's (Humphrey Bogart) fishing boat in 1944 movie *To Have and Have Not*

Queen of Diamonds

The playing card that causes Raymond Shaw (Laurence Harvey) to go into a hypnotic trance leaving him open to external suggestions (1962 movie *The Manchurian Candidate*)

Queen of Dixie

Samuel L. Clemen's (Fredric March) riverboat of which he was Captain. 1944 movie *Adventures of Mark Twain*

Queen Elizabeth

Time's Man of the Year for 1952. British liner retired to Port Everglades, Florida in 1968 as a tourist attraction

Queen Elizabeth I

Daughter of Anne Boleyn and Henry VIII: born 1533, reigned 1558-1603

Queen of Hearts

Ruler of Wonderland who demands "Off with their heads" (Lewis Carroll's *Alice's Adventures in Wonderland*). In 1933 movie played by May Robson, in 1951 Disney movie voice of Verna Felton

Queen Hippolyte

Wonder Woman's mother, who lives on Paradise Island (comic book series). In the 1975 TV movie *Wonder Woman* played by Cloris Leachman, in the TV series by Carolyn Jones

Queen Mary
   Cunard ocean liner, now moored at Pier J Long Beach, California, as a floating museum. It was bought for $3 million in 1967

Queen Tika
   Ruler of the underground city Murania (Gene Autry serial *The Phantom Empire*) played by Dorothy Christy

Queen Umpateedle
   Wife of King Guzzle, of the Kingdom of Moo (comic strip *Alley Oop*)

Queen of the West
   Dale Evans (Roy Rogers wife)

Queequeg
   Harpooner on board the "Pequod" (Herman Melville's *Moby Dick*). Played by Friedrich Ledebur in 1956 movie

Questel, Mae
   Actress who is the voice of:
   Olive Oyl, Betty Boop, Li'l Audrey, Aunt Bluebelle, etc.

Question Mark, The
   First plane to fly non-stop from Europe to the United States September 2, 1930, Paris to New York 37 hrs., 18½ minutes, pilot was Captain Dieudonné Coste; mechanic was Maurice Bellonte

Quick Carl
   Cowboy who can do everything fast but eat a Marathon Candy Bar (TV Advertisement) Marathon John played by Patrick Wayne, son of John Wayne

Quick Draw McGraw
   Horse character in Hanna-Barbera cartoons—His sidekick in Baba Looey, (voice of Daws Butler). His mother's name is Martha—He got his nickname when he was a pony for being so fast to draw mustaches on faces

Quittin' Time
   First spoken word in the 1939 movie *Gone With the Wind*. Said by a slave working in the field

Quiz and Game Shows, Television

About Faces	Ben Alexander
Across the Board	Ted Brown
Act It Out	Bill Cullen
Ad-Libbers	Peter Donald
All About Faces	Richard Hayes
Almost Anything Goes	Charlie Jones, Lynn Shakleford, Regis Philbin

Your Surprise Store ....Lew Parker
In the 1967 movie *The Graduate* the Newlywed Game is playing on the Robinson family TV. It is also the quiz show the Mayor of New York is watching in the 1971 movie *The Taking of Pelham 1–2–3*. In the 1975 movie *The Black Bird* "Let's Make a Deal" is being shown in the hotel room of a dead man

Quotations

Agent 86, Maxwell Smart: "Sorry about that, Chief"

Alphonse and Gaston (*comic strip by Frederick Burr Opper*): "You first, my dear Alphonse"; "After you, my dear Gaston"

Neil Armstrong: "That's one small step for a man, one giant leap for mankind"

P. T. Barnum: "There's a sucker born every minute"

Rhett Butler: "Frankly, my dear, I don't give a damn" (*to Scarlett O'Hara in Gone with the Wind*)

Senator Claghorn (*Fred Allen's radio show*): "That's a joke, Son"

Cool Hand Luke (*movie*): "What we have here is a failure to communicate"

Jimmy Durante: "Everybody wants to get into de act"

W. C. Fields: "Any man who hates dogs and children can't be all bad"

Greta Garbo: "I want to be alone"

Jackie Gleason (*as Ralph Kramden*): "One of these days, Alice, pow, right in the kisser"

George Gobel: "Well, I'll be a dirty bird"

Oliver Hardy: "This is another fine mess you've gotten me into" (*said to Stan Laurel*)

Gabriel Heatter: "Ah, there's good news tonight"

Al Jolson: "You ain't heard nothing yet, folks" (*The Jazz Singer*)

Little Beaver: "You betchum, Red Ryder"

Baron Munchhausen (*Jack Pearl*): 'Vas you dere, Sharlie?"

Joe Penner: "Wanna buy a duck?"

Sergeant Preston: "On, King! On, you huskies"

Chester Riley: "What a revoltin' development this is" (*Life of Riley*)

Knute Rockne: "When the going gets tough, the tough get going"

Will Rogers: "I never met a man I didn't like"

Red Ryder: "Roll, Thunder, roll"

Sam Spade (radio): "Period. End of report"

Little man in Bill Holman comic strip: "Nov Shomz Ka-pop"

Mae West: "Beulah, peel me a grape"

Mae West: "Come up and see me sometime" (*Diamond Lil*)

Ella Wheeler Wilcox: "Laugh and the world laughs with you, weep and you weep alone"

Archie on radio's Duffy's Tavern: "Hello. Duffy's Tavern, where the elite meet to eat. Archie, the manager, speaking. Duffy ain't here. Oh, hello, Duffy . . ."

Gary Cooper: "Yep"

Jackie Gleason: "The Ever Popular Mae Busch"

Ethel Barrymore from the play "Sunny": "That's all there is—there isn't anymore"

Mae West: "It's not the men in my life, it's the life in my men"

Mae West: "When I'm good, I'm very good, But when I'm bad I'm better"

Satchel Paige: "Never look back—Someone might be gaining on you"

Ben Bernie: "Yowza!, Yowza!"

Rudy Vallee: "High ho, everybody"

Lowell Thomas: "So Long until Tomorrow"

Jimmy Durante: "I got a million of em"

Jack Benny: "Now cut that out"

Humphrey Bogart: "Here's looking at you, kid"

Lauren Bacall to Humphrey Bogart 1944 movie To Have and Have Not: "If you want anything, all you have to do is whistle"

Sterling Hayden (Johnny Guitar): "I never shake hands with a left-handed gun"

Count Dracula (Bela Lugosi) Dracula: "The Children of the night, what music they make"

Rodney Dangerfield: "I don't get no respect"

Gabby Hayes as Windy to Hopalong Cassidy: "Your durn tootin', Hoppy"

Fibber McGee: "Gotta straighten out that closet one of these days"

Jack Paar: "I kid you not"

Christie Love (Teresa Graves): "You're under arrest Sugah"

George Fenneman introduction to You Bet Your Life: "Here he is, the one, the only—Groucho"

Oliver Twist: "Please Sir, may I have some more"

R

R

Initial on Archie Andrews' sweater (letter of Riverdale High)

R. A. Holmes High

Richard Allen Holmes Los Angeles High School where Chet Kincaid (Bill Cosby is the coach. TV series The *Bill Cosby Show*

Rabbi series

Written by Harry Kemelman. Adventures of Rabbi David Small of Barnard's Crossing, Massachusetts (his wife is Miriam, son Jonathan)

Novels:

Friday the Rabbi Slept Late, Saturday the Rabbi Went Hungry, Sunday the Rabbi Stayed Home, Monday the Rabbi Took Off, Tuesday the Rabbi Saw Red, Wednesday the Rabbi Got Wet, played by Stuart Margolin in 1976 TV-movie *Lanigan's Rabbi*

Rachel

Sailing ship that rescued the Pequod's lone survivor, Ishmael after Moby Dick destroyed the ship. Herman Melville's *Moby Dick*

Racing Flags

Utilized in automobile racing

Green: *Start or continue*

Yellow: *Slow down and hold your position*

Red: *Stop*

Black: *Pull into pit area*

Blue with yellow stripes: *move over so that the leaders can pass*

White: *One lap to go in the race*
Checkered: *Finish*

RKO

Radio-Keith-Orpheum, Hollywood picture company. First named FBO (Film Booking Office owned by Joseph P. Kennedy), then RKO-Pathe, then RKO Radio. Owned by Howard Hughes (1948-1955). In 1957 Desilu, Inc. bought the studios for $6,000,000

Ra II

Thor Heyerdahl's raft that sailed from Safi, Morocco, to Barbados, July 1970 (Ra I didn't complete the ocean voyage)

Racer X

Speed Racer's older brother (TV cartoon). He drives a race car called The Shooting Star (#9)

Radio Caroline

Pirate radio station (1964-1967): broadcast pop music from a ship off the east coast of England. Began March 28, 1964, others came later, radio London etc.

Raffles, (A. J.)

Gentleman burglar created by E. W. Hornung played in movies by John Barrymore, Ronald Colman, George Barraud and David Niven

Rafter

Actual name of horse which Richard Boon rode in the television series *Have Gun Will Travel*

Raggedy Anne

Cuddly rag doll from the stories by Johnny Gruelle. Her boyfriend is Raggedy Andy. Her owner is Marcella. Raggedy Anne dolls, when first made, had little candy hearts sewn in them with *I Love You* written on them

Raggin' the Scale

G8's favorite tune (pulp magazine)

Rags

Bobbie Lee Hartley's dog (movie *Ode To Billy Joe*)

Rags

Pet dog of Willy Dodger (June Havoc) on TV series *Willy*

Raggedy Andy

Raggedy Ann's boyfriend created in comic strip by Johnny Gruelle

Rags the Tiger

Crusader Rabbit's sidekick Ragland T. Tiger (TV cartoon series) Voice of Verne Loudin

Rail Splitter, The

Nickname of Abraham Lincoln

Railroads

In the game of Monopoly: Reading; Pennsylvania; B & O; Short Line

Railroad Split

The 7-10 split in bowling

Rainbow On the River

Theme song of radio series *Dr. Christian*

Rainier, Luise

Austrian actress who won Oscars for Best Actress for both 1936 and 1937

Ralph

Doorman at the Jefferson's apartment building (Ned Wertimer) (TV series *The Jeffersons*)

Ralph

Flip Wilson's invisible dog (TV *Flip Wilson Show*)

Ralph

Overstuffed man who states *"I can't believe I ate the whole thing,"* his wife yells *"You ate it, Ralph"* (TV Alka-Seltzer commercial played by Milton Moss)

Ralph 124C41+

Hero and title of science fiction novel (1911-1912 in *Modern Electrics* magazine) by Hugo Gernsback who coined the words Science Fiction, founder of *Amazing Stories* (1926), first science fiction magazine: the + in Ralph's name indicates he is one of the 10 best endowed men in the world, setting 2660 A.D.

Ralston Straight Shooters

Loyal followers of Tom Mix on radio

Rambling Wrecks, The

Nickname of Georgia Tech's football team

Rampart General

Los Angeles County Hospital that works with the Paramedic Squad Unit 51. Headed by Doctor Kelly Brackett (Robert Fuller) (TV series *Emergency!*)

Range Riders, The

Johnny Mack Brown, Raymond Hatton, Tim McCoy (movie series)

Ranger

Ship commanded by John Paul Jones when he attacked the British port of Whitehaven in Britain during the Revolutionary War. (April 23, 1778)

Ranger

Walter "Radar" O'Reilly (Gary Burghoff) pet dog back home (TV series $M*A*S*H$)

Ranger John Reid

Identity of The Lone Ranger, an ex-Texas Ranger

Ranger John Smith

Head of Jellystone Park, Yogi Bear's home (TV cartoon series). Voice of Don Messick

Rat Fink

Comic character created by custom automobile designer Ed "Big Daddy" Ross—he also built a custom car called Rat Fink—character on tee shirts, stickers etc.

Rat Pack

(see the Clan)

Raven and dove

Two birds that Noah sent out from the Ark: the raven returned, indicating that there was yet no dry land; the dove came back with an olive branch, indicating receding waters

Ray, Ed

Chowchilla, California school bus driver kidnapped, along with 26 school children July 15, 1976. He led them to safety in Livermore, California. (Hometown of this book's author)

Ray, The

Secret identity of Happy Terrill (comic books)

Raymond

Host of radio program "Inner Sanctum": played by Raymond Edward Johnson, TV voice of Paul McGarth

Raymond

Butler of Charles Foster Kane's Florida Mansion Xanadu (played by Paul Stewart) 1941 movie *Citizen Kane*

Razor

Lucas McCain's (Chuck Connors) horse (TV series *The Rifleman*)

Read Your Bible

Sign on the wall behind Judge John T. Raulston's bench at the Scopes trial, Dayton, Tennessee, 1925

Reagan, Ronald

Actor later Governor of California (1966-1974)

Married Jane Wyman (1940-1948), Nancy Davis (1952-   )

As Captain in U.S. Army he signed Major Clark Gable's

discharge papers on June 12, 1944 in Culver City, Calif.
M.C. for General Electric Theater (TV)
M.C. for Death Valley Days (TV)
Starred in number of movies
M.C.'d the first PATSY Awards
President of the Actors Union
His last movie was *The Killers* (1964)
Where's the Rest of Me?—Autobiography

Reata

Sprawling 595,000 acre Texas ranch of the Benedict family (Edna Ferber's *Giant*) Jeff Rinks land was called Little Reata

Rebel

Cowboy star Johnny Mack Brown's horse in movies

Reckless

Walton family hounddog (TV series "The Waltons")

Records

Top Singles:

"Forever and Ever," Russ Morgan Orchestra, 1949
"Goodnight, Irene," Gordon Jenkins/Weavers, 1950
"Tennessee Waltz," Patti Page, 1951
"Cry," Johnny Ray, 1952
"Song from *Moulin Rouge*," Percy Faith, 1953
"Little Things Mean a Lot," Kitty Kallen, 1954
"Rock Around the Clock," Bill Haley and the Comets, 1955
"Don't Be Cruel," Elvis Presley, 1956
"Tammy," Debbie Reynolds, 1957
"Nel Blu di Pinto di Blu (Volare)," Domenico Mudugno, 1958,
"Mack the Knife," Bobby Darin, 1959
"Theme from *A Summer Place*," Percy Faith, 1960
"Theme from *Exodus*," Ferrante and Teicher, 1961
"The Twist," Chubby Checker, 1962
"Limbo Rock," Chubby Checker, 1963
"I Want to Hold Your Hand," Beatles, 1964
"Back in My Arms Again," Supremes, 1965
"Ballad of the Green Berets," S/Sgt Barry Sadler, 1966
"The Letter," Boxtops, 1967
"Hey Jude," Beatles, 1968
"Sugar, Sugar," Archies, 1969
"Bridge over Troubled Water," Simon and Garfunkel, 1970

"Joy to the World," Three Dog Night, 1971
"First Time Ever I Saw Your Face," Roberta Flack, 1972
"Tie a Yellow Ribbon Around the Old Oak Tree," Dawn, 1973
"Seasons in the Sun," Terry Jacks, 1974
"Love Will Keep Us Together," Captain and Tennille, 1975
"Afternoon Delight," Starlight Vocal Band, 1976
Felicia Sanders is the vocalist on the 1953 hit *Song from Moulin Rouge* though she was not credited

Red
Color of gown Julie Morrison (Bette Davis) wore to the Olympus Ball in New Orleans, 1938 movie "Jezebel" The other women traditionally wore white.
Color of a bride's gown in China

Red Baron, The
Nickname of Baron Manfred von Richthofen. German aviator, top ace in World War I (80 victories). He flew a red Fokker triplane.

Red Bee, The
Secret identity of Assistant District Attorney Rick Raleigh (comic book series "The Red Bee")

Red Buck
Emmett Dalton's horse which he rode on the raid on Coffeyville October 5, 1892. Emmett was the sole survivor of the gang

Reddi-Killowat
P G & E (Pacific Gas and Electric) Little energy man

Red Fox
Outlaw Jesse James' favorite horse

Red and Blue
National Broadcasting Company's two early radio networks: Red network renamed NBC, Blue network American Broadcasting Company in 1943

Red Hot Peppers
Jelly Roll Morton's Jazz Band

Red Light Bandit
Nickname of Caryl Chessman who was executed in San Quentin. Portrayed in 1955 movie *Cell 2455, Death Row* by William Campbell and in 1977 TV-movie *Kill Me If You Can* by Alan Alda

Redlo 7

Call sign of Black and White police unit driven by Mike Danko (Sam Melville.) TV series *The Rookies*

Red River Valley

Theme song of 1940 movie *The Grapes of Wrath*, the 1943 movie *The Ox-Bow Incident* also the radio series *Our Gal Sunday*

Red Stockings

Cincinnati baseball team. First pro-team in baseball. In 1869 they won 65 games, lost 0 tied 1. In 1870 they won 130 games in a row

Red, White and Blue

Colors of the basketball used in the ABA

Red Pennington (Lt.)

Don Winslow's sidekick. Played on radio by John Gibson and Edward Davison. In 1942 serial by Walter Sande

Red Rover, U.S.S.

First United States hospital ship

Red Ryder

"From out of the west comes America's famous fighting Cowboy". Hero of comic strip by Fred Harman. Debuted in comic strips November 6, 1938. He was originally called Bronc Peeler. The outlaw Ace Hanlon killed Red Ryder's father. On radio played by Reed Hadley. Carlton KaDell, and Brooke Temple. His sidekick, Little Beaver, said, "You betchum. Red Ryder," and Red said to his horse, "Roll, Thunder, roll". Played in movies by Gordon "Wild Bill" Elliot, Jim Bannon, Allan Lane, and Don "Red" Barry. On TV played by Rocky Lane

Red Skull, The

Captain America's foe (comic book) killed off after WW2

Red-Haired Alibi, The

Shirley Temple's first movie appearance, 1932, age 3

REDUCE

Jack Lalanne's California automobile license plate

Reed, John Silas

American Journalist, founder of the American Communist Labor Party, author of *Ten Days that Shook the World* Only American buried in the Kremlin in Moscow

Reep Daggle

Chameleon Boy's real name (comic books)

Reese, Mason

Little Boy who does TV advertisements for Underwood Sandwich Spread (he has the face of a 30-year-old)

Reeves, George

American actor, real name: George Besselo; played TV's Superman; He appeared in such movies as *Gone With the Wind, From Here to Eternity* and *The Day the Earth Stood Still;* committed suicide (1959). He was buried in the grey suit he wore as Clark Kent

Reform Club

London club to which Phileas Fogg belonged (Jules Verne's *Around the World in 80 Days*)

Reggie

The raccoon you are asked to draw for Art Instruction Schools, Inc. (advertisements in magazines)

Reggie Fortune

Detective created by H. C. Bailey

Reggie Van Dough

Richie Rich's mischievous cousin (comic books)

Reginald "Reggie" Bell

Starman number One, Perry Rhodan's sidekick (Science Fiction novels)

Reggie Mantle

Archie Andrews' antagonist. Radio by Paul Gordon, TV by Mark Winkeworth

Regret

The only filly ever to win the Kentucky Derby (1915). Francis the Talking mule claims Regret as his mother. Only two fillies have won the Belmont Stakes, Ruthless (1867), first winner of the Belmont Stakes, and Tanya (1905), 5 fillies have won the Preakness

Regulation Dart Board

British: Numbers
Clockwise are:
20-1-18-4-13-6-
10-15-2-17-3-
19-7-16-8-11-14-
9-12-5

Reichenbach Falls

Cascade in Switzerland where Sherlock Holmes and Professor Moriarty grapple and apparently fall to their deaths May, 1891 (Arthur Conan Doyle's "The Final Problem") Due to public outcry Doyle was compelled to bring Holmes back. His reappearance was in *A Scandal in Bohemia* (1892)

Reindeer

The fleet of British passenger aircraft which aviation research scientist Theodore Honey (James Stewart) predicted would crash, after 1440 hours, due to metal fatigue, causing the tail section to collapse. Nevil Shute's *No Highway in the Sky* (1952 movie)

Reject

Johnny Jupiter's robot (1953 TV puppet series)

Reluctant Dragon, The

B29 in which Tim Holt served as a bombadier in the Pacific Theatre of World War II.

Reluctant, U.S.S.

Navy Cargo ship on which Lt. Douglas A. Roberts was stationed (Thomas Heggen's *Mr. Roberts*). The crew called her the Bucket. The 1955 movie was filmed on board the U.S.S. Hewell

Remembering You

Closing theme of TV series "All in the Family" (opening theme is "Those Were the Days") composed by Carroll O'Connor

Remo Williams

Real name of the Destroyer (detective novel series by Sapir and Murphy)

Renaldo

The Cisco Kid's white dog (TV series *The Cisco Kid*)

Renfield

Count Dracula's henchman. In the novel he eats flies, played by Dwight Frye in 1931 movie *Dracula*

Reno, Nevada

Once the divorce capital of the United States, farther west than Los Angeles "The Biggest Little City in the World"

Reo

Automobile built in the U.S. Between 1904-1936 by Ransom *E*li *O*lds, only man to have two automobiles named after him.

Resolute, H.M.S.

Ship from which the beams were taken in the making of the desk used by President Kennedy in the White House. Queen Victoria had the desk made for President Hayes

Resolution, H.M.S.

Captain James Cook's ship on his second and third voyages

Retired Uniform Numbers (Baseball)

Uniform Number	Player	Team	Date Retired
1	Bill Meyer	Pittsburgh (N)	1954
1	Fred Hutchinson	Cincinnati (N)	1965
3	Earl Averill	Cleveland (A)	1975
3	Babe Ruth#	New York (A)	1948
3	Harmon Killebrew	Minnesota (A)	1975
4	Mel Ott	San Francisco (N)*	1949
4	Luke Appling	Chicago (A)	1975
4	Lou Gehrig##	New York (A)	1939
5	Joe DiMaggio	New York (A)	1952
5	Lou Boudreau	Cleveland (A)	1970
6	Stan Musial	St. Louis (N)	1963
7	Mickey Mantle	New York (A)	1969
8	Yogi Berra	New York (A)	1972
9	Ted Williams	Boston (A)	1960
11	Carl Hubbell	San Francisco (N)*	1944
14	Gil Hodges	New York (N)	1972
16	Whitey Ford	New York (A)	1974
17	Dizzy Dean	St. Louis (N)	1974
19	Bob Feller	Cleveland (A)	1956
20	Frank Robinson	Baltimore (A)	1971
20	Pie Traynor	Pittsburgh (N)	1972
21	Warren Spahn	Atlanta (A)**	1965
21	Roberto Clemente	Pittsburgh (N)	1973
24	Willie Mays	San Francisco (N)	1972
27	Juan Marichal	San Francisco (N)	1975
32	Sandy Koufax	Los Angeles (N)	1972
32	Jim Umbricht	Houston (N)	1964

#—Prior to the number being retired it was worn by George Selkirk

##—First player to have his uniform number retired

*—As New York Giants

**—As Milwaukee Braves

33	Honus Wagner	Pittsburgh (N)	1956
36	Robin Roberts	Philadelphia (N)	1962
37	Casey Stengel	New York (N)	1965
		New York (A)	1970
39	Roy Campanella	Los Angeles (N)	1972
40	Don Wilson	Houston (N)	1975
41	Eddie Mathews	Atlanta (N)	1969
42	Jackie Robinson	Los Angeles (N)	1972
44	Willie McCovey	San Francisco (N)	1975
45	Bob Gibson	St. Louis (N)	1975
47	Sherry Robertson	Minnesota (A)	1970

Return to Oz
Walt Disney cartoon feature movie
Voices: Dorothy (Liza Minnelli), Cowardly Lion (Milton Berle), Tin Man (Danny Thomas), Wicked Witch (Ethel Merman), The Scarecrow (Mickey Rooney), Aunt Em (Margaret Hamilton), Glinda (Rise Stevens), Uncle Henry (Paul Ford)

Reuben
Award given to the cartoonist of the year, by the National Cartoonists Society, named for Rube Goldberg
First awarded to Milton Caniff, 1946

Reuben James
First American warship (a desteroyer) lost in World War II, sunk off Iceland by a German U-boat. October 30, 1941 (prior to Pearl Harbor attack): about 100 lives lost

Reuben "Rooster" J. Cogburn
One eyed (left) sheriff played by John Wayne in movies *True Grit* (1969) and *Rooster Cogburn* (1976). His horse is named Beau

Revere, Paul
Silversmith whose famous ride took him from Boston to near Lexington, April 18-19, 1775. He also engraved the seal of the colonies and made for George Washington his set of false teeth

Reverend Leroy
Preacher at the church of What's Happening Now (*Flip Wilson TV Show*)

Rex
Sergeant Preston's horse (originally called Blackie)

Rex
Dinosaur on board Boner's Ark (comic strip *Boner's Ark*)

588

Rex

"King of the Wild Horses." Appeared in several movie serials: *The Law of the Wild* (1934), *The Adventures of Rex and Rinty* (1935)

Rhapsody in Blue

Theme music of Paul Whiteman's orchestra

Rhedosaurus

Type of prehistoric animal found frozen in ice in the 1953 movie *The Beast from 20,000 Fathoms*"*

Rhubarb

Cat who inherits a baseball team (H. Allen Smith's *Rhubarb*). In 1951 movie played by Orangey, winner of the 1952 PATSY

Smith wrote a sequel in 1967 titled *Son of Rhubarb;* his son's name is Tiger

Rhoda

The Robot (played by Julie Newmar) on TV series *My Living Doll* starring Bob Cummings

Rhythm Boys

Bing Crosby, Harry Barris, and Al Rinker singing trio

Richard Diamond

Radio series *Richard Diamond, Private Detective*. Played by Dick Powell, TV by David Janssen

On radio Dick Powell was the only detective to sing a song at the end of each episode

Richard Henry Benson

Real name of the Avenger (detective novel series by Kenneth Robeson)

Richard M. Dixon

Real name of James LaRoe who in 1969 changed his name to Richard M. Dixon because of his very close resemblance to then President Richard M. Nixon. Mr. Dixon was once an advertising executive, now he is an entertainer

Richard Saunders

Supposed author and compiler of *Poor Richard's Almanacs,* actually written by Benjamin Franklin. Portrayed in 1938 movie *Marie Antoinette* by Walter Walker, also 1972 movie *1776* by Howard de Silva

---

*Merv Griffin is a radio announcer (voice only) in this film

Richard the Lion Heart
British King to which outlaw Robin Hood swears allegiance while Richard is away fighting in the Holy War

Richmond, Va.
Capital of the Confederacy (1861-65) after Montgomery, Al.

Rick Blaine
Humphrey Bogart's role in 1942 movie *Casablanca* Ronald Reagan was first considered for the role

Rick Jones
The lone friend of the huge green monster. The Hulk (secret identity of Bruce Banner). (Comic book series)

Rickenbacker, Captain Edward Vernon
America's top World War I ace, 26 victories (22 airplanes, 4 balloons): Medal of Honor winner, race car driver, later president of Eastern Airlines. In 1942 his plane was forced down in the Paciffc and he spent 3 weeks on a raft before being rescued. He flew for the Hat-in-the Ring Squadron. Awarded 14 honorary degrees, 19 decorations. One time owner of the Indianapolis Speedway. He produced an automobile in 1922 called The Rickenbacker, with slogan, "A Car Worthy of His Name." Autobiography about 23 days on raft *Seven Came Through*. Creator of comic strip *Ace Drummond*. He was portrayed in 1945 movie *Captain Eddie* by Fred MacMurray and in 1955 movie *The Court Martial of Billy Mitchell* by Tom McKee

Rick's Café Américain
Cafe owned by Rick Blaine (1942 movie *Casablanca*)

Rico
Caesar Enrico Bandello, gangster in movie *Little Caesar*: played by Edward G. Robinson

Riddle = Strange, Even True!
Statement using the middle names of prominent people.
Riddle—Middle name of James R. Hoffa
Strange—Middle name of Robert S. McNamara
Even—Middle name of Joe E. Brown
True—Middle name of Denton T. "My" Young

Riddler, The
Batman and Robin's foe. He leaves clues in the form of riddles. His real identity is Edward ("E") Nigma (on TV series played by Frank Gorshin)

Riegels, Roy

Center of the California Golden Bears who ran the "wrong way" in the second quarter of the 1929 Rose Bowl game, 65 yards: teammate Benny Lom stopped him 6 inches from California's own goal line. A punt on the next play was blocked for a safety, and California lost the game 8-7 to Georgia Tech

The Rifleman's Creed

U.S. Army training exercise
This is my Rifle
My Rifle is my best friend
There are many like it
But this one is mine
I must fire my rifle true
I must shoot straighter
than the enemy of my country
Who may be trying to shoot at me
My rifle and I are a team
Together we are defenders of my Country
And are dedicated to its defense
Unto Death, before God
I swear this—

Riggs, L. A. "Speed"

Lee Aubrey Riggs, auctioneer for the American Tobacco Company featured on the radio/TV series *Your Hit Parade* . . . "Sold . . . American!"

Righteous Brothers

Singing team: Bobby Hatfield, Bill Medley (replaced by Jimmy Walker)

Rijo

Tiger on television commercials for Enco Gas *Put a tiger in your tank*

Rikki-Tikki-Tavi

Teddy's pet monogoose (Rudyard Kipling's *The Jungle Book*)

Rima

The bird-girl (William Henry Hudson's *Green Mansions*). In the 1959 movie, the part was played by Audrey Hepburn

Ring Eye

Frog Millhouse's (Smiley Burnette) horse in movies. He later rode a horse named Nellie

Ringling Brothers

The brothers who founded the Ringling Brothers Circus beginning in 1882. Albert (b 1852), August (b 1854), Alfred T. (b 1862), Charles (b 1864), John (b 1866), Henry (b 1869). Joined with the Barnum & Bailey Circus to become the Greatest Show on Earth

Rinso White Girl

Little girl on radio who advertised Rinso White laundry detergent. On radio the girl who sang the jingle was the future opera star Beverly Sills

Rin Tin Tin

(Rinty) German Shepherd.
Original dog found by Lee Duncan.
Rinty was born in a trench in France during World War I
Made films for Warner Brothers in 1920's.
First: *Where the North Begins* (1923)
Voted most populad film performer of 1926. Rinty had four sons that became stars. Rinty no. 4 became the star of the TV series "Rin Tin Tin." Rin Tin Tin the first, died August 10, 1932 in the presence of his master Lee Duncan and actress Jean Harlow, a neighbor. On radio his owner (fictitious) was Francis X. Bushman. On TV series (1954-55) as Private Rin Tin Tin ("Rin Tin Tin") owned by Corporal Rusty (Lee Aaker). Starred in several movie serials. Winner of 1958 and 1959 TV PATSY awards

Rip Kirby

Scientist-detective (comic book series "Rip Kirby." Created by Alex Raymond) Debut in comic strip March 4, 1946. Desmond is his valet, Honey Dorian, his girlfriend

Rippy, Rodney Allen

Small 3½ year old joyous boy in 1972 Jack-in-the-Box TV commercial. He sings "Make life a little easier . . ." (Jack-in-the-Box is owned by Ralston-Purina)

Ritter, "Tex" (Woodward)

Singer of the theme song in 1952 movie *High Noon*. First artist to record for Capitol Records. On WSM radio he had been known as Cowboy Tom. Only member of both the Cowboy Hall of Fame (Oklahoma City) and The Country Western Music Hall of Fame (Nashville)

Ritz Brothers

Zany comedians: Al, Jimmy, Harry. Real last name is Joachim. A fourth brother George became their first manager. Their theme song was "Thanks A Million, A Million Thanks To You"

River City

Iowa town visited by Harold Hill (Meredith Wilson's *The Music Man*)

Riverdale High

School attended by Archie Andrews (comic books)

Riverfield

Town setting of radio series *Bright Horizon*

River Heights

Hometown of Nancy Drew (juvenile stories by Carolyn Keene)

Rivets

The SPCA dog mascot

"RMS Titantic, 41° 46′ North—50° 14′ West 15 April 1912 Rest In Peace"

Annual radio message sent out by the IIP (International Ice Patrol) on the anniversary of the Titanic's sinking. The organization's existence resulted from the Titanic tragedy

Road Pictures

Series starring Bob Hope, Bing Crosby, and Dorothy Lamour:

Road to Singapore, 1940 (Originally titled *The Road to Mandalay*)

Road to Zanzibar, 1941

Road to Morocco, 1942

Road to Utopia, 1946

Road to Rio, 1948 (Biggest grossing movie of 1948)

Road to Bali, 1952 (First road picture in color)

Road to Hong Kong, 1962

Jack Oakie and Fred MacMurray were planned to be in the first road film instead of Hope and Crosby

Road Runner

Large bird, Geococcyx californianus (in Warner Brothers' cartoons it says "Beep beep"). Created by Chuck Jones. He is chased by Wile E. Coyote. Voice of Mel Blanc. Does not talk in movies other than to say "Beep Beep." In comics he talks. Debut in 1948 cartoon *Fast and Furry-ous*. Debut in comic books Dell Color Comics #918, July 1958. In cartoons he spoke only once, in the Bugs Bunny 1951 cartoon *Operation: Rabbit*. He is the father of three smallest Beeps (Road Runners)

Roaring Chicken

Hekawi Indian played by Edward Everett Horton on TV series *"F Troop"*

Robe, The

20th Century-Fox 1953 movie based on novel by Lloyd C. Douglas, starring Richard Burton. It was the first Cinema Scope movie. The voice of Christ was that of Cameron Mitchell. Premiered at Grauman's Chinese Theatre, September 24, 1953. *Demetrius & the Gladiators* (1954) was the sequel. Only movie given 8 stars by the New York Daily News. 4 for process, 4 for the film. Four stars is usually the maximum given

Robby

Robot (1955 movie *Forbidden Planet;* also in 1957 movie *The Invisible Boy*). His fuel is Isotope 217, he speaks 187 languages (he cost $125,000 to build for movie). He also appeared on an episode of *The Twilight Zone* "The Brain Center at Whipples" in 1964. In Isaac Asimov's 1950 story "I Robot" he introduced a robot named Robbie which he first originated as far back as 1940. An automated radio station is called a Robby the Robot

Robert Dietrich

A pen name of E. Howard Hunt (Watergate figure)

Robin

Secret identity of Dick Grayson "The Boy Wonder" (TV series "Batman"): played by Burt Ward. Debut Detective Comics #38 June 1940. His parents John and Mary Grayson were the circus high wire act The Flying Graysons. They were killed by Bess Zucco and his mob. Dick Grayson's birthday is on November 11. Played in 1943 movie serial by Douglas Croft. In 1949 movie serial by John Duncan

Robin Hood

(Robin of Locksley or Robert of Locksley)

Hero of English folk ballads and of children's stories. Living in Sherwood Forest with his band of men clad in Lincoln Green, robbing the rich to give to the poor, and waging constant war against the Sheriff of Nottingham or the nobility personified in Guy of Gisbourne, Robin is supposedly Earl of Huntingdon. At least 5 movie versions of his adventures preceded Douglas Fairbanks, Sr.'s feature of 1922. Errol Flynn played Robin in 1938, Jon Hall in 1948, and many others as well have made it a favorite.

Richard Greene was Robin on TV, (1955) Richard Todd in a Disney movie in 1952. (Richard Greene is the grandson of William Friese-Greene, the inventor of the moving picture camera. His grandfather was portrayed in the 1951 movie *The Magic Box* by Robert Donat)

Robin Hood films:

1922—*Robin Hood*-Douglas Fairbanks, Sr.

1938—*The Adventures of Robin Hood*-Errol Flynn

1946—*The Bandit of Sherwood Forest*-Cornel Wilde (as Robin's son) (Russell Hicks payed Robin Hood)

1948—*Prince of Thieves*-Jon Hall

1950—*Rogues of Sherwood Forest*-John Derek (as Robin's son)

1952—*Tales of Robin Hood*-Robert Clarke

1952—*The Story of Robin Hood and His Merrie Men*-Richard Todd

1956—*Men of Sherwood Forest*-Don Taylor

1959—*Son of Robin Hood*-June Laverick (as Robin's daughter)

1961—*The Sword of Sherwood Forest*-Richard Greene

1962—*Triumph of Robin Hood* (Italian)-Don Burnett

1967—*A Challenge of Robin Hood*-Barrie Ingham

In the 1952 film *Ivanhoe*—Harold Warrender played Robin Hood (Locksley) in a brief appearance

Robin played by Sean Connery in 1976 movie *Robin and Marian*. On 1975 TV series "When Things were Rotten" played by Dick Gautier

In Disney (1973) cartoon feature movie, the voices were: Robin Hood (Brian Bedford), Prince John (Peter Ustinov), Little John (Phil Harris), Sir Hiss (Terry-Thomas), Allan a Dale (Roger Miller), Sheriff (Pat Buttram), Trigger (George Lindsey), Friar Tuck (Andy Devine)

Robinson, Brandbury

Halfback for St. Louis University. He threw the first legal forward pass in a football game. Jack Schneider was the receiver in a game against Carroll College (Waukeska, Wisconsin) September 5, 1906

Robinson, Jack "Jackie" Roosevelt

First Negro to play in major league baseball, Brooklyn Dodgers, 1947. Rookie of the Year, played first game April 15, 1947 against Boston Braves at Brooklyn. Prior to the Dodgers, he played for the Kansas City Monarchs, then Montreal. He previously played football for UCLA.

In 1950 *The Jackie Robinson Story* portrayed by Jackie Robinson

Robinson Crusoe

Hero of Daniel Defoe's novel of a shipwrecked sailor who spends 28 years on a island. His sole companion is a native which he named Friday. *Adventures of Robinson Crusoe* played in 1954 movie by Dan O'Herlihy

1913 movie-Robert Leonard *Robinson Crusoe*

1924 movie-Harry Myers-*Robinson Crusoe of Clipper Island* (serial; Feature version titled *Robinson Crusoe of Mystery Island*) (1936), *Robinson Crusoe on Mars* (1964) (Paul Mantee)

Robot

Series 1A1998

Robot that serves the Jupiter II's Robinson crew. Voice of Robert May. (TV series *Lost in Space*)

Robot

Word first introduced, in Samuel Butler's 1872 novel *Erehwon* (Nowhere spelled backwards)

Robotman

Secret identity of scientist Bob Crane whose Brain is transplanted into a robot. Bob Crane then changes his name to Paul Dennis (Robotman). His Robot dog is called Robbie (Robotman comic book series)

Robotrix

Female robot in Fritz Lang's *Metropolis* (1926): played by Brigitte Helm

Rob Roy and Prudence Prim

President Calvin Coolidge's two dogs (his cat was named Tiger)

Rochester (Van Jones)

Jack Benny's valet: played by Eddie Anderson, he called Benny "Boss"

Rocinante

Don Quixote's horse on which he charged windmills

Rock, The

Nickname of Alcatraz Prison, federal prison in San Francisco Bay. Alcatraz means Pelican in Spanish

Rock-A-Bye Baby

Code name for the mission to disperse deadly nerve gas in the vicinity of Fort Knox by Pussy Galore's flying circus. Lead aircraft flown by Miss Galore was called *Champagne Leader* 1964 movie *Goldfinger*

Rock Around the Clock

Theme song of 1955 movie *The Blackboard Jungle* (played by Bill Haley and his Comets). Original theme song on TV series "Happy Days"

Rockettes

Dancers at New York's Radio City Music Hall. The Roxy theatre had 30 dancers named the Roxyettes

Rockhead and Quarry Construction Co.

Gravel firm for which Fred Flintstone works. Mr. Slate is his boss (TV's *The Flintstones*). He has also worked for Bedrock Rock and Gravel Company and Slaterock Gravel Company

Rock Men and Shell Men

Two groups of prehistoric people (1940 movie *One Million B.C.* and 1966 movie *One Million Years B.C.*)

Rock 'n' Roll Groups

Lead	*"And The"*
Archie Bell	Drells
B. Bumble	Stingers
Bill Haley	Comets
Billy J. Kramer	Dakotas
Billy Ward	Dominoes
Bobby Pickett	Crypt-Kickers
Bobby Vee	Strangers
Booker T	M.G.'s
Brian Poole	Tremoloes
Buddy Holly	Crickets
Buddy Knox	Rhythm Orchids
Cliff Richard	Shadows
Country Joe	Fish
Danny	Juniors
Dave Allan	Arrows
Diana Ross	Supremes
Dicky Doo	Don'ts
Dion	Belmonts
Dr. Feelgood	Interns
Don Juan	Meadowlarks
Duane Eddy	Rebels
Eric Burdon	Animals/War
Frankie Lymon	Teenagers
Freddy	Dreamers
Gary Lewis	Playboys
Gary Puckett	Union Gap

Gene Vincent	Blue Caps
Gerry	Pacemakers
Gladys Knight	Pips
Hank Ballard	Midnighters
Harvey	Moonglows
Herman	Hermits
Huey "Piano" Smith	Clowns
James Brown	Famous Flames
Jay	Americans
Jerry Butler	Impressions
Jimmy Gilmer	Fireballs
Joey Dee	Starlighters
John Fred	Playboy Band
Johnny	Hurricanes
Jr. Walker	All-Stars
King Curtis	Kingpins
Lee Andrews	Hearts
Linda Ronstadt	Stone Poneys
Link Wray	Wraymen
Little Anthony	Imperials
Little Caesar	Romans
Little Joe	Thrillers
Lulu	Luvers
Martha	Vandellas
Maurice Williams	Zodiacs
Mitch Ryder	Detroit Wheels
Morry Williams	Kids
Paul McCartney	Wings
Paul Revere	Raiders
Question Mark	Mysterians
Rosie	Originals
Ruby	Romantics
Sam the Sham	Pharoahs
Shep	Limelites
Sly	Family Stone
Smokey Robinson	Miracles
Sonny Til	Orioles
Spanky	Our Gang
Tommy James	Shondells
Wayne Fontana	Mindbenders

Rock of Eternity

Mountain peak over which Captain Marvel flies when

entering or returning from another time period (comic book series *Captain Marvel*)

Rockwell, George Lincoln

Founder of the American Nazi Party in 1959. Originally called the Union of Free Enterprise National Socialists

Rockwell, Norman

Painted 318 Saturday Evening Post Covers. Painted for Look, Life and other magazines. Has painted every Boy Scout calendar since 1923 except two. Painted the portraits of characters in the credits of the 1966 movie *Stagecoach*

Rocky

The bobcat in the Mercury Bobcat television commercials

Rocky

Nickname of Jim Rockford's (James Garner) father, Joseph Rockford (Noah Beery, Jr.) TV series *The Rockford Files*. Played on pilot movie by Robert Donley

Rocky (Rocket J. Squirrel)

Bullwinkle's (Bullwinkle J. Moose) sidekick squirrel (cartoon series "Bullwinkle"). Voices on TV cartoons Rocky (June Foray) Bullwinkle (Bill Scott)

Rocky Fortune

Radio detective played by Frank Sinatra (1953-54)

Rocky Jones

Space Ranger, played on TV by Richard Crane (1953-1954). His Followers were called Junior Spacemen

Rodan

Flying pterodactyl monster (1957 Japanese motion picture). He hatched in the Oaski mine #8

Rodeo Big Three

Championship rodeos: Cheyenne Frontier Days, Calgary Stampede, Pendleton Roundup

Roderick Anthony

Captain of the "Ferndale" (Joseph Conrad's *Chance*)

Rodney

Cowardly knight who is the head of King ID's Army. Gwen the fair maiden has eyes for him (cartoon *Wizard of Id* by Parker and Hart)

Roger Dorn, Captain

Companion of detective Peter Quill (radio series "Peter Quill")

Rogers, Lela

Mother of actress Ginger Rogers, she played such a role in 1942 movie *The Major and the Minor*

Rogers, Roy

(Leonard Slye) Sang with the Sons of the Pioneers, called "King of the Cowboys"—Dale Evans becoming his second wife. Made his debut in *The Old Homestead* (1935) as Len Slye. Later, used pseudonym Dick Weston before Republic changed his name to Roy Rogers for his starring movie *Under Western Stars* (1938)

Roger Wilco

Message received, will comply (World War II verbal code)

Rokk Krinn

Name of Cosmic Boy (comic books) from the planet Braal

Rolex Oyster Pepetual Chronometer

Wrist watch worn by James Bond. (*On His Majesty's Secret Service* novel)

Rolfe, John

Virginia colonist (1585-1622) who married Pocahontas April 15, 1614

Rolling Stones

Original members: Mick Jagger, Brian Jones, Keith Richard, Charlie Watts, Bill Wyman. Group recorded for the British Decca label

Rollo

Rich boy ("Nancy" cartoons)

Roma

U.S. dirigible that crashed and burned at Norfolk, Virginia February 21, 1922. Captain Dale Mabry (Commander) and 33 other men died

Romance of Helen Trent, The

Radio soap opera about a fashion designer:

"The story of a woman who sets out to prove what so many other women long to prove in their own lives . . . that romance can live on at thirty-five . . . and even beyond"

Romulans

Enemies of the Federation headed by Praetor (TV series "Star Trek")

Ronald McDonald

McDonald's Hamburgers' clown. Originally played by Vito Scotti. He wears yellow shoe laces. McDonald's

600

theme song, composed by Barry Klein in 1963, is "My Favorite Clown"

Ronson

Brand name of James Bond's cigarette lighter

Rooms

In the game of "Clue" (detective board game): Ball Room, Billiard Room, Conservatory, Dining Room, Hall, Kitchen, Library, Lounge, Study (note: no bedrooms)

Rooney, Mickey

American actor born Joseph Ninian Yule, Jr. became Mickey McGuire, with Our Gang: Autobiography *I.E. An Autobiography*. Married to Ava Gardner, 1942-1943; Betty Rase (Miss Birmingham, 1944) 1944-1947; Martha Vickers, 1949-1951; Elaine Mahnken, 1952-1959; Barbara Thamason, (Miss Muscle Beach, 1954) 1959-1966; Margaret Lane, 1966-1967; Caroline Huckett, 1969-1970; Jan Chamberlain, 1975- . Adopted the name Mickey McGuire from a character in Fontaine Fox's comic strip *The Toonerville Trolley*

Roosevelt Franklin

Sesame Street little-boy muppet who celebrates his birthday on September 4th (TV's "Sesame Street")

Roosevelt, Franklin Delano

Only United States President to be elected for four terms; 1932, 1936, 1940, 1944 (respectively over Hoover, Alf Landon, Wendell Wilkie, T. E. Dewey)

The distant relative shared by him and Theodore Roosevelt was Nicholas Roosevelt, a New York politician in the early 18th century (about 1700). Portrayed by Ralph Bellamy in 1960 movie *Sunrise at Campobello* and by Captain Jack Young in 1942 movie *Yankee Doodle Dandy*

Roosevelt, Theodore

Leader (Lieutenant-Colonel) of the Rough Riders, 1st Volunteer Cavalry

Youngest man to become President of the United States: age 42 years, 10 months, 18 days, when inaugurated Sept. 14, 1901. First American to win a Nobel Prize. Portrayed in 1942 movie *Yankee Doodle Dandy* by Wallas Clark. Portrayed in 1976 movie *The Wind and the Lion* by Brian Keith. His son Brigadier General Theodore Roosevelt, Jr. was portrayed in the 1962 movie *The Longest Day* by Henry Fonda

Roosevelt boys
Sons of Franklin and Eleanor Roosevelt who served during World War II while their father was President of the United States:
James, Marine Corps, Elliot, Air Corps, Franklin, Jr., Navy, John, Navy
In the 1960 movie *Sunrise at Campobello* the sons were played respectively by Tim Considine, Pat Close, Robin Warga, Tommy Carty

Root, Charlie
Chicago Cubs' pitcher who threw the baseball in the 4th inning of the third (Oct. 1) 1932 World Series game in Chicago when Babe Ruth pointed to the centerfield bleachers and, after taking two strikes and then two balls, hit right where he indicated he would (Root denied that Babe Ruth ever pointed, but Ruth said that he did)

Root Beer
Dennis the Menace's favorite drink (especially with cookies)

Rootie Kazootie
TV puppet show, 1950-1952. Host: Todd Russell, Puppets: Rootie Kazootie, El Squeeko Mouse, Gala Poochie, Polka Dottie, Nipper

Rorschach Test
Psychological personality test utilizing "inkblots," symmetrical patterns in which the subject of the test constructs mental images

Rosabella
Mary, Queen of Scots horse

Rosa's Cantina
Saloon in El Paso where Senorita Felina danced (1960 Grammy winning "El Paso" by Marty Robbins)

Roscoe Sweeney
Buz Sawyer's friend (comic strip)

Rosebud
Citizen Kane's last word on his deathbed (1941 movie *Citizen Kane*), Rosebud being the brand of sled that he had as a child and the frame story of the movie consisting of a search for the meaning of the word. Rosebud is Joan Blondell's real first name

Rosebud
Richie Petrie's (Larry Mathews) middle name:
R   Robert = his dad's name

O	Oscar = Laura's mother's suggestion
S	Sam = Rob's father's name
E	Edward = Laura's father's brother
B	Benjamin = Rob's mother's suggestion
U	Ulysses = Rob's grandfather's suggestion
D	David = Rob's grandfather's suggestion

A compilation of names suggested by his family (TV series *Dick Van Dyke Show*)

Rosebuds

Billy Rose's eight dancing girls averaging 250 lbs each

Rosedale

Cemetery where Big Jim (Edward G. Robinson) is buried by Robbo and Guy Gisborne's gang (1964 movie *Robin and the 7 Hoods*)

Rosehill, New York

Town, location of TV serial "Love of Life". From 1951-1961 the setting was Barrowsville

Rosemary's Baby

Named Andrew John; 1968 movie, directed by Roman Polanski and starring Mia Farrow, (as Rosemary Woodhouse), John Cassavetes, and Ruth Gordon (who won an Academy Award as best supporting actress for her role as a motherly witch) about witchcraft in an urban setting

Rose of Tralee

Theme song of radio series *Backstage Wife*, performed by Chet Kingbury

Rosenkowitz sextuplets

Born January 11, 1974, in Capetown, South Africa to Susan and Colin in order of their birth: David, Nicolette, Jason, Emma, Grant, Elizabeth

Rosenthal, Joe

Photographer who won Pulitzer Prize for picture of U.S. Marines raising the American flag on Mt. Suribachi, Iwo Jima (March 15, 1945): the event was restaged so Rosenthal could get a good picture (see Iwo Jima)

Rosey

Family robot of the Jetsons (TV cartoon series "The Jetsons")

Rosie

Waitress on the Bounty paper towel ads (played by Nancy Walker)

Rosie the Riveter

World War II character created to inspire the women

who worked in the factories supposedly based on the exploits of Aircraft worker Rosina B. Bonavita, who with her co-worker riveted 3,345 rivets in 6 hours in the wing on a Grumman Avenger bomber. Title of 1941 musical starring Jane Frazee

Rose Marie

Real name: Rose Marie Curley. Radio child star, "The Darling of the Airways," later in movies, on Broadway, and on TV ("Hollywood Squares," "The Dick Van Dyke Show," among others)

Ross, Nellie

First woman governor. Elected governor of Wyoming in 1924. Fifteen days later Ma Ferguson became the Governor of Texas. In 1933, Nellie Ross became the first woman director of the mint, holding the position for the next 20 years

Rough-House

Owner of Wimpy's favorite hamburger stand (Popeye comic strip)

Rough Riders

In western movie series they were: Buck Jones, Tim Mc-Coy, Raymond Hatton

Roundhouse Junction

Town setting of 1975 movie *Bite the Bullet*

Round? Trip

Name on B17 (3463) in airplane graveyard that Capt. Fred Derry (Dana Andrews) goes through to bring back memories (1946 movie *The Best Years of Our Lives*)

Route 66

U.S. highway from Chicago to Los Angeles. Title of song composed by Bobby Troup. TV series, theme song (instrumental) by Nelson Riddle

Rover

Code name of Mrs. Roosevelt, used during World War II

Rovers Bar

Pub located at 11 Coronation Street setting of British TV series *Coronation Street*

Rover Boys, The

Boys' novels created by Edward Stratemeyer: central characters are Dick, Sam, Tom (under pseudonym Arthur M. Winfield)

Rowlf

Puppet dog (muppet) on TV series *The Jimmy Dean Show*

Roxanne

Bud Collyer's assistant on TV's game show *Beat the Clock*. Her real name is Dolores Rosedale

Roy

Country hick who shoots and kills motorcyclists Wyatt and Billy with a shotgun from the passenger side of a pickup truck (1969 movie *Easy Rider*)

Royal

Movie Theater in the film *The Last Picture Show* (1971) (The last movie shown was *Red River* (1948) starring John Wayne and Montgomery Clift). (The other movie shown was *Father of the Bride* (1950) starring Spencer Tracy and Elizabeth Taylor). In the novel the two films were *Storm Warning* (1950) and the last film was *The Kid from Texas* (1950) Audie Murphy and Gale Storm

Royal Canadians

Guy Lombardo's orchestra, established in 1923 "Sweetest music this side of heaven"

Royal Hawaiians

Harry Owens' 1940s orchestra

Royal Order of Raccoons

Lodge that Ralph Kramden (Jackie Gleason) and Ed Norton (Art Carney) belonged to (TV series *The Honeymooners*). The headman was called the Grand High Exalted Mystic Ruler

"Brothers under the pelt". Bylaw requirements

1. Public school education
2. Six months in the U.S.
3. $1.50 initiation fee

Royal Wedding

1951 movie in which Fred Astaire dances on the walls and ceiling of his room. The room was specially built to slowly rotate to account for the fantastic effect. It was so well planned by director Stanley Donen and Astaire and crew, it took only ½ day to film

Roy Earle

Killer played by Humphrey Bogart in 1941 movie *High Sierra*. The part was turned down by George Raft, Paul Muni, Edward G. Robinson and James Cagney

R. Psmith

Hero of mystery stories by P. G. Wodehouse. R. Psmith pronounces his last name Smith, the "P" being silent

Rubber Duck

Singer C. W. McCall (Bill Fries) handle beginning with his 1976 tune *Convoy*

Rubble

Neighbors of the Flintstones: Barney, Betty, Bamm-Bamm (adopted son). Betty's maiden name is Betty Jean Bricker.
Bamm Bamm is called the strongest boy in the world.
Voices: Barney (Mel Blanc), Betty (Bea Benaderet and Gerry Johnson) Bamm Bamm (Jay North)

Rubin, Barbara Jo

First North American female jockey. First rode at Aqueduct in 1969

Ruby

Apple family pet snake (TV series *Apple's Way*)

Ruby

Amos's wife ("Amos 'n' Andy"): on radio by Elinor Harriot

Ruby, Jack

Dallas night club owner (1911-1967) who killed Lee Harvey Oswald, Nov. 24, 1963. Ruby's two nightclubs were the Carousel Club and the Vegas Club

Ruby Slippers

Size 4½ shoes that Glinda, the Good Witch of the North, gave Dorothy after Dorothy's house fell on the Wicked Witch of the East (1939 movie *The Wizard of Oz*). At the 1970 M-G-M auction the slippers sold for $15,000

Rudolph

The Red-Nosed Reindeer, 1950 Hit record by Gene Autry in annual TV story narrated by Burl Ives. Rudolph is the son of Donner, his girl friend is Clarence. In comic books, his best friend was Grover Groundhog

Ruff

Dennis the Menace's dog (daily comic strip). He's afraid of cats

Ruff and Ready

Cat and bulldog (comic book series). TV voices Ruff (Don Messick), Ready (Daws Butler)

Rufus

Jim Henson's muppett dog (*The Muppetts*) he appeared on the Jimmy Dean Show

Rugby

School attended by Tom Brown (Thomas Hughes' *Tom Brown's Schooldays*, 1857)

Rum and Coca Cola

Song written about 1944, words by comedian Morey Amsterdam; subject of famous copyright suit on grounds that Lord Invader (Rupert Grant) wrote the words

Rumpelstiltskin

Dwarf who could spin straw into gold (Grimms' fairy tales)

Runnymede

Meadow on Thames River west of London where the Magna Charta was signed, June 15, 1215, by King John (it is also said that nearby Charter Island is the place of signing)

Runt

Boston Blackie's sidekick (movie series): played by George E. Stone. On radio his sidekick was Shorty

Ruptured Duck

B-25 piloted by Major Ted W. Lawson in Doolittle's raid on Tokyo. Portrayed in 1944 movie *Thirty Seconds Over Tokyo* by Van Johnson

Ruritania

European Kingdom ruled by King Rudolf V. Anthony Hope's 1894 novel *The Prisoner of Zenda*

Rushville Center

Town, location of radio serial "Ma Perkins"

Russell

Bill Cosby's brother (with whom he slept)

Russell, Harold

Handicapped veteran with two artificial hands who played in William Wyler's *The Best Years of Our Lives* (1946) in a role of a handicapped ex-serviceman. For the role he won an Oscar for best supporting actor and honorary Oscar for his courage as a veteran. He lost both hands when a dynamite charge exploded on training maneuvers in North Carolina.

Rusty B. Company

Boy in TV series "Rin-Tin-Tin": played by Lee Aaker. Adopted by Fort Apache's B Company

Rusty

Bob Steele's horse (Western B movies)

Rutgers

New Jersey college that played, Nov. 6, 1869, the first intercollegiate football game, beating Princeton 6-4 under soccer rules

Ruth

Festus's mule (TV series "Gunsmoke")

Ruth, George Herman "Babe"

"Sultan of Swat", "King of Clout," "Bambino"

Most successful slugger in major league history, one of first 5 elected to Baseball's Hall of Fame: pitcher (1914-1919) with Boston Red Sox, outfielder (1920-1934) with New York Yankees and (1935) Boston Bees. He hit 714 home runs in his career; in the 1921 season, he hit 59, passing the previous record holder, Roger Connor, who played from 1880 to 1896 in the National League and hit 137 home runs. His record fell in 1974, after nearly 40 years, when Henry Aaron of Atlanta hit his 715th home run. Ruth's 60 home runs in 1927 still stands as the 154-game season record, though surpassed by Roger Maris's 1961 "asterisked" total of 61 in 162 games. Ruth led the American League in slugging percentage (lifetime, .690) every season from 1918 to 1931, except for 1925, the year he collapsed physically and Ken Williams led; he was consistently a leader in runs batted in, and led in home runs except for 1922 (Williams with 39 to Ruth's 35) and 1925 (Meusel with 33), though he was tied in 1918 by Tilly Walker of Philadelphia (11) and in 1931 by his teammate Lou Gehrig (46). In 2503 games, Ruth struck out 1330 times and walked 2056 times; no other player has as many bases on balls.

Ruth's record as a pitcher, in a short mound career, is also impressive. For 43 years he held the World Series record for consecutive scoreless innings pitched (29⅔), broken by Whitey Ford in the 1960 and 1961 series; his World Series earned run average is 0.87 (Harry Brecheen's 0.83 is the only better mark). He hit the first home run in an All Star Game (1933).

Ruth's last home runs (713-714) were hit May 25, 1935, off Guy Bush of Pittsburgh at Forbes Field.

His "calling the shot" home run in the third game of the World Series (Oct. 1, 1932) was hit off Charlie Root of

Chicago at Wrigley Field; it was Ruth's last series homer (15: record held by Mickey Mantle, 18).

Ruth's salary of $80,000 a year in 1930-1931 was the highest ever for its time.

The answer to the question "Whose record did Ruth break when he hit 60 homers?" is of course "His own," since his 59 home runs in 1921 was then the record

Ruth starred in 1927 silent movie *The Babe Comes Home* and appeared with Harold Lloyd in 1928 silent movie *Speedy*

In 1942 movie *The Pride of the Yankees* Ruth was portrayed by Babe Ruth (himself)

In 1948 movie *The Babe Ruth Story* portrayed by William Bendix who as a boy was the bat boy with the New York Giants

Ryder Cup

Awarded to the winners in men's professional golf in British-American competition

Ryman Auditorium

Nashville, Tennessee, location of Grand Ole Opry from 1942 to 1974; known after 1961 as Grand Ole Opry House. Named for Riverboat captain Thomas Ryman. The auditorium was the setting of the TV series *The Johnny Cash Show*

Prior to being held there the Opry was held at the Nashville War Memorial Auditorium (The first performer on the Grand Ole Opry was Uncle Jimmy Thompson, a Civil War veteran)

S

6

Sides to a snowflake

6

Players on a hockey team

6

The good reporter's questions: Who, What, When, Where, Why, How

6 Seconds

Minimum time a bareback rider on bullrider must stay on his animal to qualify. A saddle bronc needs 8 seconds

Sixth Avenue

Manhattan location of the Jefferson family apartment. TV series *The Jeffersons*. Prior to this they resided at 708 Hauser Street, Queens, New York

6YZ643

License number of Fred Flintstone's car (TV series *The Flintstones*)

7

Members of a water polo team

7

Number of voyages of Sinbad the Sailor (*Arabian Nights*)

7 Against Thebes

Argive heroes who fought Thebes (Greek mythology): Adrastus, Polynices, Tydeus, Parthenopaeus, Amphiaraus, Capaneus, Hippomedon

7 Ages of Man

Jaques, philosophizing in William Shakespeare's *As You Like It* enumerates them as embodied in: Infant, Schoolboy, Lover, Soldier, Justice, Pantaloon (retirement), Second childhood ("sans everything")

7 Deadly Sins
Pride, Avarice, Wrath, Envy, Gluttony, Sloth, Lust

7 Destroyers
Ran aground in the Santa Barbara Channel, Sept. 8, 1923: U.S.S. "Chauncey," U.S.S. "Delphy," (flagship), U.S.S. "Fuller," U.S.S. "S. P. Lee," U.S.S. "Nicholas," U.S.S. "Woodbury," U.S.S. "Young," (U.S.S. "Farragut" and U.S.S. "Somers" were damaged) 22 sailors died

7 Dwarfs, The
Snow White's woodland companions (Disney cartoon feature movie): Bashful (voice: Scotty Mattraw); Doc (voice: Roy Atwell); Dopey ("Never had anything to say"); Grumpy (voice: Pinto Colvig); Happy (voice: Otis Harlon); Sleepy (voice: Pinto Colvig); Sneezy (voice: Billy Gilbert). Doc is the only one to wear glasses. In movie jam session Grumpy plays the piano, Sleepy the trumpet, Dopey the drums, Doc the bass, Sneezy, the accordian, Bashful the symbols and Happy leads the band.
Movie premiered at the Carthay Circle Theatre, Hollywood December 21, 1937

7 Hills of Rome
Aventine, Caelian, Capitoline, Esquiline, Palatine, Quirinal, Viminal

7 Little Foys
Brynie, Charlie, Dick, Eddy, Madeleine, Mary, Irving, Father: Eddie. In 1942 movie *Yankee Doodle Dandy* Eddie played by Eddy, Jr. In 1955 movie *The Seven Little Foys* Eddie portrayed by Bob Hope (Who also came from a family of seven children)

7 Mules
Linemen for the Four Horsemen on the 1924 Notre Dame football team; Ed Huntsinger, end; Charles Collins, end; Joe Bach, tackle; Edgar (Rip) Miller, tackle; Noble Kizer, guard; John Weibel, guard; Adam Walsh, center

Seven Original Astronauts
Beginning with the Mercury program (1961): Alan B. Shepard, Jr., Virgil I. Grissom, John H. Glenn, Jr., M. Scott Carpenter, Walter M. Schirra, Jr., L. Gordon Cooper, Jr., Donald K. Slayton (did not fly). Schirra was the only Astronaut to be in the Mercury, Gemini and Apollo programs

7 Saville Row
Burlington Gardens, London. Home address of Phileas Fogg, the man who went *Around the World in 80 Days*

7 Seas, The
Antarctic; Arctic; North Atlantic; South Atlantic; Indian; North Pacific; South Pacific

7 Sisters
Women's Ivy League colleges:

	Location	*Date founded*
Barnard	New York, N.Y.	1889
Bryn Mawr	Bryn Mawr, Penna.	1885
Mount Holyoke	So. Hadley, Mass.	1837
Radcliffe	Cambridge, Mass.	1879
Smith	Northampton, Mass.	1871
Vassar*	Poughkeepsie, N.Y.	1861
Wellesley	Wellesley, Mass.	1875

Actress Katherine Hepburn graduated from Byrn Mawr (She was once suspended for smoking)

7 Sisters, The
Daughters of Atlas (in the constellation Pleiades): Alcyone, Sterope, Celeno, Electra, Maia, Taygeta, Merope (dimmest star, because she married a mortal)

7 Virtues
Faith, Hope, Charity (Love), Fortitude, Justice, Prudence, Temperance

Seven Wise Men
(7 Sages of Greece) Periander of Corinth, Pittacus of Mitylene, Thales of Miletus, Solon of Athens, Bias of Priene, Chilo of Sparta, Cleobulus of Lindus

7 Wonders of the World
Antiquity
    Colossus of Rhodes
    Egyptian Pyramids (Only one still in existence)
    Hanging Gardens of Babylon
    Lighthouse (Pharos) at Alexandria
    Mausoleum at Halicarnassus
    Statue of Zeus by Phidias at Olympia
    Temple of Diana at Ephesus
Middle Ages
    Catacombs of Alexandria

---

*Now co-ed, no longer a women's college

Coliseum of Rome
Great Wall of China
Leaning Tower of Pisa
Mosque of St. Sophia at Constantinople
Porcelain Tower of Nanking
Stonehenge, Salisbury Plain, England

7 Works of Mercy, The
Bury the dead; Clothe the naked; Feed the hungry; Give drink to the thirsty; House the homeless; Tend the sick; Visit the fatherless and afflicted

Seven Years
Length of time a person must be missing before they can be declared legally dead

7B Praed Street
London, W2 house address of detective Solar Pons who becomes the successor of Sherlock Holmes. His telephone number being Ambassador 10000, his landlady is Mrs. Johnson. (Series by August Derleth)

7th
Cavalry regiment that was George Armstrong Custer's last command

7X
Coca Cola's secret ingredient

16
Number on football jersey originally worn by Mean Mary Jean (Judy Strangis) the Plymouth girl (TV commercial); later changed to 1 and in 1975 to 75

17 Cherry Tree Lane
London home of the Banks family (1964 movie *Mary Poppins*)

17 South Jackson
Home of the Goldbergs (radio series)

17 Paseo Verde
Home address of detective Joe Mannix (Mike Connors) TV series *Mannix*. His phone number is 555-6644

17 Richmond Street
Address of 35-year-old detective Mr. Parker Pyne (detective created by Agatha Christie)

17 Shore Road
Address of mansion in 1976 movie *Burnt Offering*. The family moved in on July 1

60
Home runs hit by Babe Ruth in a 154-game season 1927

(540 times at bat). Hit number 60 on September 30, 1927. (In the same game Walter Johnson made his final major league appearance, he pinch-hit). Of the 60 Ruth hit 28 in Yankee Stadium

60 Feet 6 Inches
Distance between the pitcher's rubber and home plate in baseball

61
Home runs hit by Roger Maris in a 162-game season. 1961 (590 times at bat): number 61 was hit off of Boston Red Sox pitcher Tracy Stallard. 30 of them were hit in Yankee Stadium. That year teammate Mickey Mantle hit 54. Maris' achievement is recorded in the baseball record book with an asterisk, as Ruth hit his 60 in a 154-game season, Maris had hit his 59th by the 154th game of his 162 game season.

61A Charington Gardens
London address of Margot Wendice (Grace Kelly) and —Tony Wendice (Ray Milland), 1954 movie *Dial M for Murder*. Their phone number is MAyfield 3-499

62
Velvet Brown's raffle ticket number which won the racing horse The Pie. Number 113 was originally drawn, but no such ticket was sold; number 62 being drawn next. (1944 movie *National Velvet*)

62
Self-portraits painted by Rembrandt van Rijn. (In 1936 movie *Rembrandt* he is portrayed by Charles Laughton)

63
Length in yards of longest field goal in NFL history: by Tom Dempsey (his right—kicking—foot is artificial, size 3) of the New Orleans Saints against the Detroit Lions, Nov. 8, 1970. This was the last play of the game and won for the Saints 19-17. He is also missing his right hand

64
Squares on a chess board

$64
Highest prize in CBS radio show "Take It or Leave It"

65th Precinct
New York setting of TV series "Naked City"

67
Michael Sarrazin and Jane Fonda's marathon dance number in the 1969 movie *They Shoot Horses, Don't They?*

77

Red Grange's uniform number

77 Sunset Strip

Address of private investigators Stuart Bailey (Efrem Zimbalist, Jr.) and Jeff Spencer (Roger Smith).
Next to Dinos Restaurant.
Their phone number is PRospect 4-712
Their secretary is named Suzanne Fabray (Jacqueline Beer) (TV series *77 Sunset Strip*)

77th

Infantry division to which belonged the "Lost Battalion" (1st Battalion, 308th Infantry), separated near Binarville, France, in the Meuse-Argonne offensive, Oct. 2-Oct. 7, 1918, in World War I

78 RPM records

Manufacture discontinued in 1958. In 1948 RCA Victor introduced the 45 rpm giving it the code name of Madame X

79 Wistful Vista

Home of Fibber McGee and Molly. On radio played by Jim and Marion Jordan on TV by Bob Sweeney and Cathy Lewis. All the places Fibber McGee went were located at the intersection of 14th and Oak

600

Number of cavalrymen in the Light Brigade (Alfred, Lord Tennyson's "The Charge of the Light Brigade")

600 East 32nd Street

Manhattan, New York home address of the Davis family (TV series *Family Affair*)

607 Maple Street

Home address in Springfield of the Anderson family, on TV and radio series *Father Knows Best*

623 East 68th Street

New York City address of the Mertz apartment house in which the Ricardos are tenants. (TV series *I Love Lucy*)

626 Club

Night spot where Joey Evans (Frank Sinatra) sang in the 1957 movie *Pal Joey*

627 Elm Street

Hillsdale, California home address of the Mitchell family, especially Dennis (TV's *Dennis the Menace*)

632 A.F.
Time in which is set Aldous Huxley's novel *Brave New World*. A.F. stands for After Ford (Henry Ford)

636 Carlyle Street
Santa Monica, California, home address of Grady Wilson (Whitman Mayo) TV series *Grady*

657 Hoagland Avenue
Alfalfa's parents' home address in Blainville, California, in the *Our Gang* serial titled *Alfalfa's Aunt*. His parents are John and Martha Switzer (*Our Gang* movie serial)

698 Sycamore Road
San Pueblo, California home address of the *Partridge Family* (TV series)

704 Hauser Street
Queens, New York address of the Bunkers (TV series *All In The Family*). Prior to this, the family lived on Union Street. The Jeffersons lived at 708 Hauser Street

714
Badge number of Sgt. Joe Friday (radio/TV series "Dragnet")

714
Home runs hit (1915-1935) by Babe Ruth: Ruth's first major league home run was hit off Jack Warhop of Yankees (Ruth was member of Boston Red Sox), May 6, 1915, in New York. At bat 8,399 times in 2,503 games

714 . . . 715
Hank Aaron hit his 714th home run in his first time at bat, opening day, April 4, 1974, in Cincinnati Riverfront Stadium, off Cincinnati pitcher Jack Billingham (he also pitched his 528, 636, 641, and 709 home run); ball was retrieved by policeman Clarence Williams.

Hank Aaron hit his 715th home run off Dodger pitcher Al Downing at Atlanta Stadium, April 8, 1974, 9:07 p.m., the count was one and 0, he hit a fast ball over the left center-field fence. Braves' relief pitcher Tom House retrieved the ball in the Atlanta bullpen. (Pearl Bailey sang the National Anthem before the game.) Downing, who also wore uniform number 44, also gave up Aaron's home runs 674 and 696, number 715 was hit in his 11,295th time at bat in his 2967th game

Aaron's first major league home run was hit off Vic Raschi of the St. Louis Cardinals April 23, 1954, at St. Louis. Aaron had hit a home run in St. Louis in 1965 but was called out by umpire Pete Koudas for stepping out of the batter's box. Aaron ended his baseball career with 755 home runs

723K

Theo Kojak's (Telly Savalas) automobile radio call sign (TV series *Kojak*)

730

Actual number of home runs hit by Babe Ruth in official baseball games while in the major leagues.
714 in regular season play
15 in World Series play
1 in All Star Game (1933)
730 Total Home Runs in the Major Leagues

730 Hampton Street

Milwaukee home address (Apartment A) of *Laverne and Shirley* (TV series)

732

Number of Bicentennial Minutes broadcast one each evening on CBS TV at 8:27 or 8:28 p.m. EST. Began in July 4, 1974 through July 4, 1976. Given by noted individuals. An additional Bicentennial Minute was given on Dec. 31, 1976 by President Ford

746

Ticket number under which Sam Spade checks the Maltese Falcon at the Union Bus Depot. He mails the ticket to his post office box, P.O. Box 589, Station C, where it is picked up by his secretary Effie (1941 movie *The Maltese Falcon*)

747 Bonnie Vista Road

Tarzana, California home address of the Preston family. (TV series *The New Dick Van Dyke Show*)

751

Chicago psychologist Doctor Robert Hartley's office number (TV series *The Bob Newhart Show*)

776 B.C.

First Greek Olympic games

792 Main

New York City address of Woody Allen (comic strip *Inside Woody Allen*)

1600

Address on Pennsylvania Avenue in Washington, D.C. of the White House

1616

Year in which Shakespeare and Cervantes died on April 23, which was also Shakespeare's birthday

1720 Valley Road

Los Angeles home address of the ranch of Carol (Connie Hines) and Wilbur Post (Alan Young) (TV series *Mr. Ed*)

1753 Angelo

Los Angeles home address of Jim Stark (James Dean) (1955 movie *Rebel Without A Cause*)

6939 A.D.

Date when the 1939 New York World's Fair time capsule is to be opened. By then it will have been buried for 50 centuries

7190

Number stamped on the gold bar James Bond uses as bait for Auric Goldfinger (1964 movie *Goldfinger*)

7321 years

Age of Dr. Lao (Tony Randall) (1963 movie *Seven Faces of Dr. Lao*)

$64,000 Question

Television quiz show (1955-1958) sponsored by Revlon, emceed by Hal March. A new Cadillac was the consolation prize for those who missed the big $64,000 Question. Psychologist Dr. Joyce Brothers won $64,000 in the category of boxing. Barbara Feldon won with Shakespeare

762513

Service serial number of Major Donald Craig (Rock Hudson 1967 movie *Tobruk*)

636-9970

Rob and Laura Petrie's home phone number (TV series *The Dick Van Dyke Show*)

773,692

Number of words in the English Bible (King James version)

17,576,000

Different combinations using 3 numbers and 3 letters (license plates)

S

Middle initial in Harry S Truman's name: doesn't stand for any name, therefore no period after the S

S & H

Green trading stamps founded in 1891 by Thomas Alexander Sperry and Shelley B. Hutchinson for Merchants Supply Company of Bridgeport, Conn. Takes 1200 stamps to fill a book

SAM

Surface-to-Air Missile

SALT

Strategic Arms Limitation Talks: between U.S. and U.S.S.R. at Helsinki (1970) and Geneva (1972)

SCPD

Police Department in the TV series *The Rookies* (Southern California Police Department)

SHIELD

Supreme Headquarters, International Espionage Law-Enforcement Division (comic book series Nick Fury, Agent of S.H.I.E.L.D.)

SHADO

Supreme Headquarters Allied Defense Organization: 1980's setting of TV series "UFO"

SHAPE

Supreme Headquarters, Allied Powers in Europe: military center for NATO command

SIA

Government agency (United States Intelligence Agency) for which Alexander Mundy (played by Robert Wagner) steals: agency head is Noah Bain (TV series "It Takes a Thief")

SMERSH

Soviet organization, Smyert Spionam "death to spies" that does battle with the British Secret Service for which James Bond is an agent

SNAFU

World War II slang expression watered down to mean Situation Normal All Fouled* Up (FUBAR—Fouled Up Beyond All Recognition was a spin-off)

SOS

· · · – – – · · · (distress signal), before SOS it was CQD. The first ship to use SOS was the Titanic the night she sank

SPEBSQSA

Society for the Preservation and Encouragement of Barber Shop Quarter Singing in America

---

*originally stood for 4 letter expletive

SPQR

Senatus Populusque Romanus ("The Roman Senate and People"): initials on Roman standards and elsewhere, especially during the republic

STP

Initials for the STP Corporation's "Scientifically Tested Products," in the case of the Oil Treatment it refers to "Scientifically Treated Petroleum"

SWAT

Special Weapons and Tactics Team (TV series "S.W.A.T.")

Sabena Boeing 707

Belgium national airliner in which 18 members of the U.S. Olympic skating team were killed, February 15, 1961 at Berg, Belgium

Sabrina

Teenage witch (TV cartoon). Voice of Jane Webb

Sacred Cow

C-54, first official presidential airplane, 1944. Serial number 2107451 piloted by Major Henry T. Myers

Sacred Stars of the Milky Way

Fraternal organization of which Vic Gook (Art Van Harvey) is an exalted Big Dipper in the Drowsy Venus Chapter (radio series, *Vic and Sade*)

Sad Sacks, The

The essential GI of World War II, a cartoon character by George Baker featured in *Yank* from its first issue. Debut CBS radio June 12, 1946 played by Herb Vigran. In 1958 movie *The Sad Sack* Jerry Lewis played Private Bixby

Sadie

Sad Sack's WAC girlfriend (comic strip series "Sad Sack")

Sadie Hawkins Day

First Saturday after November 11, when girls chase boys to catch a husband: originally adopted by college groups and others from recurrent event in Al Capp comic strip "Li'l Abner." Originally begun on November 13, 1939 on Sadie's 35th birthday. Sadie is the daughter of Hekzebiah Hawkins one of the founders of Dogpatch

Safety Sadie

Symbol of the U.S. Consumer Product Safety Commission. Portrayed by actress Carol Arthur

Safi

Baby monkey that rode with Thor Heyderdahl on Ra I

Sailor

Spin's horse (Spin and Marty, on TV's "Mickey Mouse Club")

Saint, The

Simon Templar, detective/adventurer created by Leslie Charteris

Saint Movies

1938 *The Saint in New York* (Louis Hayward)

1939 *The Saint Strikes Back* (George Sanders)

1939 *The Saint in London* (George Sanders)

1940 *The Saint's Double Trouble* (George Sanders)

1940 *The Saint Takes Over* (George Sanders)

1941 *The Saint in Palm Springs* (Georgia Sanders)

1942 *The Saint's Vacation* (Hugh Sinclair)

1943 *The Saint Meets the Tiger* (Hugh Sinclair)

1954 *The Saint's Girl Friday* (Louis Hayward)

Radio:

Edgar Barrier, Brian Aherne, Vincent Price, Tom Conway, Barry Sullivan

TV:

Roger Moore—drove a Volvo 1800s—sportscar

Debut in novel "Meet the Tiger" (1928)

St. Aloysius

San Diego Catholic Church where ex-policeman Father Samuel Patrick Cavanaugh (George Kennedy) is a priest (TV series *Sarge*)

St. Andrew

Patron saint of Scotland

St. Boniface

Patron saint of Germany

St. Canute

Patron Saint of Denmark

St. Denis

Patron saint of France

St. Dominic

Manhattan Catholic Church of which Father Chuck O'Malley (Gene Kelly) is assigned, Father Fitzgibbons (Leo G. Carroll) is the pastor (1962-1963 TV series *Going My Way*)

St. Francis Academy

All girls-school at which Rosalind Russell plays Mother Superior. *The Trouble With Angels* (1966), *Where Angels Go—Trouble Follows* (1968)

St. George
Patron saint of England

St. Gregory
New Orleans hotel in Arthur Hailey's *Hotel* (1967 movie)

St. James (Santiago)
Patron saint of Spain

St. Joseph's Day
March 19—Day that the swallows return to Mission San Juan Capistrano each year

St. Patrick
Patron saint of Ireland

St. Lidwina
The Patron saint of skaters

St. Mary Mead
English village in which Agatha Christie's sleuth Miss Jane Marple lives

St. Mary's Hospital
Sonoma County hospital where Robert Ironside recovered from being shot. The staff gave him his wheelchair. (TV series *Ironside*)

St. Mary's Industrial School
The Baltimore, Maryland Catholic boys' home where George "Babe" Herman Ruth grew up (1902-1914). (Al Jolson also had a brief stay there)

St. Olaf
Patron Saint of Norway

St. Patrick's Cathedral
New York City church where the Doomsday bomb is exploded destroying Earth in the 1970 movie *Beneath the Planet of the Apes*

St. Petersburg
Missouri village on the Mississippi River from which Tom Sawyer and Huckleberry Finn hail

St. Valentine's Day Massacre
The February 14, 1929, machine-gunning of 7 members of Bugs Moran's (or Dion O'Banion's) gang by 5 members of Al Capone's mob, some dressed like policemen, who arrived in a Cadillac touring car at the S. M. C. Cartage Co. warehouse, 2122 North Clark Street, Chicago. Killed were James Clark, Al Weinshank, Adam Heyer, John May, Reinhardt Schwimmer, Pete Gusenberg, Frank Gusenberg (Highball, John May's German Shepherd was present). The two machine gunners were Frank Rogers

and James Morton. George "Bugs" Moran and two other hoods missed being there by 5 minutes. No arrests were ever made

In the 1959 movie *Some Like it Hot* Tony Curtis and Jack Lemmon play two musicians who join an all girl band after witnessing the incident. In the movie George Raft plays the leader of Capone's mob.

The same day as the Massacre the Hollywood Brown Derby Restaurant opened across the street from the Ambassador Hotel on Wilshire Blvd. Designed by Cecil B. DeMille, it was in the shape of a derby hat. On the walls were caricatures of movie stars

Saki

Pseudonym of Hector Hugh Munro (1870-1916), English author of macabre humorous stories

Sal

First Sergeant Braxton Rutledge's (Top Soldier) horse of Troop D, 9th U.S. Calvary, Fort Linton (1960 movie *Sergeant Rutledge* (The Apaches called Rutledge Captain Buffalo)

Salem

Town, locale of daytime serial "Days of Our Lives"

Salem

Cat belonging to Sabrina (the teenage witch in a TV cartoon series)

Salomey

Li'l Abner's pig (comic strip) last of the Alabammus Hammus breed

Sally

Switchboard operator at Blair General Hospital in Dr. Kildare films (played by Marie Blake who later played the Grandmother on TV's *Addams Family*)

Sally

Dick and Jane's little sister. Her teddy bear is named Tim (Primary Reader)

Sally Kimball

Encyclopedia Brown's junior partner (Juvenile series)

Salt and Pepper

Charles Salt (Sammy Davis Jr.)
Christopher Pepper (Peter Lawford)
1968 movie *Salt and Papper* and 1970 Jerry Lewis directed sequel *One More Time*

"Salty" Bill Barnacle
  Popeye's sidekick (pre-1929)
Sam
  Piano player (1942 movie *Casablanca*): played by Dooley
  Wilson. Wilson could not play the piano himself. The
  music was actually played by Elliott Carpenter. Sam sang
  "As Time Goes By," "It Had To Be You," and "Knock
  on Wood"
Sam
  Dr. Sean Jamison's (Brian Keith) pet parrot (TV series
  The Little People)
Sam
  Alice's boyfriend, a butcher (Alan Melvin) TV series *The
  Brady Bunch*
Sam
  Cook at the Tides Restaurant in Bodega Bay (1963 movie
  The Birds)
Sam
  Hondo Lane's (John Wayne) pet dog in 1954 movie
  Hondo
Sam
  Longfellow Deed's (Monte Markham) dog (TV series *Mr.
  Deeds Goes to Town*)
Sam
  Sesame Street junk robot (he's made up of odds and ends).
  His birthday is on May 24th
Sam
  Taxicab driver for Vincent Parry (Humphrey Bogart) in
  the 1947 movie *Dark Passage* played by Tom D'Andrea
Sam
  Richard Diamond's switchboard operator on TV played by
  Mary Tyler Moore (but all the viewers ever saw were
  her legs) and Roxanne Brooks. Moore's legs were previ-
  ously shown as the dancing Old Gold Cigarette Pack on
  TV commercials
Sam Carraclough
  Of Greenall Bridge, Yorkshire—Lassie's first owner, his
  son Joe being the 2nd. (Eric Knight's *Lassie Come Home*)
Sam Catchem
  Dick Tracy's freckle-faced detective companion on TV
  played by Joe Devlin. Prior to Sam, Dick Tracy's partner
  was Pat Patton who became Chief of Police. Sam's wife is
  Marge, his daughter is Julie

Samford
Friend of Doctor John Watson, who introduced him to Sherlock Holmes

Sam (George Samuel) Kirk
Captain James T. Kirk's only brother who died. His wife is Aurelan, their son Peter (TV series *Star Trek*)

Sam O'Brien
The bartender of the Longbranch Saloon (played by Glenn Strange). Prior to Strange, played by Clem Fuller and Robert Brubaker (TV series *Gunsmoke*)

Sam 'n' Henry
Names of Freeman Gosden and Charles Correll in the radio series preceding "Amos 'n' Andy" (Debut on radio January 12, 1926). Broadcast on WGN radio. When they moved to WMAQ they became Amos 'n' Andy

Sam Spade
Detective created by Dashiell Hammett in the novel *The Maltese Falcon* (1930). Story originally appeared in *Black Mask Magazine*, in 1929
Debut CBS radio July 12, 1946. On radio Spade was played by Howard Duff and Steve Dunne. In the movies he was played by Humphrey Bogart in *The Maltese Falcon* (1941), by Ricardo Cortez (1931 version *Dangerous Female;* also known as *The Maltese Falcon*), and by Warren William as Ted Shayne (in 1936 *Satan Met a Lady,* a version of *The Maltese Falcon*)

Sam Spade, Jr.
Son of famous San Francisco, private eye Sam Spade. In 1975 movie *The Black Bird* played by George Segal

Samantha Stevens
Witch (TV series "Bewitched"): (played by Elizabeth Montgomery, daughter of Robert Montgomery) Her two children are Tabitha and Adam. Her maiden name is Dobson

Samantha
Pet goose (1956 movie *Friendly Persuasion*) winner of 1957 PATSY

Samson
Prince Philip's horse (Walt Disney version of *Sleeping Beauty*)

San Bernardino
California, largest county (20,117 sq. mi.) in the United States (larger than 9 states of the U.S.)

San Clemente
Site of the "Western White House" during the Nixon administration

San Francisco Beat
Title of reruns of the TV show "The Lineup"

San Francisco Opera House
Birthplace of the Charter for the United Nations, June 26, 1945. Central Hall, Westminster, London was the site of the first session of the United Nations General Assembly (1946)

San Francisco Post-Dispatch
Late edition newspaper that carried the headline: "Thursby, Archer Murders Linked!" (1941 movie *The Maltese Falcon*)

San Jobal Prison
Institution in which Alexander Mundy (Robert Wagner) spent time for robbery before being bailed out by Noah Bain. His Parole Officer is Miss Agnew (TV series *It Takes A Thief*)

San Juan Hill
Place near Santiago, Cuba, where the Rough Riders made their famous charge (on foot), July 1, 1898, under the command of Theodore Roosevelt

San Pablo
The U.S. Navy gunboat on which Jake Holman (Steve McQueen) is a crew member. 1966 movie *The Sand Pebbles*

San Quentin
California prison in which country and western singer Merle Haggard served 3 years of a 1-to-5 year term

San Remo
Southwestern cow town where Tony Petrocelli (Barry Newman) is a young lawyer (TV series "Petrocelli")

San Simeon
Location of Hearst Castle, an estate built by publisher William Randolph Hearst in California. Designed by Julia Morgan

San Tanco
Sisters of Charity Convent in Puerto Rico to which Sister Bertrille (Sally Field) belongs (TV series "The Flying Nun"). Headed by Mother Superior Plaseato (Madeleine Sherwood)

Sancho Panza
Don Quixote's squire (in Cervantes' novel)

Sanders, George
British actor, brother of actor Tom Conway
Academy award (1950) for best supporting role, Addison De Witt in *All About Eve*
Autobiography (1960): *Memoirs of a Professional Cad*

Sanders, Colonel Harlan T.
Goateed and mustached founder of Kentucky Fried Chicken. Honorary colonel in the Kentucky Guard. He made a cameo appearance in the 1967 Jerry Lewis movie *The Loud Mouth*

Sandman
Debut Adventure Comics #40, July 1939
(original version)
Secret identity of playboy Wesley Dodds who wears a gas mask and uses a gas gun. His sidekick later was Sandy (Hawkins) The Golden Boy.
(Present Version)
Debut The Sandman #1. Winter 1974—Entity that controls people's dreams with the aide of his two assistants Glob and Brute (There is also another Sandman who is one of Spider Man's nemeses)

Sandwich Islands
Former name of the Hawaiian Islands

Sandy
Orphan Annie's dog (comic strip and radio): "Arf" says Sandy (on radio voice of Brad Barker, Pierre André)

Sandy
Ostrich on board Boner's Ark (comic strip Boner's Ark)

Sandy
Tom Swift, Jr.'s sister (Juvenile series)

Sandy and Little Red
Two bloodhounds that tracked down escaped convict James Earl Ray. June 13, 1977. Ray had escaped from Brushy Mountain State Prison in Tenn. with 4 other prisoners June 10, 1977

Sandy Harbor
Town setting of radio series *Ethel and Albert* (Arbuckle)

Sandy Hawkins
The Sandman's boy sidekick (comic book series "The Sandman")

Sanford and Son Salvage
Established 1939 (TV series Sanford and Son starring Redd Foxx and Demond Wilson)

Santa Claus' reindeer
In Clement Clarke Moore's poem "A Visit from St. Nicholas" (1823); Dasher, Dancer, Prancer, Vixen, Comet, Cupid, Donner, Blitzen

Santa Fe & Disneyland
Railroad running around the perimeter of Disneyland

Engines (1870s)	Trains	Stations
C.K. Holliday	100-S.F.&D. Limited	Main Street
E.P. Ripley	200-Holiday Red	Frontierland
Fred Gurley	300-Excursion	Tomorrowland
Ernest S. Marsh	400-Holiday Green	
Lilly Bell	500-Holiday Blue	

Santa Fe Trail
Kansas City, Missouri, to Santa Fe, New Mexico

Santa Luisa
Fictitious California setting for TV series *Dan August* (Burt Reynolds)

Santa Maria
Cristobal Colon's (Christopher Columbus's) flagship, a carack, in 1492 voyage, accompanied by "Nina" and "Pinta": wrecked off Hispaniola Christmas Day 1492, Columbus left August 3, 1492 arriving October 12, 1492. Rodrigo de Triana, one of the crew of 88, was the crew member who first sighted land in the New World. Columbus portrayed in 1949 movie *Christopher Columbus* by Fredric March, also in 1957 movie *The Story of Mankind* by Anthony Dexter

Santa Mira
Small town setting of 1956 movie *Invasion of the Body Snatchers*

Santana
Name of boat that Frank McCloud (Humphrey Bogart) takes over from Johnny Rocco (Edward G. Robinson) and his gange (1948 movie *Key Largo*). Call letters A-S-A-N

Santana
Humphrey Bogart's 55 foot sailboat, purchased from William Powell for $55,000. Prior to the Santana he owned a 36 foot craft named Sluggy. Santana was also the name of his film company

Santiago

The old fisherman in Ernest Hemingway's novel *The Old Man and the Sea*. Played in 1958 movie by Spencer Tracy

Saperstein, Abe

Founder (1927) of the basketball team the Harlem Globetrotters. Portrayed in 1951 movie *The Harlem Globtrotters* by Thomas Gomez. Portrayed in 1954 movie *Go, Man, Go* by Dane Clark

Sapphire

Wife of George "Kingfish" Steven (radio/TV series "Amos n' Andy"): played by Ernestine Wade

Sarah Siddons Award

Statuette given by the Sarah Siddons Society of Chicago for best theatrical performance. Award given to Eve (Anne Baxter) in the opening scene of the 1950 movie *All About Eve*. The real society came into being *after* the movie *All About Eve*. Sarah Siddons was an actress with the English Theatre; nicknamed *The Queen of Tragedy*

Sarah Williams

Name Huckleberry Finn calls himself when dressed as a young girl. He later forgets and calls himself Mary Williams then calls himself Sarah Mary Wiliams; he then reveals his true name to be George Peters. (Mark Twain's *Huckleberry Finn*)

Saratoga

Jean Harlow's last movie (1937). She died (June 7 of cerebral edema at age 26) while filming the picture; Mary Dees replaced her in the role of Carol Clayton, with Paula Winslowe dubbing in her voice. Also long shots of Geraldine Dvorak. Harlow's next movie was to have been *In Old Chicago*

Sardi's

Famous Broadway restaurant in New York where casts traditionally celebrate the opening night of a new Broadway play

Sarek and Amanda

Mr. Spock's father Mr. Sarek (Vulcan) and mother Mrs. Sarek (human) (TV series "Star Trek"). Sarek is 102, 437 Earth years old. The average life span of a Vulcan being 250 years. He has T-negative blood. Spock and his father didn't talk to each other for 18 years. Spock's parents are played by Mark Lenard (who also played the role of a Romulan Commander) and Jane Wyatt

Sarkhan (South)
Mythical country setting of 1963 movie *The Ugly American*

Sarong Girl, The
Nickname of actress Dorothy Lamour

Sarnoff, David
(1891-1971) Born in Uzlian, Russia. Called the Father of U.S. television. First to receive S.O.S. of the ship *Titanic* when it hit an iceberg April 1912. He radioed details to world for 72 hours. President of RCA Corporation. Awarded "Emmy" among many other awards

Sasha
Bear appearing with her bearded owner and trainer, Earl Hammond, in Hamm's Beer TV commercials.

Sasha
Bird in "Peter and the Wolf"

Satchmo (Satchel Mouth)
Nickname of Louis Armstrong (July 4, 1900-1971). American musician famed for his New Orleans jazz trumpet style. In movies *The Five Pennies* (1959) and *The Glenn Miller Story* (1954) he portrayed himself. He appeared in 1969 movie *Hello Dolly*

Satellite
Jules Verne's dog

Saturday Evening Post
Magazine that claimed to have been founded by Benjamin Franklin though first issue was in August 4, 1821, more than 30 years after Franklin's death

Savoir Faire
Mischievous mouse who is the nemesis of Klondike Kat (TV cartoon series *Klondike Kat*)

Sawdust
Fictional comic strip by Chet, Al, Ray, Rick and Hap. Serial within the "Dick Tracy" comic strip.
Also *The Invisible Tribe* by Verda Alldid (he married Sparkle Plenty)
Bugs and Worms by Peanut Butter

SAYHEY
Willie Mays' California car license plate

Say-Hey Kid
Nickname of baseball player Willie Howard Mays, because as a rookie he had the habit of saying "Say Hey" because he couldn't remember the other players names. Outfielder

with New York and San Francisco Giants and New York Mets, sometimes called the best ballplayer of his time. He has never been thrown out of a ball game in his career, became first Black team captain in majors

Scamp

Puppy of The Lady and the Tramp (Disney cartoon-movie)

Scamp

President Theodore Roosevelt's dog (other household pets while he was president were):

Algonquin—(calico pony)

Gems—(Mrs. Roosevelt's dog)

Mike—Ethel's bull terrier)

Fidelity—(Ethel's pet horse)

Black Jack—(Family dog)

Scandinavia

Norway, Sweden, Denmark, Iceland, Finland

Scannell, Mary

Elevator (#7) operator in the Empire State building who survived the crash of her elevator car when it fell from the 80th floor to the basement, when a B25 bomber hit the 79th floor of the Empire State building July 28, 1945. She later appeared on the TV quiz show "I've Got a Secret"

Scar

Vint Bonner's (John Payne) horse on TV series *The Restless Gun*

Scheherazade

Wife of King Shahriar, who told tales for 1001 nights (the so-called "Arabian Nights Entertainment")

Schmoo

Animal created by Al Capp ("Li'l Abner" comic strip): lays eggs, gives milk, tastes like steak and chicken. They live in the Valley of the Schmoon

Schmoozer

Fearless Fosdick's sidekick (Comic strips)

Schnappsy

Dinglehoofer's pet dog (Comic Strip *Dinglehoofer and His Dog*). Replaced original dog, named Adolph, just before World War II

Schnoogle Paper Clip Co.

Firm for which Bugs Bunny occasionally works (comic strip series)

Schnozzola
Nickname for Jimmy Durante, because of the size of his nose or "schnozzola". Coined by Sime Silverman, founder of *Variety*

Schuber
Ship featured in 1961-1962 TV series *Follow the Sun*

Schwab's Pharmacy
Drugstore in Hollywood (8024 Sunset Blvd) where Judy "Lana" Turner was discovered at age 15 sitting on a fountain stool drinking a Coca Cola by Billy Wilkerson who worked for *The Hollywood Reporter*. He supposedly said "How would you like to be in movies?" Another story states that she was discovered in Currie's Ice Cream Parlor across the street from Hollywood High School in January 1936. Still other accounts put her outside Currie's Candy and Cigar Store

Schwabacher's Sweeteries
Malt shop where Emmy Lou, Taffy and Alvin congregate (cartoon "Emmy Lou")

Schuyler
Sky King's first name

Scorpio
Killer whom San Francisco policeman "Dirty" Harry Callahan (Clint Eastwood) is in pursuit of in 1971 movie *Dirty Harry*

Scorpion
Nuclear submarine commanded by Commander Dwight Towers (Gregory Peck) (1959 movie *On The Beach*)

Scorpion
Evil Nazi nemesis of Don Winslow, *Don Winslow of the Navy* (1941) and *Don Winslow of the Coast Guard* (1943). Also the nemesis in two serials *The Adventures of Captain Marvel* (1941) and *Blake of Scotland* (1937)

Scotch Cup
Trophy awarded for the sport of curling

Scott Jordon
Detective in stories by Harold Q. Masur

Scotty
Mark Trail's boy sidekick, on radio played by: Ben Cooper, Ronald Liss

Scout
Tonto's horse (on TV Tonto used a saddle)

Scout Law, The

A scout is: (Boy Scout)

Trustworthy	Obedient
Loyal	Cheerful
Helpful	Thrifty
Friendly	Brave
Courteous	Clean
Kind	Reverent

Scout Motto

"Be Prepared"

Scout Oath (Boy Scout)

"On my honor I will do my best: to do my duty to God and my country, and to obey the scout law; to help other people at all times; to keep myself physically strong, mentally awake and morally straight"

Scout Promise

Girl Scouts:

On my honor, I will try;

to do my duty to God and my country,

to help other people at all times,

to obey the Girl Scout Laws

Scout Slogan

"Do a Good Turn Daily"

Scrabble

Word game by Sel Right. Value of letters for scoring:

A = (1), B = (3), C = (3), D = (2), E = (1), F = (4), G = (2), H = (4), I = (1), J = (8), K = (5) L = (1), M = (3), N = (1), O = (1), P = (3), Q = (10), R = (1), S = (1), T = (1), U = (1), V = (4), W = (4), X = (8), Y = (4), Z = (10), Blank = (0)

Scraggs

Daisy Mae's maiden name (comic strip "Li'l Abner") On radio Daisy Mae was played by Laurette Fillbrandt

Scraps

Dog that co-stars with Charlie Chaplin in the 1918 movie *A Dog's Life*

Scripts

Colors used in the rewriting of scripts:

White—original; blue—first change; pink—second change; yellow—third change.

Scroll of Thoth

Sacred work containing the secret chant that brings the mummy Im-ho-tep (Boris Karloff) back to life:

"Oh! Amon-Ra, oh God of Gods,
Death is but the doorway to new life.
We live today, we shall live again.
In many forms shall we return, oh
Mighty One"
(1932 film *The Mummy*)

Scrooge
Ebenezer Scrooge—Sad, stingy old man whose dead partner, Jacob Marley, haunts him at Christmas: in 1938 movie *A Christmas Story* played by Reginald Owen; in 1951 movie by Alastair Sim; in 1970 musical *Scrooge* played by Albert Finney.
His favorite expression is Bah-humbug! Charles Dicken's *A Christmas Carol*

Scrooge McDuck, (Uncle)
Donald Duck's tight, moneyed uncle, born in Scotland. He keeps his money in a giant money bin (built by the Oso Safe Company) in Ducksburg. He is the richest duck in the world but is constantly besieged by the Beagle Boys. His chauffeur is named Bleeker (Walt Disney character)
Debut in Uncle Scrooge Comics #1 (1951)

Scruffy
Family dog of the Muirs (TV series "The Ghost and Mrs. Muir")

SCUBA
Self-Contained Underwater Breathing Apparatus

Scuba-Schooner
Glass-bottom, windowed tourist boat operating near the Catalina Islands. 1966 movie *The Glass Bottom Boat*

Scuffy and Little Toot
Cartoon tugboats in movie cartoons

Seacliff Children's Home
Orphanage where Mighty Joe Young saves a child from burning to death in the 1949 movie *Mighty Joe Young*

Sea Dart
Jetmarine (submarine) of Tom Swift, Jr. (novel series)

Seadog
Cap'n Crunch's sailor dog
(Cap'n Crunch's Breakfast Cereal)

Seagulls
Of Red Skelton (comedy routine): Gertrude, Heathcliffe

Sea Hound

Captain Silver's schooner (1947 movie serial)

Sea of Discord

Body of water between the Isle of Jazz and the Land of Symphony. It is finally breached by the Bridge of Harmony. Walt Disney's 1935 *Music Land*

Sea of Tranquility

Mare where Apollo 11 landed on the moon, July 20, 1969, at 4:17:20 p.m. EDT: "The Eagle has landed"

Search for Tomorrow

Longest running daytime serial on television—Debuted September 3, 1951 and still on the air

Sea Star Island

Floating Island ruled by William Shakespeare X, (Geoffrey Holder) where the Great Pink Sea Snail lives in 1967 movie *Doctor Dolittle* (In books the island is called "Spidermonkey Island")

Sea Tiger

U.S. submarine in which Cary Grant plays Commander Sherman in 1959 movie *Operation Petticoat*. The other movie in which Cary Grant played a submarine (U.S.S. Copperfin) skipper was in *Destination Tokyo*

Seat 23A

Global Airline Golden Argosy flight 2 to Rome. D. O. Guerrero (Van Heflin), the man who carries a bomb onboard. He took out $250,000 worth of insurance (cost $7.50). Stowaway Ada Quonsett (Helen Hayes) is seated in seat 23B (she won an Oscar for Best Supporting actress for this role)

(1970 movie *Airport*)

Seaview

Atomic submarine commanded by Admiral Nelson (Richard Basehart) TV series *Voyage to the Bottom of the Sea*

Second cousins

Presidents James Madison and Zachary Taylor: James Taylor, who died in 1729, was their great-grandfather in common

Secret Agent

TV series about adventures of British agent John Drake (Patrick McGoohan). The series theme song *Secret*

Agent Man was sung by Johnny Rivers. In England the series was called *Dangerman*

Secret Agent X-9
Identity of Mr. Corrigan, American Secret agent. Comic strip written by Dashiell Hammett and drawn by Alex Raymond. Debut January 22, 1934. Made into a movie serial twice: *Secret Agent X-9* in 1937 starring Scott Kolk, and again in 1945 starring Lloyd Bridges

Secret Identities

Pseudonym	Real Identity
Airboy	Davy Nelson
Amazing Man	John Aman
Angel, The	Warren Worthington III
Ant Man	Dr. Henry Pym
Aquaman	Arthur Curry
Atom, The	Al Pratt (Golden Age)
	Ray Palmer
Batgirl	Babs Gordon
Batman	Bruce Wayne
Beast, The	Hank McCoy
Black Bat	Tony Quinn
Black Canary	Dinah Lance
Black Cat	Linda Turner
Black Condor	Senator Tom Wright
Black Green Lantern	John Stewart
Black Hood, The	Kip Burland
Black Owl	Doug Danville
Blackout	Basil Brusiloff
Black Terror	Bob Benton
Blue Beetle	Dan Garrett
Blue Bolt	Fred Parrish
Blue Tracer	Wild Bill Dunn
Bouncing Boy	Chuck Taine
Brainiac 5	Querl Dox
Bulletgirl	Susan Kent
Bulletman	Jim Barr
Captain America	Steve Rogers
Captain Boomerang	"Digger" Harkness
Captain Cold	Len Snart
Captain Freedom	Don Wright
Captain Future	Curtis Newton
Captain Marvel	Billy Batson
Captain Marvel, Jr.	Freddie Freeman

Captain Midnight	Captain Albright
Captain Triumph	Lance Gallant
Captain Satan	Cary Adair
Captain Wings	Captain Boggs
Captain Zero	Lee Allyn
Cat Man	Barton Stone
Cat Man	David Merrywether
Catwoman	Selina Kyle
Chameleon Boy	Reep Daggle
Chandu the Magician	Frank Chandler
Chemical King	Condo Arlik
Chlorophyll Kid	Ral Benem
Clock, The	Biran O'Brien
Color Kid	Ulu Vakk
Colossal Boy	Gim Allon
Commando Yank	Chase Vale
Cosmic Boy	Rokk Krinn
Creeper, The	Jack Ryder
Crimson Avenger	Lee Travis
Cyclops	Scott Walker
Cyclops	Slim Summers
Daredevil	Brent Hill
Daredevil	Matt Murdock (Golden Age)
Deadman	Boston Brand
Dr. Fate	Kent Nelson
Doctor Mid-Nite	Dr. Charles McNider
Doctor Strange	Stephen Strange
Doll Girl	Martha Roberts
Doll Man	Darrel Dane
Domino Lady	Ellen Patrick
Dream Girl	Nura Nal
Duo Damsel	Luornu Durgo
Element Lad	Jan Arrah
Elongated Man	Ralph Dibny
Face, The	Tony Trent
Falcon, The	Sam Wilson
Ferro Lad	Andrew Nolan
Firebrand	Rod Reilly
Firefly	Harvey Hudson
Fire Lad	Stag Mavlen
Flash (Golden Age)	Jay Garrick
Flash (New Series)	Barry Allen

Gay Ghost, The	Keith Everet & Charles Collins
Ghost, The	George Chance
Ghost Rider	Johnny Blaze
Golden Arrow	Roger Parson
Golden Girl	Betsy Ross
Green Arrow	Oliver Queen
Green Hornet	Britt Reid
Green Lama	Jethro Dumont
Green Lantern (Golden Age)	Alan Scott
Green Lantern (modern version)	Hal Jordan
Hawkgirl	Shiera Sanders
Hawkman (2nd Version)	Carter Hall
Heap	Baron Von Emmelmann
Heat Wave	Mick Rory
Hourman	Rex Tyler
Hulk, The	Bruce Banner
Human Bomb	Roy Lincoln
Human Torch	Jim Hammond
Human Torch, The	Johnny Storm
Hydroman	Bob Blake
Iceman	Bobby Drake
Invisible Girl	Susan Storm
Invisible Kid	Lyle Norg
Iron Fist	Danny Rand
Iron Man	Tony Stark
Isis	Andrea Thomas
Karate Kid	Val Armorr
Kid Flash	Wally West
Kid Psycho	Gnill Opral
Light Lass	Ayla Ranzz
Lightning Lad	Garth Ranzz
Little Blue Boy	Tommy Rogers
Lone Ranger	John Reid
Madam Fatal	Richard Stanton
Manhunter	Dan Richards
Man O'Metal	Pat Dempsy
Marvel Gril	Jean Grey
Marvelman	Mickey Moran
Mary Marvel	Mary Bromfield
Masked Detective	Rex Parker

Masked Rider	Wayne Morgan
Matter-Eater Lad	Tezil Kem
Matter Master	Mark Mandrill
Metamorpho	Rex Mason
Mighty Thor	Dr. Don Blake
Minute-Man	Jack Weston
Mirror Master	Samuel Scudder
Mister Fantastic	Reed Richards
Mr. Scarlet	Brian Butler
Mr. Terrific (TV)	Stanley Beemish
Mr. Terrific	Terry Sloane
Mon-El	Lar Gand
Moon Man	Steve Thatcher
Mouthpiece, The	Bill Perkins
Night Girl	Lydda Jath
No. 711	Dan Dyce
Parasite, The	Maxwell Jensen
Penguin	Oswald Chesterfield Cobblepot
Phantom Detective	Richard Curtis Van Loan
Phantom Eagle	Mickey Malone
Phantom Girl	Tinya Wazzo
Phantom Lady	Sandra Knight
Plastic Man	Eel O'Brian
Pied Piper	Thomas Peterson
Polar Boy	Brek Bannin
Power Man	Luke Cage
Radar	Pep Pepper
Ray, The	Happy Terrill
Red Bee	Rick Raleigh
Red Torpedo	Jim Lockhard
Reverse Flash	Eobard Thawne
Riddler	Edward "E" Nigma
Robin	Dick Grayson
Robotman	Bob Crane (Paul Dennis)
Sandman	Wesley Dodds
Saturn Girl	Imra Ardeen
Scarecrow	Jonathan Crane
Shadow, The	Lamont Cranston
Shadow Lass	Tasimia Malor
Shark, The	T. S. Smith
Shield, The	Joe Higgins

Whisper, The	James Gordon
Whizzer	Bob Frank
Wildfire	Drake Burroughs
Wonder Girl	Donna Troy
Wonder Woman	Diana Prince

Sedalia, Missouri

Destination of the 1866 cattle drive, originating in Texas on TV series *Rawhide*

See, the Conquering Hero Comes

Song that a welcoming brass band played as William Hamilton arrived in San Francisco on April 14, 1860, being the last Pony Express Rider (of 30) to complete the first westward journey (see Fry, Johnny)

Seems Like Old Times

"Arthur Godfrey Time" radio theme song, one of two, the other is *In the Blue Ridge Mountains of Virginia*

Sees

Candy store chain founded by Mary Sees who began selling candy at the age of 71. Slogan *A Happy Habit*

See Threepio (C-3PO)

Metallic robot played by Anthony Daniels in 1977 movie "Star Wars"

Sehlat

Toy resembling a teddy bear that Spock played with as a child (TV series *Star Trek*)

Selenites

Creatures found on the moon by the space travelers in H. G. Wells' *The First Men In The Moon*

Selfridge, Lt. Thomas E.

First airplane fatality in the world, September 17, 1908, at Fort Myer, Virginia, in a plane piloted by Orville Wright, Selfridge was in the Army Signal Corps. Selfridge Field is where the movie *Wings* was filmed

Selkirk, Alexander

Scottish sailor (1676-1721), the original Robinson Crusoe; put ashore October 1704 on Más a Tierra, one of the Juan Fernandez Islands (uninhabited), off the coast of Chile by Captain Thomas Stradling; rescued in February 1709 by Captain Woodes Rogers after 4 years alone

Sellers, Peter

Roles in 1959 movie *The Mouse that Roared:* Count of Mountjoy (Bobo): Duchess Gloriana XII; Tully Bascomb, head of the army

Roles in 1964 movie *Dr. Strangelove:* Group Captain Lionel Mandrake; President Merkin Muffley; Dr. Strangelove. Voice of Winston Churchill in 1956 movie *The Man Who Never Was.* In 1974 movie *Soft Beds, Hard Battles* he played nine roles including Prince Kyoto of Japan, General Latour of France and Adolf Hitler

Seminole

Indian tribe which hadn't signed a peace treaty with the United States until 1975 (after their war with U.S. 1835-42)

Semper Fidelis

"Always faithful": motto of United States Marines

Semper Paratus

"Always Ready"—Motto of the U.S. Coast Guard

Senior Service

British Royal Navy

Sensurround

Audio effect (Low frequency 16-20 cycles) associated with the films *Earthquake* (1974), *Midway* (1976), *Roller Coaster* (1977)

September 3 to 13, 1752

Dates that never existed, as the Gregorian calendar replaced the Julian calendar. In order to bring the calendar up to the correct date (which was 11 days behind), September 2 was immediately followed by September 14

Sequoia

The presidential yacht of F. D. Roosevelt and Richard M. Nixon

Sequoya

Indian name of George Guess, who created (1809-1821) the Cherokee alphabet

Serapis

British warship sunk by Captain John Paul Jones while commanding the Bonhomme Richard September 23, 1779 off the coast of Scotland. When asked to surrender by the British, he replied, "We have not yet begun to fight."

Serena

Samantha's black-haired look-alike cousin (both played by Elizabeth Montgomery), TV series *Bewitched*

Sergent (Vince) Carter

Gomer Pyle's drill instructor and friend (TV series "Gomer Pyle, U.S.M.C.") : played by Frank Sutton

Sergeant Chad Smith

Police officer played by Henry Fonda on TV series *The Smith Family*

Sergeant Chip Saunders

Army sergeant played by Vic Morrow in TV series *Combat*. Before becoming a soldier of WW II he was a shoe salesman

Sergeant Cuff

Early detective in English fiction (Wilkie Collins' *The Moonstone*, 1868)

Sergeant Dan Briggs

Police officer (Ben Alexander) father of Detective Jim Briggs (Dennis Cole), TV series *Felony Squad*

Sergeant Dennis Foley

Fernwood, Ohio police officer who has eyes for Mary Hartman. Foley is played by Bruce Soloman (TV series "Mary Hartman, Mary Hartman")

Sergeant Ed Brown

San Francisco policeman, assistant to retired Police Chief of Detectives Robert Ironside. Brown is played by Don Galloway on TV series "Ironside"

Sergeant (Charles) Enright

San Francisco Police Commissioner Stewart McMillan's (Rock Hudson) right-hand man (played by John Schuck) (TV series "McMillan & Wife")

Sergeant Garcia

Fat Spanish soldier (Henry Calvin) who attempts to capture Zorro (TV series "Zorro"). His assistant was Corporal Rehmus (Don Diamond)

Sergeant (Ernest) Heath

New York City detective of the Homicide Bureau, friend of detective Philo Vance (radio/movie)

Sergeant Joe Friday

Central character of "Dragnet" (radio & TV): played by Jack Webb. His partners were officers Ben Romero (Barton Yarborough), Ed Jacobs (Barney Phillips), Frank Smith (Ben Alexander), and Bill Gannon (Harry Morgan). For one season only Friday was a lieutenant and Smith a sergeant, but they soon reverted

Sergeant John Contreras

San Francisco policeman (Johnny Seven) on TV series "Amy Prentiss"

Sergeant John M. Stryker

U.S. Marine non-com played by John Wayne in 1949 movie *Sands of Iwo Jima*

Sergeant Preston of the Yukon

"I arrest you in the name of the Crown," originated on Detroit radio station WXYZ in series *Challenge of the Yukon:* played by Richard Simmons, Paul Sutton and Brace Beemer. On TV played by Richard Simmons. Preston's first name is William

Sergeant Frank Smith

Sgt. Joe Friday's second TV partner ("Dragnet"): played by Ben Alexander

Sergeant Matt Grebb

San Francisco police inspector in radio/TV series and 1958 movie *The Line-Up*. Played on radio by Wally Maher; on TV/movie by Tom Tully

Sergeant (Morgan) O'Rourke

First Sergeant of F Troop, Fort Courage. Played by Forrest Tucker (TV series "F Troop")

Sergeant Sam MacCray

In charge of the Chase crew (played by Wayne Maunder) (TV series "Chase")

Sergeant Sam Stone

Police detective (Howard Duff) whose sidekick is detective Jim Briggs (Dennis Cole) (TV series "Felony Squad")

Sergeant (Hans) Schultz

Friendly German First Sergeant at Stalag 13. He would rather remain completely apathetic ("I see noth-ing, I know noth-ing"): played by John Banner. TV series "Hogan's Heroes." In 1942 John Banner posed for U.S. Army recruiting posters

Sergeant (Orville) Snorkel

Beetle Bailey's sergeant (cartoon series). He wears five stripes. On TV cartoon series voice of Allen Melvin

Sergeant Tibbs

Cat (1961 Disney movie *101 Dalmatians*)

Sergeant Velie

Inspector Queen's assistant: played on radio by Howard Smith, Ted de Corsica, Ed Latimer; in movies by James Burke; on TV by Tom Reese

Sergeants 3

Title of 1962 movie (*Gunga Din* in the American West)

starring, as 3 Army sergeants, Frank Sinatra (Mike Merry), Dean Martin (Chip Deal), Peter Lawford (Larry Barrett)

Service Above Self

Rotary Club motto. Organization founded February 23, 1905 by Paul P. Harris

Service Hymns

U.S. Navy - *Anchors Aweigh*
U.S. Marines - *Marine Hymn*
U.S. Coast Guard - *Semper Paratus*
U.S. Air Force - *Wild Blue Yonder*

Sesame Street

Muppets: Grover, Bert, Sherlock Hemlock, Cookie Monster, Ernie, Roosevelt Franklin

Seth

Third child of Adam and Eve, father of Enos

Seville, David

Creator of the singing Chipmunks. Real name Ross Bagdasarian, cousin of William Saroyan. He played a POW in 1953 movie *Stalag 17*

Seward's Folly

U.S. purchase of Alaska from Russia, 1867, for $7,200,000. Bill passed through Congress by a single vote

Sexton Blake

British detective created by Harry Blyth (Hal Meredith). Debut in *The Missing Millionaire*, December 1893. His dog is Pedro, his sidekick is a boy named Tinker.
Movies - C. Douglas Carlile, Douglas Payne, Langhorne Burton, George Curzon, David Farrar, Geoffrey Toone

Shadow, The

Identity secretly assumed by Lamont Cranston: on radio played by Bret Morrison, Bill Johnstone, and Orson Welles and by Robert Hardy Andrews. But see *Kent Allard*. "Who knows what evil lurks in the hearts of men? The Shadow knows." Closing: "The weed of crime bears bitter fruit - crime does not pay - The Shadow Hmmm."
Created by Maxwell Grant (Walter Gibson). Debut *Shadow Magazine* (Vol I April/June 1931). *The Living Shadow* was the first novel of 283. Shadow first appeared on radio on *Detective Story Hour*, August 1930. The Shadow was the show's host being played by Jack La Curto and Frank Readik. His other secret identities on radio

are as Lingo Queed (underground figure), Henry Arnaud (businessman) and Fritz (janitor)

Played in movies: *The Shadow* (1939 serial), Victor Jory and by Kane Richmond in *The Shadow Returns* (1946), *Behind the Mask* (1946), *The Missing Lady* (1946)

Shadow Thief, The

Hawkman's arch-enemy, his real identity is that of Carl Sands (comic books)

Shadyland Avenue

Street that the Bumstead family lives on (radio/movie/television/comic *Blondie*)

Shady Rest

Hotel (TV series "Petticoat Junction") in town of Hooterville

SHAEF

Supreme Headquarters Allied Expeditionary Force

Shaggy Dog, The

Teenager Wilby Daniels (Tommy Kirk) using an ancient spell changes back and forth from a dog (Walt Disney's 1959 movie *The Shaggy Dog*). The dog was played by Sammy's Shadow, winner of 1960 PATSY

Shamrock

Sir Thomas Lipton's yachts: in his attempts to win the America Cup, all 5 of them had the name Shamrock (I through V) (1899-1930)

Shamus

Private eye Q. T. Hush's pet dog (TV cartoon series 1960)

Shan

President Gerald Ford's Siamese cat

Shangri-La

Hidden Tibetan valley paradise (James Hilton's *Lost Horizon*)

Name under which Franklin D. Roosevelt hid the identity of the U.S. aircraft carrier "Hornet," from which Lt. Col. James Doolittle led 16 Army B-25 bombers in his raid (April 18, 1942) against Japan (Tokyo, Yokosuka, Yokohama, Nagoya)

Shangri-La

Previous name of the Presidential retreat Camp David (named for Eisenhower's father). Shangri-La was named by F.D.R.

Shannon

John F. Kennedy's Irish cocker spaniel born in 1963; given to him by the Prime Minister of Ireland, Eamon de Valera

Sharkey

Iodine Tremblechin's boyfriend (comic strip *Little Iodine*)

Sharon

Anthony Barretta's (Robert Blake) girlfriend (Madlyn Rhue) who was killed by hired hoods (first episode) (TV series "Barretta")

Sharpie

The Gillette Parrot (TV commercial); "Look sharp, feel sharp, be sharp"

Shaw, U.S.S.

Ship that exploded on December 7, 1941 at Pearl Harbor. The photograph of the Shaw exploding is one of the most famous combat photos of any war

SHAZAM

Ancient Egyptian wizard who gave the Marvel family their magic powers: in his underground throne-room (an old subway tunnel) are seven statues, "The Seven Deadly Enemies of Man": Pride, Envy, Greed, Hatred, Selfishness, Laziness, Injustice (Captain Marvel comic books)

SHAZAM

Magic word that changes Billy Batson into Captain Marvel and back again:

S	=	(Wisdom of) Solomon
H	=	(Strength of) Hercules
A	=	(Stamina of) Atlas
Z	=	(Power of) Zeus
A	=	(Courage of) Achilles
M	=	(Speed of) Mercury

SHAZAM

Magic word that changes Mary Batson into Mary Marvel and back again:

S	=	(Grace of) Selena
H	=	(Strength of) Hippolyta
A	=	(Skill of) Ariadne
Z	=	(Fleetness of) Zephyrus
A	=	(Beauty of) Aurora
M	=	(Wisdom of) Minerva

Shazam

New name of Captain Marvel after a lawsuit resulted

between National comics and Fawcett publishers stating that Captain Marvel was a copy of Superman. Noted lawyer Louis Nizer represented National. Fawcett lost the case and stopped producing comic books

Shazam!

Gomer Pyle's (Jim Nabors) favorite expression, besides *Golly!*

She

1935 movie *She* played by Helen Gahagan. 1965 *She* by Ursula Andress. Sequel: *Vengeance of She* (1968), Olinka Berova

Helen Gahagan would later become a congresswoman from California, who in 1950 was defeated by Richard Nixon for the Senate

Sheena

Queen of the Jungle. Created by S. M. Iger and Will Eisner. Debut in Jumbo Comics #1 September 1938. Played in movie/TV series by Irish McCalla

Shiek, The

Rudolph Valentino (Rudolpho Alfonzo Raffaelo Pierre Filibert Guglielmi di Valentina d'Antonguolla). Great silent actor dying at young age of 31. Two of his best films were *The Sheik* (1921) as Ahmed Ben Hassan and *Son of the Sheik* (1926). Prior to Valentino, James Kirkwood was offered, but refused, the role of the Sheik. Valentino's funeral services were held at Cambell's funeral parlor on Broadway in New York City, August 24, 25, 1926 which over 100,000 people attended. In 1951 movie *Valentino* he was portrayed by Anthony Dexter; in 1975 TV movie *The Legend of Valentino* by Franco Nero and in 1977 movie *Valentino* by Rudolf Nureyev

Shelby, Montana

Site of the heavyweight championship fight between Jack Dempsey and Tom Gibbons, July 4, 1923. Dempsey won a 15-round decision

Shell Scott

Detective in stories of Richard S. Prather. White haired, he stands 6'2", weights 206 pounds and is 30 years old. He drives a skyblue Cadillac convertible

Shelly

Turtle that advertises Kellogg's Corny Snaps cereal. Voice of Bob Hot

648

Shenandoah

(ZR-1) First U.S. Naval dirigible launched September 4, 1923. Crashed September 3, 1925 near Ava, Ohio; 14 died

Shep

George of the Jungle's elephant (TV cartoon series)

Shepard, Bert

One-legged pitcher. He played in one single game for the Washington Senators in 1945

Shere Khan

The villainous tiger in Rudyard Kipling's *The Jungle Books.* In Walt Disney's 1966 movie his voice was that of George Sanders. Voice of Roddy McDowall in TV cartoon series

Sheriff Andy Taylor

Sheriff of the North Carolina country town of Mayberry (played by Andy Griffith) (he later became its Mayor). TV series "The Andy Griffith Show." His deputy if Barney Fyfe (Don Knotts)

Sheriff Lofty Craig

Lawman in town of Diablo on TV series "Annie Oakley" (played by Brad Johnson)

Sheriff Micah Torrance

Lawman of North Fork (played by Paul Fix), he is a friend of Lucas McCain (TV series "The Rifleman")

Sheriff Mitch

Law-enforcement officer of Grover (Ewing Mitchell), TV series "Sky King"

Sheriff of Nottingham

Robin Hood's foe: played in 1938 movie *The Adventures of Robin Hood* by Melville Cooper, by Lloyd Corrigan in 1946 movie *The Bandit of Sherwood Forest*. Played on TV series "When Things were Rotten" by Henry Polic II

Sheriff Roy Coffee

Virginia City sheriff (Ray Teal) friend of the Cartwright family (TV series "Bonanza")

Sherlock Hemlock

Sesame Street's resident detective. His birthday is April 17 (TV's "Sesame Street")

Sherlock Holmes

Detective created by Sir Arthur Conan Doyle, perhaps the best-known fictional character in the world. Home address: 221B Baker Street, London, England, where he lives with Dr. John Watson (before and between Watson's marriages) and with Mrs. Hudson as landlady. (A portrait of Holmes hangs in Nero Wolfe's office directly under his wall clock.) He was named for U.S. Supreme Court Justice Oliver Wendell Holmes and a popular cricket player, Sherlock. Between cases Holmes indulged in cocaine and morphine; one of his hobbies is playing his Stradivarius. He died January 6, 1930 in his home "Windlesham" in Crowborough, Sussex, where he retired to raise bees (his death was established by the B.S.I., Baker Street Irregulars)

Movies starring Basil Rathbone as Sherlock Holmes and Nigel Bruce as Dr. Watson:

1939: *The Hound of the Baskervilles*
1939: *The Adventures of Sherlock Holmes*
1942: *Sherlock Holmes and the Voice of Terror*
1942: *Sherlock Holmes and the Secret Weapon*
1943: *Sherlock Holmes in Washington*
1943: *Sherlock Holmes Faces Death*
1944: *Sherlock Holmes and the Spider Woman*
1944: *The Scarlet Claw*
1944: *The Pearl of Death*
1945: *The House of Fear*
1945: *The Woman in Green*
1945: *Pursuit to Algiers*
1946: *Terror by Night*
1946: *Dressed to Kill*

Other actors who played Sherlock Holmes (stage, movies, radio) were: William Gillette (for 36 years on stage), John Barrymore, Raymond Massey, Clive Brook, Peter Cushing, Ed Wynn, Fritz Weaver, Robert Stephens, Ben Wright, John Stanley, Roger Moore, Nichol Williamson, Stewart Granger. There have been over 150 Sherlock Holmes movies. Debut NBC radio October 20, 1930: played on radio by William Gillette, Richard Gordon and Tom Conway. Peter Cushing and Reginald Owen have played both Holmes and Watson in movies. In the 1976 TV movie *The Great Houdinis,* Sir Arthur Conan Doyle was portrayed by Peter Cushing. In the 1939 movie *The Hound of the Baskervilles* (1939) the hound was played by a 140 pound Great Dane named Chief. The first person credited with playing Sherlock Holmes (on stage) was

Charles Brookfield. Clive Brook was the first talking Sherlock Holmes in *Return of Sherlock Holmes* in 1929. According to William S. Baring-Gould. Holmes was born on Friday, January 6, 1854 and died on Sunday, January 6, 1957.

Sherlock Jr.

1924 movie starring Buster Keaton as a movie projectionist who fancies himself a great detective

She's Only a Bird in a Gilded Cage

Theme song of Aunt Fanny (Fran Allison) on radio's *The Breakfast Club*

Sherman

Boy of Peabody (the genius dog) (cartoon series *Peabody*). Voices of TV cartoons: Sherman (June Foray), Peabody (Bill Scott)

Sherwood Forest

Haunt of Robin Hood and his band of Merry Men

Sheik

Real name of the horse Michael Ansara rode on the TV series "Broken Arrow"

Shield, The

Secret identity of Joe Higgins (comic book series *The Shield*). Debut Pep Comics #1, January 1940

Shields, Arthur

Character actor, especially in movies: brother of Barry Fitzgerald

Shiloh

Wyoming ranch on which the Virginian serves as foreman (TV series "The Virginian"), near the town of Medicine Bow

Shinbone

Western town setting in the 1962 movie *The Man Who Shot Liberty Valance*. The town paper is *The Shinbone Star*

Shine On, Harvest Moon

Ruth Etting's theme song

Ships of U.S. Navy

Naming of ships during World War II:

Battleships	named for	States
Aircraft Carriers		Battles
Cruisers		Cities
Destroyers		Dead war heroes

Submarines — Fish
Ammunition Ships — Gods of mythology
Tugs — Indian tribes

Shipwreck Kelly

Alvin Kelly, America's great flagpole sitter of the 1920's and 1930's

Shire, The

Land in the Middle Earth where the Hobbits live (J. R. R. Tolkien's *The Hobbit* and other novels). Given to the Hobbits in 1601 by King Argeleb II of Arthedian

Shirley Temple

Popular drink for children made with Ginger Ale (or 7-Up, etc.) with a dash of Grenadine and a cherry

Shoeless Joe Jackson

Chicago White Sox outfielder Joseph Jefferson Jackson involved in 1919 World Series scandal: banned in 1920 from baseball. One of the American League's best players (he batted .408 in 1911, led the league in slugging percentage in 1913, and had a lifetime batting average of .356, behind only Cobb and Hornsby), he was idolized and the principal casualty of the "Black Sox" scandal: one little boy is supposed to have brought him to tears by saying, "Say it ain't so, Joe." He was the only player to hit a home run in the 1919 World Series

Shopton

Tom Swift and Tom Swift, Jr.'s hometown

Shortstop

Position played by Snoopy on Charlie Brown's baseball team (Charles Schulz *Peanuts*)

Shorty

Boston Blackie's henchman (radio series): played by Tony Barrett (in movie serials the Runt was Blackie's sidekick)

Shotz Beer

Milwaukee Brewery where Laverne and Shirley work (TV series "LaVerne and Shirley")

Shrimp Boats Are A-'comin'

Longest-running popular tune (1951) on TV's "Your Hit Parade"

Shrine of the Little Flower

Father Charles Edward Coughlin's church in Royal Oak, Michigan. Broadcast on radio during he 1920s and 1930s. Known as *The Fighting Priest*

Shutters and Boards

Country-western song written by Audie Murphy (and Scott Turner), most decorated World War II hero and postwar movie star

Schultzy

Photographer Bob Collins' (Robert Cummings) secretary on the TV series "Love That Bob" (Schultzy played by Ann B. Davis). Her full name is Charmaine Schultz

Sic Semper Tryannis

Cry ("Thus ever to tyranny") by John Wilkes Booth as he leaped to Ford's Theater stage after shooting Abraham Lincoln. Motto of the state of Virginia

Sid

Samuel Spade's lawyer (1941 movie *The Maltese Falcon*)

Sid

Tom Sawyer's younger half-brother

Sidewalks of New York

Song played as horses are paraded before the running of the Belmont Stakes in June each year

Si-Fan

Secret evil organization over which Dr. Fu Manchu presides, its agents in every major city in the world (Sax Rohmer's *Fu Manchu* novels)

Sigerson

Sherlock Holme's smarter brother, played by Gene Wilder in the 1975 movie *The Adventures of Sherlock Holmes' Smarter Brother*

Sign of the Four, The

One of the Sherlock Holmes' more famous cases. The four are: Jonathan Small, Mahomet Singh, Abdullah Khan, Dost Akbar

Silas

Barkley family servant (played by Napoleon Whiting), TV series "The Big Valley"

Silks, Mattie

Female friend of Wild Bill Hickok who, on August 25, 1877, became engaged in the only recorded pistol duel between two women in the West. The other woman was Katie Fulton. Both women missed, but Katie's shot wounded Cort Thompson, the very man they were dueling over

Silly, little ass
Tinker Bell's favorite expression (James M. Barrie's novel *Peter Pan*), expression was not used in Disney movie

Silver
The Lone Ranger's white stallion: "Come on, Silver! Let's go, big fellow! Hi-yo, Silver! Awa-a-ay!" Silver was captured in Wild Horse Valley. In comic books Silver's father was Sylvan. In 1938 movie serial *The Lone Ranger* played by Silver King, in 1939 movie serial *The Lone Ranger Again* played by Silver Chief. In the 1939 movie *Gone with the Wind* Thomas Mitchell rides one of the Silvers. In a scene from the 1946 movie *Ziegfeld Follies* Silver appeared in a scene with Lucille Ball. The first sponsor of the Lone Ranger on radio was Silvercup Bread

Silver
Prefix initially attached to names of both the *Beatles* and the *Rolling Stones* becoming the Silver Beatles and The Silver Rolling Stones. In both cases the name was soon dropped

Silver Albatross
Jack Armstrong's Uncle Jim's airplane

Silver Buffalo
Highest award given by the Boy Scouts of America

Silver-B
Buck Jones's (Charles Gebhart's) horse, Silver Buck, another horse of his was White Eagle

Silver City, Arizona
Setting for the TV series "The Deputy" starring Henry Fonda as Marshal Simon Fry

Silver Creek
Colorado mining town from which Our Gal Sunday came. She later married Lord Henry Brinthrope and moved to his Virginia estate, Black Swan Hall (radio series *Our Gal Sunday*)

Silver Dart
Captain Midnight's airplane

Silver Dollar, The
San Francisco gambling casino owned by Duke Fergus (John Wayne) in the 1945 movie *Flame of the Barbary Coast*. His rival Tito Morrell (Joseph Schildkraut) owns the El Dorado

654

Silver King
White stallion of Fred Thompson. 1920's movie cowboy (he bought him in Ireland)

Silver Seashell Bar and Grill
Favorite hangout of Michael Lanyard (The Lone Wolf) (radio series *The Lone Wolf*)

Silver Surfer
Superhero created by Stan Lee and Jack Kirby. Debut in *Fantastic Four* comics #48, March 1966

Silverstone
The Millionaire's 60,000 acre estate (TV series "The Millionaire")

Simmons Corners
Town in which Little Orphan Annie grew up (comics)

Simon
Kangaroo that advertises Quangaroos breakfast cereal

Simon
The Partridge Family's pet dog (TV series)

Simon and Garfunkel
Paul and Art, respectively; singing team. Paul Simon's tunes "Mrs. Robinson" (excerpts only) and "The Sounds of Silence" were sung by them as background in 1967 movie *The Graduate*

Simon Legree
Evil overseer and slave-driver (Harriet Beecher Stowe's *Uncle Tom's Cabin*)

Simon Templar
Real name of the Saint (see *The Saint*)

Simone
Inspector Jacques Clouseau's wife (played by Capucine) in 1964 movie *The Pink Panther*

Simple J. Malarkey
Character drawn by Walt Kelly in his comic strip *Pogo*. He was a caricature of Senator Joseph McCarthy

Simpson, Mrs. Wallis Warfield
Baltimore, Md., divorcee for whom King Edward VIII of England abdicated his throne Dec. 11, 1936 to marry "the woman I love." "I have found it impossible to carry the heavy burden of responsibility and to discharge my duties as King as I would wish to do without the help and support of the woman I love." His brother, the Duke of York, succeeded him as George VI

Simpsonville

Town, location of radio serial *Young Widder Brown*

Sinatra, Frank

Popular baritone singer (Francis Albert Sinatra) began his singing career with The Hoboken Four, sang with Harold Arden, Harry James and Tommy Dorsey orchestras, then on radio's *Hit Parade*. Won an Oscar as best supporting actor (1953 movie *From Here To Eternity*) as Maggio (for which he only received $8,000)

His nicknames: The Voice, The Swooner, King of the Ratpack, Chairman of the Board, Ole Blue Eyes, The Leader, The Pope, The Dago, Frankie-Boy.

His wives: Nancy Sinatra (1939-1951), Ava Gardner (1951-1957), Mia Farrow (1966-1968), Barbara Marx (1976-   )

His children (with Nancy): Nancy, Frank, Jr., Christina

At birth Frank Sinatra, Sr. weighed 13 pounds. He has recorded for several major labels: Columbia, RCA Victor, Bluebird, Capitol, and five minor labels before starting his own label Reprise Records. In his marriage to Barbara Marx (ex-wife of Zeppo) Charles Freeman served as his best man

Sinbad

Pet duck on the Ra I with Thor Heyerdahl and his crew

Sinestro

Green Lantern's arch-enemy

Sing-A-Long Gang

Mitch Miller's 25-member singing group

Singers/Bands

Singer	Band
Amy Arnell	Tommy Tucker
Fred Astaire	Leo Reisman
Mildred Bailey	Paul Whiteman; Red Norvo
Bonnie Baker, (Wee)	Orrin Tucker
Art Carney	Horace Heidt
June Christy	Stan Kenton
Rosemary Clooney	Tony Pastor
Dorothy Collins	Raymond Scott
Perry Como	Ted Weems
Don Cornell	Sammy Kaye
Bing Crosby	Gus Arnheim; Paul Whiteman

Doris Day	Bob Crosby; Les Brown
Mike Douglas	Kay Kyser
Ray Eberle	Gene Krupa; Glenn Miller
Bob Eberly	Dorsey Brothers; Jimmy Dorsey
Billy Eckstine	Count Basie
Ruth Etting	Red Nichols
Dale Evans	Anson Weeks
Ella Fitzgerald	Chick Webb
Helen Forrest	Artie Shaw; Benny Goodman; Harry James
Betty Grable	Ted Fio Rito
Merv Griffin	Freddy Martin
Connie Haines	Harry James; Tommy Dorsey
Rita Hayworth	Xavier Cugat
Al Hibbler	Duke Ellington
Billie Holiday	Count Basie; Paul Whiteman; Artie Shaw; Benny Carter
Lena Horne	Noble Sissle; Charlie Barnet
Betty Hutton	Vincent Lopez
Marion Hutton	Glenn Miller
Kitty Kallen	Jack Teagarden; Artie Shaw, Harry James, Jimmy Dorsey
Priscilla Lane	Fred Waring
Rosemary Lane	Fred Waring
Peggy Lee	Benny Goodman
Tony Martin	Tom Gerun, Anson Weeks
Gordon MacRae	Horace Heidt
Marilyn Maxwell	Ted Weems; Buddy Rogers
Helen O'Connell	Jimmy Dorsey
Tony Pastor	Artie Shaw
Ginny Powell	Boyd Raeburn
Dinah Shore	Ben Bernie, Leo Reisman, Peter Dean, Beasley Smith
Joe Stafford	Tommy Dorsey
Kay Starr	Charlie Barnet; Joe Venuti
Martha Tilton	Benny Goodman; Will Bradley
Mel Torme	Artie Shaw

Sarah Vaughn	Georgie Auld; Earl Hines; Billy Eckstine
Harry VonZell	Charlie Barnet
Bea Wain	Larry Clinton
Helen Ward	Benny Goodman
Frances Wayne	Woody Herman
Edythe Wright	Tommy Dorsey
Nan Wynn	Hal Kemp

(Marilyn Maxwell, who was the first actress to entertain U.S. troops in Korea, was born Marvel Marilyn Maxwell) The following female vocalists married their band leaders: Dorothy Collins (Raymond Scott), Harriet Hilliard (Ozzie Nelson), Ann Richards (Stan Kenton), Georgia Carroll (Kay Kyser), Irene Daye (Charlie Spivak), Ginny Powell (Boyd Raeburn), Jo Stafford (Paul Weston). Bob and Ray Eberle are brothers. Bob changed the spelling of his name to Eberly.

In movies: *The Gene Krupa Story* (1959) Krupa was portrayed by Sal Mineo; *The Five Pennies* (1959) Red (Ernest Loring) Nichols was portrayed by Danny Kaye, Jimmy Dorsey portrayed by Ray Anthony and Glenn Miller portrayed by Ray Daley: *The Glenn Miller Story* (1954) Glenn Miller was portrayed by James Stewart; in *The Benny Goodman Story* (1955) Goodman was portrayed by Steve Allen; in 1972 movie *Lady Sings the Blues* Diana Ross portrayed Billie Holiday

Singing Brakeman, The
Nickname of country singer Jimmie Rodgers, also nicknamed The Father of Country Music and The Blue Yodeller

Singing in the Rain
Only movie in which Gene Kelly and Donald O'Connor appeared together (1952)

Singing Nun, The
Belgian nun Soeur Sourire: sang the 1963 hit record "Dominique." Portrayed by Debbie Reynolds in 1966 movie *The Singing Nun*

Singing Sam
The Barbasol Man, radio singer Harry Frankel

Singin' Sandy
Sandy [Saunders] role played by John Wayne in a series of movies: *Riders of Destiny* (1933) *Sagebrush Trail* (1933), *The Lucky Texan* (1934) etc; allegedly Smith

Ballew sang the part for John Wayne, who mouthed the words

Sinister Six
Evil group of villains that does battle against the super hero Spider Man. They are: Dr. Octopus, Mystero, Vulture, Electro, Kraven the Hunter, Sandman

Sir Dennis Nayland Smith
Scotland Yard detective who pursues Doctor Fu Manchu. In 1940 movie serial played by William Royle

Sir Gallahad III
Thoroughbred that sired 3 Kentucky Derby Winners: Gallant Fox—(1930), Gallahadion—(1940), and Hoop Jr.—(1945)

Sir Henry Merrivale
Detective created by John Dickson Carr. He is head of the Ministry of Miracles (nickname of the Central Office 8 of the Metropolitan police), debut in 1934 novel *The Plague Court Murders*

Sir-Love-A-Lot
Frank Harmon's (William Holden) dog in 1973 movie *Breezy*. Directed by Clint Eastwood. The canine was played by Earle

Sir Percy Blakeney
Secret identity of the Scarlet Pimpernel. From the play *The Scarlet Pimpernel* (1905), the pimpernel being a flower. In movies played by Leslie Howard (1935), Barry K. Barnes (1941), David Niven (1948): on radio, Marius Goring

Sirius
Orion's dog: the Dog Star

Six Crises
1962 autobiographical book of Richard M. Nixon's political career. The six crises he refers to are: The Hiss Case, (Alger Hiss); The Fund (campaign fund); The Heart Attack, (Eisenhower's); Caracas (his trip); Khrushchev (debate); The Campaign of 1960 (Presidential race)

Sitting Bull
Leader of the Sioux Indians. Portrayed in two movies by J. Carroll Naish: *Annie Get Your Gun* (1950) and *Sitting Bull* (1954). In 1965 movie *The Great Sioux Massacre* by Michael Pate

Skate, U.S.S.

First submarine to surface at the North Pole, 1959

Skeeter

Tom Swift, Jr.'s helicopter (novel series)

Skeeter

Tailspin Tommy's best friend played in 1934-1935 movie serials by Noah Berry, Jr. Played by Milburn Stone in features from 1939

Skeezix

Adopted son of bachelor Walt Wallet. He was found on Walt's doorstep on Valentine Day, February 14, 1921 (comic strip *Gasoline Alley*)

Skeleton Island

Island just south of Treasure Island, actual location of the buried treasure put there by Captain Flint, dug up by Ben Gunn (Robert Louis Stevenson's *Treasure Island*)

Skelton, Red

Richard Skelton, his radio and TV roles: Bolivar Shagnasty, Cauliflower McPugg, Clem Kadiddlehopper, Freddie the Freeloader, George Appleby, J. Newton Numskull, Junior, the Little Kid (3-year-old mean widdle kid), San Fernando Red, Willie Lump Lump, Sheriff Deadeye, Ludwick von Humperdoo, Cookie the Sailor

Skipper

Jungle Jim's son (TV series "Jungle Jim")

Skipper

Controversial toy doll that becomes taller, gets a smaller waist and larger breasts, when you turn her arms

Skull Cave

Place where the Phantom's large treasure is kept in the Bengali jungle (comic strip/book series *The Phantom*)

Skull Island

King Kong's (and his son's) home, from which he was brought to New York aboard the ship "Venture." It's located 1,753 miles from DaKong, southwest of Sumatra in the Indian Ocean. In the 1962 Japanese movie *King Kong vs. Godzilla*, Pharoah Island is his home. In the 1976 version of *King Kong* the ship used is the "Susanne Onstad"

Skull Island

Location of buried treasure in 1952 movie *Abbott and Costello Meet Captain Kidd*

Skully Nell

Dummy of Max Terhune in vaudeville

Skycycle X-2

Rocket on which Robert Craig Evel Knievel attempted to cross the Snake River (September 8, 1974), Snake River Canyon, Twin Falls, Idaho. He banked $6,000,000 for his failure

Sky Hound

Captain Silver's airplane

Sky King

"America's Favorite Flying Cowboy" Texas Ranger, Schyler King, pilot of the Twin Cessna *Songbird*. Played on TV by Kirby Grant: radio, Jack Lester, Earl Nightingale, Roy Engel. His niece was Penny (TV Gloria Winters, radio Beryl Vaughn). His nephew was Clipper (radio Jack Bivens). They lived on the Flying Crown Ranch. Kirby Grant later married Gloria Winters

Sky Queen

Tom Swift, Jr.'s flying lab (novel series)

Skyrocket

Marty Marham's horse (Spin and Marty *Mickey Mouse Club*)

Skytruck

Type of airplane from which the *Phoenix* was made (Elleston Trevor's novel *The Flight of the Phoenix*). The plane crashed on March 17th, owned by Arabco Oil Company

Slazenger I

Golf ball used by Auric Goldfinger when he played against James Bond (1964 movie *Goldfinger*). In Ian Fleming's novel, Goldfinger used a Dunlop 65 Number One (British golf balls are smaller than American: 1.62 inches in diameter compared to 1.68)

Sleeping Beauty

Princess Aurora, who had become Briar Rose and then went into a deep sleep until Prince Philip awakened her with a kiss (1959 Walt Disney cartoon movie *The Sleeping Beauty*). It is her castle that is located in Disneyland

Sleuth

Hardy Boys' boat (novel series)

Slightly Read Bookshop

"Papa" David Soloman's (Ralph Locke) establishment in the radio soap opera *Life Can Be Beautiful*

Slim
Name Harry Morgan (Humphrey Bogart) calls Marie Browning (Lauren Bacall) in 1944 movie *To Have and Have Not*. In the movie Marie is 22 years old—actually Miss Bacall was 19, this being her first movie. Marie calls Harry, Steve

Slinky
Toy spring that walks up and down stairs

Slivers
Little Nemo's dog (comic strip *Little Nemo*)

Sloan Guaranty Trust Company
Organization of which John Putnam Thatcher is senior vice-president in novels by Emma Lathem (Mary J. Latis and Martha Hennissart)

Slovik, Eddie D.
Private in U.S. Army (36896415) who was executed on January 31, 1945—the only U.S. soldier executed for desertion since 1864. Portrayed in TV movie *The Execution of Private Slovik* by Martin Sheen

Slue-Foot Sue
Wife of Pecos Bill (American folklore)

Sluggo
Nancy's bald-headed boyfriend (comic strip)

Slump
Deputy Mitchell's (Stuart Margolin) dog (TV series "Nichols")

Smallville, Illinois
Town in which Superboy was raised by Mr. and Mrs. Kent. Population 5012. Clark Kent lived on Main Street. He was a cub reporter for The Sentinel. He left for Metropolis at age 26

Smart Money
1931 film, only movie starring both Edward G. Robinson and James Cagney

Smaug
Evil fire-breathing dragon that lives in the lonely mountains, he is slain by Bard the Archer. J.R.R. Tolkein's *The Hobbit*

Smee
Captain Hook's companion (James M. Barrie's *Peter Pan*), in Disney movie voice of Bill Thompson

Smell-O-Vision

Special theater gimmick introduced by Michael Todd, Jr. for the movie *Scent of Mystery* (1959)

SMERSH

Smyert Spionam (Death to Spies), evil Soviet organization that preceeded SPECTRE in Ian Fleming's James Bond novels

Smiley

Baxter family shaggy dog (TV series "Hazel")

Smilin' Ed

Ed McConnell, children's radio and TV host and singer

Smilin' Jack

Comic strip series created in 1933 by Zack Mosley, originally called *On the Wings* (debut Sunday comics October 1, 1933). December 31, 1933 title was changed to *Smilin' Jack*. About adventures of aviator Jack Martin who in 1940 marries his girlfriend Joy

Smith

Most common name in the United States, followed by Johnson, Williams, Jones and Brown

Smith Brothers

Cough drops: William, Andrew (on radio they were called Trade and Mark because the words appeared under their pictures on the box in which the drops were sold). Andrew has the longest beard

Smith, Captain Edward J.

Captain of the "Titanic" April 14, 1912, when she struck an iceberg and sank on her maiden voyage. Portrayed by Brian Aherne in 1953 movie *Titanic*

Smith, Captain John

His life, according to legend, was saved by Powhatan's daughter Pocahontas. President (1608-1609) of the Virginia colony, he was largely responsible for its success. In the 1953 movie *Captain John Smith and Pocahontas* the pair were portrayed by Anthony Dexter and Jody Lawrence

Smith, Jeff

Motorcycle stunt man that performed the hazardous stunts for Steve McQueen in the 1963 movie *The Great Escape*. He made the jump over the fence and piled up into the barbed wire fence. McQueen did some of the other driving

663

Smithers

Mr. Lodge's (Veronica's father) butler (*Archie* comics)

Smoke Rings

Theme song of Glen Gray's Casa Loma Orchestra

Smokey

Drunken horse (Lee Marvin's) (1965 movie *Cat Ballou*)

Smokey the Bear

U.S. Forest Service symbol for their fire-prevention program since 1950. Voice of Jackson Weaver (1950-1976). A real bear cub nicknamed Smokey the Bear was discovered in the burnt-out forest of New Mexico's El Capitan Mountains in 1950. Meanwhile, the bear is kept at the National Zoo in Washington, D.C. (Gag line is that "The" is Smokey's middle name.) In 1975 Smokey was retired from service as his age equals 70 human years, the mandatory retirement age for Federal employees. His mate at National Zoo had been Goldie, but no cubs were born. His personal Zip Code is 20252. In the 1973 movie *The Ballad of Smokey the Bear* made by the Forest Service, James Cagney is the voice of Smokey

Smokey the Bear's motto

"Only you can prevent forest fires"

Smothers Brothers

Dick and Tom, popular singers and entertainers; their TV show's satire slew so many sacred cows it was canceled in 1969

Snagglepuss

TV cartoon lion whose favorite phrase is "Exit Stage Left" and "Heavens to Mergatroyd." Voice of Daws Butler, his twin brother is Snaggletooth

Snap, Crackle, and Pop

Kellogg's Rice Krispies (3 little elf-type men). Snap is the blonde. Voices of Daws Butler, Paul Winchell and Don Messick

Snark

Yacht built to Jack London's order and on which he lived 1906-1908 sailing the high seas. In the 1943 movie *Jack London*, London is portrayed by Michael O'Shea

Snidely Whiplash

Arch-enemy of Dudley Do-Right (cartoon series), voice of Hans Conried

Sniffles

Little mouse friend of Mary Jane (comic book series)

Snoop Sisters

Ernesta (played by Helen Hayes) and Gwen ("G" played by Mildred Natwick) (TV series): the sisters get involved in and solve crimes

Snoopy

Charlie Brown's pet, a beagle, who pretends to fly a Sopwith Camel against the Red Baron, tries writing novels, etc. (Charles Schulz's comic strip *Peanuts*). Snoopy hates cocoanut candy and gets weed claustrophobia. Charles Schulz was originally going to call him Sniffy until he discovered that name used in another comic strip. In movie cartoons Bill Melendez, the director of the movies, did the voice of Snoopy. In late 1960's The Royal Guardsmen had a hit record with *Snoopy Versus the Red Baron*

Snoopy

Apollo 10 lunar module: it descended to 9 miles from the lunar surface, then docked with its command module. Charlie Brown was the command module

Snow Baby

Admiral Robert Peary's daughter, Marie, born (1893) in the Arctic Circle at Inglefield Gulf

Snowball

Albino dolphin: only one known to exist (Miami Seaquarium, 1962)

Snowbirds

Canadian Air Force's aerobatic team

Snow White and the 7 Dwarfs

1937 Walt Disney movie: premiered at the Carthay Circle Theater, Hollywood, December 21, 1937. Voice of Adrienne Caselotti, Margery Belcher (later Marge Champion) modeled for Snow White. In 1938 Walt Dsiney won an Honorary Academy Award for *Snow White*. Shirley Temple presented him with one normal Oscar and 7 miniature statuettes (see *7 Dwarfs*). 1941 movie *Ball of Fire* with Barbara Stanwyck used the same theme. Again remade in 1948 as *A Song Is Born* with Virginia Mayo (with Benny Goodman, Louis Armstrong, Lionel Hampton, Charlie Barnet, Danny Kaye). A silent version of the movie had previously been made in 1917

Snowy

Tintin's little white dog (comic series by Hergé)

Snuffles
 Quick Draw McGraw's dog friend, he'll do anything for a dog biscuit (TV cartoon)

Snuffleupagus
 Large elephant-like blue animal seen only by Big Bird (TV series "Sesame Street"). His birthday is on August 19th

Soccer
 World Cup
  The Jules Rimet Trophy, first played for in 1930, representing the world's championship, contested every 4 years (even non-Olympics years): candidate teams are grouped in 4 divisions and playoffs are by a complex system controlled by the International Federation of Football Associations (FIFA)
 World Cup Winners
  1930 - Uruguay
  1934 - Italy
  1938 - Italy
  1950 - Uruguay
  1954 - West Germany
  1958 - Brazil
  1962 - Brazil
  1966 - England
  1970 - Brazil
  1974 - West Germany

Sock-It-To-Me-Girl
 Judy Carne of the TV comedy series "Laugh-In"

Softy
 Little girl doll who advertises Zee's Nice 'n Soft tissues

Solar Council
 United planet organization comprising the planets of Mars, Pluto, Jupiter, Venus, Saturn and Eos (TV series "Captain Video")

Solar Pons
 London detective called *The Sherlock Holmes of Praed Street* who lives at 7B Praed Street, his assistant is Doctor Lyndon Parker (series by August Derleth)

Solar Scouts
 Buck Rogers' listeners' fan club (radio)

Solar Year
 365.242127 days (the Mayans estimated it as 365.24219)

666

Soldiers Three
Story collection (1889) by Rudyard Kipling: the soldiers are Learoyd, Mulvaney and Ortheris, serving with the British Army in India

Solly Brass
Annie Fanny's agent, who resembles Phil Silvers (comic strip *Annie Fanny*)

Solna, Minnesota
Town in which the Scandinavian family The Larsens settle in 1858 (TV series "The New Land")

Somebody Up There Likes Me
1956 movie starring Paul Newman as Rocky Graziano. One of two movies that Paul Newman and Steve McQueen appear together in (McQueen received $19 a day as an extra). The other film is *The Towering Inferno*. James Dean was to play Graziano before his death

Someday I'll Find You
Them song of radio series "Mr. Keen, Tracer of Lost Persons" composed by Noël Coward

Somerset
The British war ship mentioned in Henry Wadsworth Longfellow's poem *Paul Revere's Ride*

Something's Got to Give
Movie on which Marilyn Monroe was working (1962) at the time of her death. Her last appearance was on her birthday, June 1, 1962, at age 36. The movie was later retitled *Move Over Darling* in 1963 starring Doris Day

Sommerset Winterset
Pseudo-intelligent character made famous on TV by Sid Caesar. A parody of author Somerset Maugham

Song-writing teams
Leiber and Stoller (Jerry and Mike)
Lennon and McCartney (John and Paul)
Henderson, De Sylva, and Brown (Ray, Buddy, Lew)
Rodgers and Hart (Richard and Lorenz)
Schwartz and Dietz (Arthur and Howard)
Gilbert and Sullivan (William and Arthur)
Rodgers and Hammerstein (Richard and Oscar)
Kern and Hammerstein (Jerome and Oscar)
Loewe and Lerner (Frederick and Alan Jay)
Ira and George Gershwin
Burt Bacharach and Hal David

Dubin and Warren (Al and Harry)
Weill and Brecht (Blitzstein) (Kurt and Bertolt)
Movie portrayals:
In British movie *The Story of Gilbert and Sullivan* portrayed by Robert Morley and Maurice Evans respectively
In the 1945 movie *Rhapsody in Blue* George Gershwin was portrayed by Robert Alda (Mickey Roth as a boy) and Ira Gershwin was portrayed by Herbert Rudley (Darryl Hickman as a boy)
In the 1946 movie *The Jolson Story* Oscar Hammerstein was portrayed by Edwin Maxwell
In the 1948 movie *Words and Music* Richard Rodgers was portrayed by Tom Drake and Lorenz Hart portrayed by Mickey Rooney

Songbird
Sky King's 1953 Twin Cessna (C310B) airplane. The first Songbird was a Cessna T-50

Songbird of the South
Nickname of Kate Smith

Song of Bernadette, The
Theme song of radio soap *Against the Storm*

Sonja
Duck (Prokofiev's *Peter and the Wolf*)

Sonny Boy
Title of song sung by Al Jolson in his second talking picture *The Singing Fool* (1928). Becoming the title of his next film (1929)

Son of
(movies)
Son of Ali Baba (1952)
Son of Belle Star (1953)
Son of Captain Blood (1962)
Son of Dracula (1943)
Son of Dr. Jekyll (1951)
Son of Frankenstein (1939)
Son of Fury (1942)
Son of Godzilla (1969)
Son of Hercules (1962-1963), series
Son of Kong (1953)
Son of Lassie (1945)
Son of Monte Cristo (1940)
Son of Paleface (1952), Bob Hope

Son of Robin Hood (1959)*
Son of Sinbad (1955)
Son of the Sheik (1926)
Son of Spartacus (1962)

Son of a Gun
Actor/TV host Joey Bishop's yacht

Sons of the Desert
Fraternal organization to which Stan Laurel and Oliver Hardy belonged (movie series). Stan and Ollie belong to Oasis 13, the Los Angeles chapter. The head man of the organization is called The Exalted Exhausted Ruler. The International Laurel and Hardy Fan Club is known as Sons of the Desert, the head man being the Grand Sheik. They give out the annual Fine Mess Award for the year's greatest fiasco

Sothern, Ann
Played Susie Camille MacNamara in TV series "Private Secretary." The voice (Mrs. Abigail Crabtree) of the car (TV series, 1965, "My Mother the Car")

Sounder
The Calloway family dog (Walt Disney's 1965 movie *Those Calloways*)

Souphead
Jughead Jones' little cousin who closely resembles him (*Archie* comics)

Soupy Sales
Nickname of television comedian Milton Hines, who has had a substantial number of pies thrown in his face. He starred in 1966 movie *Birds Do It*

Soupy Sales Show
Four supporting puppets: Black Tooth, Hippy, Pookie, White Fang. In his store lives Hobart and Reba

Sour Apple
Award given by the Hollywood Women's Press Club for the least cooperative actor or actress of the year. The Golden Apple is awarded for the most cooperative

South High
(Old South High) High School attended by Annette (Mickey Mouse Club serial)

South Philadelphia
Area from where these singers originated: Mario Lanza,

---

*Is actually Robin Hood's daughter, Daring Hood

Eddie Fisher, Bobby Rydell, Frankie Avalon, James Darren, Fabian Forte, and Chubby Checker, among others

Southwest High
Stockton, California High School (Spartans) featured in TV series "Sons and Daughters"

Spacecraft/Ship movements
Pitch (up-and-down motion of the nose or bow)
Roll (side-to-side movement around the long axis)
Yaw (angular motion of the nose or bow away from the line of flight)

Spacely Space Sprockets
Company which employed George Jetson (TV cartoon show "The Jetsons")

Spaulding
Manufacturer of the baseballs used in both the American and National Leagues until 1976. Present manufacturer is now Rawlings

Spar
Female member of the U.S. Coast Guard: from the service's motto, Semper Paratus

Spare-Ribs
Toots and Casper's pet dog (comic strip)

Sparkle Plenty
Daughter of Gravel Gertie and B.O. Plenty (*Dick Tracy* cartoon series)

Spark Plug
Barney Goggle's horse, always in a blanket (comic strip by Billy DeBeck)

Sparrow, The
Killed Cock Robin (nursery rhyme)

Sparta, Mississippi
Locale of movie *In the Heat of the Night*

Spartan Apartment Hotel
Home of the fictitious detective Sheldon (Shell) Scott (Shell Scott series by Richard S. Prather) located on North Rossmore, Hollywood (2nd Floor), 3 rooms and bath bachelor apartment

Spear, Sammy
Jackie Gleason's late orchestra leader. Gleason called him "The Flower of the Music World"

670

Spear-T Ranch

Montana cattle ranch near Lewiston, setting of radio soap *Lone Journey*

SPECTRE

Special Executive for Counterintelligence, Terrorism, Revenge and Extortion (James Bond series). Ernst Starvo Blofeld is the Chief of SPECTRE, Emilio Largo is SPECTRE 2

Spectre, The

Secret identity or ghost of detective Jim Corrigan (comic book series *The Spectre*), debut More Fun Comics #1 (Feb. 1935)

Spectrum

The rainbow colors: Violet, Indigo, Blue, Green, Yellow, Orange, Red: mnemonic Roy G. Biv

Speech, parts of

Traditioal in English: Noun, Pronoun, Verb, Adverb, Adjective, Preposition, Conjunction, Interjection

Speed Airlines

Airline company that Selina Kyle (Catwoman) was a stewardess with (*Batman* comic books)

Speedwell

Ship that was not seaworthy enough to accompany the "Mayflower" in 1620

Speedwell Boys

Children's novels: Billy, Dan

Speedy

Alka-Seltzer boy (TV commercial): created in 1952 by Robert Watkins. He has red hair and blue eyes. Voice of Richard Beals, who is also the voice of Speedy's South American twin Pron-Tito

Speedy Gonzales

Mexican mouse (Warner Brothers movie cartoon): "The fastest mouse in all of Mexico." He lives in Guadalajara. Voice of Mel Blanc. 1955 cartoon *Speedy Gonzales* won an Oscar for Best Short Subject. In 1962 Pat Boone had a hit record titled *Speedy Gonzales*

Spellbinder

Villainous cartoon character who distorts words. Letterman eventually comes to the rescue and puts the words straight (TV series "The Electric Company")

Spider

"Msater of Men" created by Grant Stockbridge (Norvel

Page): debut "The Spider Strikes" (Spider Magazine, October 1933). Movies serials—Warren Hull, secret identity of Richard Wentworth. His fiancee is Nita Van Sloan. Movie serials; *The Spider's Web* (1938) (15), *The Spider Returns* (1941) (15). He keeps his seals in his cigarette lighter. His chauffeur is Ram Singh, a Hindu, his car a Lancia, his plane a Northrop

Spider Man (Spidey)
Secret identity of Peter Parker (comic book series *Spider Man*). In animated TV series voice of Bernard Cowan and Paul Sols. On 1977 TV series by Nick Hammond. Debut in Amazing Fantasy Comics #15 (August 1962), created by Steve Ditko and Stan Lee. Peter Parker lives with his Aunt May. It was when his Uncle Ben was killed by a burglar that Parker decided to become a crime fighter

Spike
Charles Schulz's dog who appeared in a Ripley's Believe It or Not! column. The dog had eaten many unusual items

Spike
Fonzie's tough little cousin (Danny Butch), TV series "Happy Days" (he calls him his nephew)

Spike
Snoopy's brother (comic strip *Peanuts*)

Spike
Tubby's nemesis, Spike is leader of the Westside Boys (comic strip *Tubby* by Marge)

Spin and Marty
Adventure series on the Mickey Mouse Club (boys stayed on the Triple R Ranch during the summer. Martin (Marty) Markham and Spin Evans by Tim Considine and David Stollery

Spinach
Food that gives Popeye all of his super-strength. He almost always carries a can or two. Prior to Spinach he used garlic (according to his cartoons)

Spindrift
Jack Armstrong's Uncle Jim's yacht

Spindrift
Airship on Flight 612 (Flight 703 in novel), Los Angeles to London, piloted by Captain Steve Burton, that crashes in the Land of the Giants (TV series "Land of the Giants")

SPIRIT

License plate of the Magician's white Corvette. Nickname of the private Boeing 737 of Anthony Blake, the Magician (TV series "The Magician"). Named Anthony Dorian in pilot movie. His home address is 315 Vinewood, Los Angeles

Spirit, The

Super-crimefighter Denny Colt, who was "killed" when Dr. Cobra threw chemicals on him. In a sleep resembling death, he was buried in Wildwood Cemetery, but awoke and broke out as the Spirit (comic book series *The Spirit*): created by Will Eisner (debut June 1940)

Spirit of America

Racing driver Craig Breedlove's jet-powered car

Spirit of Ecstasy

Hood ornament on a Rolls Royce

Spirit of St. Louis

Charles Lindbergh's N-X-211 Ryan monoplane on his Atlantic flight, May 20-21, 1927. It was also the first airplane in which Henry Ford, Sr. ever flew (August 17, 1927, a 10 minute flight over Detroit)

Spirit of '76

Air Force One: Presidential airplane

Spitz

Dog that is Buck's deadly rival (Jack London's *The Call of the Wild*). In the 1935 Clark Gable movie Buck's rival is Prince

Spitz, Mark

U.S. swimmer who won 7 gold medals (more than any athlete before him) in the 1972 Munich Olympics. The events: (individual: all world's record performances) 100-meter freestyle, 200-meter freestyle, 100-meter butterfly, 200-meter butterfly: (relay) 400-meter freestyle, 800-meter freestyle, 400-meter medley. Spitz, who won 2 gold medals in the 1968 Olympics, is tied with Paavo Nurmi at 9 for most total gold medals in the Olympics, the latter having won his in the 1920, 1924, 1928 Olympics

Sponsors

Radio programs:
The Aldrich Family: Jell-O
Amos 'n' Andy: Rinso Soap
Jack Armstrong: Wheaties

Jack Benny: Canada Dry, Chevrolet, Jell-O, Lucky Strike

Edgar Bergen and Charlie McCarthy: Chase & Sanborn Coffee

Burns and Allen: Maxwell House Coffee

Jimmy Durante Show: Rexall

The Falcon: Gem Blades

Buck Jones: Grape Nuts Flakes

Spike Jones: Coco-Cola

Little Orphan Annie: Ovaltine

Fibber McGee and Molly: Johnson's Wax

Tom Mix: Ralston

Sergeant Preston: Quaker Puffs

The Shadow: Blue Coal

Superman: Kellogg's

Terry and the Pirates: Quaker Puffs

Your Hit Parade: Lucky Strike

Spook

Prisoner in the dungeon of the Kingdom of Id. He has been in the dungeon for 34 years for calling the King a clod. He is guarded by Turnkey (comic strip *The Wizard of Id* by Johnny Hart and Brant Parker)

Spooky

Fenwick Flooky's cat (the comic strip *Spooky* appeared right under Bill Holman's *Smokey Stover*—it was signed Scat Holman). Debut in *Smokey Stover* comic strip March 10, 1935

Sportlight

Grantland Rice's newspaper sports column

Sportsmen

Singing group featured on radio's *The Jack Benny Program.* They also appeared on *The Eddie Cantor Show*

Spot

Dick and Jane's black and white dog (school primary book)

Spot

The household dragon of the Munsters (TV series "The Munsters")

Spot

Dog of board Boner's Ark (comic strip *Boner's Ark*)

Spot

Hong Kong Phooey's pet cat (TV cartoon series *Hong Kong Phooey*)

Spot

Woody Allen's pet ant that his parents gave him as a child as they couldn't afford a dog (comedy skit)

Spot

Confederate soldier's pet dog in 1950 movie *Rocky Mountain*

Spouter Inn

New Bedford, Massachusetts lodging where Ishmael met Queequeg prior to their sailing on the Pequod (1841), Herman Melville's *Moby Dick*. Inn run by Peter Coffin

Spray

Sandy and Bud Ricks' pet dog (TV series "Flipper")

Spring City

Setting of radio series *Those Websters*

Springdale

Town setting of radio series *Rosemary*

Springfield

The home town of the Anderson family (TV series "Father Knows Best". Their phone number is SPringfield 2274. Also setting for 1959 movie *The Shaggy Dog*)

Springfield

Town location of TV serial "The Guiding Light."

SPringfield 4682

Phone number of Gillis Grocery Store at 285 Norwood Street in Springfield, owned by Dobie Gillis' father (Frank Faylen) TV series "The Many Loves of Dobie Gillis"

Springfield College, Mass.

Location of basketball's Hall of Fame: basketball invented here 1891 by James Naismith

Spruce Goose, The

Nickname of Howard Hughes' $58 million 8-engine flying boat (Hughes HK-1 "Hercules" NX37602): flown only once, 1,000 yards, in November 3, 1947

Spud Stavins

Tim Tyler's sidekick (cartoon series "Tim Tyler's Luck")

Spunky

Cute little cartoon mouse that readers are asked to draw for Art Instruction Schools, Inc (magazine ad). Charles Schulz, before becoming a free-lance comic strip writer, worked for this school

Spunky

Shirley Temple's horse in the 1935 movie *Curly Top*. The horse was given to her to keep

Sputnik I
First satellite in orbit, launched by U.S.S.R. October 4, 1957: flight ended January 4, 1958

Spy Smasher
World War II fighter of evil. Secret identity of millionaire Alan Armstrong (*Whiz* comics). Republic movie serial (1942) Kane Richmond—12 episodes. He fought the AXIS powers during World War II

Squadron of Justice
Captain Marvel's three Lieutenants: Tall Billy, Hill Billy, Fat Billy (comic books)

Squadron of Peace
Don Winslow's evil-fighting organization (radio series *Don Winslow of the Navy*)

Squeaky
Smilin' Ed's pet mouse (radio and TV)

S.S. Hurrah
Backdrop ship on stage in the 1942 movie *Yankee Doodle Dandy* starring James Cagney as George M. Cohan

Stage Show
TV show, starring the Dorsey brothers, on which Elvis Presley made his TV debut (January 28, 1956)

Stagg, Amos Alonzo
Football coach, died 1965, aged 103 years: "The Grand Old Man of Football": a Yale All-American, coached for 57 years, especially at Chicago, 1892-1932, and College of the Pacific, 1933-1946, winning 314 games, more than any other coach (Glenn Warner won 313, through there are those who say Warner won 316 and Stagg 311). Member of National Football Hall of Fame. He is also a member of the Basketball Hall of Fame. Elected in 1959 as a contributor. Six major league baseball teams also made him an offer to pitch for them.

Stalactite
Limestone deposit hanging from roof of cave

Stalag 13
German prison camp (TV series "Hogan's Heroes"), from which no prisoner has ever escaped. The code name of the allied soldiers in the camp is Goldilocks, the code name of their submarine contact is Mama Bear

Stalagmite
Limestone deposit rising from floor of cave

Stalin, Joseph

Pseudonym of Iosif Dzhugashvili, premier of U.S.S.R.; *Time* magazine's "Man of the Year" for 1939 and 1942

Standish Arms Hotel

Clark Kent's (Superman) Metropolis apartment home, Apartment 5H; he later moved to 344 Clinton Street

Standish, Miles

Sent John Alden to propose for him to Priscilla Mullins: Priscilla answered, "Why don't you speak for yourself, John?" (H. W. Longfellow's "The Courtship of Miles Standish"). Historically, Standish, one of the "Mayflower" settlers (1620), was captain of the Pilgrims military forces: a widower, he remarried in 1623, about a year after John Alden and Priscilla married. John Alden was the last survivor of those 41 males who signed the Mayflower Compact November 11, 1620. In the 1952 movie *Plymouth Adventure* Dawn Addams portrays Priscilla Mullins while Noel Drayton portrays Miles Standish

Standish Sanitarium

Hospital that Dr. Hugo Z. Hackenbush (Groucho Marx), a horse doctor, heads (1937 movie *A Day at the Races*)

Stanford Axe

Trophy awarded to the winner of the annual Stanford-California football game

Stanley Cup

National Hockey League's trophy, won by annual champions since 1911-1912 season: originally (1893) bought for 10 pounds donated by Frederick Arthur Stanley, Baron Stanley of Preston. First won by Montreal·AAA

Stanwood

Town location of radio serial *When a Girl Marries*

Star City

Town where Oliver Queen (Green Arrow) lives

Stardust

Spaceship of Major Perry Rhodan, Peacelord of the Universe (*Perry Rhodan* series by Walter Ernsting and K. H. Scheer)

Stardust I

NASA spaceship in which Astronaut Captain Tony Nelson (Larry Hagman) was in when, after landing, he found Jeannie (Barbara Eden) in a bottle (TV series "I Dream of Jeannie")

677

Stardust Dance Hall

Dance hall where 35-year-old butcher Marty Pilletti (Ernest Borgnine) meets 29-year-old Clara Snyder (Betsy Blair), a chemistry teacher at Benjamin Franklin High School (1955 movie *Marty*)

Star Fleet Ships

(TV series "Star Trek")

Belonging to the United Federation of Planets:

Constellation Class

Constellation NCC 1017 (Captain Matt Dekker)

Republic NCC 1371 (Captain Finner)

Constitution NCC 1700

Enterprise NCC 1701 (Captain Kirk)

Farragut NCC 1702 - Lost in Action (Captain Garrovick)

Lexington NCC 1703 (Captain Wesley)

Yorktown NCC 1704

Excalibur NCC 1705 (Captain Harris)

Exeter NCC 1706 (Captain Ronald Tracey)

Hood NCC 1707

Intrepid NCC 1708 - Lost in Action (Vulcan Captain Satak)

Valiant NCC 1709 - Lost in Action

Kongo NCC 1710

Potenkin NCC 1711

Star Spear

Tom Swift, Jr.'s rocket ship (novel series)

Star Trek

Science-fiction Hugo Award-winning TV series created by Gene Roddenberry. Crew members (part of the ship's complement of 430) of the U.S.S. "Enterprise":

Role		*Actor*
Captain James T. Kirk	Captain	William Shatner
Commander Mr. Spock	First Officer	Leonard Nimoy
Lt. Commander Leonard McCoy	Doctor	DeForest Kelley
Lt. Commander Montgomery Scott "Scotty"	Chief Engineer	James Doohan
Lt. Sulu	Helmsman	George Takei
Lt. Uhuru	Communications	Nichelle Nichols
Ensign Pavel Chekov	Navigator	Walter Koenig
Christine Chapel	Nurse	Majel Barrett

Majel Barrett also played Captain Pike's first officer Number One. She is the voice of the Enterprise's computer and is married to the show's producer, Gene Roddenberry

The series lasted from September 8, 1966 to April 4, 1969 when it was cancelled by NBC. Thousands of letters were sent in protest, including the entire Princeton graduation class

Starbuck

First mate of the "Pequod" (Herman Melville's *Moby Dick*): played by Leo Genn in 1956 movie *Moby Dick*

Stars and Bars

The Confederate flag

Stars and Stripes Forever, The

March composed (1897) by John Philip Sousa: traditional song played by circus bands as a distress signal to warn all circus performers that there is an emergency. Song was played July 6, 1944 at Hartford, Connecticut when the Ringling Brothers Circus tent caught fire, killing 168 people. In the 1952 movie *Stars and Stripes Forever* Sousa was portrayed by Clifton Webb

Stars Over Broadway

Theme song of the TV series "Your Show of Shows"

Star-Spangled Banner, The

Words by Francis Scott Key set to tune "To Anacreon in Heav'n"; became U.S. National Anthem on March 3, 1931

State Fair - Omaha

Inscription on the Giant Balloon that the Wizard of Oz (Frank Morgan) came to and left the Land of Oz, in 1939 movie *The Wizard of Oz*

Staten Island Ferries

Richmond - Bayonne

Holland Hook - Elizabethport

Linoleumville - Carteret

Tootenville - Perth Amboy

STate 1096

Elliott Ness' (Robert Stack) office phone number. Office located in Room 308, Federal Bldg. 913 Dearborn Street, Chicago (TV series "The Untouchables")

States

Last three admitted to the Union:

Arizona	48th state	February 1912
Alaska	49th state	January 1959
Hawaii	50th state	August 1959

Steamboat Willie

Mickey Mouse's (and Walt Disney's) first sound cartoon film, debut at the Colony Theatre in New York City, November 8, 1928. Mickey does variations on "Turkey in the Straw": preceded by silent Mickey shorts *Plane Crazy* and *Gallopin' Gaucho,* but Steamboat Willie was released first. Mickey's last cartoon was *The Simple Things* (1953)

Steamboat Willie

Billy Batson's (Captain Marvel) Black valet (1950's comic books)

Stella Dallas

"The true-to-life sequence, as written by us, to the world famous drama of mother love and sacrifice" (radio series *Stella Dallas* — played by Anne Elstner). Filmed twice: (1926) with Belle Bennett and again in 1937 with Barbara Stanwyck

Stephens, Alexander Hamilton

Southern patriot (1812-1883) from Georgia vice-president (1861-1865) of the Confederacy under President Jefferson Davis of Mississippi (there was also a General Jefferson Davis who fought for the Union during the Civil War)

Stepin Fetchit

Stage name of movie actor Lincoln Theodore Monroe Andrew Perry. He adopted the name Stepin Fetchit from the name of a racehorse by which he made some money

Steptoe and Son

British TV series on which the American series "Sanford and Son" is based

Sterling Morris

Bill Batson's boss at radio station WHIZ (*Captain Marvel* comic books)

Stern, Bill

The Colgate Shave Cream man, highly imaginative sports broadcaster: announced the first remote sports broadcast, on NBC radio, May 1939, in a baseball game between Columbia and Princeton at Columbia. He also announced the first pro telecast (NBC) of a baseball game, New York Giants and St. Louis Cardinals at the Polo Grounds

Steve Aloysius McGarrett

Detective lieutenant on Honolulu police force: played by Jack Lord (TV series "Hawaii Five-O")

Steve Canyon

(Col. Stevenson Burton Canyon) Comic strip character created by Milton Caniff (TV-played by Dean Frederick, 1950). Steve married Summer Smith Olsen April 1970

Stevenson Aircraft

Los Angeles aviation company for which Chester A. Riley works as a riveter (radio/TV series *The Life of Riley*)

Steve Trevor

Wonder Woman's boyfriend (comic books): he is an Army Captain (later Major) and pilot stationed at Camp Merrick near Washington, D.C. He was killed off by Dr. Cyber in Wonder Woman comics #180, January 1969. In 1974 TV series *Wonder Woman*, played by Lyle Waggoner

Steve Wilson

Editor of the "Illustrated Press" (radio/TV series "Big Town"): played on radio by Edward G. Robinson, Edward Pawley, and Walter Greaza: on TV by Mark Stevens and Pat McVey. His society editor was Lorelei Kilbourne

Steven Kiley

Colleague of Doctor Welby (TV series "Marcus Welby, M.D.")

Stiller and Meara

Comedians Jerry Stiller and Anne Meara

Stone, Dwight Eliott

Last person drafted into the U.S. Armed Forces prior to the expiration of the Selective Service Act on June 23, 1973

Stone Mountain

Granite dome (650 feet above the level around it) near Atlanta, Georgia, on which appear deep-relief sculptures (90 feet high, 190 feet long) of Jefferson Davis, Robert E. Lee, Stonewall Jackson. Begun by Gutzon Borglum, who later did the heads on Mt. Rushmore, the work was taken over by Henry Augustus Lukeman, who destroyed the head of Lee that Borglum had finished; the project, after 47 years of work, was finished by Walker Hancock

Stonewall

Nickname of Confederate General Thomas Jonathan Jackson (1824-1863): called "Stonewall" by Gen. B. E. Bee for the firm stand of his troops at the first battle of

Bull Run, July 21, 1861; killed by his own troops at the Battle of Chancellorsville

Stormy

Gordon "Wild Bill" Elliot's horse (movie series)

Story of Suicide Sal, The

Famous poem composed by Bonnie Parker (who was nicknamed Suicide Sal). It was published in newspapers throughout the country while she and Clyde Barrow were still fugitives. She also composed the poem *The Legend of Bonnie and Clyde*

Stradivarius

Antonio Stradivarius (1644-1739), Italian violinmaker. Violin owned by sleuth Sherlock Holmes which he bought for a mere 55 shillings. Jack Benny owned one valued at $25,000

Straight Arrow

Secret identity of Steve Adams (comic books), owner of the Broken Bow cattle ranch. Fury is his golden palomino. On radio played by Howard Culver

Straight Flush

B-29 photographic and weather-reporting plane (#91) that took pictures of the atomic bomb explosions on Hiroshima and Nagasaki: piloted by Major Claude Eatherly

Straight Pass

Private-eye Tony Rome's (Frank Sinatra) private houseboat (1967 movie *Tony Rome*)

Straight Shooters

Tom Mix's radio fan club (sponsored by Ralston): listening boys and girls were invited to join

Stratemeyer, Capt. Edward L.

(1862-1930) Creator of juvenile series under pseudonyms: *Tom Swift* (Victor Appleton), *Bobbsey Twins* (Laura Lee Hope), *Rover Boys* (Arthur W. Winfield), *Hardy Boys* (Franklin W. Dixon), *Motor Boys, Bomba the Jungle Boy, Nancy Drew* and many of the other series were written by his daughter Harriet S. Adams under the pen name of Carolyn Keene after his death. Other series of his were: *Dana Girls, Happy Hollisters, Honey Bunch, Curly Tops, Bunny Brown,* and others.

Strathfield

Town setting of television soap opera *From These Roots*

Strawberries and Cream
Traditional food served at Wimbledon each year
Strawberry 9
PBY plane that first spotted the Japanese fleet (1976 movie *Midway*)
Streaky
Superman's super cat (comic books)
Street, Gabby
Washington Senator catcher who caught a baseball thrown off the top of the Washington Monument (over 500 feet high), August 21, 1908, by Pres Gibson, catching the 13th ball thrown
Strelka and Belka
Two soviet dogs in orbit brought safely back to Earth on August 20, 1960. Their names mean "Little Arrow" and "Squirrel"
Stretch Cunningham
Archie Bunker's co-worker (played by James Cromwell) (TV series "All in the Family")
Stretch Snodgrass
Not-too-smart student at Madison High School: played by Leonard Smith (radio series *Our Miss Brooks*)
Strip
Tiger's dog (comic strip *Tiger* by Bud Blake)
Stromboli
The evil puppeteer who captures Pinocchio and keeps him in a cage (Walt Disney 1940 movie *Pinocchio*): voice of Charles Judels
Strong Legs Run That Weak Legs May Walk
Slogan of football's East-West game (college seniors) held annually in San Francisco. Proceeds go to the Shrine's Hospital for Crippled Children. First game was played in 1926
Stuart, Jeb
James *E*well *B*rown Stuart, Confederate cavalry general (1833-1864): portrayed by Errol Flynn in 1940 movie *Santa Fe Trail*
Stuart, Mary
Mary, Queen of Scots, rival of Elizabeth I for the throne of England, mother of James I of England
Studs Lonigan
Trilogy of novels by James T. Farrell: *Young Lonigan*, 1932; *The Young Manhood of Studs Lonigan*, 1934;

Judgment Day, 1935: played in movies by Christopher Knight

Study in Scarlet, A

Novel in which Sherlock Holmes first appeared, 1886, by Sir Arthur Conan Doyle, for which he received 25 pounds

Sub-Mariner

Super villain/hero man of the sea whose real name is Prince Namor. He is the son of Princess Fen and Commander Leonard McKenzie. Created by William Everett, debut *Marvel Mystery* comics #1 November 1939

Submarines

Names of submarines in Disneyland underwater adventure: D301: Nautilus, D302: Seawolf, D303: Skate, D304: Skipjack, D305: Triton, D306: George Washington, D307: Patrick Henry, D308 Ethan Allen

Sugar Babe

Luke McCoy's (Richard Crenna) nickname for his wife Kate (Kathy Nolan), TV series "The Real McCoy's"

Sugar Bear

Advertises Post's Super Sugar Crisp cereal (TV cereal box ad)

Sugar Blues

Theme song of Clyde McCoy's band

Sugarfoot

Tom Brewster (TV series "Sugarfoot"): played by Will Hutchins. The series was titled *Tenderfoot* for British TV

Sugar Fox

Culprit who attempts to steal Sugar Bear's Sugar Crisp Breakfast Cereal (TV commercials)

Suicide Is Painless

Theme song of movie and TV series "M*A*S*H"

Suicides

Cleopatra: bitten by an asp
Hannibal: poison
Ernest Hemingway: gunshot
Adolf Hitler: gunshot
Judas Iscariot: hanged
Mark Antony: his own sword
Nero: cut throat
Freddie Prince: gunshot
Vincent Van Gogh: gunshot
Ivar Kreuger: gunshot
George Eastman: gunshot

Meriwether Lewis: gunshot
George Sanders: overdose
James Forrestal: jumped out of window
Virginia Woolf: drown
Ernest Hemingway's father, Doctor Clarence Hemingway, also died from suicide when he shot himself in 1928

Suite 1221
Room in the St. Francis Hotel in San Francisco where Roscoe "Fatty" Arbuckle supposedly raped Virginia Rappe on September 5, 1921. She died September 10. After 3 trials, Arbuckle was acquitted

Sullivan, Anne
American teacher (Anne Mansfield Sullivan Macy), chosen (1887) to teach Helen Keller, a child left blind, deaf and dumb by scarlet fever: they became lifelong friends. In the 1962 movie *The Miracle Worker*, Sullivan was played by Anne Bancroft, Keller by Patty Duke. In the 1962 movie, Anne Bancroft won an Oscar for Best Actress, Patty Duke won an Oscar for Best Supporting Actress

Sullivan Award
Given to the year's Outstanding American Amateur Athlete (male or female)

Sultana
Captain Dan Tempest's (Robert Shaw) pirate ship. 1956 television series "The Buccaneers"

Summer of '42
Trio of boys (novel/1971 movie): Benjie (Oliver Conant), Hermie (Gary Grimes), Oscy (Jerry Houser); also in 1973 sequel movie *Class of 44'*

Sun
Advertises Kellogg's Raisin Bran cereal. Voice of Bob Bowker

Sun Bonnets, The
Walt Disney characters (young female bears in Disneyland): Beulah, Bubbles, Bunny

Sunbonnet Sue
Theme song of radio series *David Harum*

Sundance Kid
Pseudonym of western outlaw Harry Longbaugh: portrayed by Robert Redford in 1969 movie *Butch Cassidy and the Sundance Kid*

Sunflower
Little Hiawatha's sister (Walt Disney comics)

Sun-Maid

Brand of popular boxed raisins. Collett Peterson is the girl who, in 1914, posed for the portrait of the Sun-Maid Raisin girl on the raisin boxes

Sunny

Crazy bird that loves Cocoa Puffs breakfast cereal. Voices of Chuck McCann (General Mills TV commercial)

Sunny Dell Acres

B. O. Plenty, Gertie and Sparkle's house. At the intersection of Bliss Avenue and Joy Court (*Dick Tracy* comics)

Sun Records

Memphis, Tennessee, recording company: founded by Sam Phillips in 1951, located at 706 Union St. Between 1954 and 1957 these stars recorded under the Sun label: Elvis Presley, Johnny Cash, Jerry Lee Lewis, Carl Perkins, Roy Orbison, Charlie Rich, also Conway Twitty under his real name Harold Jenkins

Sunrise, Colorado

Setting of TV series "Bus Stop"

Sunset Handicap

Annual horserace run at Hollywood Park

Sunshine State

Nickname of Florida, South Dakota and New Mexico

Super Bowl

Professional football's championship game; played 1967-1970 between American Football League and National Football League, since 1971 between winners of American and National Conferences in National Football League

Game		Winner	Loser	Score
I	1967	Green Bay Packers	Kansas City Chiefs	35-10
II	1968	Green Bay Packers	Oakland Raiders	33-14
III	1969	New York Jets	Baltimore Colts	16-7
IV	1970	Kansas City Chiefs	Minnesota Vikings	23-7
V	1971	Baltimore Colts	Dallas Cowboys	16-13
VI	1972	Dallas Cowboys	Miami Dolphins	24-3
VII	1973	Miami Dolphins	Washington Redskins	14-7
VIII	1974	Miami Dolphins	Minnesota Vikings	24-7
IX	1975	Pittsburgh Steelers	Minnesota Vikings	16-6
X	1976	Pittsburgh Steelers	Dallas Cowboys	21-17
XI	1977	Oakland Raiders	Minnesota Vikings	32-14

The first Super Bowl touchdown was scored by Max McGee

Superboy

Adventures of *Superman* as a boy in the town of Smallville—his girlfriend was Lana Lane. Debut: *More Fun Comics* #101 Feb. 1945; in his own comic book in *Superboy Comics* #1 (March 1949); in a 1962 short-lived series *The Adventures of Superboy* played by John Rockwell. Became a member of Legion of Super Heroes in *Adventure Comics* Vol. 380 May 1969

Super Circus
TV series:
Ringmaster: Claude Kirchner
Clowns: Cliffy the Tramp, Scampy the box clown, Nick Francis, the fat clown
Leader of the Super Circus Band: Mary Hartline

Supercalifragilisticexpialidocious
Magic word in song sung by Julie Andrews (1964 Disney movie *Mary Poppins*)

Supergirl
Secret identity of Linda Lee Danvers, Superman's cousin (comic book series): she was called Kara when she was born on the planet Krypton. Her parents were Zor-El and Allura. Created by Mort Weisinger and Otto Binder, she debuted in *Action Comics* #252 (May 1959). She was sent to Earth in a rocketship from the city of Argo on the planet Krypton. She was raised at the Midvale Orphanage, adopted on Earth by Fred and Mary Danvers. She attended Stanhope College. She is a member of the Legion of Super Heroes

Superman
"The Man of Steel," identity assumed secretly by Clark Kent. He was born Kal-El (comic strip and book movie series/TV series): played on radio by Clayton "Bud" Collyer and Michael Fitzmaurice; in movies and TV by George Reeves (George Besselo)
Debut: *Action Comics* #1, June 1938: writer, Jerry Siegel; artist, Joe Shuster.
His first appearance did not mention his origin, which was finally explained in *Superman Comics* #1. A year later Siegel and Shuster sold their rights to Superman for $130
The first use of "Superman" in literature was in George Bernard Shaw's 1903 comedy *Man and Superman*. In 1942 George Lowther wrote the novel *Superman*. Debut as a newspaper comic strip January 16, 1939. In movie serials, Superman was played by: *Superman* (1948) Kirk Alyn (Clark Kent as a boy by Alan Dinehart III, Clark

Kent as a teenager by Ralph Hodges); *Atomic Man vs Superman* (1950) Kirk Alyn
In 1951 movie *Superman and the Mole Men* (1951) George Reeves
In 1941-1943 Max Fleisher produced Superman movie cartoons for Paramount
In 1966 Broadway musical *It's A Bird, It's A Plane, It's Superman* with Bob Holiday
On TV cartoon series the voice of Superman is that of Clayton "Bud" Collyer. Played in 1977 movie *Superman* by Christopher Reeve
In the TV series (108 episodes) debut April 15, 1953
    Superman/Clark Kent (George Reeves)
    Lois Lane (Phyllis Coates and Noel Neill)
    Perry White (John Hamilton)
    Jimmy Olsen (Jack Larson)
(See: *Superboy, Metropolis, Kents, Krypton*)
"Faster than a speeding bullet, more powerful than a locomotive, able to leap tall buildings at a single bound, look! Up in the sky! Is it a bird? Is it a plane? It's Superman!!"

Super Mex
Nickname of pro-golfer Lee Trevino

Supersnipe
Secret identity of 8-year-old Koppy McFad (debut October 1942 in comic books). He has the biggest comic book collection in the world

Supreme Governor
Highest position attained in the Loyal Order of Moose Lodge

Supremes
Very successful female singing group for Motown Records in 1960's (beginning in 1957). Original members: Diana Ross, Mary Wilson and Florence Ballard. Cindy Birdsong replaced Ballard (1967). Name of group became Diana Ross and the Supremes, finally Ross departed the group (1970), leaving Mary Wilson, Cindy Birdsong and Jean Terrell (sister of fighter Ernie Terrell)

Surak
Considered to be the Father of Cvilization on the planet Vulcan (TV series "Star Trek")

Surratt, Mary E.
First woman executed by hanging in U.S. (July 7, 1865)

for implication in Lincoln assassination plot, which was said to be formed in her house in Washington, D.C.

Surrender Dorothy

The message that Wicked Witch of the West (Margaret Hamilton) writes in the sky with her broom outside of the City of Oz (1939 movie *The Wizard of Oz*)

Suspects

In the name of "Clue": Colonel Mustard, Miss Scarlett, Mr. Green, Mrs. Peacock, Mrs. White, Professor Plum

Susquehanna Hat Company

Place of business that Eddie Harrington (Lou Costello) and Albert Mansfield (Bud Abbott) are in search of in 1944 movie *In Society*. Every time Eddie asks directions to Bagel Street, the person he asks breaks one of the hats he is to deliver there

Susy

Little blue car (1952 Disney movie cartoon). Her license plate number is 711

Swamp Fox, The

Nickname of General Francis Marion (about 1732-1795), Revolutionary War guerrilla leader in the South

Swaythling Cup

Trophy awarded for the sport of Table Tennis

Swedish Nightingale, The

Nickname of Jenny Lind (1820-1887), opera and concert singer; client of P. T. Barnum in her American tour

Swee' Pea

Popeye's adopted son. On radio he adopted a boy named Matey (see *Popeye*)

Sweet Apple, Ohio

The town where Conrad Birdie (Jesse Pearson) comes for his farewell appearance before being inducted into the U.S. Army (1963 movie *Bye Bye Birdie*)

Sweet Georgia Brown

Theme song of the Harlem Globetrotters basketball team, composed by Ben Bernie

Sweethearts of the West

Billing given to the team of Roy Rogers and Mary Hart (later she called herself Lynne Roberts)

Sweet Polly Purebred

Underdog's girlfriend and news reporter (TV cartoon series): voice of Norma McMillan

Sweety Face
   Wallace Wimple's fat wife (radio's *Fibber McGee and Molly*)

Swiftwater
   Town in which the Calloway Family lives (Walt Disney 1965 movie *Those Calloways*)

Swimming Hall of Fame
   Located at Fort Lauderdale, Florida. Founded in 1965, the first member elected was Johnny Weissmuller

Swordfish
   Password used by both Groucho and Chico to enter a speakeasy located at 42 Elm Street (1932 movie *Horse Feathers*)

Sycamore Springs
   Hometown of Nick Charles (William Powell), 1944 movie *The Thin Man Goes Home*

Sydenstricker
   Pearl S. Buck's middle name (another of her names is Comfort). Winner of 1931 Pulitzer Prize and 1938 Nobel Prize in literature. Her 1954 autobiography is titled *My Several Worlds*

Sylvester
   Professor Marvel's horse (1939 movie *The Wizard of Oz*)

Sylvester Cat (Sylvester P. Pussycat)
   Lisping cat who tries to catch Tweety Pie (Warner Bros. cartoon). Voice of Mel Blanc; "Thuffering Thucatash"

Sylvester, Johnny
   (1926 Essex Falls, N.J.) 11-year-old lad who seemed to have lost his will to live after an operation. Babe Ruth sent him a telegram promising to hit a homerun for him in the next day's World Series game against St. Louis. The next day Ruth hit three home runs. It apparently gave Johnny the inspiration he needed for he went on to recovery

Symbols
   Of the Evangelists: St. Matthew, Angel: St. Mark, Lion: St. Luke, Ox: St. John, Eagle

Syndics of the Cloth Hall, The
   Rembrandt's painting (1661) embossed in lining of Dutch Masters cigar boxes (the man on the far left of the painting was left out of the Dutch Masters reproduction)

T

2

The only even prime number

2:00

Time on clock that Captain Hook throws in the crocodile's mouth in 1952 movie *Peter Pan*

2X

The special vitamin that gave the Blue Beetle his special powers (comic books)

2X2L

Call letters of the last ham radio operator to broadcast message in H. G. Wells' *War of the Worlds* as adapted by Orson Welles on the Mercury Theatre's broadcast of October 30, 1938. "Isn't there anyone on the air? Isn't there anyone . . . 2X2L—"

2 thieves

Crucified with Jesus: Dismas, Gestas, they were tied to the cross, Jesus was nailed

2 Years

Length of time doctors gave Paul Bryan (Ben Gazzara) to live (even though the series lasted 3 years) (TV series "Run for Your Life")

2:45

Time on the clock on building that Harold Lloyd climbs in the 1923 silent movie *Safety Last*. Also the approximate time that Dorothy lands in Munchkinland, on the Mayor's clock (*The Wizard of Oz*)

3 B's

Great composers of classical music:
Bach (Johann Sebastian, 1685-1750);

Beethoven (Ludwig van, 1770 or 1772-1827);
Brahms (Johannes, 1833-1897)

In 1969 movie *Chronicles of Anna Magdalena Bach* was portrayed by Gustav Leonhardt

In 1960 movie *The Magnificent Rebel* Beethoven was portrayed by Carl Boehm

In 1947 movie *Song of Love* Brahms was portrayed by Robert Walker

3 Caballeros, The

Panchito, Jose Carioca, Donald Duck (Walt Disney 1944 cartoon feature movie *Saludos Amigos, The Three Caballeros*). The voices respectively are: Joaquin Garay, Jose Olveira and Clarence Nash

3 cardinal virtues

Faith, Hope, Charity. Compare *7 virtues*

3 Fates

Lachesis (who determined the fate)
Clotho (who spun the thread of life)
Atropos (who cut the thread)

3 Furies

Alecto (the unresting), Megaera (the jealous), Tisiphone (the avenger)

3 Good Fairies

Mistress Flora (wears red, voice of Verna Felton), Mistress Fauna (wears green, voice of Barbara Jo Allen), and Mistress Merryweather (wears blue, voice of Barbara Luddy), who befriend Sleeping Beauty (Walt Disney cartoon feature movie *Sleeping Beauty*, 1958)

3 Graces

Aglaia, Thalia, Euphrosyne: sisters, daughters of Zeus and Eurynome

Three Haircuts

Wig-wearing singing group takeoff on current popular artists. Performed by Sid Caesar, Carl Reiner, and Howard Morris (TV series "Caesar's Hour"). Their favorite song is *You Are So Rare To Me*

3 Hours

Time Wendy, Michael and John spent in Never Never Land with Peter Pan. When they left, Big Ben showed 8; when they returned it showed 11

Three Laws of Robotics

1. A robot may not injure a human being, or, through inaction, allow a human being to come to harm

2. A robot must obey the orders given it by human beings except where such orders conflict with the First Law

3. A robot must protect its own existence as long as such protection does not conflict with the First or Second Law Handbook of Robotics, 56th Edition, 2058 A.D. (Isaac Asimov's novel *I, Robot*)

3 Little Maids
Yum-Yum, Peep-Bo, Pitti-Sing: three schoolgirl sisters, wards of Ko-Ko (Gilbert and Sullivan's operetta *The Mikado*)

Three Little Pigskins
1934 Three Stooges short, co-starring Lucille Ball. The three stooges play football players in game of the Cubs against the Tigers. On their jerseys are these symbols: ½ - Larry, ? - Curly, H_2O_2 - Moe

3 men in a tub
Butcher, Baker, Candlestick Maker (nursery rhyme)

Three Mesquiteers
Republic movie series, based on the books of William Colt MacDonald. Original members of the cowboy trio in the Republic series: Syd Saylor as Lullaby Joslin, Bob Livingston as Stony Brooke, Ray Corrigan as Tucson Smith. Other members: John Wayne, Tom Tyler, Duncan Renaldo (played Cisco Kid), Bob Steele, Raymond Hatton, Rufe Davis, Jimmie Dodd (host of Mickey Mouse Club), Ralph Byrd (played Dick Tracy), Harry Carey, Hoot Gibson, Max Terhune, Guinn Williams

3 Musketeers
Athos, Porthos, Aramis (Alexander Dumas' novel *The Three Musketeers*): D'Artagnan later becomes a member of the group
Movie versions in 1911, 1913, and 1914
1921 movie: Leon Barry, George Siegmann, Eugene Pallette
1936 movie: Walter Abel, Moroni Olsen, Paul Lukas, Onslow Stevens
1939 movie: Don Ameche and the three Ritz Brothers
1948 mvoie: Gene Kelly, Gig Young, Van Heflin, Robert Coote
1973 movie: Oliver Reed, Michael York, Frank Finlay, Richard Chamberlain
In 1956 TV series: Jeffrey Stone, Peter Trent, Paul Campbell

3 Musketeers' motto

"All for one, one for all"

3:00

Time of the clock on Independence Hall; reverse side of the bicentennial 1776-1976 half dollar

3 R's

Elements of learning
Reading, Writing, 'Rithmetic
New Deal program
Relief, Recovery, Reform

3 Stable Mews

London address of John Steed's (Patrick Macnee) apartment (license number of his motor car is YT3942). Steed prefers his tea with 3 lumps of sugar stirred counterclockwise (TV series "The Avengers")

3 Stooges

Originally Ted Healy and His Stooges in the 1920s.
Larry Fine and the brothers Moe and Curly Howard.
Shemp Howard, another brother, replaced Curly Howard in 1947; Joe Besser replaced Shemp Howard in 1955; Joe DeRita (Curly Joe) replaced Joe Besser in 1958. Their first movie was *Soup to Nuts* (1930)

3 Wise Men

Gaspar, Melchior, Balthasar: the "3 kings of Orient" who came to worship the baby Jesus in Bethlehem

3 wise monkeys

Japanese Little Apes of Nikko
Mizaru: See no evil
Mikazaru: Hear no evil
Mazaru: Speak no evil

3-1/3 minutes

How long James Bond likes his eggs boiled (novel series)

3T808

Oklahoma automobile license number of Duke Mantee's (Humphrey Bogart) getaway car (1936 movie *The Petrified Forest*)

3X2(9YZ)4A

Formula spoken by Johnny Chambers to change himself into superhero Johnny Quick (comic book series *Johnny Quick*)

10

B. D.'s football jersey number (comic strip *Doonesbury*)

10

Members on a Lacrosse team

10

Notches found on the pocket watch carried by Pretty Boy Floyd (Charles Arthur Floyd) when shot by the F.B.I. They represented the people he had killed

10

Height in feet of basket ring in basketball; also height of crossbar on goal post in football

10

Number on football jersey worn casually by Mary Tyler Moore (as Mary Richards) (TV series "The Mary Tyler Moore Show")

$10

Reward for Dingus Magee (Frank Sinatra) on wanted posters (1970 movie *Dirty Dingus Magee*)

10-2-4

Numbers on Dr. Pepper bottle, suggest right time for a Dr. Pepper break

Ten Commandments of the Cowboys

Created by Gene Autry:

1. Fair Play
2. Truthfulness
3. Patriotism
4. Respect for Women
5. Respect for Parents
6. Respect for Animals
7. Respect for Old Folks
8. Religious and Racial Tolerance
9. Cleanliness of Thought
10. Cleanliness of Speech

10:00 P.M.

Time at which Taps are blown

10 plagues of Egypt

Water becomes blood
Frogs
Lice
Flies (swarms)
Cattle murrain
Sores (boils)
Hail and fire
Locusts

Darkness
Slaying of Egyptian first-born (Exodus 7-12)

12

Number of pints of blood in the average human body

12

Number of children fathered by Hawaiian detective Charlie Chan

12

Members on a Canadian football team

Twelve Angry Men

Play, later movie by Reginald Rose. First presented on TV series "Studio One," broadcast September 20, 1954. Then made into a movie in 1957. The cast of both as follows (clockwise around table):

Juror	Actor (Studio One)	Actor (Movie)	Occupation
1	Norman Fell	Martin Balsam	High School Coach
2	John Beal	John Fiedler	Bank Clerk
3	Franchot Tone	Lee J. Cobb	Head of a Message Service
4	Walter Abel	E. G. Marshall	Stockbroker
5	Lee Philips	Jack Klugman	Mechanic
6	Bart Burns	Edward Binns	House Painter
7	Paul Hartman	Jack Warden	Salesman
8	Robert Cummings	Henry Fonda	Architect
9	Joseph Sweeney	Joseph Sweeney	Retired
10	Edward Arnold	Ed Begley	Garage Owner
11	George Voskovek	George Voskovek	Watch Maker
12	Will West	Robert Webber	Advertising Executive

12 Apostles

The immediate disciples of Jesus Christ: Peter, James, John, Andrew, Philip, Bartholomew, Matthew, James (son of Alphaeus), Thomas, Simon, Judas Iscariot, Thaddeus (or Judas [Jude] son of James)

12 astrological houses

The House of Life, The House of Fortune and Riches, The House of Brethren, The House of Parents and Relatives, The House of Children, The House of Health, The House of Marriage, The House of Death, The House of Religion, The House of Dignities, The House of Friends and Benefactors, The House of Enemies

12 Days of Christmas

Carol in which "My true love gave to me: a partridge in a pear tree, two turtle doves, three french hens, four calling birds, five golden rings, six geese a-laying, seven swans a-swimming, eight maids a-milking, nine ladies dancing, ten lords a-leaping, eleven pipers piping, twelve drummers drumming"

12 hours

The gestation period of a Tribble (TV series "Star Trek")

12 labors of Hercules

1. The killing of the Nemean lion
2. The killing of the Hydra
3. The killing of the Erymanthian boar
4. The capture of the Cerynean hind (or stag)
5. The killing of the birds of Stymphalus
6. The cleansing of the Augean stables
7. Capturing the Cretan bull
8. Capturing the man-eating horses of Diomedes of Thrace
9. Obtaining the girdle of Hippolyta, Queen of the Amazons
10. Capturing the oxen of Geryon
11. Bringing of Cerberus, the three-headed dog, up from Hades
12. Bringing back the apples of the Hesperides

12th Precinct

New York City Police Department. Manhattan 6th Street Precinct that is the setting for TV series "Barney Miller"

13

A baker's dozen (many bakers still sell 13 to the dozen)
The size of Scarlet O'Hara's waist in Margaret Mitchell's novel *Gone with the Wind* is 13 inches

13

Age of Huckleberry Finn in Mark Twain's novel

13

Number that is a symbol for marijuana (M being the 13th letter of the alphabet). Used by the Hell's Angels Motorcycle Club

13

Universally accepted unlucky number. Few office buildings and hotels have a thirteenth floor, numbering from 12 to 14. Fear of the number 13 is called triskaidekaphobia

13 Dwarfs

Who escort Bilbo Baggins from the Shire to the Lonely Mountains:
Balin (son of Fundin), Bifur, Bofur, Bombur, Dori, Dwa-

lin, Fili Perish (youngest), Gloin, Kili Perish, Nori, Oin, Ori, Thorin Oakenshield

They were accompanied by Gandalf the Wizard (J.R.R. Tolkien's *The Hobbit*)

13 Minutes

Theater box offices barred viewers from entering the theater during the last 13 minutes of the 1961 movie *The Naked Edge*

20 Broad Street

(New York City) Address of the New York Stock Exchange

20 Questions

Quiz game is which panel members were given the initial clue of whether it was animal, vegetable or mineral

20 Years Old

Age Buck Rogers was when he was knocked out from gas in an abandoned mine near Pittsburgh, Pennsylvania, waking up in the year 2430 after 500 years of sleep (comic strip *Buck Rogers*)

21 Beacon Street

Boston address of private eye David Chase (Dennis Morgan) (TV series "21 Beacon Street")

$21.98

Amount unaccountable after the Dalton's raid on two banks in Coffeyville, Kansas, October 5, 1892. The Condon bank lost $20, the First National Bank lost $1.98. The Dalton gang lost all but Emmett

22

Roulette number that Rick Blaine (Humphrey Bogart) has a Bulgarian refugee play twice in a row in order to win enough money for him and his wife to travel to America (1942 movie *Casablanca*)

Number ball lands on rigged roulette wheel causing Hooker (Robert Redford) to lose $3,000 (1973 movie *The Sting*)

22 Wood Avenue

Metropolis home address of Lois Lane (TV series "The Adventures of Superman")

23

Number of station house commanded by Captain Spike Ryerson (James Drury) TV series "Firehouse"

23g Gresham Terrace, W.I.

London apartment address of the Honorable Richard

Rollison (The Toff) and his valet Jolly (John Creasey's *The Toff* detective series)

23rd

Century in which TV series "Star Trek" is set, and 1976 movie/TV series *Logan's Run*

24

Estimated dollar value of beads and trinkets paid for Manhattan Island by Peter Minuit to the Indians in 1626

24 Dock Street

Address of William "Rocky" Sullivan's (James Cagney) apartment building. 1938 movie *Angels with Dirty Faces*. His favorite solicitation was "Hello—what do you hear, what do you say"

24 Maple Drive

Fairview Manor, Connecticut home address of the Banks family (TV series "Father of the Bride")

24 St. Anne's Place

Apartment house address in Greenwich Village, New York of the Norths, Pam and Jerry (radio series *Mr. and Mrs. North*)

24 Sussex Drive

Address of the Prime Minister of Canada

24 Walnut Avenue

Home address of police chief Ramsbottom whose house Officers Laurel and Hardy raid in 1933 short film *Midnight Patrol*

24 years

Added years of pleasure and all knowledge at his command, for which Dr. Johann Faust sold his soul to the devil (*Faust* by Goethe)

25th

Century to which Buck Rogers, a 20th century native, is transported

26

Age at which George Armstrong Custer became a general during the Civil War. Marquis de Lafayette previously became a Major General in George Washington's Army a month prior to his 20th birthday

26

Letters in the English alphabet

26

Number of innings in longest major league baseball

699

game: both starting pitchers, Leon Cadore of the visiting Brooklyn Robins and Joe Oeschger of the Boston Braves, pitched all the way (3 hours, 50 minutes) to a 1 to 1 tie, May 1, 1920; Boston tied the score in the sixth inning and then there were 20½ scoreless innings

26 Bar Ranch
John Wayne's ranch in Arizona

26 miles, 385 yards
Distance from Marathon to Athens: length of Olympic marathon race. The first running (1896) of the race was over a 25-mile course

27
Wives married by the Mormon leader Brigham Young. In the 1940 movie *Brigham Young - Frontiersman* he was portrayed by Dean Jagger

27A Wimpole Street
London house address of Professor Henry Higgins (play by Alan Jay Lerner, movie *My Fair Lady*)

27-QRX
Secret formula swallowed by Roy Lincoln turning him into the Human Bomb (comic books)

27th Precinct
New York City police department precinct featured on TV series "N.Y.P.D."

28
Years spent by Frank Faraday (Dan Dailey) in a Caribbean prison before obtaining his freedom (precisely 28 years, 4 months, 13 days) (TV series "Faraday and Company")

28
Velvet Brown's racing number at the Grand National Steeplechase when she rode The Pie to victory only to be disqualified (1944 movie *National Velvet*)

28 years, 2 months, 19 days
Time that Robinson Crusoe spent on his island. Shipwrecked, September 30, 1659: he left December 19, 1686

30
Pieces of silver Juda Iscariot was paid for betraying Jesus (Matthew 26:15)

30
Number of fences horses jump in the Grand National Steeplechase, at Aintree, England. The horses go around

the track twice, the first time jumping 16 hurdles; the second, 14

30-Foot Bride of Candy Rock, The
Only movie (1959) made by Lou Costello without Bud Abbott. Dorothy Provine plays the 30-foot bride

30th Century
Metropolis setting of the Legion of Super Horses (*D.C. Comics* series)

31 Flavors
Baskin-Robbins Ice Cream. 31, standing for a flavor for each day of the month (actually they have over 450 flavors). Chain founded by Irvine Robbins in 1945

$32.50
Weekly salary that Fred Derry makes as a salesman at Midway Drugs after the war (1946 movie *The Best Years of Our Lives*)

33 hours, 30 minutes, 29.8 seconds
Charles Lindbergh's New York-to-Paris flight time, May 20-21, 1927. On September 1, 1974, a new world's record was set for a New York-to-Paris flight. An SR-71 flew it in 1 hour, 56 minutes with refueling

33 Rue Dunot, Faubourg St. Germain
Paris home address of detective C. Auguste Dupin (created by Edgar Allan Poe)

35 Hillview Drive
East Valley, California home address of the Howard family (TV series "Jimmy Stewart Show")

35 Plus
Helen Trent's age (radio serial) *The Romance of Helen Trent*. "The story of a woman who sets out to prove to herself what so many other women long to prove in their own lives . . . that romance can live on at 35 and beyond"

37
Age of New York born Rick Blaine (Humphrey Bogart) in 1942 movie *Casablanca*

37
Lucas "Cool Hand Luke" Jackson's (Paul Newman's) prison number at the Division of Correction Road Prison 36, where he is one of 50 prisoners (1967 movie *Cool Hand Luke*). He is serving a 2-year sentence for cutting the heads off of parking meters

39

Age Jack Benny claimed for years (actually born 1894 in Waukegan, Ill. on Valentine's Day)

39 Crenshaw Street

Tuckahoe, New York home address of the Findlays and daughter Carol (TV series "Maude")

39 Stone Canyon Way

Bedrock home address of the Fintstones in the 5th Precinct. Family: Fred, Wilma and Pebbles (TV cartoon)

206

Number of bones in the human body

211

(Armed Robbery) Crime in progress announced to Adam-12 by the police dispatcher in the opening scenes of the TV series "Adam-12"

212-A West 87th Street

New York City home address of Ellery Queen, detective

217 Elm Street

Summerfield home of Throckmorton P. Gildersleeve (Willard Waterman) (TV series "The Great Gildersleeve")

219 Primrose Lane

Los Angeles home address of the Smith family (featuring Henry Fonda) (TV series "The Smith Family")

220 yards

Distance of one furlong

221 North Holstead Street

Chicago home address of Luigi Basco (radio/TV series *Life with Luigi*)

221B Baker Street

London address of Sherlock Holmes, with Dr. Watson at various times his roommate and Mrs. Hudson as the housekeeper. Prior to moving there, Holmes lived on Montague Street near the British Museum. Holmes and Watson moved to Baker Street in January 1881. There are 17 steps to their second story flat

222APL

British license plate of John Lennon's psychedelic Rolls Royce

228 Circle Avenue

Ridgemont, New York home address of the Nash family (TV series "Please Don't Eat the Daisies")

237

Weight in pounds of Brad Runyon, radio's *The Fat Man*

250

Age of the High Lama of Shangri-La, Father Perrault (James Hilton's *Lost Horizon*): played in 1937 movie by Sam Jaffe and in 1973 movie by Charles Boyer

258

The first U.S. draft lottery number to be drawn by Secretary of War Newton Baker July 20, 1917

258 GPP

California automobile license number of Matt Helm's (Tony Franciosa) red Thunderbird sports car (TV series "Matt Helm")

263 Princengracht

Address of Amsterdam house in which Anne Frank and 7 others hid from the Nazis for 2 years and a month (1942-1944): *Anne Frank: The Dairy of a Young Girl*. It is now the Anne Frank Museum. Portrayed in the 1959 movie *The Diary of Anne Frank* by Millie Perkins, the Oscar that Shelley Winters won for Best Supporting Actress in the movie was dedicated by her to the museum

275JLH

California license plate hanging on the door to the storeroom of Ed Brown's garage (TV series "Chico and the Man")

303 Oak St.

Home address of Elmer J. Fudd (comic books, cartoons)

307 Marshall Road

Washington, D.C. home address of the Morley family (TV series "The Farmer's Daughter")

310 Elm

Home address of Winnie Woodpecker in town of Puddleberg

312 Maple Drive

Beverly Hills home address of the Burns family on TV series "The Burns and Allen Show." Their next door neighbors, the Mortons, live at 314

313

License number of Donald Duck's car

315 Vinewood

Los Angeles home address of Anthony Blake (Bill Bixby) on TV series "The Magician"

321 Bundy Drive

Sheridan Falls home address of Liz (Lucille Ball) and

George Cooper (Lee Bowman, Richard Denning) radio series *My Favorite Husband*

328 Chauncey Street
Bensonhurst, Brooklyn address of the apartment house where the Kramdens and Nortons live (TV series "The Honeymooners")

331
U.S. Military R.R. train engine that pulled President Abraham Lincoln's funeral train. It traveled from Washington, D.C. to Springfield Illinois, so slowly that the trip took two weeks. The armorplated car was built especially for the President but never used until it became a part of the funeral train

332 W. 64th Street
Apartment building address of both Rhoda and her sister Brenda (TV series "Rhoda")

335
School that Henry attends (cartoon *Henry* by John Liney)

336
Dimples on a golf ball

336 North Camden Drive
Home address of Jack Benny and Rochester's house (radio series *The Jack Benny Program*)

340
Number of lights in Cullan Hall, West Point. A piece of trivia that all plebes are expected to remember when questioned by upper classmen

343 Brockner Street
Woodland Hills, Fernwood, Ohio home address of Mary and Tom Hartman (TV series "Mary Hartman, Mary Hartman")

344 West 78th Street
New York City address of Ann Marie (Marlo Thomas), apartment 4D (TV series "That Girl")

345 Laurel Drive
Home address in Los Angeles of Joan (Joan Davis) and Judge Bradley J. Stevens (Jim Backus) (TV series "I Married Joan")

345 Stone Cave Road
Barney Rubble's home address (TV series "The Flintstones")

348

License number of Andy Gump's car (comic strip *The Gumps*)

348 Temple Drive

Home address of Elwood P. Dowd, his sister Veta and his Pooka, Harvey. Mary Chase's novel/movie *Harvey*

351 Ellis Park Road

Los Angeles city address of private eye Peter Gunn (Craig Stevens), TV series "Peter Gunn"

738 North State Street

Chicago address of gangster Dion O'Banion's flower shop where he was murdered in November 10, 1924 by Al Capone's gang. His funeral had $50,000 worth of flowers

1038-5th Ave.

New York City home address of Weston Liggett (Laurence Harvey) in 1960 *Butterfield 8*

1049 Park Avenue

New York City (apartment 1102) home of Felix Ungar and Oscar Madison (TV series "The Odd Couple")

$1200

Money Bob Hope owes the Soviet Union (1963 autobiographical novel *I Owe Russia $1200*)

1200 Glenview Road

Los Angeles home address of the Robinson family (1967 movie *The Graduate*)

1313

Los Angeles Yellow Cab driven by Augustus "Red" Perdy (Red Skelton). Cab phone number is MAdison 1234 (1950 movie *The Yellow Cab Man*)

1313 Blueview Terrace

Chester A. Riley's Los Angeles address ("Life of Riley")

1313 Harbor Blvd.

Anaheim, California address of Disneyland

1313 Mockingbird Lane

Home address of the Munsters (TV series "The Munsters")

1313-13th Street

Sad Sack's civilian home address (comic books)

$2000

Rent for Boardwalk with a Hotel (£2000 in British version) (Game board *Monopoly*)

2000 A.D.

Setting of Edward Bellamy's (actor Ralph Rexford Bellamy is one of his descendants) novel *Looking Backward* recalling back to 1887 when the book was written

2000 Ridgeway Avenue

Home address of David Starsky (Paul Michael Glaser), TV series "Starsky & Hutch"

2001

:A Space Odyssey

Most striking part of musical score was part of Richard Strauss' *Thus Sprach Zarathustra*

2,130

Consecutive baseball games played by New York Yankees' Lou Gehrig (began June 1, 1925, until May 2, 1939): he replaced Wally Pipp and was replaced by Babe Dahlgren. Mickey (James B.) Vernon holds the AL record for most games played at first base, 2227

2133 A.D.

Setting of Gene Roddenberry's 1973 TV movie *Genesis II*

2149

Setting of TV series "Captain Video" (22nd Century). Last two digits corresponded with show's year of showing

2149 = 1949

2150 = 1950

2150

Officer Dan Matthew's (Broderick Crawford) unit number (TV series "Highway Patrol")

2355

Year in which TV series "Tom Corbett, Space Cadet" is set. The last two numbers correspond with the year of the series being shown, i.e.

2355 = 1955

2356 = 1956

2,357

Number of pies used in the eight days of shooting for the Pie Throwing scene in Blake Edwards 1965 movie *The Great Race* (biggest pie throwing scene on film). The movie *Dr. Strangelove* had a large pie-throwing scene in the war room but was edited out of final print

2430

Year in which Buck Rogers, World War I pilot, awoke after 500 years of suspended animation (comic strip/ books, radio series *Buck Rogers in the 25th Century*, 1939 movie serial; all drawn from Philip Nowlan's 1928 novel *Armageddon 2419 A.D.*). In the novel Anthony

Rogers falls asleep in the year 1927 at age 29 and awakens in the year 2419 being in a state of suspended animation for almost 500 years

3600 Prospect Street

Georgetown, Washington, D.C., ivory-covered brick town-house home of Regan MacNeil (Linda Blair) in 1973 movie *The Exorcist*

3955

Year the U.S. astronauts return to Earth to find the planet ruled by intelligent apes (*Planet of the Apes* movie series)

20,000

Number of pounds bet by Phileas Fogg that he could go "Around the World in 80 Days"

20500

Zip Code of the White House

29,028

Elevation of Mt. Everest above sea level

33298

James Riddle Hoffa's prisoner number while he spent time at Lewisburg, Pa. in 1967. He was later pardoned by Richard Nixon

246772

Navy service serial number of Lt. Kenneth Braden (James Garner) in 1959 movie *Up Periscope* on board the submarine *U.S.S. Barracuda*

381-813

Montag's (Oskar Werner) identification with the 451 (fire department that burns books) in 1966 movie *Fahrenheit 451*

232-0799

Harry Orwell's (David Janssen) phone number (TV pilot movie "Harry O")

362-0224

Ex-Police Chief Robert T. Ironside's telephone number at his office

234-0-567

Social Security number never issued to anyone because of the song *I'm In Love With 234-0-567* written by Hillie Bell and Willard Egloff

$10,000,000

Price United States paid Mexico in the Gadsden Purchase. 45,535 sq. mi. (1853)

$25,000,000

United States paid Denmark for the Danish Virgin Islands, 1917

202-456-1414

Phone number of the White House

T

Middle initial of Agent James West (Robert Conrad) (TV series "Wild Wild West") and of Captain James Kirk (William Shatner) (TV series "Star Trek")

T-5678

License plate number of the tiny fire engine ridden by the Texaco Fire Chief himself, Ed Wynn (1933 film *The Chief*)

TBI

Initials on Kodak cameras: T=time; B=bulb; I=instantaneous

T.C.

Top Cat (cartoon character), voice of Arnold Stang

T.H.E. Cat

Thomas Hewett Edward Cat (TV series): starred Robert Loggia

T-M Bar Ranch

Tom Mix's ranch, located in Dobie Township (radio series)

TNT

Trinitrotoluene, explosive chemical

T-N-T (Taylor and Turner), publicity for the Robert Taylor and Lana Turner 1941 movie *Johnny Eager*

TOE

Tony, Oscar and Emmy winners:

Jack Albertson, Paul Scofield, Melvyn Douglas, Thomas Mitchell, Ingrid Bergman, Shirley Booth, Helen Hayes, and Liza Minnelli

TRASH 3

License number of the El Paso city garbage truck in which Carter "Doc" McCoy (Steve McQueen) and Carol McCoy (Ali McGraw) are trapped (1973 movie *The Getaway*)

T.S.O.P.

Instrumental hit song that was a version of the theme song of TV series "Soul Train." T.S.O.P. = The Sound of Philadelphia. Recorded by M.F.S.B. = Mothers, Fathers, Sisters, Brothers (a studio group)

TU-144

First supersonic transport (SST) to fly (Russian-built)

TW3

Nickname for TV series (1964-1965) "That Was The Week That Was" featuring Nancy Ames

TWA

Transcontinental & Western Airways known during 1930's as the Lindbergh Line because of Charles Lindbergh's investment in the company. Howard Hughes later gained control of the airlines, 1936. Later renamed Trans World Airlines

Tabard Inn, The

Inn in Geoffrey Chaucer's *Canterbury Tales* where the pilgrims begin and end their journey: Harry Baillie, the host, joins the pilgrims for their good company. Journey began April 3, 1387

Tabitha

Samantha and Darrin Stephen's little witch daughter (TV series "Bewitched"): played by Erin and Diane Murphy (twins). On 1977 TV series Tabitha as a grownup played by Lisa Hartman

Tackhammer

Woody Woodpecker's dog foe (comic books)

Taffy Trumbull

Emmy Lou's best girlfriend (cartoon)

Taft Hotel

Los Angeles hotel where Benjamin Braddock (Dustin Hoffman) and Mrs. Robinson (Anne Bancroft) carry on their affair. On the first meeting, Benjamin signs the register *Mr. Gladstone* and is given room 568 (1967 movie *The Graduate*)

Taft, William Howard

First U.S. President to throw out the baseball to open the baseball season (April 14, 1910, Philadelphia at Washington). Walter Johnson won the game by pitching a one hitter. Johnson pitched a total of 14 opening day games, each time having the President autograph a baseball
Appearing in a baseball game in Washington, Taft stood up to stretch in the seventh inning, thus creating a tradition. Taft was the heaviest U.S. President, weighing between 300 to 340 pounds. He became a Supreme Court Justice after being President

Tagg

Annie Oakley's younger brother ("Annie Oakley" TV series played by Jimmy Hawkins)

Taia

Ibis the Invincible's girlfriend (comic strips)

Tailspin Tommy

(Tommy Tompkins) 1930's comic strip and book hero created by Glenn Chaffin, artist Hal Forest (1929)

In movie series played by Maurice Murphy, Clark Williams and John Trent

Taliaferro

Booker T. Washington's middle name (pronounced Tolliver). He was the first Black to have his portrait on a U.S. postage stamp (10 cent stamp in 1940)

Talmadge Sisters

Norma (1897-1957), Constance (born 1898), Natalie (1899-1969). Norma was the first actor to leave a mark in the cement outside Grauman's Chinese Theater when, in 1927, she stumbled accidentally onto a freshly laid sidewalk; press-agentry soon made it a distinction and a tradition. Natalie married Buster Keaton

Tamba

Ape in "Jungle Jim" movie series/TV series: played by Peggy

Tammany

Tiger who lives with Pogo in the Okefenokee Swamps (comic strip *Pogo*)

Tana leaves

Substance which rejuvenated Kharis (*The Mummy* played by Tom Tyler). Three leaves brought him back to life, nine leaves gave him movement (*The Mummy's Hand,* 1940)

Tang, U.S.S.

U.S. submarine that sank itself with its own torpedo, October 1944 (nine crew members survived to tell the tale)

Tango

Captain Christopher Pike's horse in his youth (TV's "Star Trek")

Tania

Name that Patricia Hearst began calling herself after supposedly joining the SLA (Symbionese Liberation Army)

Tank Tinker

Hop Harrigan's mechanic (radio series/movies). Radio: Kenny Lynch, Jackson Beck; movies: Summer Getchell

Tantor

Elephant friend of Tarzan

Taos

New Mexico town from which Marshal Sam McCloud (Dennis Weaver) lived prior to moving to New York City (TV's "McCloud")

Tara

Scarlet O'Hara's Georgia plantation (Tara Hall) in Margaret Mitchell's *Gone with the Wind*. The home has 4 rectangular columns in front. The name "Tara" comes from the ballad by Sir Thomas More (Mitchell's working name was Fontenoy Hall). *Tara's Theme* is the recurring theme song throughout the 1939 movie

Taratupa

South Pacific island where McHale and his crew is stationed (TV series "McHale's Navy")

Target

Annie Oakley's horse (TV series)

Tarleton twins

Stuart (Fred Crane) and Brent (Grorge Reeves): 1939 movie *Gone With the Wind*

Tarots

22-card deck (larger deck has 56 additional cards in 4 suits):

I	The juggler	XII	The hanging man
II	The high priestess (Popess)	XIII	Death (often unlabeled
III	The empress	XIV	Temperance
IV	The emperor	XV	The devil
V	The hierophant (Pope)	XVI	Lightning (The tower)
		XVII	The stars
VI	The lovers	XVIII	The moon
VII	The chariot	XIX	The sun
VIII	Justice	XX	Judgment
IX	The hermit	XXI	The world
X	Fortune (the wheel of)	XXII	The fool (often unnumbered
XI	Strength		

Tarzan

Fictional jungle hero (Lord of the Jungle) created (1914) by Edgar Rice Burroughs in *Tarzan of the Apes:* next to Sherlock Holmes as the most widely known character in fiction in English comic strip by Harold Foster, begun January 7, 1929 (Buck Rogers debuted the same day) and continued by Rex Maxon, Burne Hogarth and others; one of the first strips to tell a consecutive adventure story and one of the first to appear in modern comic books. Jungle identity of Tarzan is John Clayton (Lord Greystoke). Tarzan means "White Skin" in ape language. Tarzan was born November 22, 1888. First story appeared in *All Story* magazine October 1912 (bought for $700)

Novels: *Tarzan of the Apes*
The Return of Tarzan
The Beasts of Tarzan
The Son of Tarzan
Tarzan and the Jewels of Opar
Jungle Tales of Tarzan
Tarzan the Untamed
Tarzan the Terrible
Tarzan and the Golden Lion
Tarzan and the Ant Men
The Tarzan Twins (juvenile)
Tarzan, Lord of the Jungle
Tarzan and the Lost Empire
Tarzan at the Earth's Core
Tarzan the Invincible
Tarzan Triumphant
Tarzan and the City of Gold
Tarzan and the Lion Man
Tarzan and the Leopard Men
Tarzan's Quest
Tarzan and the Forbidden City
Tarzan the Magnificent
Tarzan and the Foreign Legion
Tarzan and the Tarzan Twins (juvenile)
Tarzan and the Madman
Tarzan and the Castaways

Tarzan and the Valley of Gold by Fritz Leiber (only non-Burroughs authored Tarzan novel authorized)

In the movies, played by:

Elmo Lincoln (silents)
Gene Polar (silents)
P. Dempsey Tabler (silents)
James Pierce (silents)
Frank Merrill (silents
Johnny Weissmuller
Herman Brix (Bruce Bennett)
Buster Crabbe
Glenn Morris
Lex Barker
Gordon Scott
Denny Miller
Jock Mahoney
Mike Henry
Ron Ely (TV), debut NBC September 8, 1966
Charlie Chase (1932 comedy)
Unauthorized:
Peng Fei (Chinese), 1940
Joe Robinson (Italian), 1963
Vladimir Korenev (Russian), 1963
Don Bragg, 1964 (Olympic medal winner)
Darasingh (India), 1963-1965
Ralph Hudson (Italian), 1964

Clint Walker in 1954 Bowery Boys movie *Jungle Gents*. On radio played by James Pierce (his wife Joan Burroughs, also daughter of Edgar Rice Burroughs, played Jane), Carlton Kardell, Lamont Johnson. In 1921 Broadway play *Tarzan of the Apes* Ronald Adair played Tarzan, Greta Kemble Cooper played Jane

In the first Tarzan movie, *Tarzan of the Apes* (1918), 10-year-old Gordon Griffith played Tarzan as a boy, thus becoming the first person to play Tarzan in the movies. In the same movie Elmo Lincoln (Otto Elmo Linkenhelt) played Tarzan as an adult. Winslow Wilson was first chosen to play Emo Lincoln's role but he joined the Army when World War I broke out instead.

In 1938 Lou Gehrig turned down the offer to play Tarzan. In the 1960 movie *Tarzan the Magnificent* starring Gordon Scott as Tarzan, a future Tarzan appeared, Jock Mahoney. In the 1942 movie *Tarzan's New York Adventure* starring Johnny Weissmuller as Tarzan, Elmo Lincoln appears in the film as a roustabout

Four Tarzans have won Olympic medals: Johnny Weiss-

muller, Herman Brix, Buster Crabbe and Glenn Morris
The first Tarzan to give the Tarzan yell was Frank Merrill.
Johnny Weismuller's Tarzan yell was the combination of a
violin G-string, a hyena's howl, a dog's growl, a camel's
bleat, all combined together. Ron Ely used the same yell
on TV. Giving the Tarzan yell became a regular gag
routine by Carol Burnet on TV

Tarzan
Ken Maynard's horse (movies). Ken Maynard was the
movies' first singing cowboy. Singing in the 1930 movie
Songs of the Saddle

Tasmanian Devil
Speedy little monster that travels in cyclonic motions. He
loves to eat rabbits, thus causing trepidation for Bugs
Bunny; voice of Mel Blanc. Debut: *Devil May Hare*
(1953) (Warner Brothers cartoons)

Tate
College where events occur in 1947 MGM musical *Good
News*

Tatooine
Home planet (two moons) of Luke Skywalker (Mark
Hamill), 1977 movie *Star Wars*

Tattoos
Of James Bond (they are actual tattoos on the right wrist
of actor Sean Connery); "Mum and Dad" and "Scotland
Forever"
In *Peter Pan*, the tattoo on Smee's chest reads "Mother,"
in a heart

Taxi Boys, The
Ben Blue and Billy Gilbert (comedy team in movie shorts)

Taylor, Elizabeth Rosemond
English-born American actress in movies: Academy
Awards as best actress for Gloria Wandrous in *Butter-
field 8* (1960) and Martha in *Who's Afraid of Virginia
Woolf?* (1966)
Her husbands: Conrad Hilton, Jr., 1949-1951; Michael
Wilding, 1952-1957; Michael Todd, 1957-1958; Eddie
Fisher, 1959-1964; Richard Burton, 1964-1974; Richard
Burton, 1975; John Warner, 1976-
She married both Wilding and Todd on February 21
John Warner is the former Secretary of the Navy

714

Taylor-Burton movies

Elizabeth Taylor and Richard Burton appeared together in:

Cleopatra (1963)
The V.I.P.s (1963)
The Sandpiper (1965)
Who's Afraid of Virginia Woolf? (1966)
The Comedians (1967)
The Taming of the Shrew (1967)
Boom! (1968)
Dr. Faustus (1968)
Under Milkwood (1971)
Hammersmith Is Out (1972)
Divorce His; Divorce Hers (1973)

Elizabeth Taylor made a non-billed cameo appearance as a reveler in 1969 movie *Anne of the Thousand Days* in which Richard Burton starred

T. Banacek Restorations

Sign on the door of Thomas Banacek's brick mansion on Beacon Hill in Boston (TV series "Banacek")

Tea Cup

Trophy awarded to the winner of the annual Clemson-South Carolina football game

Teachers

Socrates taught Plato
Plato taught Aristotle
Aristotle taught Alexander the Great

Teakettle, U.S.S.

Patrol craft (PC1168) featured in 1951 movie *You're in the Navy Now*. Both Charles Bronson's and Lee Marvin's film debut

Team of horses

In the 1939 movie *Stagecoach* two teams of horses were used to pull the Overland Stage
The six horses in the first team were: Bessie, Bonnie, Blackie, Bill, Queenie, Sweetheart
Only the names of four horses are mentioned in the second team: Bridesmaid, Baby, Honey Chile, Sweetheart (again)

Teapot Dome

Navy oil reserve in Wyoming: Harding's Secretary of the Interior Albert B. Fall was found guilty (1929) of having been bribed to grant oil leases to private individuals

Tecumseh
 Annapolis Academy's God of 2.5 (2.5 being the passing grade)

Teddy
 Mack Sennett's Great Dane dog, trained to do tricks in Sennett comedies

Teddy Bear, The
 Cuddly toy bear named after President Theodore Roosevelt, created by Morris Michton in 1902. The original bear is now in the Smithsonian

Teddy Bear Picnic, The
 Theme song of radio series "Big Jon and Sparkie"

Teela
 Gunga Ram's (Nino Marcel) elephant (TV series "Andy's Gang")

Teen Titans
 Group of Super Heroes:
 Robin, Aqualad, Wonder Girl, Kid Flash, Speedy (comic books)

Teenie
 Paul Bunyan's daughter

Teeth
 Human (32 teeth):
  Incisors: 8
  Cuspids (canines): 4
  Bicuspids (premolars): 8
  Molars: 12

Tehani
 Tahitian girl in love with Fletcher Christian (Clark Gable). Played in 1935 version of *Mutiny on the Bounty* by Movita (Maria Castenada) who became Marlon Brando's second wife. Brando played Fletcher Christian in the 1962 version of *Mutiny on the Bounty*

Telemachus
 Son of Odysseus and Penelope (Homer's *Odyssey*): he helped his father kill Penelope's suitors

Telstar I
 First U.S. communications satellite (A.T.&T. Co.) to amplify radio and TV signals (launched July 10, 1962)

Temple, Shirley
 Youngest person to be listed in *Who's Who*. Her two stand-ins as a child actress were: Marilyn Granas and

Mary Lou Isleib. Once married to actor John Agar. Shirley Temple Black later became U.S. Ambassador to Ghana

Templemer City
Captain Nemo's underwater city in the 1969 movie *Captain Nemo and the Underwater City*

Tenafly
Harry Tenafly, black detective (TV series "Tenafly"): played by James McEachin

Tenderfoot
A beginning Boy Scout prior to being sworn in as a full-fledged Scout

Tenderly
Theme song of Jackie Gleason's Pool Soul Character TV series *The Jackie Gleason Show*

Ten Little Indians
Title of 1939 Agatha Christie novel *And Then There Were None* (originally titled *Ten Little Niggers*); also called *The Nursery Rhyme Murders*. In movies: *And Then There Were None* (1945); *Ten Little Indians* (1966); *Ten Little Indians* (1975)

Tennessee Plowboy, The
Nickname of country singer Eddy Arnold

Tennessee Tuxedo
Penguin who lives with his sidekick Chumley, a walrus, at the Megopolis Zoo. Don Adams is Tennessee's voice (TV cartoon series *Tennessee Tuxedo and His Tales*)

Tennessee Waltz
Ballad recorded by Cowboy Copas in 1950 and Patti Page in 1951 (top record in 1951). The song was originally offered to, but turned down by, Frank Sinatra. Became the official song of the state of Tennessee (since 1965)

Tennis Big Four (Grand Slam)
Championship tournaments:
Australian Open
French Open
Wimbledon (English)
Forest Hills (U.S.)

Tennis Hall of Fame
Located at Newport, Rhode Island

Teresa (Tracy) Draco
James Bond's wife for a brief time (1½ hours) (Ian Fleming's novel *On Her Majesty's Secret Service*). 1962 movie Teresa played by Diana Rigg

Terhune, Max

One of the Three Mesquiteers. His sidekick was the dummy Elmer Sneezeweed

Terra V

Commander Buzz Corey's spaceship. He had Terra I through IV shot out from under him (TV series "Space Patrol")

Terrified Typist, The Case of the

Only case Perry Mason ever lost in court: after the guilty verdict, Attorney Mason convinced Judge Hartley that a retrial was in order, since there were two Duane Jeffersons, one his client and the other the accused

Terrytown

Mighty Mouse's hometown (cartoons/comic series)

Teterboro Airport

New Jersey control tower that Arthur Godfrey buzzed in his DC 3 in January 1954. His license was suspended over this incident

Terry Lee

Hero of Milt Caniff's comic strip *Terry and the Pirates:* he was the young sidekick of Pat Ryan (name originally suggested for Terry was Tommy Tucker). Comic strip debuted October 22, 1934. On radio, Terry Lee played by Jackie Kelk, Cliff Carpenter, Owen Jordon. In 1940 movie serial played by William Tracy

Tess Trueheart

Dick Tracy's wife. In comic strips Tess was Tracy's fiancee for 18 years. Tired of waiting, she married a wealthy ex-baseball player, Edward Nuremoh (homerun spelled backwards) in 1939. The marriage only lasted one day as he committed suicide. Tess played: on radio by Helen Lewis, in movies by Anne Gwyne

Texas, The

Confederate locomotive that chased the stolen locomotive "The General" in the Great Locomotive Chase of the Civil War (April 12, 1862). The Texas raced backwards, driven by Captain William A. Fuller, the engineer of the General (portrayed by Jeff Hunter in 1956 Disney movie *The Great Locomotive Chase*)

Texas Theatre

Dallas movie house in which Lee Harvey Oswald was captured November 22, 1963. The movies playing were *Cry of Battle* and *War is Hell*

Thaddeus B. Sivana, Jr.
The World's Wickedest Boy (comic books)

Thalia Menninger
Cute, blonde girl (played by Tuesday Weld) whom Dobie Gillis (Dwayne Hickman) chased after in TV series "The Many Loves of Dobie Gillis"

Thanks for the Memory
Bob Hope's theme song, sung with Shirley Ross in the 1938 movie *The Big Broadcast* aboard the ship *S.S. Art Deco*. The song won an Oscar

"Thanks, King"
Jim Thorpe's reply to Sweden's King Gustav V's statement after the 1912 Olympic Games in which the King said, *"You, sir, are the greatest athlete in the world"*

The Answer
Harry Orwell's boat
TV series starring David Janssen, "Harry O"

The Buck Stops Here
Sign on President Truman's desk, now used by President Carter

Theodore
Hamm's Beer's bear (cartoon)

Theodore Horstmann
$200-a-week, 135-pound orchid nurse employed by detective *Nero Wolfe*

There's One Born Every Minute
Elizabeth Taylor's first movie appearance, 1942, age 10 years. Carl "Alfalfa" Switzer appeared in the film

"The Rain in Spain Stays Mainly in the Plain"
Phrase that phonetics expert Professor Higgins teaches Eliza Doolittle to say in order to rid her of her cockney accent (play/movie *My Fair Lady*)

There She Is
Theme song of the annual Miss America Pageant

"There's No Place Like Home"
Phrase Dorothy repeats as she clicks the heels of her Ruby Slippers together three times in order to return to Kansas (1939 movie *The Wizard of Oz*)

"The Stuff that Dreams are made of"
Sam Spade's (Humphrey Bogart) reply to Detective Tom Polhaus (Ward Bond) when asked, "What is it?" referring to the Maltese Falcon. It is the last line of the 1941 movie *The Maltese Falcon*. Very similar to the line in

719

Shakespeare's *The Tempest*. "We are such stuff as dreams are made on"

They All Kissed the Bride
Movie Carole Lombard was to make when she was killed in an aircraft accident. Joan Crawford took the role, giving her salary to the Red Cross and other charities

They Only Kill Their Masters
Last movie made (1972) on the MGM lot

Thimble Theatre
Original comic strip (beginning 1919) by E. C. Segar (Elzie Crisler Segar) that featured Olive Oyl, Castor Oyl, Popeye, Alice the Goon, Blozo, Eugene the Jeep, Poopdeck Pappy, Sea Hag, Swee' Pea, Toar, Wimpy, George W. Geezil, Pooky Jones, Bluto, Harold Ham Gravy (debut comic strip December 7, 1919)

Thin Man, The
Novel (1932) by Dashiell Hammett (the Thin Man was the victim, Clyde Miller Wynant, an inventor). In the 1934 movie *The Thin Man* Clyde Wynant was played by Edward Ellis, therefore Edward Ellis played the Thin Man in the 1934 movie *The Thin Man*, not William Powell
On radio and TV it was the title of a series about the adventures of Nick and Nora Charles (Charalambides), inadvertent mystery-solvers
On radio Nick Charles was played by Lester Damon, Les Tremayne, Joseph Curtin, and David Gothard and Bill Smith; Claudia Morgan was Nora
In movies Nick and Nora were played by William Powell and Myrna Loy (1937-1946); Nick Jr. played by Dickie Hall and Dean Stockwell. In 1975 TV movie *Nick and Nora Charles* played by Craig Stevens and JoAnn Pflug
On TV they were played by Peter Lawford and Phyllis Kirk

Thin Man Movies
Starring William Powell and Myrna Loy:
The Thin Man (1934), *After the Thin Man* (1936), *Another Thin Man* (1939), *Shadow of the Thin Man* (1941), *The Thin Man Goes Home* (1944), *Song of the Thin Man* (1947), and 1975 TV movie *Nick and Nora* starring Craig Stevens and JoAnn Pflug

Thing

Living hand belonging to the Addams family (TV series "The Addams Family")

Thing, The

Member of the Fantastic Four crime-fighting team. His real identity is that of Ben Grimm (like Mickey Mouse, he has only 4 fingers). His blind girlfriend is Alicia Masters (comic books)

Thing, The

Volkswagen model that is designed for rough roads and fun

Thing, The

Song recorded in 1950 by Phil Harris. The identity of The Thing was never revealed

Thing, The

Eight-foot carrot-like alien plant played by James Arness (brother of Peter Graves) in the 1951 movie *The Thing* (from science-fiction story "Who Goes There?" by John W. Campbell, writing as Don A. Stuart). The Thing has green blood

Think

Motto of IBM (International Business Machines)

Thinker, The

"Le Penseur" statue created by Rodin, intended to have been Dante. When Dobie Gillis wants to contemplate, he sits under this statue and asks the TV audience, "Now I ask you . . . (TV series "The Many Loves of Dobie Gillis")

Thinking Machine

Professor Augustus S. F. X. Van Dusen, Ph.D., LLD, F.R.S., M.D., M.D.S., detective created by Jacques Futrelle. He wears a size 8 hat. Martha is his housekeeper. His best friend is Hutchinson Hatch, a newspaper reporter for the *Daily American*

Thinking of You

Theme song of Kay Kyser's orchestra (Kay Kyser, born James King Kern Kyser, was once a football coach at the junior high school at Rocky Mount, North Carolina)

This Could Be The Start of Something Big

Steve Allen's theme song, which he wrote

This Is It

Bugs Bunny's theme song (TV cartoon)

This Is It

Theme song of comedy radio series *The Aldrich Family*

This Old Man

Children's marching song (sung by Chinese children in the 1958 movie *Inn of the Sixth Happiness*)

"This old man he played (—),
He played nick-nack on my (—)":

one . . . drum	six . . . sticks
two . . . shoe	seven . . . oven
three . . . tree	eight . . . gate
four . . . door	nine . . . line
five . . . hive	ten . . . hen

Thomas, Lowell

News commentator, narrator of Fox's Movietone News, narrator of "This is Cinerama," first Cinerama movie which debuted September 30, 1952 at the Broadway Theatre, in New York City

Thomas Cup

Trophy awarded for the sport of badminton

Thomas Howard

Assumed name taken by Jesse James when he was with his wife and children. His brother Frank went under the alias of B. J. Woodson. They were also nicknamed in their youth Dingus and Buck respectively

Thompson

Ernie's (played by Barry Livingston) last name prior to him being adopted by the Douglas family on TV series "My Three Sons"

Thomson, Bobby

New York Giants' third baseman, known as the Flying Scot (born in Glascow, Scotland), wearing No. 23, who hit a three-run home run off pitcher Ralph Branca, wearing No. 13, in the last half of the ninth inning of the third playoff game (October 3) at the Polo Grounds to win the 1951 National League pennant. Final score of the game: New York Giants, 5; Brooklyn Dodgers, 4

Branca had just relieved Don Newcombe* after Alvin Dark singled and Don Mueller did the same, sending Dark to third, and then Monte Irvin popped out, Whitey

---

*Don Newcombe was the first winner of the Cy Young Award in 1956

Lockman doubled, scoring Dark and sending Mueller to third. Mueller hurt his leg sliding into third and Clint Hartung came in to run for him. Rather than give Thomson an international walk (rookie Willie Mays was in the on-deck circle), Manager Charlie Dressen ordered Branca to pitch to Thomson, who hit the second pitch over the left-field fence. Larry Jansen, who had relieved Sal Maglie in the 8th inning, was the winning pitcher. Called the "shot heard around the world" and the "little miracle at Coogans Bluff," sportscaster Russ Hodges made his famous outburst "The Giants have won the pennant, the Giants have won the Pennant, the Giants have won the pennant, the Giants have won the pennant." That same evening Bobby Thomson appeared on Perry Como's TV show

Thor

Pet dog of Manhunter (comic books)

Thorny (Mr. Thornberry)

Ozzie and Harriet's neighbor (radio and TV): on radio played by John Brown, TV by Don DeFore

Thorpe, Jim (James Francis Thorpe)

American Indian (Sac and Fox) athlete (1888-1953—Indian name: Bright Path—won both the pentathlon (4 firsts) and the decathlon (8412.96 points out of possible 10,000) in the 1912 Stockholm Olympics. Forced to return prizes in 1913 when his history of having played baseball for money was discovered; Olympic records expunged. The teams were Rocky Mount and Fayetteville of the Eastern Carolina League, where he played in 1909-1910

Voted (1950) greatest athlete and football player of first half of 20th Century

Played football under Glenn "Pop" Warner at Carlisle Indian School, helping beat Harvard and Army

Professional football for Canton Bulldogs and baseball for the New York Giants, Cincinnati Reds, and Boston Braves

At the 1912 Olympics, King Gustavus of Sweden presented his trophy saying, "You, sir, are the greatest athlete in the world." Thorpe replied, "Thanks, King." He had a twin brother (Charles) who died in his youth. Dwight Eisenhower wrenched his knee during a football game at West Point while trying to tackle Thorpe

Jim Thorpe was the first member elected to the Pro Football Hall of Fame (1963)

In the 1951 movie *Jim Thorpe—All American* Thorpe was portrayed by Burt Lancaster. Jim Thorpe played a prisoner in the 1949 movie *White Heat*, played a Navajo Indian in the 1944 movie *Cheyenne Autumn* and the Captain of the guards in the 1935 movie *She*

Those Were the Days

Opening theme of TV series "All in the Family" (closing theme "Remembering You"). Sung by Carroll O'Connor and Jean Stapleton. *Those Were the Days* was re-recorded in 1975 season so that the words could be better understood

Three Blind Mice

Theme song of the Three Stooges comedy team

Three Faces of Eve

Her real name was Chris Sizemore. Three distinct personalities manifested in one person (from true accounts documented by Doctors Thigpen and Cleckley): Eve White, Eve Black, Jane (1957 movie made of this story featured Joanne Woodward as Eve in an Oscar-winning performance). Eventually 22 different personalities would emerge. Ironically, Joanne Woodward would play the psychiatrist to a girl with 16 different personalities in the 1976 TV movie *Sybil*. Sally Field portrayed Sybil

Three Little Pigs

1932-33 Oscar-winning short cartoon by Walt Disney: the houses of the 3 pigs (huffed and puffed by the Big Bad Wolf) were made of straw, sticks, bricks. The story comes from an English fairy tale traced by Joseph Jacobs to one of the Grimms' tales. The song *Who's Afraid of the Big Bad Wolf* was written by Frank Church in only five minutes

Three Little Words

Theme song of radio's *Double or Nothing*

Three Oaks Medical Center

Hospital where Dr. Jerry Malone worked (radio series *Young Dr. Malone*)

Three Soldiers

Dan Fuselli, Chrisfield, John Andrews (novel by John Dos Passos, 1921). John Dos Passos died the same day as Gamal Abd-Al Nasser of Egypt, Sept. 28, 1970

Three Stars (Will Shine Tonight)

Theme song of TV series "Dr. Kildare"; recorded by Richard Chamberlain

Thresher and Scorpion

U.S. nuclear submarines lost at sea:

Thresher, April 10, 1963 (#593)

Scorpion, May 21, 1968

Throckmorton P.

First name and middle initial of The Great Gildersleeve, a character played on radio by Hal Peary (real name: Harold Jose Pereira de Faria) and Willard Waterman: (they both played Sheriff Mike Shaw on radio's *Tom Mix Show*) originally on "Fibber McGee and Molly" (where he owned the Gildersleeve Girdle Works) and then on "The Great Gildersleeve." On TV he was played by Willard Waterman, and his nephew Leroy by Ronald Keith

THRUSH

The Technological Hierarchy for the Removal of Undesirables and the Subjugation of Humanity (evil society in TV series "The Man from U.N.C.L.E.")

Thumper

Rabbit (1942 Disney feature cartoon movie *Bambi*): voice of Peter Behn

Thun

King of the Lion Men on the planet Mongo. In *Flash Gordon* movie serial played by James Pierce

Thunda

King of the Congo, name given to Captain Roger Drum (Buster Crabbe) by the Rock People (1952 Columbia movie serial *King of the Congo*)

Thunder

Red Ryder's horse (movies, cartoons and radio): "Roll, Thunder, roll"

Thunderbolt Grease Slapper

Racing car of Tom Slick (voice of Bill Scott), TV cartoon show "George of the Jungle"

Thunderhead

Pony sired by Flicka (1945 movie *Thunderhead–Son of Flicka*); sequel to *My Friend Flicka*, 1943, starring Roddy MacDowall

Thunder Holding Corporation

Company run by Walter Andrews (Walter Brennan), TV series "The Tycoon" (1964-1965)

Thunderbirds

U.S. Air Force's aerobatic team. Begun in 1953, their home base is Nellis AFB, Nevada. The five positions are: leader, left wing, right wing, solo, slot

Aircraft they have flown are:

Republic F84G Thunderjet

Republic F84F Thunderstreak

Republic F100 Super Sabre (several series)

Republic F105 Thunder Chief (back to F100s)

McDonald F4 Phantom

Northrop T38 Talon

Thunderbolt

Johnny West's horse (toy doll)

Thunder Martin

Lone Ranger and Tonto's comical sidekick on radio, played by Paul Hughes. He was foreman of Clarabelle Hornblow's ranch (Clarabelle is the only woman to know the Lone Ranger's true identity)

Thunder Riders

Evil residents of Murania who sometimes came above ground (Gene Autry serial *The Phantom Empire*)

Tibbets, Paul, Jr.

Colonel who piloted the B-29 "Enola Gay" that dropped the atomic bomb on Hiroshima, August 6, 1945

Tic Toc Base

Secret location of the Time Tunnel in 1966 TV series "The Time Tunnel"

Ti-d-bol Man

Man who floats in the toilet tank in a small boat; played on TV advertisements by Fred Miltonberg

Tides Restaurant

Wharf restaurant where citizens of Bodega Bay take refuge from the attack of the birds (1963 movie *The Birds*)

Tiffany

Poodle girlfriend of Benji the dog (movie *Benji*)

Tiffany Jones

Comic strip debut November 11, 1964: played in 1973 movie *Tiffany Jones* by Anouska Hempel

Tige

Buster Brown's bulldog (comic strip and radio)

"I'm Buster Brown and I live in a shoe

This is my dog Tige, and he lives there too"
On radio Bud Tollefson was the voice of Tige's barks

Tiger
The Brady family's pet dog (TV series "The Brady Bunch")

Tiger Lily
Indian maiden, daughter of the chief of the Piccaninnies, rescued by Peter Pan (James Barrie's *Peter Pan*): in 1924 silent movie played by Anna May Wong

Tiger Shark
Submarine commanded by Commander White (William Holden) in 1952 movie *Submarine Command*

Tigger
Winnie-the-Pooh's Tiger Friend: "Hi, I'm Tigger" (movies/TV): voice of Paul Winchell

Tiki
Yacht piloted by Captain Adam Troy (TV series "Adventures in Paradise")

Tilda
The Gumps' maid (comic strip): played on radio by Bess Flynn

Till Death Do Us Part
BBC TV series on which the American series "All in the Family" is based. The series featured Alf and Elsie Garnett of London's East End

Time's Man of the Year
Title first conferred in 1927 on Charles Lindbergh

Times of Your Life, The
Commercial jingle written by Paul Anka for Kodak Cameras. Paul recorded the song in 1975 and it became a hit

Time zones
U.S. and possessions: Atlantic Time, Eastern Time, Central Time, (Rocky) Mountain Time, Pacific Time, Yukon Time, Alaska-Hawaii Time, Bering Time (from 60th to 165th meridians of longitude)

Timmy Tinkle
Robot handyman who works at radio station WHIZ along with Billy Batson (Captain Marvel) (comic books)

Timor Island
South Pacific island where Captain William Bligh and the few members left of his loyal crew landed after traveling almost 4,000 miles in 45 days in the longboat of the

Bounty after being put adrift by the mutineer Fletcher Christian

Timothy Q. Mouse

Dumbo's friend and manager (1941 Disney cartoon feature movie *Dumbo*): voice of Edward Brophy

Tin Goose

Nickname of Ford trimotor passenger airplane of the 1930's: an adaptation from Tin Lizzie

Tin Lizzie

Nickname of the Ford Model T automobile (1908-1927): 15,456,868 were built, all black

Tinker

Detective Sexton Blake's boy assistant (novels by Harry Blyth)

Tinker Bell

Peter Pan's companion, a fairy for whose fading light Peter always successfully appeals to the audience to believe in fairies. Walt Disney studios used Marilyn Monroe's figure as their model for Tinker Bell

Tinker to Evers to Chance

Chicago Cubs' famous double-play trio (1903-1910): Joe Tinker, shortstop; Johnny Evers, 2nd baseman; Frank Chance, 1st baseman (the third baseman was Harry Steinfeldt). They completed only 54 double plays in 4 years, never setting any records. All three became managers of the Chicago Cubs, all three are in the Baseball Hall of Fame

F.P.A.'s poem ("Baseball's Sad Lexicon" by Franklin Pierce Adams):

These are the saddest of possible words:
"Tinker to Evers to Chance."
Trio of bear cubs and fleeter than birds,
Tinker and Evers and Chance.
Ruthlessly pricking our gonfalon bubble,
Making a Giant hit into a double—
Words that are heavy with
Nothing but trouble:
"Tinker to Evers to Chance."

In the 1949 movie *Take Me Out to the Ball Game* the double play trio for the St. Louis Wolves was: Dennis Ryan (Frank Sinatra), Eddie O'Brien (Gene Kelly) and Nat Goldberg (Jules Munshin). They sang a song titled *O'Brien to Ryan to Goldberg*

Tinkerbelle

Robert Manry's 13½-ft. sailboat: crossed Atlantic Ocean in 78 days (1965). Falmouth, Mass. June 1 to Falmouth, England August 17. His registration number is OH7013AR

Tinsel Town

Nickname of Hollywood. Coined by Oscar Levant in his statement "strip the phony tinsel off Hollywood and you'll find the real tinsel underneath"

Tin Woodman

Name given to the all-metal man in L. Frank Baum's novel *The Wizard of Oz*. In movie versions he is referred to as the Tin Man or Tin Woodsman. In 1925 movie version played by Oliver Hardy: in 1939 movie version played by Jack Haley

Tiny

Cute little cartoon mouse that readers are asked to draw for Art Instruction Schools, Inc. (magazine ad)

Tiny

Li'l Abner's 15½-year-old brother who had been lost most of his life (comic strip)

Tiny

One of Gene Autry's sidekicks played by Alan Hale, Jr. (TV series "The Gene Autry Show")

Tiny Tim

Bob Cratchit's crippled son (Charles Dickens' *A Christmas Carol*)

Tiny Tim

Pseudonym of "camp" performer and falsetto singer Herbert Buckingham Khaury. Title of his first album was *God Bless Tiny Tim*. His biggest hit record was *Tip Toe Through the Tulips* (1968)

Tip

*T*o *I*nsure *P*romptness: an acronym

Tip

Young lad hero of the Land of Oz (short for Tippetarius). He was actually born a girl named Ozma, changed to a boy and was later changed back to a girl. He/she is the son/daughter of King Pastoria who ruled Oz prior to the Wizard (novel/animated movie *Return to Oz*)

Tippecanoe, U.S.S.

Aircraft carrier from which Buz Sawyer and Roscoe

Sweeney flew missions during World War II (comic strip *Buz Sawyer*)

Tippy
Turtle's head the reader is asked to draw for Art Instruction School's ads in magazines

Titan
Largest moon of Saturn, home of Saturn Girl (Imra Ardeen), where all citizens have the power of ESP (comic book series)

Titanic
A supposedly unsinkable White Star liner, she hit an iceberg at 25 m.p.h. and sank April 15, 1912, south of Newfoundland on her maiden voyage: "Carpathia" answered "Titanic's" radio distress call. The "Titanic's" call letters were MGY. The "Titanic's" builder Thomas Andrews, John Jacob Astor and author Jacques Futrelle all perished along with over 1,500 other passengers. Author Graham Greene in his autobiography *A Sort of Life* states that he dreamt about a ship sinking the night the Titanic was lost; he was 5 years old. He also states that years later he again dreamt about a ship sinking and again it came true. Previously in 1898 novelist Morgan Robertson wrote a story in which an 800 foot long liner hits an iceberg on her maiden voyage and sinks. The vessel's name was the Titan

Titusville, Pa.
Site of first oil well (drilled by Edwin Drake) August 27, 1859 (Seneca Oil Company). The well first produced the next day at a depth of 69½ feet

Toad Hall
Village where J. Thaddeus Toad, Cyril the horse, Winky and other animals live. Kenneth Grahame's *The Wind in the Willows*

To Anacreon in Heav'n
Tune used for "The Star-Spangled Banner," words by Francis Scott Key: music by John Stafford Smith

Toastmaster General
Title conferred on George Jessel (George Jessel, Eddie Cantor, and Walter Winchell had been singing members of the *Newsboy's Sextet*)

To Be Or Not To Be
1942 movie starring Jack Benny and Carole Lombard.

Carole Lombard's last picture before she died in a plane crash. In the movie Carole said to Benny, "What can happen in a plane?" Because of the tragedy, the line was cut out

To Hell and Back

Autobiography of Audie Murphy, the most decorated United States soldier of World War II. Also title of 1954 movie in which Audie Murphy portrayed himself

Toast of the Town

Ed Sullivan's (1901-1974) TV show, broadcast from the Maxine Elliott Theatre in New York City. Those appearing June 20, 1948, the opening night:

Singing Fireman John Kokoman

Pianist Eugene List

Comedian Jim Kirkwood

Comedians Jerry Lewis and Dean Martin

Dancer Kathryn Lee

Composers Richard Rogers and Oscar Hammerstein II

Fight Referee Ruby Goldstein

Comedian Lee Goodman

Singer Monica Lewis

Ray Block's orchestra

It was the longest running TV variety show. It played each Sunday night at 8:00 p.m. on CBS. Title changed to *The Ed Sullivan Show* in September 1955. The show lasted until 1971. Wayne and Shuster made more appearances on the program than anyone else. When he had the Beatles on in 1964, he polled 82 per cent of the viewers. Show was originally to be called *You're the Top*

Toastettes

Dancers on Ed Sullivan's TV program "Toast of the Town." The six original dancers were the June Taylor girls

Tobor

"Robot" spelled backwards

Captain Video's evil foe (TV series)

Space-traveling robot in 1954 science-fiction movie *Tobor the Great*. Crime fighting robot in 1965 TV cartoon series *Eighth Man*

Toby

Kunta Kinte's slave name (1977 TV series "Roots")

Toby

Dog in the "Punch and Judy" puppet show

Tocata und Fugue d-moll

Musical selection by Johann Sebastian Bach. Played by Captain Nemo in the 1954 movie *20,000 Leagues Under the Sea* and also played by the Phantom in the movie *Phantom of the Opera*

Tod Stiles

One of the automobilists in TV's "Route 66": played by Martin Milner

Today Is Tonight

Novel written by Jean Harlow (with aid of Carey Wilson) in the early 1930's

Today's World

San Francisco magazine for which Doris Martin works (TV series "The Doris Day Show")

Todd-AO

Wide screen film process introduced by Michael Todd, first shown in the 1955 movie *Oklahoma!* and second in the 1956 movie *Around the World in 80 Days*

AO = American Optics

Toff, The

Adventures of the Honorable Richard Rollison (John Creasey's *Toff* series). His valet is named Jolly. His two cars are a Rolls-Bentley and an Austin. His flat is on Gresham Terrace, London. Movies starring John Bentley as the Toff: *Salute the Toff, Hammer the Toff*. Novel debut: *Introducing the Toff* (1938)

To J.R.M.

Dedication in novel *Gone with the Wind* by Margaret Mitchell (1936). J.R.M. is her husband John Robert Marsh

Tokens

Used in the game of "Monopoly" (metal): Thimble, Iron, Shoe, Dog, Battleship, Top Hat, Cannon, Race Car. In the British edition they are tractor (orange), automobile (red), tank (green), motorcycle and rider (gray), train engine (blue) and sailing ship (gold)

Toklas, Alice B.

Gertrude Stein's secretary. *I Love You, Alice B. Toklas* (1968) movie starring Peter Sellers and Leigh Taylor-Young (her cookbook had a recipe for psychedelic hashish pudding on page 273 *The Alice B. Toklas Cookbook*)

Tokyo Rose

Pseudonym of Iva Ikuko Toguri d' Aquino, World War II propaganda agent on Japanese radio. Broadcasts from Germany and Italy were made by Axis Sally. She was pardoned by President Ford on his last day of office January 20, 1977. She was 60 years old

Tom and Jerry

Rock 'n' roll duet, 1950's: name originally used by Simon and Garfunkel. *Hey Schoolgirl* on Big Records in 1957 was their only hit

Tom and Jerry

MGM cartoon featuring Tom (cat) and Jerry (house mouse), created by Hanna and Barbera. The cartoons have won 7 Academy Awards:

Debut: *Puss Gets the Boot* (1939) in which Tom was named Jasper

Jerry (without Tom) danced with Gene Kelly in *Anchors Aweigh* (1945). They were both Esther Williams' swimming partners in *Dangerous When Wet* (1953)

Tom, Dick and Harry

Three escape tunnels dug by the P.O.W.'s at Stalag Luft North, Harry being the tunnel through which 76 men escaped, 50 were captured and executed, in violation of the Geneva Convention.

Tom - From Hut 104, 335' to woods

Dick - From Kitchen

Harry - From Hut 105 - Used for escape

(1963 movie *The Great Escape*), Paul Brickhill's novel on which the movie is based, mentions a 4th tunnel named George

Tom Dooley

Gay Langland's (Clark Gable) pet dog (1961 movie *The Misfits*)

Tom Kitten

Kennedy family's White House pet cat

Tom Quartz and Slippers

President Franklin D. Roosevelt's two pet cats

Tom Sawyer

Mischievous young lad created by Mark Twain: appeared in *The Adventures of Tom Sawyer* (1878), *The Adventures of Huckleberry Finn* (1884), *Tom Sawyer Abroad* (1894), *Tom Sawyer, Detective* (1896)

Played in films *The Adventures of Tom Sawyer:*

Jack Pickford (1917), Gordon Griffith (1920), Jackie Coogan (1930), Tom Kelly (1938), Johnny Whitaker (1972)

Tom Sawyer, Detective (1938) Billy Cook

Tom Sawyer's gang
Tom Sawyer, Hubkleberry Finn, Joe Harper, Ben Rogers, Tommy Barnes

Tom Swift
and His . . . (boys' novels, created by Edward Stratemeyer, 1862-1930): he lives in town of Shopton. His girlfriend and eventual wife is Mary Nestor
Electric Locomotive
Flying Machine
Motor Boat
Air Ship
Photo Telephone
Air Scout
Motorcycle
(list not exhaustive)

Tom Swift, Jr.
and His . . . (boys' novels in the 1950's by Victor Appleton II): 18-year-old inventor, son of Tom Swift and Mary Nestor Swift
Flying Lab
Jetmarine
Rocket Ship
Giant Robot
Atomic Earth Blaster
Outpost in Space
Diving Seacopter
Ultrasonic Cycloplane
Deep-Sea Hydrodome
Space Solartron
Electronic Retroscope
Spectromarine Selector
Electronic Hydrolung
Triphibian Atomicar

Tom Thumb
First American steam locomotive (Baltimore and Ohio Railroad), built by Peter Cooper in 1830 at Canton Iron Works, Baltimore, Md.

Tom Thumb, "General"
Nickname of Charles Sherwood Stratton (1838-1883),

American dwarf, 36 inches tall, married (February 10, 1863) Lavinia Warren (Mercy Lavinia Bump), who stood 32 inches tall: both worked for P. T. Barnum. Tom Thumb died July 15, 1883. P. T. Barnum had a dwarf who was smaller yet, named Admiral Dot, whose nephew was called Major Atom

Toma, David

Newark, N.J., detective on whose real-life exploits the TV series "Toma" is based. Toma is played by Tony Musante, but the real David Toma makes cameo appearances in many episodes

Tomania

Warring nation that Adenoid Hynkel (Charles Chaplin) is dictator of, allied with Bacteria. They plan to invade the neighboring country, Austerlich. 1940 movie *The Great Dictator* (see Bacteria)

Tomboy

Actor/singer Stuart Hamblen's horse which he rode in movies

Tombstone

Town setting of the TV series "The Life and Legend of Wyatt Earp" starring Hugh O'Brien

Tommy and Arthur

Rock operas created by the groups *The Who* (Pete Townshend) and *The Kinks* (Ray Davies) respectively. Tommy Walker is a pinball wizard

Tommy Anderson

Dennis the Menace's little friend (played by Tommy Booth on TV series)

Tommy Atkins

Nickname for the British soldier

Tommy Hambledon

Detective created by Manning Coles

Tomorrow

Magazine of which Tom Corbett (Bill Bixby) is editor on the TV series "The Courtship of Eddie's Father"

Tonight Show

M.C.'s: Steve Allen, Jack Paar, Johnny Carson. José Melis was Jack Paar's bandleader, then Skitch Henderson, and finally Doc Severinsen. Groucho Marx introduced Johnny Carson on his first night hosting *The Tonight Show* Oct. 1, 1962

Tonight We Love
   Theme song of Freddy Martin's orchestra. Adapted from Tchaikovsky's piano concerto

Tonto
   The Lone Ranger's faithful Indian companion: on radio played by John Todd; on TV played by Jay Silverheels; in movies played by Chief Thundercloud (real name Victor Daniels, a full-blooded Cherokee). Tonto was a member of the Potawatomi tribe. Tonto debuted on the 10th radio episode. Jay Silverheels is a Mohawk Indian and one time professional Lacrosse player in Canada. In comic books Tonto has a pet eagle named Taka

Tonto's horse
   Scout; earlier, also, White Feller, Paint. On radio Tonto originally rode double with the Lone Ranger on Silver

Tony
   Tom Mix's horse. In movies: there was also Tony, Jr., Tony I, Tony II and Old Blue

Tony Award
   Annual award for theatrical excellence, given in several categories: named for Antoinette Perry, American theater producer who died in 1946

Tony Rome
   Miami private eye (Frank Sinatra) who lives on his sailboat, the Straight Pass. Movies: *Tony Rome* (1967), *Lady In Cement* (1968)

Tony the Tiger
   Advertises Kellogg's Sugar Frosted Flakes: voice of Thurl Ravenscroft ("They're G-G-Great!). A member of the Johnny Mann singers

Tony the Tiger, Jr.
   Son of Tony the Tiger: advertises Kellogg's Frosted Rice: voice of Jackie Haley, Jr.

Too-Too
   Doctor Do-little's owl

Toot-Toot-Tootsie Goodbye
   Only song that Al Jolson and Eddie Cantor ever sang together, on the radio program *The Eddie Cantor Show* May 6, 1946

Top
   Cyrus Smith's pet dog that traveled in the balloon with its 5 passengers to Lincoln Island (Jules Verne's *The Mysterious Island*)

Topac

Trans-Orient-Pacific Airlines, airline company flight 420 from Hawaii to San Francisco, DC-4 N 8104H, number 4 engine catches fire. Piloted by Captain Sullivan (Robert Stack) 1954 movie *The High and the Mighty*

Topo

Aquaman's octopus (comic book series *Aquaman*)

Top of the World, Ma!

Arthur "Cody" Jarrett's (James Cagney) final words as he dies in the explosion of a gas tank in the 1949 movie *White Heat*

Topo Gigio

Mechanical Italian mouse that spoke with a heavy accent as part of a comedy routine with Ed Sullivan on his TV show: "Hey, Eddie, kees me goodnight." His girlfriend is Rosy. He was featured in 1965 movie *Magic World of Topo Gigio*

Topper

Hopalong Cassidy's white horse

Topps

Largest maker of baseball cards (Topps Chewing Gum Company). Produced their first card in 1951. Producer of Bazooka Gum. The first baseball cards were introduced by Old Judge Cigarettes in 1886

To Protect and To Serve

Motto on the side of Adam-12 police car (Los Angeles Police Dept.) (TV series "Adam-12")

Topsy

Young slave girl who jes' grewed (Harriet Beecher Stowe's *Uncle Tom's Cabin*)

Torch Bearer

Highest rank held as a Camp Fire Girl

Torchy Blane

Movie series starring Glenda Farrell, Lola Lane and Jane Wyman. Her boyfriend is Lieutenant Steve McBride (Barton MacLane, Allen Jenkins & Paul Kelly)

Tornado

Zorro's black horse (TV series). Phantom was his white horse

Toro

The Human Torch's sidekick (*The Flaming Kid* comic

books). He was orphaned when his parents were killed in a train wreck

Torrin, H.M.S.

Desroyer commanded by Captain Kinross (Noel Coward) (1942 movie *In Which We Serve*)

To the Egress

Sign over an exit door to the street in P. T. Barnum's New York City Museum. People who were curious to find out what an egress was, found themselves out of the museum. This helped to alleviate congestion in the building

Toto

Dorothy's dog (1939 movie *The Wizard of Oz*)

Toucan Sam

Parrot that advertises Kellogg's Froot Loops breakfast cereal: voice of Paul Frees

Touchdown Twins

Fullback Felix "Doc" Blanchard (Mr. Inside) and halfback Glenn Davis (Mr. Outside): Army Cadets football team, 1944-1946, and both All-Americans for those 3 years

Towering Inferno, The

1974 movie starring Paul Newman and Steve McQueen. The movie was adapted from a combination of two separate novels *The Tower* by Richard M. Stern and *The Glass Inferno* by Thomas Scortia and Frank Robinson

Town Hall Quartet

Male singing group on radio's *The Fred Allen Show*

Track 29

On which the "Chattanooga Choo Choo" leaves, from the Pennsylvania Station at a quarter to nine

Tracy-Hepburn movies

Spencer Tracy and Katharine Hepburn appeared together in:

Woman of the Year (1942)
Keeper of the Flame (1942)
Without Love (1945)
The Sea of Grass (1947)
State of the Union (1948)
Adam's Rib (1949)
Pat and Mike (1952)
The Desk Set (1957)

Guess Who's Coming to Dinner (1967) (for which she got an Oscar; it was Tracy's last film)

Spencer Tracy has been nominated for an Oscar 9 times. He won two years in a row for Best Actor with *Captains Courageous* (1937) and *Boys Town* (1938). He narrated the 1963 movie *How the West was Won*

Katharine Hepburn has been nominated for an Oscar 11 times, a record. She is the only actress to win an Oscar three times for Best Actress: *Morning Glory* (1932/33), *Guess Who's Coming to Dinner* (1967, co-winner with Barbra Streisand for *Funny Girl*), and *The Lion in Winter* (1968). She has never accepted an Oscar in person

Trail Seeker

A beginning Camp Fire Girl prior to being sworn-in as a full-fledged member

Train Whistle signals

. = *Short toot*

- = *Long toot*

. = Apply Brakes. Stop

. . . = Stop at the next station

. . . . . = Warning to get off of the tracks

- . . . = Flagman, protect the rear of the train

- -.- = Approaching a road crossing

Tramp

Family's pet dog (TV series "My Three Sons"): also name of family dog on TV series "Room for One More." Tramp of "My Three Sons" has won the 1961, 1962, 1963 and 1964 TV PATSY

Trans-America

Airline company whose plane (Trans-America 2 flight Lincoln to Rome) is blown up but lands safely (Arthur Hailey's novel *Airport*) (See Trans Global for movie version)

Trans-American

New York City detective agency that Mr. Nick Charles once worked for (TV series "The Thin Man")

Trans Global

Airline company that has one of their aircraft bombed. It was the Golden Argosy flight 281 to Rome (Beoing 707, plane no. 324) with 110 passengers. 1970 movie *Airport*. Passengers boarded at Gate 33, Concourse D at Lincoln International Airport

739

Trans Global 45
Flight (B707) that gets stuck in the snow, closing runway 29 at Lincoln International Airport. Aircraft were forced to use runway 22 (1970 movie *Airport*)

Trans State Airlines
Airline company (TSA) flight 17 (DC-7) piloted by Captain Dick Barnett (Dana Andrews) that collided with Navy Jet (T33) 8255, piloted by Commander Dale Heath (Efrem Zimbalist, Jr.) on Victor 16 airways (1960 movie *The Crowded Sky*). In the novel written by Hank Searls it is Pacific Central Airlines flight 7

Transylvania
Homeland of Count Dracula (Bram Stoker's *Dracula*): actually an area in Romania in Carpathian Mountains

Trask Engineering
Corporation that employs Henry Mitchell on TV series "Dennis the Menace"

Traveler
Robert E. Lee's horse

Travis McGee
Detective created by John D. MacDonald, all the novels have a color mentioned in the title, beginning the *Long Long Lavender Look*. Travis McGee lives on a houseboat named the Busted Flush. Played by Rod Taylor in 1970 movie *Darker than Amber*

Treaty of Versailles
Treaty signed June 28, 1919, at end of World War I (not ratified by United States), resulting from conference attended by the Big Four: Woodrow Wilson of the United States, Lloyd George of the United Kingdom, Georges Clemenceau of France, Vittorio Orlando of Italy

Trespassers W
Piglet's grandfather (actually it is the remains of a sign by piglet's tree house). Piglet thinks it's short for Trespassers William (*Winnie-the-Pooh* stories)

Trevi Fountain
Fountain in Rome where tourists make wishes after tossing coins into it: featured in 1954 movie *Three Coins in the Fountain,* from a novel by John Secondari

Tribbles
Small furry animals that reproduce at a very high rate (episode "Trouble with Tribbles," TV series "Star Trek")

Trieste

Bathyscaphe, built by Jacques Piccard and his father Auguste, that descended to 35,800 feet: it explored the lowest part of the Marianas Trench in the Pacific, January 13, 1960, carrying Don Walsh and the younger Piccard

Trigger

Roy Roger's palomino horse of the movies and TV. Called "the smartest horse in movies," Trigger could count and do the hula, among other tricks. In the 1938 movie *The Adventures of Robin Hood*, Maid Marian (Oliva de Havilland) rode Trigger prior to Roy Roger's becoming his owner. Then he was called Golden Cloud. Trigger won the 1953 PATSY. On July 3, 1965 Trigger died at age 33, after which Roy Rogers had him stuffed and put on display at his Double R-Bar Ranch in Apple Valley, California

Triple Crown

Baseball: Highest batting average, most home runs, most runs batted in

Won by: Ty Cobb (1909), Heinie Zimmerman (1912), Rogers Hornsby (1922, 1925), Jimmy Foxx (1933), Chuck Klein (1933), Lou Gehrig (1934), Joe Medwick (1937), Ted Williams (1942, 1947), Mickey Mantle (1956), Frank Robinson (1966), Carl Yastrzemski 1967)

Horse racing: (so named since 1930)

Kentucky Derby (Churchill Downs, Louisville, Kentucky): 1¼ miles, 1½ miles 1875-1895 (first run May 17, 1875)

Preakness (Pimlico, Baltimore, Maryland): 1 3/16 miles

Belmont Stakes (Belmont Park, Elmont, Long Island, New York): 1½ miles (held at Acqueduct 1963-1967)

Winner	*Jockey*	*Year*
Sir Barton	John Loftus	1919
Gallant Fox	Earle Sande	1930
Omaha	W. Saunders	1935
War Admiral	Charlie Kurtsinger	1937
Whirlaway	Eddie Arcaro	1941
Count Fleet	John Longden	1943
Assault	Willie Mehrtens	1946
Citation	Eddie Arcaro	1948

| Secretariat | Ron Turcotte | 1973 |
| Seattle Slew | Jean Cruquet | 1977 |

(Seattle Slew was the first unbeaten Triple Crown winner).

Whirlaway was nicknamed Mr. Longtail

The Kentucky Derby is run on the first Saturday in May, called "Run for the Roses." The Preakness has been run at Pimlico since 1909. The race (since 1873) is named after a two-year-old horse that won the Dinner Party Stakes at Pimlico. The Belmont Stakes was established in 1867, run in June, "The Test of Champions," named for August Belmont, first president of the American Jockey Club. Not named for Belmont Park, which was also named for Mr. Belmont. The songs played before each race are: Kentucky Derby, "My Old Kentucky Home"; The Preakness, "Maryland, My Maryland"; Belmont Stakes, "Sidewalks of New York"

The winners: Gallant Fox, the father of Omaha, were both owned by William Woodward. Whirlaway and Citation were both owned by Warren Wright Secretariat was the first horse to finish the Kentucky Derby in under two minutes (1:59.4). He is the son of 1957 Preakness winner Bold Ruler

Triple Crown

Harness Racing:

Little Brown Jug (Delaware, Ohio)

William H. Cane Futurity (Yonkers Raceway)

Messenger Stakes (Roosevelt Raceway)

Triple-R

Ranch at which Spin and Marty stay during the summer. It is owned by Mr. Logan. The phone number is PIedmont 7-5321 (TV's Mickey Mouse Club)

Triplets, The

Dance routine in which Fred Astaire, Nanette Fabray and Jack Buchanan dance and sing on their knees dressed as infants. Miss Fabray's role was originally meant for Oscar Levant (1953 movie *The Band Wagon*)

Triskaidekaphobia

Unnatural fear of the number 13. Alfred Hitchcock's first and only uncompleted movie is titled *Number 13* (1922). The number 13 is producer Darryl F. Zanuck's favorite number. He had the 1946 movie title *32 Rue Madeleine* changed to *13 Rue Madeleine*. Many buildings do not have a thirteenth floor

Trixie

Hi and Lois Flagston's youngest daughter (comic strip)

Trooper Duffy

Frontier soldier (TV series "F Troop"): played by Bob Steele

Tropicana

Nightclub at which Ricky Ricardo (Desi Arnaz) was the band leader (TV series "I Love Lucy")

Tropis

Little half-human, half-ape-like animals found in the jungles of New Guinea in the 1970 Burt Reynolds movie *Skullduggery*. One couple, Morris and Topazi, have a baby (delivered dead in room "Happy" of the Snow White Motel) which becomes a cause célèbre. Pat Suzuki plays Topazi

Trotting Horse Hall of Fame

Located in Goshen, New York

Trudy

Guitarist/singer José Feliciano's seeing eye dog

Trudy

Hubert's wife (comic strip *Hubert* by Dick Wingert)

Trusty

Old bloodhound (1955 Disney cartoon feature movie *Lady and the Tramp*)

Trylon and Perisphere

Symbol of the 1939-1940 New York World's Fair

Tubby Tompkins

Little Lulu's boyfriend (comic books): he collected doorknobs. He is the leader of a boy's gang that consists of Iggy, Eddie and Willy

Tubby Watts

Superhero Johnny Quick's assistant

Tudbury's

Blondie Bumstead's favorite department store (comic strip)

Tuesday

Recommended meatless day - during World War II

Tuesday Club

Professional club to which sleuth Miss Jane Marple and her nephew, writer Raymond West, are members (detective novels)

Tuffy

Jerry's mouse cousin; he's a little gray mouse that wears a pair of diapers ("Tom and Jerry" cartoon series)

Tukutese quintuplets

Born Feb. 6, 1966, in Mdantsane, South Africa:

Tandeka, girl, "well-beloved"

Zoleka, girl, "serenity"

Tandekile, boy, "I've got it" (also called Mbambile)

Tembekile, boy, "trusted"

Kululekile, boy, "happy"

Tulsa, Oklahoma

Hometown of Mike Doonesbury (comic strip)

Turk, The

Character who advertises Camel Cigarettes. He is a night-time repairman for the New York Telephone Company. George Kozul is also seen in Camel Cigarette advertisements *Meet the Turk*. He is a look-alike for Mark Spitz

Turner, Captain William

Captain of the "Lusitania" when it was sunk by the German submarine U-20, May 7, 1915. He was torpedoed again in another ship in 1917

Turner, Lana

Julia Jean Mildred Frances Turner Shaw Crane Topping Barker May Eaton Dante

Her husbands: Artie Shaw (1940-1941), Stephen Crane (1942-1944), Bob Topping (1948-1952), Lex Barker (1953-1957), Fred May (1960-1962), Robert Eaton (1965-1969), Ronald Dante (1969)

In Hollywood Lana Turner was nicknamed the Sweater Girl. Judge George E. Marshall married her to both Artie Shaw and Stephen Crane. She married, divorced, married, divorced Stephen Crane (therefore she was married 8 times to 7 husbands). It was Lana and Stephen Crane's daughter Cheryl who killed Lana's boyfriend Johnny Stompanato with a butcher knife on Good Friday, April 4, 1958 (see *Schwab's*)

Turtle

First submarine: invented by David Bushnell in 1775

Tuskegee Institute

Founded by Booker T. Washington in 1881

Tusk, Tusk

Character that advertises Kellogg's Coca Krispies cereals. Voice of Joel Cory

Tuxedo Junction

Theme song of Erskine Hawkins' orchestra. Also the name of Glenn Miller's orange grove in Monrovia

Tweety Pie

Warner Brothers' cute little yellow canary cartoon character, who is chased by Sylvester the cat; "I tawt I taw a puddy tat," *Tweedy Pie* won an Academy Award for Best Short Subject in 1947. Voice of Mel Blanc. Debut: *Birdie and the Beast* (1944)

Twelve Oaks

The Wilkes family plantation (Margaret Mitchell's *Gone With the Wind*), where the barbecue was held. The home had round columns. On the sundial on the plantation is inscribed "Do Not Squander Time, that Is the Stuff Life Is Made Of"

Twiggy

Nickname of British fashion model Lesley Hornby. She starred in the 1971 movie *The Boy Friend*

Twin Cities

Minneapolis and St. Paul, Minnesota

Twin Oaks

Highway diner where Cora Smith (Lana Turner) and Frank Chambers (John Garfield) meet. (1946 movie *The Postman Always Rings Twice*)

Twins

Syndicated advice columnists Ann Landers (Esther Pauline) and Abigail Van Buren (Pauline Esther): nicknamed Eppie and Popo, born July 4, 1918

Two-Face

One-time handsome Harvey "Apollo" Kent until acid was thrown on exactly half of his face (left side). Enemy of Batman. Decided to be a criminal by the flip of a two-headed coin

Two Guitars

Theme song of radio program *The A & P Gypsies*, performed by Harry Horlick's Orchestra

Typhoid Mary

Mary Mallon, carrier of typhoid in New York City in 1906. A cook, she continued to cook for many institutions and households, thus spreading the disease

U

U-2

Reconnaissance plane flown by Francis Gary Powers, departed Peshawar, Pakistan, for Bodo, Norway (shot down over the Soviet Union) May 1, 1960

U19

Old German submarine that Frank Lauffnauer (Frank Sinatra) rebuilds to attack the British passenger ship "Queen Mary" (1966 movie *Assault on a Queen*)

U-20

German submarine under the command of Kapitan Lieutenant Schwieger, that sank the "Lusitania" May 7, 1915

U78

German submarine that was destroyed along with the allied ship in the 1944 movie *Lifeboat*. Walter Slezak played the U-boat Captain

U505

German submarine captured on the high seas by the U.S.S. Pillsbury June 4, 1944. It was the first enemy ship captured by the U.S. Navy on the high seas since 1815

U.N.C.L.E.

United Network Command for Law and Enforcement, headed by Mr. Waverly (Leo G. Carroll) (TV series "The Man From U.N.C.L.E." and "The Girl From U.N.C.L.E.")

Section I	Policy and Operations
Section II	Operations and Enforcement
Section III	Enforcement and Communications

UL
Underwriters Laboratories: seal of approval attached to some electrical apparatus or appliances

Ugly Duckling, The
One nickname of baseball player Lawrence Peter "Yogi" Berra

Ujiji, Tanganyika
Where Henry Stanley found David Livingstone, November, 1871. *"Dr. Livingstone I Presume"*

Ulanga
African River on which Charlie Allnut (Humphrey Bogart) and Rose Sayer (Katharine Hepburn) ride in the 30-foot launch *The African Queen*. The Ulanga later changes into the Bora River. 1951 movie *The African Queen*

Ultra-Man
Japanese science fiction TV serial. Iyata, using the Beta-Capsule, turns himself into the super-hero Ultra-Man

Ulysses
Freighter in which Jack Lemmon is trapped after collision (1957 movie *Fire Down Below*)

Uncas
Son of Chingachgook the last of the Mohicans (James Fenimore Cooper's *The Last of the Mohicans*), Played in movies: 1922 movie by Albert Roscoe, 1932 movie by Frank Coghlan, Jr., and on TV by Lon Chaney, Jr.

Uncle Arthur
Samantha's warlock uncle (Paul Lynde) (TV series "Bewitched")

Uncle Fester
Weird member of TV's "Addam's Family." Played by child star Jackie Coogan, who was instrumental in creating the Coogan Act (Child Actors Bill). The act controlled the earnings of child stars

Uncle Henry
Dorothy's uncle (1939 movie *The Wizard of Oz*)

Uncle Joe
Self-appointed manager of the Shady Rest Hotel and Chief of the train Cannonball (Edgar Buchanan) (TV series "Petticoat Junction")

Uncle Miltie

Nickname of comedian Milton Berle. Title of his autobiography *Always Leave Them Laughing* was made into a 1949 movie

Uncle Remus

Negro character who narrates tales in Joe Chandler Harris's stories. Played in 1946 Disney movie *Song of the South* by James Baskett for which he was awarded an honorary Oscar. Played on radio by Fred L. Jeske

Uncle Sam

Comic book hero, whose sidekick is Buddy (debut *National Comics* #1, July 1940)

Uncle Wiggily

Central character of children's books by H. R. Garis

Uncola, The

7 Up (soft drink)

Underdog

Secret identity of Shoeshine Boy (TV cartoon series): voice of Wally Cox

Unicorn

Mythological animal resembling a horse with a horn growing from its forehead

Union Triad

Three fraternal organizations founded at Union College, Schenectady, New York

Kappa Alpha (1825), Sigma Phi (1827), Delta Phi (1827)

Union Jack

Flag of Great Britain created on May 1, 1707, consists of superimposed

English flag of St. George

Scottish flag of St. Andrew

Irish flag of St. Patrick

Unit 51

Los Angeles County rescue unit (TV series "Emergency"). Also police unit on TV series "Police Woman." On "Emergency," the team drives a Dodge truck, license 999007, with call letters KMA367

United Artists Corporation

Founded in 1919 by Mary Pickford, Douglas Fairbanks, D. W. Griffith, Charles Chaplin

United Kingdom

Of Great Britain (Isle of Man, Channel Islands) and Northern Ireland (since 1921)

United Nations

Security Council (permanent members): United States, Soviet Union, United Kingdom, France, China

United Planets E-X Craft 101

First spaceship launched on the 7th of Sextor, 2351 to the Planet Altair IV. The ship was nicknamed "Bellerophon" on exploratory mission 83. Second space cruiser sent into outer space to the planet Altair IV was the United Planets Cruiser C57D. Captained by Commander John J. Adams (Leslie Nielsen) and a crew of 20. Ship departed Earth on the 7th of Sextor, 2371, (1956 movie *Forbidden Planet*)

United States Coins

In circulation 1978:

Coin	Portrait (obverse)
Cent	Abraham Lincoln
	(first president on a coin, 1909)
Nickel	Thomas Jefferson
Dime	Franklin D. Roosevelt
	(118 grooves on its edge)
Quarter	George Washington
	(119 grooves on its edge)
Half Dollar	John F. Kennedy
Dollar	Dwight D. Eisenhower

United States Currency (6⅛ × 2 9/16″)

Portraits:

$1	George Washington
$2	Thomas Jefferson
$5	Abraham Lincoln
$10	Alexander Hamilton
$20	Andrew Jackson
$50	Ulysses S. Grant
$100	Benjamin Franklin
$500	William McKinley
$1,000	Grover Cleveland
$5,000	James Madison
$10,000	Salmon P. Chase
$100,000	Woodrow Wilson

The only female whose portrait has appeared on U.S. currency was that of Martha Washington on a One Dollar Silver Certificate in 1891

For the 1976 Bicentennial the $2 bill was re-introduced

depicting John Trumbull's portrait of the signing of the Declaration of Independence

United States Flag

7 red stripes, 6 white stripes, 50 stars in 9 alternating rows of 6 and 5 stars. Authorized to fly day and night at the Capitol Building, Grave of Francis Scott Key, the World War Memorial and at Fort McHenry.

United States Presidents

Who died in office (every President elected in a year ending in 0 since 1840):

President	Elected	Died
Harrison	1840	April 4, 1841
Taylor	1848	July 9, 1850
Lincoln	1860	April 15, 1865
Garfield	1880	September 19, 1881
McKinley	1900	September 14, 1901
Harding	1920	August 2, 1923
F.D. Roosevelt	1940	April 12, 1945
Kennedy	1960	November 22, 1963

United States Savings Bonds

Portraits:

$25	George Washington
$50	Thomas Jefferson
$75	John F. Kennedy
$100	Grover Cleveland
$200	Franklin D. Roosevelt
$500	Woodrow Wilson
$1,000	Abraham Lincoln
$10,000	Theodore Roosevelt

Univac I

First commercially sold electronic computer, 1951

Universal Import and Export

Cover organization for the British secret 000 operations of which James Bond is a part (Ian Fleming's James Bond novels)

University of Illinois

School to which Lt. Col. Henry Blake went (TV series "M*A*S*H"): he wears the school jersey whenever possible. Played by McLean Stevenson

University College

(London University) Grover Street, London, where Sherlock Holmes' loyal friend John H. Watson received his degree in medicine in 1878

University of Pittsburgh
First football team to use uniform numbers, December 5, 1908

Unknown Soldier
Tomb of the Unknown Soldier, Arlington Cemetery, Virginia, in which, since November 11, 1921, one unknown serviceman has been buried from U.S. Wars: W. W. I, W.W. II, Korean War (Vietnam produced no Unknown Soldier)
Inscription: "Here rests in honored glory an American soldier known but to God"
The naval ship *U.S.S. Olympia* brought from France the body of America's first unknown soldiers after WWI. The British Unknown Soldier is buried in Westminster Abbey

Untouchables, The
Federal group of crimefighters under the U.S. Treasury Department. In 1959-1963 TV series played by Elliot Ness (Robert Stack), Enrico Rosi (Nicholas Georgiade), Bill Youngblood (Abel Fernandez) and Lee Hobson (Paul Picerni). The role of Ness was first offered to Van Heflin and Van Johnson. In the pilot movie *The Scarface Mob* Elliot Ness marries Betty Anderson (Pat Crowley). Elliot Ness' office is number 208. (Robert Stack was the national 20 gauge rifle champion in 1937 and once held the world's record of 354 consecutive hits)

Upset
Only horse to beat Man O'War: Sanford Memorial Stakes, Saratoga, August 13, 1919 by half a length. In that race, Man O'War ran his fastest six furlongs (1:11 1/5)

Ural Mountains
Separate Asia from Europe

Useless
Sundance's (Earl Holliman) pet dog (TV series "Hotel de Paree")

Utopia
Sir Thomas More's imaginary island in his 1516 work *Utopia*. In the 1966 Oscar winning film *A Man for All Seasons* More was portrayed by Paul Scofield

V

V-E Day
> May 8, 1945, end of World War II in Europe

V-J Day
> August 15, 1945 (U.K.), September 2, 1945 (U.S.): end of war with Japan

Vagabond Lover
> Nickname of Rudy Vallee (Hubert Prior Vallee) from his theme songs, "I'm Just a Vagabond Lover" (title of 1929 movie) and "My Time Is Your Time"

Valhalla
> The great hall where Odin lives and receives heroes fallen in battle (Norse mythology)

Valiant Lady
> Radio daytime serial adventures of Joan Hargrave-Scott

Valley Falls High
> School attended by Chip Hilton where he is a super-athlete ("Chip Hilton" sports series by Claire Bee, circa 1950)

Valley Forge
> Name of American Airlines space vehicle in which Lowell Freeman (played by Bruce Dern) tries to save the last of the Earth's trees and plants with the aid of 3 drones he names Dewey (#1), Huey (#2), Louie (#3) (1972 movie *Silent Running*). The drones were played by handicapped actors: Steve Brown, Cheryl Sparks, Mark Persons and Larry Wisenhurt

Valley of the Blue Moon
> Tibetan valley where the magic city of Shangri-La is located (James Hilton's *Lost Horizon*)

Valse Triste
By Sibelius—theme song of radio series *I Love a Mystery*

Vampires
Dead humans who turn into blood-sucking bats at night. They cannot stand the smell of garlic and fear crucifixes. They can be destroyed with holy water, a stake through the heart, or by being exposed to the light of day or a silver bullet. They have no shadow, nor reflection, can't abide running water. They cannot stand wolfbane

Vanilla
Dog on radio's *Amos 'n' Andy* series

Van Nuys High School
California high school attended by Jane Russell, Stacy Keach, Diane Baker, Robert Redford, Marilyn Monroe and Natalie Wood, among others

Vassar
School whose eight members of the 1933 graduation class make up "The Group" (Mary McCarthy's *The Group*)

Valda
Secretary to private eye Mike Hammer

Velvet Fog, The
Early nickname of singer-crooner Mel Torme

Venture
Ship that carries King Kong from Skull Island (1933 movies *King Kong* and *Son of Kong*). In the 1976 version of *King Kong* it's the Petrox Explorer

Venus
Belle Starr's black horse

Venus
The planet that Abbott and Costello land on in the 1953 movie *Abbott and Costello Go to Mars*

Vera
Captain Herr Thiele's ship (Katherine Anne Porter's *Ship of Fools*)

Veronica and Betty
Archie Andrew's girlfriends Veronica Lodge and Betty Cooper (Ronnie is Veronica's nickname) (comic books) Veronica is the brunette, Betty is the blonde. Betty's dog is Fluffy, Veronica's cat is Al E. Played on radio: Veronica—Vivian Smolen and Gloria Mann; Betty—Doris Grundy, Joy Geffen, Rosemary Rice. Played on TV: Veronica—Hillary Thompson, Betty—Audrey Landers

Very Thought of You, The
   Theme song of Ray Noble's orchestra
Very, Very Nice
   Mr. Moto's favorite expression
Vesta
   Ship on which Renfield brings his master, Count Dracula to England, inside of a coffin. He takes up a home at Carfax, Abbey (1931 movie *Dracula*). In Bram Stocker's novel he travels to England on the ship "Demeter" and leaves for home on the *Czarina Catherine*, arriving on Oct. 29
Veterans' Day
   Name by which Armistice Day has been observed since 1954
Vic
   General Custer's horse (see *Comanche*)
Vice-Presidents of the United States

	Under President
John Adams	George Washington
Thomas Jefferson	John Adams
Aaron Burr	Thomas Jefferson
George Clinton	Jefferson/James Madison
Elbridge Gerry	Madison
Daniel D. Tompkins	James Monroe
John Caldwell Calhoun	J. Q. Adams/
	Andrew Jackson
Martin Van Buren	Jackson
Richard Mentor Johnson	Martin Van Buren
John Tyler	W. H. Harrison
George Mifflin Dallas	James K. Polk
Millard Fillmore	Zachary Taylor
William Rufus	Franklin Pierce
Devane King	
John Cabell Breckinridge*	James Buchanan
Hannibal Hamlin	Abraham Lincoln
Andrew Johnson	Lincoln
Schuyler Colfax	U. S. Grant
Henry Wilson	Grant
William Almon Wheeler	Rutherford Hayes
Chester Alan Arthur	James Garfield
Thomas Andrews	Grover Cleveland
Hendricks	
Levi Parsons Morton	Benjamin Harrison

Adlai Ewing Stevenson	Cleveland
Garret Augustus Hobart	William McKinley
Theodore Roosevelt	McKinley
Charles Warren Fairbanks	Theodore Roosevelt
James Schoolcraft Sherman	W. H. Taft
Thomas Riley Marshall	Wilson
Calvin Coolidge	W. G. Harding
Charles Gates Dawes	Coolidge
Charles Curtis	Herbert Hoover
John Nance Garner	F. D. Roosevelt
Henry Agard Wallace	F. D. Roosevelt
Harry S Truman	F. D. Roosevelt
Alben William Barkley	Truman
Richard Milhous Nixon	Dwight Eisenhower
Lyndon Baines Johnson	J. F. Kennedy
Hubert Horatio Humphrey, Jr.	Johnson
Spiro Theodore Agnew	Nixon
Gerald Rudolph Ford	Nixon
Nelson Aldrich Rockefeller	Ford
Walter Frederick Mondale	Jimmy Carter

Vicki, Miss

Victoria May Budinger, wife of Tiny Tim (Herbert Khaury), married on TV's "Tonight" show, Dec. 17, 1969. Tulip is their daughter (The couple was divorced October 24, 1977)

Vicky

Richard Nixon's French poodle

Victor

Dan Reid's horse, a descendant of the Lone Ranger's horse Silver

---

*He later became a Confederate General during the Civil War. Vice president John C. Calhoun resigned in December 1832 to become a Senator. Spiro J. Agnew (real last name Anagnostopoulos) resigned October 9, 1973 under dishonorable conditions. Vice president William King took the oath of office while dying of tuberculosis in Cuba. Presidents who had no vice president were: John Tyler, Millard Fillmore, Andrew Johnson, Chester Arthur, as they succeeded to the presidency due to the death of the President.

Victoria

Balloon in Jules Verne's novel *Five Weeks in a Balloon*

Victoria

Ship in Ferdinand Magellan's fleet of 5: first ship to circumnavigate (1519-1522) the world (piloted by Juan Sebastian del Cano)

Victory

Admiral Nelson's flagship at the Battle of Trafalgar, Oct. 21, 1805, in which he was killed

Victory at Sea

TV documentary series covering World War II: scored by Richard Rodgers, narrated by Leonard Graves. A 1959 movie was narrated by Alexander Scourby

Video Ranger

Captain Video's boy sidekick (played on TV by Don Hastings) (1951 movie serial by Larry Stewart)

Vincent Van Gopher

Rodent friend of Deputy Dawg (TV cartoons)

Violins

Subject on which Jack Benny won $64 on the TV quiz show "$64,000 Question" when he answered the question, "Who is the famous eighteenth century violin maker whose first name was Antonio?"—Answer by Jack was "Stradivarius." He took the $64 and quit

Virgil Tibbs

Pasadena, California, police officer who travels to Wells, a city in one of the Carolinas, and solves a murder there for police chief Bill Gillespie (John Ball's novel *In the Heat of the Night*). Philadelphia detective (played by Sidney Poitier) who travels to a small Mississippi town, Sparta (Rod Steiger as Chief Gillespie) (1967 movie)
Virgil Tibbs then appeared in the two sequel movies *They Call Me Mr. Tibbs* (1970) and *The Organization* (1970) as a San Francisco police lieutenant

Virginia

The Old Dominion state is also called the Mother of Presidents; 8 United States Presidents were born there: Washington, Jefferson, Madison, Monroe, W. H. Harrison, Tyler, Taylor, Wilson

Virginia

Virginia O'Hanlon, 8-year-old girl who wrote a letter to the *New York Sun*, asking if there was a Santa Claus; she received the answer (published Sept. 21, 1897): "Yes, Virginia, there is a Santa Claus . . ." from Francis Pharcellus Church. Virginia lived at 115 West 95th Street in New York

Virginian, The

Hero, known only by that name, of Western novel (1902) by Owen Wister; his reply to Trampas: "When you call me, that, *smile!*"

Played in movies by Dustin Farnum (1914), Gary Cooper (1929), Joel McCrea (1945)

Played in TV series "The Virginian" by James Drury: the first Western series to run 90 minutes

Vivian

The Coca-Cola girl played by Jessica Dragonette (radio series *The Musical Comedy Hour*)

Vodka Martini

James Bond's favorite beverage. He prefers it very dry, shaken rather than stirred

"Voice of Canada"

Nickname of actor Lorne Green when he was a disc-jockey on Canadian Radio. He later starred in "Bonanza" and had a hit recording on RCA Victor, "Ringo" (1964)

Von Zell, Harry

Announcer of the Eddie Cantor radio show and George Burns and Gracie Allen Show on radio and TV. He had replaced Bill Goodwin. He was originally a singer with Charlie Barnet's band. He once introduced President Herbert Hoover on radio; "Ladies and Gentlemen, the President of the United States, Hoovert Heever"

Voodoo

McDonnell F-101 jet fighter

Vulcan

Jean Laffite's pirate ship in movie *The Buccaneer*. In the 1938 movie *The Buccaneer* portrayed by Fredric March. In the 1958 movie *The Buccaneer* by Yul Brynner

Vulcania

Captain Nemo's secret headquarters (1954 movie *20,000 Leagues Under the Sea*)

Vulgaria

Country that tries to steal Caractacus Potts' automobile Chitty Chitty Bang Bang, there children are forbidden (1968 movie *Chitty Chitty Bang Bang*)

Vultura

Evil ruler of the planet Atoma to which Captain Video goes in an attempt to defeat him. In the 1951 movie serial played by Gene Roth

W

WA 5-0434

Betty Cooper's phone number (*Archie* comics)

WB'BY

Radio station where Mark "Megaphone" Slackmeyer is a
D.J. (comic strip *Doonesbury*)

WCPD

West California Police Department in the TV series
"S.W.A.T."

WGBS-TV

Television station in Metropolis where Clark Kent (Superman) works as a reporter (after quitting his newspaper
job at the *Daily Planet*). Galaxy Broadcasting System

WHIZ

Radio station owned by Sterling Morris for which Billy
Batson (Captain Marvel) worked (comic book series).
Amalgamated Broadcasting. Actually a radio station in
Zanesville, Ohio

WIN

Whip Inflation Now

President Ford's anti-inflation slogan (1974). Began a
short-lived WIN button craze

WJM

Fictional TV station, channel 12, Minneapolis, for which
Mary Richards (Mary Tyler Moore) works (TV's "Mary
Tyler Moore Show"). The six clocks in the newsroom
were (left to right) one of these cities: Tokyo, Los
Angeles, Chicago, Minneapolis-St. Paul, New York, Lon-
don

WLA285

California license plate number of Michael McCord (The California Kid's) hot rod. Played by Martin Sheen (1974 TV movie *The California Kid*)

WSM

Nashville radio station that broadcasts Grand Ole Opry. WSM = We Shield Millions was the motto of the National Life and Accident Insurance Co. who originally owned the radio station. WSM-FM became the first licensed FM station in the U.S., beginning in 1941 (see *Ryman Auditorium*)

WWJ

First commercial radio station (Detroit, August 20, 1920); KDKA, Pittsburgh, Pa., began broadcasting August 31, 1920, and made the first regular scheduled broadcasts beginning Nov. 2, 1920

WXYZ

Radio station for which Alan Scott (The Green Lantern) is program director (comic books). Actually, WXYZ is a Detroit radio station on which the radio series "The Lone Ranger" (1933), "The Green Hornet" (1936), and "Challenge of the Yukon" (1947) premiered

WZAZ

1950's Milwaukee TV station on TV series "Happy Days"

W. C. Fields

William Claude Dukinfield

W. C. joke

Four-minute toilet (w.c.) story cut by NBC from Jack Paar's "Tonight" show of February 10; he walked off the show at 11:41 P.M. Eastern Standard Time, February 11, 1960, as a result. He returned to the show on March 7, after a trip to Hong Kong

Waggles

Captain B. J. Hunnicut's (Mike Farrell) dog back home (TV series M*A*S*H)

Wagner, (Honas) John Peter

Hall of Fame baseball shortstop. A pillar stands in Forbes Field in his honor. His picture is on what is considered the rarest of all baseball trading cards. On back of 1909 package of Ty Cobb Cigarettes (only cigarette ever named for a baseball player). Now valued at $3,000 plus

Wags

Dickie Dare's dog (comic strip *Dickie Dare* by Milton Caniff)

Wainwright College

College that Andy Hardy (Mickey Rooney) attends after he returns from World II (1946 movie *Love Laughs at Andy Hardy*)

Wa saba ani mako, o Tar Vey, Rama Kong

Chant of the witch doctor on Skull Island when Ann is tied to two pillars and offered to King Kong as a bride (1933 movie *King Kong*): translation "Thy bride is here, O mighty one, great Kong"

Walden Pond

Small lake near Concord, Mass., where Henry David Thoreau lived from July 4, 1845 to September 6, 1847 in a small cabin

Waldo

Dog in TV series "Nanny and the Professor"

Waldo

Mr. Magoo's nephew (movie cartoons): voice of Jerry Hausner. Another of his nephews on TV was Presley

Waldo Binny

Chester A. Riley's neighbor whose hobby is inventing (played by Sterling Holloway) (TV's "Life of Riley")

Walker, Clint

6'6" actor who appeared in TV series *Cheyenne* and *Kodiak*. His first movie with a speaking part was as Tarzan in the 1954 Bowery Boys movie *Jungle Gents* in which he was billed as Jett Norman. He, along with Montgomery Clift, and Errol Garner, has a twin sister. She's named Lucille

Walker, Mary Edwards

Only female to win the Medal of Honor. She served as a doctor during the Civil War, being presented the medal in 1865

Walker Cup

Awarded to the winners in men's amateur golf in British-American competition

Wallace, De Witt

American publisher, founder of the *Reader's Digest* in 1922

Walls of Jericho, The

Name given by Clark Gable to the blanket that separated

him and Claudette Colbert in their motel room in the 1934 movie *It Happened One Night*

WALL ST. LAYS AN EGG
Headline on *Variety* (Wednesday, October 30, 1929), the weekly theatrical newspaper, after the Stock Market crash which occured the day before on Black Tuesday

Wally
Beaver's older brother (TV series "Leave It To Beaver"): played by Tony Dow

Wally
Oswald the Rabbit's not-so-friendly next-door neighbor (cartoons)

Wally's Filling Station
Gas station where Gomer Pyle (Jim Nabors) worked in town of Mayberry (TV series "The Andy Griffith Show")

Wally Walrus
Woody Woodpecker's sidekick (cartoon/movie characters by Walter Lanz)

Walnetto
Candy that the dirty old man (Arte Johnson) many times offers to Gladys Ormphby (Ruth Buzzi); "Want a Walnetto?" (TV's "Laugh In")

Walrus
Captain Flint's ship (Robert Louis Stevenson's *Treasure Island*)

Walt Whitman High
High school on TV series "Room 222"

Walter
Swiss patriot William Tell's son from whose head he shot off an apple. On TV series "The Adventures of William Tell" played by Richard Rogers, William by Conrad Phillips

Walter Denton
Student at Madison High School that is a favorite of English teacher Constance Brooks (TV radio series *Our Miss Brooks*): played on radio/TV by Richard Crenna

Walter Johnson High School
High school named for baseball Hall-of-Famer Walter Johnson. Only school in the world named for a baseball player (Bethesda, Maryland)

Walters, Barbara
First female news broadcaster on network news program. She signed a $5 million, 5-year contract with ABC TV as

the new evening anchorwoman. She accepted the offer on April 22, 1976

Waltz King, The
Nickname of Wayne King

Waltz You Saved For Me, The
Theme song of Wayne King's orchestra

Waltzing Matilda
Australia's national song, first published 1903: words by A. B. Paterson (1864-1941), music by James Barr (1779-1860)

Walz, Jacob
Prospector (died 1891) who discovered (1870) the "Lost Dutchman" mine in Arizona, perhaps in the Superstition Mountains, only to have its location become lost

Wambsganss, William
Cleveland Indians' second baseman who performed the only unassisted triple-play in World Series history, in a game against the Dodgers in the World Series of 1920

Wameru
Doctor Marsh Tracy's (Marshall Thompson) game preserve (TV series "Daktari")

Wanda Von Kreesus
Heroine of *Oh, Wicked Wanda* comic strip by Frederick Mullally and Ron Embleton in each issue of *Penthouse* magazine

Wanderer
Ship that brought King Kong from Skull Island to New York (novelization). In the movies the ship is "Venture"

Wanderer of the Wasteland
1924 movie of Zane Grey novel. First movie to use the Technicolor process
Heroine of *Oh, Wicked Wanda* comic strip by Frederick
Last name of brothers who played in Pittsburgh Pirates' outfield from late 1920's to 1940's: Paul, known as Big Poison, led the National League in batting 3 times; Lloyd, known as Little Poison, also has a lifetime batting average of over .300

War Babies
1932 one-reel film in which Shirley Temple made her debut (part of "The Baby Burlesks" series). "Mais oui, mon cher!" was her first line. *Red-Haired Alibi* (1932) was her first full-length movie, although she only had a small part

762

War Paint

Kansas City Chief's football team mascot (a horse)

War Winds

Leslie Lynnton Benedict's (Elizabeth Taylor) horse in 1956 movie *Giant*

Ward, U.S.S.

Destroyer; first American ship to fire at Japanese at Pearl Harbor (Dec. 7, 1941); sunk in December 1944 during Philippines invasion (Ormoc Bay, Leyte) acting as transport

Warner Brothers

Motion picture studio founded 1923 by Russian-born brothers Albert, Harry, Jack and Samuel. Jack's autobiography is *My First Hundred Years in Hollywood*

Warp factor

Indicator of the speed of Star Ship "Enterprise" (TV series "Star Trek"): Warp drive was first used in 2018

Warp Factor One = the speed of light

Warp Factor Three = 24 times the speed of light

Warp Factor Six = 216 times the speed of light*

Warp Factor Eight = 512 times the speed of light

The other means of power is impulse drive

Wash

Washington Jefferson Lincoln Lee, Tom Mix's Negro cook (radio series). On radio, voice of Vance McCune and Forrest Lewis

Washington Merry-Go-Round

Drew Pearson's (1897-1969) syndicated newspaper column. After Pearson's death, the column was taken over by Jack Anderson

Wasp

Nemesis of Mandrake the Magician (comic strip)

Watch on the Rhine

Song that a group of German officers sing in Rick's Cafe as a group of Frenchmen attempt to drown them out with their singing of "Le Marseillaise" (1943 movie *Casablanca*)

Water

The one word that Helen Keller (played by Patty Duke) attempts to say in the 1962 movie *The Miracle Worker*. It was also the last word uttered by Ulysses S. Grant

---

*Maximum saf cruising speed of "Enterprise"

Watergate Seven
James W. McCord, E. Howard Hunt, G. Gordon Liddy, Jr., Bernard L. Barker, Eugenio R. Martinez, Frank A. Sturgis, Virgilio R. Gonzalez: arrested June 17, 1972, breaking into the Democratic Campaign Headquarters at Watergate building, Washington, D.C. The resulting cover-up and crisis led eventually to the resignation of President R. M. Nixon, August 9, 1974

Wayback Machine
Time machine that sends Mr. Peabody (the dog) and his Watchword of the Boy Scouts, *We'll Be Loyal Scouts*

Wayne Manor
Estate home of millionaire Bruce Wayne (Batman). The Bat Cave is located under the manor, 14 miles from Gotham City

Way You Look Tonight, The
Theme song of radio series "Mr. and Mrs. North"

We
First word of the United States Constitution (text)

We
Title of Charles A. Lindbergh's autobiographical account (1936) of his flight across the Atlantic: "We" are Lindbergh and his plane, "The Spirit of St. Louis"

We
1924 Russian Utopian novel by Zamyatin, set in 2600 A.D.

We belong dead
Last words of the monster before he blows up the laboratory destroying himself and his intended mate (1935 movie *The Bride of Frankenstein*)

We Learn to Do by Doing
Motto of the 4H Club

Weapons
Used in the game of "Clue": knife, revolver, wrench, lead pipe, rope, candlestick

Weary Willie
Sad-faced clown portrayed by Emmett Kelly. In the 1952 movie *The Greatest Show on Earth* Emmett Kelly portrayed himself

Web, The
Secret identity of crimefighter Professor John Raymond whose wife is named Rose (comic books)

Webb, Matthew

(1848-1883) First person to swim the English Channel. Dover to Calais in 21 hrs., 45 min. (August 24-25, 1875)

WEBELOS

Watchword of the Boy Scouts, *We'll Be Loyal Scouts*

Weber City

Amos 'n' Andy's hometown prior to moving to New York

Webster Webfoot

Jimmy Weldon's puppet duck (TV series "Funny Boners") (1950's)

"We Burn them to Ashes and then burn the ashes"

Motto of the 451 Fire Department, Ray Bradbury's *Fahrenheit 451*

We Buy—We Sell—We Trade

Slogan of a pawn shop. Original meaning of the three balls usually hung in front of the store

We Do Our Part

Slogan of the NRA (National Recovery Administration, 1933-1936)

Weight limits

Professional boxer can weigh no more:

Flyweight	112 lbs.
Bantamweight	118 lbs.
Featherweight	126 lbs.
Lightweight	135 lbs.
Welterweight	148 lbs.
Middleweight	160 lbs.
Light Heavyweight	175 lbs.
Heavyweight	Over 175 lbs.

In the Junior Divison:

Middle -	154 lbs.
Welter -	140 lbs.
Light -	130 lbs.

Weissmuller, Johnny

American swimmer and actor (born 1904)

He was the sixth actor to play Tarzan, the first in talkies, the role he is best known for and which he played 12 times, also playing Jungle Jim

In 1922, he became the first man to break 1 minute in the 100 meters (58.6 seconds)

In 1923, he became the first to break 5 minutes for the 400 meters (4:57)

At the 1924 Paris Olympics, he won gold medals in the 100-meter and 400-meter freestyle races (:59) (5:04.2) In 1928 Olympics at Amsterdam he won a gold medal in the 100-meter freestyle (:58.6)

Welcome Home, Admiral Dewey, Hero of Manila
Sign on the rear fender of Wolf J. Flywheel's (Groucho Marx) automobile (1941 movie *The Big Store*)

"We'll Meet Again"
Song sung by Vera Lynn as a number of nuclear explosions occur in the closing scene of 1964 movie *Dr. Strangelove*. During WWII Vera Lynn was nicknamed "Sweetheart of the Forces" by the British Tommies

Weller, Charles E.
Originated "Now is the time for all good men to come to the aid of the party" as a typing exercise

Wellingtons
Singers of the Ballad of Gilligan's Island (TV series "Gilligan's Island")

Wells, Alice
First policewoman, sworn in September 12, 1910. She worked for the Los Angeles Police Department

Wells, Floyd
Kansas State Penitentiary inmate whose statement led to the arrest of Perry Smith and Richard Hickock who killed the Clutter family on their River Valley farm in Holcomb, Kansas. Wells received the reward for their capture. Wells once worked for Herbert Clutter

Wells, H. G.
Herbert George Wells (1886-1946), English novelist

Wendy
"The Good Little Witch"; girlfriend of Casper, the friendly ghost (comic book series)

Wendy Moira Angela
The older Darling girl (Sir James Barrie's *Peter Pan*). Actress Wendy Barrie (born Marguerite Jenkin) changed her first name to Wendy after the character and her last name to Barrie after Peter Pan's creator

We Never Sleep
Motto of the Pinkerton National Detective Agency

We're Here
Schooner in Rudyard Kipling's *Captains Courageous*, commanded by Disko Troop

Werewolves

Monsters who, in legend, are afraid of garlic and wolf-bane. They can be killed with silver bullets, a silver cane or any other item containing silver. Their ring finger is their longest finger. In the palm of their hand is a pentagram (see *The Wolf Man*)

We Serve

Motto of the Lions Club

Wessex

Thomas Hardy's dog

Westdale

High school for which Greg Brady (Barry Williams) plays football (TV series "The Brady Bunch")

West Egg

Long Island home of Jay Gatsby (F. Scott Fitzgerald's *The Great Gatsby*)

West 35th Street

New York location of Nero Wolfe's four-story old brownstone house, which he bought in 1930

Western Hockey League (1968-1969)

Seattle (Totems)

Portland (Buckaroos)

Vancouver (Canucks)

San Diego (Gulls)

Phoenix (Roadrunners)

Western outlaws, fraternal section

Younger brothers: Cole (Thomas), Bob, Jim, John

Dalton brothers (cousins to James brothers and Younger brothers and related to Johnny Ringo): Bob, Grat, Emmett, Bill

Reno brothers: John, Clinton (not in the gang), Frank, Simon ("Slim"), William

Harpe brothers: Micajah ("Big Harpe"), Wiley ("Little Harpe")

James brothers: Jesse Woodson, Alexander Frank

Outlaws Jesse and Frank James, John Wesley Hardin, and Al Jennings were the sons of ministers. The Dalton brothers all at once served as deputy marshals; one of them Frank, was a marshal for Judge Isaac C. Parker. Emmett Dalton later wrote his autobiography *When the Daltons Rode* which, in 1940, was made into a movie starring Randolph Scott. Jesse James, Frank James, Cole Younger and Jim Younger all rode with Quantrill's Raiders. It was the Reno brothers who, on October 6, 1866, committed the first train robbery in U.S. history. They robbed the Ohio and Mississippi Railroad at Seymour, Indiana for $10,000. On December 11, 1868 the brothers were hanged by a lynch mob. It was Thomas "Cole" Younger who was the father of Belle Starr's (Belle Shirley's) daughter Pearl. Frank James never spent time in jail; he was acquitted of all his crimes

Westerns on TV

Series	Central Role	Actor
Adventures of Jim Bowie	Jim Bowie	Scott Forbes
Adventures of Kit Carson	Kit Carson	Bill Williams
Alias Smith and Jones	Hannibal Heyes (Joshua Smith)	Peter Duel/ Roger Davis
	Jed "Kid" Cury (Thaddeus Jones)	Ben Murphy
Annie Oakley	Annie Oakley	Gail Davis
Bat Masterson	Bat Masterson	Gene Barry
Big Valley	Victoria Barkley	Barbara Stanwyck
Black Saddle	Clay Culhane	Peter Breck
Bonanza	Ben Cartwright	Lorne Greene
Branded	Jason McCord	Chuck Connors
Broken Arrow	Tom Jeffords	John Lupton
Bronco	Bronco Lane	Ty Hardin
Buckskin	Jody O'Connell	Tommy Nolan
Californians, The	Matt Wayne	Richard Coogan
Cimarron City	Matt Rockford	George Montgomery
Cimarron Strip	Jim Crown	Stuart Whitman
Cisco Kid, The	Cisco Kid	Duncan Renaldo
Colt .45	Christopher Colt	Wayde Preston
Cowboy G-Men	Pat Gallagher	Russell Hayden
Custer	George A. Custer	Wayne Maunder
Daniel Boone	Daniel Boone	Fess Parker
Deputy, The	Simon Fry	Henry Fonda
Destry	Harrison Destry	John Gavin
Dundee and the Culhane	Dundee	John Mills
Empire	Jim Redigo	Richard Egan
Frontier Doctor	Dr. Bill Baxter	Rex Allen

Gene Autry Show, The	Gene Autry	Gene Autry
Guns of Will Sonnett, The	Will Sonnett	Walter Brennan
Gunslinger	Cord	Tony Young
Gunsmoke	Matt Dillon	James Arness
Have Gun, Will Travel	Paladin	Richard Boone
High Chaparral	John Cannon	Leif Erickson
Hondo	Hondo Lane	Ralph Taeger
Hopalong Cassidy	Hopalong Cassidy	William Boyd
Iron Horse, The	Ben Calhoun	Dale Robertson
Hotel de Paree	Sundance	Earl Holliman
Jefferson Drum	Jefferson Drum	Jeff Richards
Johnny Ringo	Johnny Ringo	Don Durant
Judge Roy Bean	Roy Bean	Edgar Buchanan
Kung Fu	Caine	David Carradine
Lancer	Murdoch Lancer	Andrew Duggan
Laramie	Jess Harper	Robert Fuller
Laredo	Reese Bennett	Neville Brand
Lawman, The	Dan Troop	John Russell
Legend of Jesse James, The	Jesse James	Chris Jones
Life and Legend of Wyatt Earp	Wyatt Earp	Hugh O'Brian
Long Ranger	Lone Ranger	Clayton Moore
Loner, The	William Colton	Lloyd Bridges
MacKenzie's Raiders	Ranald MacKenzie	Richard Carlson
A Man Called Shenandoah	Shenandoah	Robert Horton
Man From Blackhawk	Sam Logan	Robert Rockwell
Man Without A Gun	Adam MacLean	Rex Reason
Maverick	Bret Maverick	James Garner
Monroes, The	Clayt Monroe	Michael Anderson, Jr.
Outlaws	William Foreman	Don Collier
Overland Trail	Kelly	William Bendix
Pony Express	Brett Clark	Grant Sullivan

Range Rider	Range Rider	Jock Mahoney
Rawhide	Rowdy Yates	Clint Eastwood
Rebel, The	Johnny Yuma	Nick Adams
Restless Gun, The	Vint Bonner	John Payne
Rifleman, The	Lucas McCain	Chuck Connors
Roy Rogers Show, The	Roy Rogers	Roy Rogers
Shane	Shane	David Carradine
Sheriff of Cochise, The	Frank Morgan	Scott Brady
Sky King	Sky King	Kirby Grant
Stagecoach West	Luke Parry	Wayne Rogers
Steve Donovan, Western Marshall	Steve Donovan	Douglas Kennedy
Stoney Burke	Stoney Burke	Jack Lord
Sugarfoot	Tom Brewster	Will Hutchins
Tales of the Texas Rangers	Jack Pearson	Willard Parker
Tales of Wells Fargo	Jim Hardie	Dale Robertson
Tall Man, The	Pat Garrett	Barry Sullivan
Tate	Tate	David McLean
Temple Houston	Temple Houston	Jeffrey Hunter
Texan, The	Bill Longley	Rory Calhoun
Tombstone Territory	Clay Hollister	Pat Conway
Trackdown	Hoby Gilman	Robert Culp
26 Men	Tom Rynning	Tris Coffin
Two Faces West	Rick and Ben January	Charles Bateman
Virginian, The	Owen Wister	James Drury
Wagon Train	Major Seth Adams/ Chris Hale	Ward Bond/ John McIntire
Wanted Dead or Alive	Josh Randal	Steve McQueen
Westerner, The	Dave Blasingame	Brian Keith
Whispering Smith	Tom Smith	Audie Murphy
Wichita Town	Mike Dunbar	Joel McCrea
Wide Country	Mitch Guthrie	Earl Holliman
Wild Bill Hickok	Bill Hickok	Guy Madison

Wild Wild West	Jim West	Robert Conrad
Yancy Derringer	Yancy Derringer	Jock Mahoney

Westmacott, Mary

Pseudonym of mystery writer Agatha Christie

Westminster Abbey

London church, parts of which date to the 13th century: coronation place of the kings of England; burial place of the notables of England

Westwood High

School which Keith (David Cassidy) attends (TV series "The Partridge Family")

"We've Only Just Begun"

Popular song hit by the Carpenters in 1970. Originated as a TV commercial theme for Crocker Citizens Bank in California (written by Paul Williams and Robert Nichols); Williams was part of the singing group in TV ad. The song is now played at many weddings replacing "I Love You Truly"

What A Way To Go

1964 movie starring Shirley MacLaine as Louisa Foster. Her five husbands were:

Edgar Hooper - Dick Van Dyke

Larry Flint - Paul Newman

Rod Anderson - Robert Mitchum

Jerry Benson - Gene Kelly

Leonard Crowley - Dean Martin

What Happened to Mary?

First movie serial, in 1913, starring Mary Fuller

"What'll I Do"

Song played in opening scene in the 1975 version of *The Great Gatsby*. Composed by Irving Berlin in 1924. First person to record the song was actor Walter Pidgeon

What's My Line

TV game show:

M.C.: John Charles Daly

Panel (1950 to 1965): Dorothy Kilgallen, Arlene Francis, Bennett Cerf, and guest (such as Hal Block or Fred or Steve Allen). The original panelists were: Louis Untermeyer, Harold Hoffman, Dr. Richard Hoffman and Arlene Francis. The first mystery guest appeared in February 1950; he was Phil Rizzuto (later broadcaster for the New York Yankees). Bennett Cerf was the founder of Random House Publishers. Dorothy Kilgallen completed an around-the-world flight in 1936 on commercial airlines beating other female reporters. She completed the trip in 24 days, 12 hours and 52 minutes. She told the story in her book *Girl Around the World*

When *What's My Line* was later shown in syndication 1968-1973 the M.C.'s were Wally Bruner and Larry Blyden

Wheatfield with Crows

Painting upon which Van Gogh was working when he shot and killed himself (1890)

When

First word of the Declaration of Independence (text)

When Irish Eyes Are Smiling

Theme song of radio series *Duffy's Tavern*

When It's Round-Up Time in Texas

Tom Mix's theme song

When you call me that, smile!

The Virginian to Trampas (Owen Wister's *The Virginian*). In the 1929 movie *The Virginian* the Virginian's (Gary Cooper) line is "If you want to call me that, smile" said to Trampas (Walter Huston)

"When the Moon Comes Over the Mountain"

Theme song of Kate Smith, who in 1976 was the Grand Marshal for the Tournament of Roses parade

"Where the Blue of the Night Meets the Gold of the Day"

Bing Crosby's theme song; his 1953 autobiography is titled *Call Me Lucky*

"Whipped Cream"

Theme song for the TV game show "The Dating Game": a hit song by Herb Alpert and the Tijuana Brass

Whisky A Go Go

Los Angeles nightclub on the Sunset Strip at which singer Johnny Rivers appeared and recorded a number of albums (1960's)

Whistler, The

Radio program: introduction, "I am the Whistler, and I know many things, for I walk by night. I know many strange tales hidden in the hearts of men and women who have stepped into the shadows. Yes, I know the nameless terrors of which they dare not speak"

On radio: played by Bill Forman (also on TV), Marvin Miller, and Everett Clark (Dorothy Roberts did the whistling on radio and TV as she was the only person available who could reach a two octave range)

Movies starring Richard Dix (all but the last) as the Whistler:

The Whistler (1944)
Mark of the Whistler (1944)
Power of the Whistler (1945)
Voice of the Whistler (1945)
The Mysterious Intruder (1946)
The 13th Hour (1947)
Secret of the Whistler (1947)
Return of the Whistler (1948) Michael Duane

Whistler's Mother

Popular title of James McNeill Whistler's painting "Arrangement in Grey and Black." His mother Anna McNeill posed for the picture when she was 65 years old. The painting hangs in the Louvre

White Flash

Tex Ritter's horse

WHitehall 1212

London telephone number of New Scotland Yard Superintendent William Gryce, friend of detective Richard Rollison (*the Toff*) (John Creasey's *Toff* series)

White Way Hotel

New York City Times Square hotel where the 1938 Marx Brothers novie *Room Service* occurs

Whitewind

Golden Arrow's horse (comic book series *The Golden Arrow*)

Whitey

Hoot Gibson's horse (movies)

Whitey

White Owl Cigars' owl

Whitey

President Zachary Taylor's favorite horse. They both served in the Mexican War at Buena Vista, Palo Alto. Whitey served in his master's funeral parade

Whitey

Boston Blackie's little black terrier on TV's "Boston Blackie"

Whitfield and Kimberly Publishers

Firm that publishes Ellery Queen's (Jim Hutton) novels on TV series "Ellery Queen"

Whiz Kids

Nickname of the 1950's Philadelphia Phillies baseball team

"Who's Afraid of the Big Bad Wolf?"

Popular 1932 hit song, from the Walt Disney animated movie *The Three Little Pigs* (in film the song was sung by Mary Modler, Pinto Colvig and Dorothy Compton). *The Three Little Pigs* won an Academy Award for Best Short Subject (animated) (1932-1933)

Who's buried in Grant's Tomb?

Tomb located on Riverside Drive in New York City, popular consolation prize question asked by Groucho Marx on his TV show "You Bet Your Life," in hopes that no one would miss it (some people did). Hiram Ulysses Simpson Grant is buried there. A fact that very few people know is that his wife Julia Boggs Dent Grant was also buried there 17 years after Hiram's death

Other consolation questions were: When did the War of 1812 start? How long do you cook a 3 minute egg? What color is an orange?

Who's on First?

Well-polished Abbott and Costello comedy routine used by them in 1945 movie *The Naughty Nineties*, Abbott as Dexter Broadhurst of the St. Louis Wolves and Costello as Sebastian Dinwiddle

First base	Who
Second base	What
Third base	I Don't Know
Shortstop	I Don't Care
Catcher	Today
Pitcher	Tomorrow
Left Field	Why
Center Field	Because

(No right fielder is mentioned in the routine)

A copy of the film is kept at the Baseball Hall of Fame

"Why don't you come up and see me sometime"

Line never said by Lady Lou (Mae West) to Captain Cummings (Cary Grant) in 1933 movie *She Done Him Wrong*. The line she did use was: "Why don't you come sometime 'n' see me?"

Wicked Witch of the East

Witch killed when Dorothy's house fell on her; Dorothy

774

got the magical red shoes from her (1939 movie *The Wizard of Oz*)

Wicket Gate, The
Entrance to the road which leads to the Celestial City; over the door is written: "Knock, and it shall be opened unto you" (John Bunyan's *The Pilgrim's Progress*)

Widener Cup
Trophy awarded for the sport of Horseracing

Widener Handicap
Annual horserace at Hialeah

Widow Maker
Pecos Bill's horse (American folklore)

Wiere Brothers
Comedy team: Harry, Herbert, Sylvester

Wightman Cup
Trophy awarded to the winners in lawn tennis in British-American competition

Wilbur
Fern's small pig, saved by Charlotte A. Cavatica, a large grey spider (E. B. White's *Charlotte's Web*). In 1973 movie, voice of Henry Gibson

Wild Bill Hickok
James Butler Hickok (1837-1876), Western gunfighter and lawman; killed by Jack McCall August 2, 1876, while holding the famous "dead man's hand" of aces and 8's

Wildcat
Secret identity of Ted Grant, motorcycle-riding crime-fighter (comic book series)

Wild Goose, The
Name of John Wayne's yacht

Wile E. Coyote
Pursuer of the Roadrunner (Warner Brothers cartoon): voice of Mel Blanc. Prior to the roadrunner, the Coyote was teamed with Ralph the Sheepdog

Wilhelmina
Nickname for Nick Carter's 9mm Luger (*Nick Carter-Killmaster* series)

Wilkes-Barre, Pennsylvania
Joe Palooka's hometown (comic strip)

William Goodrich
Pseudonym of Roscoe "Fatty" Arbuckle as a director. Used by him after the scandal involving the death of

Virginia Rappe. The name Will B. Good was suggested by Buster Keaton as an alternative to William Goodrich

"William Tell Overture"

Theme song of the Lone Ranger (composed by Gioacchino Rossini). Also known as "The Mickey Mouse Overture," Mickey having conducted it in a Disney short cartoon. William Tell was the legendary Swiss hero who shot an apple from his son Walter's head

Williams, Saundra

First Miss Black America, winning title September 8, 1968

Williams, (Tennessee)

Thomas Lanier Williams. Plays of his made into movies: *The Glass Menagerie* (1950), *A Streetcar Named Desire* (1951), *The Rose Tattoo* (1955), *Baby Doll* (1956), *Cat on a Hot Tin Roof* (1958), *Suddenly, Last Summer* (1959), *The Fugitive King* (1960), *Summer and Smoke* (1961), *The Roman Spring of Mrs. Stone* (1961), *Sweet Bird of Youth* (1962), *The Night of the Iguana* (1964), *Boom* (1968). *A Streetcar Named Desire* won the 1947 Pulitzer Prize. His 1976 autobiography is titled *Memoirs*

Williamsburg

Harry S Truman's presidential yacht

Willie

Penguin on the pack of Kool cigarettes

Willie (William) Chan

Honolulu detective sergeant Charlie Chan's cousin who is captain of the all-Chinese baseball team (Earl Derr Bigger's *Charlie Chan* novel series)

Willie and Joe

Bill Mauldin's World War II GI cartoon characters. Played in 1951 movie *Up Front* by Tom Ewell and David Wayne. In 1952 movie sequel *Back at the Front* (retitled: *Willie and Joe at the Front*) by Tom Ewell and Harvey Lembeck

Willie Gillis

U.S. Army private who appeared on the cover of the *Saturday Evening Post* magazine eleven times beginning in October 4, 1941 edition. Created by Norman Rockwell whose neighbor, Robert Buck, posed for Willie

Willie Loman

Brooklyn salesman in Arthur Miller's play *Death of a*

Salesman. Played by Lee J. Cobb in 1949 Pulitzer Prize winning play. Played by Fredric March in 1951 movie

Willie Stark
The southern governor (Broderick Crawford) who ran his state with an iron hand. Based on the life of Louisiana's Huey Long. The 1949 movie *All the King's Men* won an Oscar for best picture as did Crawford for best actor

Willie the Actor
Nickname of infamous bank robber Willie Sutton. He has spent over 35 years in prison and stolen more than $2 million (according to him)

Willig, George
Man who climbed the 110 story (1350′) South Tower of the World Trade Center, May 26, 1977. It took him 3½ hours. He was fined $1.10 by Mayor Abraham Beame. Newspapers nicknamed him The Spiderman

"Will You Love Me In December As You Do In May?"
Song composed in 1905 by Ernest R. Ball and James J. Walker, also known as *Beau James* the Mayor of New York City. His life was portrayed in the 1957 movie *Beau James* by Bob Hope. He also married Billy Rose to Fanny Brice when he was Mayor

Wills, Frank
Janitor who discovered the break-in at the offices of the Democrats in the Watergate building, June 17, 1972

Wilma Deering, (Lt.)
Buck Rogers' girlfriend: played on radio by Adele Ronson, in 1939 movie serial *Buck Rogers* by Constance Moore and on TV by Lou Prentis

Wilson, Clerow "Flip"
His television roles: Geraldine Jones; Freddie Johnson, the Bachelor; Marvin Latimer; Danny Danger; Herbie the Ice Cream Man; Reverend Leroy (TV's "The Flip Wilson Show")

Wilson, Samuel
The original Uncle Sam, a meatpacker during the War of 1812 who stamped his kegs "U.S."

Wimpy (J. Wellington Wimpy)
Popeye's hungry friend always munching on a hamburger. His favorite line is "Gladly pay you Tuesday for a hamburger today." Played on radio by Charles Lawrence

Winchell, Paul
Ventriloquist and inventor. He holds more than 30

patients, one on a successful artificial heart. His dummies: Jerry Mahoney, Knucklehead Smiff, Irving the Mouse. Voice of Tigger (Winnie-the-Pooh)

Winchell, Walter

New York newspaperman, 34 years with the *New York Daily Mirror* (1897-1972), noted for his Broadway column in which he invented words widely adopted

Radio's "The Jergens' Journal" reporter: "Good evening, Mr. and Mrs. North and South America and all the ships and clippers at sea." Another version: "Good evening, Mr. and Mrs. America and all the ships at sea, let's go to press"

Narrator of TV series "The Untouchables" for $25,000 an episode. He spoke at a rate of 197 words per minute. As a columnist he hung out at Sherman Billingsley's Stork Club during the 1940's. He always sat at table 50 in the Cub Room. There was even a Winchellburger on the menu

Winchester House

Rambling "mystery" house in San Jose, California, built by Sarah L. Winchester, heir to the Winchester Arms fortune. She believed that as long as she kept building onto the house, she would keep living. The house has 160 rooms, 200 doors, 10,000 windowpanes, 47 fireplaces, stairways to nowhere, secret passages. Originally named Llanda Villa Estate, the house was constructed between 1884 and 1922 costing $5,500,000 of her $20,000,000 inheritance

Windy Wales

Bobby Benson's sidekick

Winfield, Darrell

Marlboro cowboy on 1960's TV commercials and magazine ads. He was the most popular, having appeared in 85 per cent of the commercials (others were Dick Hammer, Dean Myers, Robert Norris, Tom Mattox)

Wingfoot Express

Walt Arfons' J-46 jet-powered car: driven (1965) by Tom Green

Wings

First movie to win an Academy Award (1928): starred Charles "Buddy" Rogers and Clara Bow (Gary Cooper appeared in the movie). Only silent movie to win Best Picture

Winkie Country

Part of the Land of Oz where the Wicked Witch of the West (Margaret Hamilton in the movie) lives in L. Frank Baum's *The Wizard of Oz*. The Winkies are the people in the western country of Winkie, later ruled by the Tin Man (*Land of Oz*). Originally ruled by the Wicked Witch of the West

Winky, Blinky and Noddy

The three comical sidekicks of The Flash (original version comic books)

Winky Dink

TV cartoon boy; the show "Winky Dink and You" was narrated by Jack Barry: voice of Mae Questel. His friends are Dusty Dan and Mike McBein

Winnie Woodpecker

Woody Woodpecker's girlfriend (comic books)

Winnie Mae

Lockheed Vega (N-105-W) piloted by Wiley Post (using a Sperry automatic pilot), first world solo flight, July 22, 1933: 15, 596 miles in 7 days, 18 hours, 49½ minutes

Winnie-the-Pooh

Teddy bear of Christopher Robin's: central character of A. A. (Alan Alexander) Milne's *When We Were Very Young* (1924), *Winnie-the-Pooh* (1926), *Now We Are Six* (1927), *The House at Pooh Corner* (1928). Books illustrated by Ernest H. Shepherd. In cartoons Winnie's voice is that of Sterling Holloway

Winston

Hector Heathcoat's dog (cartoon)

Winters, Jonathan

His characters in comedy routines: Maynard Tetlinger, Winslow G. Flydipper, Elwood P. Suggins, Chester Hunnihugger, Maude Frickett, Lance Loveguard

Winton Flyer

1905 yellow automobile stolen by the chauffeur, Boon (Steve McQueen) in the 1969 movie *The Reivers*

Wise Guys (Little Wise Guys)

Comic book series featured with "Daredevil": Jock C. H. Herendeen, Meatball (later Curley), Pee Wee (later Slugger), Scarecrow. Created by Charles Biro, debut in *Daredevil Comics* #13 (October 1942)

Wishbone
    The cattle-drive cook (Paul Brinegar) (TV series "Raw-hide")
Wives of Henry VIII
    Catherine of Aragon (Married 1509; divorced 1533; mother of Mary Tudor; his brother's widow)
    Anne Boleyn (married 1533; beheaded 1536; mother of Elizabeth I, born 1533)
    Jane Seymour (married 1536; died in childbirth 1537; mother of Edward VI, born 1537)
    Anne of Cleves (married and divorced 1540)
    Catherine Howard (Married 1540, beheaded 1542)
    Catherine Parr (married 1543; survived him)
    Henry VIII portrayed in movies:
    The Private Life of Henry VIII (1933) Charles Laughton
    Young Bess (1953) Charles Laughton
    A Man For All Seasons (1966) Robert Shaw
    Ann of the Thousand Days (1969) Richard Burton
    Anne Boleyn portrayed in movies:
    Anne of the Thousand Days (1969) Genevieve Bujold
    A Man For All Seasons (1966) Vanessa Redgrave
Wizard of Menlo Park
    Nickname of Thomas A. Edison, whose laboratory was at Menlo Park, New Jersey. Portrayed in 1940 movie *Young Tom Edison* by Mickey Rooney, also in 1940 movie *Edison, the Man* by Spencer Tracy
Wizard of Oz, The
    Novel (*The Wonderful Wizard of Oz*, 1900) by Lyman Frank Baum (1856-1919) in 38 sequel Oz books
    It was staged as early as 1901, and was made into silent movies in 1910 and 1924 (with Larry Semon)
    In 1939 it became a musical film with Judy Garland as Dorothy Gale, Jack Haley as the Tin Woodsman (Hickory), Ray Bolger as the Scarecrow (Hunk), Bert Lahr as the Cowardly Lion (Zeke), Margaret Hamilton as the Wicked Witch (Miss Elvira Gulch), Frank Morgan as the Wizard (Professor Marvel), and Billie Burke as the Good Witch, Glinda
    The movie premiered at Loew's Capitol Theater in New York on August 18, 1939. The first 18 minutes of the movie is in black and white, also ending in black and white. Movie is shown annually on TV since 1956. The original casting for the movie was: Dorothy (Shirley

Temple), Tin Man (Buddy Ebsen), The Wizard (W. C. Fields). In the movie Frank Morgan played 5 roles: Professor Marvel, Wizard of Oz, Coachman, Guard at the door of Emerald City, and Guard at the doorway to the Wizard's chamber

Wodehouse, P. G.

Pelham Grenville Wodehouse (born 1881), English author, notably of the "Jeeves" novels and of plays and musicals. He composed the song "Bill" for the 1936 movie *Show Boat*

Wohelo

Watchword of the Campfire Girls, made up of the first letters of *WO*rk, *HE*alth, *LO*ve

WOL

Winnie-the-Pooh's friend the Owl spells his name this way

Wolf

John F. Kennedy's wolfhound born in 1963

Wolf

Rip Van Winkle's dog

Wolf City

1894 Wyoming town, setting for 1965 movie *Cat Ballou*

Wolf Larsen

The "Sea Wolf," captain of the schooner "Ghost" (Jack London's *The Sea Wolf*)

Wolf Man

Lawrence (Larry) Stewart Talbot (played by Lon Chaney, Jr.) in 1941 movie *The Wolf Man*: a werewolf (makeup by Jack Pierce). The character of the Wolf Man appeared in later pictures. In the earlier *The Werewolf of London* (1935) Henry Hull had played Wilfred Glendon, who changes to a werewolf at the full moon

Played by Oliver Reed in 1961 movie *The Curse of the Werewolf*

Wolfman Jack

Pseudonym of disc jockey Robert Smith, whose program is syndicated to 1,453 radio stations. Began on radio station XERP in Mexico

Wolf von Frankenstein, Baron

Son of Dr. Henry Frankenstein (1936 movie *Son of Frankenstein*): played by Basil Rathbone

Wolves

Baseball team for which Dennis Ryan (Frank Sinatra)

and Eddie O'Brien (Gene Kelly) play (1949 movie *Take Me Out to the Ball Game*)

Women's Hall of Fame
Founded at Seneca, New York in 1973

Wonderful World
Cedric Wehunt's (Chester Lauck) favorite greetings, radio's *Lum 'n Abner*

Wonder Girl
Identity of Drusilla Prince (Debra Winger), the younger sister of Wonder Woman (TV series "Wonder Woman")

Wonder Warthog
Secret identity of mild-mannered Philbert Desenex (comic book character drawn by Gilbert Shelton)

Wonder Woman
Secret identity of Diana Prince. Debut in *All Star Comics* #8 December 1941. Created by William Moulton Morston (pen name Charles Moulton), inventor of the polygraph (lie detector). Wonder Woman's (who was "born" on March 22) real name is Diana, who took the name Diana Prince from an Army nurse who went to South America to get married. On TV series played by Lynda Carter. Wonder Woman possesses: The Beauty of Aphrodite, The Wisdom of Athena, The Strength of Hercules, The Speed of Mercury

Wood
Material immune to power of the original Green Lantern (*All Star* and *All American Comics*)

Woodbridge
Town location of TV serial "The Secret Storm"

Woodlawn Vase
Trophy presented to the winner of the Preakness horse race at Pimlico

Wood Memorial
Annual horserace run at Aqueduct

Woodstock
Snoopy's bird friend/secretary (Charles Schulz's "Peanuts" cartoon strip), introduced in 1970

Woodsy Owl
Symbol of the anti-pollution movement: "Give a hoot; don't pollute"

Woody Woodpecker
Slightly -mad bird character in Walter Lantz cartoon shorts and comic books: niece, Knothead; nephew, Splin-

ter. Voice of Mrs. Grace Lantz speeded up: his laughter is Mel Blanc's

Woodward, Robert and Carl Bernstein

Two *Washington Post* reporters who exposed the Watergate coverup. In 1976 movie *All the President's Men*, portrayed by Robert Redford and Dustin Hoffman respectively

Woody

The Mod Squad's Mercury station wagon (license 188458), wrecked in one of their episodes (TV series "Mod Squad")

Woofer

Winky Dink's dog (TV cartoon series "Winky Dink and You")

Woola

Captain John Carter's pet Martian hound (*Martian Series* by Edgar Rice Burroughs)

Wooley, Sheb

Entertainer who recorded one of 1958's big hits "The Purple People Eater"

Recorded comedy albums under pseudonym Ben Colder

Played on TV in series "Rawhide" as Pete Nolan

Woolworth, F. W.

Frank Winfield Woolworth (1852-1919), five-and-dime store magnate. He opened his first store in Utica, New York in 1879. Prior to the completion of the Empire State Building, the Woolworth Building in New York City was the tallest building in the world (1913-1931)

Woozy Winks

Plastic Man's partner (comic books): debut *Police Comics* #13, November 1942

World Football League (defunct)

Western Division
    Honolulu Hawaiians
    Southern California Sun
    Portland Storm
    Houston Texans
Central Division
    Chicago Fire
    Birmingham Americans
    Memphis Southmen
    Detroit Wheels
Eastern Division
    Philadelphia Bell

        Florida Blazers
        New York Stars
        Jacksonville Sharks
    Other teams were the Charlotte Hornets, Shreveport
    Steamers, San Antonio Wings
World Hockey Association
    Members teams are:

Calgary	Cowboys
Cincinnati	Stingers
Cleveland	Crusaders
Denver	Spurs
Edmonton	Oilers
Houston	Aeros
Indianapolis	Racers
Minnesota	Fighting Saints
New England	Whalers
Phoenix	Roadrunners
Quebec	Nordiques
San Diego	Mariners
Toronto	Toros
Winnipeg	Jets

World Tennis teams
    (original teams)
Pacific Division
    Golden Gaters
    Los Angeles Strings
    Hawaii Leis
    Denver Racquets
Gulf Plains Division
    Minnesota Buckskins
    Houston E. Z. Riders
    Florida Flamingos
    Chicago Aces
Central Division
    Cleveland Nets
    Detroit Loves
    Pittsburgh Triangles
    Toronto Royals
Atlantic Division
    Philadelphia Freedoms
    Boston Lobsters
    Baltimore Banners
    New York Sets

The Denver Racquets were the first champions in 1974
Teams (as of 1977)

- Boston Lobsters
- New York Apples
- Indiana Loves
- Cleveland Nets
- Soviets
- Phoenix Racquets
- Golden Gaters
- Seaport Cascades
- San Diego Fryers
- Los Angeles Strings

"World is Waiting for the Sunrise"

The song that Stan Laurel plays on the bedsprings in his jail cell (1939 movie *The Flying Deuces*)

The World of Tomorrow

Theme of the 1939 New York's World's Fair. It opened Sunday, April 30, 1939 in Flushing Meadow, Queens, N.Y. Grover Aloysius Whalen was the Fair's president

World Series and Rose Bowl

Only two men have played in both. Jackie Jensen for the New York Yankees (MVP) and for USC (All American) and Charles Essigian for the Los Angeles Dodgers and Stanford

(Earl Neale played for Cincinnati in 1919 World Series but his participation in the Rose Bowl was as coach for Washington)

"World Turned Upside Down, The"

Tune played as Cornwallis surrendered at Yorktown, October 19, 1781

World Wide Wickets

Company headed by J. B. Biggley in the 1961 play, 1967 movie *How to Succeed in Business Without Really Trying* (Biggley played by Rudy Vallee in play and movie)

World's Wonder Horse

Title given to Gene Autry's horse, Champion

Worthless

Mule belonging to Dirty Sally Fergus (Jeanette Nolan) (TV series "Dirty Sally")

Worth's Law

"When something fails to work and you demonstrate it for a repairman, it works better than ever, as if it never failed to work at all": first appearance of this law in print

Wrenn, Roger

Photographer who took the famous picture of General Douglas MacArthur wading ashore in the Philippines, October 1944

Wright Whirlwind

9 cylinder J-5C engine, 223 h.p. (serial no. 7331) on Charles Lindbergh's Ryan monoplane "Spirit of St. Louis" when he solo-hopped the Atlantic Ocean, May 20-21, 1927. The engine was designed by Charles Edward Taylor. The Wright Brothers' airplane was given patent number 821393

Wrightsville

Town invaded by two rival motorcycle gangs, one led by Johnny (played by Marlon Brando), leader of the Black Rebels, and the other led by Chino (Lee Marvin) (1954 movie *The Wild One*, based on the actual takeover of the California town of Hollister by a motorcycle gang on July 4, 1947)

Wrigley Field

National League ball park in Chicago (1060 West Addison St.), only major league baseball stadium not equipped with lights for night baseball

Wynken, Blynken, and Nod

Sailed in a wooden shoe (from Eugene Field poem "A Dutch Lullaby")

X

X214

South Pacific Japanese-infested island to which construction chief Wedge Donovan (John Wayne) and the Seabees travel to make an air field (1944 movie *The Fighting Seabees*)

X-757

U.N.C.L.E.'s explosive that is put on the toenails much like nail polish, when wadded up it can be used as an explosive (TV series "The Girl from U.N.C.L.E.")

XB70

Experimental bomber destroyed in a midair collision June 8, 1965. In a publicity shot for General Electric, the XB70 (10107) was flying formation with an F104, F4 and F5. A Lear jet flew along to take the photographs. Joe Walker's F104 collided with the XB70, killing Walker and the GB70's co-pilot Carl Cross; Al White, the GB70 pilot, escaped injury. The only other XB70 built was retired to the Air Force Mseum

XP-59

First United States jet-propelled airplane (1942), manufactured by Bell

Xanadu

Citizen Kane's Florida mansion, on a 49,000-acre estate (1941 movie)

Xanadu

Mandrake the Magician's secret mountain hideaway (comic series)

Xanthu

Star Boy's (Thom Kallor) parents' planet of birth. Star

Boy was born on an orbiting space station (comic books)

X-Ray vision

Super ability which allows Superman to see through objects. The reason that Clark Kent's glasses didn't melt is that they are made from the windshield of the space capsule in which he came to earth

Xantippe

Socrates' shrewish wife

Y

Yachts

  Dragoon - Ronald Colman

  Infanta - John Barrymore

  Jobella - Harry Cohn

  Moonraker - William Conrad

  Oneida - William R. Hearst

  Pilar - Ernest Hemingway

  Santana - Humphrey Bogart

  Seward - Cecil B. DeMille

  Sirocco/Zacca - Errol Flynn

  Temptress - John Gilbert

  The Zacca was the yacht on which Peggy Satterlee claimed
  Errol Flynn raped her

  The Oneida was the yacht upon which producer/director
  Thomas H. Ince, "Father of the Western," was mysteriously killed

  The Pilar was used during World War II as a Navy patrol
  boat

Yahoos

  Human-like dumb animals in the land of Houyhnhnms (intelligent, rational horses) (Jonathan Swift's *Gulliver's
  Travels*)

Yahtzee

  A dice game by E. S. Lowe. Any 5 of a kind is called a
  Yahtzee and scores 50 points

Yakky Doodle

  Baby duck friend of the bulldog Chopper (TV cartoon):
  voice of Jimmy Weldon

Yale

University attended by Flash Gordon, where he played polo. It was also the school of Frank Merriwell

Yamamoto and Musashi

Two largest battleships ever built, Japanese, World War II. The 72,000 ton Yamamoto was Admiral Isoro Ku Yamamoto's flagship. It was the larger of the two

Yankee Clipper

Apollo 12 command module; landing module was "Intrepid"

Yankee Clipper

Nickname of baseball player Joe DiMaggio, coined by broadcaster Arch McDonald. It became the name of DiMaggio's yacht

Yankee Clipper

Name given to the Pan American Airway's Boeing 314 Seaplanes in 1934. They began the first transatlantic scheduled air mail service on May 20, 1939. NC18603 was the aircraft that began the service

Yankee Doodle

Character that advertises Kellogg's Mini-Wheats cereal. Voice of Leonard Wienrib

Yankee Doodle Dandy

Biographical film (1942) about George M. Cohan: James Cagney played, sang, and danced the title role (Henry Blaire at age 7, Douglas Croft at age 13;. Cagney again portrayed George Michael Cohan in the 1955 movie *Seven Little Foys*

Yankee Soup

Only soup served each and every day in the Congressional cafeteria, by law making the entrée mandatory. Yankee Soup is bean soup

Yankee Stadium

"The House that Ruth built" (coined by sportswriter Fred Lieb): New York Yankees' home ball park at River Ave. and 161 St. in the Bronx: opened in 1923. Memorial plaques in centerfield to Miller Huggins, Lou Gehrig, and Babe Ruth. Ruth hit the first home run in Yankee Stadium. The first game was played on April 18, 1923 (Yankees beat the Boston Red Sox 4-1). On June 13, 1948 at the 25th Anniversary of the Stadium, Babe Ruth made his farewell speech

Yehoodi

The little man who pushes the next Kleenex tissue up in the Kleenex box. As created by Bob Hope on his radio program

Yehudi

Non-existing character created on radio by Jerry Colonna. He's never heard or seen

Yellow

Color that takes away Green Lantern's power (*All-Star* comics); also detective Nero Wolfe's favorite color (he dislikes red and purple). Also, color of Dick Tracy's raincoat and hat

Yellow Kid, The

First comic strip type cartoon, created (May 6, 1895) by Richard Outcault for New York *World*. The Yellow Kid lived in Hogan's Alley

Yellow Submarine

(Model 37-A087799B6 Mod) Cartoon movie featuring the singing and voices of the Beatles' Lonely Hearts Club Band in the war between the folks of Pepperland and the Blue Meanies. Old Fred was the Lord Admiral of Pepperland and Captain of the Yellow submarine. The crew consisted of the Beatles and Jeremy Hilary Boob (Story written by Erich Segal)

Ygam

The fantastic planet ruled by androids named Draags (1973 movie *Fantastic Planet*)

Yogi

Nickname of New York Yankee catcher (later manager) Lawrence Berra. Jack Maquire (son of Cardinal Scout Jack, Sr.) conferred the nickname on Lawrence after seeing a Hindu fakir in a movie

Yogi Bear

Cartoon bear (voice of Daws Butler) who lives in Jellystone National Park. His hobby is stealing picnic baskets; "Smarter than the average bear." Hanna-Barbera TV cartoon (1958-63). His little sidekick is Boo Boo Bear (voice of Don Messick)

Yojo

Queequeg's wooden god that he carries with him (Herman Melville's *Moby Dick*)

Yokum

Family name of Li'l Abner. Mammy's maiden name was Pansy Hunks prior to marrying Lucifer Ornamental Yokum

York

Lt. William Clark's slave on their expedition to the Pacific Ocean

Yorktown, U.S.S.

Aircraft carrier sunk by the Japanese, June 7, 1942, in the Battle of Midway

Yosemite Sam

Ornery Warner Brothers cartoon character that debuted in the 1944 movie *Hare Trigger:* voice of Mel Blanc

"You Are My Sunhine"

Song written by two-time governor of Louisiana Jimmie Davis (with Charles Mitchel). Jimmie Davis' white horse was named Sunshine

"You Came A Long Way from St. Louis"

Song sung by Peggy Lee in 1955 movie *Abbott and Costello Meet the Mummy*

You have been in Afghanistan, I perceive?

After stating "How are you?" those were the first words Sherlock Holmes spoke to Doctor John H. Watson when they first met

Young Allies

Comic book characters: Henry "Tubb" Tinkle, Toro, Bucky, Knuckles, Jefferson Worthington Sandervilt, Whitewash Jones

Young Defenders

Crimefighters (comic book series): Joanie, Lefty, Slim, Whitey (replaced later by Beanie). Captain Freedom watches over them.

Your Hit Parade

On radio from 1935 with many soloists and orchestras: sponsored by Lucky Strike cigarettes, thus the Lucky Strike Hit Parade

On TV: 1950—Raymond Scott's Orchestra, announcer Andre Baruch, Eileen Wilson, Snooky Lanson, Russell Arms, June Valli; Dorothy Collins replaced Wilson, and Gisele MacKenzie replaced Valli. 1957—original group replaced by Tommy Leonetti, Jill Corey, Alan Copeland, Virginia Gibson. Show went off the air in 1958. 1959—

Dorothy Collins, Johnny Desmond. 1974—Kelly Garrett, Sheralee, Chuck Woolery

Your Show of Shows

TV variety program starring Sid Caesar and Imogene Coca, originally titled *Admiral Broadway Revue Your Show of Shows*

Yukon King

Sgt. Preston's Alaskan husky dog (radio series *Challenge of the Yukon*): King was raised by a wolf named Three Toes

Z

0001 North Cemetery Ridge
Home address of the Addams family (TV series)

0767884
Captain A. Bronkov's (Jack Palance) Army serial number. He was imprisoned at Stalag 21 during part of WWII; this was years before he became a police lieutenant for the Ocean City police department (TV series "Bronk")

Z5
Secret international organization which Dr. Stanislaus Alexander Palfrey heads ("Dr. Palfrey" detective series by John Creasey)

Zaharias, Mildred Babe Didrikson
Best-known woman athlete of 20th century, who concentrated on golf but competed in track and field (4 world's records broken in 1932 Olympics), swimming, diving, baseball, boxing, basketball, and many other sports. She was the first U.S. born golfer to win the British Women's Open (1947). She was nicknamed Babe after Babe Ruth. She appeared in the 1952 movie *Pat and Mike*. Her autobiography is titled *This Life I've Led*. She was portrayed in the 1975 movie *Babe* by Susan Clark

Zaire
African country where Muhammad Ali defeated George Foreman to regain the World Heavyweight Boxing Championship, October 29, 1974

Zangara, Giuseppe (Joe)
On February 15, 1933 in Miami in an attempt to assassinate President-elect Franklin D. Roosevelt, he shot Chicago Mayor Anton J. Cermak (killing him). Wounded

were Mrs. Joseph H. Gill (of Miami); William J. Sinnott (of New York); Miss Margaret Kruis (of Newark, N.J.); and Russell Caldwell (of Coconut Grove, Florida). He was executed at Florida State Prison at Raiford on March 21, 1933

Zapruder, Abraham
Bystander who filmed the assassination of President John F. Kennedy, November 22, 1963, in Dallas

Zarkov, Dr.
Flash Gordon's companion: played by Frank Shannon in movies

Zebec
Name of the Karras family's motor home (TV series "Three for the Road")

Zebra
A white animal with black stripes; in the 1966 movie *The Bible* a pair of zebras were the first animals to enter Noah's Ark

Zed
Last letter in the English (British) alphabet. In the United States it is pronounced *zee*

Zeke (Ezekial)
Li'l Bad Wolf's father (comic books)

Zelda Gilroy
High school girl (played by Sheila James) who chases after, but never catches, Dobie Gillis (Dwayne Hickman) (TV series "The Many Loves of Dobie Gillis")

Zener Cards
Deck of cards used in experiments to determine ESP (Extra Sensory Perception) abilities
25 cards, 5 symbols: Square □, Circle ○, Cross ×, Star ☆, Wavy Line ∼

Zenn-La
Super-hero Silver Surfer's planet of birth (comic books)

Zenith
Hometown of George Babbitt; he is a member of the Zenith Athletic Club (Sinclair Lewis' *Babbitt*): played in 1924 movie by William Louis and in 1934 movie by Guy Kibbee

Zephyr
America's first streamlined train, ran on the Burlington route, 1934

Zero

Annie Rooney's dog (comic strip series *Annie Rooney*)

Zero

World War II Japanese fighter. Copy of Howard Hughes' H-1 airplane which the U.S. Army turned down in 1937

Ziggy

The 6¼-ton elephant that had been chained indoors for over 30 years in the Brookfield, Ill., Zoo and was unchained July 4, 1973

Zip

Zoning Improvement Plan (post office system) introduced in 1962

Zippie

Roller-skating chimpanzee (TV in 1950's)

Zodiac

	Sun enters
Aries, The Ram	March 21
Taurus, The Bull	April 20
Gemini, The Twins	May 21
Cancer, The Crab	June 21
Leo, The Lion	July 23
Virgo, The Virgin	August 23
Libra, The Balance	Sept. 23
Scorpio, The Scorpion	Oct. 23
Sagittarius, The Archer	Nov. 22
Capricorn, The Goat	Dec. 22
Aquarius, The Water Carrier	Jan. 20
Pisces, The Fish	Feb. 19

Zor-El and Allura

Supergirl's (Linda Lee Danvers) father and mother who she left on the planet Krypton when it exploded (comic book series *Supergirl*)

Zorro

Don Diego de Vega, a California Robin Hood type (a milksop until he dons his mask), created by Johnston McCulley in the story, "The Curse of Capistrano." (Retitled *The Mark of Zorro*) In movies played by Douglas Fairbanks, Sr., who played both Zorro and Don Q., the son of Zorro; Robert Livingston; John Carrol, who played the great-grandson of the original Zorro; Tyrone Power; Reed Hadley; George Turner; Clayton Moore; Gordon Scott
On TV played by Guy Williams (as Don Diego de la Vega)

The name means "fox" in Spanish

In the novel Zorro carves the letter Z on the cheeks of his foe; this was toned down in movies and on TV. In the novel Zorro is finally pardoned by the governor, reveals his identity and weds Señorita Lolita Pulido

Bernardo, his deaf-mute servant, was the only other person to know of Zorro's identity. Don Diego's home was located at Reinade, Los Angeles

Movies:

1920 - *The Mark of Zorro* - Douglas Fairbanks

1940 - *The Mark of Zorro* - Tyrone Power

1960 - *The Sign of Zorro* - Guy Williams

1962 - *Zorro and the Three Musketeers* - Gordon Scott

Movie serials:

1937 - *Zorro Rides Again* - John Carrollas (James Vega, Zorro's great grandson)

1939 - *Zorro's Fighting Legion* - Reed Hadley

1944 - *Zorro's Black Whip* - Linda Sterling (as Barbara Meredith)

1947 - *Son of Zorro* - George Turner

1949 - *The Ghost of Zorro* - Clayton Moore

TV: 1958 TV series starring Guy Williams (theme song sung by The Chordettes became a hit record)

Zyra

Satellite planet of the star Bellus (which crashes into and destroys earth). The lone 40 survivors escape via rocket ship to Zyra to start a new life (1951 movie *When Worlds Collide*)

ZVBXRPL

Horse racing tip written on a piece of paper sold to Hugo Z. Hackenbush (Groucho Marx) by Tony (Chico Marx) the Tootsie-Frootsie Ice Cream Man for $1.00. The message is in code, for which a code book is sold to Hackenbush for another dollar (printing cost). A Master code book is then sold to him for $1.00 (to cover delivery)*. Then a Breeder's Guide (4 for $5.00). The code gives the name of the jockey Burns, for which he buys 10 more books for $10. He finally discovers that Burns is to ride Rosie but it's too late to place his bet and Sun-Up wins the race (1937 movie *A Day at the Races*)

---

*Groucho beats him down from $2.00

ZZ

The operating initials of this book's author Fred L. Worth as an air traffic controller with the Federal Aviation Administration

More Mindbending Books
from WARNER

KNOCK YOUR SOCKS OFF!!!
FROM WARNER BOOKS

GRAFFITI IN THE BIG 10
by Marina N. Haan & Richard B. Hammerstrom
(V37504, $4.95)

See what campus life is like from the *inside.* To gather these immortal scrawlings, our researchers penetrated to the ultimate inner sancta—the toilet stalls—plumbing the very depths of the thinking of students at the universities of the Upper Midwest. Here is the collection—profane, profound and profuse. And FUNNY!!!